ATLANTIC OCEAN

• Kunda

• Tollund
• Aamosen
Svaerdborg
Gallehus •

• Star Carr
York •
Rothwell • • The Lunt
Nonsuch • • Brandon
Danebury • • Hoxne
Stonehenge • • Clacton
• • Swanscombe
Kent's Cavern • • Neanderthal
Winchester • Meer II • Koln Lindenthal
Maiden Castle • • • Mezhirich •
Butser Hill • St. Acheul
Abbeville • Somme R.
• Speyer • Dolní Věstonice
Carnac •

Grand Pressigny • • Hallstatt
Solutré • Wasserburg •
Combe Grenal • • La Tène
Abri Pataud •
Lascaux • • Dordogne R.
Cassegros •
Altamira •

BLACK
SEA

Douro R.

Terra Amata •

Herculaneum •
• Pompeii
Samothrace •
THESSALY
MITANNI
• Troy

Aphrodisias •
Hacilar •
Olympia • Mycene •

MEDITERRANEAN SEA

Qsar Es-Segitir •

Knossos •

—— Ice limit at height of Weichsel Glaciation

Archaeological Sites in Europe

IN THE BEGINNING

An Introduction to Archaeology

SEVENTH EDITION

Brian M. Fagan

University of California, Santa Barbara

HarperCollins*Publishers*

Sponsoring Editor: Alan McClare
Project Editor: Karen Trost
Design and Cover Coordinator: Mary Archondes
Cover Design: Wanda Lubelska Design
Cover Illustration/Photo: The ceremonial purification of Sennufer and his
wife Meretjj, from Sennufer tomb at Thebes. New
Kingdom, 18th dynasty. Courtesy of Hirmer
Fotoarchiv, Munich.
Production: Willie Lane/Sunaina Sehwani
Compositor: ComCom Division of Haddon Craftsmen, Inc.
Printer and Binder: R. R. Donnelley & Sons Company
Cover Printer: New England Book Components, Inc.

In the Beginning: An Introduction to Archaeology, Seventh Edition

Library of Congress Cataloging-in-Publication Data

Fagan, Brian M.
  In the beginning: an introduction to archaeology/Brian M.
Fagan.—7th ed.
    p.   cm.
  Includes bibliographical references and index.
  ISBN 0-673-52134-6
  1. Archaeology—Methodology.   2. Archaeology—History.   I. Title.
CC75.F34 1991   90-39409
930.1'028—dc20   CIP

90   91   92   93   9 8 7 6 5 4 3 2 1

Contents

PART THREE
DATA AND CONTEXT   67

Chapter 7
The Archaeological Record   140

PART FOUR
RECOVERING ARCHAEOLOGICAL DATA   163

Chapter 8
Doing Archaeological Research   165

Chapter 9
Finding Archaeological Sites   176

Chapter 15
Settlement Archaeology and Spatial Analysis   386

Chapter 16
Trade, Social Organization, and Religious Life   426

To the Reader

Many people think of archaeology as a romantic subject, a glamorous pastime spent with pyramids, mysterious inscriptions, and buried treasure. This stereotype originated in the nineteenth century, when both archaeologists and the ancient civilizations they uncovered became legendary. Today, more than 150 years of archaeological investigations have turned archaeology into a meticulous scientific discipline. But the excitement is still there, in the many diverse and highly detailed reconstructions of life in the past from finds that sometimes seem trivial. Archaeologists have established the direction of the wind during a bison hunt on the Great Plains about eight thousand years ago, learned which plants made up the wreaths created for Tutankhamen's funeral, and even examined the garbage produced in modern urban America. In this book I describe how archaeologists make and study such finds to illuminate the human past.

In the Beginning introduces the history and methods of archaeology and its significance today. I discuss archaeological concepts and procedures and show how archaeologists describe cultures as part of time and space to interpret the prehistoric past. One objective in this book is to provide a comprehensive summary of the field for people who have little or no experience with it. A second objective is to alert you to a major crisis facing archaeology in our time. All archaeological sites are finite records of the past; once destroyed, they can never be replaced. But treasure hunting by individuals and an explosive increase in the construction of buildings, roads, dams, and the like have destroyed thousands of archaeological sites all over the world. Without access to intact sites, we cannot possibly complete a picture of the human past. The crisis of site destruction is, in its way, as important as the ecological crisis we face. *In the Beginning* is meant to alert you to the need for living responsibly with your cultural heritage.

Archaeology has become a highly sophisticated, "high-tech" discipline in recent years, and there are many more professional archaeologists working in the field than even a decade ago. The result has been not only a knowledge explosion but also the development of ever more sophisticated and fine-grained methods for studying the past. We cannot examine even a small fraction of these elaborate, often expensive, and invariably fascinating methods within the compass of this relatively short book.

Nor do we delve deeply into the powerful statistical methods and computerized approaches that are commonplace in archaeology today. This book focuses on the basic principles of our discipline, on the fundamental tenets that are as important whether one uses a trowel, a laser recording system, or a complicated computer graphics program in pursuit of the past. I hope that you will pursue the topics that interest you in more advanced and specialized archaeology courses or in the many excellent books and articles listed in the Bibliography at the back of the book or in the Guide to Further Reading at the end of each chapter.

The chapters close with summaries highlighting the major themes and concepts. Whenever practicable, drawings and photographs illustrate the subjects the text describes in words. I use specialized terminology as little as possible and define every new term when it first appears. In addition, a Glossary at the back of the book provides definitions of the words used in the book as well as of some words you may encounter in other reading.

I have written this book from predominantly English-language sources for two main reasons. First, my reading in the vast archaeological literature has been necessarily selective and mostly in English. Second, for most of you, English is your native tongue. Although linguistic abilities and time have thus biased this volume toward the achievements and writings of English-speaking archaeologists, archaeology is indeed a global activity, conducted with great energy and intelligence by every nation and in every corner of the world.

Brian M. Fagan

To the Instructor

When I started writing the first edition of this book in 1968, I had no idea that I would be revising it for the seventh time more than twenty years later. *In the Beginning* has been in print during a period of profound change in archaeology. One has only to glance through the first edition and then through this one to see just how much it has changed in the 1970s and 1980s. Hundreds of instructors have assigned the first six editions, and thousands of students have used them. Some respected teachers have even told me that they were introduced to archaeology by *In the Beginning*, which indeed reflects the passage of years. They and many others have helped improve the book by writing to me with suggestions, criticisms, even reprints of their own work. Of course, the seventh edition also reflects my own perceptions of contemporary archaeology and of the way in which the discipline is evolving. Archaeology's many traits, interacting variables, and different forms of feedback make it almost as much a cultural system, evolving multilinearly, as the many cultures it studies.

The seventh edition of *In the Beginning* reflects a number of important trends in archaeology in the past five years, including these:

- An explosion of archaeological data from all over the world, resulting from a vastly expanded community of archaeologists everywhere. This growth has led to a mountain of archaeological literature in dozens of languages, making the task of keeping up-to-date even more challenging.
- A growing emphasis on regional studies, cultural resource management, and nondestructive ways of investigating the past. Remote sensing and computers are increasingly important in archaeology today, for destructive excavation is now seen as a strategy of last resort in many areas.
- Renewed emphasis on multidisciplinary research, especially in the general area of geoarchaeology, placing human activities within an environmental context.
- Vastly increased use of instrumentation and highly scientific approaches to the past. Almost no archaeological research is carried out in this day and age without a battery of equipment and scientific

instruments. These sophisticated tools can include remote-sensing devices such as ground-penetrating radar, lasers, and electron microscopes. Thus the cost of archaeological research is rising. Quantitative methods are now common, with computers applied to create huge data banks on local, regional, state, and even national archaeology.

- Increasing specialization among archaeologists. As the theoretical problems facing archaeology become ever more challenging and frustrating, many scholars have turned to increasingly arcane specializations, specializations that involve them in minute reconstructions of tiny portions of the past. So esoteric are some of these specialties that they seem to bear little relevance to the main objectives of archaeology outlined in this text.

- Quickened interest in site formation processes and middle-range theory. Interpretation of the archaeological record is now a major theoretical debate.

- Ever more precise archaeological fieldwork. Excavation and analysis are becoming more and more accurate, data recovery ever more fine-grained, resulting in some astonishingly minute reconstructions of prehistoric culture, not only from recent settlements but also from early hominid meat caches more than 1.75 million years old.

- New theoretical debates over evolutionary archaeology and "post-processual" archaeology. A new generation of theoretical debate pursues an ever-elusive goal—a unifying body of distinctive archaeological theory.

- Potentially most important, a profound change in archaeology itself. At the start of the 1980s, most archaeologists were academic scholars in universities, colleges, or museums. At the start of the 1990s, most American archaeologists are involved with conservation and management, known as cultural resource management. We are now a more professional discipline, undergoing a revolution that geology, for example, underwent some decades ago. This switch in our ways of thinking about and teaching archaeology is likely to affect us profoundly.

- Last of all, a vanishing archaeological record. In fact, our remnants of the past continue to disappear at an astonishing rate, prey to massive industrial development worldwide and to hordes of looters, vandals and pothunters. Within a generation, much of the archaeological record in more developed parts of the world will have vanished forever.

These are but a few of the fascinating trends in contemporary archaeology that help to form this edition of *In the Beginning*. This is an interesting time in archaeology, for the "new" archaeology of the 1960s and 1970s is no longer new. Then it set out some bold and promising objectives:

imposing great scientific rigor, creating a body of archaeological theory, and searching for general laws of cultural behavior. At first the new archaeologists attacked every concept in archaeology. Today, the level of bombast has subsided, to be replaced by better-focused theoretical debate about everything from style and function to ethnographic analogy. But there is frustration, too, and a widespread feeling that the new archaeology has not delivered its promised advances, that some of its high-minded objectives will never be fulfilled. In part, many of those who are disappointed feel that way because they believed that creating a new body of archaeological theory would be much easier than it has proved to be. It is also because the interpretative problems of much regional and spatial archaeology are obdurate, sophisticated, and difficult, especially when approached with borrowed concepts. Archaeology has spent two decades borrowing such concepts as general systems theory and cluster analysis from other disciplines. These ideas have often proved inadequate or inappropriate for archaeological application, except in the most general way. At the moment, we are midway in a long period of transition, with archaeologists divided into a minority engaged in intensive theoretical debate and the remainder carrying out the same forms of empirical research, albeit in more scientific ways, that were commonplace before processual archaeology came along. Those who believe that this dichotomy will endure are false prophets! What is happening in archaeology has already happened in many mature sciences and is still taking place in much of biology: the development of distinctive and scientific archaeological methods and theories that not only enrich our understanding of the past but add to our understanding of ourselves. We may hope that the short remainder of this century will see archaeology achieve this lofty goal; it depends on the work and cooperation of archaeologists of all theoretical and methodological persuasions. Please encourage your students to think of archaeology as one enterprise, not as dozens of unrelated activities!

One of the fascinating things about revising this book is spotting emerging trends and the cutting-edge research that blazes a new trail in the field. The period since the sixth edition has seen no startling breakthroughs. We are ending a period of consolidation, perhaps of mild despair, marked by signs of a return to basics and much wasted theoretical verbiage that grasps at archaeological straws. There are signs, however, in the renewed debate over evolutionary archaeology that the beginnings of a new theoretical chapter are emerging, some valuable, if extremely challenging, approaches that may yield rich dividends in the 1990s and beyond. In the meantime, it is business as usual, with a continuing proliferation of highly specialized studies, some extremely worthwhile, others esoteric and too expensive, more marginal to the field. It is as if some scholars are running away from the seemingly intractable theoretical problems of archaeology and the parlous state of the archaeological record by burying themselves in arcane research instead. This is not to say that such research is valueless; it is not. But there is a real danger that we will trivialize our discipline and lose sight of the basic goals of archaeology and its important role in twentieth-century society.

I have changed about 25 percent of this edition, mostly by updating discussions of methods, theories, and case examples. Part One covers the significance, goals, and current crisis in archaeology; the historical chapters in Part Two have been shortened in the interests of space and clarity—and because many readers have suggested this! However, they still cover the early origins of archaeology and its development into the science it is today. Part Three covers the basic concepts of archaeology. I have retained the format and coverage of earlier editions at the request of reviewers, as a good introduction to Part Four, which deals with the recovery of archaeological data. Here I have added new material on site formation processes and fresh examples, and I have rewritten the sections on the preservation of the archaeological record. Part Five contains new coverage on lithic technology and on ceramics.

The second half of *In the Beginning* retains its organization from earlier editions, but it has been substantially updated. Chapters 15 to 19 now include new theoretical advances, and I have redrafted coverage of cultural resource management to reflect recent legislation and the complex reburial controversy. As in earlier editions, I recommend further reading selections for readers who wish to delve deeper into topics treated briefly in this book. Space restrictions prevent me from adopting any other approach.

This is a long book and a complex one. But it is still too short, for one could easily write a thousand-page text on archaeology. Thus I have had to skate over some topics, such as population carrying capacity, in almost indecent haste. I have also firmly omitted discussion of some of the more exotic experimental methodologies that now litter the pages of archaeological literature. Many of them are fascinating, even innovative, ways of researching the past. To my mind, however, they are best left to the advanced student and the specialist, for few of them are strictly relevant to the basic goals of archaeology outlined in these pages. I leave it to each of you to fill in details on topics that you think are given inadequate treatment. I urge you, however, to give full coverage to one vital topic: the growing crisis of site destruction. This subject demands full factual and moral coverage in introductory courses, where many students arrive with the notion of finding buried treasure or collecting beautiful artifacts. Many of us have firsthand experience with treasure hunters and with tragically bulldozed sites. Every course in archaeology must place responsibility for preserving the past emphatically on the public. It is for this reason that the book ends with a stark statement of basic archaeological ethics for everyone.

In the Beginning is a comprehensive introductory look at contemporary archaeology. With the very first edition, I decided not to espouse any one theory of archaeology but to give each instructor a basis for amplifying the text with his or her own viewpoint and theoretical persuasion. This decision has turned out to be endorsed by many users. A reviewer said many editions ago: "This is the fun with the book." Long may it continue to be so.

As always, this edition is the result of input and advice from many people, both professional archaeologists and students. Their comments have always been challenging and provocative, at times even flattering. I only hope that my efforts to navigate between conflicting viewpoints and priorities meet with their approval. I am deeply grateful to my distinguished colleague Hester Davis for her advice on cultural resource management and for the counsel of George Michaels on quantitive methods.

Finally, a word of profound thanks to the dedicated production staff at HarperCollins who made the seventh edition a reality. I am deeply grateful for their skills.

Brian M. Fagan

PART One

BACKGROUND TO ARCHAEOLOGY

*Like earnest mastodons petrified in the forests of their own
apparatus the archaeologists come and go, each with his pocket
Odyssey and his lack of modern Greek. Diligently working upon the
refuse-heaps of some township for a number of years they erect on
the basis of a few sherds or a piece of dramatic drainage, a sickly
and enfeebled portrait of a way of life. How true it is we cannot
say; but if an Eskimo were asked to describe our way of life,
deducing all his evidence from a search in a contemporary refuse
dump, his picture might lack certain formidable essentials.*

Lawrence Durrell
Prospero's Cell

*W*hy study archaeology? What is the importance of this popular and apparently romantic subject? We begin to answer these questions by looking at the place of archaeology in the twentieth-century world, at its important role in our cultural enrichment and in the writing of world history. Unfortunately, the discipline faces a crisis brought about by rapid destruction of important sites by industrial development and treasure hunting. Furthermore, the credibility of archaeologists is undermined by all sorts of pseudo-archaeologies purporting to tell the truth about lost worlds, ancient astronauts, and sunken continents.

The reality of archaeology is much less romantic but just as fascinating. We define archaeology by placing it within its broad context as part of anthropology and history.

Chapter
1

Introducing
Archaeology

*A*rchaeology has always been thought of as a romantic subject. In fact, however, modern archaeology is a rigorous and demanding scientific discipline. We use the word *discipline* because archaeology consists of a broad range of scientific methods and techniques for studying the past, used carefully and in a disciplined way. In this chapter we explore archaeology's role in the twentieth-century world and the crisis of destruction that archaeology faces; define archaeology in relation to anthropology and history; and look at the different types of archaeologists.

WHY STUDY ARCHAEOLOGY?

Many people associate archaeologists with buried treasure, the Great Pyramid, and grinning skeletons. They believe archaeologists are romantic heroes, like the film world's Indiana Jones. Cartoonists depict them as elderly, eccentric scholars in sun helmets digging up inscribed tablets in the shadow of Egyptian temples. They are thought to be typical absent-minded professors, so deeply absorbed in the details of ancient life that they care little for the pressures and frustrations of modern life. Archaeology is believed to open doors to a world of romance and excitement, to discoveries like the spectacular tomb of the Egyptian pharaoh Tutankhamun, opened by English archaeologists Howard Carter and Lord Carnarvon in 1922. Even today, many people believe that archaeologists spend their lives solving great mysteries and finding lost civilizations. Any course or lecture on archaeology is filled with people who are indulging their fascination with the past. I hope you are reading this book for the same reason.

Few archaeologists are fortunate enough to discover a royal burial or a forgotten civilization, however. Most of them excavate for a lifetime finding nothing more spectacular than some fine pottery or delicately made stone tools. But archaeology is still a fascinating subject that captures the imagination of scholar and public alike. British archaeologist Stuart Piggott called archaeology "the science of rubbish," and there is much truth in that statement. Archaeologists spend their lives investigating the surviving and abandoned remains of ancient societies. It is not gold or fine objects that interest them, though, but the information that comes from digging up finds and properly recording them. The archaeologist today is as interested in why people lived the way they did as in the objects they made and the buildings they erected.

On the face of it, the study of archaeology, however fascinating, seems a luxury we can ill afford in a world beset by economic uncertainties and widespread poverty and famine. But to regard archaeology in such a way would be to treat the entire cultural heritage of humanity as irrelevant and unnecessary to the quality of our lives; in reality, it is integral (White, 1974; Trigger, 1984a).

Early Archaeologists

The first people to study archaeology did so because they enjoyed digging into the past (Daniel, 1981; Fagan, 1985; Trigger, 1989), both out of curiosity and for fun. In the 1800s, archaeology was no more than a lighthearted pastime (Marsden, 1984). People would gather from far and wide to witness the unbandaging of an Egyptian mummy or the excavation of an ancient burial mound. "Eight barrows were examined," wrote Englishman Thomas Wright (1852) of an archaeological picnic in 1844. "Most of them contained skeletons, more or less entire, with the remains of weapons in iron, bosses of shields, urns, beads, brooches, armlets, bones, amulets, and occasionally more vessels." The day's festivities ended with a "sumptuous repast" and a tour through the landowner's "interesting collection of antiquities" (Figure 1.1).

The first archaeologists to dig in Egypt, as well as those who discovered the Maya and the Assyrians, were no more than amateurs (Fagan, 1975, 1979; Willey and Sabloff, 1980). Normally ardent travelers, they learned how to dig as they went along, their objective being to discover and remove as many spectacular finds as they could in the time they had. Englishman Austen Henry Layard was in his twenties during the mid-1840s when he dug into the ancient mounds of the biblical cities of Calah and Nineveh in Iraq. He discovered the lost civilization of the Assyrians—and gave up archaeology by the time he was thirty-five (Layard, 1849). The Mayan civilization of Mexico and Guatemala was first described by American travel writer John Lloyd Stephens, who traveled in the forests

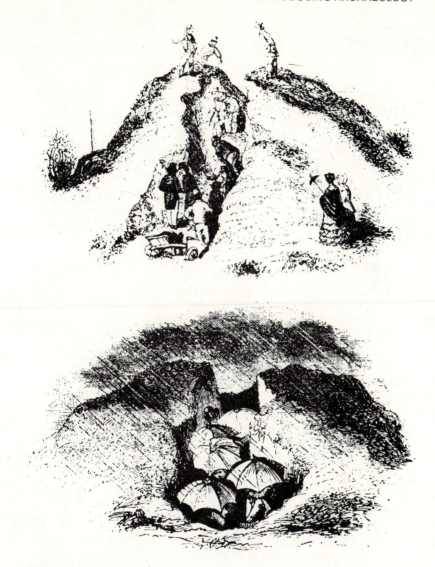

Figure 1.1 A nineteenth-century barrow excavation as depicted in *Gentlemen's Magazine,* 1840.

of the Yucatán with artist Frederick Catherwood in 1839 (Figure 1.2). His *Incidents of Travel* (Stephens, 1841) was an instant bestseller. Both Layard's and Stephens's works were as much volumes of travel and adventure as they were archaeological reports. One has the impression that they had great fun on their travels. "The reader is perhaps curious to know how old cities sell in Central America. Like other articles of trade they are regulated by the quality in the market and the demand," wrote Stephens. "I paid fifty dollars for Copán . . . for which Don José Maria thought me only

Figure 1.2 A lithograph by Frederick Catherwood of the Mayan site, Chichén Itzá.

a fool; if I had offered more, he would probably have considered me something worse."

The foundations of modern archaeology lie not only in the adventure-some spirit but also in the intellectual curiosity of the early travelers and archaeologists. None was more single-minded than Heinrich Schliemann, a German businessman who made several fortunes before retiring and devoting the remainder of his life to searching for the cities that were described in Homer's poems (Ceram, 1953; Wood, 1985). In his early forties he gave up business, married a young Greek woman, and set out to find Homer's legendary city of Troy. His feverish search ended at the mound of Hissarlik in northwestern Turkey. Schliemann always worked on a large scale. He recruited 150 men and moved 325,000 cubic yards of soil in his early seasons. His excavation techniques were modeled on those used to dig the Suez Canal in Egypt some years earlier. By 1873, Schliemann had found no fewer than seven cities and a great gold trea-sure, which he proudly displayed on his wife's neck (Ceram, 1953; Deuel, 1977). But his archaeological methods were brutal—he destroyed almost as much as he discovered.

Until the last decades of the nineteenth century, archaeological exca-vations still resembled treasure hunts—and that they often were. Early excavators in Egypt, such as the notorious Giovanni Belzoni, a strongman turned tomb robber, literally mined the ancient Egyptians for gold. Bel-zoni would push his way into mummy caves and even sit down on a corpse to rest. "When my weight bore on the body of an Egyptian, it crushed like a bandbox," he recalled (Fagan, 1975). The losses to science from such activities were incalculable. How often do we read that such and such a find "crumbled to dust," or that exposed to the open air the object "dissolved before our very eyes"?

Most early archaeologists were interested in carrying away precious objects for display in foreign museums and minimally in preserving the great sites they dug for future generations. But their depredations did lead to the popular fascination that archaeology holds for many today.

Archaeology as Entertainment

Scientific archaeology began over a century ago but has become a serious and popular field of investigation only within the past half century. Popular interest in the past has sharply increased in recent decades, sparked in part by an explosion of popular literature on archaeology. Colorful, imaginative reconstructions of early human beings camping on the African savannah appear in the pages of *National Geographic.* Spectacular archaeological discoveries merit prominent headlines in many newspapers. Archaeology is as much a part of popular culture as football or the automobile. Thousands of people read archaeology books for entertainment, join archaeological societies, and flock to popular lectures on the past.

The jetliner and the package tour have helped make archaeology a medium of popular entertainment as well. Fifty years ago only the wealthy and privileged could take a tour up the Nile, visit the Greek temples, and explore Mayan civilization. Now package tours can take you to Egypt, to the Parthenon, and to Teotihuacán. The jumbo jet and the air-conditioned bus can take you to such remote sites as Petra in Jordan or the Inca cities in Peru. The famous sites of antiquity give the modern traveler a sense of time that dwarfs the day-to-day cares of the twentieth century. The immense Pyramids of Giza in Egypt, and the prodigious labor that built them; the white columns of the Temple of Poseidon at Sounion, Greece, touched with pink by the setting sun; the ruins at Tikal bathed in the full moon's light—as sights alone, these overwhelm the senses. Tutankhamun's golden mask or a giant stone idol with an oversized head (Figure 1.3) lifts us to a realm where achievement endures and perceptions seem of a higher order. It is this sense of physical reality carried from the past that holds our human secrets, if only we could read its meaning, and draws people to archaeology—a casual interest for some, but for others a consuming passion.

Archaeology and Cultural Heritage

Every society on earth has some form of the origin myth: folklore that is the official, sanctioned account of how it came into being. Our own society is no exception. "And God said, 'Let us make man in our image, after our likeness: and let them have dominion over the fish of the sea, and over the

Figure 1.3 A stone idol with oversized head attributed to the Olmec site at La Venta, Mexico, now in the Olmec archaeological park in Villabermose, Veracruz. Made of basalt, Middle Formative period, c. 900 to 500 B.C.

fowl of the air, and over the cattle, and over all the earth, and over every creeping thing that creepeth on the earth.' "—thus reads the first chapter of Genesis in the biblical Old Testament, a majestic account of the Creation that was accepted as the authorized version of human origin for centuries.

Origin myths, such as that of Genesis, developed in response to humanity's deep-seated curiosity about its origins. For more than two thousand years, Westerners have speculated about their ancestry and tried to develop theoretical models to explain their origins. Some of these models are purely philosophical; others are based on scientifically collected data. Much of these data come from archaeological surveys and excavations. Archaeology is fascinating because it enables us to test theoretical models of evolving societies: why some people have flourished, others have vanished without a trace, and still others have sunk into obscurity.

Our curiosity about the past stems not only from preoccupation with our ultimate origins but from strong feelings of nostalgia as well. We live in a world of rapid change and diminishing natural resources, in a crowded, overpopulated urban environment. As population increases and ecological problems deepen, we find ourselves nostalgic for simpler, earlier times. The life of prehistoric peoples, determined by the seasons of vegetable foods and the movements of game, is perceived as a time of natural simplicity. Archaeology gives insight into those less complicated societies of the past (for discussion, see Trigger, 1984a).

Archaeology also contributes valuable information to our collective cultural heritage. Most American Indian groups came into contact with literate Western civilization only in the past three centuries. Before European contact, North American Indian history was not written; it consisted mostly of oral traditions handed down from generation to generation. Archaeology and archaeological sites are the only other possible sources for American Indian history. Only as archaeologists probe into their ancestry will the first chapters of American history be written.

One of the most remarkable examples of archaeology's ability to reveal the history of the Indian comes from Ozette, Washington, where Richard Daugherty has excavated the remains of a Makah Indian village that was buried by mud slides about five hundred years ago (Kirk, 1974). Conditions for preservation at the site were so exceptional that archaeologists were able to recover complete details of the village's plank houses and their contents, down to stored food and whalebone harpoons. By working closely with the Tribal Council, Daugherty was able not only to interpret the objects found on the site but also to help the council raise a large sum of money for a local museum in which to display the finds. In this way he brought the hitherto forgotten history of the Makah into the consciousness of the Indians themselves and of the public as well (Fagan, 1978). Though scientific monographs on this site have yet to appear, the public is fully informed on the results of the excavation.

The Ozette example is by no means unique, for more and more archaeologists are working closely with American Indian communities, and southwestern groups, among others, have retained archaeologists and anthropologists to work on land claim cases currently in the courts. E. Charles Adams has excavated at the Hopi village of Walpi in the Southwest, with the cooperation of the local people.

In Florida, Kathleen Deagan has excavated the site of Fort Mose, the first free black community in North America. This tiny hamlet of some thirty-seven families, two miles from Spanish St. Augustine on the Atlantic coast, was founded in 1738, overrun by the British in 1740, and rebuilt in 1753. A walled fort enclosed a large church, the priest's house, a well, and guardhouses, while the villagers lived in 22 thatched houses. Many of the inhabitants were of West African origin, and excavations have recovered military artifacts and domestic items, offering the prospect that one day archaeologists will be able to identify what African, English, Indian, and Spanish cultural elements the black inhabitants retained. Fort Mose was occupied until the Spanish abandoned Florida in 1763. Other excavations in the South and the Southeast have investigated plantation life and slave communities, a rich archaeological record of culturally very diverse African American populations.

Political Uses of Archaeology

Many newly independent nations, eager to foster nationalism, are encouraging archaeological research as the only way to uncover the early roots of the peoples who lived there before colonial times. For years the Tanzanian and Zambian governments in Africa have sponsored excavations, whose results soon appear in university textbooks and schoolbooks. The primary goal of archaeology there, as in many parts of the world, is to write unwritten history, not from archives and dusty documents but from long-abandoned villages and rubbish heaps (Trigger, 1984a). That this type of archaeology is essential is clear from the remarks by President Kenneth Kaunda of Zambia, when presented with a book on Zambian history written by a group of archaeologists and historians. With intense pride he said, "This is our history. Now we can look people from other countries in the face and tell them that we have a history and a national identity to be proud of." It is difficult to convey the feeling that came through in his remarks.

In a far less admirable way, a number of governments have used archaeology for political ends. With it the Nazis produced "evidence" for the evolution of a master race in Europe (J.G.D. Clark, 1939). During the late 1960s, the government of Rhodesia in southern Africa claimed that the Zimbabwe ruins, a famous complex of stone buildings, were the work of Phoenician colonists who had settled south of the Zambezi River more than two thousand years ago. They chose to ignore half a century and more of archaeological research that showed Zimbabwe had been built by indigenous African peoples between A.D. 1000 and 1500. The reason for the claim was easily discerned: a Phoenician date for Zimbabwe would be evidence for white settlement in southern Africa long before the local people arrived (Garlake, 1973). Oddly, the controversy has a new twist now that Zimbabwe is an independent nation. Local politicians accuse white archaeologists of not understanding the true significance of the site, even though they had proved it was built by Africans. Only locally born scholars, they argue, have adequate "cultural background" to interpret the symbolism in the ruins.

As Don Fowler has recently pointed out (1987), interpretations of the past are rarely value-neutral. Nation-states have long used and manipulated the past for their own needs, as the Aztec rulers of Mexico did early in the sixteenth century (Fagan, 1984a). Inevitably, archaeologists themselves bring to their work values and perspectives from their own culture, even if they are much more conscious of this than they were a generation ago (Shanks and Tilley, 1987a). Such subliminal biases are very different from the deliberate use of archaeology to establish historical fact and to support claims against governments or nationalist goals. Today archaeology is being pressed into service in support of American Indian land claims in British Columbia and elsewhere and is deeply involved in bitter political controversies over demands for reburial of skeletons of native Americans and Australian aborigines (Chapter 19). It is also proving to be of vital use in economic development in South America. As early as 1000 B.C., farmers living on the *altiplano* along Lake Titicaca in southern Peru were beginning to use raised fields, elevated planting surfaces that were used to grow crops in areas that were subject to seasonal flooding (Erickson, 1985). The soils are rich, and by elevating them and building a canal network, prehistoric cultivators were able to grow potatoes, quinoa, and other indigenous crops with impressive yields. The raised fields were abandoned before the Spanish conquest, and the modern economy of the same environment is based on pastoralism. Archaeologists' experiments with reconstructions of ancient raised gardens showed that excellent crop yields could be obtained from the prehistoric plots, in areas considered marginal by modern agricultural authorities. Working with more than five hundred local farmers, about ten hectares of abandoned raised fields had been rehabilitated by 1986. The archaeologists also participated in training schemes devoted to traditional agricultural systems, and their work has now begun to have an impact on government-sponsored development projects. The traditional system has many advantages—high yields, no need for fertilizer, and much reduced risks of frost or flood damage. Furthermore, high yields can be obtained with local labor, local crops, and no outside capital. This project is one of several in the Americas that are leading to a revival in traditional methods that help solve local food supply problems.

Archaeology as a Social Science

Archaeologists bring a unique tool to the social sciences of which they are a part: a perspective that enables them to understand how people have dealt with the world around them from the earliest times. This facility contributes to a much better understanding of our own history, as well as that of the environment, the world climate, and the landscape. The long-abandoned settlements that archaeologists study are repositories of precisely dated geological, biological, and environmental data that can add a vital time depth to studies of the contemporary world. In the dry pueblos of Arizona, preservation conditions are so good that wood, fossil pollen grains, and other environmental evidence are found in abundance. It is proving to be possible to study the gradual evolution of southwestern agriculture through many centuries and determine how the local people responded to uneven rainfall and other environmental changes. Information from such research is extremely valuable to students of agriculture who are trying to expand crop production in the desert.

In addition, archaeological sites are storehouses of information for a host of natural and physical sciences. Chemists and physicists have made great contributions to the study of the past by developing such approaches as radiocarbon dating and spectrographic analysis for studying prehistoric trade. As our pages show, geologists, botanists, and zoologists, among many other scientists, have made vital contributions to the study of the past as well.

Destruction of Archaeological Sites

Pothunters and treasure hunters have left thousands of archaeological sites looking like rabbit burrows and have so damaged them that archaeological inquiry is impossible. The ravages of industrial activity, strip mining, and agriculture have also taken their catastrophic toll on many sites.

In some parts of the United States, damage of sites is an uncontrolled epidemic. Those of us alive today may be the last to see undisturbed archaeological sites in North America (McGimsey, 1972). Quite apart from the ravages of the industrial society, professional looters and amateur pothunters reap havoc with archaeological sites large and small. In a recent scandalous episode, an undisturbed late prehistoric site at Slack Farm, close to the Ohio River in Kentucky, was looted by a group of pothunters who paid the landowner a large sum for the right to dig up Indian burials and the valuable grave goods associated with them. It was two months before their nefarious activities were halted, by which time the site looked like a battlefield (Fagan, 1991a).

Federal legislation now requires that archaeological impact studies be done on all government-funded development projects to ensure that any damage done to archaeological resources during construction work is minimal. This legislation has massively expanded archaeological work throughout North America (see Chapter 19). It is designed to protect the finite database of archaeological sites that are studied by archaeologists and by scientists from many other disciplines.

Archaeology has also worked directly for contemporary American society, especially in the management of resources and waste. University of Arizona archaeologist William Rathje has studied the garbage dumps in Tucson for a long time (Rathje, 1974). He examines patterns in garbage disposed of by Tucson households, analyzes evidence from the dump with the latest archaeological research designs and techniques, and joins to it data gleaned from interviews with householders and other sources. His study has revealed startlingly wasteful habits in Arizona households of many economic and social backgrounds, information that could be used to suggest better strategies for consumer buying and resource management.

Rathje argues that such studies of modern garbage can supply unique knowledge about ourselves as well as about the past. Because the objects we use shape our lives in many ways, we need to understand how they affect us to learn about the past and anticipate the future (Rathje and Ritenbaugh, 1984b).

The archaeologist's task, then, is significant in the modern world, in which we must understand other cultures if we are to survive. To say that archaeology is a luxury is to deny the cultural achievements of our predecessors and to deprive many millions of the opportunity to learn about their roots and ancestry. As more and more non-Western societies abandon their traditional ways of life to become part of modern technological civilization, archaeologists have to be guardians of the world's dying cultures. People move from their traditional village sites into cities or modern housing, leaving their old settlements to crumble to the ground. Only with the archaeologist's spade, combined with oral tradition and the work of early anthropologists, can we hope to recover many details about the dying culture. Richard Lee and others made remarkable anthropological studies of San hunter-gatherers in the Kalahari desert of southern Africa, to learn about the living people and their recently abandoned campsites (Yellen, 1977). In this and other field studies, the archaeologist and the anthropologist together hurry to describe a society that is slowly becoming extinct as it reacts to pressure from the outside world.

In short, archaeology also satisfies our intellectual curiosity about the nature of humanity. Perhaps its greatest achievement is to have established the tremendous antiquity of human existence on earth. With their broad perspective on time and circumstance, archaeologists are as much part of our lives as are historians, anthropologists, physicists, and any army of more exotic specialists. Archaeology is the only source of cultural history for some societies.

THE CRISIS IN ARCHAEOLOGY

Unfortunately, archaeological sites are an endangered species. As we have mentioned, sites that cry out to be investigated are being destroyed so rapidly that a sizable portion of the world's archaeological heritage has already vanished forever. Unlike trees or animals, archaeological sites are a finite resource. Once a bulldozer or a treasure hunter moves in, archaeological evidence is wiped out. The archaeologist's archives are buried in the soil, and the only way to preserve them is to leave them alone, intact, until they can be investigated with rigorous scientific care. Both human nature and the world's growing populations' insatiable needs have wrought terrible destruction on the archaeological record everywhere.

Collectors and the Morality of Collecting

Our materialistic society greatly emphasizes wealth and the possession of valuable things. Many people feel an urge to possess the past, to keep a piece of antiquity on the mantel. Projectile points, prehistoric hand axes,

Benin bronzes, or Maya pots add an exotic touch to the prosaic American living room. Many archaeological artifacts, such as those Benin bronzes, have high antique and commercial value. They are "buried treasure," valued as museum pieces and by the world's major collectors, commanding enormous prices at auction and in salesrooms. Glorious finds of antiquity are displayed without context, often because their archaeological associations are unknown. High commercial prices and the human urge to own have incited unscrupulous treasure hunting and a flourishing illegal trade in antiquities, resulting in the rape of sites for gold and other precious ornaments, as well as pottery, sculpture, and all other artifacts that today's covetous collectors seek to own and sell.

The destruction of archaeological sites for commercial ends has grown to alarming proportions, but it is nothing new. The dilettantes of eighteenth-century Italy, Giovanni Belzoni in Egypt, and Lord Elgin in Greece were merely the best known of those who satisfied the educated European's lust for antiquities. In the Americas, the thirst for pre-Columbian antiquities goes back at least a century. The only difference is that today the traffic in tomb robbing and illegal antiquities is better organized, more lucrative, and fueled by inflation, greed, and the aggressive policies on acquisition of heavily endowed public and private museums.

The pressure to acquire objects of interest and value has escalated in the twentieth century as more museums compete for fewer and fewer valuable and authentic pieces. In some countries, such as Italy and Costa Rica, tomb robbing is a full-time, if technically illegal, profession. The Italian *tombaroli* concentrate on Etruscan tombs (Hamblin, 1970). Their finds command high prices from foreign dealers, and the government does little to control either the looting or the export trade. Entire Inca cemeteries have been dug up for gold ornaments. Thousands of Egyptian tombs have been rifled for papyri and statues. And the problem is not confined to ancient civilizations. North America bristles with pothunters who think nothing of ravaging sites for their projectile points and potsherds. Looting even one projectile point destroys a small part of our nation's limited archaeological resource. The cumulative effect of treasure hunting, pothunting, and metal detectors is catastrophic.

Why do people collect antiquities? In 1921, Henri Codet, a French medical doctor, wrote a pioneering dissertation on collecting. He concluded that it has four underlying motives: "the need to possess, the need for spontaneous activity, the impulse to self-advancement, and the tendency to classify things" (Meyer, 1977). Another Frenchman said of collecting: "It is not a pastime, but a passion and often so violent that it is inferior to love or ambition only in the pettiness of its aims." People collect everything from beer-bottle caps to oil paintings, and anything collectible is considered by collectors to be portable and private—and it is their duty to preserve it. It follows that everything has a market value and can be purchased, the market value depending on the demand for the category of artifact or its rarity or aesthetic appeal. The archaeological context of the artifact is often quite unimportant, and information about the people who made it is usually irrelevant: all that matters is the object itself (Figure 1.4).

Protecting antiquities is complex and incredibly difficult, for in the final analysis, it involves appealing to people's moral values and requires almost unenforceable legislation that ultimately would take away a potential source of livelihood, however illegal, from thousands of poverty-stricken peasants and more prosperous intermediaries who have some political influence. Many countries are now feeling more nationalistic about their past and their own archaeological sites. When collecting began, such countries as Egypt or Turkey had no museums to house the finds of early archaeologists. Now most countries have museums, and many have antiquities services and stringent laws controlling the export of archaeological finds—at least in theory. The trouble is that the laws cost a fortune to administer and enforce, and even relatively developed countries as Mexico are unable to police even the most famous sites. But public opinion in Egypt and other countries shows some pride in the national heritage. It is galling to see the prized sculptures and antiquities of one's past adorning museums in distant capitals. Yet the tide of public opinion cannot stem the collectors' mania or the ruthless policies of some museums. Perhaps the most notorious example of questionable acquisition by a large museum was perpetrated by the Metropolitan Museum of Art in New York when it purchased a Greek painted vase priced at no less than a million dollars in 1972 (Hess, 1974). The Euphronios vase dates to the sixth century B.C. and is one of the finest examples of its type ever found (Figure 1.5). The Met claimed that the vase came from a private collection that had been intact for almost half a century. But others suspected that the vase was found in an illegal excavation of an Etruscan tomb north of Rome and sold by tomb robbers. The controversy continues. Fortunately, some universities and museums have adapted more stringent acquisitions policies, although it is too early to say whether they have had any effect. Changing public attitudes, more cautious policies, and a shortage of fine antiquities may slow the traffic, but significant damage has already been done.

PSEUDO-ARCHAEOLOGIES

Modern archaeology is highly technical and—let us be honest—sometimes rather dull. In contrast, the flood of "pseudo-archaeologies" that has appeared in recent years positively drips with romance and excitement, with "unexplained" secrets, lost civilizations, and great temples buried in dense rain forests. The Lost Continent of Atlantis, the Ten Lost Tribes of Israel,

Figure 1.4 The wrong and the right way to dig. Archaeology is a hobby for both these groups, but the top group is destroying evidence of the past by their digging "techniques," whereas the bottom group is preserving it. The latter, alas, happens all too rarely.

Figure 1.5 The Euphronios vase, sixth century B.C., showing dead Sarpedon being carried by Thanatos and Hypnos. (Height, 18 inches; diameter, $21\frac{11}{16}$ inches)

expeditions in search of Noah's Ark—all provide superb raw material for the armchair adventurer.

Pseudo-archaeologies are not new, and they have always been lucrative businesses. In the mid-nineteenth century, thousands of Americans bought books that described great mound-building civilizations that flourished and did battle in the Midwest. Their descendants have supposedly moved from earth into space. Perhaps the most notorious pseudo-archaeology of recent times was perpetuated in the early 1970s by a popular writer with dubious archaeological credentials named Erich von Däniken. He took advantage of general fascination with space to argue that people from other worlds have lived on earth long before our civilization arose. With his books and films he earned millions of dollars by arguing that "foreign astronauts visited the earth thousands of years ago. The crew of the spaceship soon realized that the earth could support intelligent life" (von Däniken, 1970, 1971). They found primitive humans on earth and fertilized some of the females. Millennia later the spacemen returned and found *Homo sapiens* scattered over the earth. They repeated their breeding experiment and eventually produced a "creature intelligent enough to have the rules of society imparted to it" (von Däniken, 1970). These new beings started art and agriculture and eventually their own civilizations, regarding their progenitors as "benevolent gods who were interested in their welfare." But soon warfare began, and people began to destroy many of the sacred places. Centuries later, people started to excavate these ancient temples. The astronauts' influence on prehistoric people, argues von Däniken, was about equivalent to that of Captain Cook and his mariners on the Tahitians—devastating.

The world at large adored von Däniken's incredible hypotheses, but archaeologists were puzzled. His extravagant theories—they are nothing less—are a superb example of misused archaeological data. Most scholars find it impossible to follow von Däniken's reasoning, for his archaeological "evidence" is laced with biblical allusions, in one of which he claims that Sodom and Gomorrah were destroyed by an atomic bomb! The Ark of the Covenant, he contends, was an electrified transmitter that enabled Moses to communicate with the astronauts.

Von Däniken's brand of pseudo-archaeology is unusual only because he has moved into space for his heroes. Like his predecessors, and like many people fascinated by escapism and space fiction, he is intoxicated with the mystery and lure of vanished tribes and lost cities engulfed in swirling mists (Wauchope, 1972; Harrold and Eve, 1987). Of course, the pseudo-archaeologists do not all turn to space for their explanations. In order to answer the intense controversy that surrounds the question of early settlements in the Americas, Barry Fell and other authors have alleged that North America was settled by foreigners long before the Vikings and Christopher Columbus arrived (Fell, 1977). They use as evidence isolated artifacts and alleged inscriptions that are sometimes little more than crude forgeries and are invariably without well-documented archaeological contexts. Many of their theories bear no resemblance whatsoever to archaeological reality.

Flamboyant nonarchaeology of the type espoused by von Däniken and Fell will always appeal to people who are impatient with the deliberate pace of science and to those who believe in faint possibilities. Some of these "cult archaeologies" show all the symptoms of becoming personality cults, even religious movements (Cole, 1980). The theories espoused by the leaders become articles of faith, the object of personal conversion. They are attempts to give meaning to being human and are often steeped in symbolism and religious activity. Almost invariably the cultists dismiss archaeologists as "elitists" or "scientific fuddy-duddies" because they reject wild theories that are unsupported by scientifically gathered evidence. Until recently, archaeologists made little effort to popularize their findings, leaving a clear field for the bizarre and the eccentric.

The credibility of modern archaeology depends on archaeologists' ability to communicate the results of their scientific research to wide audiences in intelligible and enjoyable forms. They have a formidable task, for as we have seen, popular attitudes toward archaeology tend toward the romantic and the exotic. Today's archaeology is far from exotic, and although it is highly technical, it is still extremely fascinating. This book will give you an understanding of how scientific archaeologists go about their work.

ARCHAEOLOGY, ANTHROPOLOGY, AND HISTORY

Anthropology and Archaeology

Anthropology is the scientific study of humanity in the widest possible sense. Anthropologists study human beings as biological organisms and as people with a distinctive and unique characteristic—culture. They carry out research on contemporary human societies and on human development from the very earliest times. This enormous field is divided into subdisciplines:

Physical anthropology involves the study of human biological evolution and the variations among different living populations. Physical anthropologists also study the behavior of living nonhuman primates, such as the chimpanzee and the gorilla, research that can suggest explanations for behavior among the earliest human beings.

Cultural anthropology deals with the analysis of human social life, both past and present. It is primarily a study of human culture and how culture adapts to the environment. A number of specialists work within cultural anthropology:

> *Ethnographers* spend most of their time describing the culture, technology, and economic life of living and extinct societies.

> *Ethnologists* engage in comparative studies of societies, a process that involves attempts to reconstruct general principles of human behavior.

> *Social anthropologists* analyze social organization, the ways in which people organize themselves.

Linguistics, the study of human language, sometimes has an important role to play in the study of the past. Many early archaeologists were deeply concerned with such major problems as the origins of the Indo-Europeans, speakers of primeval European languages.

Many of the archaeologist's objectives are the same as those of the cultural anthropologist, one difference being that archaeologists study ancient societies. Thus one could describe an archaeologist as a special type of anthropologist, one who studies the past. This definition is somewhat inadequate, however, for archaeologists use many theoretical frameworks to link their excavated evidence to actual human behavior and do far more than merely use evidence different from that of their anthropological colleagues.

Archaeology

Archaeologists both build theories and apply scientific techniques and theoretical concepts in studying the material remains of culture (Deetz, 1967; Fagan, 1991a; Sharer and Ashmore, 1987). They cover all of human history, from the time of the earliest human beings right up to the present.

To understand what archaeology involves requires some knowledge of the material evidence we examine. As we shall see in Chapter 7, some raw materials survive much longer than others. Stone and clay vessels are nearly indestructible; wood, skin, metals, and bone are much more friable. In most archaeological sites, only the most durable remains of human material culture are preserved for the archaeologist to study. Any picture of life in the prehistoric past derived from archaeological investigations is likely to be very one-sided. As a result, the unfortunate archaeologist is like a detective fitting together a complicated collection of clues to give a general impression and explanation of prehistoric culture and society. Much effort has gone into developing sophisticated methods for studying the prehistoric past. Often, it can be like taking a handful of miscellaneous objects—say, two spark plugs, a fragment of a china cup, a needle, a grindstone, and a candleholder—and trying to reconstruct the culture of the people who made these diverse objects on the basis of these objects alone.

Some people think that archaeology is an assortment of techniques, such as accurate recording, precise excavation, and detailed laboratory analysis. This narrow definition, however, deals only with "doing archaeology," the actual work of recovering data from the soil. Modern archaeology is far more than a gathering of techniques, for it involves not only recovering, ordering, and describing things from the past but also interpreting the evidence from the earth. In fact, it is an *interactive* discipline, striking a balance between practical excavation and description and theoretical interpretation.

Theory in Archaeology

The word *theory* has many uses among social scientists. In archaeology it is the overall framework within which a scholar operates. Theory is still little developed in archaeology, as in the other social sciences, partly because working with variable human behavior is difficult and also because of inadequate research methods. Normally, archaeologists work within procedural rules and a classification system that is also used by other scholars with the same basic theoretical leanings. Truly interactive archaeology is a constant dialogue between theory and observation, a more or less uniquely self-critical procedure that is very much based on inferences about the past, in turn built on phenomena found in the contemporary world. Theoretical approaches to archaeology are numerous; these are some of them:

> *Cultural materialism* seeks the causes behind sociocultural diversity in the modern world. Thus technoeconomic and technoenvironmental conditions exert selective pressures on society and its ideologies (Harris, 1968). Cultural materialism is closely associated with the teachings of Engels and Marx. It is especially attractive to archaeologists because it stresses technology, economy, and environ-

ment, data for which survive in the archaeological record. The majority of archaeologists would probably consider themselves cultural materialists (Chapter 1).

Structural approaches treat human cultures as shared symbolic structures that are cumulative creations of the human mind. Structural analyses are designed to discover the basic principles of the human mind, an approach associated in particular with famed French anthropologist Claude Lévi-Strauss. The difficulty with this approach for archaeologists is that the intangibles of the human mind are difficult to verify from the archaeological record (Chapter 18).

Ecological approaches stress the study of ancient societies within their ecosystems (Chapter 15). They are fundamental to contemporary archaeology.

Evolutionary approaches have been popular in archaeology since the nineteenth century. The concepts that form multilinear cultural evolution are inextricable from modern archaeological research (Chapters 3 and 18).

A broad definition of archaeology includes not only the subject matter but also the techniques used to describe and explain it. More than a century and a half of work all over the world has developed a battery of methods and techniques for describing and explaining the past. But these are not enough; they are related to a body of theory that provides both a framework and a means for archaeologists to look beyond the facts and material objects for explanations of events that took place during our long history.

Much archaeological research and theory is strongly influenced by contributions made by people in other academic disciplines, such as specialists in other fields of anthropology and in biology, chemistry, geography, history, physics, and computer technology. Multidisciplinary research is essential to modern archaeology, but much of it does not handle the archaeological record itself and is meaningless unless combined with such data.

Archaeology and Prehistory

The term *archaeology* originally embraced the study of ancient history as a whole, but the word was gradually narrowed to its present definition— the study of material remains and human cultures using archaeological theory and techniques (Daniel, 1981).

In 1833, French scholar Paul Tournal (1805–1872) coined the name *période anti-historique* for the period of human history extending back before the time of written documents (Grayson, 1983). In time, this phrase shrank to *prehistory* and now encompasses the enormous span of human cultural evolution that extends back at least three million years. This is the time frame studied by prehistoric archaeologists.

Archaeology and History

The earliest known written records were compiled on the banks of the Tigris and Euphrates rivers where Iraq is now, about five thousand years ago. There *history*, the study of human experience in written documents, begins.

Archaeology is our primary source of information for 99 percent of human history. Written history describes less than one-tenth of 1 percent of that enormous time span. Although written records extend back five thousand years in the Near East, the earlier portions of that period are but dimly illuminated by the documents. In other parts of the world, prehistory ended much later. Continuous written history in Britain began with the Roman conquest some two thousand years ago; decipherable records in the New World commenced with Christopher Columbus, even though the Maya had long had a record-keeping system and a form of calendar. Some parts of the world did not come into contact with Western society until much more recently. The pastoral Khoi Khoi of the Cape of Good Hope came out of prehistory in 1652 and were first known to the outside world when Portuguese explorer Bartholomeu Dias met them in the late fifteenth century. The tribes of the Central African interior had their first outside contact with David Livingstone in 1855. Continuous government records in this area did not begin until late in the nineteenth century, and parts of New Guinea and the Amazon basin are still in the process of leaving their prehistoric past.

Documentary history contrasts sharply with the view of our past as it is reconstructed from the archaeological record. First, historians work with accurate chronologies (Dymond, 1974). They can date an event with certainty to within a year, possibly even as closely as to the minute or the second. Second, their history is that of individuals, groups, governments, and even several nations interacting with each other, reacting to events, and struggling for power. They are able to glimpse the subtle interplay of human intellects, for their principal players have often recorded their impressions or deeds on paper. But the historian's record often has gaps. Details of political events are likely to be far more complete than those of day-to-day existence or the trivia of village life, which often mattered little to contemporary observers. Such minor details of past human behavior do absorb students of ancient society, especially archaeologists interested in broad patterns of human change and early cultures, and it is here that the archaeologist may be useful to the historian (Deetz, 1977, 1988).

DIVERSITY OF ARCHAEOLOGISTS

Because no one could possibly be expert in the entire time span of archaeology, most archaeologists specialize, pursuing one of the following specialties.

Prehistoric archaeologists (prehistorians) study prehistoric times, from the day of the earliest human beings right up to the frontiers of documentary history. Their dozens of specialties include paleoanthropologists, who are experts in the living floors and artifacts of the earliest human beings. This specialty requires close cooperation with physical anthropologists interested in human biological evolution and with geologists studying the complex strata in which the earliest human dwellings are found. Others are experts in stone technology, studying the early peopling of the world and the subsistence strategies used by prehistoric hunter-gatherers. Those who specialize in the origins of agriculture and literate civilization work with ceramics, domesticated grains and animal bones, and a wide range of site types and economic lifeways. Because modern prehistoric archaeology covers the globe, it is divided between New and Old World archaeologists, each focusing on specific regions such as the North American Southwest, Mesoamerica, or Peru. Even these large areas are too big for specialist researchers to work alone, and so they tackle a specific region, site, or detailed problem within a larger site, region, or area. Our knowledge of world prehistory today was gathered by hundreds of archaeologists working in all parts of the world, on small problems or larger ones, on a regional survey or a ten-year excavation at one settlement. And of course, some prehistorians are experts on soil analysis, ancient animal bones, computer applications and statistical methods in archaeology, or simply excavation itself.

Classical archaeologists study the remains of the great Classical civilizations of Greece and Rome (Figure 1.6). Many of them work closely with historians, amplifying documentary records and filling in details of architectural and art history. Traditionally, Classical archaeologists have given much attention to art objects and buildings, but some are now

Figure 1.6 The Parthenon in Athens. Most Classical archaeologists give much attention to art history and architecture.

beginning to study the types of economic, settlement, and social problems, of interest to prehistoric archaeologists, that are discussed in this book (Snodgrass, 1987; Soren and James, 1988).

Egyptologists and Assyriologists are among the many specialist archaeologists who work on specific civilizations or time periods. These specialties require unusual skills. Egyptologists must acquire a fluent knowledge of hieroglyphs to help them study the ancient Egyptians, and Assyriologists, experts on the Assyrians of ancient Iraq, must be conversant with cuneiform script.

Historical archaeologists study archaeological sites in written records. They examine Medieval cities, such as Winchester and York in England; they excavate Colonial American settlements (Figure 1.7), Spanish missions, and nineteenth-century forts in the West; and they study a range of interesting historical artifacts, from bottles to uniform buttons (Deetz, 1977; Noël Hume, 1969, 1982; South, 1977).

Both historical and archaeological data are such that gaps always remain in the reconstruction of the past. Even on sites where historical records are exceptionally complete, though, archaeology can provide valuable information to amplify them (Schuyler, 1978). For example, archaeologists have worked closely with historians from the University of Mary-

Figure 1.7 Foundations for the Public Hospital for the Insane at Colonial Williamsburg in Virginia, which were revealed by archaeological excavation in 1972.

land on a citywide exploration of the Historic District of Annapolis (Leone and Potter, 1984). The excavations investigated a tavern, eighteenth-century residences, and many other sites, including a lot now occupied by a modern hotel. This property was first occupied about 1690; bottles, cups, and plates dating to that decade have come from the site. The archaeologists revealed intricate layers of occupation, including a timber house of the early 1700s. Governor Calvert's brick house, whose first floor now forms part of the modern hotel, was subsequently built on the same site in the 1720s. Most of this structure was drastically rebuilt in the nineteenth century, but the walls were preserved within the Victorian building. The excavations also revealed a brick heating system for channeling hot air to a greenhouse. This was partly torn up in the 1760s and filled with domestic refuse before being covered over by an addition to the 1720 house. The refuse proved a rich treasure trove for the archaeologist; it included bones, pins, buttons, hair, pieces of paper, cloth, and fish scales. The Calvert House site is unusual in that archaeologists were able to recover complete layers of Annapolis history virtually intact.

European cities like Winchester and York offer magnificent opportunities to combine historical records such as title deeds with excavations, making it possible to identify the owners of individual Medieval houses (Selkirk and Selkirk, 1970; Keene, 1985). One of the most vivid discoveries in historical archaeology comes from the fortress of Masada in Israel. The first-century historian Josephus Flavius describes how the Romans besieged a group of Jewish patriots in the fortress in A.D. 73. The defenders chose to commit mass suicide rather than surrender. Excavations in the mid-1960s revealed minute details in the daily lives of the besieged and their heroic deaths. Thus archaeology and history combined painted a vivid and surprisingly complete picture of the siege.

Historical archaeology comes into its own in studies of the past five thousand years, for which abundant documentary records are available. But historical records can also be important in telling us about societies that had limited written records. The Classic Maya civilization, which flourished in Mesoamerica between about A.D. 200 and 900, had developed a complex writing system. With it the Maya could record religious, political, and astronomical events with elaborate glyphs sculpted on stone and wood and set down in large books. Although still only partly deciphered, these records are beginning to provide a valuable new perspective on a civilization hitherto known almost entirely from archaeological investigations (Hammond, 1982; Schele and Miller, 1986).

Underwater archaeologists study sites and ancient shipwrecks on the sea floor and lake bottoms, even under rapids in Minnesota streams (Bass, 1988). Scuba-diving archaeologists now have an array of specialist techniques for recording and excavating these underwater sites. There is a tendency to think of underwater archaeology as something different, but in fact it is not. The objectives of such archaeology remain the same—to reconstruct and interpret ancient cultures. The fact that the data for doing so are underwater is almost irrelevant (Bass, 1986; Gould, 1983). Some modern underwater excavations, such as the excavations at Fort Royal in Jamaica and the reconstruction of the Kyrenia Ship from northern Cyprus, are superb examples of scientific archaeology.

Biblical archaeologists study the archaeology of the Old and New Testaments, linking the historical accounts in the Bible with archaeological sites in the Near East. This complex specialization requires a detailed knowledge not only of history and several languages, but of archaeology as well.

Industrial archaeologists study buildings and other structures dating to the Industrial Revolution or later, such as Victorian railway stations, old cotton plantations, windmills, and even slum housing in England (Hudson, 1982; Clark, 1987). Anyone entering this field needs at least some training as an architectural historian.

Ethnoarchaeologists study living societies as a way of better understanding and interpreting the past. They examine the dynamics of modern hunter-gatherer, horticultural, and peasant societies and collect empirical data on the present that can be used to interpret the archaeological record. Ethnoarchaeologists examine such phenomena as recently abandoned campsites and the hunter-gatherer's ways of acquiring food at different seasons. This type of "middle-range" research is gaining importance in archaeology (Chapter 14).

These are but a few of the specialties in archaeology. The modern science is so complex as to have experts in dozens of aspects of the subject, from mouse bones to soil profiles to techniques in ancient metallurgy. All are unified by their common interest in studying humanity in the past.

GOALS OF ARCHAEOLOGY

Whether they concentrate on the most ancient human societies or those of more recent centuries, most archaeologists agree that their research has four broad goals:

Studying sites and their contents in a context of time and space, to reconstruct descriptions of long sequences of human culture. This descriptive activity reconstructs cultural history.

Reconstructing past lifeways.

Studying cultural process (Trigger, 1978), explaining *why* culture change takes place.

Understanding sites, artifacts, food remains, and other aspects of the archaeological record as they relate to our contemporary world.

By no means would every scholar agree that all four of these objectives are equally valid or indeed that they should coexist. In practice, however, each objective usually complements the others, especially when archaeologists design their research to answer specific questions, rather than merely digging as a precursor to describing rows of excavated objects.

Culture History

The expression *culture history* means, quite simply, the description of human cultures as they extend backward thousands of years into the past. An archaeologist working on the culture history of an area describes the prehistoric cultures of that region. Culture history is derived from the study of sites and the artifacts and structures in them in a temporal and spatial context. By investigating groups of prehistoric sites and the many artifacts in them, it is possible to erect local and regional *sequences* of human cultures that extend over centuries, even millennia (see Chapters 11 and 17). Most of the activity is descriptive, accumulating minute chronological and spatial frameworks of archaeological data as a basis for observing how particular cultures evolved and changed through prehistoric times. Culture history is reconstructed by building up local sequences of archaeological sites into regional and even larger frameworks of changing human cultures. It is an essential preliminary to any work on lifeways or cultural process (see Chapter 18).

Many archaeologists who work on culture history feel inhibited by poor preservation of artifacts and sites about making inferences on the more intangible aspects of human prehistory, such as religion and social organization. They argue that archaeologists can legitimately deal only with the material remains of ancient human behavior. Unfortunately, this rather narrow view of culture history has sent many people off in unprofitable directions, into a long and painstaking preoccupation with artifact types and local chronologies that turned much of archaeology into a glorified type of classification.

Past Lifeways

The study of past lifeways—the ways in which people have made their livings in the past—has developed into a major goal since the 1930s. This new purpose for archaeology became evident as people realized that the prehistory of humankind was played out against a complicated background of changing environments. Every human culture was, they realized, a complex and constantly changing adaptation to specific environmental conditions.

Prehistoric lifeways were first studied in their environmental contexts by Grahame Clark at Star Carr and other sites in Europe (Chapter 3) and by Julian Steward and others in the United States (Clark, 1954; Steward, 1955; Steward and Setzler, 1977). These scholars realized that artifacts and structures without environmental context give a one-sided view of humanity and its adaptations to the environment. They began to concentrate on reconstructing ancient subsistence patterns from animal bones, carbonized seeds, and other food residues recovered in meticulous excavation. They called for assistance by pollen analysts, soil scientists, and botanists so that they could look at archaeological sites in a much wider, multidisciplinary context. The context of such studies was still descriptive archaeology, preoccupied with space and time, but the emphasis was different: the contexts supplied by space and time related to changing patterns of human settlement, subsistence strategies, and ancient environments.

Robert Braidwood took with him a team of scientists from other disciplines when he started work on the early history of agriculture in the Zagros Mountains of the Near East (Figure 1.8). He recovered evidence of domesticated animals as early as 6000 B.C. and based a new theory for the origins of food production on more precise environmental data than ever before (Braidwood and Braidwood, 1983). Richard MacNeish worked closely with botanists as he traced the early history of maize in the Tehuacán Valley in Mexico (MacNeish, 1970). Conditions there were so dry that he was able to show how settlements of the Tehuacán people had slowly changed as they relied more heavily on maize cultivation after 5000 B.C. As long ago as 1948, Gordon Willey surveyed in detail the coastal Virú Valley in Peru, where he plotted the distributions of hundreds of prehistoric sites from different chronological periods against the valley's changing environment (Willey, 1953). This was a pioneer attempt at recon

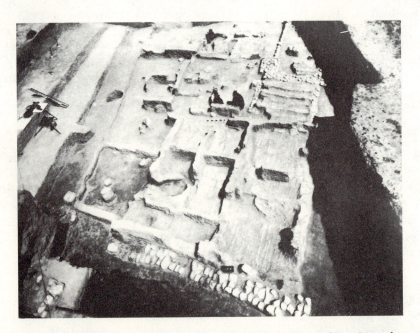

Figure 1.8 Robert Braidwood's excavation at the village of Jarmo in the Zagros Mountains of the Near East was among the first team investigations to study early agriculture.

structing prehistoric patterns of settlement, obviously a key part in any attempts to reconstruct prehistoric lifeways.

Such factors as population density and carrying capacity of agricultural land are clearly required to understand ancient lifeways. The intent in this goal of archaeology is still, however, descriptive, within a theoretical framework that saw human cultures as complicated, ever-changing systems. These systems interacted not only with others but with the natural environment as well.

Cultural Process

A third archaeological goal in the past twenty-five years not only describes the past but also explains culture change in prehistory. Archaeologists with this goal attempt to explain cultural change, process, and evolution in prehistory, topics that we explore more fully in Chapter 18 (definitions are in the Glossary). The ultimate goal of these prehistoric archaeologists is to explain why human cultures in all parts of the world reached their various stages of cultural evolution. Human tools are seen as part of a system of related phenomena that include both culture and the natural environment. Prehistoric archaeology, they argue, is a science in which research methods must be much more rigorous than hitherto. Archaeologists should design their research work within a framework of testable propositions that may be supported, modified, or rejected when they review all the excavated and analyzed archaeological data.

This approach to archaeology, once called the "new archaeology," is primarily meant to find out the "ways in which human populations (in their own way) do the things other systems do" (Binford, 1968). The many archaeologists of this persuasion believe that the past is inherently knowable, provided that rigorous research methods and designs are used and that field methods are impeccable. They feel strongly that archaeology is more than a descriptive science and that archaeologists can explain cultural change in the past (Binford, 1983a; Meltzer and others, 1986).

This activity is often called "processual archaeology," a label that emphasizes its concentration on cultural process and explanation of the past.

Understanding the Archaeological Record

"The archaeological record is here with us in the present," writes Lewis Binford (1983a). He emphasizes how much a part of the contemporary world the artifacts and sites that make up the remains of our past are. Our observations about the past are made today, in the 1990s, for we are describing sites and artifacts as they come from the soil today, centuries, often millennia after they were abandoned. In this way the archaeologist differs from the historian, who reads a document written in, say, 1492, which conveys information written by a contemporary observer that has not changed since that year. The archaeological record is made up of material things and arrangements of material objects in the soil. The only way we can *understand* this record is by knowing something about how the individual finds came into being. Binford likens archaeological data to a kind of untranslated language that has to be decoded if we are to make statements about human behavior in the past. "The challenge that archaeology offers, then, is to take contemporary observations of static material things and, quite literally, translate them into statements about the dynamics of past ways of life and about the conditions in the past which brought into being the things that have survived for us to see," writes Binford (1983a). Archaeologists must be deeply aware of phenomena in the contemporary world if they are to make inferences about the past. They cannot study it directly but must consider it with reference to the present. For this reason, controlled experiments, observations of contemporary hunter-gatherers and horticulturalists, and the formulation that Binford and others call "middle-range theory" are vital to archaeologists (Chapter 14).

Differing Goals: New and Old World Archaeologists

Not only do disagreements about goals divide archaeologists as a whole, but American scholars have a viewpoint different from that of many Old World prehistorians as well. In the United States, archaeologists have long considered their discipline as part of anthropology. European archaeologists, by contrast, lean toward defining archaeology as part of history. In the Old World, the arts of excavation have been highly developed by a historical tradition that began with A. H. L. Fox Pitt-Rivers and continued with Sir Mortimer Wheeler and many post–World War II archaeologists. Both British and Continental prehistorians have greatly emphasized recovery of data from the ground, tracing settlement patterns and structures, reconstructing economics, and analyzing in detail artifact types and complicated typologies. Many European archaeologists have acquired international reputations for their skill as excavators or museum people. The archaeologist is seen as an artisan with diverse skills, not the least of which is effective reconstruction of the past, both to amplify the written record and to create a historical story, albeit incomplete, for periods when no archives record the deeds of chiefs or the attitudes of individuals.

One reason for the difference in approach may be that European archaeologists think of prehistory as their own history, whereas prehistorians in the Americas are conscious that they are studying prehistoric peoples from a background completely different from their own, a non-Western tradition.

But for all the differences in approaches and goals, every archaeologist, of whatever viewpoint, would agree that we cannot hope to carry out archaeological research without a body of sound theory, good descriptive archaeology, and detailed information from both the contemporary world and prehistoric lifeways. Above all, the present and the phenomena of the world we live in are there to help us achieve better understanding of the major issues in archaeology:

- What were our earliest ancestors like, and when did they come into being? How old is "human" behavior, and when did such phenomena as language evolve? What distinguishes our behavior from that of other animals?
- How and when did humanity people the globe?
- What were the conditions and when and how did human beings begin to abandon the hunter-gatherer lifeway and domesticate animals and plants, becoming sedentary farmers?
- What brought about civilization, and what caused complex societies to evolve—the urban societies from which, ultimately, our own industrial civilization grew?
- Last, a long-neglected question: how did the expansion of Western civilization affect the hunter-gatherer, agricultural, and even urban states of the world that it encountered after Classical times? As more and more of the world's hunter-gatherer and peasant societies are assimilated into the fringes of our industrialized economy, archaeology is becoming the primary way of studying the tragic, closing centuries of prehistory between A.D. 1400 and our own era.

In the Beginning is not meant to describe these major developments in world prehistory. Rather, I summarize the multitude of methods and theoretical approaches that archaeologists have used to gain a better understanding of our long past.

SUMMARY

- Modern archaeology is the scientific study of past cultures and technologies—whether ancient or recent—by scientific methods and theoretical concepts devised for that purpose.
- Archaeology covers the human past, from the earliest peoples up to modern times.
- Archaeology had its origins in treasure hunting, Renaissance classicism, and grave robbing, but it has evolved into a highly precise discipline. It has become an integral part of twentieth-century life as a component of popular culture and modern intellectual curiosity.
- Archaeology provides the only viable means of discovering the history of many of the world's societies whose documented past began in recent times. As such, it is a vital support for nationalist feeling and for fostering cultural identity.
- Archaeologists have major contributions to make to the resolution of modern land disputes and to modern management of resources.
- The destruction of sites, fostered by greedy collectors and industrial development, is the crisis that archaeology is faced with today. Archaeological sites are a finite resource that can never be replaced. If the present rate of destruction continues, the danger is real that

few undisturbed archaeological sites will remain by the end of this century.

- Archaeologists also face a challenge from people who promote "pseudo-archaeologies" purporting to explain the past, such as extravagant theories that ancient Egyptians or Phoenicians landed in the New World thousands of years before Columbus.
- Archaeology is part of the science of anthropology, which is the study of humanity in the widest possible sense. Archaeologists use a battery of special methods and techniques to examine human societies of the past.
- There are many types of archaeologists. Prehistoric archaeologists study prehistory, that is, human history before written records; historical archaeologists use archaeology to supplement documentary history; and Classical archaeologists study ancient Greece and Rome.
- Modern archaeology has three basic goals: studying culture history, reconstructing past lifeways, and explaining cultural process.
- In contrast to American archaeologists, many Old World scholars think of archaeology as extending documentary history into the remote past.

GUIDE TO FURTHER READING

These books may be helpful as general reading about archaeology today, but I advise you to consult a specialist before starting in on them:

Binford, Lewis R. *In Pursuit of the Past.* New York: Thames and Hudson, 1983. A closely argued essay on archaeology that integrates ethnoarchaeology with the archaeological record. Recommended for more advanced readers.

Ceram, C. W. *Gods, Graves, and Scholars.* New York: Knopf, 1953. A classic account of early archaeologists; a wonderful introduction to the heroic days of archaeology.

Deetz, James. *In Small Things Forgotten.* Garden City, N.Y.: Anchor/Doubleday, 1977. An admirable essay on historical archaeology for beginners.

Fagan, Brian M. *Archaeology: A Brief Introduction,* 4th ed. New York: Harper-Collins, 1991. A short primer on the fundamentals of archaeology.

Meltzer, David J., Don D. Fowler, and Jeremy A. Sabloff, eds. *American Archaeology Past and Future.* Washington, D.C.: Smithsonian Institution Press, 1986. A series of essays on American archaeology that range over many of the topics in this chapter.

Sharer, Robert J., and Wendy Ashmore. *Discovering Our Past.* Palo Alto, Calif.: Mayfield, 1988. A short introduction to methods and theory in archaeology.

PART
Two

A SHORT HISTORY OF ARCHAEOLOGY
Sixth Century B.C. Through 1990

The Four Stages of Public Opinion

I (Just after publication)
  The Novelty is absurd and subversive of Religion & Morality.
  The propounder both fool & knave.

II (Twenty years later)
  The Novelty is absolute Truth and will yield a full & satisfactory
  explanation of things in general—The propounder man of
  sublime genius & perfect virtue.

III (Forty years later)
  The Novelty won't explain things in general after all and
  therefore is a wretched failure. The propounder a very ordinary
  person advertised by a clique.

IV (A century later)
  The Novelty a mixture of truth & error. Explains as much as
  could reasonably be expected. The propounder worthy of all
  honour in spite of his share of human frailties, as one who has
  added to the permanent possessions of science.

Thomas Huxley
Notes, 1873

*N*o one can fully understand modern scientific archaeology without having some notion of its roots. The first archaeologists were little more than philosophers and antiquarians who were searching for curiosities, buried treasure, and intellectual enlightenment. These treasure hunters were the predecessors of the early professionals, scholars who concentrated on site description and believed that human society evolved through simple stages, the final stage being modern civilizations. Since World War II, archaeology has undergone a major transformation, from a basically descriptive discipline into a many-sided activity that is greatly absorbed in trying to understand how human cultures changed and evolved in the past. If there is one major lesson to be learned from the history of archaeology, it is that no development in the field took place in isolation. All innovations in archaeology are the result of steady advances in the quality of scientific research.

Chapter
2

The Beginnings of Scientific Archaeology

Sixth Century B.C. to the 1950s

*T*his chapter examines the early development of archaeology from its beginnings in the philosophical speculations of the Greeks to the development of radiocarbon dating and theories of cultural ecology in the 1950s. We begin with the early philosophers and excavators, then see how a close relationship between the new disciplines of anthropology and archaeology in the late nineteenth century led to evolutionary approaches to the interpretation of the past. The first half of the twentieth century saw tremendous strides in archaeology, but a preoccupation with classification, description, and chronology gave a somewhat narrow view of prehistory. New approaches after World War II took into account environmental change and the relationships between human cultures and ecological processes. These innovations led archaeology in new directions, away from simple descriptions toward multilinear evolutionary frameworks for prehistoric times.

BEGINNINGS

People have speculated about human origins and the remote past for thousands of years. As early as the eighth century B.C., the Greek philosopher Hesiod wrote about a glorious, heroic past of kings and warriors. He described five great ages of history, the earliest one of Gold, when people "dwelt in ease." The last was an Age of War, when everyone worked hard and suffered great sorrow (Daniel, 1981). Speculations of this type were widespread in Classical and early Chinese writings.

The centuries of the Renaissance saw a quickened intellectual curiosity not only about humanity but about the Classical world as well. People of wealth and leisure began to travel in Greece and Italy, studying antiquities and collecting examples of Classical art. Soon collecting became a major passion of the wealthy and powerful and the study of Greek and Roman art a major scholarly preoccupation. A new era in Classical archaeology began with the first archaeological excavations into the depths of the famed Roman city of Herculaneum in 1783 (Ceram, 1953; Fagan, 1985). The Herculaneum excavations revealed incredibly full details of one of several Roman towns buried by ash from an eruption of Vesuvius in A.D. 79. They transported archaeology and its practitioners into spectacular artistic realms. At Pompeii, the choking ash preserved the bodies of people fleeing the eruption in panic (Figure 2.1).

Wealthy collectors made a beeline for Mediterranean lands, while their less wealthy colleagues stayed at home and speculated about ancient European history, and about the builders of burial mounds, fortifications, and occasionally more spectacular monuments such as Stonehenge in southern England (Figure 2.2). How old were the builders of such structures? Had they resembled the American Indians, South Sea islanders, and

Figure 2.1 Body of a beggar smothered by volcanic ash outside the Nucerian Gate at Pompeii.

Figure 2.2 Stonehenge, the Bronze Age ceremonial center in southern England that was an early focus of antiquarian interest. This picture was taken before restoration of the stones in 1958.

other living nonliterate peoples (Figure 2.3)? There was only one way to find out—excavate ancient sites.

These eighteenth-century excavations yielded a mass of stone and bronze axes, strange clay pots, gold ornaments, and skeletons buried with elaborate objects. This jumble was confusing. Some graves contained gold and bronze, others held only stone implements, and still others housed cremated remains in large urns. Many questions were unanswered. Which burials were earliest? Who had deposited the bodies, and how long ago? No one yet had a way of putting in order the thousands of years of prehistoric times that preceded the Greeks, Romans, and ancient Egyptians of biblical fame (Daniel, 1981). Prehistory was little more than a confusing grab bag of exotic objects.

SCRIPTURES AND FOSSILS

One reason that early archaeologists were confused was that they had no idea how long people had been living on earth. They had no means of dating the finds from their crude excavations. At the same time, most people believed that Genesis, chapter 1, told the true story of the Creation. God had created the world and its inhabitants in six days. The story of Adam and Eve provided an entirely consistent explanation for the creation of humankind and the peopling of the globe. In the seventeenth century, Archbishop James Ussher used the genealogies in the Old Testament to calculate that the world was created on the night preceding October 23, 4004 B.C. (Grayson, 1983). Ussher's widely ac-

Figure 2.3 An Australian aborigine with his lightweight tool kit. (Nineteenth-century engraving)

cepted chronology allowed approximately six thousand years for all of human history. It became theological dogma, a chronological yardstick for all of prehistory.

At the time when antiquarians were digging into European burial mounds, Captain James Cook and other Western navigators were exploring the Americas and the Pacific, bringing back new information about all manner of primitive societies flourishing at various levels of cultural development, none of them as advanced as eighteenth-century Europe. A few scholars began to put prehistory in a new perspective, in terms of human progress over time, from the simple to the more complex. But could all this progress have occurred within a mere six thousand years?

At the same time, new archaeological discoveries were casting doubt on biblical chronologies. The bones of tropical animals such as the elephant and the hippopotamus began to be found in the gravels of European rivers. Soon the same types of bone were turning up in the same strata as carefully chipped stone axes of obvious human manufacture (Figure 2.4). Few scientists claimed that these finds were more than six

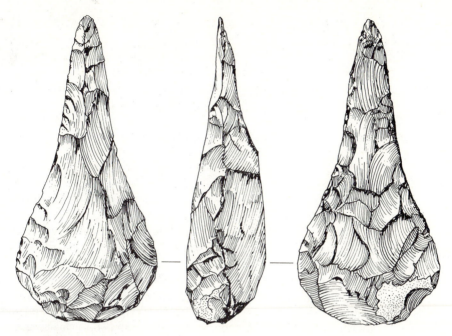

Figure 2.4 A stone hand axe of the type found by John Frere at Hoxne, England, in 1797.

thousand years old. Even the most eminent scholars believed that humanity had inhabited the world for six thousand glorious years, a beautiful world that "teemed with delighted existence." Until the 1860s, the shackles of theological dogma confined human existence within a few millennia.

THE ANTIQUITY OF HUMANKIND

The eighteenth century saw an awakening of interest in archaeology, geology, and the natural sciences. A knowledge explosion in science coincided with the Industrial Revolution. Geologists were in the forefront, their field studies stimulated by deep cuts into the earth resulting from vast engineering projects such as railroad and canal building. William "Strata" Smith (1769–1839) was one of many field observers who studied these exposures, identifying geological strata and fossil animal types that appeared and disappeared at the same time everywhere on earth. Smith emphasized that the rocks of the earth had been formed by continuous natural geological processes. Every gale that battered the coast, every flash flood or sandstorm, and every earthquake movement was among the natural phenomena that had gradually shaped the earth into its modern form. Thus, as James Hutton (1726–1797) argued in his *Theory of the Earth,* the earth was formed by entirely natural processes, not by divine intervention or catastrophic floods that earlier scientists had considered the nemesis of such animals as the dinosaurs.

Hutton's and Smith's theories of what became known as "uniformitarianism," caused a furor, for they attacked the very essence of the Ussherian chronology with their arguments that the earth was formed by long-term natural processes and not by divine intervention. If one accepted the new theories, one accepted the notion that humankind had lived on earth for many thousands of years. The debate over the antiquity of humankind culminated in 1859 with two major scientific developments—the publication of Darwin's theory of evolution and natural selection and the verification of the contemporaneity of humans and extinct animals.

Charles Darwin began to formulate his theories as a result of a five-year scientific voyage around the world aboard H.M.S. *Beagle* in 1831–1836. Back in England, Darwin delved more deeply into what he called the "species question." He realized that his theory would imply that accumulated favorable variations in living organisms over long periods must result in the emergence of new species and the extinction of old ones. Darwin was a timid man, and he procrastinated in publishing his results. Evolution, even more than uniformitarianism, flew right in the face of the sacrosanct interpretation of the account of the Creation in Genesis. He sat on his ideas for twenty years until another biologist, Alfred Wallace, sent him an essay that reached much the same conclusions. Reluctantly, Darwin penned a "preliminary sketch," as he called it, in 1859—*On the Origin of Species.*

This scientific classic described evolution and natural selection, giving a theoretical explanation for the diversity of both living and fossil forms. Evolution by natural selection does not, of course, entirely explain biological phenomena, but natural selection does provide a direct way of accounting for biological change as time passed. Predictably, Darwin's theories caused a furor, horrifying many people by assuming that human beings were descended from apelike ancestors (Figure 2.5). But they were soon widely accepted by the scientific community and formed a theoretical background for some important contemporary archaeological discoveries.

Discoveries of human artifacts in association with extinct animals were nothing new by 1859, for many such finds had been reported over the years, mostly at the hands of enthusiastic amateur diggers. One of the most persistent was French customs officer Jacques Boucher de Perthes, who collected stone tools and animal bones from sealed gravels of the Somme River near Abbeville, in northern France, between 1837 and the 1860s. The pompous and sometimes eccentric Boucher de Perthes was ridiculed by the scientific establishment when he claimed that the makers of his axes had lived before the biblical flood. But he persisted, and his collections had

Mr. Bergh to the Rescue
The Defrauded Gorilla. "That *Man* wants to claim my Pedigree. He says he is one of my descendants."
Mr. Bergh. "Now, Mr. Darwin, how could you insult him so?"

Figure 2.5 A period cartoon by Thomas Nast lampooning Darwin's linking apes with human beings.

reached an impressive size by 1859. Rumors of his finds reached the ears of antiquarian John Evans and geologist Joseph Prestwich. They visited de Perthes and examined his collections and sites. In one place John Evans actually removed a hand axe from the same sealed level as a hippopotamus bone. The two visitors were convinced that Boucher de Perthes's many finds were proof of long antiquity for humankind, something that the new theories of uniformitarianism and evolution made intellectually possible. As John Evans said: "This much appears established beyond doubt, that in a period of antiquity remote beyond any of which we have hitherto found traces, this portion of the globe was peopled by man." Rapid scientific acceptance of the long antiquity of humankind followed rapidly, an established antiquity that is one of the intellectual and practical foundations of all scientific archaeology (Grayson, 1983).

If the Somme hand axes and other such finds were of great antiquity, who were the people who had manufactured and used them? Were they modern-looking humans or apelike beings that were closer to apes than people? Part of what was soon to become an intricate fossil jigsaw came to light in a cave near Düsseldorf in Germany's Neanderthal ("Neander Valley") region in 1856 when quarry workers unearthed a primitive-looking human skull (Figure 2.6). It had a huge, beetling brow ridge and a squat skull cap that were quite unlike the smooth, rounded cranium of modern *Homo sapiens* (Huxley, 1863). Scientists were of two opinions.

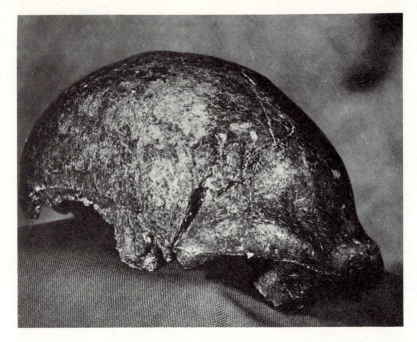

Figure 2.6 The Neanderthal cranium from western Germany, found in 1856.

Many dismissed the Neanderthal skull as that of a modern pathological idiot. But a minority, among them the celebrated English biologist Thomas Huxley, believed that the skull was from a primitive human being, perhaps one of those who had made early stone tools. Huxley himself not only championed the theories of evolution but also expressed what has become one of the fundamental questions archaeologists confront to this day: "the ascertainment of the place which man occupies in nature and of his relations to the universe of things" (Huxley, 1863). At the time Huxley wrote these words, scientists were finally realizing that the past before written records was knowable and that humanity had evolved both biologically and culturally over a very long period of time indeed. (For a treatment of archaeology, evolution, and biblical theories of creation, see Spuhler, 1985).

HUMAN PROGRESS: EVOLUTIONISM

As we have seen, human progress was no new idea. Popular in the eighteenth century, it declined in favor during the Napoleonic wars, when civilization seemed, philosophically, to have come apart. But the spectacular social and economic changes generated by the Industrial Revolution in the nineteenth century renewed interest in progress. In 1850 the sociologist Herbert Spencer (1820–1903) was already declaring that "progress is not an accident, but a necessity. It is a fact of nature" (Spencer, 1855). Darwin's theories of evolution seemed to many people a logical extension of the doctrines of social progress. The new theories opened up enormous tracts of prehistoric time for Victorian archaeologists to fill. The oldest finds were Boucher de Perthes's crude axes from the Somme Valley. Later in prehistory, apparently, other people started to live in the great caves of southwestern France, at a time when reindeer, not hippopotamuses, were living in western Europe. And the famous "lake dwellings," abandoned prehistoric villages found below the water's edge in the Swiss lakes during the dry years 1853 and 1854, were obviously even more recent than the cave sites of France (Daniel, 1981). What was the best theoretical framework for all these finds? Could notions of human progress agree with the actual archaeological discoveries? Did prehistoric peoples' technology, material culture, and society develop and progress uniformly from the crude tools of the Somme Valley to the sophisticated iron technology of the much more recent La Tène culture in Europe? Had cultures evolved naturally along with the biological evolution that lifted humanity through all the stages from savagery to civilization?

Many archaeologists began to treat prehistoric peoples as geological artifacts. Intoxicated by thousands of stone tools and archaeological sites of unbelievable richness, they gaily cataloged their finds into a long series of epochs, like geological eras, stages through which every human society would ultimately pass. It was a logical step, they thought. The universal progress of humanity enjoyed the status that one French archaeologist called a "Great Law" (de Mortillet, 1867; Sackett, 1981). But as archaeological research extended beyond Europe and into the New World, the incredible diversity in early human experience became visible in the archaeological record. The great civilizations of the Near East were recovered by Henry Layard and others, and the great Mesoamerican religious complexes were described anew (Layard, 1849; Stephens, 1841). Upper Paleolithic art was accepted as authentic some years after the Altamira paintings were discovered in northern Spain in 1879 (Figure 2.7) (Cartailhac, 1901). Yet many parts of North America and Africa showed no signs of higher civilizations. Furthermore, the New World civilizations and European cave art seemed to imply that humanity sometimes "regressed." The great religious centers of Mesoamerica had been abandoned, for instance, and art equal to that from the French caves did not reappear there for many thousands of years. Scientists became less and less certain that people had a common, consistently progressing universal prehistory. Obviously, humankind had progressed considerably overall since the remote millennia of its simple origins, and life had improved for humanity—for the Victorians, at any rate.

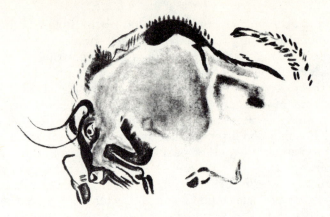

Figure 2.7 Bison in a polychrome cave painting in Altamira, Spain. The Altamira style is the ultimate artistic
achievement of the Upper Paleolithic hunter-gatherers
of western Europe, about 12,000 B.C.

Edward B. Tylor (1832–1917)

Archaeologists were not the only people thinking about human progress
(Harris, 1968; Hatch, 1973). The early anthropologists, pioneers of a discipline that developed from a strong Victorian interest in human institutions, were evolutionists, too. E. B. Tylor, one of the fathers of anthropology in the English-speaking world, avidly believed in human progress
(Tylor, 1871). He surveyed human development in all its forms, from
crude stone axes of the Somme Valley in France to Maya temples to
Victorian civilization. The origins of civilized institutions, he argued,
might be found in the simpler institutions of ruder peoples. If the stone
axes made by Australian natives were like those found in ancient European river terraces, then perhaps marriage customs of the native Australi-
ans were similar to those among the Paleolithic inhabitants of Europe.
Most of his data came from two sources: accounts of contemporary primitive peoples and archaeological findings from the past. He arranged these
to reflect a three-level sequence of human development: from simple
hunting *savagery,* as he called it, through a stage of simple farming, which
he called *barbarism,* to *civilization,* the most complex of human conditions (Figure 2.8).

Lewis Henry Morgan (1818–1881)

American anthropologist Lewis Morgan went even further than Tylor. He
outlined no fewer than seven ethnic periods of human progress in his
famed book *Ancient Society* (1877). Like Tylor, however, Morgan's stages
began with simple savagery and had human society reaching its highest
achievements in a "state of civilization" (Willey and Sabloff, 1980). His

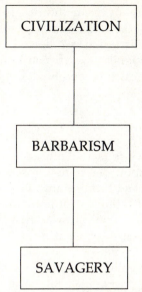

Figure 2.8 E. B. Tylor's sequence of human development.

seven stages, he said, had developed quite rationally and independently in different parts of the world.

The theories of Lewis Morgan strongly influenced Karl Marx and Friedrich Engels, communist social philosophers. They drew on his ideas of primitive communism—the notion that people shared available resources—and proceeded to say that this type of sharing was gradually eroded by the growing forces of industrial civilization (Harris, 1968). His work was also to influence modern North American archaeology, with its strong evolutionary bias.

Such notions of human progress were easy to defend in a world whose frontiers were still being explored. There was no such thing as a "world prehistory" in the 1870s, merely thousands of scattered archaeological finds, most of them from Europe, the Mediterranean, or North America. Nearly all were from thoroughly unscientific excavations that would make a modern archaeologist shudder. Even expert scientists turned to the comfortable framework of biological and social evolution to explain the astonishing human diversity.

UNILINEAR EVOLUTION AND DIFFUSIONISM

The spectacular discoveries of the late nineteenth century took place when anthropology was coming of age as one of the social sciences. British social anthropologist Sir James Frazer laid out the long-term objectives of anthropology in 1890. Anthropologists, he said, were assigned the task of discovering the general laws that regulated human history in the past and would continue to control human development in the future. They were to study "the origin, or rather the rudimentary phases, infancy, and childhood of human society" (Frazer, 1890). His remarks reflected growing professional rigor among students of humanity, which coincided with gradual refinement in methods of excavation and ways of classifying the past.

Unilinear Evolution

Anthropology formed from several diverse intellectual philosophies (Harris, 1968). These included biological evolution, the notion of social progress, and the idea of cultural evolution. A most important influence was the constant contact between Western civilization and other human societies with completely different social institutions. It was easy for anthropologists, corresponding as they did with missionaries and pioneer settlers from all over the world, to argue that Victorian civilization was the pinnacle of human achievement. The huge volume of anthropological and archaeological data they collected was used to build a universal scheme of *unilinear cultural evolution.* In other words, all human societies had the potential to evolve from a simple hunter-gatherer way of life to a state of literate civilization, but many of them had never made it.

Today unilinear evolution seems far too simple an explanation for evolving society. But one must remember that every generation of archaeologists looks at the world through its own perceptions of the social and political environment around it. The early archaeologists were no exception, assuming that their own civilization was the contemporary high point of human achievement. As more and more data accumulated from anthropological research and archaeological excavations all over the world, however, it became clear that a universal scheme of unilinear evolution was a totally unrealistic way of interpreting world history.

Diffusion and Diffusionists

As archaeological knowledge blossomed late in the nineteenth century—and in America, particularly, early in the twentieth—slowly the great human cultural diversity during prehistoric times was recognized. But scholars still faced many hard questions. What were the origins of human culture? When and where was metallurgy introduced? Who were the first farmers? If people did not develop according to universal evolutionary rules, how, then, *did* culture change and cultural diversity come about? Archaeologists began to expect that population movements, migrations, and invasions would explain prehistory.

The *diffusion* of ideas and objects from one people to another was recognized early as a valid explanation for cultural change in prehistory. It was especially popular with late nineteenth-century archaeologists, who reacted against the idea that cultures changed uniformly and also realized that culture change could be explained by outside influences. The newly discovered Near Eastern civilizations raised problems that might be explained by diffusion. What were the origins, for instance, of such peoples as the Mycenaeans, found by Heinrich Schliemann in the 1870s (Fagan, 1985)? Many archaeologists began to go along with diffusionist theories when they tried to explain why Near Eastern civilizations were so much richer than the apparently poor European cultures of the same period. Furthermore, they argued, how could the brilliant New World civilizations in Mexico and Peru have arisen if not by long-distance migration from the civilized centers in the Near East?

In its more extreme forms, diffusionism is the assumption that many major human inventions originated in one place and then diffused to other parts of the world by trade, migrating populations, cultural contact, or bold explorers. Simple diffusionist ideas were very popular late in the nineteenth and early in the twentieth centuries. They had the advantage of being easy to formulate and understand, and there was something romantic in the idea of vast migrations of adventurous people from one end of the world to the other. Early in the twentieth century, British anatomist Elliot Grafton Smith became obsessed with the techniques of Egyptian mummification, sun worship, and monumental stone architecture. The achievements of ancient Egyptian civilization were so unique, he argued in *The Ancient Egyptians,* published in 1911, that all of world civilization and much of modern Western culture diffused from the Nile Valley. It was the People of the Sun who had achieved all this, people who were not afraid of voyaging all over the globe in search of gold, shells, and precious stones. Everywhere they went, they took their archaic civilization with them. Thus the practice of sun worship and the techniques of irrigation, agriculture, metallurgy, and stone architecture—among many others—spread over the world.

Smith's diffusionist views of human history were much oversimplified and at least as inadequate as unilinear cultural evolution. Slowly, the first professional archaeologists of the twentieth century realized that they were dealing with very complex problems. Fortunately, they set aside attempts to write universal histories and concentrated on collecting basic data from archaeological sites.

Diffusionist theories have remained popular, albeit in a modified form. In their most extreme manifestations, they still reach incredible heights of absurdity, as in seeking to prove that black Africans colonized America before Columbus or that the Vikings settled Minnesota thousands of years ago.

DESCRIPTIVE ARCHAEOLOGY

The first professional archaeologists and anthropologists lived when the traditional cultures of non-Western societies were being erased by modern technological civilization. They felt their overwhelming priority to be collecting basic information about vanishing cultures. These data were an essential preliminary to the elaborate theoretical approaches used in archaeology today (Stocking, 1968; Fagan, 1984b).

Franz Boas (1858–1942)

American anthropologist Franz Boas was among those who insisted on far more detailed field research (Hatch, 1973). He and his students helped establish anthropology—and by implication, archaeology along with it—as a form of science, by applying more precise methods to collecting and classifying data. They collected an incredible quantity of data on pot designs, basketry, and thousands of other cultural details. Artifacts and customs were meticulously studied and used as the basis for explanations of the past.

American ethnographers in the 1920s collected enormous inventories of cultural traits, such as types of moccasins and designs of bows and arrows. These collections led to some quite false interpretations of American Indian culture, later disproved by archaeological research. Ethnologists of this period saw the European arrival, especially with domestic horses, as of unparalleled importance, causing the Great Plains to become filled with nomadic buffalo hunters and raiders of the type made familiar to us by Hollywood films. They described the Plains as having been sparsely populated up to that time because water was scarce and plows were not available to till the soil. They were partly right, for the Plains population did indeed swell rapidly as horses came into use. But subsequent work by such archaeologists as W. D. Strong, who dug at Signal Butte, Nebraska, revealed that the Great Plains had been inhabited by hunter-gatherers and horticulturalists for many hundreds of years before the Europeans and horses turned the Plains into a carnival of nomads (Strong, 1935). Archaeology, then, became a source of information against which one checked the historical reconstructions produced by ethnologists.

Vere Gordon Childe (1892–1957)

Perhaps the most brilliant of these archaeologists was an Oxford-trained Australian, Vere Gordon Childe. A gifted linguist, he acquired an encyclopedic knowledge of the thousands of prehistoric finds in museums from Edinburgh to Cairo. Once he had mastered the data, a task made easier by his language skills, Childe (1925) set out to describe European prehistory in outline. He meant to distill from archaeological remains "a preliterate substitute for the conventional politico-military history with cultures, instead of statesmen, as actors and migrations instead of battles" (Childe, 1958).

Gordon Childe classified cultures by the surviving culture traits—pots, implements, house forms, ornaments—known to be characteristic because they were constantly found together. Such cultures were the material expression of "peoples." Not supplying a chronological record for themselves, the cultures might have widespread or limited distribution in time and space. Cultural successions were reconstructed within limited geographic areas and compared with those from neighboring regions; the culture traits—presumed to have spread from one area to another—were carefully checked. This type of methodology spread in the 1930s and 1940s, when archaeology was still mainly a descriptive discipline. But Childe went further, for he was one of the few archaeologists who realized that cataloging artifacts was useless unless conducted with some frame of reference. He therefore used data from hundreds of sites and dozens of cultures to formulate a comprehensive viewpoint of Old World prehistory that became a classic. The origins of agriculture and domestication and of urban life were, he felt, two great revolutionary turning points in world history. He described two major stages, the Neolithic and urban revolutions. Each so-called revolution saw new and vital inventions that could be identified in the archaeological record by characteristic artifacts. The Neolithic and urban revolutions were really a technological and evolutionary model, combined with an economic one, so that the way people got their living was the criterion for comparing stages of world history. Childe dominated archaeological thinking in Europe until the late 1950s. But his ideas were less influential in the New World because Childe himself never studied or wrote about American archaeology (for an extended treatment, see McNairn, 1980; Trigger, 1980).

CULTURE HISTORY

Boas, Childe, and their disciples made collecting data a primary objective in both New and Old World archaeology. But archaeology itself evolved somewhat differently on each side of the Atlantic.

Old World Archaeology

The Europeans were studying their prehistoric origins, concentrating on constructing descriptive, historical schemes tracing European society from its hunter-gatherer origins up to the threshold of recorded history. The earliest sites were the Abbevillian and Acheulian hand axe sites in the Thames and Somme river valleys, followed by Lartet and Christy's cave dwellers in southwestern France that showed that the Neanderthalers were followed by modern humans with a much more sophisticated hunter-gatherer culture. A similar culture history sequence was postulated for all of Europe and the Near East as well. As Gordon Childe showed, the later prehistoric peoples of the Near East and temperate Europe were the logical ancestors of the Greeks, Romans, and other civilizations. It was no coincidence that Arnold Toynbee and other world historians adopted Childe's universal schemes when they made prehistoric times the first chapter in their great historical syntheses.

The New World: The Direct Historical Approach

New World archaeologists were in a very different position. Their most logical way to work was from the known, historical Indian cultures backward into prehistoric times (Fagan, 1990; Willey and Sabloff, 1980). This approach was pioneered in the 1880s by Cyrus Thomas of the Bureau of American Ethnology. He and fellow archaeologists from other institutions excavated dozens of earthworks in the Ohio Valley, using pottery and other small finds to demonstrate the continuity between prehistoric and modern Indian culture. The early Southwestern archaeologists adopted a similar approach in their 1890s research tracing modern Indian pottery styles centuries back into the past. This work culminated in the excavations at Pecos Pueblo carried out by Harvard archaeologist A. V. Kidder between 1915 and 1929 (Kidder, 1924). These excavations established a cultural sequence still used in modified form today. Later researchers, such as W. D. Strong, applied similar methods to Plains archaeology with great success (Strong, 1935).

This *direct historical approach*—working from known, historic sites to unknown, prehistoric settlements, preferably those of known peoples— has strict limitations, however. It works satisfactorily as long as one is dealing with the same cluster of finds, such as pottery forms. Once one excavates sites occupied by people with totally different cultures, however, continuity is lost, and the direct historical approach can no longer be used.

The Midwestern Taxonomic System

Franz Boas's influence was strong from the 1920s to the 1950s among archaeologists who concentrated on collecting and classifying enormous numbers of prehistoric finds from hundreds of sites all over the Americas. They began to arrange these in increasingly elaborate regional sequences of prehistoric cultures but ran into trouble because no two archaeologists could agree on how to classify the pottery and other objects. Thus no one could compare one area to another using common terminology. Fortunately, a group of scholars headed by W. C. McKern prepared definitions that soon became known as the "Midwestern taxonomic system" (McKern, 1939). This system was an attempt to unify sequences of prehistoric cultures all over the Midwest by finding similarities between collections of prehistoric artifacts. By correlating sequences of artifacts and hundreds of sites through long prehistoric periods, using seriation methods (Chapter 5), users of the system were able to compare cultural sequences throughout the Midwest and the eastern United States. The system was highly effective in linking cultural sequences but was limited as a means of interpreting the past, simply because it relied on artifacts and stratigraphic evidence, paying little attention to food remains and other lines of evidence about the past.

The Midwestern taxonomic system was put to wide use over much of the central and eastern United States, partly by extensive surveys undertaken as public works during the Great Depression of the 1930s. By the 1940s, James Ford, James Griffin, and Gordon Willey had begun to look farther afield than local regions. At their disposal was a mass of unpublished archaeological data from hundreds of sites excavated during the Depression (Ford and Willey, 1941; Griffin, 1946). Their studies in the eastern United States revealed steady development in prehistoric material culture over many thousands of years. They distinguished periods within which broad similarities in prehistoric culture could be found and designated those as developmental stages.

Just as the Midwestern taxonomic system was reaching the potential limits of its effectiveness, Gordon Willey and Philip Phillips extended earlier survey work in a landmark monograph that applied essentially the same techniques to the entire New World. Most important, they devised developmental stages for the whole continent (Willey and Phillips, 1958). These proposed stages were defined by technology, economic data, settlement patterns, art traditions, and social factors rather than by chronology, which, to their way of thinking, was a less important consideration.

Chronology and Time Scales

No question worried the archaeologists of the 1920s to the 1950s more than establishing an age for their sites and finds. Once they reached the limits of direct historical ties, they had no means of dating early American cultures. The first breakthrough came in the early years of this century, when University of Arizona astronomer A. E. Douglass started his now-famous studies of annual growth rings in southwestern trees (see Chapter 5). By 1929, Douglass had developed an accurate chronology for southwestern sites that was eventually extended back from modern times into the first century B.C. Unfortunately, however, tree-ring dating could be used only in the dry areas of the Southwest, where trees had a well-defined annual growth season. (It has now been applied with success to northern areas.)

Elsewhere, archaeological chronology was mostly done by intelligent guesswork until 1949, when University of Chicago scientists J. R. Arnold and W. F. Libby (1949) described the radiocarbon method for dating organic materials from archaeological sites (Libby, 1955). Within a few years, radiocarbon dates were processed from hundreds of sites all over the world. For the first time, a widely accepted chronological framework for New World prehistory superseded the guesswork of earlier years. Archaeologists could finally compare widely separated sites and cultures with an unbiased time scale. They could now deemphasize chronology and classification and concentrate, instead, on *why* American and Indian cultures had changed in the past. (Dating techniques are described in Chapter 6.)

CULTURAL ECOLOGY

After radiocarbon dating arrived, the new emphasis in archaeology was on interpretation, based on carefully studied regional sequences. One conclusion was obvious: human material culture and social organization had developed from the simple to the infinitely complex. From then on, many accounts of world prehistory or broad syntheses of large culture areas allowed for the general notion of progress in prehistory. Childe with his revolutions, Robert J. Braidwood in the Near East, and Gordon Willey in North America all attempted to look at culture history with the knowledge that human culture is constantly and dynamically related to its environment and to other factors that interact with it (Braidwood and Braidwood, 1983; Childe, 1942; Willey, 1966, 1971).

Julian Steward: Multilinear Evolution

At about this time, anthropologist Julian Steward started asking himself, Are there ways of identifying common cultural features in dozens of societies distributed over many cultural areas (Steward, 1955)? Disagreeing with the ardent evolutionists, who insisted that all societies passed through similar stages of cultural development, Steward assumed that certain basic culture types would develop in similar ways under similar conditions. Very few actual concrete features of culture, though, would appear among many human societies in a similar, regular order repeated again and again. In other words, cultural evolution was multilinear; that is, it had proceeded on many courses and at different rates, not just on one universal track, as Tylor and others had believed.

Before Steward, such people as Alfred Kroeber, Lewis Morgan, and Leslie White had long thought of culture as like a layered cake, with technology as the bottom layer, social organization the middle, and ideology the top (White, 1949). Steward not only added the environment to the cake but also looked to it for causes of cultural change. To do so, he developed a method for recognizing the ways in which such change is caused by adaptation to the environment.

Calling his study of environment and culture change *cultural ecology,* Steward began by making several points:

> Similar adaptations may be found in different cultures in similar environments.
>
> No culture has ever achieved an adaptation to its environment which has remained unchanged over any length of time.

> Differences and changes during periods of cultural development in any area
> can either add to societal complexity, or result in completely new cultural
> patterns. (Steward, 1955)

Steward used these principles as a basis for studying cultures and culture change in widely separated areas. To study different cultures, he would isolate and define distinguishing characteristics in each culture, a nucleus of traits he called the *cultural core*. He observed that African San, Australian aborigines, and Fuegian Indians were all organized in patrilineal (descent through the father) bands, forming a cultural type. Why? Because their ecological adaptation and social organization were similar. Although their environments differed greatly, from desert to cold and rainy plains, the practical requirements of the hunting and gathering lifeway grouped all these people in small bands, each with its own territory. In each area, the social structure and general organization of the bands were very similar, and their adaptation to their environment was fundamentally the same, despite many differences in detail. Steward used his cultural-core device to isolate and define distinguishing characteristics of the hunter-gatherer and of other specific culture types from all the miscellaneous data he had.

Steward spent much time studying the relationships between environment and culture that form the context and reasons for critical features of culture. Though a culture trait, be it a new type of house or a form of social organization, might be found at one location because it diffused there, that did not explain why the people accepted the trait in the first place. Steward applied cultural ecology to such questions and also to problems such as why the adjustment of human societies to different environments results in certain types of behavior. To diffusion and evolution he added a new concept: changing adaptations to the natural environment. In other words, the study of culture change involved studying human cultures and their changing environmental conditions as well.

A STUDY OF ARCHAEOLOGY

When Steward's work appeared, American archaeology was completely preoccupied with chronology and artifacts. Every issue of each archaeological journal was crowded with arid reports of pottery chronologies that seldom referred to their context or meaning as human implements. It was as if archaeologists were classifying insects or collecting postage stamps. Then, in 1948, archaeologist W. W. Taylor published his famed work *A Study of Archaeology,* a devastating critique of American archaeologists' preoccupation with chronology.

Taylor called for a "conjunctive approach" to archaeology, shifting emphasis from chronological sequences and distributions to detailed, multilevel studies of individual sites and their features, such as cultural layers, floors, or hearths. The conjunctive approach brought together all possible sources of evidence on a site—technology, style, ecological evidence, architecture, and information on social life—to focus on the people who lived at the site and on the changes in their culture.

Studying the people meant seeing their artifacts in context, as products of entire cultural systems, and reconstructing these systems as completely as possible, including even the less tangible parts, such as their social organization and religious institutions. This view contrasted with that of Childe and his contemporaries on the other side of the Atlantic, who preferred to limit their study to artifacts. Taylor tried to introduce into archaeology a view of culture envisaging the discipline as integral to anthropology. He felt that the disciplines should work together to arrive at general truths about human culture (Kluckhohn, 1940).

All this was a far cry from the simple evolutionary and diffusionist schemes of earlier decades. Julian Steward's and W. W. Taylor's research brought twentieth-century archaeology to the threshold of great theoretical change. They established, once and for all, the close relationship between archaeology and anthropology. *A Study of Archaeology* showed, with incisive clarity, that one of archaeology's primary goals must be to develop adequate explanations for human prehistory, an aim far more sophisticated than mere excavation, collection, and description.

SUMMARY

- Archaeology has its origins in the intellectual curiosity about the past felt by a number of Classical writers, such as Hesiod, who engaged in much speculation about the stages in early human history.
- With the Renaissance this curiosity about the past, which manifested itself in excavations at Herculaneum and elsewhere, was renewed. But speculations about early prehistory were shackled by the dogma of the Christian church.
- With greater knowledge of human biological and cultural diversity late in the eighteenth century, people began to speculate about the relationships among different groups and about the notion of human progress from simple to complex societies.
- Proof that humanity had existed for more than six thousand years was the discovery in the Somme Valley, France, and elsewhere, of the bones of extinct animals directly associated with tools made by human beings. These discoveries could not be placed in a scientific context, however, until both uniformitarian geology—the new science of paleontology—and the theory of evolution by natural selection were created.
- The notion of human social evolution followed that of biological evolution. Many archaeologists thought of prehistoric cultures as arranged in stratumlike layers of progress from the simple to the

complex. A simple form of unilinear evolution was espoused by such pioneer anthropologists as Sir Edward B. Tylor and Lewis Morgan, who portrayed humanity as having progressed from simple savagery to complex, literate civilization.

- Unilinear evolution was recognized by early twentieth-century archaeologists as far too simple a scheme to satisfactorily explain prehistory. Some scholars began to turn to diffusionist schemes, assuming that many cultural innovations had emanated from ancient Egypt and similar centers of higher civilization.
- These diffusionist explanations proved just as unsatisfactory. Influenced by Franz Boas and Vere Gordon Childe, archaeologists began to describe artifacts and sites much more precisely and preoccupied themselves with culture history and chronologies.
- American archaeologists extensively used the direct historical approach to prehistory, working back in time from known historical cultures to prehistoric societies. This system was first developed in the Southwest, most notably by A. V. Kidder. Standard taxonomic systems were also developed in the 1930s and were widely used. Radiocarbon dating arrived in the late 1940s, coinciding with greater interest in the natural environment and the study of human ecology. Anthropologist Leslie White devised a theory of multilinear evolution to explain the past, and his colleague Julian Steward formulated the principles of cultural ecology, studying the relationships between human cultures and their natural environments.
- W. W. Taylor's *Study of Archaeology*, published in 1948, was a landmark critique of American archaeology, chiding archaeologists for preoccupation with description and chronology rather than with cultural change. This pioneer work and the research of Julian Steward and of Leslie White established once and for all the close relationship between archaeology and anthropology.

GUIDE TO FURTHER READING

Brace, C. Loring. *The Stages of Human Evolution,* 2d ed. Englewood Cliffs, N.J.: Prentice-Hall, 1979. A good summary of the history of evolutionary theory.

Campbell, Bernard G. *Humankind Emerging,* 4th ed. Boston: Little, Brown, 1985. A definitive college text on human evolution.

Daniel, Glyn, ed. *The Origins and Growth of Archaeology.* Baltimore: Pelican, 1967. Extracts from the writings of early archaeologists that amplify the other readings in this guide.

Fagan, Brian M. *The Adventure of Archaeology.* Washington, D.C.: National Geographic Society, 1985. A lavishly illustrated account of the history of archaeology that is ideal for beginners.

Grayson, Donald. *The Establishment of Human Antiquity.* Orlando, Fla.: Academic Press, 1983. A definitive and scholarly study of human antiquity based on contemporary sources. Strongly recommended for the advanced reader.

Meltzer, David J., Don D. Fowler, and Jeremy A. Sabloff, eds. *American Archaeology Past and Future: A Celebration of the Society for American Archaeology, 1935–1985.* Washington, D.C.: Smithsonian Institution Press, 1986. A set of essays that review the development of American archaeology since the 1930s. An admirable adjunct to this chapter.

Trigger, Bruce G. *A History of Archaeological Interpretation.* Cambridge: Cambridge University Press, 1989. A brilliant and definitive intellectual history of archaeology. A seminal resource.

Willey, Gordon, and Jeremy Sabloff. *A History of American Archaeology,* 2d ed. New York: Freeman, 1980. A detailed account of New World archaeology from the Spanish occupation until recent times.

Chapter
3

Science, Ecology, and Decoding the Past

The 1950s to the 1990s

*A*rchaeology, like the other social sciences, has changed almost beyond recognition in four decades. The digital computer, statistical methods, and the philosophy of science have transformed archaeology from a primarily descriptive discipline into a much more comprehensive system. Chapter 3 starts with these developments and shows how more sophisticated ecological and evolutionary approaches and the greater application of deductive scientific methods and theory building took archaeology in new directions. Scholars such as Lewis Binford, Kent Flannery, Albert Spaulding, and Julian Steward recognized the major trends in social science and began the difficult task of applying them to archaeology. The chapter ends with a brief glance at the major approaches to processual archaeology, which is described in more detail in Part Seven.

SCIENCE AND ARCHAEOLOGY

Statistical Methods

Statistical methods began to change archaeology and anthropology in the 1950s. Although archaeologists had been counting tools and other finds for years, Albert Spaulding (1960b), the pioneer in this field, mentioned only a few instances of people using chi-square (χ^2) and other statistical techniques in an early paper he wrote on the subject. Both changing interests among researchers and application of the digital computer to order and handle enormous numbers of tools brought about this new approach to archaeological evidence. Statistical methods rapidly came into fashion as archaeologists realized that with these they could prepare far more meticulous and detailed descriptions of finds than had ever been carried out without them. Spaulding forecast that archaeology's future depended on how successful we are in applying quantitative methods to archaeological data (for quantitative methods, see Chapter 11).

Lewis Binford and the Scientific Method

Doing graduate work at the University of Michigan, Lewis Binford came into contact with eminent scholars who had done much to develop archaeology in the 1940s and 1950s. Among them were James Griffin, who taught him descriptive archaeology; Albert Spaulding, who introduced him to statistical techniques for handling specific problems; and Leslie White, who exposed him to logic and urged him to steep himself in the philosophy of science. Binford learned the importance of theory and recognized the close links between archaeology and ethnography. The ultimate objective of archaeology, he discovered, was a search for universal laws that govern cultural change.

In the 1960s, Binford wrote closely reasoned, classic papers that caused ferment in archaeological circles. He advocated more rigorous scientific testing. Statements about the significance of the archaeological record used to be evaluated according to how far back our knowledge of contemporary peoples could be projected onto prehistoric contexts and according to our judgment of how professionally competent and honest the archaeologists interpreting the past were (Binford, 1962, 1972, 1983a). Inferences about the archaeological record had been made by simple induction, along with guidance from ethnographic data and experimental archaeology. Binford argued that although induction and inferences are perfectly sound methods for understanding the past, the real need was for independent methods for testing propositions about the past, and these must be far more rigorous than the time-honored value judgments arrived at by assessing professional competence. His approach was soon called the "new archaeology."

With a scientific approach providing interaction among old data, new ideas, and new data, we can approach a research problem from a collection of observed data that enable us to pose research hypotheses. Some general problems may have to do with change: How and why did the hunter-gatherers of the Near East turn to agriculture and domestic animals for their livelihood? Or the problems may touch on cultural relationships: Did a new pottery type suddenly appearing in a Midwest cultural sequence get there by trade, population movement, or independent invention?

Working hypotheses were nothing new in archaeology. Binford's approach was different because he advocated that these hypotheses be tested explicitly against archaeological data collected in the field and against other alternatives that have been rejected. Once a hypothesis is tested against raw data, it can join the body of reliable knowledge upon which further hypotheses can be erected. And these in turn may require additional data or even entirely new approaches to the excavation and collection of archaeological information. Binford suggested that the explicit scientific method commonly used in science should now be applied to archaeological research.

Binford's papers, lectures, and seminars provoked interest among many American archaeologists, of whom numbers joined him in reevaluating the scientific methods of archaeology. He and his disciples challenged the assumption that because the archaeological record is incomplete, reliable interpretation of the nonmaterial and perishable components of prehistoric society and culture were impossible. All artifacts found in an archaeological site functioned at one time in a particular culture and society. They occur in meaningful patterns that are systematically related to the economies, kinship systems, and other contexts within which they were used. Moreover, all these artifacts were at the mercy of transient factors such as fashion or decorative style, each of which itself has a history of acceptance, use, or rejection within the society. Thus artifacts are far more than mere material items; rather, they reflect many of the often intangible variables that went into determining the actual form of the objects preserved. Binford (1968) argued that "data relevant to most, if not all, of the components of past sociocultural systems *are* preserved in the archaeological record." The archaeologist's task is to devise methods for extracting this information that deal with *all* determinants in the society or culture being studied.

Lewis Binford was not alone in this thinking. In the 1960s, British archaeologist David Clarke wrote a monumental critique of prehistoric archaeology, arguing for more explicit scientific methods, greater rigor, and a body of theory to replace "the murky exhalation that represents theory in archaeology" (Clarke, 1968). Clarke deeply influenced European archaeology, but unfortunately, he died before reaching the peak of his career (Hodder and others, 1981).

LIVING ARCHAEOLOGY (ETHNOARCHAEOLOGY)

A spin-off from this drive for greater scientific rigor was renewed interest among archaeologists in living peoples. Lewis Binford was not, of course, the first archaeologist to look at ethnography, for many scholars were worrying about the extinction threatening preindustrial societies all over the world (Binford, 1968; Sollas, 1911; Thompson, 1956). As early as 1865, Lord Avebury had urged his archaeological colleagues to compare Stone Age cultures with modern hunter-gatherer peoples. The direct historical approach evolved from American archaeologists' recognition that modern Indian cultures had long roots in prehistory.

Binford (1977, 1978, 1983a) urged, however, that once researchers choose different comparisons, they should explicitly state the implications and then test each against archaeological data. Conditions for making such tests were best in the field, observing cultural adaptations among living hunter-gatherers and subsistence agriculturalists. Before long, he argued, archaeology would be the only source of explanations for cultural variations among nonindustrial societies. Binford really cared most about how the archaeological record came into existence and how it, as a static phenomenon, was linked to ever-changing human systems (1983a).

Richard Lee was among the anthropologists who studied the !Kung San of the Kalahari, realized the archaeologists' difficulties, and arranged to take a prehistorian with them to study the remains of long-abandoned campsites and compare them to modern settlements (Lee and De Vore, 1976; Yellen, 1977) (Figure 3.1). Richard Gould, an anthropologist who worked among the Australian aborigines, deliberately went out of his way to gather information on abandoned campsites that could be useful to archaeologists (Gould, 1977). Lewis Binford himself has worked among the Nunamiut Eskimo and the Navajo on variability in adaptation systems, seeking viable analogies between living cultures and archaeological materials and trying to develop workable models of culture as rigorous yardsticks for studying variability (Binford, 1978). (See Chapter 14 for further discussion.)

Figure 3.1 An anthropologist making a plane table survey of a San camp in the Kalahari. Data from such surveys are of great value in interpreting the archaeological record.

SYSTEMS THEORY AND ECOLOGY

Systems Theory

Another element creating a more scientific archaeology was the influence of both philosophers of science, such as Thomas Kuhn (1970) and Carl Hempel, and of general systems theory (Gibbon, 1984; Watson and others, 1984; Redman, 1973). As archaeologists moved away from simple explanations and unilinear evolution toward much more elaborate theories, they began to examine the delicate and complex relationships between human societies and their ever-changing environments. Systems approaches involved thinking of human cultures as complicated systems of interacting elements, such as technology and social organization, which interacted, in turn, with the ecological systems of which they were a part (see Chapter 18). The systems approach has strongly influenced archaeology because of intense interest in relationships between prehistoric peoples and their environments. (More on systems theory in Chapter 6.)

Ecology and Archaeology

Ecological thinking about archaeology has a long history. Much of it is based on the assumption that human cultures could affect their environments, and vice versa (Trigger, 1971). One school of thought, environmental determinism, held that forms in nature, which are active, determined human culture, which is passive. Franz Boas and other anthropologists went so far as to argue that the environment was passive and that human culture developed because some environmental possibilities were selected and others ignored (Hams, 1968).

Modern ecology, with its distinctions among various ecosystems, caused these simple notions to be rejected in favor of more holistic views of culture and environment. In these new approaches, it is assumed that cultural ecology studies the whole picture of the way in which human populations adapt to and transform their environments (Dunnell, 1980). Human cultures are thought of as open systems because it is acknowledged that their institutions may be connected with those of other cultures and with the environment. Open-system ecology is very realistic, assuming a great deal of variation between individual modern and archaeological cultures. Any explanation of culture has to be able to handle the real patterns of variation found in living cultures, not just the artificial ones erected by classifiers of archaeological cultures. So many factors influence cultural systems that order can be sought only by understanding the system that Bruce Trigger (1971) calls "those processes by which cultural similarities and differences are generated." Many complex factors are external to the culture and cannot be controlled by the archaeologist; one cannot reconstruct the whole cultural system from only one part of it (in archaeological cultures, the surviving artifacts and food residues). Every facet of the cultural system has to be reconstructed separately, using the evidence specifically relevant to that facet, making available, in time, a picture of the whole cultural system, as comprehensive as possible. The issue is a society's total adaptation to both its natural and cultural environments. Trigger (1971) points out: "Developments affecting any one aspect of the culture can ultimately produce further adjustments throughout the system and affect the system's relationship with the natural environment."

Studying prehistoric societies in context—in their natural environments—involves examining the relationships between prehistoric settlements and their surrounding landscape. Important studies in Mexico have assumed that the patterns of human settlement throughout time provide a reliable way of studying the changing adaptations of human cultures to an environment over a long period (Flannery, 1976; Sanders and others, 1979) (see Chapter 15). Such studies can be conducted only with detailed background knowledge of the specific environment in which the culture flourished, changed, and eventually died. One of the brightest prospects for archaeology lies in studying human cultural systems in the changing economic, demographic, and social variables interacting within an environmental setting over long periods. Some of the most sophisticated research in archaeology is being done in the open-system ecology format as archaeologists wrestle to develop a meeting ground between a broad view of cultural change and the need to look at each changing culture and its microadaptation to a dynamic environment; both are clearly needed (Flannery, 1976).

DECODING THE PAST

The emphasis on systems theory, scientific method, and new approaches to ecology changed the tactics in archaeological research in the 1960s and 1970s. The result was a state of ferment, a fascinating intellectual climate in which practically every familiar theory in archaeology was challenged. Much of the debate was about the goals of the discipline; some people argued that archaeology was a science, the objective of which was to study basic laws of human behavior. But other archaeologists viewed archaeology as examining the activities of past human beings, as a discipline that was less a science than a historical discipline with its own limitations, resources, and explanatory methods (Flannery, 1973a; Spaulding, 1973). Everyone agrees, however, that mathematical models, statistical approaches, and rigorous scientific methods will be more and more vital in archaeology. We can be certain, too, that future archaeology will incorporate the evidence and valid empirical generalizations of history (Spaulding, 1973).

The fervor of debate and controversy quieted somewhat in the 1980s, partly because many basic tenets put forward by Lewis Binford and other scholars had by then been accepted. The pressure of demography has meant that most younger archaeologists practicing today were trained by scholars brought up in the new thinking. The scientific method is widely used; research designs are far more sophisticated than those of a generation ago; highly technical scientific techniques like remote sensing are common. But frustration remains, for most of the rich theoretical expectations of the 1960s remain unfulfilled (Dunnell, 1982). Archaeologists today seem divided into two camps: a smaller group who write about "theoretical" issues and concentrate on concepts, methods, and techniques, which are occasionally applied to a body of data, and a much larger group who carry out empirical studies of the same type that have been done for generations. More "scientific" methods may be used, true, but the effect is mostly superficial. Little integration seems to link the two groups. In this sense, the "new" archaeology of the 1960s has failed. Many archaeologists wonder whether archaeology is, in fact, an atheoretical discipline. They must be wrong, for it seems to be undergoing the change that occurred in biology a generation ago and is now taking place throughout the social sciences—a serious attempt to assemble a body of theory for archaeology as distinctive as those of physics and the other established sciences. The innovators who started the revolution in archaeology in the 1960s had no idea the task they were undertaking was so enormous (Meltzer and others, 1986).

What exactly has been achieved, and where do we go from here? Some of the achievements of archaeology since the 1960s are indeed impressive: an explosion in raw data, a new emphasis on regional surveys, and widespread use of quantitative methods. Ecological theory and human ecology itself are fundamental parts of archaeology in the 1980s. The "new" archaeology, not coincidentally, is no longer called that. Its most important and rigorous elements have survived. Other elements, such as the search for general laws of human behavior and the more extreme manifestations of general systems theory, have less significance. No one would now question that human cultures should be thought of as ever-changing systems interacting with their natural environment and one another. The difference today is that archaeologists are thinking much more profoundly about the archaeological record itself and how it came into being. As we said in Chapter 1, archaeology is unique in depending on inference for interpreting the past. We can study that past only by means of material evidence that has been changed by centuries, even millennia, underground. How do we explain the archaeological record? This is the question that must be tackled before we try to interpret the past itself; that record itself is perhaps *the* question for archaeologists in the 1990s.

Experimental archaeology and the discipline often called ethnoarchaeology grew in popularity in the 1970s. Much of this research focused on obvious problems like the tree-felling power of stone axes or the cultural ecology of modern hunter-gatherers in the Kalahari, often referred to in these pages. But these projects have led a number of investigators to ask the question of questions: How can the present, with all its rich data on modern subsistence, climate, soil qualities, and a myriad of other phenomena, be used to interpret the past? Not only that, under our world with its varied landscape lies the archaeological record—thousands of sites and artifacts buried since they were abandoned by their makers. Theoretically at any rate, we have a wealth of data that could be used to interpret the past, to bridge the gap between sites and peoples as they were in prehistoric times and the surviving archaeological record of the 1990s. Some people are puzzled as to why archaeologists are busy studying modern Australian aborigines or the city dump in Tucson, Arizona. The reason is that for the first time archaeologists are investigating the relationship between the static archaeological record and the dynamic, ever-changing world in which we live—and they are doing it while simultaneously developing a new body of archaeological theory, which Binford (1983a) names *middle-range theory.*

Middle-range theory is best defined as a body of theoretical constructs designed to bridge the gap between the archaeological record in the past and the modern world (see Chapter 14). In the final analysis, archaeological research is an interaction between observed facts (the archaeological record) and research to give meaning to these observations (by means of experimental archaeology, ethnoarchaeology, and historical documents). This interaction involves the archaeologist in all manner of seemingly exotic inquiries: Eskimo subsistence in the 1990s, patterns of wear on the edges of prehistoric tools and modern replicas, and the effects of various geological deposits on the survival of animal bone parts. Much of this research, dealing with basic global problems in the origins of humanity or of more complex societies, must be worldwide in scale. Certainly the sort of research carried out by the archaeologist in 2020 will differ from that of a colleague in the 1990s, but middle-range theory and studies of the contemporary world will continue to be important themes in archaeological research at least for the remainder of the twentieth century (Meltzer and others, 1986).

The "new" archaeology of the 1960s and 1970s is no longer new. Some archaeologists have reacted strongly against the ardent materialism of the new archaeology and have embarked on a search for "meaning" or "structure" in the archaeological record (Leone, 1986). They believe that people are like actors, assuming an active role in the shaping of their culture, their society. Thus one must search for the structure behind the artifacts, the overarching patterns that guided people in their interactions with their own culture. Structural archaeology of this type is still little more than an idea (see Chapter 18), with some of the most notable research coming from studies of the cosmology of the ancient Mayan civilization of Central America (Friedel and Schele, 1987).

At the same time, more and more archaeologists are thinking hard about the role that archaeology plays in contemporary society, about the ideologies that they, as active members of contemporary society, seek to impose on their interpretations of the past (Chapter 18). They realize that the past can be interpreted in many different ways, including some that actually manipulate archaeology for political and other ends.

Contemporary archaeology is in considerable theoretical turmoil, as those on the cutting edge of contemporary thinking about the past search for a body of original theory that is effective as a way of studying and interpreting prehistory. So far the search has been largely unsuccessful. It is possible that many inspirations will come from recent advances in evolutionary biology, for, as Kent Flannery has pointed out, archaeology is second to none as a discipline for studying evolution (Flannery and Marcus, 1983; Mithen, 1989). In the meantime, archaeology has come a long way since the antiquarian digs of eighteenth-century Britain. Techniques for recovering data that were a pipe dream a generation ago are now everyday reality. The cartoon stereotype of the pith-helmeted archaeologist digging up pyramids is fading rapidly as the prehistorian of today pursues ever more eclectic and wide-ranging research, much of it far from the familiar excavations and artifact laboratories. In the pages that follow I will describe some of the approaches that are leading the archaeologist ever more rapidly from pith helmet dusty with ancient soil to the computer and the contemporary world, still seeking to understand the past.

SUMMARY

- In the 1950s, statistical methods long used in the natural and physical sciences began to be used in archaeology. With the new approaches these techniques engendered, archaeologists could perform far more meticulous and detailed descriptions and manipulate larger quantities of data.
- Lewis Binford, strongly influenced by Leslie White, Julian Steward, and Albert Spaulding, formulated a new archaeological method and theory using explicitly scientific methods. He proposed that archaeological data be tested against formal hypotheses and that careful research designs be used for planning all inquiries.
- This more scientific archaeology went beyond applying the formal scientific method; one advance was a new interest in living archaeology—ethnoarchaeology. Studying surviving hunter-gatherers gives insight into prehistoric societies. Before long, it was clear, archaeology would be the only means for explaining cultural variations in nonindustrial societies.
- With the development of a more scientific archaeology, increasing attention was paid to the works of philosophers of science, such as Thomas Kuhn, and to the principles of general systems theory. Moving away from simple explanations of the past, archaeologists chose systems approaches to help them depict a human culture as a complicated system of interacting elements that in turn interacted with the ecological system of which it was a part.

- Systems approaches developed hand in hand with cultural ecology, that is, with studies of the changing relationship between prehistoric societies and the environments in which they flourished. Settlement archaeology depended heavily on statistical methods and computers to order large quantities of field data.
- A new emphasis on scientific approaches has set off a debate as to whether archaeology is among the humanities or the sciences.

GUIDE TO FURTHER READING

Binford, Lewis R. *In Pursuit of the Past.* New York: Thames and Hudson, 1983. A superb, clearly written account of archaeology in the 1980s, with a personal record of intellectual developments in recent years.

————. *Working at Archaeology.* Orlando, Fla.: Academic Press, 1983. Binford's major papers arranged in historical order. Read in conjunction with *In Pursuit of the Past.*

Flannery, Kent V., ed. *The Early Mesoamerican Village.* Orlando, Fla.: Academic Press, 1976. A volume of essays with fascinating dialogues about the various approaches to archaeology.

Redman, Charles L., ed. *Research and Theory in Current Archaeology.* New York: Wiley Interscience, 1973. Essays with a critique of the way in which processual archaeology evolved. Those by Kent Flannery and Albert Spaulding are especially important.

Watson, Patti Jo, Steven Le Blanc, and Charles L. Redman. *Archaeological Explanation,* 2d ed. New York: Columbia University Press, 1984. A fundamental source on the development of processual archaeology.

PART Three

DATA AND CONTEXT

Time which antiquates antiquities, and hath an art to make dust of all things.

Sir Thomas Browne
Hydriotaphia, 1658

*P*art Three describes the truly basic concepts behind archaeological research, those of culture and context. Every archaeological site and every find has a context, not only within some long-extinct culture but also in time and space. In this section of the text, we examine the concept of culture in archaeology, the nature of archaeological data, and the ways in which people have established archaeological contexts. Fundamental to context are methods of defining human activities in space and, especially, for measuring prehistoric time. We describe the various methods that have been devised for dating prehistoric cultures from the very earliest times.

Chapter
4

Culture, Data, and Context

*T*he concepts of culture, space, and time in archaeology (basic units of investigation in the discipline) are inseparable. Accurate measuring of age in calendar years and of spatial context lie at the very core of all archaeological research. Indeed, as Albert Spaulding points out, a minimal definition of archaeology describes it as the study of interrelations between the form of artifacts found in a site and their data and spatial location relative to the problem being studied (Spaulding, 1960a).

In this chapter we introduce you to some basic concepts of archaeological research, to culture, to data in the form of artifacts, and to the matrix, provenience, and context of the data. The provenience and context of all archaeological data are based on the two fundamental laws, superposition and association. From basic concepts, we move on to discuss spatial context—not the limitless frontiers of the heavens, but a precisely defined location for every find made during an archaeological survey or excavation.

THE CONCEPT OF CULTURE

In Chapter 1, I stated that "anthropologists study human beings as biological organisms and as people with a distinctive and unique characteristic— culture. . . . Archaeologists are, in fact, a special type of anthropologist, specializing in past human culture." Few concepts in anthropology have generated as much controversy and academic debate as those expressed in that statement (Kroeber and Kluckhohn, 1952). All definitions of this most elusive of theoretical formulations are a means of explaining cultures and human behavior in terms of the shared ideas a group of people may hold. One of the best definitions was written by the great Victorian anthropologist Sir Edward Tylor more than a century ago. He stated that culture is "that complex whole which includes knowledge, belief, art, morals, law, custom, and any other capabilities and habits acquired by man as a member of society" (Tylor, 1871). To that definition, modern archaeologists would add the statement that culture is our primary means of adapting to our environment.

Culture is a distinctively human attribute, for we are the only animals to use our culture as our *primary* means of adapting to our environment (Keesing, 1974). It is our adaptive system. Although biological evolution has protected the polar bear from arctic cold with dense fur and has given the duck webbed feet for swimming, only human beings make thick clothes and igloos in the Arctic and live with minimal clothing under light, thatched shelters in the tropics. We use our culture as a buffer between ourselves and the environment that became more and more elaborate through the long millennia of prehistory. We are now so detached from our environment that removal of our cultural buffer would render us almost helpless and probably lead to extinction of the human race in a very short time. Thus human cultures are made up of human behavior and its results; they obviously consist of complex and constantly interacting variables. Human culture, never static, is always adjusting to both internal and external change, whether environmental, technological, or societal (Deetz, 1967; Dunnell, 1971). Increasingly, humans have modified the natural environment to such an extent that they have created their own.

The Nature of Culture

Culture can be subdivided in all sorts of ways—into language, economics, technology, religion, political or social organizations, and art. But human culture as a whole is a complex, structured organization in which all our categories shape one another. All cultures are made up of myriad tangible and intangible traits, the contents of which result from complex adaptation to a wide range of ecological, societal, and cultural factors. Much of human culture is transmitted from generation to generation by sophisticated communication systems that permit complex and ceaseless adaptations to aid survival and help rapid cultural change take place—as when less advanced societies come into contact with higher civilizations.

Everyone lives within a culture of some kind, and every culture is qualified by a label, such as "middle-class American," "Eskimo," or "Masai." The qualification conjures up characteristic attributes or behavior patterns typical of those associated with the cultural label. One attribute of a middle-class American might be the hamburger; of the Eskimo, the kayak; of the Masai, a long-handled, fine-bladed spear. Our mental images of cultures are associated with popular stereotypes, too. To many Americans, Chinese culture conjures up images of paper lanterns and willow-pattern plates; French culture, good eating and fine wines. We are all familiar with the distinctive "flavor" of a culture that we encounter when dining in a foreign restaurant or arriving in a strange country. Every culture has its individuality and recognizable style, which shape its political and judicial institutions and morals (Frankfort, 1951; Renfrew, 1975). Archaeologists think of culture as possessing three components:

The individual's own version of his or her culture, the diversified individual behavior that makes up the myriad strains of a culture.

Shared culture: elements of a culture shared by everyone. These can include cultural activities like human sacrifice or ritualized warfare or any shared human activity, as well as the body of rules and prescriptions that make up the sum of the culture (Figure 4.1). Language is critical to this sharing; so is the cultural system.

The cultural system, the system of behavior in which every individual *participates*. The individual not only shares the cultural system with other members of society but also takes an active part in it.

Culture, then, can be viewed as either a blend of shared traits or a system that permits a society to interact with its environment. To do anything more than merely work out chronological sequences, the archaeologist has to view culture as complex, interacting components. These components remain static unless the processes that operate the system are carefully defined. Archaeologists are deeply involved with "cultural process," the processes by which human societies changed in the past.

Figure 4.1 The Mayan city of Palenque, viewed from the north, with the palace in the foreground and the Temple of the Inscriptions in the background. This is a place where Maya Indians shared cultural activities and public ceremonies.

A *cultural system* was well defined by archaeologist Stuart Struever (1971): "Culture and its environments represent a number of articulated [interlinked] systems in which change occurs through a series of minor, linked variations in one or more of these systems." For example, an Eskimo cultural system is part of a much larger Arctic ecosystem. The cultural system itself is made up of dozens of subsystems: an economic subsystem, a political subsystem, and many others. Let us say that the climate changes suddenly. The Eskimo now switch from reindeer hunting to fishing and sealing. The change triggers all sorts of linked shifts, not only in the economic subsystem but in the technological and social subsystems as well. A cultural system is in a constant state of adjustment within itself and with the ecosystem of which it is a part. The concept of cultural systems is derived from general systems theory, a body of theoretical concepts formulated as a means of searching for general relationships in the empirical world (Watson and others, 1984). The action of cultural systems has come into use in archaeology purely as a general concept to help us understand the ever-changing relationship between human cultures and their environment.

Many of the interacting components of culture are highly perishable. So far, no one has been able to dig up a religious philosophy or an unwritten language. Archaeologists have to work with the *tangible* remains of human activity that still survive in the ground. But these surviving remains of human activity are radically affected by intangible aspects of human culture. For example, the Hopewell people of the American Midwest traded finely made ornaments fashioned out of hammered copper sheet over enormous distances 1,800 years ago. These ornaments turn up in Hopewell burial mounds. The copper technology that made them was simple, but the symbolism behind the artifacts was not. They were probably exchanged between important individuals as symbolic gifts, denoting kin ties, economic obligations, and other social meanings that are beyond the archaeologist's ability to recover (Fagan, 1990). So the archaeologist faces much greater limitations in research than the ethnographer, who works with living societies and can talk to individuals in society.

NORMATIVE, FUNCTIONAL, AND PROCESSUAL MODELS OF CULTURE

Normative Models

Anthropologist Franz Boas had a profound influence on early American archaeology, for he developed what is often called a "normative" view of culture. This was the first concept of culture to be applied to archaeology, the notion that all human behavior is patterned, the forms of the patterns being determined very largely by culture. Under this rubric are a set of rules, or norms for behavior, within any society that pass from one generation to the next. There are, of course, individual variations, for all the norms do is to define the range of acceptable behavior.

Boas applied the normative view of culture to contemporary societies, but archaeologists often use it to examine societies evolving over long periods of time. Anthropologists try to abstract the norms of human behavior by observing societies over many months, even years. They are searching, as it were, for the "grammar" of a society. Archaeologists use the material remains of the archaeological record, such as pottery or stone tools, to infer human behavior, arguing that such durable artifacts represent norms of technological behavior, if nothing else. It is argued that implicit rules governed the manufacture of all kinds of artifacts over many generations.

This descriptive approach allowed archaeologists to reconstruct and observe variations and changes in what they called behavioral norms. It has been very successful in working out detailed, descriptive outlines of human prehistory at the local and regional levels. However, it does not address two critical goals of archaeology—reconstructing past lifeways and explaining cultural change.

Functional Models

Bronislaw Malinowski was one of the great anthropologists of the twentieth century, famous not only for his observations of the Trobriand Islanders in the western Pacific but also for his functional model of culture. Culture to Malinowski was "inherited artifacts, goods, technical processes, ideas, habits, and values." He went much further than Boas, arguing that each human culture was a set of closely interrelated mechanisms designed to satisfy both social and survival needs, not just for individuals but for society as a whole. To Malinowski and other anthropologists of the functionalist school, culture was a way of responding to human needs of all kinds, and the nature of that society could be understood only by looking at the network of complex relationships that formed the underlying structure of that society. Each component of a cultural system, living or prehistoric, has a specific function, be it stone technology, ways of growing crops, or residence rules after marriage. Each function is connected to a myriad of others by a network of relationships, forming an ever-adjusting cultural system.

Functionalism can be a somewhat ahistorical way of looking at human societies, but archaeologists have found it of considerable use in examining individual artifacts and cultural traits as part of a much larger network of functional relationships. However, in one aspect functionalism diverges greatly from more recent ecological models of culture, which view cultural systems not as self-regulating but as undergoing constant change as they adapt to their natural environments.

Processual Models

The ultimate goal of archaeology, as we have stated, is to explain how and why human cultures changed in the past. Two models of culture have been developed since the 1950s to explain cultural process. These cultural ecological and multilinear evolutionary models were described in Chapter 3.

The changing models of culture in archaeology reflect a gradual shift in emphasis from mere description of the past through inductive research to much more sophisticated models based on deductive, hypothesis-testing strategies. It would be a mistake to think of our cultural models as static, for they are not, responding as they do to ever more sophisticated and fine-grained methods and theoretical approaches to the past.

CULTURAL PROCESS

Systems theory deals with relationships and variations in relationships; in other words, it deals with precisely the phenomena involved in explaining the processes by which cultures change. Modern scientific archaeology analyzes the causes of cultural change, that is, the cultural process.

The word *process* implies a patterned sequence of events that leads from one state of affairs to another. This patterned sequence is determined by a decision-making process that sets the order of events. A forty-foot sailing yacht starts as a pile of materials—wood, aluminum, copper, bronze—and then a patterned sequence of manufacturing events turns the material into a gleaming new ship. Archaeology is a process, too. It involves designing the research project, formulating the hypothesis, collecting and interpreting the data, testing the data, and, finally, publishing the results.

Causes are events that force people to make decisions about how to deal with new situations. As such, they are distinct from the actual process of decision making—the mechanisms that lead to any kind of change. A change in the natural environment from year-round rainfall to a seasonal pattern is a cause.

In archaeology, *cultural process* refers to the "identification of the factors responsible for the direction and nature of change within cultural systems" (Sharer and Ashmore, 1987). *Processual archaeology* is analysis of the causes of culture change, which involves looking at relationships between variables that could lead to cultural change. These possible causes are then tested against actual archaeological data, sometimes in a systems theory context.

As more and more archaeological data have become available, the older, simplistic explanations of cultural process in prehistory, such as universal evolutionism and diffusionism, fail to reflect accurately the situations as we now see them. Clearly, no one element in any cultural system is the primary cause of change; instead, a complex range of factors—

rainfall, vegetation, technology, social restrictions, population density—interact and react to changes in any element in the system. It follows, then, that human culture, from the ecologist's viewpoint, is merely one element in the ecosystem, a mechanism of behavior whereby people adapt to an environment (Figure 4.2) (Dunnell, 1980).

ARCHAEOLOGICAL DATA

The cultures archaeologists study are reconstructed from archaeological data. Archaeological data consist of any material remains of human activity—a scatter of broken bones, a ruined house, a gold mask, a vast temple plaza. Archaeologists have names that define these remains for research purposes.

Figure 4.2 A San hunter-gatherer in the Kalahari searches the bole of a tree for water. Human culture is, from the ecologist's viewpoint, merely one element in the ecosystem.

The *archaeological record* is the general name denoting the more or less continuous distribution of artifacts over the earth's surface, in highly variable densities. Variations in artifact densities reflect the character and frequency of land use, making them an important variable that the archaeologist can measure (Dunnell and Dancey, 1983). Some high-density clusters of artifacts may be subsumed under *site.* Although *archaeological record* refers specifically to distributions of artifacts, these can include:

1. *Artifacts:* in the strict sense, objects manufactured or modified by humans (Figure 4.3).
2. *Features:* artifacts and artifact associations that cannot be removed intact from the ground, such as post holes and ditches.
3. *Structures:* houses, granaries, temples, and other buildings that can be identified from patterns of post holes and other features in the ground.
4. *Ecofacts:* sometimes refers to food remains, such as bones, seeds, and other finds, which throw light on human activities.

Data are the natural materials recognized by the archaeologist as significant evidence, all of which are collected and recorded as part of the research. Archaeological data are sometimes referred to as *evidence.*

Archaeological data do not consist of artifacts, features, structures, and ecofacts alone, however; they consist also of their *context* in space and time. Lewis Binford (1972) says that "data relevant to most, if not all, the components of past sociocultural systems are preserved in the archaeologi-

Figure 4.3 A magnificent Iron Age helmet from the River Thames in London (20.5 cm diameter at base). Objects like this are useful for cross-dating archaeological sites all over Europe.

cal record. . . . Our task, then, is to devise means for extracting this information."

MATRIX AND PROVENIENCE

All scientifically collected or excavated archaeological finds, be they a complete site or a lone object, occur within a matrix and have a specific provenience.

The *matrix* is the physical substance that surrounds the find. It can be gravel, sand, mud, or even water. Most archaeological matrices are of natural origin—passing time and external phenomena, such as wind and rainfall, create them. The early bone caches at Olduvai Gorge in Tanzania were at the edge of a shallow and ever-fluctuating lake 1.75 million years ago. The scatter of tools and bones left by the departing hominids was soon covered by a layer of thin lake sand carried by advancing shallow water. This matrix preserved the tools in their original positions for thousands of millennia (Leakey, 1971). An archaeological matrix can also be humanly made, such as the huge earthen platforms of Hopewell burial mounds in the Midwest (Fagan, 1990).

Provenience (or provenance) is the precise three-dimensional position of the find within the matrix as recorded by the archaeologist. It is derived from accurate records kept during excavations and site surveys, from evidence that is inevitably destroyed once a site is dug or artifacts are collected from a surface site.

Every human artifact has a provenience in time and space. The provenience in time can range from a radiocarbon date of $1,400 \pm 60$ years before the present for a Mayan temple to a precise reading of A.D. 1988 for a dime released by the United States Mint. Frequently, it can simply be an exact position in an archaeological site whose general age is known. Provenience in space is based, finally, on associations between tools and other items that were results of human behavior in a culture. Provenience is determined by applying two fundamental archaeological laws: the law of association and the law of superposition.

The Law of Association

The archaeological law of association (Figure 4.4) was first stated by Danish archaeologist J. J. A. Worsaae in 1843. Working with prehistoric burials, Worsaae stated the principle clearly:

> The objects accompanying a human burial are in most cases things that were in use at the same time. When certain artifact types are found together in grave association after grave association, and when more evolved forms of the same tools are found in association with other burials, then the associations provide some basis for dividing the burials into different chronological groups on the basis of association and artifact styles.

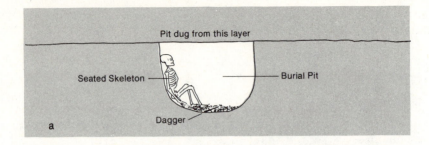

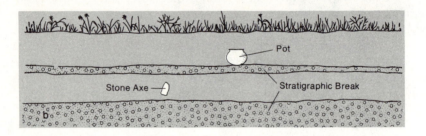

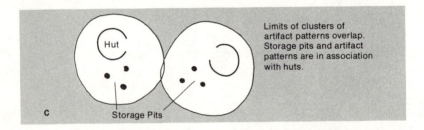

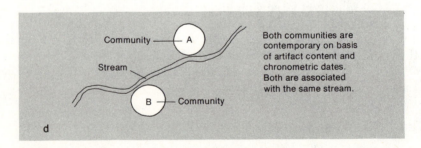

Figure 4.4 Some instances of archaeological associations. (a) The burial pit, dug from the uppermost layer, contains not only a skeleton but also a dagger that lies close to its foot. The dagger is associated with the skeleton, and both finds are associated with the burial pit and the layer from which the grave pit was cut into the subsoil. (b) In contrast, a pot and a stone axe are found in two different layers, separated by a sterile zone, a zone with no finds. The two objects are not in association. (c) Two different household clusters with associated pits and scatters of artifacts. These are in association with each other. (d) An association of two contemporary communities.

Worsaae eventually proved the chronological validity of the law of association by stratigraphic excavations in dozens of burial sites (Harris, 1989).

Instances of archaeological associations are legion. The first evidence of high antiquity for humankind came from associations of stone axes and the bones of extinct animals discovered in the same geological layers. Many early Mesoamerican farmers' houses are associated with storage pits for maize and other crops. In this and many other cases, the horizontal association between artifacts and houses, dwellings and storage pits, or artifacts and food residues provide the archaeological association. Unassociated artifacts, examined deprived of association with other finds, yield relatively little worthwhile information. Much of the most valuable archaeological data are derived from precise studies of associations between different finds in the ground.

The Law of Superposition

The time dimension of archaeology is erected on basic principles of stratigraphic geology set down by the uniformitarians early in the nineteenth century. "Strata" Smith's classic studies of British geology were based on the law of superposition (Daniel, 1981). It was easy for archaeologists to adopt this law, for many of their most important finds were made within geological layers or contexts.

The law of superposition states that the geological layers of the earth are stratified one upon another, like the layers of a cake. Cliffs by the seashore and quarries are easily accessible examples. Obviously, any object found in the lowermost levels, whether a stone or something humanly made, was deposited there before the upper levels were accumulated. In other words, the lower strata are *earlier* than the upper strata. The same law applies to archaeological sites: the tools, houses, and other finds in the layers of a site can be dated relative to the layers by their association with the stratum in which they are found (Figure 4.4).

The basis of all scientific archaeological excavation is the accurately observed and carefully recorded stratigraphic profile (Wheeler, 1954).

We will return to stratigraphy and superposition in Chapter 5.

ARCHAEOLOGICAL CONTEXT

Archaeological context is derived from careful recording of the matrix, provenience, and association of the finds. Context is far more than just a find spot, a position in time and space. It involves assessing how the find got to its position and what has happened since its original owners abandoned it. Anyone wanting to reconstruct human behavior or ancient cultural systems must pay careful attention to the context of every find.

Context is affected by three factors:

1. The manufacture and use of the object, house, or other find by its original owners. The orientation of a house may be determined by the position of the sun on summer afternoons. Because the archaeologist's objective is to reconstruct ancient *behavior,* this aspect of context is vital.

2. The way in which the find was deposited in the ground. Some discoveries, like royal burials or caches of artifacts, were deliberately buried under the ground by ancient people; others vanished as a result of natural phenomena. Dilapidated houses that have been abandoned are slowly covered by blowing sand or rotting vegetation. The Roman city of Herculaneum in Italy, however, was buried quickly by a catastrophic eruption of Vesuvius in August of the year A.D. 79.

3. The subsequent history of the find in the ground. Was the burial disturbed by later graves, or was the site eroded away by water?

Primary and Secondary Context

The context of any archaeological find can be affected by two processes: the original behavior of the people who used or made it and events that came later.

Primary context is the original context of the find, undisturbed by any factor, human or natural, since it was deposited by the people involved with it. The Iron Age warrior depicted in Figure 4.5, who was buried at Maiden Castle in A.D. 43, died from his wounds in a battle against a Roman legion. The survivors buried him swiftly in a shallow grave. The skeleton survived intact in its primary context until Sir Mortimer Wheeler excavated the undisturbed burial late in the 1930s (Wheeler, 1943).

Secondary context refers to the context of a find whose primary context has been disturbed by later activity. Very frequently, excavators of a burial ground will find incomplete skeletons whose intrusive graves have been disturbed by deposition of later burials. As in the tomb of Pharaoh Tutankhamun, tomb robbers may disturb the original grave furnishings, frantically searching for gold or precious oils. The latter were highly prized as fragrances by the Egyptian nobility. In still other instances, finds can be shifted by the natural forces of wind and weather. Many of the Stone Age tools found in European river gravels have been transported by floodwaters to a location far from their original place of use. All these disturbed finds are in a secondary context.

Spatial Context

Spatial context is important to archaeologists because it enables them to determine the distance between different objects or features, between entire settlements, or between settlements and key vegetational zones and landmarks. Important distances can be a few inches of level ground between a dagger and the associated skeleton of its dead owner, a mile

Figure 4.5 An iron arrowhead embedded in the backbone of a skeleton from a battle cemetery at Maiden Castle, Dorset, England. The artifact comes from a Roman cultural context; the skeleton, native British. Nevertheless, they are associated in the archaeological record.

separating two seasonal camps, or a complicated series of interrelated distance measurements separating dozens of villages that are part of an elaborate trading system carrying luxury goods through several geographic regions hundreds of miles apart.

One can identify four levels of spatial context, each of them coinciding with an actual level of human behavior.

1. *Artifacts:* individual human activity.
2. *Structure:* household or group activities (structures can, of course, include public buildings, such as temples, which are used by more than one household).
3. *Site:* community activity, groups of contemporary houses, stores, temples, and other structures.
4. *Region:* the activities of groups of people reflected by sites distributed on the landscape. These are sometimes referred to as a settlement pattern.

These four levels of spatial context are closely tied to actual cultural behavior (Figure 4.6). An artifact itself can provide valuable information

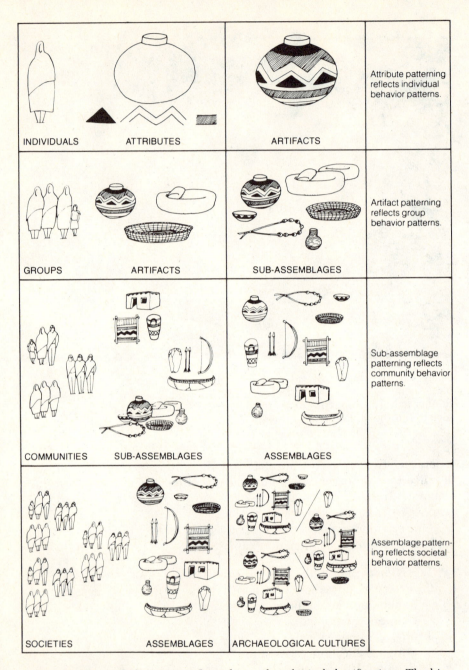

INDIVIDUALS **ATTRIBUTES** **ARTIFACTS**

Attribute patterning reflects individual behavior patterns.

GROUPS **ARTIFACTS** **SUB-ASSEMBLAGES**

Artifact patterning reflects group behavior patterns.

COMMUNITIES **SUB-ASSEMBLAGES** **ASSEMBLAGES**

Sub-assemblage patterning reflects community behavior patterns.

SOCIETIES **ASSEMBLAGES** **ARCHAEOLOGICAL CULTURES**

Assemblage patterning reflects societal behavior patterns.

Figure 4.6 Human behavior as reflected in archaeological classifications. The hierarchy begins with attributes and artifacts and ends with entire archaeological cultures.

on technology and actual use. But to infer cultural behavior we must know the artifact's association, both with other artifacts and with the matrix in which it was found. The patterning of artifacts in space around an abandoned iron smelting furnace or near the bones of a slaughtered bison kill is tangible evidence for specific human behavior. An unassociated projectile point will never give you anything more specific than the inference that it was used as a weapon. But a patterning of projectile points, scraping tools, and large boulders associated with a bison skeleton has a context in time and space that allows much more detailed inferences.

The basic assumption behind all studies of artifacts in space is that they were used for rational purposes and that characteristic groups of them were used for specific activities, such as ironworking, butchery, and hunting. It follows that similarly patterned groups of artifact types found on other sites resulted from similar activities, even if they show differences in detail. During the earlier millennia of the Stone Age, people enjoyed much the same level of hunting and gathering culture throughout Africa, Europe, and India. This parallel is reflected in thousands of similar-looking stone axes found in sites as widely separated as the Thames Valley in England and the Cape of Good Hope in South Africa.

ARTIFACTS, SUBASSEMBLAGES, AND ASSEMBLAGES

Artifacts

Artifacts are commonly defined as items that exhibit "any physical attributes that can be assumed to be the result of human activity" (Dunnell, 1971). This definition implies that the term *artifact* covers every form of archaeological find, from stone axes, bronze daggers, and clay pots to butchered animal bones, carbonized seeds, huts, and all other manifestations of human behavior that can be found in archaeological sites. Some archaeologists define artifacts by breaking them down into four categories: portable artifacts, features, structures, and ecofacts (forms of archaeological evidence that we will cover in more detail later in this book).

Whichever definition is preferred, all assume that any object or any event of manufacture or consumption is a product of human activity if its location or any other of its features cannot be accounted for by natural processes. In other words, artifacts are compared to natural objects and distinguished from them, not by individual features but by a patterning of different, human-caused features. It is this patterning that is important. A simple flake removed from an elaborate ceremonial obsidian knife blade may not necessarily show evidence of human modification. But the patterned, consistently repeated removal of several dozen or hundreds of small flakes—the pattern forming a knife—is highly diagnostic of human activity. Normally there is no difficulty at all in telling artifacts made or caused by humans from those caused by water action, fire, animal kills, or other natural phenomena.

Subassemblages

An artifact, such as an arrowhead or a basket, is made up of a combination of attributes (see Chapter 12), which make up a constant pattern of behavior reflected in the finished artifact. When such artifacts are found in patterned associations reflecting the shared cultural behavior of minimal groups, they are commonly classified in *subassemblages* (Deetz, 1967). A hunter uses a bow, arrows, and a quiver; a blacksmith uses hammers, tongs, and bellows to make hoes or spears; and so on. Subassemblages represent the behavior of individuals.

Assemblages

When a number of subassemblages of artifacts—say, a collection of hunting weapons, baskets, pounders, and digging sticks, traces of windbreaks, and stone vessels—are found in a contemporary association, they reflect in their patterning the shared activities of a total community and are known as *assemblages*. With assemblages, one is looking at the shared behavior of a community as a whole, which frequently is reflected in the remains of houses, the features associated with them, and community settlement patterns.

ARCHAEOLOGICAL SITES

Archaeological sites are places at which traces of past human activity are to be found. Sites are normally identified by the presence of artifacts. They can range in size from a large city, such as Teotihuacán, in the Valley of Mexico, to a tiny scatter of hunter-gatherer artifacts in Death Valley, California. There are millions of archaeological sites in the world, many of them still undiscovered. Some were occupied for a few hours, days, or weeks; some were occupied for a generation or two and then abandoned forever. Other localities, such as Mesopotamian occupation mounds, or *tells*, were reoccupied again and again for hundreds, even thousands, of years and contain many stratified layers (Figure 4.7). In contrast, the occupation site may contain little more than a surface scatter of potsherds or stone tools or an occupation layer buried under a few inches of topsoil. Archaeological sites can consist of a simple association (an isolated burial and one pot), many associations making up an assemblage of artifacts representing one community, or a series of assemblages stratified one above another.

Figure 4.7 In the background, a Mesopotamian tell, a site that was occupied over thousands of years.

Classifying Sites

Archaeological sites can be classified in these ways:

By archaeological context. The context of artifacts in the site can be used to distinguish between sites such as surface locations, single-level occupations, and stratified settlements.

By artifact content. The site is labeled according to its specific artifact content: pottery, stone tools, milling stones, and so on. The associations, assemblages, and subassemblages of artifacts in the site are used to label it as Stone Age, Mayan, and so on.

By geographic location. Most human settlements have been concentrated in well-defined types of geographic locations, and these sites can be referred to as cave sites, valley bottom sites, foothill sites, and the like.

By artifact content related to site function. Because subassemblages reflect individual human behavior, sites can be classified by the characteristic patterning of the artifacts found in them, such as kill sites and habitations.

Common Site Functions

These are some common site functions:

Living or *habitation sites* are the most important sites, for they are the places where people have lived and carried out a multitude of activities. The artifacts in living sites reflect domestic activities, such as food preparation, as well as toolmaking. Dwellings are normally present. The temporary camps of California fisherfolk are living sites, as are Stone Age rockshelters, southwestern pueblos, and Mes-

Approximate age	Geological epoch	Three-age terminology	Important events
3000 B.C. - 7800 B.C. -	HOLOCENE	Iron Age Bronze Age Neolithic Mesolithic	Writing in the Near East Origins of food production
8000 B.C. - 35,000 B.P. -	END OF PLEISTOCENE	Upper Paleolithic	Settlement of the Americas Origins of blade technology
70,000 B.P. - 400,000 B.P. -	PLEISTOCENE	Middle Paleolithic	Emergence of *Homo sapiens* (150,000 B.P.) Hand axes in widespread use
1.75 million B.P. - 5 million B.P. -		Lower Paleolithic	Origins of toolmaking (2 million B.P.)
13 million B.P. -	PLIOCENE		
25 million B.P. -	MIOCENE		No humans
34 million B.P. -	OLIGOCENE		

Note: This figure is for general reference throughout the text.
B.P. = "before the present."

Figure 5.1 Some nomenclature of Old World archaeology and geology.

NEW WORLD CHRONOLOGY

The three-age system of the Scandinavians was not adopted in North America. Systematic archaeological research flourished in the New World after 1859, but early attempts to find Paleolithic sites there were unsuccessful. The complicated cultural strata of the European rivers, with their rich storehouses of hand axes, did not exist, but relationships between the Indian population and the finds of the archaeologist were soon established. Stratigraphic observations and local cultural sequences did not preoccupy American archaeologists as they did the Europeans. Few researchers bothered to apply meticulous excavation techniques to later New World archaeological sites, in which, in any case, almost no metals were found (Willey and Sabloff, 1980).

Not until 1914 did chronology and detailed stratigraphic observation of the past become important in American archaeology when N. C. Nelson (1914), and later A. V. Kidder, began to use potsherds in southwestern sites as stratigraphic indicators. Kidder's classic excavations at the Pecos Pueblo (1924) brought about a conference there in 1927, which delineated eight sequential stages of Pueblo culture. With that event the foundations of accurate stratigraphic and chronological studies in American archaeology were soundly laid in the classic archaeological laboratory of the Southwest (Willey and Sabloff, 1980).

As we saw in Chapter 2, the direct historical approach and the development of tree-ring dating in the southwestern United States provided at least one area of the Americas with an accurate chronological framework. Most other regions were without precise time scales in calendar years until radiocarbon dating was begun in the 1950s.

CHRONOMETRIC (ABSOLUTE) AND RELATIVE DATING

Prehistoric chronologies cover enormous periods of time—millennia and centuries. Some idea of the scale of prehistoric time can be gained by piling up a hundred quarters. If the whole pile represents the time the human race has been on earth, the length of time covered by historical records would equal considerably less than the thickness of one quarter.

Archaeologists commonly refer to dates expressed in years as chronometric or absolute dates. Julius Caesar landed in Britain in 55 B.C.; Washington, D.C., was founded in A.D. 1800. The current chronometric dates for the earliest humans begin around four million years ago. Though not nearly as precise as the date for Caesar, they are nevertheless expressed in years. Dating experts draw widely on techniques invented by chemists and physicists and used by geologists for chronometric dating (see Chapter 6).

Relative dates correlate prehistoric sites of cultures with one another by their relative age. They are based on the law of superposition.

Relative dates are simpler to establish than chronometric dates. If I place a book on the table and then pile another on top of it, clearly the upper of the two was placed on the table at a later moment in time than the original volume. The second book became part of the pile after the first—though how long afterward we have no way of telling.

Stratigraphy and Superposition

Most relative chronology in archaeology has its basis in large- or small-scale stratigraphic observations in archaeological sites of all ages. As the eminent British archaeologist Sir Mortimer Wheeler (1954) argues, the basis of scientific archaeological excavation is the accurately observed and carefully recorded stratigraphic profile.

Superposition is fundamental in studying archaeological sites, for many settlements, such as Near Eastern mounds, Indian villages in the Ohio Valley, or cave sites, contain multilevel occupations whose decipherment is the key to their relative chronology. Wheeler (1954) describes the process of human occupation as applied to stratigraphy:

The human occupation of a site normally results in the accumulation of material of one kind or another on and about the area occupied. Objects are lost or discarded and become imbedded in the earth. Floors are renewed and old ones buried. Buildings crumble and new ones are built on the ruins. A flood may destroy a building or a town and deposit a layer of alluvium on its debris and later, when the flood has subsided, the level site may be reoccupied. Sometimes, the process is in the reverse direction. Evidences of occupation may be removed as in the deepening of an unsurfaced street by traffic, or the digging of a pit for the disposal of rubbish or for burial. . . . In one way or another the surface of an ancient town or village is constantly altering in response to human effort or neglect; and it is by interpreting rightly these evidences of alteration that we may hope to reconstruct something of the vicissitudes of the site and its occupants.

Stratigraphy, as applied to archaeological sites, is on a much smaller scale than that of geology, but it is often correspondingly more complicated (Harris, 1989). Most archaeological relative chronology employs careful observation of sequences of occupation levels as well as correlation of these with cultural sequences at other sites in the same area. Successive occupation levels may be found at the same spot, as in a cave, fort, or mound site, where many generations of settlers lived within a circumscribed or restricted area. In other sites, however, the chronological sequence can be horizontal, as when economic or political conditions dictate regular movement of villages when fields are exhausted or residence rules modified. In this case, a cultural sequence may be scattered throughout a series of single-level occupation sites over a large area and can be put together only by judicious survey work and careful analysis of the artifacts found in the different sites.

The artifacts, food bones, or other finds recovered from the layers of a site are as critical as the stratigraphy itself. Each level in a settlement, however massive or small, has its associated artifacts, the objects that the archaeologist uses as indicators of cultural and economic change. Indeed, the finds in each layer—and their associations—often provide the basic material for relative chronology. Furthermore, the relative dating of many sites is complicated by other questions. Has the site been occupied continuously? Do stratigraphic profiles reflect continuous occupation over a long time or a sequence that has been interrupted several times by warfare or simple abandonment of the site? Such problems can be resolved by careful examination of excavated profiles (Figures 5.2, 5.3, and 5.4).

Another factor that may affect interpretation of stratigraphy is the breaks or disruptions in the layering caused by human activity and by natural phenomena. These disruptions in a site form a vital part of the context of archaeological data.

Cultural transformations are those resulting from human behavior. For example, later occupants of a village may dig rubbish pits or graves into earlier strata. Cattle may be kept on the site, their hooves removing

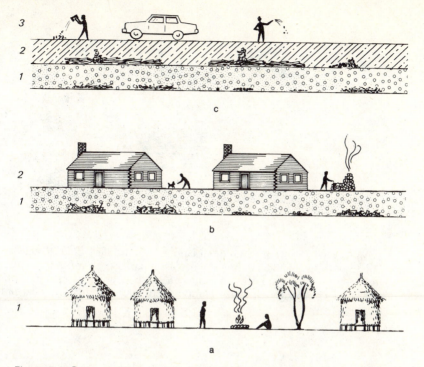

Figure 5.2 Superposition and stratigraphy: (a) A farming village flourishes five thousand years ago. After a time, the village is abandoned, and the huts fall into disrepair. Their ruins are covered by accumulating earth and vegetation. (b) After an interval, a second village is built on the same site, with different architectural styles. This village in turn is abandoned; the houses collapse into piles of rubble and are covered by accumulating earth. (c) Twentieth-century people park their cars on top of both village sites and drop litter and coins that when uncovered reveal to the archaeologist that the top layer is modern. An archaeologist digging this site would find that the modern layer is underlain by two prehistoric occupation levels; that square houses were in use in the upper of the two, which is the later (law of superposition); and that round huts are stratigraphically earlier than the square ones here. Therefore, village 1 is earlier than village 2, but when either was occupied or how many years separate village 1 from village 2 cannot be known without additional data.

the soil and disturbing the upper levels of the underlying horizons; this disturbance may also be caused by later people cultivating the rich soils of an abandoned village site. Building activities may cause foundation trenches and even stone walls to be sunk into earlier levels. The local inhabitants' technological level has a direct bearing on their ability to destroy evidence of earlier occupation. The inhabitants of a Near Eastern city are obviously more likely to have destroyed evidence of earlier occupation with constant rebuilding than a group of farmers without metal tools who merely reoccupy earlier village sites, minimally disturbing the

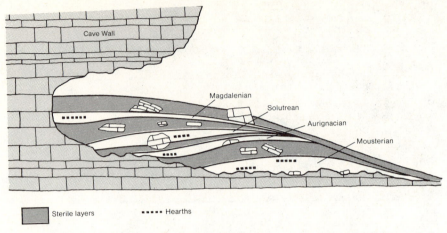

Figure 5.3 An idealized section through an Upper and Middle Paleolithic cave in France. The four archaeological culture layers are separated by sterile layers, the Mousterian being earlier than the Aurignacian, and so on. Most stratigraphic sequences are, of course, much more complicated than this hypothetical one. (After Oakley)

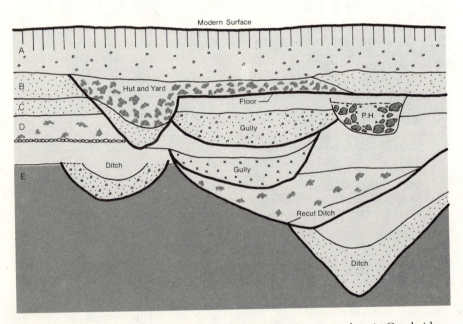

Figure 5.4 A stratigraphic section through the original town nucleus in Cambridge, England, showing profiles of prehistoric and Roman enclosures and huts with a post pole (P.H.), gullies, and ditches. The complex stratigraphy is interpreted by correlating the various features with their horizontal layers, a difficult task in this case because of the jumbled layers. The lowest ditch was cut into bedrock (E) and was truncated by a later ditch. ($\frac{1}{32}$ actual size)

underlying levels. Modern construction activity, road building, or deep plowing can also disturb a site and its contents, as can depredations by pot and treasure hunters, who care not at all about scientifically collected data.

Natural transformations are those caused by natural phenomena. A sudden flood can cover an abandoned village with a thick layer of mud. Volcanic ash buried Roman Herculaneum in A.D. 79. Burrowing animals, too, enjoy archaeological sites, working their way through the soft, organic soils of caves and village sites and disrupting stratigraphy over large areas of the settlement. Natural transformations are vital, for they determine the preservation of data. Preservation conditions differ widely from site to site and must be assessed carefully for each location. We must understand conditions of both cultural and natural transformation to interpret archaeological data precisely.

ARTIFACTS AND RELATIVE CHRONOLOGY

Manufactured artifacts are the fundamental data with which archaeologists study human behavior in the past. These artifacts are reflections of ancient human behavior and how it has changed throughout time. You need only look at the simple stone chopper of the earliest human beings and compare it to the latest and most sophisticated computer to get the point. Most artifact changes in prehistory, however, are extremely gradual. They are cumulative, minor changes in such elements as, say, shape, decoration, or lip angle of clay pots that lead ultimately to a vessel quite different in form, hardly recognizable as related.

Early Artifact Studies

Early archaeologists closely considered how objects evolved throughout time and studied minute details in these changes. If animals evolved, they argued, why not artifacts as well? As early as 1849, John Evans described the *stater* of Philip II of Macedon (Figure 5.5) and its progressive alteration in the hands of British coiners who had little interest in the Greek prototype. Evans noticed the degeneration in the design and used it to devise a chronological sequence for the coins. But he and others soon found that in tool design many variables affected changes, among them improved efficiency, stylistic degeneration, or simply popularity. British General Pitt-Rivers was the first to apply *typology*—a method used in natural science to work out relationships in the form and structure of organisms within an evolutionary sequence—to analysis of human-made objects (Thompson, 1977). Pitt-Rivers's typologies were based on another important principle: some technological trends are irreversible. An obvious example is an aeronautical enthusiast who, given a series of photographs of aircraft types dating from the beginnings of aviation up to the present, could place them in approximately correct order, even if he had no idea

Figure 5.5 Derivation of the British stater from the stater of Philip II of Macedon, as studied by Sir John Evans. The faces of the original Macedonian coins are at the far left.

of the dates of the photographs. It would simply be impossible to envision a typological sequence in which the earliest aircraft was a supersonic jet and the latest a 1912 Blériot monoplane: the modifications needed would be both illogical and incredible.

Another scholar, Egyptologist Sir Flinders Petrie, also contributed much to early study of artifact chronology. In 1902 he wanted to arrange a large number of pre-Dynastic tombs from the Nile Valley in chronological order. He eventually placed them in sequence by studying groups of pots found with the skeletons, so arranging the vessels that their stylistic differences reflected gradual change (Petrie, 1889). The handles on the jars were particularly informative, for they changed from functional appendages into more decorative handles and, finally, degenerated into painted lines. Petrie built up a series of pottery stages at Diospolis Parva to which he assigned "sequence dates," the fifty stages running from SD 30 to SD 80. The SD 30 was the oldest in the group. Petrie started his sequence with the number 30 because he assumed correctly that the earliest of his wares was not, in fact, the most ancient Egyptian pottery. His sequence dates were subsequently applied over wide areas of the Nile Valley, providing an admirable relative chronology for early Egyptian pottery that remained in use for many years. When a pot of a known type in the sequence date series was found, the pot itself and all objects associated with it could be dated to that stage in the sequence.

Seriation

In the past half century *seriation*, a technique for ordering items by their morphology, has evolved swiftly. Archaeologists generally use seriation to study relative chronology (Johnson, 1968; Marquardt, 1978). Recent studies of seriation are based on the assumption that popularity for any artifact or culture trait is transient. The miniskirt becomes the midi or maxi, dancing styles change from month to month, records hit the top forty but are forgotten in a short time, and each year's "brand new" automobile model is soon relegated to the secondhand lot. Other traits may have far longer lives. The chopper tools of the earliest people were a major element in early tool kits for hundreds of thousands of years. Candles were used for centuries before kerosene and gas lamps came into fashion. But each had its period of maximum relative frequency, or popularity. Figure 5.6 shows how such popularity distributions are made up with bar graphs plotted against strata or other archaeological associations. Each distribution of artifacts or culture traits plotted has a profile that has been described as resembling a battleship's hull viewed from the air.

The technique of seriation is based on the assumption that popularity of pottery types, forms of stone artifacts, and other culture traits peaks in a battleship curve, the widest part of the graph representing the period of maximum popularity. Thus it is argued that sites within a restricted and uniform geographic area showing similar plots of pottery or other artifact types are of broadly the same relative date. A series of sites or surface

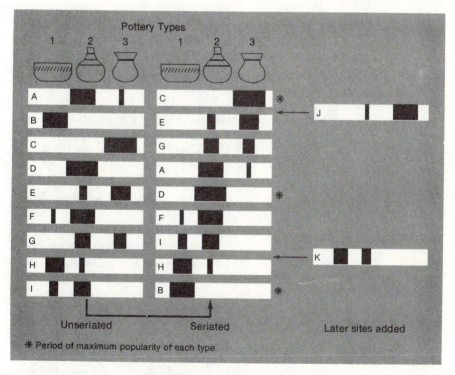

Figure 5.6 At the left, nine excavated sites (A to I) contain different percentages of three distinct pottery types. At the right, the nine sites have been seriated by rearranging the bars of type percentages into battleship curve order. At the far right, later excavations are eventually fitted into the sequence.

collections can be linked in a relative chronology (even though, without chronometric dates, one cannot tell when they were occupied) provided that the samples of artifacts used are statistically reliable. Edwin Dethlefsen and James Deetz tested the battleship curve assumption against some historical data, using a series of Colonial gravestones from a New England cemetery (Deetz, 1967; Dethlefsen and Deetz, 1966) (Figure 5.7). The gravestones, dated by the inscriptions on them, show three decorative styles—death's head, cherub, and urn and willow—that yield an almost perfect series of battleship curves following one upon the other. Seriation is also applied to stylistic change in a single series of artifacts that may in themselves form a battleship curve. The same principle used by Petrie with his pre-Dynastic jars applies, and a battleship curve results. Once the sequence of artifact types has been established, it is possible to insert new sites or single components from multilevel settlements into the carefully correlated sequence of seriated artifact types. These are added simply by comparing the percentages of types found in the new site with those in the correlated sequence as a whole. The new site is inserted into the sequence with considerable precision, on the assumption that closely similar artifacts were made at approximately the same time and that the lifetime of these tools coincides, albeit approximately, at all sites in a restricted culture area. If the collections are radiocarbon-dated, the seriation can also be given an accurate date in years (Dunnell, 1970).

The so-called battleship curve seriation method has been widely applied in American archaeology, especially by the late James Ford (1962), who used it extensively in the southeastern United States. Figure 5.8 illustrates a fine example of a seriated pottery sequence, from the Tehuacán Valley in Mexico, famed for its evidence of early cultivation of maize in Mesoamerica (MacNeish, 1970). It shows how three distinctive phases of Tehuacán culture were ordered in a relative chronology with the seriated counts of many pottery types.

You will notice that Figure 5.8 contains no absolute dates; the illustrated seriation is based on changing pottery forms and nothing else. In fact, of course, the chronological validity of the Tehuacán sequence has been confirmed by radiocarbon dating. Today's seriators use sophisticated statistical techniques to produce the seriation and to test the viability of their conclusions (Hole and Shaw, 1967; Johnson, 1968; Le Blanc, 1975; Marquardt, 1978). Sound sampling procedures are obviously essential if seriation is to be used extensively, and so it is necessary to establish that the samples collected were selected randomly (see Chapter 8).

Although seriation can work well with undated artifact sequences, it works even better when radiocarbon dates or other accurate dating methods are available. When artifact types change rather predictably throughout a period and these changes are well documented and dated in such a way that the direction of change is established, it is possible to assign undated sites with similar artifacts to an approximate relative position on the crude time scale. This is the approach pioneered by John Evans. It

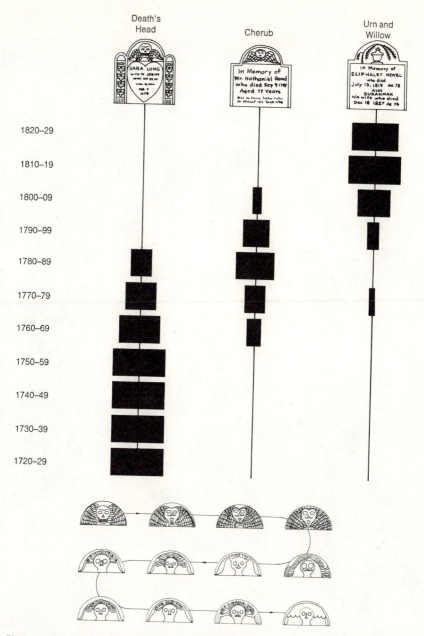

Figure 5.7 (top) Deetz's seriation of stylistic sequences of gravestones in Stoneham, Massachusetts. These dated battleship curves prove that all objects have a period of maximum popularity. (bottom) Seriation of a stylistic change within one New England gravestone motif. This type of seriation deals with the minute changes in a motif and shows how cultural traits change very gradually over time.

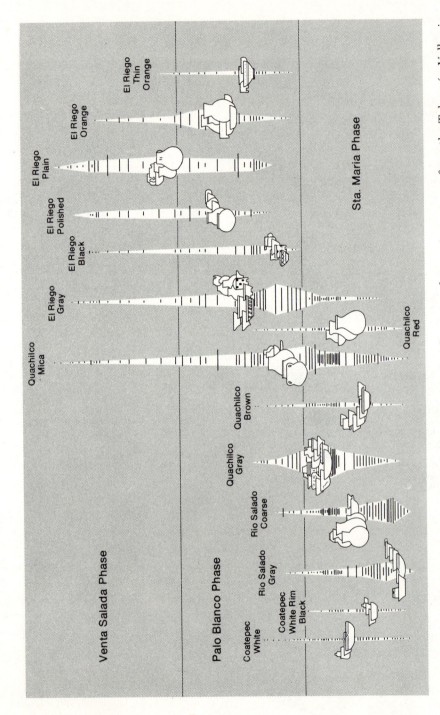

Figure 5.8 The battleship curve principle was used to develop this seriated ceramic sequence from the Tehuacán Valley in Mexico.

works well, of course, only when the artifacts being studied are of a type that changed in a distinctive and readily identifiable way.

Cross-Dating

One of the classic relative dating techniques of archaeological research, cross-dating has been applied to many sites in the New and Old Worlds. In its classic application, cross-dating is based on dated objects, such as coins or pottery types, whose precise ages are known in the localities of ultimate origin (Childe, 1956).

When a dated artifact, such as a coin, turns up in an otherwise undated prehistoric occupation level far from its place of origin, it is safe to conclude that the horizon was laid down no earlier than the date of the article of known age. An Indian village site in Virginia that yielded an Elizabethan coin bearing the date 1588 obviously dates to 1588 or later.

Such items as Chinese porcelain, Roman glass vessels, faience or glass beads, cotton and flax fabrics, bronze daggers, and Greek wine amphorae were luxuries that were diffused widely throughout the Old World, often to the barbarian tribes on the fringe of the unknown. The dates of styles of Chinese porcelain or Greek vases, changing according to fashion's dictates, are firmly established in historical records. Such objects are found hundreds and even thousands of miles from the source of manufacture in undated prehistoric camps or trading centers. Because the date of the import is known at its source, the settlement in which it is found can be relatively dated to a period contemporary with, or younger than, the exotic object of known age (Garlake, 1973; Piggott, 1965).

Cross-dating has also been widely applied to sites where objects of known age are absent. In these instances, a well-studied sequence of different artifacts, whose development throughout time has been established by excavation, seriation, and stratigraphy, can be used to fit sites in neighboring areas into the master sequence simply by taking the artifacts in them and matching them with the dated collections from the central area. Perhaps the largest recent study of this type was conducted in the Tehuacán Valley in Mexico, where the excellent artifacts and seriations from Richard MacNeish's many excavations were combined with radiocarbon dates to fix the chronological time span of each cultural phase in the valley (MacNeish, 1970). Armed with the precise chronological sequence, MacNeish's team was able to fit new sites and their artifactual contents into the sequence by both radiocarbon dating and cross-dating of the seriated artifacts in the site. In some instances, the relative chronology established by cross-dated artifacts was more accurate than a radiocarbon date that was out of line with the master chronology established on the massive Tehuacán sequence. This sequence was used as a cross-dating yardstick to correlate sites and cultural sequences all over Mexico. Obviously, individual trade artifacts with a short life at Tehuacán are best for such cross-datings, for their short life gives the cross-dating considerable precision. Artifacts such as ceramics or stone tools give less accurate re-sults, for entire pottery styles may be copied only in part by others or may take time to spread from one area to another. But approximations are better than no relative chronology at all.

Readers interested in the working details of both seriation and cross-dating are referred to the specialist literature (Marquardt, 1978).

Most methods of establishing relative chronology are coarser than is desirable, especially for more complicated sites—and what archaeologi-cal site is not complicated? Some researchers have experimented with an exciting new technique, *obsidian hydration,* to sort out associations, artifact orderings, and stratigraphic layers on many kinds of sites. This method, which also has chronometric applications, is described in Chap-ter 6.

PLEISTOCENE GEOCHRONOLOGY: THE ICE AGE

Most people have heard of the Great Ice Age, known to geologists as the Pleistocene, a period of recent geological time when much of Europe and North America experienced a bitter, arctic climate (Butzer, 1974, 1982). It was during this period that most of human prehistory was played out—against a background of complex and often dramatic climatic change that radically affected the pattern of human settlement. The science of Pleisto-cene geochronology (from the Greek *geos,* "earth"; *chronos,* "time") al-lows us to develop relative chronologies for early prehistory, and to at-tempt paleoenvironmental reconstructions (Dincauze, 1987).

The Ice Age began about 1.6 million years ago, during a long-term cooling trend in the world's oceans (Nilsson, 1983). These years have been ones of constant climatic change. The Pleistocene is conventionally di-vided into three subdivisions: the Lower, Middle, and Upper Pleistocene.

Lower Pleistocene times lasted until about 700,000 years ago. Deep sea cores tell us that climatic fluctuations between warmer and colder regi-mens were still relatively minor. These were critical millennia, for it was during this long period that archaic humans emerged in Africa and spread from tropical regions into temperate latitudes in Europe and Asia.

Middle Pleistocene times began with a reversal in the earth's polarity about 730,000 years ago, just about the time when humans first spread from Africa into Europe. This important event, the so-called Matuyama-Brunhes boundary, has been recognized in deep sea cores and in land deposits in many parts of the world. Since then, there have been at least eight cold (glacial) and warm (interglacial) cycles, the last cold cycle end-ing about 12,000 years ago. (Strictly speaking, we are still in an interglacial today). These cycles were so constant that it can be said that the world's climate has been in transition from cold to warm and back again for over 75 percent of the past 700,000 years. Typically, cold cycles have begun gradually, with vast continental ice sheets forming on land—in Scan-dinavia and on the Alps and over the northern parts of North America.

These expanded ice sheets locked up enormous amounts of water, causing world sea levels to fall by several hundred feet during glacial episodes. Thus the geography of the world changed dramatically, and large continental shelves were opened up for human settlement. When a warming trend began, deglaciation occurred very rapidly, and rising sea levels flooded low-lying coastal areas within a few millennia. During glacial maxima, glaciers covered a full third of the earth's land surface; they shrank to their present size during interglacials.

Throughout the past 700,000 years, vegetational changes have mirrored climatic fluctuations. During glacial episodes, treeless arctic steppe and tundra covered much of Europe and parts of North America but gave way to temperate forest during interglacials. In the tropics, Africa's Sahara Desert may have supported grassland during interglacials, expanding dramatically during dry, cold spells.

Upper Pleistocene times began about 128,000 years ago, with the beginning of the last interglacial. This lasted until about 118,000 years ago, when a slow cooling trend brought full glacial conditions to Europe and North America. This Würm glaciation, named after a river in the Alps, lasted until about 10,000 years ago, when there was a rapid return to more temperate conditions.

The final Würm glaciation was a period of constantly fluctuating climatic change, with several episodes of more temperate climate in northern latitudes. It serves as the backdrop for some of the most important developments in human prehistory, notably the spread of anatomically modern *Homo sapiens sapiens* from the tropics to all parts of the Old World and into the Americas (Fagan, 1991b). Between about 25,000 and 15,000 years ago, northern Eurasia's climate was intensely cold, and a series of brilliant Stone Age hunter-gatherer cultures evolved both on the open tundra and in the sheltered river valleys of southwestern France and northern Spain, cultures famous for their fine antler and bone artifacts and exceptional artwork.

The world's geography was dramatically different 20,000 years ago, and the differences had a major impact on human prehistory. One could walk from Siberia to Alaska across a flat, low-lying plain, the Bering Land Bridge (Figure 5.9). This was the route by which humans first reached the Americas more than 12,000 years ago (Fagan, 1987). The low-lying coastal zones of Southeast Asia were far more extensive 15,000 years ago than they are now, and they supported a thriving population of Stone Age hunter-gatherers. The fluctuating distributions of vegetational zones also affected the patterns of human settlement and the course of human history (Loew and Walker, 1985).

From the archaeological perspective, the major climatic events of the past 1.5 million years provide a broad framework for a relative chronology of human culture. Although almost no human beings lived on, or very close to, the great ice sheets that covered so much of the Northern Hemisphere, they did live in regions affected by geological phenomena associated with the ice sheets: coastal areas, lakes, and river floodplains.

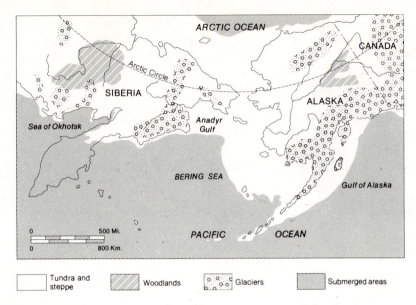

Figure 5.9 The Bering Land Bridge as reconstructed by the latest research. (After Jason Smith)

When human artifacts are found in direct association with Pleistocene geological features of this type, it is sometimes possible to tie in archaeological sites with the relative chronology of Pleistocene events derived from geological strata. And thanks to sophisticated geochronological methods like pollen analysis, it is often possible to reconstruct local environments during the Ice Age with remarkable precision (a comprehensive description will be found in Nilsson, 1983).

RECONSTRUCTING THE ICE AGE

Deep Sea Cores

Until the 1960s, scientists reconstructed the climatic events with the use of land-based phenomena such as ice sheets and vegetational sequences obtained from Pleistocene swamps and lake beds. Dramatic advances in oceanography, especially in the study of deep sea core borings, have revolutionized our knowledge of the Ice Age. Sediments from these cores provide something that has never been found on land—a *continuous* stratigraphic record of Pleistocene events. These events have been fixed at key points by radiocarbon dates (see Chapter 6) and by studies of paleomagnetism (ancient magnetism). The Matuyama-Brunhes reversal of 730,000 years ago is a key stratigraphic marker, which can be identified both in sea cores and in volcanic strata ashore, where it can be dated precisely with potassium argon samples (Chapter 6).

Deep sea cores produce long columns of ocean floor sediments that include skeletons of small marine organisms that once lived close to the ocean's surface. These planktonic foraminifera consist largely of calcium carbonate. When alive, their minute skeletons absorb organic isotopes. The ratio of two of these isotopes—oxygen 16 and oxygen 18—varies as a result of evaporation. When evaporation is high, more of the lighter oxygen 16 is extracted from the ocean, leaving the plankton to be enriched by more, heavier oxygen 18. When great ice sheets formed on land during glacial episodes, sea levels fell as moisture was drawn off for continental ice caps. During such periods, the world's oceans contained more oxygen 18 in proportion to oxygen 16, a ratio reflected in millions of foraminifera. A mass spectrometer is used to measure this ratio, which does not reflect ancient temperature changes but is merely a statement about the size of the oceans and about contemporary events on land. It is possible to confirm climatic fluctuations by using other lines of evidence as well. You can analyze the changing frequencies of foraminifera and other groups of marine microfossils in the cores. By using statistical techniques, and assuming that relationships between different species and sea conditions have not changed, climatologists have been able to turn these frequencies into numerical estimates of sea surface temperatures and ocean salinity over the past few hundred thousand years and produce a climatic profile of much of the Ice Age.

The core that serves as the standard reference for events during the past 700,000 years comes from the Solomon Plateau in the Pacific Ocean, core V28-238 (Figure 5.10) (Shackleton and Opdyke, 1973). The Matuyama-Brunhes boundary occurs at a depth of 39.3 feet (1200 cm) in the core. Above it a sawtoothlike curve identifies eight complete glacial and interglacial cycles, a far more complicated picture of the Middle and Upper Pleistocene than comes from land sediments. Scientists believe that these changes are triggered by long-term astronomical changes, especially in the earth's orbit around the sun (Covey, 1984). These affect the seasonal and north-south variations of solar radiation the earth receives.

Glaciations, Interglacials, and Sea Levels

The glaciers and ice sheets that make up the framework for geochronological studies were formed in mountainous, high-latitude areas and on continental plains during the Pleistocene. Prolonged periods of arctic climate and abundant snowfall caused glaciers to form over enormous expanses of northern Europe, North America, and the Alpine areas of France, Italy, and Switzerland. Many times during this period, arctic conditions prevailed over the Northern Hemisphere. These alternated with shorter interglacial phases, when world climate was considerably warmer than it is today.

Every ice sheet had a *periglacial zone*, an area affected by glacial climatic influences. Some 25,000 years ago, the persistent glacial high pressure zone centered over the northern ice sheet caused dry, frosty

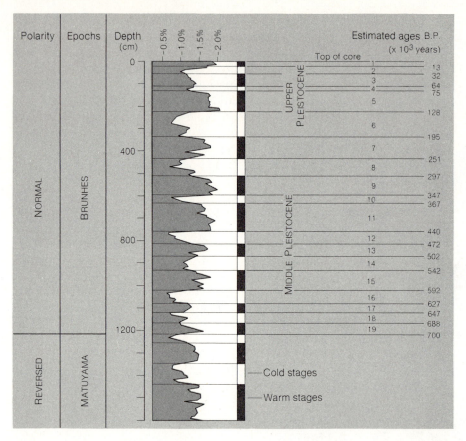

Figure 5.10 Stratigraphic record of the Pleistocene from deep sea core V28-238. The Matuyama-Brunhes boundary occurs at about 730,000 years ago. The sawtoothlike profile chronicles the relative size of the world's oceans and ice caps. (After Shackleton and Opdyke, 1973)

winds to blow over the periglacial regions. The dry winds blew fine particles of dust, known as *loess,* onto the huge, rolling plains of central and eastern Europe and northern America.

The loess plains of central and eastern Europe were inhabited by hunter-gatherers who preyed on mammoths and other big game (Soffer, 1985). They lived in long houses built of bones and skins that, when excavated, were found at least partially sunk in the loess soil (Figure 5.11). The relative dates of these settlements have been established by correlating the occupation levels with the different periods of loess accumulation that took place during the Pleistocene. Much later, in about 6000 B.C., Danubian peoples, the first farmers of temperate Europe, settled almost exclusively on these same light loess soils, for they were eminently suitable for the simple slash-and-burn agriculture practiced by these pioneer farmers (Champion and others, 1984).

Figure 5.11 Reconstruction of 18,000-year-old Stone Age houses from Mezhirich in the western USSR. The dwellings were built of a framework of mammoth bones, carefully arranged in intricate patterns. The frame was covered with hides and probably sod.

The ice sheet growing on land had effects beyond formation of loess plains. The water that falls as snow to form the ice sheets and glaciers ultimately comes from the oceans. When large areas in the northern latitudes were covered with ice, enormous quantities of water—enough to reduce the general level of the oceans by many meters (more than 90 meters at the height of the last glaciation 18,000 years ago)—were immobilized on land. This *eustatic effect* was accompanied by an *isostatic* effect as well. The sheer dead weight of the massive ice sheets sank the loaded continental blocks of the land masses into the viscous underlying layers of the earth that lie some ten kilometers (six miles) below the surface. The isostatic effect was obviously confined to ice-covered areas, but the eustatic effect was felt all over the world. At their maximum, the sea levels of the world may have been lowered as much as 200 meters (660 feet), causing major geographic changes. Until roughly 4500 B.C., Britain was joined to the continent by a strip of marsh, covering the area that is now the North Sea and part of the English Channel (Figure 5.12).

Many prehistoric settlements occupied during periods of low sea level are, of course, buried deep beneath the modern oceans. Numerous sites on ancient beaches have been found dating to times of higher sea level. American archaeologist Richard Klein excavated a coastal cave at Nelson Bay in the Cape Province of South Africa that now overlooks the Indian Ocean (Klein, 1983). Large quantities of shellfish and other marine animals are found in the uppermost levels of the cave. But in the lower levels, occupied roughly 11,000 to 12,000 years ago, fish bones and other marine resources are very rare. Klein suspects that the seashore was many miles away at that time, for world sea levels were much lower during a long period of arctic climate in northern latitudes. Today the cave is only 45 meters (50 yards) from the sea.

Ice Age Animals

Throughout the millennia of the Ice Age, humans subsisted on game animals and plant foods. Until relatively recently, perhaps as recently as 250,000 years ago, people scavenged much of their large game meat from predator kills, perhaps killing only smaller, less formidable mammals—this issue is still in dispute. By 30,000 years ago, however, humans had become

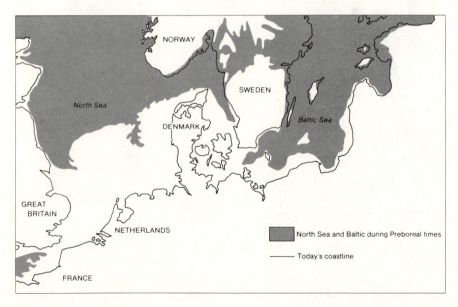

Figure 5.12 Great Britain and Scandinavia at the end of the Pleistocene, showing sea levels around 7000 B.C.

highly efficient big-game hunters, not afraid of animals as large and formidable as the bison and the mammoth, the arctic elephant. But throughout prehistory, hunters' weapons and butchery tools are found in association with the fragmented bones of animals large and small. Throughout the Ice Age, these prey were often extinct species, such as the giant pigs and buffalo found at Olduvai Gorge in Tanzania, East Africa. Paleontologists have classified Pleistocene faunas from many localities and have tried to build up relative chronologies of the Ice Age from evolutionary changes in such animals as the elephant. Such sequences are of some use, but animal bones suffer from many disadvantages as a dating tool. Mammals vary greatly in their sensitivity to climatic change. Some, like horses, are tolerant of both cold and warm climates; others prefer warm weather but can stand extremely cold temperatures with remarkable resilience. Furthermore, so many factors affect the distribution of mammals and the success of one species at the expense of another that it is very difficult to be sure that one is dealing with a chronological difference and not an environmental one. The climatic data derived from pollen analysis offers many more opportunities for precise measurement of climatic change.

At several points during the Ice Age, large-scale extinctions of mammals large and small occurred. The most dramatic of these extinctions occurred at the end of the Pleistocene, some 11,000 years ago, when many large arctic mammals like the woolly rhinoceros and more than 50 other species of American animals vanished within a short time. The whole question of faunal extinctions during the Ice Age is much debated, especially the role that human beings played in the demise of large animals like the mastodon and the mammoth in the Americas (Martin and Klein, 1984).

Plants and Pollen Analysis

If hunting was important during prehistory, foraging for wild plant foods was even more so, and it remains significant among hunter-gatherer societies to this day. Vegetation is one of the best indicators of ecological change, for it depends on climate and soil for survival and is a sensitive barometer of climatic alteration. Pollen analysis, or *palynology,* is a comprehensive way of studying ancient vegetation; it was developed in 1916 by a Swede, Lennart van Post, who used forest trees. Subsequently, this analysis was extended to all pollen-liberating vegetation. The principle of pollen analysis is simple (Dimbleby, 1985). Large numbers of pollen grains are dispersed in the atmosphere and have remarkable preservative properties if deposited in an unaerated geological horizon. The pollen grains can be identified microscopically (Figure 5.13) with great accuracy and can be used to reconstruct a picture of the vegetation that grew near the spot where they are found.

Pollen analysis begins in the field. The botanist visits the excavation and collects a series of closely spaced pollen samples from the stratigraphic sections at the site. Back in the laboratory, the samples are examined

Chapter
6

Time: Chronometric Dating

*M*ore effort has been devoted to inventing methods of chronometric dating in archaeology than to almost any other aspect of the subject (Bailey, 1983). The reason for this interest is that fundamental questions about the past are involved. How old is this tool? How long ago was that site occupied? Are these villages contemporary? These are probably the first questions asked by anyone curious about an artifact or a prehistoric village, as well as by the archaeologist. They remain among the most difficult to answer.

We now have an impressive array of chronological techniques for dating the past. Some have become well established and are reliable. Others, after a brief vogue, have been ejected into academic oblivion when someone discovers a fatal flaw. In practice, the huge span of human cultural history is dated by a number of scientific methods; the chronological span is shown in Figure 6.1. Potassium argon dating provides a somewhat generalized chronology for the first two-thirds of human history, its recent limits reaching up some 20,000 years ago (it is less precise after 100,000 years). The other major radioactive technique, radiocarbon dating, covers a period from approximately 75,000 years ago up to as recently as A.D. 1500, when the standard errors become too large for the small time spans.

As for recent periods, historical documents provide a fairly accurate chronology for kings and political events going back more than five thousand years in the Near East and shorter periods elsewhere in the world. In the New World, prehistory ends with European settlement of the Americas in the fifteenth century. Frequently in these more recent periods, archaeology can be used in conjunction with historical

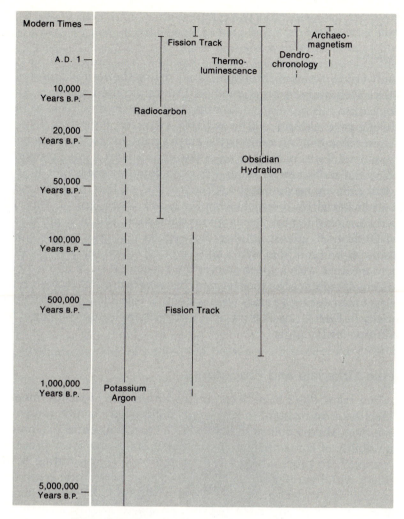

Figure 6.1 Chronological spans of major chronometric methods in archaeology. B.P.: "Before the present."

documents or oral records, which are covered by many other dating methods, including imported objects of known historical date and dendrochronology. Dates in years not only tell how old a site is but also illuminate the relationships among communities, cultures, or larger geographic or social units.

Let us now look at the principal methods of chronometric dating used to develop absolute chronologies for world prehistory. Our discussion starts with the chemical and physical methods used to date the earlier millennia of prehistory and ends in modern times with objects of known age.

from Koobi Fora in northern Kenya, dated to about 1.85 million years, one of the earliest dates for human artifacts (Curtis, 1975).

Limitations

Potassium argon dates can be taken only from volcanic rocks, preferably from actual volcanic flows. The laboratory technique is so specialized that only a trained geologist should take the samples in the field. Archaeologically, it is obviously vital that the relationship between the lava being dated and the human settlement it purports to date be worked out carefully. The standard deviations for potassium argon dates are so large that greater accuracy is almost impossible to achieve.

Chronological Limits

Potassium argon dating is accurate from the origins of the earth up to about 100,000 years before the present.

RADIOCARBON DATING

Principles

Radiocarbon dating is the best known and most widely used of all chronometric dating methods. J. R. Arnold and W. F. Libby (1949) published a paper in *Science* describing the dating of organic samples from objects of known age by their radiocarbon content. The paper caused an archaeological furor, but once checked, it was soon applied to organic materials from prehistoric sites hitherto undatable by any reliable chronometric method. More than forty years have elapsed since the radiocarbon dating method became a regular part of the archaeologist's tool kit. For the first time we begin to have a world chronology for prehistory, based almost entirely on dates obtained by Libby's technique.

The radiocarbon dating method is based on the fact that cosmic radiation produces neutrons that enter the earth's atmosphere and react with nitrogen. They produce carbon 14, a carbon isotope with eight rather than the usual six neutrons in the nucleus. With these additional neutrons, the nucleus is unstable and is subject to gradual radioactive decay. Willard Libby calculated that it took 5,568 years for half the carbon 14 in any sample to decay, its so-called half-life. (The half-life is now more accurately measured to be 5,730 years.) He found that the neutrons emitted radioactive particles when they left the nucleus, and he arrived at a method for counting the number of emissions in a gram of carbon.

Carbon 14 is believed to behave exactly like ordinary carbon from a chemical standpoint, and together with ordinary carbon it enters into the carbon dioxide of the atmosphere. The tempo of the process corresponds to the rates of supply and disintegration. Because living vegetation builds up its own organic matter by photosynthesis and by using atmospheric carbon dioxide, the proportion of radiocarbon present in it is equal to that in the atmosphere. As soon as an organism dies, no further radiocarbon is incorporated into it. The radiocarbon present in the dead organism will continue to disintegrate slowly, so that after 5,730 years only half the original amount will be left; after about 11,100 years, only a quarter; and so on. Thus if you measure the rate of disintegration of carbon 14 to nitrogen, you can get an idea of the age of the specimen being measured. The initial amount of radiocarbon in a sample is so small that the limit of detectability is soon reached. Samples earlier than 75,000 years contain only minuscule quantities of carbon 14 (Grootes, 1978).

Datable Materials and Procedures

Radiocarbon dates can be taken from samples of many organic materials. About a handful of charcoal, burnt bone, shell, hair, skin, wood, or other organic substance is needed. The samples themselves are collected with meticulous care during excavation from particular stratigraphic contexts so that an exact location, specific structure, or even a hearth is dated. Several dates must be taken from each level, because one or more may have been contaminated by a variety of factors. Modern rootlets, disturbances in the stratigraphy, and even packing with cotton wool or newspaper can introduce younger carbon into an ancient sample, although some of the more obvious contaminations are eliminated by careful laboratory treatment.

The first stage in the dating procedure is physical examination of the sample. The material is then converted into gas, purified to remove radioactive contaminants, and then piped into a proportional counter (Figure 6.3). The counter itself is sheltered from background radiation by massive iron shields. The sample is counted at least twice at intervals of about a week. The results of the count are then compared with a modern count sample, and the age of the sample is computed by a formula to produce the radiocarbon date and its statistical limit of error.

A date received from a radiocarbon dating laboratory is in this form:

3,621 ± 180 radiocarbon years before the present (B.P.)

The figure 3,621 is the age of the sample (in radiocarbon years) before the present. With all radiocarbon dates, A.D. 1950 is taken as the present by international agreement. Notice that the sample reads in *radiocarbon years*, not calendar years. Corrections must be applied to make this an absolute date.

The radiocarbon age has the reading ± 180 attached to it. This is the *standard deviation*, an estimate of the amount of probable error. The figure 180 years is an estimate of the 360-year range within which the date falls. Statistical theory provides that there is a 2 out of 3 chance that the

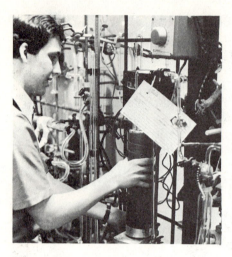

Figure 6.3 A radiocarbon laboratory at the University Museum, University of Pennsylvania. Left: The equipment used to purify the sample and convert it to gas. Right: The equipment used for measuring radioactivity.

correct date is between the span of one standard deviation (3,441 and 3,801). If we double the deviation, chances are 19 out of 20 that the span (3,261 and 3,981) is correct. Most dates in this book are derived from carbon 14–dated samples and should be recognized for what they are—statistical approximations.

The conventional radiocarbon method relies on measurements of a beta-ray decay rate to date the sample. A number of laboratories are now experimenting with an ultrasensitive mass spectrometer to count the individual carbon 14 atoms in a sample instead. This exciting new approach has numerous advantages and promises to overcome many disadvantages in the traditional method. One can date much smaller samples—as small as a fragment of straw in a potsherd—and the results will be more accurate than conventional readings. It takes only a few minutes to measure samples that hitherto took hours to study. The practical limits of radiocarbon dating with beta decay approaches are between 40,000 and 60,000 years.

Accelerator mass spectrometry allows radiocarbon dating to be carried out by direct counting of carbon 14 atoms, rather than by counting radioactive disintegrations (Gowlett, 1987). This has the advantage that samples up to 1/1,000 the size can be dated, especially for the time span between 10,000 and 30,000 years ago. Accelerator dating distinguishes between carbon 14 and carbon 12 and other ions through its mass and energy characteristics, requiring far smaller samples to do so. Even more important, the problem of background radiation is eliminated, and the sample sizes are the same for all time periods, the small quantity of organic material required allowing retesting if this proves necessary. The samples needed are so small that it is possible, for example, to date an individual tree ring or an actual artifact. The method is much faster, for relatively modern samples can be dated within thirty minutes or so, as opposed to the many hours required for the conventional system.

Accelerator dating is especially useful for dating the amino acids from bone collagen, but almost any material can be dated, even tiny wood fragments preserved in the haft sockets of metal spearheads, for example. The technique has been used for dating Upper Paleolithic sites in Europe, where charcoal is rare, and is especially useful as a method for dating series of burials from mass graves and other circumstances where great precision is required. At present, about a third of all radiocarbon dates are coming from this new approach (Gillespie and others, 1984).

Archaeological Applications

Radiocarbon dates have been obtained from African hunter-gatherers' settlements as long as 50,000 years before the present, from Paleo-Indian bison kills in the American Plains, from early farming villages in the Near East and the Americas, and from cities and spectacular temples associated with early civilizations. The method can be applied to sites of almost any type where organic materials are found, provided that they date to between about 40,000 years ago and A.D. 1500.

Limitations

Radiocarbon dates can be obtained only from organic materials, which means that relatively few artifacts can be dated. But associated hearths with abundant charcoal, broken animal bones, and burnt wooden structures can be dated. Artifacts contemporary with such phenomena are obviously of the same age as the dated samples. The context of any dated sample has to be established beyond all doubt, and having a block of samples from the same division is preferable so that they can be treated statistically and tested for probable degree of accuracy. It is the moment of death of an organism that is dated. All radiocarbon dates are, of course, statistical computations and if uncalibrated, merely the radiocarbon age that is statistically most likely.

Calibration of Radiocarbon Dates

Just when archaeologists thought they had found an accurate and reliable means for dating the past, radiocarbon dates for tree rings of the California bristlecone pine were published. The readings were consistently younger for trees before 1200 B.C. because Libby made a false assumption when he originally formulated the radiocarbon method. He had argued that the concentration of radiocarbon in the atmosphere remained constant as time passed, so that prehistoric samples, when alive, would have contained the same amount of radiocarbon as living things today.

In fact, changes in the strength of the earth's magnetic field and alterations in solar activity have considerably varied the concentration of radiocarbon in the atmosphere and in living things. Thus samples of six thousand years ago were exposed to a much higher concentration than are living things today. It is possible, fortunately, to correct radiocarbon dates by using accurate dates from tree rings. Since 1966, dendrochronology experts have been systematically applying radiocarbon analysis to tree-ring samples of known age and have plotted calibration curves, which are used for converting radiocarbon dates into actual dates in years. A task force of radiocarbon experts has recently produced tables that match radiocarbon ages with calibrated dates (Klein and others, 1982). This tool is likely to receive universal acceptance in coming years; it calibrates dates between A.D. 1950 and 6500 B.C. The discrepancies between radiocarbon and calibrated dates are wide. Here is an example: 10 B.C. ± 30 has a calibrated interval of 145 B.C. to A.D. 210. British archaeologist Colin Renfrew calibrated radiocarbon dates for European prehistory some years ago. He claimed that, as a result, many long-accepted chronological relationships are now reversed (Renfrew, 1971). According to him, the famous megalithic stonebuilt tombs of western Europe are older than the pyramids of Egypt, supposedly their predecessors. The final layout of Stonehenge (the complex of prehistoric stone circles in southern Britain) constructed in 1600 B.C., was originally thought to have been inspired by Mycenaean designs. When the calibrated dates were released, it was found that the earliest stages of Stonehenge dated to before 1800 B.C., much older than the Mycenaean civilization in question. The new, calibrated radiocarbon chronology for Europe, argues Renfrew, allows us to think of distinctive European societies that developed their own institutions without the Oriental influence favored by so many archaeologists. Few prehistorians jumped so whole-heartedly into the new chronologies as Renfrew, but widespread calibration of radiocarbon dates is certain to be a reality within a few years. In the meantime, most people think of radiocarbon dates as nothing more than *radiocarbon ages,* not dates in actual years. Earlier dates are still uncalibrated, but recently scientists have used a new, highly accurate technique based on the decay of uranium into thorium to date fossil coral near Barbados in the Caribbean. They compared these dates to radiocarbon results, and found that dates between 10,000 and 30,000 years ago may be as much as 3,500 years too recent. Earlier radiocarbon ages, then, are of unknown accuracy, but the new coral researches may provide more accurate chronologies for much of the late Ice Age in the future.

Chronological Limits

Carbon 14 dating is accurate from around 40,000 years B.P. to A.D. 1500.

FISSION TRACK DATING

Principles

Fission track dating is a new chronometric method that promises to have important archaeological applications in the future. The principle of the method is that many minerals and natural glasses, such as obsidian, contain very small quantities of uranium that undergo slow, spontaneous decay. Most uranium atoms decay by emitting alpha particles, but spontaneous fission causes the decay of about one atom in every two million, the fission decay rate and its extent are constant, and the date of any mineral containing uranium can be obtained by measuring the amount of uranium in the sample, which is done by counting the *fission tracks* in the material. These tracks are narrow trails of damage in the material caused by fragmentation of massive, energy-charged particles. The older the sample, the more tracks it has. It is possible to examine fission tracks under high magnification and to calculate the sample's age by establishing the ratio between the density of the tracks and the uranium content of the sample.

Datable Materials and Procedures

Two counts of fission tracks are needed for each sample. The materials used, which must have a high uranium content, can be either volcanic rock, as in lava flows that originated more recently than the beginnings of prehistory, or manufactured materials, such as certain types of artificial glass. In rocks, it is the time of origin of the rocks that is being dated, not the time of their utilization. An optical microscope is used to examine the tracks in the sample, which have first been etched with hydrofluoric acid. This procedure enlarges the tracks to make them more visible. The first count establishes the density of the tracks; the second, by inducing fission of uranium 235 through neutron irradiation, makes a count of the uranium content in the sample. The age of the sample is the ratio of the number of observed tracks resulting from natural fission to those resulting from induced fission.

Archaeological Applications

The fission track dating technique is still new to archaeology, but it promises to become a fairly precise means of dating samples between 100,000 and one million years old. The method can be used to date many mineralogical materials, but in archaeology it is applicable only to sites that were subjected to volcanic activity just before, during, or shortly after occupation. Sites overlain or underlain by lava can be given upper or lower age limits by dating the lava. Because many early sites are found in volcanic areas, such as the Great Rift Valley of East Africa, the method has obvious applications.

Few results from the fission track method have been published, but volcanic pumice from Bed I at Olduvai Gorge, where the early hominid fossils were found, was dated to 2.03 ± 0.28 million by the fission track method. This reading was in reasonably close agreement with Leakey's original date of about 1.8 million years, obtained from potassium argon readings for the same stratum. Modern manufactured glass with high uranium content, used to make a nineteenth-century candlestick, has been dated accurately to the last century (Brill, 1964; Fleischer, 1975).

Limitations

The limitations of fission track dating are much the same as those of potassium argon dating. Only volcanic rocks contemporary with a human settlement and formed at the time the site was occupied can be used.

Chronological Limits

Fission track dating is accurate from one million to 100,000 years before the present. Some limited application to historic artifacts is possible as well.

OBSIDIAN HYDRATION

Principles

Obsidian is a natural glass substance formed by volcanic activity. It has long been prized for its sharp edges and other excellent qualities for toolmaking. Projectile heads, hand axes, blades, and even mirrors were made from this widely traded material in both the New World and the Old. A new dating method makes use of the fact that a freshly made surface of obsidian (and no other known artifact material) will absorb water from its surroundings, forming a measurable *hydration layer* that is invisible to the naked eye. Because the freshly exposed surface has a strong affinity for water, it keeps absorbing until it is saturated with a layer of water molecules. These molecules then slowly diffuse into the body of the obsidian. This hydration zone contains about 3.5 percent water, increasing the density of the layer and allowing it to be measured accurately under polarized light. Each time a freshly fractured surface is prepared, as when a tool is being made, the hydration begins again from scratch. Thus the depth of hydration achieved represents the time since the object was manufactured or used (Leute, 1987).

Hydration is observed with microscopically thin sections of obsidian sliced from artifacts and ground down to about .003 inch. The thickness of the layer is measured through the microscope at eight spots, the mean value being calibrated into units of microns (micrometers). These thickness readings can be used in both absolute and relative chronologies (Taylor and Meighan, 1978; Friedman and Trembour, 1983). Unfortunately, this promising dating method has some problems, mostly because we still do not fully understand hydration. Little is known about how temperature changes or chemical composition affect hydration, and so it is impossible to use the method without calibrating it against tree-ring dates or some other established archaeological procedure. Researchers are working hard to solve these problems so that obsidian hydration can become an economical and widely applicable dating method in the future.

po
jig
sou
de
the
cla
rec

or

Ar

Fro
app
ear
dip
acc
Ge
atte
chr
rea
tho
tion
be
and

Ch

Arc
to t

CA

Cal

A ca
of d
chro
anci
Yuca
Cale
Egy]
life i

cale

Archaeological Applications

Obsidian hydration is a useful way of ordering large numbers of artifacts in relative series, simply by positioning each in the series according to its micron reading, such as 1.5 or 2.0. Provided one has control over such constants as chemical composition, one can place artifacts in order with great precision. This approach was first tried at the Mammoth Junction site in Colorado, which served not only as a quarry site but also as a residential settlement and hunting station. By assigning some 450 artifacts such as projectile heads and scrapers positions in a series, the investigators were able to find the order in which 37 types of projectile point came into fashion and disappeared. The chronological data could be linked to attributes like weight or length: all six of the latest styles weighed less than a gram, as if they had been used not for spears but for much lighter arrows.

Obsidian hydration is extremely useful for sorting out the cultural content of sites like shell middens, in which the stratigraphic layers are often indistinct and the site is excavated in arbitrary levels. By plotting the hydration values from obsidian artifacts against the excavated layers on a three-dimensional scatter diagram, you can sometimes identify how much the arbitrary excavation has mixed artifacts from different levels. Another possible application has researchers using hydration readings to associate artifacts found on a living surface with one another in groups. Using arbitrary ranges of hydration readings, say, 1.5 to 1.9, one can group obsidian tools into units useful for analysis, with little or no possibility of contamination with other tools. This technique is particularly useful on surface sites.

Applications of obsidian hydration to chronometric chronology are still in their infancy (Meighan, 1983). If one can determine the rate of hydration in a population of artifacts, there is a chance that one can assign each artifact a date in years. More than two thousand obsidian dates were obtained from 520 test trenches at the city of Kaminaljuyu in Guatemala. These, and a further two thousand samples from surrounding sites, were used to piece together dozens of phases in the complicated residential history of the site and its satellite communities. Many of the dated artifacts came from surface sites, where they were the only possible source of chronological information. The same approach was used at the Aztec site of Chiconautla in the Basin of Mexico. This was known to be an important Aztec community. But the excavators were able to use obsidian hydration to show that the large numbers of rasp-ended scrapers found at Chiconautla were in fact used for maguey cactus cultivation long before the Aztec community flourished on the site (Michels and Tsong, 1980).

Limitations

Obsidian hydration is potentially as useful as radiocarbon dating, but it still suffers from grave limitations, especially when dealing with very early

Figure 6.6 Many Mayan *stelae* (carved stone monuments) record important dates in the lives of their rulers. This stela carries a date equivalent to A.D. 771.

dating their own civilization in years started from a mythical date long before their own society was in being. Known as the Long Count, the system is recorded on many stelae, along with inscriptions that signal important events or transfer of priestly power. Attempts that have been made to link the Long Count and the Christian calendar place the span of the Mayan calendar from about 3113 B.C. to A.D. 889. Much of this time is, of course, long before the Maya themselves were a fully fledged state. But the Long Count stelae are a useful check on the dates of such well-known Mayan sites as Tikal and Palenque.

The most reliable chronometric dates are, of course, those obtained from historical documentation of archaeological sites. We know that King Henry VIII began to build his palace at Nonsuch, England, in A.D. 1538, as well as the chronology of Plimoth Plantation in Massachusetts, from contemporary records, and our primary interest lies in discovering details of settlement layout or day-to-day life. Many later sites yield easily dated artifacts, such as coins dropped by the inhabitants on the floors of buildings or elsewhere in the settlement's strata. Such objects can provide accurate dates for the earliest age of the archaeological sites being investigated.

Objects of Known Age

Objects of known age found in African, North American, and European prehistoric sites include a bewildering array of artifacts, from dated coins and glass bottles to Chinese porcelain and all manner of imported ceramics. The latter include American domestic tableware, English imported china, and Spanish majolica vessels in historic sites in North America. Ivor Noël Hume (1969) has compiled an extremely valuable compendium of artifacts from Colonial America that is a useful source book for anyone interested in such objects. Some of these types of finds can act as artifacts for cross-dating prehistoric sites.

One of the most useful Colonial American artifacts is the imported English kaolin pipe (Figure 6.7). Not only were pipes manufactured, imported, smoked, and thrown away within a very short time, but also the shape of the pipe body changed in an easily recognizable evolutionary chain. Clay pipes were so cheap that everyone, however poor, used and discarded them almost like cigarettes. Not only the bowl but the length of the stem and the diameter of the hole changed between A.D. 1620 and 1800, and these characteristics have been used to date these artifacts and the sites associated with them with considerable precision.

Stanley South and others have used statistical techniques to study the relationships between eighteenth-century English imported pottery and historic sites in North Carolina. They argued that once enough percentage relationships had been worked out, they would be able to date sites of unknown age by using the frequencies of imported pottery types (South, 1972). Surprisingly good correspondence was found between the calculated median dates and the known historical dates of the pottery forms.

Roger Grange (1972, 1981) has taken this method a step further and applied the ceramic dating formula to the Pawnee and Loup Loup ceramic tradition of the Great Plains. This tradition was estimated, from historical data and archaeological cross-dating, to date from the period A.D. 1825 to 1846, when Pawnee potmaking died out, back to about A.D. 1500. Grange calculated median dates with archaeological data derived

1730-1770

1780-1820

1800-1830

Figure 6.7 Representative evolutionary changes in the designs on the bowls of English tobacco pipes dating to between 1730 and 1830.

from seriation, which gave the range of types. He found fair correspondence between the median dates and those obtained by more conventional analyses, especially when the greatest peaks of popularity for different pottery types were used as the basis for calculations. Formula dating of this type may have much potential in areas where tree-ring chronologies or calibrated radiocarbon dates provide a basis for accurate calculations of median age. And the advantages for cross-dating of newly discovered sites are obvious.

The potential range of historic objects that can be dated to within surprisingly narrow chronological limits is enormous. Many people collect beer cans, bottle caps and openers, barbed wire, firearms, uniform buttons, even horseshoes. All these artifacts, to say nothing of such prosaic objects as forks, electrical switch plates, and scissors, can be dated to within a few years with mail order catalogs, U.S. patent records, and a great deal of patient detective work. Bernard Fontana (1968) points out that bottles, buckets, and horseshoes may be the unrespectable artifacts of archaeology but, unlike many of their prehistoric equivalents, they can be dated with great accuracy. What better way to learn about archaeology than to study and date our own material culture!

SUMMARY

- Although historical records provide a fairly accurate chronology for much of the past five thousand years, archaeologists rely heavily on chemical and physical chronometric dating methods.
- Potassium argon methods are used for dating the earliest human beings. These can be used to determine dates from the origins of the earth up to about 400,000 years ago. This radioactive counting method is based on measuring accumulations of argon 40 in volcanic rocks. It has been used to date Olduvai Gorge and other early sites to between one and three million years ago.
- Radiocarbon dating is the most widely used method. It can be applied at sites from between 75,000 and four hundred years ago. Based on the rate at which carbon 14 decays to nitrogen in organic objects, it can be used to date many such materials as charcoal and bone and even skin and leather. The accuracy of radiocarbon dating is subject to statistical errors, owing to past variations in the carbon 14 content of the atmosphere, and thus has to be calibrated against tree-ring chronologies.
- Fission track dating is done by measuring the uranium content of many minerals and volcanic glasses and examining the fission tracks left in the material by fragmentation of massive concentration of energy-charged particles. It can be applied in sites between a million and 100,000 years old, where volcanic rocks are found in human-occupied levels.

- Thermoluminescence may prove to be a method for dating potsherds, in which the baked clay has trapped electrons; these are released for measurement by sudden and intense heating under controlled conditions. The visible light rays emitted during heating are known as thermoluminescence. This method is still highly experimental.
- Dendrochronology (tree-ring dating) has its principal application in the American Southwest. It provides an accurate chronology for about two thousand years of southwestern prehistory and has many uses on more recent sites in Europe and elsewhere. Dendrochronologists count the annual growth rings in trees such as the bristlecone pine and correlate them into long sequences of growth years that are joined to a master chronology. Wooden beams and other archaeological wood fragments are correlated with this master chronology to provide accurate dates for pueblos and other sites.
- Archaeomagnetic dating can be used to date clay samples from furnaces and other features by measuring the thermoremanent magnetism of the clay and correlating it with records of changes in the earth's magnetic field.
- Historical records and calendars developed by such people as the Ancient Egyptians and the Maya are of immense value for dating their literate civilizations. A great deal of valuable chronological information can also be obtained from objects of known age, such as clay pipe or coins. But again, these objects are confined to the most recent periods of human history.

GUIDE TO FURTHER READING

The literature on chronometric dating is enormous, but these volumes can be of great use to the student.

Fleming, Stuart J. *Dating in Archaeology.* New York: St. Martin's Press, 1976. An introduction to archaeological chronology that is good on basic principles.

Leute, Ulrich. *Archaeometry.* Weinheim, West Germany: VCH, 1987. A useful summary of dating techniques and science in archaeology. Quite technical in orientation.

Michels, J. W. *Dating Methods in Archaeology.* New York: Science Press, 1973. Probably the most widely read book on dating presently available. A good follow-up to this chapter.

Taylor, R. E., and C. W. Meighan, eds. *Chronologies in New World Archaeology.* Orlando, Fla.: Academic Press, 1978. Essays on New World chronological problems.

Chapter
7

The Archaeological Record

*T*he archaeological record is incomplete, for complex and still little understood processes have transformed the abandoned artifacts, structures, and sites of our forebears. Our interpretations of the archaeological record depend, ultimately, not only on how representative the surviving stone implements, pottery, or other objects are of past human behavior; they also depend on our knowledge of the complex processes that formed the remains of human behavior *after they were abandoned to the elements.*

There was a time when archaeologists assumed that their knowledge of the past would always be incomplete. Many argued that the reliability of our statements about the past depended on how strongly we can believe that the nonmaterial elements of society and culture are reflected in the incomplete archaeological record that has come down to us.

In this chapter, we examine the nature of the archaeological record, site formation processes, and the nature of archaeological data.

ARCHAEOLOGICAL DATA

The traditional cautionary arguments have been challenged by American archaeologist Lewis Binford and other prehistorians, who refuse to accept the assumption that archaeology yields information only on material culture. The distinction between material culture (artifacts, houses, and the products of human culture) and nonmaterial culture (kinship, social organization) is regarded as totally artificial, for every aspect of a human sociocultural system interacts with many other complex variables. According to Binford (1968), "Data relevant to most, if not all, the components of past sociocultural systems *are* preserved in the archaeological record." The archaeologist's task, then, as he sees it, is to develop means for extracting such information from the data recovered from excavations and archaeological surveys.

This school of thought refuses to attribute the limitations in our knowledge about the past to the quality of the archaeological record and the state of its preservation in the soil. The limitations, they say, lie in our methodological naiveté, in the various methodologies that many archaeologists are seeking to improve by means described at intervals in this book.

Archaeological data result from two processes. The first is human behavior, the results of human activity. The other is what are often called transformational processes. As we have seen, the archaeologist is concerned to identify and reconstruct ancient human behavior, such as the occupation of a hunting camp. The hunting band decides on a location, gathers building materials—sticks, brush or sod, mammoth bones—erects a dwelling, occupies it, then destroys or just abandons the settlement. Archaeologists reconstruct sequences of ancient human behavior not only from archaeological data itself but also from the circumstances under which they are found.

Human behavior is the first stage in the formation of the archaeological record. But what happens when the site is abandoned? The remains of brush shelters, a scatter of stone tools, the remains of a ceremony are abandoned as being of no further use to their owners. All manner of natural processes take hold. The bodies of the buried dead decay; toppled brush shelters rot away in the sun. Subsequently, a nearby lake may rise and cover the remains, or windblown sand may accumulate over the stone artifacts. Another group may come and build a farming village on the same spot or may simply pick up and reuse some of the artifacts left by the earlier occupants. All of these cultural and noncultural developments are transformational processes—continuous, dynamic, and unique processes that vary with each archaeological site. Of course, there are wide differences in the preservation of various artifacts, raw materials, and other finds. Thus the archaeologist's data are always biased and incomplete, altered by a variety of transformational, or site transformation, processes. It follows that anyone investigating an archaeological site has to look closely at both natural and human agents of transformation. For example, World Wars I and II destroyed thousands of archaeological sites, whereas wet conditions in Scandinavian bogs have preserved prehistoric corpses in excellent condition.

SITE FORMATION PROCESSES

"The time machine, which has enchanted generations of readers and moviegoers, is a fictional artifact for transporting people through time. Although archaeologists would welcome a time machine, we are satisfied by the remarkable fact that objects made, used, and deposited in the past survive into the present. We need not go to the past, for it comes to us" (Schiffer, 1987). Michael Schiffer's point is well taken, for the objects from the past that survive come down to us in two forms, either as historically documented artifacts, such as Orville and Wilbur Wright's first airplane, or in the archaeological record as culturally deposited artifacts that are no longer part of a living society. This past, in the form of artifacts, does not come down to us unchanged, for complex processes have acted on these objects, be they tools, dwellings, burials, food remains, or other humanly manufactured or modified items. Archaeologists have not only to study these artifacts but to untangle the many events and processes that contribute to the great variability in the archaeological record as we record it today (Butzer, 1982; Schiffer, 1983, 1987; Stein, 1983).

It is very easy to assume that archaeological sites encompass ancient human behavior in simple, direct ways. In fact, they do not. Anyone seeking to study the past, to examine ancient human behaviors, has to take into account many complex factors that have introduced great variability into the records of both history and archaeology. These factors that create the historic and archaeological records are known as site formation processes (Schiffer, 1987).

Site formation processes are those agencies, natural or cultural, that have transformed the archaeological (or historical) record since a site was abandoned. There are two basic forms of site formation process: cultural and noncultural.

Cultural transformations are ones where human behavior has transformed the archaeological record. They can vary widely in their impact and intensity. For example, later occupants of a surface that was a hunter-gatherer camp in the Near East may have been farmers and goatherds rather than hunters. The foundations of their houses cut deeply into underlying strata, while the hooves of their penned goats trample on and scatter small stone artifacts lying on the surface. And, of course, the archaeologist's excavations are cultural processes, too.

On a more specific level, people reuse artifacts—to conserve precious tools and valuable raw materials, changing the use of an artifact from a knife to a scraper, recycling a projectile point to another use. Sometimes prestigious or valuable objects become prized heirlooms passed down from generation to generation or buried with the dead, as soapstone pipes and other precious artifacts were with Hopewell kin leaders in the Midwest more than two thousand years ago. Reuse, especially of such commodities as building materials, can become a potent factor on settlements that are occupied for longer periods of time, where people recycle old bricks and other materials for new dwellings. Then there is the dumping of trash, some of it underfoot, much of it elsewhere, in secondary locations where trash heaps may form. These heaps often tend to cluster in specific locations that can be used for many generations, perhaps using a convenient, abandoned storage pit or an old dwelling. Disposal of the dead can be viewed as another form of discard behavior. It is a great mistake to think of any form of human discard behavior as random. The archaeologist must decipher the complicated behavioral processes—perhaps the logic, if you will—behind the accumulation of trash heaps, the disposal of the dead, and many other activities.

In short, the archaeological record is not a safe place for artifacts, for a myriad of human activities can disturb them after deposition—plowing, mining, digging of foundations, land clearance, even artillery bombardment, to say nothing of pothunting and site looting.

Noncultural processes are the events and processes of the natural environment that affect the archaeological record. The chemical properties of the soil or bacteria may accelerate the decay of organic remains such as wooden spears or dwellings or may even increase the chances of superb preservation. Rivers may overflow and inundate a settlement, mantling the abandoned remains with fine silt. A great earthquake can topple a settlement in a few minutes, as happened to the Roman port at Kourion in Cyprus on July 21, 365 (Soren and James, 1988). Windblown sands, ice disturbances, even the actions of earthworms can disturb the archaeological record.

Whether site formation processes are cultural or noncultural, the important point is that one can never take the archaeological record at face value. In other words, what you see in the ground is not necessarily a direct reflection of human behavior. The archaeologist must not only record, analyze, and interpret the archaeological record at face value but also investigate the formation processes that altered the record from the moment of its deposition. One has to allow for the effects of these processes through systematic investigation of the factors that have affected a site since it came into being.

Site formation processes are always important in archaeology, but they assume special importance under circumstances when it is necessary to document precise associations between, say, human activity and extinct animals. Of no controversy is this more true than the ongoing debates about the date of the first human settlement of the Americas (Fagan, 1987). The earliest well-attested occupation of the Americas dates to about 12,000 years ago, perhaps a couple of millennia earlier, documented by an archaeological record that is beyond question. It is a different matter with earlier claims, claims as early as 30,000 years ago or more, notably from sites in South America. The Boqueirão da Furada site in northeastern Brazil is claimed to contain evidence of human occupation, including hearths, dating to before 25,000 years ago. However, the excavators have failed to scrutinize the site formation processes that have acted on the alleged artifacts from the lower levels of the site. What natural geological processes formed the deposits in which the artifacts were found? Are there ways in which the few tools from the cave could have been formed by natural means—for example, by falling from a sheer cliff above the site? And how were the hearths claimed to exist in the deposits formed? Through human behavior or by, say, natural brushfires? At present, the archaeologists responsible for the excavations have not attempted to document the natural or cultural processes that could have formed this tantalizing archaeological record (Guidon and Delibrias, 1986).

The environment is a hostile place for human artifacts, for the process of interacting with it causes deterioration and drastic modification of the many properties of artifacts, affecting everything from color and texture to weight, shape, chemical composition, and appearance. The environmental agents of deterioration can be grouped into chemical, physical, and biological categories (Dowman, 1970; Schiffer, 1987). Chemical agents are universal, for the atmosphere contains water and oxygen, which create many chemical reactions—corrosion of some metals is an example. Different water temperatures, irradiation of materials by sunlight, and atmospheric pollutants all cause chemical reactions. Buried objects are often subject to rapid chemical change, especially as a result of dampness. Soils also contain reactive compounds such as acids and bases that contribute to many deterioration processes. Acid soils dissolve bones, for example. Many archaeological deposits are somewhat salty, a condition caused by salts derived from wood ash, urine, and the neutralization of acids and bases. Such saline conditions can retard some decay, but copper, iron, and silver can decay severely.

Physical agents of deterioration are also universal, agents such as water, wind, sunlight, and earth movement. Water is especially potent, for it can tumble artifacts on the shores of oceans or lakes or from riverbank encampments, even sometimes fracturing them in ways that suggest human manufacture. Rainwater can cascade off roofs and tunnel deep grooves into walls. The cycle of wetness followed by drying cracks many woods and causes rot; melting and freezing ice cracks rocks, even concrete. Physical agents operate on small scale and large. For example, the effects of the Kourion earthquake not only flattened the small port but also affected the landscape for miles around.

Living organisms are the main agents of biological decay. Bacteria occur almost everywhere and are usually the first to colonize dead organic matter and begin the processes of decay. Fungi also occur widely and are especially destructive to wood and other plant matter, particularly in damp, warmer climates. Beetles, ants, flies, and termites infest archaeological sites, especially middens and abandoned foods. Animals such as dogs and hyenas chew, gnaw, and scavenge bones and other organic materials from the surfaces of abandoned sites and game kills.

Not only artifacts but also archaeological sites are affected by the processes within the natural environment of which they are a part. Archaeologists who spend most of their time in the field are often known as "dirt archaeologists" because they are always working with one of the primary constituents of an archaeological site, the soil. The first human activity at any site took place on a natural surface, on natural sediments themselves sitting on underlying bedrock. Sometimes this underlying sediment was weathered over a long time and may contain pollen grains, plant remains, or other sources of environmental information. For in-⁹ stance, some Bronze Age burial mounds in Europe were erected on undisturbed soils that contained forest pollen grains, giving a picture of the local environment at the time of construction. After the site is abandoned, additional sediments usually accumulate on top of the archaeological remains due to the action of wind or water, such as the windblown sands that accumulate in the rooms of southwestern pueblos. Human feet or animal paws, burrowing animals, earthworms, wall flakings from overhanging cliffs, and the deteriorating elements of artifacts and structures contribute to the alteration of archaeological deposits. Upper Palaeolithic rockshelters in southwestern France, for example, were occupied intermittently by hunter-gatherer groups between 30,000 and 15,000 years ago. Some of the larger ones contain densely packed layers of hearths, ash accumulations, boulders, and decaying structures. Untangling how these levels were formed is a complex process. A myriad of different environmental processes contribute to site formation and can transform the archaeological record in ways that can be mistaken for traces of human behavior.

The study of site formation processes is still in its infancy, but we know that the human past has been created in the archaeological record by a variety of cultural and noncultural processes that have a wide variety of effects on what archaeologists recover from the soil. The site formation processes at each individual site must be considered separately, usually within the context of different deposits within it. The first stage is to identify the specific cultural and noncultural formation processes that created each deposit or set of deposits. This involves thinking of the artifacts in these deposits as an integral part of them. The investigator records and analyzes such phenomena as reductions in size, patterns of damage, and distribution within the deposit as one way of trying to understand the complex "package" of evidence about cultural and environmental materials that makes up that deposit. In other words, the archaeologist has to establish what cultural and noncultural processes led to the formation of each deposit in the site. The fundamental point about studying site formation processes is that they have to be identified before behavioral or environmental inferences can be made about any archaeological site. The identification of specific site formation processes is difficult, even under ideal circumstances, and involves not only geoarchaeological research but also data acquired from ethnoarchaeology, controlled experiments, and other sources. It is not enough, then, to observe conditions of unusually good preservation or to describe the complex layers of a prehistoric rockshelter. One must also analyze and interpret the ways in which the archaeological record was formed—site formation processes. "The real time machine, then, is the archaeological process: the principles and procedures that we as scientists apply to material traces in the historical and archaeological records. If we desire to obtain views of the past that are closer to reality . . . we must build into our time machine a thorough understanding of formation processes" (Schiffer, 1987, where a comprehensive survey of the topic will be found).

THE MATRIX: PRESERVATION AND HUMAN ACTIVITY

All archaeological finds, from a humble stone chopper to an Egyptian pharoah's tomb, occur within a physical matrix (Chapter 4). The matrix in an archaeological site can result from natural phenomena such as a river flood or from human behavior such as the building of a new community on top of an older one. The chemistry and physical characteristics of the matrix can have a profound effect not only on the provenience of an archaeological find but also on its context and association with other subjects. For example, the physical characteristics of the deposits in which they were found tell us that fast-running waters of the River Thames in England rolled dozens of Stone Age hand axes downstream from where they were originally dropped by their makers and deposited them in river gravels, to be recovered by archaeologists over 250,000 years later. Human behavior also determines the context and provenience of archaeological finds in the matrix. Many Hopewellian culture burials of 1,800 years ago were deposited in mound platforms in the Ohio Valley. Careful excavation of the surrounding deposits shows that many people were laid to rest before a large earthwork was erected over the sepulchral platform where the dead lay.

Evaluating the natural formation processes that have contributed to the archaeological record involves geoarchaeological research (Chapter 15). Deciphering human activities from artifact patterns in the matrix requires careful evaluation of many subtle behaviors from the remote past. The following are some common instances where human activity has affected the archaeological record.

Discards

The patterns of artifact discard can be very subtle; understanding them often requires knowledge that is still beyond our grasp.

Cozumel At the Mayan trading center on Cozumel, off the coast of the Yucatán, the people invested very little material wealth in temples, tombs, or other permanent monuments (Friedel and Sabloff, 1984). Their capital in obsidian (volcanic glass) was kept fluid and on hand, an investment in resources different from that found at other Mayan ceremonial centers, which invested heavily in religious monuments and tangible displays of wealth. The different investment in resources reflected the activities and significance in each type of locality. Interpreting such patterns of discard, the remains that are left for interpretation after the long centuries and millennia of natural destruction have taken place, presents huge difficulties for archaeologists.

Fulani   In a fascinating discussion of thirty-six modern, inhabited Fulani compounds in northern Cameroon, West Africa, Nicholas David (1971) attempted to show the "fit" between the houses in the compounds and their Fulani inhabitants. He found that so many variables affected the layout of the compounds that only the most general observations were possible. The huts in the compound could sometimes be used to estimate the numbers of adult women or male family heads. But what about bachelors or children? Fish-drying ovens of puddled mud and large hearths were signs of economic specialization and of evening classes for study of the Koran in the modern settlements. But had an archaeologist dug up the compound centuries after its abandonment, only the ovens would have survived. The house of the chief musician gave no clue to his profession, nor did those of many part-time specialists. The granaries used to store grain supplies were not built on stone foundations that were likely to survive: the only sign of the basic subsistence economy in the archaeological record might be the special grinding huts in the compound. Furthermore, though in prehistoric times the compounds might have reflected the status of different families—wealthy people, poor, free Fulani, and slaves—today they have no slavery and a far more homogeneous society. Above all, in earlier times wealth was not necessarily reflected in house size. All houses were of about the same size, a dimension dictated, so David found, by white ant infestation. When insecticides became available in the late 1960s, houses started to get larger. The absolute limits of archaeological inference were soon met when David attempted to fit the material culture and houses to social structure. He found that in modern country villages, people build houses to suit their precise needs. Land is abundant and free. But in modern towns, where the Fulani have to buy land and modify their property for their needs within a much tighter framework, people either have to move to new quarters or adapt their life-style to fit their limited space. The constraints are far more severe.

Any archaeologist working anywhere has to face the peculiar problems that David demonstrated with his Fulani compounds. What are the distorting effects of human discard patterns on the archaeological record, on surface site survey, and on the limits to which we can take the interpretation of sites and finds? These are questions that few archaeologists have yet tackled head-on, but they form a critical facet of the preservation question.

Recycling

People discard artifacts, and they recycle them as well. A stone axe can be resharpened again and again until the original, large artifact is just a small stub that has been recycled into extinction. It takes a great deal of effort to build a mud-brick house from scratch. Very often, an old house is renovated repeatedly, its precious wooden beams used again in the same structure or in another building. Such recycling can distort the archaeological record, for what appears to be a one-time structure can in fact have been used again and again. Tree-ring dating of pueblos in the Southwest is complicated by the constant reuse of wooden beams. Sometimes, too, the Indians would cut beams and stockpile them for later use.

Not only individual artifacts but also entire archaeological sites can be recycled. A settlement flourishes on a low ridge in the Near East. After a generation or two the site is abandoned, and the inhabitants move elsewhere. Later, people return to the site, level the abandoned houses, and build their own dwellings right on top of the site. This type of recycling can result in the sealing and preserving of earlier levels, but it can also result in the reuse of building materials from earlier houses.

Heirlooms

Successive generations may also find a structure or an artifact so valuable that they consciously preserve it for the benefit of their descendants.

Eridu   The great temple, or *ziggurat*, of the city of Eridu in Mesopotamia was first erected around 5000 B.C. This important shrine was visible for miles around and was rebuilt on the same site time and time again for more than two thousand years. Tracing the complex history of this structure has consumed many hours of excavation time. Reconstructing the sequence of mud-brick construction through generations of recycling of successive structures involves understanding how mud-brick architecture came into being and how it decays (Lloyd, 1963).

Ceremonial Artifacts   Many prehistoric societies valued ritual objects, such as masks, ceremonial axes, and other symbolic artifacts that were associated with ancestor worship. These ceremonial artifacts were sometimes buried with a dead priest or leader, as with Tutankhamun and some of the Mayan leaders. It is easy enough to tell their age and association with a grave dug at a particular period. In other instances, ceremonial artifacts can be treasured for generations, being displayed only on special occasions or kept in a special relic hut. An interesting example of such heirlooms is that of the sacred relics of the Bemba tribe in Central Africa, which included ceremonial iron gongs and bow stands that were at least two hundred years old (Richards, 1937). Tragically, these were destroyed by political protesters in the early 1960s, causing great trauma among the older Bemba. By treasuring such objects, however, the owners can unwittingly distort the archaeological record. Fortunately, in most cases it is possible to identify instances of *curation,* or preservation, by the style of the artifacts. In Tutankhamun's tomb, Carter found among the grave furniture objects that had belonged to earlier pharaohs. Presumably, they had been placed in the tomb to fill in gaps in the royal inventory caused by the pharaoh's unexpected death.

Deliberate and Accidental Destruction

The many other potential causes of human distortion of the archaeological record can include deliberate destruction of cemeteries, erasure of inscriptions from temples at royal command, or the ravages of warfare, both ancient and modern. The trench warfare of World War I did terrible damage to archaeological sites. Even more destructive are depredations by treasure hunters and antiquities dealers supplying the greed of museums and private collectors (Meyer, 1977).

PRESERVATION CONDITIONS: INORGANIC AND ORGANIC MATERIALS

We must now examine preservation conditions, some of the circumstances under which the archaeological record comes down to us in exceptional condition. Under highly favorable circumstances, many kinds of artifactual materials are preserved, including such perishable items as leather containers, basketry, wooden arrowheads, and furniture. But under normal circumstances, only the most durable artifacts usually survive. Generally, the objects found in archaeological sites are of two broad categories: inorganic and organic materials.

Inorganic objects are of such materials as stone, metals, and clay. Prehistoric stone implements, such as the choppers of the earliest humans, made more than two million years ago, have survived in perfect condition for archaeologists to find. Their cutting edges are just as sharp as they were when abandoned by their makers. Clay pots are among the most durable human artifacts, especially if they are well fired. It is no coincidence that much of prehistory is reconstructed from chronological sequences of changing pottery styles. Fragments (potsherds) of well-fired clay vessels are practically indestructible; they have lasted as long as 10,000 years in some Japanese sites.

Organic objects are made of living substances, such as wood, leather, bone, or cotton. They rarely survive in the archaeological record. When they do, the picture of prehistoric life they give us is much more complete than that from inorganic finds. Organic materials formed a vital part of most societies' tool kits. Hunter-gatherers of southwestern France made extensive use of antler and bone for hunting tools and weapons (Champion and others, 1984). Some of their finest artistic achievements were executed on fragments of these organic materials with flint engravers. The preservation of organic materials depends heavily on local environmental conditions.

ORGANIC MATERIALS AND THE ARCHAEOLOGICAL RECORD

Most of the world's archaeological sites preserve little more than the inorganic remains of the past, the most durable artifacts to survive the centuries and millennia. Sometimes, however, especially favorable preservation conditions result in the survival of highly informative organic materials—artifacts, food remains, and environmental data.

Waterlogged Environs and Wetlands

Waterlogged or peat-bog conditions are particularly favorable for preserving wood or vegetal remains, whether the climate is subtropical or temperate. Tropical rain forests, such as those of the Amazon Basin in South America and Zaire in Africa, are far from kind to wooden artifacts. In contrast, a significant number of archaeological sites occur near springs or in marshes where the water table is high and perennial waterlogging of occupation layers has occurred since they were abandoned (Coles, 1984; Purdy, 1988).

Wetlands look like dreary, waterlogged countryside, far from appealing. In prehistoric times, wetlands were often just used for hunting or were traversed by pathways. Others were exploited for crops, for grazing, even for settlement and such industries as gathering thatching grass. Wetlands come in an infinite variety, each type formed by different depositional processes, with a highly varied archaeological content. Many wetland sites have been well protected from the ravages of animal and human scavengers and from the severe noncultural processes that have acted on more exposed locations. In some cases, as in the Somerset Levels of southwestern England, archaeologists have been able to reconstruct entire landscapes traversed by wooden walkways, using not only walking but also aerial photographs, remote sensing, and subsurface boring (Coles and Coles, 1986).

Somerset Levels Perhaps the most famous wetland sites are in the Swiss lake region, notably Lake Neuchâtel, where a combination of land and underwater excavation has yielded farming settlements dating from Neolithic times right up to the Iron Age, as well as Roman boats and traces of Medieval settlement (Coles and Coles, 1989). The finds include not only valuable information on settlement layout and economic life but also such artifacts as sickles and their sandstone molds, complete wooden-handled adzes with deer antler mount and polished stone blade, even basketry, as well as a wealth of animal bones and plant remains.

The Somerset Levels in England were once a bay of the nearby Severn River, a bay filled with thick peat deposits between 6,000 and 1,500 years ago (Coles and Coles, 1986). Conditions on the Levels fluctuated constantly, so the inhabitants built wooden trackways that traversed their traditional routes across the Levels (Figure 7.1). Some six thousand years ago, the Neolithic builders of the Sweet Track needed a raised walkway to cross a reedy marsh. They felled trees on dry ground, prepared them as required, and carried the wood to the marsh edge. Then they placed long poles end to end on the marsh surface along the preferred route, usually alder, ash, or hazel trunks pegged into the underlying wet ground with stout stems about every three feet. The pegs were driven in obliquely in pairs, crossing over the poles in a V shape. The builders then lodged

Figure 7.1 Neolithic track in the Somerset Levels, southwestern England.

planks into these crossed pegs on top of the poles, forming a walkway about sixteen inches wide and about the same height above the poles. The Sweet Track extended for over a mile, joining a small island with a larger islet in the middle of the Levels. The Sweet Track excavations have provided a unique opportunity not only for paleoenvironmental reconstruction but also for tree-ring analyses. A chronology from the ash trees has established that the entire timber for the track was expertly felled at one time, with the track being used for about ten years. So detailed were the investigations that the excavators were able to show that part of the track, over a particularly wet portion, was repaired several times. Wooden wedges, wooden mallets, and stone axes were used for splitting the planks; other artifacts came from the crevices of the track, among them stone arrowheads, complete with traces of shaft, glue, and binding, hazelwood bows, and imported stone axes. Several other tracks have also been excavated from the Somerset Levels.

Tollund Man   Danish bogs have yielded a rich harvest of wood-hafted weapons, clothing, ornaments, traps, and even complete corpses, such as that of Tollund man (Glob, 1969). This unfortunate individual's body was found by two peat cutters in 1950, lying on his side in a brown peat bed in a crouched position, a serene expression on his face and eyes tightly closed (Figure 7.2). Tollund man wore a pointed skin cap and a hide belt—nothing else. We know that he had been hanged, because a cord was found knotted tightly around his neck. The Tollund corpse has been shown to be about two thousand years old and to belong to the Danish Iron Age. So excellent were preservation conditions in the acidic bog soil that much of his skin survives, and his peaceful portrait has been included in many archaeological volumes. A formidable team of medical experts examined his cadaver, among them a paleobotanist who established that Tollund man's last meal consisted of a gruel made from barley, linseed, and several wild grasses and weeds, eaten twelve to twenty-four hours before his death. He is thought to have been a sacrificial victim of a fertility cult, hanged to ensure successful crops and continuation of life.

Ozette   Richard Daugherty of Washington State University worked at the Ozette site on the Olympia Peninsula in the Pacific Northwest for more than a decade (Kirk, 1974). The site first came to his attention in 1947 as part of a survey of coastal settlements. Ozette had been occupied by Makah Indians until twenty or thirty years before, and traces of their collapsed houses could be seen on top of a large midden. It was not until 1966 that Daugherty was able to start excavations at the site, which was being threatened with obliteration by wave action and mud slides. A trial trench revealed large deposits of whale bones and yielded radiocarbon samples dating back 2,500 years. Most important, the muddy deposits had preserved traces of wooden houses and the organic remains in them. Then, in 1970, a call from the Makah Tribal Council alerted Daugherty

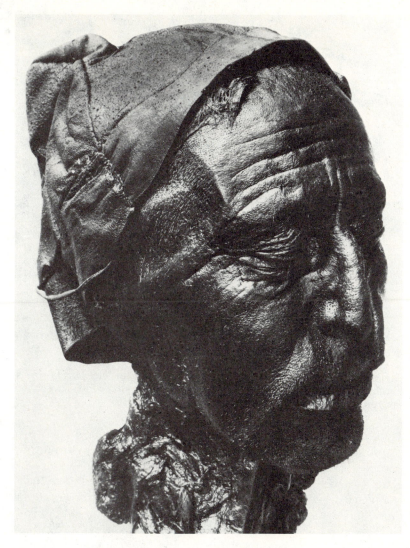

Figure 7.2 Tollund man, preserved for two thousand years in a Danish bog.

to a new discovery. High waves had cut into the midden and caused the wet soil to slump, revealing traces of wooden fishhooks, boxes, and even a canoe paddle. A cursory glance showed that the Ozette site contained the remains of collapsed wooden houses buried under an ancient landslide.

Daugherty and his colleagues worked for more than ten years to uncover the remains of four cedarwood longhouses and their contents (Figure 7.3). The excavations were fraught with difficulty, and high-pres-

Figure 7.3 Ozette, Washington. Excavation of the walls, sleeping benches, and planks of a prehistoric house uncovered by a mud slide. The water-logged conditions preserved wood and fiber perfectly.

sure hoses and sprays were needed to clear the mud away from the delicate woodwork. All the finds were then preserved with chemicals before final analysis. The wet muck that mantled the houses had engulfed them suddenly in a dense, damp blanket that preserved everything except flesh, feathers, and skins. The houses were perfectly preserved, one uncovered in 1972 measuring sixty-nine feet long and forty-six wide. There were separate hearths and cooking platforms, and hanging mats and low walls served as partitions. More than 40,000 artifacts came from the excavations, including conical rain hats made of spruce roots, baskets, wooden bowls still impregnated with seal oil (Figure 7.4), mats, fishhooks, harpoons, combs, bows and arrows, even fragments of looms, and ferns and cedar leaves. A fine artistic tradition in wood excited the excavators: the trove included a whale fin carved of red cedar and inlaid with seven hundred sea otter teeth. No one had ever seen one of these objects before, although Captain Cook had illustrated one in his report of a voyage to the Northwest coast in 1778.

The Ozette site is a classic example of how much can be recovered from an archaeological site in waterlogged conditions. But Ozette is important in other ways, too, for the Makah Indians who lived there had a

Figure 7.4 A bowl for oil from the Ozette site carved in the form of a man is complete even to a braid of human hair.

tangible history, extending back at least two thousand years before the whites came. Oral traditions and written records for the Makah go back no further than A.D. 1800. The Makah abandoned Ozette only in modern times, to move nearer a school in the 1920s. The archaeological excavations have traced the continuity of this village of whale catchers and fisherfolk far back into prehistory, giving a new sense of identity to the Makah of today. The excavation was finally closed in 1981.

Dry Conditions

Very arid environments, such as those of the American Southwest or the Nile Valley, are even better for preservation than waterlogged localities.

The Tomb of Tutankhamun   Undoubtedly one of the most famed of all archaeological discoveries is the amazing tomb of Tutankhamun (c. 1345 B.C.), unearthed by Lord Carnarvon and Howard Carter in 1922 (Carter and others, 1923–1933). The undisturbed burial chamber was opened, revealing the grave furniture in exactly the same state as it had been laid out by the king's mourners. Gilded wood chests, cloth, ivory caskets, models of chariots and boats, and the mummy were all perfectly preserved, together with a bewildering array of jewelry and paintings shining as brightly as the day they were painted, even showing the somewhat hasty execution accorded them by the artist. Tutankhamun's sepulcher provides as vivid a glimpse of the past as we are ever likely to obtain. Papyrus texts too have been preserved by the dry Egyptian conditions in many Nile Valley cemeteries, giving an unrivaled picture of the ancient Egyptian world (Kemp, 1989).

Hogup   C. Melvin Aikens spent many years excavating the Hogup cave in Utah, where deep, dry deposits contain a record of human occupation that began at least 9000 B.P. and lasted into historic times (Aikens, 1970). Preservation conditions are so good that Aikens and his colleagues were able to recover stone artifacts, basketry, netting fragments, bone artifacts, and the remains of large and small animals. The early deposits of the cave were strewn with the chaff of pickleweed seeds; the seeds were also found in human feces from the site. During the earlier periods of occupation, open water and marshland lay not too far from the cave, which is known by the discovery of plentiful waterfowl bones and marsh plants in the deposits. After 3000 B.P. the waterfowl disappeared and the pickleweed declined sharply, demonstrating that the marshes were flooded by lake water. The drier environment that evolved in modern times increased exploitation of vegetable foods and small mammals. Few sites contain a wider range of evidence for hunting and food gathering than that in Hogup. And it is precisely these basically dry conditions, which have persisted over the West since the end of the Pleistocene, that have preserved this evidence so well.

Arctic Conditions

Arctic sites, too, are excellent for preserving the human past. The circumpolar regions of Siberia and the New World have acted like a giant freezer, in which the processes of decay have been held in check for thousands of years. Close to the Arctic Ocean, dozens of deep-frozen mammoth carcasses have survived thousands of years in a state of perennial refrigeration. Perhaps the most famous is the Beresovka mammoth, which became enmired on the swampy banks of a Siberian river one spring some 10,000 years ago. The Soviet expedition that recovered the carcass in 1901 found the meat so fresh that the scientists fed it to their dogs. The mammoth's hair was perfectly preserved, and the remains of its last meal were found on its tongue and in its stomach (Digby, 1926).

Pazyryk   Refrigerated sites are common in the Arctic and even in areas far south of the permafrost zones of Siberia. A series of 2,300-year-old burial mounds at Pazyryk, not far from the Chinese and Mongolian borders, were permanently frozen by a special microclimate within them created by the heat-conducting properties of the stone cairn that formed the core of each tumulus (Rudenko, 1970). Preservation conditions were so perfect that the warriors' linen shirts adorned with braid, leather-decorated caftans, and felt and leather headdresses survived. So did body tattoos, one chieftain bearing a lively picture of a monster like a lion-griffin. Deer, birds, and carnivores also adorned his trunk and limbs. Wooden trolleys, emaciated horses, even carpets and felt wall hangings survived in near-perfect condition.

Franklin Expedition, Canadian Arctic   On May 19, 1845, veteran Arctic explorer Sir John Franklin left London in command of the most completely equipped Arctic expedition ever to search for the famed Northwest Passage across far northern Canada. H.M.S. *Erebus* and H.M.S. *Terror* sailed into the remote north from western Greenland in July of the same year and were never seen again. It was a couple of years before concern was felt, as the ships were equipped for a prolonged absence. By 1850, however, several expeditions were combing the Hudson Bay region for traces of the missing explorers. Three graves were found on remote Beechey Island, close to where the searchers discovered traces of the expedition's first winter camp, but these were of men who had died before the expedition ran into trouble. It was not until 1859 that other searchers on King William Island at the root of the Boothia Peninsula, the western arm of Hudson Bay, came across a cairn and an abandoned ship's boat filled with dead sailors, who had perished while on a last desperate journey to safety. Sporadic searches until the 1880s yielded occasional European artifacts and nonnative human bones. No records of the expedition were ever recovered, and it was assumed that Franklin and his men had perished from malnutrition, for they refused to take advantage of Inuit survival techniques that would have provided them with food even in the depths of winter.

Anthropologist Owen Beattie is an expert in forensic anthropology who has worked on many criminal cases in his native Canada. In 1981 he mounted the first of a series of field trips in search of new evidence for the demise of the Franklin expedition. At first he concentrated his search in the King William Island area but recovered little more than some startling evidence for cannibalism among the last survivors of the expedition. He also recovered a skeleton from the boat site that displayed unusually high lead levels, to the point where he suspected that its owner had suffered from chronic lead poisoning.

Could lead poisoning have contributed to the tragedy? Beattie needed more complete anatomical information. So he applied for permission to exhume the graves of the three men who had been interred on Beechey Island—Petty Officer John Torrington, Able Seaman John Hartnell, and Marine Private William Braine. It was a spectacular exercise in cold-climate archaeology and forensic medicine, which furnished new clues as to the fate of the Franklin expedition.

The wooden coffins of the three men were well preserved, Torrington's covered with blue wool fabric decorated with white tape. A hand-painted, wrought-iron plaque, perhaps fashioned from a tin can, bore the inscription "John Torrington, died January 1st, 1846, aged 20 years." The excavators had to thaw ice around the coffin lid and shear the nails. The body was encased in a block of ice that was melted with buckets of heated water. Soon Torrington's perfectly preserved toes and the front of his shirt came into view. The head was covered with a fold of blue wool. When the cloth was drawn back with tweezers, John Torrington's perfectly preserved countenance stared at them (Figure 7.5). For the first time, scientists gazed not at a crude drawing or a primitive photograph of their forebears but at the face of an actual nineteenth-century human being. It was a startling and emotional experience.

Figure 7.5 John Torrington.

John Torrington had been buried in simple, gray linen trousers. He wore a white shirt with blue stripes with a high collar and a pleated waist. A white, polka-dotted kerchief covered his medium-brown hair. An on-site autopsy revealed that he had stood five feet four inches tall and had been very emaciated at the time of his death. Laboratory tests on his organs told a tale of serious medical problems for such a young man. His lungs were blackened by inhalation of coal dust and smoke and other atmospheric pollutants. Since Torrington was a stoker, this is hardly surprising. He was suffering from emphysema and tuberculosis and had probably died of pneumonia. However, the real cause of death was probably the severe mental and physical problems caused by lead poisoning, for trace element analyses of his hair gave readings of more than six hundred parts per million, evidence of acute lead poisoning.

The bodies of John Hartnell and William Braine, exhumed in 1986, also bore signs of serious lead poisoning. Beattie's detailed autopsies painted a picture of an expedition plagued by catastrophic health problems, almost certainly resulting from lead poisoning. Loss of energy and poor appetites, neurotic and illogical behavior, acute depression—these symptoms, especially the mental ones, were deadly in the stressful conditions of the Arctic. The lead concentrations probably came from the solder used to seal the tinned foods consumed by the expedition, and many of the foods may have been spoiled owing to poor sealing into the bargain.

There were, of course, many causes for the ultimate failure of the Franklin expedition, but the near-perfect preservation conditions of the

Arctic have provided modern science with a possible underlying cause for one of the great tragedies of nineteenth-century exploration (Beattie and Geiger, 1986).

Tragedy at Utqiagvik   Another spectacular discovery, this time from a bluff overlooking the Arctic Ocean near Barrow, Alaska, also records a tragedy, this from recent prehistory. Two Inupiat women, the one in her forties, the other in her twenties, were asleep in a small driftwood-and-sod house on a bluff overlooking the ocean on a stormy night in the 1540s (Dekin, 1987). A teenage boy and two young girls slept nearby. The sea ice was crashing against the shore, the pack driven against the coast by high waves. Suddenly, a giant mass of ice chunks broke free in a violent surge and was carried over the bluff, crashing tons of ice down on the tiny house. The roof collapsed, killing the inhabitants immediately. At dawn, the neighbors found the house silent and left it buried under the ice. Later, other members of the family removed some utensils and food from the ruins, and the timber uprights projecting through the ice were salvaged. The rest was undisturbed for five centuries, deep-freezing a prehistoric tragedy.

Five centuries ago, Utqiagvik was a sizable settlement, but it is now buried under much of an expanding Barrow, Alaska. There are at least sixty house mounds. In 1982 the remains of a Inupiat winter house came to light, intact and still mostly frozen. The house was formed of hand-hewn driftwood used for both floor boards and wall panels. Everything was held together with a matrix of frozen earth and insulated with a sod roof. The well-preserved bodies of the women were autopsied. Both had been in reasonably good health, although their lungs were blackened with anthracosis, a condition caused by inhaling smoke and oil lamp fumes in closed-in winter houses. They ate a heavy diet of whale and sea blubber, which had narrowed their arteries and caused atherosclerosis. The older woman had given birth about two months before the disaster and was still lactating. Both of them had suffered periods of poor nutrition and illness. The older had recovered from pneumonia and a painful muscle infection called trichinosis, perhaps contracted from eating raw polar bear meat.

The women had slept naked under their bed robes, probably to avoid moisture buildup in their daily garments that would freeze when they went outside. Outside, they had worn caribou parkas, snow goggles, and mittens, also waterproof sealskin inner boots, all found in the entrance tunnel to the house. Much of their time was spent making and repairing clothing, and repairing the hunting gear that was well preserved in the ruins. There were bone harpoon heads for hunting seals and other sea mammals, also remains of a bola, a sinew throwing device weighted with bone weights used to snare birds in flight. A wooden bucket stitched together with baleen and a wood and bone pick for clearing ice were recovered near the house entry.

Ipiutak   The Utqiagvik site is one of many well-preserved prehistoric locations in the Arctic, sites that have refrigerated wooden objects, bone and ivory artifacts, even clothing. The famous Ipiutak site near Point Hope on the Alaskan coast of the Chukchi Sea, dated to the first few centuries A.D., contains more than sixty semisubterranean dwellings, with a nearby cemetery (Collins, 1937). A series of skeletons buried close to the surface were found partially disarticulated, lying in a deposit of wood fragments, which included some flamboyant ivory carvings and midden soil. The excavators inferred that the dead had been deposited on the ground, enclosed in a wooden frame or a pile of logs. Elaborate ivory carvings were invariably associated with the surface burials at Ipiutak, preserved by the cold that has persisted at the site since its abandonment. Ipiutak art is dominated by small sculptures of bears, walruses, and other animals; composite masks and delicate spiral ornaments were probably fastened to the grave coverings. It is sobering to realize that under temperate conditions only stone artifacts and the outlines of the Ipiutak houses and bed platforms would have survived the two thousand years since the settlement was occupied (Dumond, 1987).

An archaeologist must always evaluate the preservation conditions at every site investigated to determine the preservation factors, both human and natural, that have affected the integrity of the archaeological record.

SUMMARY

- Traditionally, archaeologists have argued that the archaeological record is incomplete, because many items of material culture have been lost to decay and destruction.
- Lewis Binford and others have refused to accept the assumption that archaeology yields information only on material culture. They argue that data on all components of past sociocultural systems are preserved in the archaeological record and that much depends on the methods of recovery used to obtain archaeological data.
- Site formation processes are factors that create the historic and archaeological records, natural or cultural agencies that have transformed the archaeological record during and since a site was abandoned.
- There are two basic types of site formation processes. Cultural transformations are those wherein human behavior has transformed the archaeological record by such acts as rebuilding houses or reusing artifacts. Noncultural processes are events and processes of the natural environment that affect the archaeological record, such as the chemical properties of the soil and natural phenomena such as earthquakes and wind action.

- Later human activity can radically affect archaeological preservation. People may selectively discard some types of artifacts, and many variables can affect the layout of settlements and other considerations. The Fulani compounds in West Africa demonstrate the difficulties of interpretation.
- Some people, such as the southwestern Indians, recycled wooden beams and other materials, distorting the archaeological record. Sites are reused, lower strata are often disturbed, and succeeding generations may preserve an important building, such as a temple, for centuries. Modern warfare, industrial activity, even deep agriculture and cattle grazing can affect the preservation of archaeological remains.
- Preservation conditions depend mostly on the soil and general climatic regime in the area of a site. Inorganic objects, such as stone and baked clay, often survive almost indefinitely. But organic materials, such as bone, wood, and leather, survive only under exceptional conditions, such as in dry climates, in permafrost areas, and when waterlogged. The surviving picture of the past obtained from excavations is often confined to inorganic materials.
- Waterlogged and peat-bog conditions are especially favorable for preserving wood and vegetal remains. In this chapter we discussed the Danish bog corpses and the Ozette site in Washington State as sites of these types.
- Dry conditions can preserve almost the full range of human artifacts, the best examples being the remarkably complete preservation of ancient Egyptian culture and the comprehensive finds made in desert caves, such as Hogup cave in Utah, in the American West.
- Arctic conditions can literally refrigerate organic materials in the soil. We described the survivors of the Franklin expedition and the light they threw on the fate of that celebrated explorer, as well as Arctic sites in Alaska.

GUIDE TO FURTHER READING

Beattie, Owen, and John Geiger. *Frozen in Time: The Fate of the Franklin Expedition.* London: Bloomsbury Publishing, 1986. A popular account of the excavation of the graves of three members of the Franklin expedition. Gives an excellent description of the difficulties of excavating in Arctic environments.

Coles, Byrony, and John Coles. *Sweet Track to Glastonbury.* New York: Thames and Hudson, 1988. An exemplary account of the Coles' excavations in England's Somerset Levels. Excellent illustrations.

Purdy, Barbara, ed. *Wet Site Archaeology.* Caldwell, N.J.: Telford Press, 1988. A series of essays on wet site excavations in various parts of the world. Excellent on methodological problems.

Rukenko, S. *Frozen Tombs of Siberia.* Trans. by M.W. Thompson. Berkeley: University of California Press, 1970. Vivid descriptions of prehistoric burial mounds on the Siberian steppe, including tattooed corpses. A minor classic of archaeology.

Schiffer, Michael. *Formation Processes of the Archaeological Record.* Tucson: University of Arizona Press, 1987. A valuable synthesis of site formation processes in archaeology and some of the research problems associated with them. Comprehensive bibliography.

PART Four

RECOVERING ARCHAEOLOGICAL DATA

A mere hole in the ground, which of all sights is perhaps the least vivid and dramatic, is enough to grip their attention for hours at a time.

P. G. Wodehouse
A Damsel in Distress

Archaeology is the only branch of anthropology where we kill our informants in the process of studying them.

Kent V. Flannery
The Golden Marshalltown

*P*art Four deals with the ways in which archaeologists acquire data in the field. As we stressed earlier, acquiring such data depends on a sound research design and on formulating specific hypotheses before reconnaissance, site survey, or excavation can be begun. Our knowledge of the past is limited, not only by preservation in the ground but also by our own methods for recovering data. Chapters 8 through 10 describe some of the fundamental principles and processes of archaeological fieldwork, as well as some of the many special problems encountered by archaeologists in the field. And rather than draw on a single case study, we have chosen to give many examples, relying on your instructors to use case studies derived from their own experience.

Chapter 8

Doing Archaeological Research

*"T*he excavator without an intelligent policy may be described as an archaeological food-gatherer, master of a skill, perhaps, but not creative in the wider terms of constructive science," wrote Sir Mortimer Wheeler in his classic 1954 description of archaeological research. This chapter shows just how true his remarks were. Modern archaeology makes use of scientific methods developed not only by archaeologists themselves but also by scientists in many other disciplines. It is a complex process involving research design, field surveys, and actual excavation, as well as lengthy laboratory analysis of many types of finds. Above all, modern archaeological research is a multidisciplinary effort, ideally involving a closely knit group of researchers with many and diverse skills.

After discussing the qualifications of a good archaeologist, we look at the relationship between science and archaeology, at inductive and deductive reasoning, and then examine the process of archaeological research itself. This short chapter is an important preliminary to the discussions of archaeological data acquisition that follow.

THE ARCHAEOLOGIST'S SKILLS

Early archaeologists needed few qualifications beyond a liking for the past, some experience in excavation, and an ability to classify artifacts. Sir Leonard Woolley, famed excavator of Ur-of-the-Chaldees in Mesopotamia in the 1920s, was completely self-trained and learned excavation in a few seasons in the Sudan. In an interview with an Oxford college president, he was told: "*I* have decided that you shall become an archaeologist!" Fortunately for science, Woolley obeyed him (Fagan, 1979).

The archaeologists of the 1990s, however, require specialist training in administrative, technical, and academic skills of many types. Modern archaeology has become so complex that few individuals can possibly master all the skills needed to excavate a large city or even a medium-sized settlement where preservation conditions are exceptionally complete. In the 1920s, Woolley excavated Ur with a handful of Europeans, three expert Syrian foremen, and several hundred workers. An expedition to an equivalent site today would consist of a carefully organized team of experts whose skills reflect the precise hypotheses about the site that were to be tested in the field.

Let us examine, then, some of the basic skills an archaeologist needs.

Theoretical Skills

The archaeologist must be able to define research problems in their context: everything that is known about them. This knowledge includes not only the current status of research on a specific problem, such as the origins of humanity or the earliest human settlement of Ohio, but also the latest theoretical and methodological advances in archaeology that could affect the definition and solution of the problem.

The research problem will be defined by the specific objectives to be achieved. The archaeologist must have the expertise to formulate the precise hypotheses to be tested in the research. As the research proceeds, he or she will have to be able to evaluate and put together the results of the work in the context set by the original objectives.

Methodological Expertise

Every archaeologist must have the ability to plan the methods to be used in the research to achieve the theoretical goals initially laid out. Methodological skills include being able to select between methods of data collection and to decide which analytical methods are most effective for the data being handled. Excavating sites requires a large range of methodological skills, from deciding which sampling and trenching systems to use to devising recording methods to dealing with special preservation conditions where fragile objects have to be removed intact from their matrix.

One important aspect of methodological expertise requires selecting and working with specialists from other disciplines. This task involves understanding multidisciplinary research and knowing the uses and limitations of the work done by, say, geologists or zoologists for the specific problems one is investigating.

Technical Skills

Methodological and technical skills overlap, especially in the field. The scientific excavation of any site or a large-scale field survey requires more than the ability to select a method or a recording system; one needs also to execute it under working conditions. Archaeological excavations require great precision in measurement and excavation, deployment of skilled and unskilled labor, and implementation of find-recovery systems that keep artifacts in order from the moment they are found until they are shipped to the laboratory for analysis. At issue here is provenience of the artifacts and features and of the associated ecofacts. (An ecofact consists of nonartifactual materials such as food residues and other finds that throw light on human activities.) The field archaeologist has to assume the roles of supervisor, photographer, surveyor, digger, recorder, writer, and soil scientist, as well as be able to deal with any unexpected jobs, such as uncovering the delicate bones of a skeleton or setting up details of a computer program. On large sites, expertly trained students or fellow archaeologists may assume such specialist tasks as photography; on small sites, the archaeologist must often perform this and all other tasks single-handedly.

Administrative and Managerial Skills

Modern archaeology requires—or actually demands—that its practitioners exercise high-grade administrative and managerial skills. Today's archaeologist has to be able to coordinate the activities of specialists from other disciplines, organize and deploy teams of volunteer students and paid laborers, and raise and administer research funds obtained from outside sources. He or she must always be aware of all aspects of a research project as it progresses, from arranging for permits and supplies of stationery and digging tools to doing the accounts.

Above all, anyone working on an archaeological project has to be an expert in human relations, in keeping people happy at demanding work, which is often carried out under difficult and uncomfortable conditions. The diplomatic side of archaeological excavations is often neglected. But the folklore of archaeology abounds with stories of disastrous excavations run by archaeologists with no sensitivity to their fellow workers. A truly happy excavation is a joy to work on, a dig on which people smile, argue ferociously over interpretations of stratigraphic profiles through an endless day, and enjoy the companionship of a campfire in the evenings.

Writing and Analytical Skills

If there is one basic lesson to be learned at the beginning of any archaeological endeavor, it is that all excavation is destruction of finite archives in the ground that can never be restored to their original configuration. Every archaeologist is responsible not only for analyzing his or her finds in the laboratory but also for preparing a detailed report on the fieldwork that has been done—an important part of the permanent record of archaeological research. Regrettably, the shelves in museums all over the world are filled with finds from sites that have been excavated but never written up. An unpublished site is effectively destroyed.

At first glance, the list of qualifications a professional archaeologist needs can be formidable. In practice, though, sound classroom training combined with a great deal of fieldwork experience can provide the necessary background.

ARCHAEOLOGY, SCIENCE, AND THE SCIENTIFIC METHOD

At various places we have referred to scientific archaeology, the scientific method, and the testing of hypotheses against data collected in the field (Kelley and Hanan, 1988). It is now time to ask the Damocletian question: Is archaeology a science? The answer is a qualified yes. In the sense that archaeologists study human societies of the past by scientifically recovering and analyzing data that consist of the material remains of these societies, it is a science. But in the sense that archaeology, as part of anthropology, studies the intangible philosophic and religious beliefs of a society, it is not a science.

What do we mean by *scientific*? Science is a way of acquiring knowledge and understanding about the parts of the natural world that can be measured. It is a disciplined and carefully ordered search for knowledge, carried out in a systematic manner. This is a far cry from the ways in which we acquire our personal experience of religious philosophies, social customs, or political trends. Science involves using methods of acquiring knowledge that are not only cumulative but also subject to continuous testing and retesting. Over the years, scientists have developed the general procedures for acquiring data, known as the scientific method, which have come into wide use. Even though the scientific method may be applied in somewhat different ways in botany, zoology, and anthropology, the basic principles are the same: the notion that knowledge of the real world is both cumulative and subject to constant rechecking. The scientific method has many applications to archaeological data, and its use classifies much of archaeology as a science.

The Scientific Method

Science establishes facts about the natural world by observing objects, events, and phenomena. In making these observations, the scientist proceeds by using either inductive or deductive reasoning.

Inductive reasoning takes specific observations and makes a generalization from them. I once found nearly 10,000 wild vegetable remains in a 4,000-year-old hunter-gatherer camp in central Zambia. More than 42 percent of them were from the *bauhinia,* a shrub prized for its fruit and roots, which flowers from October to February. The *bauhinia* is still eaten by San hunter-gatherers in the Kalahari today. From this knowledge I induced that *bauhinia* has been a preferred seasonal food for hunter-gatherers in this general area for thousands of years (Fagan and Van Noten, 1971).

Deductive reasoning works the other way around. That is, the observer starts with a generalization and proceeds to form specific implications. In the Kalahari, I would have formulated a hypothesis (or series of hypotheses) about *bauhinia* eating by San and prehistoric hunter-gatherers and then tested it with ethnographic fieldwork and archaeological investigations. My hypothesis would then be confirmed, rejected, or refined.

A classic example of applying both inductive and deductive approaches comes from field studies done in the Great Basin in the western United States by anthropologist Julian Steward, who spent much of the 1920s and 1930s working on Shoshonean ethnography. The mass of field data that he collected led him to inductive generalizations about the ways in which the Shoshoneans moved their settlements throughout the year (Steward, 1938).

In the late 1960s this pioneer work was greatly refined by David Hurst Thomas, who approached the Shoshoneans' settlement patterns deductively. First, he took Steward's theory about the settlement patterns and devised hypotheses about the densities and distributions of artifacts in the various ecological zones of the Great Basin. "If the late prehistoric Shoshoneans behaved in the fashion suggested by Steward, how would the artifacts have fallen on the ground?" he asked (Thomas, 1969, 1973, 1983b). He constructed more than one hundred hypotheses relating to Steward's original theory. Next, he devised tests to verify or invalidate his hypotheses. He expected to find specific forms of artifacts associated with particular types of activity, such as hunting, in seasonal archaeological sites where hunting was said to be important. Aware of local preservation conditions, he strongly emphasized the distribution and frequency of artifact forms. Then he collected in the field the archaeological data needed for his tests. Finally, Thomas tested each of his hypotheses against the field data and rejected about 25 percent of his original hypotheses. The remainder were supported by the data and provided a major refinement of Steward's original generalization. Later fieldwork gave him abundant opportunities to refine his original hypotheses and to collect more field data to confirm them further.

Thomas's Great Basin research is a good example of the cumulative benefits of deductive reasoning and the scientific method in archaeological research.

Most early archaeological research was inductive, and much contemporary work still is. At present, the tendency is to dismiss all inductive research as scientifically unsound, for it involves some insight or intuition rather than precise application of the scientific method. Such a dismissal is totally unrealistic, however, for it means rejecting all the early archaeological knowledge acquired by scholars who did not use the scientific method.

The importance of the scientific method, however, should not be overestimated. A balanced view is this: "Science advances by disproof, proposing the most adequate explanations for the moment, knowing that new and better explanations will later be found. This continuous self-correcting feature is the key to the scientific method" (Sharer and Ashmore, 1987; see also Doran, 1987).

THE PROCESS OF ARCHAEOLOGICAL RESEARCH

The archaeology of today is becoming more and more explicitly scientific and sophisticated. To achieve this sophistication, we must formulate much more specific research designs. In this section we describe the process of archaeological research from formulation of the research design to publication of the final report.

Research Designs

Lewis Binford was among the first archaeologists to see the necessity for highly specific research designs (Binford, 1964). To this end, he called for more regional studies, for investigations in which the archaeologist would aim at solving specific problems, and for testing of hypotheses with representative samples of data drawn from a well-defined region. Such research is so complex that without highly specific research designs, it could not be executed. Under this approach, the research problem itself often determines the sites to be investigated.

A research design, whether simple or complex, is a formal procedure whose purpose is to direct the carrying out of an archaeological investigation. It has two objectives: to ensure that the results will be scientifically valid and to carry out the research as efficiently and economically as possible. The process of archaeological research, then, is controlled by the research design, which takes the project through stages. These stages, to be described shortly, are by no means common to all research projects; for although "research design" sounds rigid and inflexible, in practice the design for any project has to be flexible enough to allow changes in the overall project as field research proceeds.

Formulation

Any archaeological research begins with fundamental decisions about the problem or area to be studied. A research problem can be as grandiose as determining the origins of agriculture in the Southwest—a truly enormous project—or as specific as determining the date of the second phase in Stonehenge's construction. The initial decisions will identify both the problem and the geographic region in which it will be investigated. The latter can be one site or an entire region. These decisions immediately limit the scope of the research design.

Once the problem and the area are identified, the researcher must do a great deal of background research, involving both library work and field investigations. He or she must read up on previous archaeological research on the problem and study the geology, climate, ecology, anthropology, and general background of the area. Several field visits are essential, both to examine fieldwork conditions and to get a feel for the region. Water supplies, campsites, and sources of labor have to be identified. Landowners' permissions to dig and survey are essential, and government permits may be needed. At least some preliminary fieldwork is needed to aid in formulating the research design, especially in areas where no archaeology has been carried out before.

The objective directing all this preliminary work is to refine the problems being investigated until the archaeologist can begin to define the specific research goals. These goals will almost inevitably include testing specific hypotheses, which can be related to earlier research carried out by previous investigators, or entirely new hypotheses that come out during the preliminary formulation of the research problem. Yet others will be added as the research work proceeds. Generating hypotheses at this stage is vital, for they determine the types of data that will be sought in the field. These types must be defined, at least in general, before one goes into the field.

Let us take two hypotheses designed as part of a research project into early food production in Egypt:

> The earliest cereal agriculture near Kom Ombo developed among hunter-gatherers who had been exploiting wild vegetable foods very intensively. The emergence of agriculture came about as a result of the intensification of gathering and rapid population growth, causing shortages of wild cereals. So people began to grow wild cereals for themselves.

What sorts of data would be needed to test these hypotheses at Kom Ombo? The archaeologist formulating the project of which this hypothesis is a part would be looking for:

1. Sites in areas where wild cereals could have grown, where preservation conditions would allow for survival of vegetal remains
2. Food residues in the form of carbonized and discarded vegetable foods and the bones of domesticated animals
3. Implements used for harvesting and processing both wild and domesticated grains—grindstones, sickles, and so on
4. Evidence for such features as storage pits or baskets, indicating deliberate conservation of food supplies
5. Sites that were occupied longer than the relatively short periods favored by most hunter-gatherers, since farmers have to watch over their crops

Armed with both hypotheses and lists of the types of evidence likely to be encountered in the field, the archaeologist can plan for the equipment, facilities, and people needed to carry out the job. Even more important, the project can be formulated with advice from experts, whose specialist knowledge will be needed either in the field or in the laboratory. The necessary contacts with experts are best made before the fieldwork begins and funds are obtained. A surprising number of specialists are needed for even quite simple investigations. The Kom Ombo hypothesis could ideally require the long- or short-term services of these specialists:

1. A geologist to assist in geological dating of sites in the Nile Valley
2. A soil scientist to study occupation levels and organic soils
3. A radiocarbon dating laboratory to date carbon samples
4. A botanist to supervise recovery of vegetal remains and to identify them
5. An expert on pollen analysis to work on any such samples recovered in the excavations
6. A zoologist to study the animal bones

The larger-scale project may take an integrated team of experts from several disciplines into the field—an expensive enterprise that often yields important results. The study of early agriculture in the Near East was revolutionized by Robert Braidwood of the University of Chicago in the 1950s when he took such a team of experts with him to the Zagros Mountains. The research team was able to trace agriculture and animal domestication from their beginnings among nomadic hunter-gatherers on the highlands more than nine thousand years ago (Braidwood and Braidwood, 1983).

Research design has a critical part in cultural resource management (Chapter 19). Regional research designs for large areas such as the San Juan Basin in Colorado provide a long-term framework for hundreds of minor environmental impact studies and research projects. These designs are not cast in concrete; they are ever-changing documents that are brought up to date regularly to accommodate changing methodologies and new circumstances in the field (Fowler, 1982).

The final stage in formulating the research project is acquiring the necessary funding. This can be frustrating and time-consuming work, for sources of monies for archaeological fieldwork are always in short supply. Most excavations organized in the Americas are funded either by the National Science Foundation or, if within the United States, by some other government agency, such as the National Park Service. Some private organizations, such as the National Geographic Society or the Wenner Gren Foundation for Anthropological Research, support excavations. Some foundations limit their support to studies on specific topics. The L. S. B. Leakey Foundation of Pasadena supports only research into primate behavior and the origins of humankind and some types of urgent anthropological fieldwork. Few archaeologists are experts at fund-raising, for it requires a great deal of time. But some excavations, such as the regular seasons at Aphrodisias in Turkey or Crow Canyon in the American Southwest, rely heavily on private donations. The organizers spend considerable time raising private gifts to support each field season and the laboratory work that follows it.

Data Collection

Once the field team is assembled and the funds are in hand, actual implementation of the project begins. The first stage is to acquire equipment, set up camp, and organize the research team in the field. Once that procedure is complete, actual collecting of archaeological data can begin.

This collection of data involves two basic processes: locating and surveying sites and scientifically excavating carefully selected sites.

Locating archaeological sites is obviously the first stage in collecting data. As we will see in Chapter 9, reconnaissance can be carried out on foot, in vehicles, even on the back of a mule. A variety of techniques are used to ensure that a representative sample of sites is located and investigated before excavation. Then the surfaces of the sites are carefully examined and samples of artifacts lying at ground level are collected, to record as much as possible about the location without the expense of excavation. This recording can include photographs, some surveying and measurement, and even some probing of the site with borers or remote sensing devices. Obviously, much less information is collected from surface surveys than from excavations.

Archaeological excavations are ultimately a recording of subsurface features and the provenience, or precise relationships, of the artifacts within the site. Varied techniques are used to collect and record archaeological data from beneath the ground, as described in Chapter 10. Obviously, the scope of archaeological excavation can range from a small test pit to a large-scale investigation at a site such as the Meadowcroft rockshelter in the Ohio Valley, where excavation went on for many seasons (Adovasio and others, 1975, 1984).

Data Processing, Analysis, and Interpretation

The end products of even a month's excavation on a moderately productive site are a daunting accumulation. Box upon box of potsherds, stone tools, bones, and other finds are stacked in the field laboratory and must be cleaned, labeled, and sorted. Hundreds of slides and photographs must be processed and cataloged. Rolls of drawings with important information on the provenience of finds from the trenches must also be cataloged. Then there are radiocarbon and pollen samples, burials, and other special finds that need examination by specialists. The first stage in processing the data, then, occurs at the site, where the finds are washed, sorted, and given preservation treatment sufficient to transport them to the archaeological laboratory for more thorough examination.

The detailed analysis of the data is carried out, often for many months, in a laboratory that has the facilities for such research work. These analyses include not only classifying artifacts and identifying the materials from which they were made but also studying food remains, pollen samples, and other key sources of information. All these analyses are designed to provide information for interpreting the archaeological record. Some tests, such as radiocarbon dating or pollen analysis, are carried out in laboratories with the necessary technical equipment. We describe various approaches to archaeological analysis in Chapters 11 through 16.

Interpreting the resulting classified and thoroughly analyzed data involves not only synthesizing all the information from the investigation but also final testing of the basic hypotheses formulated at the beginning of the project. These tests produce models for reconstructing and explaining the prehistory of the site or region. We look at some of these models and interpretations in Part Seven.

Publication

The archaeologist's final responsibility is publishing the results of the research project. Archaeological excavation destroys all or part of a site; unless the investigator publishes the results, vital scientific information will be lost forever. The ideal scientific report publishes not only the research design and hypotheses that have been formulated but also the data used to test them and to interpret the site or region so that the same tests can be replicated by others (Grinsell and others, 1970).

All archaeological research is cumulative, in the sense that everyone's investigations are eventually superseded by later work, which uses more refined methods of recovery and new analytical approaches. But unless every archaeologist publishes the results of his or her completed work, the chain of research is incomplete, and a fragment of human history will vanish into oblivion. It is sad that the pace of publication has been far behind that of excavation. The reason is not hard to discern: excavation is far more fun than writing reports!

SUMMARY

- Modern archaeology makes use of scientific methods devised by archaeologists and also by scientists in many other disciplines.
- A well-qualified archaeologist commands many skills, both in archaeological method and theory and in practical methodology. This expertise includes the ability to select and work with specialists in other academic disciplines. Practical fieldwork experience and considerable administrative and managerial skill are also required on even the smallest research project. All archaeologists have to ac-

quire precise analytical and writing skills that enable them to communicate their results and record them for posterity.

- Archaeologists use science as a means for acquiring knowledge and understanding about the parts of the natural world that can be observed. They do so by working with two forms of reasoning: inductive reasoning, which takes specific observations and makes a generalization from them, and deductive reasoning, which starts with a generalization and proceeds to specific implications.
- The process of archaeological research begins with formulating highly specific research designs that are flexible enough to allow changes in the overall project as field research proceeds.
- The research project is formulated to fit the problem to be investigated and the geographic area involved. Formulation means carrying out background research and then developing hypotheses to be tested against data acquired in the field.
- Once the field team is assembled, members begin to acquire data by reconnaissance, site survey, and excavation. This acquisition requires them to record provenience, archaeological context, and a great deal of basic information about the site, its natural environment, and its archaeological finds.
- The processing of archaeological data requires analyzing and interpreting the archaeological finds, which involves sorting, classifying, and ordering the finds, and then testing the hypotheses developed as part of the research design.
- The final stage in archaeological research is publishing the results for posterity.

GUIDE TO FURTHER READING

Binford, Lewis R. "A Consideration of Archaeological Research Design," *American Antiquity* 29 (1964): 425–441. Binford summarizes the key points about sound archaeological design.

Dancey, H. S. *Archaeological Field Methods: An Introduction.* Minneapolis: Burgess, 1981. Probably the best and most up-to-date manual on American field methods around. Especially good on research design.

Hester, Thomas R., Harry J. Shafer, and Robert F. Heizer. *Field Methods in Archaeology.* Palo Alto, Calif.: Mayfield, 1987. A basic field manual on survey and excavation for the beginner.

Schiffer, Michael B., and George J. Gumerman. *Conservation Archaeology.* Orlando, Fla.: Academic Press, 1977. Essays on research design. The chapter by Mark Raab on the Santa Rosa Work Project is especially useful.

Thomas, David Hurst. *Predicting the Past: An Introduction to Anthropological Archaeology.* Fort Worth: Holt, Rinehart and Winston, 1974. A short account of the basic methods of anthropological archaeology that provides valuable background for this chapter.

Chapter
9

Finding Archaeological Sites

Numerous writers have spoken lyrically about time's ravages on the monuments of antiquity, some with pathos, some with humor. W. S. Gilbert, in the second act of *The Mikado*, in 1885, said:

> There's a fascination frantic
> In a ruin that's romantic
> Do you think you are sufficiently decayed?

There was a sense of romance in the antique and the decayed, a sense experienced by every visitor to the Parthenon in Athens or to the Pyramids. Time has transformed the abandoned sites of our ancestors in many ways. Some sites, such as Stonehenge and the Pyramids of Giza in Egypt, have never passed into oblivion. People have always realized that they were the work of earlier human beings. Others, like the thousands of sites in the Great Basin and in Australia, have vanished almost without a trace. It takes a trained archaeological eye to identify them.

Until fairly recently, archaeologists paid relatively little attention to the techniques for locating archaeological sites and interpreting them without actual excavation. A new emphasis on regional archaeological studies, innovative remote-sensing techniques, and above all the urgent need to save and record sites before they are destroyed by twentieth-century development has changed all this. In the pages that follow we review some of the archaeologist's techniques for locating and studying archaeological sites without digging them.

Two basic processes are involved in locating archaeological sites:

Archaeological reconnaissance, which is the systematic attempt to locate, identify, and record the distribution of archaeological sites on the ground and against the natural geographic and environmental background.

Site survey, which is the collecting of surface data and evaluating of each site's archaeological significance.

IDENTIFYING SITES

The competent fieldworker can identify archaeological sites with an ease born of experience that can astound the lay onlooker. I remember being astonished when, on a survey in the Zambezi Valley in Central Africa in 1959, my senior and very experienced colleague stopped suddenly and picked up half a stone flake from a gravel bed covered with Stone Age artifacts. "This is the other half of a flake I found here in 1938," he told me. I flatly disbelieved him. But he was right. We located the original in the local museum collections, and the two halves were reunited. My colleague's archaeological memory was astounding, but it was also a result of long experience with local conditions.

Let us examine some key indicators of archaeological sites.

1. Conspicuous earthworks, stone ruins, or other surface features are among the most obvious indicators. Good examples are the Adena and Hopewell burial mounds of the Ohio Valley, the pueblos of the American Southwest, and the fortified *pa,* or defensive earthworks, built by the Maori in New Zealand (Davidson, 1984). One of the most extensive settlement surveys ever undertaken was that in the Basin of Mexico in the 1960s and 1970s. It was designed to locate every surviving site in the area and to establish relationships among them (Sanders and others, 1979).

2. Vegetational cover is a useful indicator, for grass may grow more lushly on areas where the subsoil has been disturbed or the nitrogen content of the soil is greater. Conversely, many California shell middens are covered with stunted vegetation caused by the artifact-filled, alkaline soil, which contrasts sharply with the surrounding green grass at the end of the rainy season. They can be spotted from miles away. Sometimes specific types of trees or brush are associated with archaeological sites. One is the breadnut, or *ramon,* tree, which was once cultivated by the Maya. These trees are still common near ancient sites and have been used as guides in locating many archaeological sites.

3. Soil discolorations are a sign of archaeological sites. In many cases, the dark, organic soils of long-abandoned villages show up in plowed land as dark zones, often associated with potsherds and

other artifacts. Burrowing animals living in such areas leave telltale traces in the form of organic earth and artifacts, which their activities bring to the surface.

4. Surface finds of artifacts, broken bones, and other materials may show up in dry areas as dense concentrations of debris that stand out from the surrounding ground. In some cases, millennia of wind erosion may remove the soil mantling the artifacts and leave them exposed on the surface.

CHANCE DISCOVERIES

The ingenious people who calculate such things estimate that something like a quarter of the world's archaeological sites have been discovered by chance as a result of natural or human activity. Whole chapters of the past have been exposed by accidental discoveries of sites, spectacular artifacts, or skeletons. Plowing, peat cutting, road making, and other day-to-day activities have been a fruitful source of archaeological discoveries. Industrial activity, highway construction, airport expansion, and other destructive actions by twentieth-century humanity have unearthed countless archaeological sites, many of which have to be investigated hurriedly before the bulldozers remove all traces. Deep plowing, highway construction, and urban renewal are bitter enemies of the past. Yet dramatic discoveries have resulted from our despoiling of the environment. Some states require highway contractors to allocate a proportion of their contract budgets for investigating any archaeological sites found in the path of their roadways—this precaution at least permits some investigation of accidentally discovered settlements. But many construction programs pay little heed to the pleas of the archaeologist and bulldoze away the past with minimal sorrow (see Chapter 20).

The excavation for Mexico City's Metro (subway) provided a unique opportunity for accidental discoveries of archaeological sites. The shallow tunneling, which extended more than twenty-six miles under the city, yielded a wealth of archaeological material. Mexico City is built on the site of Tenochtitlán, the capital city of the Aztecs. Tenochtitlán, destroyed by the Spanish under Hernando Cortés in 1521, was a wonderful city whose markets rivaled those of most major Spanish cities in size. Little remains of Tenochtitlán on the surface today, but the contractors for the Metro found more than forty tons of pottery, 380 burials, and even a small temple dedicated to the Aztec god of the wind, Ehecatl-Quetzalcoatl (Figure 9.1). The temple is now preserved on its original site in the Pino Suárez station of the Metro system, part of an exhibit commemorating Mexico City's ancestor. The tunneling operations, happily, were under the constant supervision of a large group of archaeologists under the direction of Jorge Gussinyer of the world-famous National Museum of Anthropology. The archaeologists were empowered to halt digging whenever an archaeologi-

Figure 9.1 The temple of Ehecatl-Quetzalcoatl, found during the excavations for the Pino Suárez subway station, Mexico City.

cal find of importance was made. As a result, many newfound sculptures and artifacts were saved from destruction for the national collections (Fagan, 1984a).

Hydroelectric schemes and flood control programs in North America and elsewhere have destroyed thousands upon thousands of archaeological sites without a trace—and have accelerated the discovery of others. Some of these projects have stimulated much intensive surveying. The Aswan Dam scheme in Nubia provided a rare opportunity for intensive investigation of Pleistocene geology and Stone Age sites in the area to be flooded by Lake Nasser (Wendorf and others, 1968). Nearer home, the flood control schemes initiated by the Tennessee River Valley Authority and by the Army Corps of Engineers elsewhere in the agriculturally rich South have led to many river basin surveys (for example, see Bareis and Porter, 1984).

Nature itself sometimes uncovers sites for us, which may then be located by a sharp-eyed archaeologist looking for natural exposures of likely geological strata. Erosion, flooding, tidal waves, low lake levels, earthquakes, and wind action can all lead to exposure of archaeological sites. One of the most famous sites to be exposed in this manner is Olduvai Gorge in Tanzania, a great gash in the Serengeti Plains where nature, by earth movement, has sliced through hundreds of feet of Pleistocene lake bed to expose numerous site locations of early humans (Leakey, 1951). Fossil animal bones were found in the gorge's exposed strata by Professor Wilhelm Kattwinkel as early as 1911, which led to a fossil-hunting expedition under Professor Hans Reck and ultimately to Louis and Mary Leakey's long and patient investigations in the gorge. The results of their excavations are spectacular—a series of sites stratified one above another, in which hominid fossils, broken animal bones, and stone implements have been found and dated to ages ranging from 400,000 years for *Homo erectus* to 1.75 million years before the present for locations in the earliest bed of the gorge.

In late 1957 another remarkable discovery was made, this time in semiarid country in southeastern Colorado (Wheat, 1972). Wind erosion exposed what appeared to be five piles of bison bones in an arroyo near Kit Carson. Some projectile points were found with the bones. The bone bed, known as the Olsen-Chubbuck site, lay in a filled buffalo trail, of a type that crisscrossed the plains in early frontier days (Figure 9.2). The bones were carefully excavated and shown to come from *Bison occidentalis*, an extinct species. Separate piles made up of different bone types, such as limb bones or pelvic girdles, gave a clue to the hunters' butchery techniques. They had cut up the carcasses systematically, piling the detached members in the arroyo in separate heaps, dismembering several bison at a time. The remains of nearly two hundred bison came from the arroyo, but only some were fully dismembered. Clearly, the arroyo was a trap into which the beasts had been stampeded. (Bison have a keen sense of smell but poor vision; a lumbering herd of these gregarious beasts can be readily stampeded into an abrupt declivity, and the leaders have no option but to plunge into the gully and be immobilized or disabled by the weight of those behind them.) So vivid a reconstruction of the Paleo-Indians' hunt could be made that the excavators were even able to guess at the direction of the wind on the day of the stampede. The vivid traces of this hunt of 8,500 years ago were buried in the arroyo by nature and exposed again in our time to be discovered by the vigilant eye of an amateur archaeologist.

ARCHAEOLOGICAL RECONNAISSANCE

Famous archaeological sites like the Parthenon have never been lost. The Acropolis at Athens was remembered even when Athens itself had become an obscure Medieval village. The temples of Ancient Egyptian Thebes were famous as long ago as Roman times and have never vanished from historical consciousness (Fagan, 1975). Other sites, such as Homeric Troy, were remembered in Classical literature, but their precise locations were rediscovered only by prolonged archaeological investigation. In 1870, Heinrich Schliemann started excavations at the large mound known

Figure 9.2 A layer of excavated bison bones from the Olsen-Chubbuck site in Colorado, a kill site found by a cowboy.

as Hissarlik in northwestern Turkey. Within a few seasons, he located the remains of several prehistoric towns, one of which, he claimed, was Priam's Troy (Fagan, 1977; Wood, 1985).

Of course, most of the world's archaeological sites are far less conspicuous than the Pyramids, and unlike Troy, they have no historical records to testify to their existence. The early antiquarians discovered sites primarily by locating burial mounds, stone structures, hill-forts, and other conspicuous traces of prehistoric human works on the European landscape. The tells of the Near East, occupied by generation after generation of city dwellers, were easily recognized by early travelers, and the temples and monuments of ancient Egypt have attracted antiquarian and plunderer alike for many centuries. New World archaeological sites were described by some of the first conquistadores. Later, in 1576, Copán, the ruined Mayan city, was studied by García de Palacio. Mayan sites were vividly cataloged by John Lloyd Stephens and Frederick Catherwood in the mid-nineteenth century, and the wonders of Mesoamerican civilization were laboriously recovered from the rain forest that engulfed them (Figure 9.3) (Fagan, 1985).

Archaeological reconnaissance did not become a serious part of archaeology until field archaeologists began to realize that people had enacted their lives against the background of an ever-changing natural landscape, modified both by climatic and other ecological changes and also by human activities. Thus all that remained for archaeology to find, as expressed by Francis Bacon, was "some remnants of history which have casually escaped the shipwreck of time." In the Southwest late in the nineteenth century, the immortal Adolph F. Bandelier, historian, archaeologist, ethnographer, and novelist, walked thousands of miles in search of archaeological sites. The early twentieth century brought much more of this more systematic field archaeology in Europe. J. P. Williams Freeman and O. G. S. Crawford, among others, traced Roman roads and ancient field systems, walking and bicycling over the countryside in search of known and unknown sites. In Bolivia and Peru, Max Uhle, a German, was among those who pioneered systematic field survey in the New World. The techniques these scholars invented and perfected form the basis for much archaeological fieldwork today (Crawford, 1953).

Most early archaeological reconnaissance sought individual sites for eventual excavation. But as archaeologists have grown more and more intent on studying variability in the archaeological record, they have come

Figure 9.3 Copán in Honduras, a conspicuous archaeological site found by a Spanish priest in 1576 and made known by Stephens and Catherwood in the nineteenth century. This photograph shows the reconstructed ball court.

to deal with entire regions rather than individual sites (Binford, 1964). The objectives of reconnaissance too have shifted, in part. Although archaeologists still search for sites to excavate, most do so within an entirely different theoretical framework. Those following the more traditional approaches tend to think of a survey area as a group of sites rather than a unit of space in which prehistoric peoples lived. Thus the modern regional survey is more properly defined as "some specified unit of space within which archaeological sites and other relevant variables are tabulated" (Dunnell and Dancey, 1983). This approach makes surface surveying a much more important component of archaeological investigation than ever. Before considering the surface survey, let us examine the more traditional reconnaissance methods.

GROUND RECONNAISSANCE

Most archaeological sites are discovered by careful field surveying and thorough examination of the countryside for both conspicuous and inconspicuous traces of the past (Willey, 1953). A survey can vary from searching a city lot for historic structures or a tiny side valley with a few rockshelters in its walls to a large-scale survey of an entire river basin or water catchment area—a project that would take several years to complete. For all these, the theoretical ideal is the same: to recover all traces of ancient settlement in the survey area. Often a survey intended to recover all or nearly all sites in a region is called a *complete survey* or *comprehensive reconnaissance*.

Archaeological sites manifest themselves in many ways: in the form of tells, which are mounds of occupation debris; middens, which are mounds of food remains and occupation debris; or conspicuous caves or temples. But many others are far less easily located, perhaps displaying no more than a small scatter of stone tools or a patch of discolored soil. Still other sites leave no traces of their presence above the ground and may come to light only when the subsoil is disturbed, like the temple of Ehecatl-Quetzalcoatl, found during excavation of Mexico City's Metro line (Figure 9.1). Thus it can be seen that no surface survey, however thorough and however sophisticated its remote sensing devices, will achieve complete coverage. The key to effective archaeological surveying lies in proper research designs and in rigorous sampling techniques to provide a reliable basis of probability for extending the findings of the survey from a sample zone to a wider region.

The comprehensiveness of any survey is affected by other factors, too. Many surveys are carried out in intensively populated areas or on private farmland. Some landowners may refuse access to their lands. To their credit, most farmers or landlords do not. Indeed, owners may recall past discoveries on their land, hitherto unsuspected by archaeologists. Inaccessibility can be further complicated by such factors as dense vegetation, crops, and floodwaters. In many parts of Mexico and California, the obvious months for site surveys are at the end of the dry season, when the vegetation is dry or even burned off. But in lush, lowland floodplains, such as those of the American South, large tracts of the survey area may be totally inaccessible all year. Only the most conspicuous sites, like mounds, show up under such conditions. And of course, thousands of sites are buried under tract housing and parking lots, or countless huge earth-moving operations that have radically altered the landscape.

A great deal depends, too, on the intensity of the survey in the field. The survey area can be traversed by automobile, horseback, mule, camel, bicycle, or—most effectively—foot. Most well-known field archaeologists of this century have been avid walkers. In fact, one used to boast that he had walked the feet off of all his students and colleagues in pursuit of the past! Footwork is important, for it enables the archaeologist to train an eye for topography and the relationships of human settlement to the landscape.

Michael Schiffer of the University of Arizona identifies four basic types of intensive ground reconnaissance (Schiffer and House, 1976):

1. Conspicuous and accessible sites are located by superficial survey, such as that by Catherwood and Stephens with Mayan sites in the Yucatán in the 1840s. The investigator visits only very conspicuous and accessible sites of great size and considerable fame. These operations, however, hardly scratch the archaeological surface.

2. In the next level of survey, assisted by local informants such as landowners, relatively conspicuous sites at accessible locations are discovered. This approach was used frequently in the 1930s for the classic river basin surveys in the lower Mississippi Valley. It can be very effective, but it gives a rather narrow view of the archaeological sites in an area.

3. Limited-area reconnaissance involves very comprehensive door-to-door inquiries, supported by actual substantiation of claims that a site exists by checking the report on the ground. This type of survey, with its built-in system of verification, may yield more comprehensive information on sites. But it still does not give the most critical information of all, data on the ratios of one site type to another, nor does it assess the percentage of accessible sites that have been found. When archaeologists need a total inventory of archaeological sites in an area, such information is vital.

4. In the last type, the foot survey, a party of archaeologists covers an entire area by walking over it, perhaps with a set interval between members of the party. This is about the most rigorous method of reconnaissance, but it does work, as evidenced by the Cache River project in Arkansas. There, selected zones of the basin were surveyed by people walking sixty meters apart (Schiffer and House, 1976). When Paul Martin and Fred Plog surveyed 5.2 square miles

of the Hay Hollow Valley in east-central Arizona in 1967, they supervised a team of eight people who walked back and forth over small portions of the area (Martin and Plog, 1973). Each worker was nine meters from the next, their pathways carefully laid out with compass and stakes. Two hundred and fifty sites were recorded by this survey, at the cost of thirty person-days per square mile. One would think that every site would have been recorded. Yet two entirely new sites were discovered in the same area in 1969 and 1971, prehistoric irrigation canals were spotted by an expert on some aerial photographs, and some sandstone quarry sites were found.

As we have said, the chances of any archaeological survey recording every site in even a small area are remote. Obviously, though, total survey of an area is desirable, and sometimes nearly total coverage can be achieved by combined remote sensing and ground reconnaissance. William Sanders and his colleagues carried out a long-term archaeological survey of the Basin of Mexico in which they elected to try locating every site in the area over many seasons of fieldwork. At the end of the project, Sanders argued that this approach was far more effective than any sampling of the area, for it gave a much clearer picture of site variability on the ground (Sanders and others, 1979). Undoubtedly he is right, *if* one has the time and the money. In these days of limited budgets and short-term archaeological contracts dictated by impending site destruction, the archaeologist has turned to both remote sensing and statistical sampling to achieve goals of the survey.

REMOTE SENSING

More and more archaeologists are relying on technology and elaborate instrumentation to help them discover the past. Some archaeologists are beginning to talk about "nondestructive archaeology," the analysis of archaeological phenomena without excavations or collecting of artifacts, both of which destroy the archaeological record. The major methods in this approach are generally labeled *remote sensing* (Colwell, 1983; Drager and Lyons, 1983; Ebert, 1984; Parrington, 1983). These techniques include aerial photography, various magnetic prospecting methods, and side-scan radar.

Aerial Photography

The potential of aerial photography for archaeological reconnaissance was first recognized during World War I by O. G. S. Crawford in western Europe and by German archaeologists serving in the Sinai. The latter photographed ancient fields, streets, buildings, and other features, which showed up with astonishing clarity (Crawford and Keiller, 1928). The aviation pioneer Charles Lindbergh flew Alfred Kidder over areas of Arizona and New Mexico searching for ancient village sites. These pioneer flights were followed by hundreds of later sorties. Archaeological photography has also benefited from technological advances made during World War II and by space exploration. Today, thousands of hitherto unknown sites have been plotted on maps, whole field systems and roadways have been incorporated into panoramas of prehistoric or Roman landscapes in Italy and North Africa, and well-known sites such as Stonehenge and the many Mesoamerican and South American temples have been photographed in the context of their landscapes (Figure 9.4).

Aerial photography gives an unrivaled overhead view of the past. Sites can be photographed obliquely or vertically, at different seasons or times of day, and from many directions. Numerous sites that have left almost no surface traces on the ground have come to light through the all-embracing eye of the air photograph (Vogt, 1974; Wilson, 1983; Riley 1987).

Shadow Sites   Many earthworks and other complex structures have been leveled by plow or erosion, but their reduced topography clearly shows up from the air. The rising or setting sun can set off long shadows, emphasizing the relief of almost-vanished banks or ditches, so that the features of the site stand out in the oblique light. Such phenomena are sometimes called *shadow sites.*

Crop and Soil Marks   These are found in areas where the subsoil is suitable for revealing differences in soil color and in the richness of crop growth on a particular soil (Figure 9.5). Such marks cannot be detected

Figure 9.4 Aerial photograph of Chan Chan in coastal Peru shows the general layout of this remarkable settlement, occupied around A.D. 1200.

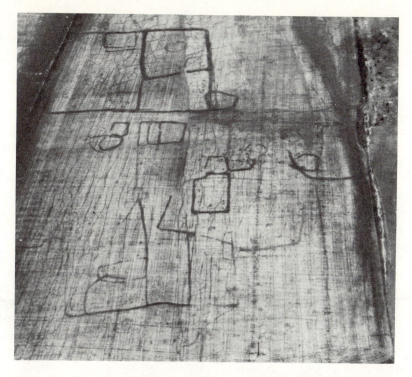

Figure 9.5 A crop mark site, from Thorpe, Achurch, Huntingdonshire, England. Under favorable circumstances, such marks can be seen clearly from the air.

easily on the surface, but under favorable circumstances they can be seen clearly from the air. The principle on which the crop mark is based is that the growth and color of a crop are mainly determined by the amount of moisture the plant can derive from the soil and the subsoil. If the soil depth has been increased by digging features, such as pits and ditches, and then filling them in or by heaping up additional earth to form artificial banks or mounds, crops growing over such abandoned structures are tall and well nourished. The converse is true where topsoil has been removed and the infertile subsoil is near the surface or where impenetrable surfaces, such as paved streets, are below ground level and crops are stunted. Thus a dark crop mark can be taken for a ditch or pit, and a lighter line will define a more substantial structure. Soil marks result from plowing soil from such features as banks and show up as a color lighter than that of the darker, deeper soil around them. Soil marks are useful in chalk country, where subsoil is a brilliant white.

Recently, archaeologists have tried combining remote sensing with phosphate testing of the soil. Certain materials associated with human activity contain compounds such as phosphate, calcium, and nitrogen. These are present in human excreta, also in bones, and in some types of refuse. Testing for bone phosphate in particular is useful, especially at ancient cemeteries where the bones may have vanished, but subsurface disturbances and high phosphate levels can still reveal the locations of long-forgotten burials.

Examples of Aerial Photography   A classic application of air photography was provided by Gordon Willey, who used a standard Peruvian Air Force mosaic of cultivated valley bottoms and margins of the Virú Valley in northern coastal Peru to survey changing settlement patterns there (Willey, 1953). Employing these photographs as the basis for a master site map of the valley, Willey was able to plot many archaeological features. Three hundred and fifteen sites in the Virú Valley were located, many of them stone buildings, walls, or terraces that showed up quite well on the mosaics. Some much less conspicuous sites were also spotted, among them midden heaps without stone walls, refuse mounds that appeared as low hillocks on the photographs, and small, pyramidal mounds of insignificant proportions. Adobe houses did not show up as clearly as stone structures. An enormous amount of time was saved that would otherwise have been spent walking over rough countryside. The aerial photographs enabled Willey and his team to pinpoint many sites before going out in the field. The finds were later investigated on the spot. The result was the fascinating story of shifting settlement patterns in Virú over many thousands of years, a classic of its kind. (See also INAH, 1980.)

The Virú surveys were made with standard aerial survey coverage taken from a high altitude. Such coverage has the advantage of minimal distortion, but, as Michael Parrington (1983) points out, the time of year and even time of day when the photos were taken is of great importance, especially when an area is in intensive use today. He cites the example of Valley Forge National Historical Park in Pennsylvania, where an aerial survey probed for traces of a Revolutionary War encampment. Unfortunately, a Boy Scout Jamboree in 1964 had been held on the site the year before. Ninety water stations, 3,900 latrine pits, thirty shower facilities, and underground utility lines left a maze of crop marks that showed up on the photograph (Figure 9.6). They effectively obscured earlier activity. Despite problems of this nature, aerial surveys have been used effectively in many areas, especially to plot prehistoric and later occupation directly onto maps. This approach was used at Chaco Canyon, New Mexico, where a prehistoric road system was plotted, using both side-scan radar and aerial photographs (Ebert and Hitchcock, 1980; Sever and Wiseman, 1985).

Most aerial photographs are taken with black-and-white film, which gives definition superior to that of color film and is much cheaper to buy and reproduce than color. The wide range of filters that can be used with black-and-white give the photographer great versatility in the field.

Some valuable experiments have been made with color photography, which is useful in detecting natural rather than cultural features. But it has the disadvantage of being more expensive and less tolerant of the photographer's errors.

Figure 9.6 Vertical aerial photograph of Valley Forge National Historical Park taken on May 13, 1965. The white marks are crop marks caused by subsurface disturbances for the Boy Scout Jamboree in 1964.

Infrared film, which has three layers sensitized to green, red, and infrared, detects reflected solar radiation at the near end of the electro-magnetic spectrum, some of which is invisible to the human eye. The different reflections from cultural and natural features are translated by the film into distinctive "false" colors. Bedrock comes up blue on infrared film, but vigorous grass growth on alluvial plains shows up bright red. Experiments at the famous Snaketown site in the American Southwest, a great Hohokam Indian pueblo, trade center, and ceremonial center, did not show up new cultural features, but tonal contrasts within a color indicated various cultural components. Vigorous plant growth showing up red on infrared photographs has been used to track shallow subsurface water sources where springs were formerly used by prehistoric peoples. The infrared data could lead the archaeologist to likely areas for hunting camps and villages where few surface indications now remain (Harp, 1978).

No archaeological aerial photography is fully effective unless the re-sults are checked on the ground. Even an expert can make many errors in interpreting surface features from air photographs. (For discussion, see Ebert, 1984.)

Nonphotographic Methods

Archaeological sites can be detected from the air, even from space, by nonphotographic techniques as well. But aerial photography is the last of the "do it yourself" types of remote sensing, a technique whose cost is within the reach of even a modest archaeological expedition. Aerial sensor imagery, using aircraft, satellites, and even manned spacecraft, involves instrumentation that is astronomically expensive by archaeological stan-dards. Thus these exciting techniques are only occasionally used, and then when the collaboration of NASA and interested experts can be enlisted.

Aircraft-borne Sensor Imagery   Aircraft-borne instrumentation of sev-eral types can be used to record images of the electromagnetic radiation that is reflected or emitted from the earth's surface. A multispectral scan-ner, for example, measures the radiance of the earth's surface along a scan line perpendicular to the aircraft's line of flight. A two-dimensional image is processed digitally. Multispectral scanners are ideal for mapping vegeta-tion and for monitoring bodies of water when more complete data are needed than can be obtained from aerial photographs. Thermal infrared line scanners were originally used for military night reconnaissance but now have many applications in the environmental sciences. The line scan-ners have thermal devices that record an image on photographic film. The temperature data obtained from such scans is combined with aerial photo-graphs to reveal tiny thermal patterns that may indicate different crop uses, the distribution of range animals, or variations in soil moisture and groundwater, both ancient and modern.

Sideways-looking Airborne Radar (SLAR)   This technique senses the terrain to either side of an aircraft's track. It does this by sending out long pulses of electromagnetic radiation. The radar then records the strength and time of the pulse return to detect objects and their range from the aircraft. SLAR has great potential for archaeology because it is not dependent on sunlight. The flying aircraft enables the observer to track the pulse lines in the form of images, no matter what obscures the ground. The SLAR images are normally interpreted visually, using radar mosaics or stereo pairs of images, as well as digital image processors. SLAR was originally used for oil exploration, geology, and geomorphology, in applications that could justify its high cost. It is useful for mapping surface soil moisture distributions, something that has great potential for the study of ancient Maya agriculture.

SLAR can show where many changes in topography have taken place or the subsoil of large sites has been disturbed. It can also be applied to underwater sites to locate wrecks on the sea floor. So far, applications of this exciting technology to the past have been few and far between, but experiments in the Mesoamerican lowlands have hinted that SLAR may be able to identify buildings beneath dense rain forest canopy. Scans of the Maya lowlands have shown that areas of wet-season swamp often have irregular grids of gray lines in them, multitudes of ladder, lattice, and curvilinear patterns. These have been compared to known ancient canal systems and are thought to represent long-forgotten large-scale irrigation schemes (Adams and others, 1981). The investigators believe that nearly all swamp edges in the Petén, the rain forest lowlands of northern Guatemala, once were extensively canalized for agriculture and communication purposes. They may have provided food supplies for much denser populations than today's.

The field testing of data from this remote-sensing technique has hardly begun. But surface investigations at Pulltrouser Swamp in northern Belize have shown that Maya farmers exploited the edges of seasonally flooded swamps between 200 B.C. and A.D. 850. A rising population of farmers brought under cultivation more than three hundred hectares of raised field plots, linked with interconnecting canals. These fields were hoed, mulched, and planted with maize, perhaps cotton, and amaranth (Turner and Harrison, 1983).

Satellite Sensor Imagery   This method is well known for its military applications, but earth resources technology satellites, both manned and unmanned, have proved extremely valuable for environmental monitoring. The most famous of these satellites are the Landsat series, which scan the earth with readers that record the intensity of reflected light and infrared radiation from the earth's surface. The data from scanning operations are converted electronically into photographic images and from these into mosaic maps. Normally, however, these maps are taken at a scale of about 1:1,000,000, far too imprecise for anything but the most general archaeological surveys. The pyramids and plazas of Teotihuacán in the Valley of Mexico might appear on such a map, but certainly not the types of minute archaeological distribution information that the average survey seeks. The Landsat imagery offers an integrated view of a large region and is made up of light reflected from many components of the earth: soil, vegetation, topography, and so on. Thus the stratified images obtained from Landsat tell the archaeologist a great deal about the environment as a cohesive whole. Computer-enhanced Landsat images can be used to construct environmental cover maps of large survey regions that are a superb backdrop for both aerial and ground reconnaissance for archaeological resources.

Aircraft and satellite scanning imagery is likely to become more commonly used in archaeology as the technology matures and becomes cheaper. These approaches are likely to become of first-rate importance for the study of archaeological sites against their background environments and landscapes and for cultural resource management. For the foreseeable future, however, most archaeologists will continue to rely on aerial photographs for most of their remote sensing.

Subsurface Detection

Once sites have been located, it is often possible to learn much about them by geophysical methods, most of which involve mechanical devices for subsurface detection of buried features (Weymouth, 1986). Many of these relatively new techniques were developed for oil or geological prospecting. Most are expensive; some are very time-consuming. But their application can sometimes save many weeks of expensive excavation and on occasion aid in formulating an accurate research design before a dig begins.

Nonmechanical Detection

In this method, the surface of the site is thumped with a suitable heavy pounder. The earth resonates in different ways, so much so that a practiced ear can detect the distinctive sound of a buried ditch or a subsurface stone wall. Dowsing, more an art than a geophysical method, really works—with practice. The author has used it on several occasions to detect buried walls.

The Auger, or Core Borer   This is a tool used to bore through subsurface deposits to find the depth and consistency of archaeological deposits lying beneath the surface. This technique has its value during an excavation, but it has the obvious disadvantage that the probe may destroy valuable artifacts. Augers were used quite successfully at the Ozette site in Washington to establish the depth of midden deposits (Kirk, 1974). Some specialized augers are used to lift pollen samples. Augers with a camera attached to a periscope head are also used to investigate the interiors of Etruscan tombs (Figure 9.7). The periscope is inserted through a small hole in the roof of the tomb to inspect the interior. If the contents are undisturbed, excavation proceeds. But if tomb robbers have emptied the chamber, many hours of labor have been saved.

Mechanical Detection

Three types of mechanical detection are resistivity survey, magnetic survey, and pulse radar.

Resistivity Survey   The electrical resistivity of the soil provides some clues to subsurface features on archaeological sites (Carr, 1982; Leute, 1987). Rocks and minerals conduct electricity, mainly because the deposits have moisture containing mineral salts in solution. A resistivity survey meter can be used to measure the variations in the resistance of the ground to an electric current. Stone walls or hard pavements obviously retain less dampness than a deep pit filled with soft earth or a large ditch that has silted up. These differences can be measured accurately so that disturbed ground, stone walls, and other subsurface features can be detected by systematic survey. To survey a site, all that is needed is the meter, which is attached to four or five probes. A grid of strings is laid over the site, and the readings taken from the probes are plotted as contour

Figure 9.7 A periscope being used to investigate an Etruscan tomb.

lines. These show the areas of equal resistance and the presence of features such as ditches and walls (Figure 9.8). This method has been used with great success in North America and was recently employed to identify subsurface features at the Late Woodland and Early Historic Howorth-Nelson site in Southwestern Pennsylvania (Adovasio and Carlisle, 1988; see Chapter 19).

Magnetic Survey   Magnetic location is used to find buried features such as iron objects, fired clay furnaces, pottery kilns, hearths, and pits filled with rubbish or softer soil (Leute, 1987). The principle is simple: any mass of clay heated to about 700°C and then cooled acquires a weak magnetism. Rocks, boulders, and soil will also acquire magnetism if iron oxides are present when they are heated. When the remanent magnetism of fired clay or of other materials in a pit or similar feature is measured, it will give a reading different from that of the intensity of the earth's magnetic field normally obtained from undisturbed soils. The proton magnetometer is the instrument most commonly used to detect archaeological features by magnetic detection. A site is surveyed by laying out fifty-foot-square units, each of them divided into a grid of five-foot squares. The measurement is taken with a staff to which are attached two small bottles filled with water or alcohol enclosed in electric coils. The magnetic intensity is measured by recording the behavior of the protons in the hydrogen atoms in the bottle's contents. The magnetometer itself amplifies the weak signals from the electrical coils. Features are traced by taking closely spaced measurements over areas where anomalies in the magnetic readings are found. Magnetic detection has been used very successfully to record pits, walls

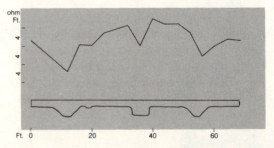

Figure 9.8 An electrical resistance survey across a Bronze Age burial site at Dorchester, Oxford, England. The upper curve represents the traverse made across the site with the instrument, with the probes set four feet apart. The lower line is a schematic section across the site; the dips indicate the two outer ditches and the burial pit, the positions of which were subsequently confirmed by excavation.

and other features in the middle of large forts or fortified towns, where total excavation of a site is clearly uneconomical. This method has been used widely in Europe and on earthen pyramids at La Venta, Mexico, but it is subject to some error because of such modern features as barbed wire fences, electric trains, and electric cables (Steponaitis and Brain, 1976; Kaczor and Weymouth, 1981).

Computers are now being used to record the field data and to convert them into a display on a TV screen or a printout. Sophisticated software allows the operator to screen out nonarchaeological variations in soil magnetism. Since a hectare of site requires at least 10,000 magnetometer readings, the use of a computer saves hours of time.

Pulse Radar   The pulse induction meter applies pulses of magnetic field to the soil from a transmitter coil. This instrument is very sensitive to metals and can be used to find pottery and metal objects and graves containing such objects. A soil conductivity meter can be used to detect subsoil features by measuring changes in the conductivity of the soil. Anomalies spotted by the instrument can be plotted with good accuracy, and pits as small as thirty centimeters in diameter and ten centimeters deep have been located. Individual metal objects can also be detected by this method, which holds great promise for the future.

The application of radar and other electronic devices is proliferating in archaeology. Ken Weeks and a team of fellow Egyptologists have embarked on a long-term project to map all the royal tombs in Thebes's Valley of Kings. They are using a hot-air balloon, X rays, and sonic detectors to map subterranean features and hidden chambers in royal tombs. High technology has come to historical archaeology, too. Joel Grossman was faced with the problem of investigating a buried seventeenth- and eighteenth-century port at Raritan, New Jersey, in three short months before a major sewer project butchered the site. Forced to carry out a year's worth of excavation in one-quarter the time, Grossman carried out a ground-penetrating radar survey of the site's buried features. The excavation was conducted with an infrared transit with computerized data recording that automatically provided provenience coordinates for every find. The technology used in the survey, excavation, and analysis of the site was very complicated, and the excavators needed considerable technical skill to operate it smoothly (Grossman, 1982). The cost of ground-penetrating radar precludes its wider use (Vaughan, 1986).

Recording Sites

Archaeological reconnaissance is useless unless one records the exact geographic location of the archaeological phenomena revealed by the survey. It is here that remote sensing comes into its own. Some of the larger projects in cultural resource management in the western United States make extensive use of remote sensing to record and manage archaeological sites (see Chapter 19). Except for rainfall patterns, all the environmental information required for many surveys can be plotted with information obtained from aerial maps. Although large archaeological sites such as road systems or major cities can be located on aerial photographs, very small phenomena such as scattered artifacts or cattle enclosures are generally impossible to find on even the most detailed maps. Aerial photographs can be used, however, to mark the locations of any archaeological phenomena once they have been located on the ground. The recording was taken a stage further in the San Juan Basin, where known types of sites and locations were plotted on aerial photographs marked up with environmental data obtained from Landsat images. Density values for different types of sites were then determined against each environmental zone and were used to suggest concentrations of sites in unsurveyed areas (Drager and Lyons, 1983). The zones involved were then sampled on foot to establish their site concentrations. This method is very effective in large-scale surveys in which only parts of the region will be disturbed by agriculture, mining, oil exploration, or other activities.

The primary purpose of many remote-sensing surveys is to map concentrations of sites and, on larger projects, to identify where maximal efforts in ground surveying and excavation should be concentrated. This decision requires not only remote-sensing data but a comprehensive record of all sites known from the survey area as well. It is not enough, however, just to plot a site on a good map and record its precise latitude, longitude, and map grid reference. Special forms are used to record the location of the site, as well as information about surface features, the landowner, potential threats to the site, and so on. Every site in the United States is given a name and a number. Sites in Santa Barbara County, California, for example, are given the prefix CA-SBa- and are numbered sequentially.

So many sites are now known in North America that most states and many large archaeological projects have set up computer data banks containing comprehensive information about site distributions and characteristics. Arkansas has a statewide computer bank that is in constant use for decisions on conservation and management, and the SJBRUS site file used in the San Juan Basin is a vital tool for mapping and predicting site concentrations. The project managers make their predictions by combining site data from both totally and partially surveyed two-kilometer grid squares with environmental zones, then measuring them with a digital planimeter. After arbitrarily eliminating zones in which less than 4 percent of the area had been surveyed, the project staff divided the number of sites in the data bank for each square in each zone and found a value for the number of sites per hectare for twenty-one of the forty-eight zones in the basin. This procedure is arbitrary, but it is a valuable planning tool when estimating time and budget expenditures for an archaeological survey.

SAMPLING IN ARCHAEOLOGICAL SURVEY*

Partly because regional studies have become more fashionable and partly because of the growing demands of cultural resources management, archaeologists have become deeply interested in economical methods for collecting survey data. Many of them have sought refuge in statistical sampling methods. Statistical sampling theory occupies an important place in archaeological research, and some statistical training is now integral to every professional's training. Unfortunately, many of the sampling applications used so far have been downright poor, so much so that one archaeologist has been moved to remark that "the literature on sampling . . . resembles in some respects a battlefield littered with pieces of machinery that have broken down" (Ammerman, 1981). It behooves us to examine sampling and archaeological survey in some detail (Redman, 1987).

Sampling has been defined as the "science of controlling and measuring the reliability of information through the theory of probability." Systematic and carefully controlled sampling of archaeological data is essential if we are to rely heavily, as we do, on statistical approaches in the reconstruction of past lifeways and cultural process. If we are interested in past adaptations to environmental conditions, we must systematically sample many types of sites in each environmental zone, not merely those that look important or seem likely to yield spectacular finds. Sampling techniques enable us to ensure a statistically reliable basis of archaeological data from which we can make generalizations about our research data. Because these generalizations are often estimates of probability, they must be based on unbiased data.

Sampling Terminology

Sampling design is integral in the formulation of a research project and a research design and must be fitted specifically to the problem posed by the researcher. For the data to be most useful, it is necessary to define clearly, and in highly specific words, what the sample will actually represent. Because relatively little can be known about the populations with which one is dealing, probability sampling of archaeological data can be very misleading in a strictly statistical sense. Sampling approaches are useful in reducing bias and as aids to making decisions about data collection, but their value as precise statements of probability is much more limited.

The objectives of sampling in archaeological survey can range from such simple goals as estimating average densities of archaeological phenomena in a region or sampling area to efforts to estimate the meaning

---

*This section on sampling is somewhat technical for many beginning courses and may be omitted at the instructor's discretion.

of these densities. Nance (1983) argues that whatever the objectives of the sampling, there are two constants: the methods used must lead to *effective* discovery of cultural remains and to efficient estimation of the "quantitative properties" in what is discovered.

Several questions arise from these constants. Effective archaeological survey is designed to locate hitherto unknown sites. How confident, then, can one be that one's sampling methods will lead to such discoveries? This doubt has led archaeologists into the concepts of discovery model sampling and discovery probability, the likelihood that archaeological remains will be detected within a sampling unit given a specified level of sampling effort (Nance, 1983). The variables influencing the probability of discovering sites are easily recited, among them the size and conspicuousness of the site (the Pyramids of Giza lie at one end of the spectrum, an isolated concentration of stone chips at the other, and the chances of finding the latter lie near zero). The sampler's problem is working out the probability of discovering most of the sites that lie between these extremes. To do so, one requires both several ways of assessing statistical probability and a wide range of empirical data.

Discovery model sampling deals with the problem of finding examples of the archaeological record. Statistical precision models are used to try to infer something about the total quantitative properties of a large body of information (a population) from our studies of only a statistical sample of that entity. Statistical precision methods work well when estimating the commonly occurring characteristics, such as some types of artifacts or site forms. Most archaeological sampling, whether applied to site survey or to artifact analyses, requires at least some use of statistical precision models.

Some Basic Concepts

The first stage in any sampling design is defining the boundaries of the area being investigated, the data universe.

The *data universe* is the unit that is chosen for investigation. It can be a single site; portions of a settlement; a well-defined geographic region, such as a river valley; or a chronological period, as between 1000 B.C. and A.D. 350 in Ohio.

Sample elements are members of a population that is of interest. Observations about a sample of elements provide a way of obtaining information about the population of which they are a part.

Sample units are the units chosen for investigating the data universe or a population. A sample element and a sample unit may be the same thing, depending on the problem being researched. A grid of square sampling units is imposed over a river valley. To estimate the density of sites in each sampling unit, the investigator chooses a sample of grid squares and observes the number of sites occurring in each. But if we want to examine the properties of the sites in the area—their size, for instance—a sampling unit may contain more than one element of the population.

Nonarbitrary units are sample units that might coincide with obvious, quite natural units, such as rooms in a pueblo, graves in a cemetery, or highly distinctive local environments. *Arbitrary units* are just that—spatial units chosen to subdivide an area into convenient sections for investigation. These can be of any shape or size. Some of the most common are grid squares or *quadrats;* long rectangular units, which are almost like pathways across an area, often known as *transects;* and simple site locations, or *points.* Sample units are purely a research tool, and as such, they contain archaeological data. The only assumption made, whether arbitrary or nonarbitrary units are used, is that the data in each are similar enough or complementary enough to allow comparison of one unit to the other.

A *population* is the sum of all sampling units. It is not the same as the data universe, which is a definition of a research area. Sample units may be devised to survey only the southern part of a river valley, for example. These units, perhaps transects across a densely forested plain, form a population. But the population of sample units is only a small part of the data universe. In many cases, however, the population may end up yielding data that are applicable to the universe as a whole.

The *data pool* is the *potential* information available to the researcher within the data universe. Sampling methods are designed to collect as much of the data pool as possible, the data acquired coming from sample units within the populations of the data universe. Even without using formal sampling methods, the amount of information that can be obtained from a data pool is limited. Sampling methods are designed to maximize data acquisition and to do so on a statistically sound basis.

Sampling frames are the lists of chosen units that form the sample of the total population to be tested. The sample frame is compiled as a means for proceeding to the selection of units for investigation. The units are listed in order and form the *sample size.* There has been much debate about the desirable size of archaeological data samples (Asch, 1975). Obviously, the ideal sample is a total population, but in practice dictates of time and funds make samples much smaller. Obviously, too, the larger the sample, the smaller the chance of missing an important variation in the population.

Sampling the Data

A data universe is easy enough to define on paper and in theory. But the reality of access in the field may be very different. Funds and people may be limited, and access to the area may be restricted by landowners, rugged landscape, vegetational cover, or even political events. And in a site chosen for excavation, one should always leave a portion undisturbed so that

later generations of archaeologists can check the work, using more sophisticated methods. The sampling of the data universe depends, finally, on
both the amount of the universe accessible and the method used to sample
the population of the sample units set up.

Nonprobabilistic sampling selects the sample units to be investigated
using intuitive or pragmatic criteria chosen by the investigator. These can
include such realistic considerations as access to only a few sites being
possible in a dense rain forest, the precedent of generations of earlier
research that lead one to concentrate on certain types of conspicuous sites,
or simply the archaeologist's long experience. This type of sampling is fine
for many specific tasks, provided that the sample units, the data universe,
and the population being investigated are clearly defined ahead of time.
Without such precise terms of reference, it is difficult to assess whether the
sample data collected are truly representative of the data universe as a
whole. Nonprobabilistic sampling often concentrates on the more conspicuous sites. Is one justified, for instance, in arguing that the burial practices
in one Hopewell burial mound were similar to those at a site three miles
away and at another twenty miles away? The answer is no, unless one's
terms of reference for making generalizations are carefully defined ahead
of time.

Probabilistic sampling is much more effective and appropriate where
one is seeking to generalize about a large data universe from a small
sample population. The discipline of statistics and statistical theory makes
considerable use of probability theory, a means of relating small samples
of data in mathematical ways to much larger populations. The classic
example is the political opinion poll, which is based on a tiny sample
(perhaps 1,500 people) used to draw much more general conclusions about
national feelings on an issue. In archaeology, probabilistic sampling im-
proves the chance that the conclusions reached on the basis of the samples
are relatively reliable. This outcome depends, however, on very carefully
drawn research designs and precisely defined sample units.

Probabilistic sampling involves the use of probability theory. It maxi-
mizes the probability that the site distribution in a chosen sample area is
similar to that for the area as a whole. This type of approach has the
advantage of allowing researchers not only to project the total number of
sites in a research area but also to calculate the proportion of large sites
to smaller ones, and so on, information vital in the study of evolving
human settlement patterns (see Chapter 15).

Probabilistic sampling in archaeology is difficult, for the peculiarities
of archaeological data, compared with, say, those of physics, make the
development of sampling strategies difficult (Mueller, 1975). Once the
sampling units have been carefully defined and chosen, the archaeologist
can elect to take a sample of individual units or of statistical clusters of
them, often a decision of convenience. One example of clusters of sample
units is a series of transects that lie close to one another yet are assumed

to include the range of data variability found in the entire population. It is obviously cheaper to survey such a cluster than to travel among several individual sample units scattered over a data universe of thousands of square miles.

Probabilistic Sampling Schemes

Archaeologists rely on three basic probability sampling schemes:

1. *Simple random sampling* takes the sample frame, determines the sample size, and then randomly selects the number of units required from the frame. The actual selection of numbered units can be done by referring to a table of random numbers until the requisite number of units has been selected. Any method, like drawing cards from a hat, will do, as long as the selection is absolutely random. This method is used when it is not necessary to take into account such variables as landscape or site topography or sometimes when an absolutely virgin area is being worked. This approach treats all samples as equal, without referring to any external variables that may affect an individual sample.
2. *Systematic sampling* is a refinement of simple random sampling. One unit is chosen, and then others are selected at equal intervals from the first one. One might excavate every fifth square on a grid of equal-sized squares laid out across a shell midden. This approach is useful for studying artifact patterning, but it is less effective when studying such situations as, say, the rooms of a pueblo, where a regular pattern of human behavior may cause one accidentally to sample only a portion of the activities at a site.
3. *Stratified sampling* is used when sample units are not uniform. The population is divided into separate groups, or strata, which reflect the observed range or variation within the population. Strata can be different ecological zones, occupation layers, artifact classes, or groups of trenches. Such units permit intensive sampling of some units and less detailed work on others.

Sampling distribution is a fundamental concept in statistical inference. If you have a constant population and draw repeated samples of similar size from it, you can observe what happens to some sample property of the population, say, a type of enclosure wall, over these repeated samplings. The sample estimates will differ from sample to sample, are variables, and will have sampling distributions. As long as the sample size remains constant, the items are selected randomly and independently of one another, and the probability remains invariant, you will end up with a binomial probability distribution (Nance, 1983). The sampling distribution has a number of properties important to archaeologists, permitting them to answer questions such as these:

1. Is the average value of the sampling distribution equal to the population parameter, or does it consistently overestimate or underestimate it?
2. Is the distribution of the sample estimate symmetrical or skewed?
3. What degree of variability, or spread about the average value, is displayed by the distribution?
4. Of paramount importance to archaeologists, what factors were responsible for producing the characteristics of the distribution?

Clusters and Elements

Archaeological surveying involves three statistical populations: sampling units defined by area, sites, and artifacts. It is of paramount importance to be very explicit about how these populations constitute samples (Mueller, 1974; Thomas, 1976). Two major types of sampling are commonly used in archaeological surveying: element sampling and cluster sampling.

Element Sampling In element sampling, you establish a sampling frame and select the sample by a random and independent selection method. This approach is used only on very large populations—typically, in archaeology, those for which arbitrary sampling units are used. You might use element sampling when estimating the density of archaeological sites over a sampling area. This is a simple approach, for the variables in this exercise would be the number of sites occurring within each of a specified number of sample units.

Cluster Sampling Archaeologists engaged in survey work are commonly interested in populations of sites, artifacts, or features lying within a region or sample area. A survey may be made up of areal (arbitrary) survey units, a sample of which is examined for traces of archaeological remains. Any given sampling unit may contain a "cluster" of elements. One can then collect a sample of sites, artifacts, or features by means of a cluster sample, in which each sampling unit is a collection (cluster) of elements. Thus your statistical population is made up of a number of clusters, each with a specific number of elements, the cluster size. This size can vary considerably from cluster to cluster. This type of approach is used when we wish to examine the properties of sites, not those of an arbitrary grid unit. What is the proportion of sites with seashells in the Preclassic Valley of Oaxaca, Mexico? What is the average site area of settlements within the sampling area? and so on.

Simple questions are tackled with single-stage cluster sampling, more complex ones with two-stage sampling, where the second stage involves selecting only a sample of elements in the cluster for closer examination. You may elect to study a river basin that you divide into 500-square-foot quadrats. Each of these units contains 250,000 potential one-foot test units. You might select one hundred test units for examination out of each quadrat in your second-stage cluster sampling.

Most archaeological sampling involves simple cluster sampling designs, but the difficulties in obtaining empirical observations that are adequate for testing theoretical propositions are still enormous. We need to know more about the spatial distribution of archaeological remains, about the formation processes that affect the archaeological record, and such factors as the density of vegetational cover, the precision of dating surface sites, and the very obtrusiveness of the features, sites, and artifacts that make up the archaeological record. (For a detailed discussion of the difficulties of archaeological sampling, see Nance, 1983.)

Few modern archaeological surveys fail to make use of sampling, for archaeologists are only too aware that many site distributions reflect the distribution of archaeologists rather than an unbiased sampling of the archaeological record. This bias applies particularly in densely vegetated areas such as the Mesoamerican and Amazonian rain forest, where the cover is so thick that even new roads are in constant danger of being overgrown. It is no coincidence that most archaeological sites found in rain forests are near well-trodden roads and tracks. The early archaeologists located sites by following narrow paths through the forest cut by *chicleros,* local people who collected resin from forest trees and guided researchers to sites. Even today, archaeologists can pass right through the middle of a large site in the forest or within a few feet of a huge pyramid and see nothing (Chartkoff, 1978). Sophisticated remote-sensing techniques have revolutionized survey in rain forest areas, however, and provided new insights into the swamp agricultural techniques used by the Maya. We can expect increasing use of both remote sensing and more sophisticated sampling techniques to change survey techniques beyond recognition in the coming years, even if they never completely supersede the traditional task of the archaeologist: investigating archaeological sites on the ground.

SITE SURVEY

One objective of archaeological surveying is to pinpoint site locations. Once this process has been completed, new sites are surveyed carefully, with these objectives in mind:

1. To collect and record information on subsurface features, such as walls, buildings, and fortifications, traces of which may be detected on the surface. Such features may include ancient roads, agricultural systems, and earthworks, which are first detected from the air and then investigated on the ground (Bradford, 1957).
2. To collect and record information on artifacts and other finds lying on the surface of the site.

3. To use both these categories of data to test hypotheses about the age, significance, and function of the site.

Teotihuacán

Site surveys can be as complex as those covering large areas. Perhaps the largest site survey project ever undertaken was the Teotihuacán Mapping Project directed by George Cowgill and René Millon. Teotihuacán lies northeast of Mexico City and is one of the great tourist attractions of the Americas. This great pre-Columbian city flourished from about 250 B.C. until A.D. 700. Up to 150,000 people lived in Teotihuacán at the peak of its prosperity. Huge pyramids and temples, giant plazas, and an enormous market formed the core of the well-organized and well-planned city. The houses of the priests and nobles lay along the main avenues; the artisans and common people lived in crowded compounds of apartments and courtyards (Millon, 1973).

The size of Teotihuacán is overwhelming, and a detailed survey of its hundreds of structures and alleyways was a monumental undertaking. Cowgill and Millon realized that the only effective way to study the city was to make a comprehensive map of all the precincts, for without it they would never have been able to study how Teotihuacán grew so huge. Fortunately, the streets and buildings lay close to the surface, unlike the vast city mounds of the Near East, where only excavation yields settlement information.

The mapping project began with a detailed ground reconnaissance, conducted with the aid of aerial photographs and large-scale survey maps. The field data were collected on 147 map data sheets of 500-meter squares at a scale of 1:2,000.

Intensive mapping and surface surveys, including surface collections of artifacts, were then conducted systematically within the twenty-square-kilometer limits of the ancient city defined by the preliminary reconnaissance. Ultimately, the architectural interpretations of the surface features within each 500-meter square were overprinted on the base map of the site. These architectural interpretations were based not only on graphic data but also on a mass of surface data collected on special forms and through artifact collections, photographs, and drawings. Extensive use of sophisticated sampling techniques and quantitative methods was essential for successful completion of the map.

By the end of the project more than five thousand structures and activity areas had been recorded within the city limits. The Teotihuacán maps do not, of course, convey to us the incredible majesty of this remarkable city, but they do provide, for the first time, a comprehensive view of a teeming, multifaceted community with vast public buildings, plazas, and avenues, and thousands of small apartments and courtyards, which formed individual households and pottery, figurine, and obsidian workshops, among the many diverse structures in the city. The survey also revealed that the city had been expanded over the centuries according to a comprehensive master plan. (For more on Teotihuacán, see Chapter 15.)

Mapping

Archaeological surveying on any scale depends, as in the case of Teotihuacán, on precise mapping (Ebert, 1984). Maps are a convenient way of storing large quantities of archaeological information. Mapping specialists, called cartographers, have developed many effective and dramatic ways of communicating information graphically, devices that are very useful inclusions in archaeological reports (Figure 9.9).

Topographic Maps   The distributions of archaeological sites are plotted on large-scale topographic maps that relate the ancient settlements to the basic features of the natural landscape (Figure 9.9, left). This master base map can be overlain with plots that show vegetational cover—either prehistoric or modern—soil types, and even prehistoric trade routes.

Planimetric Maps   These are commonly used to record details of archaeological sites. They relate different archaeological features to each other and contain no topographic information (Figure 9.9, right).

Site Plans   These are specially prepared maps made by archaeologists to record the horizontal provenience of artifacts, food residues, and features. Site plans are keyed to topographic and other surveys from a carefully selected point (datum point), such as a survey beacon or a landmark that appears on a large-scale map. This datum point provides a location from which a grid of squares can be laid out over the area of the site, normally open-ended so that it can be extended to cover more ground if necessary. The grid provides a system of coordinates for recording provenience. The arms of the grid are normally oriented, using true north.

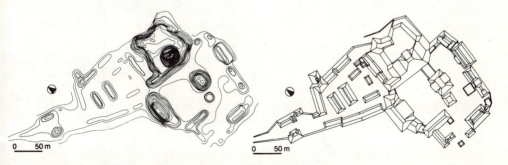

Figure 9.9 Examples of archaeological maps. Left: A topographic map that shows the relationship between sites and the landscape. Right: A planimetric map showing the features of a site. Both maps are of Nohmul, a Mayan ceremonial center.

A site grid is critical during excavation for use in three-dimensional recording. It is also vital in recording surface finds during the initial survey
process.

Readers interested in surveying and mapping techniques as they relate to archaeology are referred to the specialist literature (Hester and
others, 1987; Barker, 1983).

Surface Collection

The artifacts and other archaeological finds discovered on the surface of
a site are a potentially vital source of information about the people who
once lived there (Redman, 1987). Surface collection has these objectives:

1. To gather representative samples of artifacts from the surface of
   the site to establish the age of the area and the various periods of
   occupation.
2. To establish the types of activity that took place on the site.
3. To gather information on the areas of the site that were most
   densely occupied and that might be most productive for either total
   or sample excavation.
4. To locate major structures that lie, for the most part, below the
   surface.

Limitations   Many archaeologists distrust surface collection, arguing
that artifacts are easily destroyed on the surface and can be displaced from
their original positions by many factors. But this viewpoint neglects a
truth: *all* archaeological deposits, however deep, were once surface
deposits, subject to many of the same destructive processes as those out-
cropping on the surface today (Dunnell and Dancey, 1983). With the
increased emphasis on regional surveys and settlement archaeology in
recent years, many fieldworkers have demonstrated that surface deposits
can provide much information on artifact distributions and other phenomena also found underground, provided, of course, that they have not been
subjected to catastrophic industrial activity, strip mining, or other drastic
modifications.

Like buried deposits, surface levels contain abundant information
about artifact patternings if one can separate true patterns from those
caused by formation processes that have occurred since the site was abandoned. The same influences have affected both surface and buried deposits: natural weathering, erosion, rainfall, and human activity for years,
which may result in the comminution (pulverizing) of potsherds, stone
tools, and bone fragments. But surface data have two major advantages:
they are a body of information that can be obtained on a regional scale,
not site by site, and the cost of obtaining the data is but a fraction of that
for excavation. Increasingly, archaeologists are thinking of surface data as

primary archaeological information essential to understanding regional prehistories (Lewarch and O'Brien, 1981; Aldendorfer and Hale-Pierce, 1984; Hope-Simpson, 1984).

Methods   There are various ways of collecting artifacts from the surface of a site. Some archaeologists collect everything from the surface, take their finds home to the laboratory, and then analyze them at leisure. This approach is commonly used in areas where little archaeological research has been carried out before.

When dealing with a well-known area or with sites containing distinctive artifacts, it is possible to collect only diagnostic artifacts, such items as potsherds, stone artifacts, or other characteristic finds that are easily classified and identified. These key finds may enable one to assess what periods of occupation are represented at the site. Surface collections should be made, however, only in such a way that the provenience of the finds is plotted on a map at the time of collection.

Another way is random sampling. Because total collecting is impossible on sites of any size where surface finds are abundant, some type of sampling technique is used to obtain a valid random sample of the surface artifacts. A common random-sampling approach involves laying out a grid of squares on the surface of the site and then collecting everything found in randomly selected units. Once such a "controlled collection" has been made, the rest of the site is covered for highly diagnostic artifacts. Rigorous sampling techniques are essential to obtain even a minimal sample of finds at the individual site level. Surface collection and sampling are often combined with small test-pit excavations to get preliminary data on stratigraphic information (see also South and Widmer, 1977).

Evidence of the activities of a region's inhabitants can be obtained from surface collections, but only where the relationship between remains found on the surface and those found below the ground is clearly understood. Sometimes, the surface finds may accurately reflect site content; at other times, they may not. This problem is compounded not only by natural erosion and other factors but also by the depth of the occupation deposits on the site. Obviously, almost no finds from the lowest levels of a thirty-foot-deep village mound will lie on the surface today, unless erosion, human activity, or animal burrows bring deeply buried artifacts to the surface (McManamon, 1984).

With shallow sites, such as Teotihuacán and many prehistoric settlements in the American West, it is a reasonable assumption that the artifacts on the surface accurately reflect those slightly below the surface (Millon, 1973; Yellen, 1977). This assumption provides a basis for studying activities from surface finds. Any conclusions derived from surface collections, however, have to be verified by subsequent excavation.

Examples of effective site surveys are legion in modern archaeology. William Sanders and a team of archaeological colleagues spent many field seasons surveying the archaeological record of the Basin of Mexico. They relied heavily on surface finds for dating individual sites and for identifying the character of individual settlements (Sanders and others, 1979). The Rio Grande region of the Southwest has been the subject of intensive regional and site surveys as part of a major cultural resource management project (Plog and Wait, 1982). James Judge and Jerry Dawson were able to study hunting and living patterns among Paleo-Indian cultures of about eight thousand years ago (Judge and Dawson, 1972). They used stone tools to define different site types, distinguishing between general localities where no diagnostic tools were found and specific sites (Figure 9.10). In this area were found base camps and processing sites, where hunting tools were predominant. By using these site types as the basis for artifact collections, Judge and Dawson showed how older Paleo-Indian sites were much farther from large bodies of water than later settlements and campsites, which were closer to the greatly reduced streams and rivers of later, more arid times.

Site survey has the great advantage of being much cheaper than exca-

Figure 9.10 Paleo-Indian fluted projectile points from the Great Plains. Judge and Dawson used such surface collections to trace changing site distributions.

vation, provided that the methods used are based on explicit research designs. Many of the most exciting recent studies of cultural process and changing settlement patterns have depended heavily on archaeological reconnaissance and site survey.

SUMMARY

- Two processes are involved in locating archaeological sites: reconnaissance and site survey.
- Many archaeological sites are discovered by accident, industrial activity, modern agriculture, or natural happenings, such as floods and earthquakes.
- Many famous archaeological sites, such as the Pyramids, have never been lost to human knowledge. But other, less conspicuous locations are found only by planned ground reconnaissance. Archaeological sites manifest themselves in many ways: in the form of mounds, middens, caves, and rockshelters. Many more are much less conspicuous and are located only by soil discolorations or surface finds.
- Ground reconnaissance is done at one of several levels of intensity, ranging from general surveys leading to location of only the largest sites down to precise foot surveys aimed at covering an entire area in detail. Even these are not totally effective, and all reconnaissance is, at best, a major sampling of the research area.
- In most cases, total survey is impracticable, and so archaeologists rely on probabilistic and nonprobabilistic sampling methods to obtain unbiased samples of the research area.
- Key indicators of archaeological sites include conspicuous aboveground features, vegetational coverage, soil colors, and surface finds.
- A battery of new reconnaissance techniques involves aerial photography and remote sensing. Photographs taken from the air can be used to locate sites spread over huge areas. Pioneer efforts have been made with side-scan aerial radar and scanner imagery.
- Subsurface features are often detected with resistivity surveys, which measure the differences in electrical resistivity of the soil between disturbed and undisturbed areas. Proton magnetometers are used to locate iron objects, fired clay furnaces, and other features.
- Site survey is designed to obtain information on subsurface features at previously located sites, as well as to collect and record artifacts and other surface finds. These categories of data are used to test hypotheses about the age, significance, and function of the site.
- Site survey depends on accurate mapping. The Teotihuacán project in Mexico illustrates the results that can be obtained with a site survey.

- Surface collections may be made by gathering every artifact on the surface of the site, by selecting for diagnostic artifacts, or by random sampling. Surface collections are used to establish the activities that took place on the site, to locate major structures, and to gather information about the most densely occupied areas of the site.
- Surface survey is much cheaper than excavation and is highly effective, provided the methods used are based on explicit research designs and the results are checked by precise excavations.

GUIDE TO FURTHER READING

Colwell, Robert N., ed. *Manual of Remote Sensing,* 2d ed. Falls Church, Va.: Society of Photogrammetry, 1983. A basic manual of widespread application.

Millon, René. *The Teotihuacán Map: Urbanization at Teotihuacán, Mexico,* vol. 1. Austin: University of Texas Press, 1973. A prime example of a complicated survey and mapping project.

Mueller, James A., ed. *Sampling in Archaeology.* Tucson: University of Arizona Press, 1975. Useful essays on problems in field survey sampling, for the advanced reader.

Nance, Jack D. "Regional Sampling in Archaeological Survey: The Statistical Perspective," *Advances in Archaeological Method and Theory* 6 (1983): 289–356. A useful survey that updates Mueller and reviews basic concepts.

Sanders, William T., Jeffrey R. Parsons, and Robert S. Santley. *The Basin of Mexico: Ecological Processes in the Evolution of a Civilization.* Orlando, Fla.: Academic Press, 1979. The best description of a long-term survey project and of survey problems.

Sever, Thomas, and James Wiseman. *Remote Sensing and Archaeology: Potential for the Future.* Picayune, Miss.: NASA Earth Sciences Laboratory, 1985. A short report that assesses the potential for remote sensing in archaeology.

Wilson, D. R. *Air Photo Interpretation for Archaeologists.* New York: St. Martin's Press, 1983. A useful, practical manual for archaeologists on interpreting aerial photographs.

Chapter
10

Archaeological Excavation

*E*xcavation! The very word conjures up romantic images of lost civilizations and royal burials, of long days in the sun digging up inscriptions and gold coins. Yet, though the image remains, the techniques of modern excavation are far less romantic than they are rigorous and demanding, requiring long training in practical field techniques. Excavation is the major way in which archaeologists acquire data about the past. Unlike reconnaissance and surface survey, excavations recover data from beneath the surface of the ground—where conditions for preservation are best— and accurate information on provenience, context, and association can be recovered intact. In this chapter we discuss some of the basic principles of archaeological excavation: the organization, planning, and execution of a scientific dig.

A SHORT HISTORY OF EXCAVATION

The earliest archaeologists were little more than treasure hunters, who thought nothing of excavating several burial mounds in one day (Fagan, 1985). At the same time, the great civilizations of the Near East and Egypt were being unearthed from millennia of oblivion by such nineteenth-century diggers as Henry Layard and Heinrich Schliemann, who were hastily uncovering and removing literally tons of antiquities from their proper archaeological contexts.

In 1780, Thomas Jefferson, third president of the United States and author of the Declaration of Independence, had spent time investigating Indian burial mounds in Virginia, which were rumored to be huge sepulchers. He decided to excavate one "to satisfy myself whether any and which of these opinions was just," he wrote. Here, for the first time, was a deliberate archaeological excavation undertaken to verify one of several hypotheses about Indian mounds. Jefferson cut a perpendicular trench through the mound "so that I might examine its internal structure." The trench was dug down to the natural soil and was wide enough to allow Jefferson to record the different layers of the mound. He was able to recognize at least three layers of human bones, horizons where the Indians had gathered together dozens of bones before piling stones on top of them. His *Notes on the State of Virginia,* published in 1784, contains a description of his excavations and conclusions. It is one of the first recorded instances of stratigraphic observation in archaeology (Fagan, 1977; Willey and Sabloff, 1980).

Not until nearly a century later was scientific excavation applied anywhere. The first truly scientific digs were carried out by Austrian and German archaeologists working in Greece in the 1870s. One of these was the Austrian Alexander Conze, who began excavating at the Sanctuary of the Great Gods on the island of Samothrace in 1873, with a team of scientists that included a photographer and two architects. The dig lasted two years, and the resulting monograph was beautifully illustrated and full of accurate plans. Another, the German Ernst Curtius, began excavations in 1875 at Olympia that lasted six seasons. His excavations were conducted with Teutonic thoroughness; he made careful plans of the architecture and detailed studies of the stratigraphy, and he developed new methods of digging and recording that eventually came into use in excavations all over the Near East (Fagan, 1985).

The sense of purpose and discipline that the Austrians and Germans introduced into the digging was also practiced by a military gentleman in England. General Augustus Lane Fox, who retired from active duty in 1880, inherited the Rivers estate in southern England and changed his name to Pitt-Rivers. He devoted the last twenty years of his life to a detailed exploration of the archaeological sites on or near his estate. Pitt-Rivers's methods were elaborate and painstaking; he recorded every object found in his trenches in such a manner that its exact find spot could be identified in the future, with reference to sections and plans of the dig. Three-dimensional recording was a cornerstone of his excavations, as were accurate stratigraphic profiles with the finds recorded on them, a large and competent staff, and prompt and meticulous publication of his results. The General is a colossus in the history of archaeological excavation; the labor involved in producing the elegant blue and gold monographs describing his excavations must have been prodigious (Thompson, 1977).

American archaeologists became involved in scientific investigation of pre-Columbian sites at about the same time. Beginning with Cyrus Thomas in the Ohio Valley and Adolph Bandelier in the Southwest, archaeologists started to develop the direct historical method, working back from the known to the unknown (Fagan, 1977; Willey and Sabloff, 1980).

Scientific archaeology advanced most rapidly in the Southwest. Much early research consisted of cleaning up many of the major pueblos after the massive treasure-hunting depredations late in the nineteenth century. A small team of archaeologists, including N. C. Nelson and A. V. Kidder, spent season after season preparing precise chronological and stratigraphical frameworks for the area.

N. C. Nelson, a robust and earthy Scandinavian, was one of the first persons to use potsherds for establishing southwestern chronology. He took a cluster of sites in the Galisteo Basin of New Mexico and dug small stratigraphic trenches through their deposits. The resulting chronological sequence of pottery forms began with the Basketmaker period dating to the first millennium A.D. Harvard-trained archaeologist A. V. Kidder carried Nelson's work to its logical conclusion with large-scale excavations at Pecos pueblo from 1915 to 1926. His studies of potsherds and stratigraphic profiles led him to delineate a long sequence of southwestern prehistory that "owes to outside sources little more than the germs of its culture" (Kidder, 1924). Kidder's cultural sequence has withstood the test of time, even though detailed modifications have been made in his scheme.

It took a long time for the lessons of Pitt-Rivers, Nelson, and others to be learned by the archaeological community. European archaeologists were generally quicker to apply the rigorous principles enumerated by the General than were Americans. A great exponent of the art of scientific excavation was the Englishman Sir Mortimer Wheeler, whose short *Archaeology from the Earth* (1954) is an elegant and lively monograph that belongs in any archaeologist's library. He and his contemporaries refined and applied Pitt-Rivers's methods with consistent energy. With them, the emphasis in excavation shifted from finding objects to designing a strategy for an excavation campaign oriented toward solving archaeological problems rather than discovery for its own sake. Precise digging and recording methods invented in England and Scandinavia were soon being applied as far afield as India and South Africa (Daniel, 1981).

Modern scientific excavation owes a great deal to such people as Wheeler, who realized that good fieldwork depends on careful organization, multidisciplinary teamwork, and very accurate methods of recording and excavation.

In recent years, archaeologists have become increasingly reluctant to excavate a site except when they have a specific hypothesis to test or research problem to investigate. The reason is that the finite archaeological record is being destroyed at such a rate by industrial civilization that there is a real danger that little will be left for scientists of the future unless every effort is made to conserve undisturbed sites now. A new emphasis on regional surveys, increasing use of remote sensing to probe sites before excavation, and application of sophisticated sampling methods combined make today's excavations even more effective than those of a generation ago. They are a far cry from the popular stereotype of archaeology as a frenzied treasure hunt, as we will show in the following pages.

ORGANIZING ARCHAEOLOGICAL EXCAVATIONS

The twentieth century has witnessed a total transformation of archaeology, from treasure hunting and curiosity to scientific investigation and problem-oriented excavation. As a result, organizing an excavation has become increasingly complex.

In the early days, someone like Heinrich Schliemann or Austen Henry Layard would supervise huge teams with several hundred workers. Even as late as the 1920s, Leonard Woolley excavated the ancient Mesopotamian city of Ur-of-the-Chaldees with only a handful of qualified scholars and up to three hundred unskilled laborers. Today's excavation is limited by ever-rising costs and by the sheer complexity of the data that can now be recovered from a site. Some of the more elaborate sites are dug by teams of specialists with very little unskilled help. Others are staffed by volunteer laborers, interested amateurs, and students who gain practical experience in all aspects of excavation, from using a shovel to recording a complicated stratigraphic profile.

The director of a modern archaeological field expedition needs skills beyond those of a competent archaeologist. He or she also has to be able to fill the roles of accountant, politician, doctor, mechanic, personnel manager, and even cook. On a large dig, though manual labor may not be the director's responsibility, logistic problems are compounded, and he or she will head a large excavation team of site supervisors, artists, photographers, and numerous minor functionaries (Atkinson, 1953; Dancey, 1981; Joukowsky, 1981). Above all, the field director has to be the leader of a multidisciplinary team of specialist fieldworkers.

Multidisciplinary Research Teams

Modern archaeology is so complex that all excavation projects now require multidisciplinary teams of archaeologists, botanists, geologists, zoologists, and other specialists who work together on closely integrated research problems, such as the origins of food production. The team approach is particularly important where environmental problems are most pressing, where the excavations and research seek the relationships between human cultures and the rest of the ecosystem.

A good interdisciplinary or multidisciplinary study is based on an integrated research design bringing a closely supervised team of specialists together to test carefully formulated hypotheses against data collected by all of them. Notice that we say "data collected by all of them." Many archaeologists pay lip service to the need for multidisciplinary research teams but then recruit a few experts to act as highly paid technicians on the excavation, that is, merely to do such jobs as identifying animal remains and plant fragments or recording and interpreting geological layers. There have been cases of natural scientists excavating archaeological sites that were rich in, say, vegetable remains and then retaining an ar-chaeologist to interpret the artifacts in the site! An effective multidiscipli-nary archaeological team must be just that—a team—whose combined findings are used to test specific hypotheses.

Multidisciplinary research teams have been employed with great suc-cess at early hominid sites in East Turkana, Kenya, where geologists pro-vided the background environmental data; zoologists, the identifications and interpretations of fossil animals found in the sites; and archaeologists, the data on surviving cultural remains; while physical anthropologists studied the human remains found in the 2 to 2.5 million-year-old sites. This approach is logical, but it is rarely carried to its logical extreme, where the experts would design their research together, share an integrated field mission, and communicate daily about their findings and research prob-lems. Much of the East Turkana research has been carried out by carefully selected teams of specialist experts, whose research experience is not in, say, Pleistocene geology as a whole but in the specific types of geological deposits and stratigraphic and ecological problems in East Turkana (Isaac and McKown, 1977; Isaac and Isaac, 1989).

The criteria, then, for selecting members of multidisciplinary research teams include not only academic skills but also the ability to communicate with people in other disciplines, highly specific specialist qualifications, and, above all, a willingness to work closely with a group of scholars who are all committed to solving common problems. Such people are hard to find, and thus truly effective interdisciplinary research teams are few and far between. More loosely knit team approaches in which each member of a group pursues his or her own research but contributes to more general overall goals are far more common. The well-known Southwest Archaeo-logical Group, whose members meet annually before the field season to reach consensus on directions and research methods, is an excellent exam-ple of this approach (Brown and Struever, 1973).

Excavation Staff

Large, elaborate excavations that take several seasons to complete are staffed by a director and other specialist experts and by several other technicians as well. Among the technicians are these:

Site supervisors. Skilled excavators are responsible for excavating trenches and recording specific locations. The large-scale digs of Medieval York in northern England are divided into localities, each with a skilled excavator who supervises the volunteers doing the actual digging.

Recording experts. Some very large excavations will have a full-time surveyor, who does nothing but draw and record the stratigraphic profiles and structures found in the dig. Expert archaeological pho-tographers are in great demand and will make thousands of slides and black-and-white prints during even a short season. Their task is to create a complete record of the excavation from beginning to end (Dorrell, 1989).

Artifact and small-finds staff. Even a small excavation can yield a flood of artifacts and floral and faunal remains that can overwhelm the staff of a dig. A basic laboratory staff to bag the finds and wash, rough-sort, and mark them for eventual transport to the laboratory is essential on any but the smallest excavation. Some knowledge of preservation techniques is essential as well. Many excavations, such as the Koster site in Illinois, employ computerized data processing to handle the analysis of the finds (Struever and Holton, 1979).

Foremen. Paid foremen can become skilled archaeological excavators in their own right, but their primary responsibility is managing paid laborers, especially on overseas excavations. Some devote their entire working lives to archaeology. Perhaps the most famous archaeological foremen are found in Egypt and Iraq, where successive generations of families have served on excavations for decades. Sir Leonard Woolley worked with the same foreman, Sheikh Hamoudi, from 1912 to 1941. Hamoudi, who became almost a part of Woolley's family, was famous for his invective and for his sensitivity to the moods of the workers (Fagan, 1979).

In these days of rising costs and financial stringencies, most excavations are conducted on a comparatively small scale. There will usually be a team of students or paid laborers under the overall supervision of the director and perhaps one or two assistants; the assistants may be graduate students with some technical training in archaeological fieldwork who can take some of the routine tasks from the director's shoulders, allowing him or her to concentrate on general supervision and interpretative problems. But on many sites, the director will not only be in charge of the research and arrangements for the excavation but will also personally supervise all trenches excavated. On that one person, therefore, devolve the tasks of recording, photography, drawing, measurement, and supervision of labor. The director may also take a turn at recovery of fragile burials and other delicate objects that cannot be entrusted to students or workers; he or she is also responsible for maintaining the excavation diaries and find notebooks, storage and marking of artifacts, and the logistics of packing finds and shipping them to the laboratory.

So varied are the skills of the excavator that much of a professional archaeologist's training in the field is obtained as a graduate student working at routine tasks and gaining experience in the methods of excavating and site survey under experienced supervision. For the director, such students provide not only useful supervisory labor but also an admirable hone upon which to try out favorite theories and discuss in ruthless detail the interpretation of the site. Many an elaborate and much-cherished theoretical model has been demolished over a disputed profile at an evening campfire! Opportunities to gain excavation experience are always open, and notices of digs can be found on many college and university bulletin boards. You can also obtain information on field schools from the Society for American Archaeology's *Field School Catalog* from the American Anthropological Association, or watch issues of *Archaeology* magazine for field opportunities. The camaraderie and happiness of a well-run, student-oriented excavation is one of the most worthwhile experiences of archaeology.

PLANNING AN EXCAVATION

Excavation is the culminating step in the investigation of an archaeological site. It recovers from the earth data obtainable in no other way (Barker, 1986; Dancey, 1981). Like historical archives, the soil of an archaeological site is a document whose pages have to be deciphered, translated, and interpreted before they can be used to write an accurate account of prehistory. If there is one general remark about the history of archaeological excavation that is applicable to all areas of the world, it is that methods of data recovery have been far too crude. Today's archaeologists are presented with the reality that their excavation methods are becoming more and more precise and slow-moving, just as the destruction of archaeological sites is proceeding at a record pace.

The first lesson that budding excavators learn is that their work is destructive. Excavation is destruction—the archaeological deposits so carefully dissected during any dig are destroyed forever and their contents removed. Here, again, there is a radical difference between archaeology and the sciences and history. A scientist can readily re-create the conditions for a basic experiment; the historian can return to the archives to reevaluate the complex events in a politician's life. But all that we have after an excavation are the finds from the trenches, the untouched portions of the site, and the photographs, notes, and drawings that record the excavator's observations for posterity. Thus accurate recording and observation are overwhelmingly vital in the day-to-day work of archaeologists, not only for the sake of accuracy in their own research but also because they are creating an archive of archaeological information that may be consulted by others (Alexander, 1970). Archaeological sites are nonrenewable resources, and much of the present effort in archaeology is directed at the need to conserve most rigorously the undisturbed sites that still survive.

Austen Henry Layard, Heinrich Schliemann, and the other pioneers were looking for archaeological treasure; Thomas Jefferson, by contrast, spent many summer days excavating for information about the inhabitants of Virginian burial mounds. Today, we follow in Jefferson's footsteps and search for the past in the widest sense, excavation being but one method at our disposal, even though it is a vital one. Thousands of observations can be made, even on a small-scale excavation. Unfocused excavation is useless, for the manageable and significant observations are buried in a mass of irrelevant trivia. A focused problem is essential for every excavation to hold the observations to a reasonable and controllable limit. Any excavation must be conducted from a sound research design intended to solve specific and well-defined problems.

Research Plans

"Problem-oriented" research has become a platitudinous catchword used by almost every archaeologist, even if his or her research designs are far from explicit. As archaeology becomes more explicitly scientific and more sophisticated, much more specific research designs are essential (Figure 10.1). Lewis Binford, who wrote about the need for sound research design in archaeological research, argues that archaeologists have no explicit criteria for selecting "important" sites. Excavations are traditionally conducted on larger sites, on sites that look more productive, or on sites that are nearest to roads. These criteria bear no resemblance to the goal that is actually required, which is representative and unbiased data to answer a particular problem—a problem whose limits are ultimately defined by

Figure 10.1 An organized horizontal-grid excavation on the Iron Age hill fort at Danebury, England.

available money and time. Unbiased data, which do not reflect the investigator's idiosyncrasies, can properly yield probabilistic estimates of the culture from which the samples were drawn. This kind of information requires explicit sampling procedures, not only to select a few sites from an area to excavate but also to control reliability of the information by using probability and statistics.

Excavation costs are so great that problem-oriented digging is now the rule rather than the exception, with the laboratory work forming part of the continuing evaluation of the research problem. The large piles of finds and records accumulated at the end of even a small field season contain a bewildering array of interdigitating facts that the researcher has to evaluate and reevaluate as inquiry proceeds, by constantly arranging propositions and hypotheses, correlating observations, and reevaluating interpretations of the archaeological evidence. Finds and plans are the basis of the researcher's strategy and affect fieldwork plans for the future. The days when a site was excavated because it "looked good" or because sheer lack of imagination precluded development of a research strategy are passing; unfocused excavation is slowly being replaced by constant reevaluation of research objectives.

The need for sound planning and design is even more acute in ecological research in archaeology, where archaeologists try to understand changes in human culture in relation to human environmental systems. Let us take the example of the Koster excavation in Illinois, one of the largest and most complex digs ever undertaken in North America.

The Koster Site

In the lower Illinois Valley lies the site, a deep accumulation of twenty-six prehistoric occupation layers extending from about 10,000 years ago to around A.D. 1100 to 1200 (Struever and Holton, 1979). The wealth of material at Koster first came to light in 1968 and has been the subject of extremely large-scale excavation. The dig involved collaboration by three archaeologists and six specialists from such other disciplines as zoology and botany, as well as use of a computer laboratory (Figure 10.2).

Even superficial examination of the site showed that a very careful research design was needed, both to maximize use of funds and to ensure adequate control of data. In developing the Koster research design, James Brown and Stuart Struever (1973) were well aware of the numerous, complex variables that had to be controlled and the need to define carefully their sampling procedure and the size of the collecting units.

They faced a number of formidable difficulties. Thirteen of the Koster cultural horizons are isolated from their neighbors by a zone of sterile slopewash soil, which makes it possible to treat each as a separate problem in excavation and analysis—as if it were an individual site—although, in fact, the thirteen are stratified one above another. Because the whole site is more than thirty feet deep, the logistical problems are formidable, as in

Figure 10.2 General view of the Koster excavations.

all large-scale excavations. One possible strategy would have been to sink test pits, obtain samples from each level, and list diagnostic artifacts and cultural items. But this approach, though cheaper and commonly used, is quite inadequate to the systems model that the excavators drew up to study the origins of cultivation in the area and cultural change in the lower Illinois Valley. Large-scale excavations were needed to uncover each living surface so that the excavators could not only understand what the living zones within each occupation were like but also, after studying in detail the sequence of differences in activities, make statements about the processes of cultural change.

From the large scale of the excavations, Brown and Struever saw the need for immediate feedback from the data flow from the site during the excavation. Changes in the excavation method would no doubt be needed during the season's fieldwork to ensure that maximum information was obtained. To accomplish this flexibility, both excavation and data-gathering activities were combined into a data flow system (Figure 10.3) to ensure feedback to the excavators that would be as close to instantaneous as possible. The categories of data—animal bones, artifacts, vegetable remains—were processed in the field, and the information from the analyses was then fed by remote access terminal to a computer in Evanston, Illinois, many miles away. Pollen and soil samples were sent directly to specialist laboratories for analysis. The effects of the data flow system are highly beneficial. The tiresome analysis of artifacts and food residues is completed on the site, and the data are available to the excavators in the field in a few days, instead of months later, as is usual. The research design can be modified in the field at short notice, with ready consultation be-

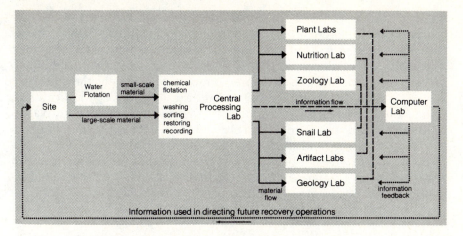

Figure 10.3 Data flow system of the Koster site.

tween the team members in the field. A combination of instant data retrieval; comprehensive and meticulous collecting methods involving, among other things, flotation methods (see Chapter 13); and a system approach to both excavation strategy and research planning have made the Koster project an interesting example of effectively used research design in archaeology.

In many projects, excavation is only part of the overall research design. As a method, it should be used sparingly, for the end result is always destruction of a site (Barker, 1986). Under these circumstances, no one can challenge the necessity for highly specific, problem-oriented excavation at all times.

TYPES OF EXCAVATION

Archaeological excavation is designed to acquire as much raw data as possible with available financial and other resources. Its ultimate objective is to produce a three-dimensional record of an archaeological site, in which the various artifacts, structures, and other finds are placed in their correct provenience and context in time and space. The process of excavation, described below, involves the archaeologist in constant choices about the methods to be used, the types of trenches to be laid out, and the tools to be used, to mention only a few of the decisions to be made.

Total and Selective Excavation

As we saw in Chapter 8, not only the size and character of a site but also sampling techniques can be important in deciding which excavation methods are used. In the early days of archaeology, many sites were excavated completely. *Total excavation* of a site has the advantage of being comprehensive, but it is expensive and leaves none of the site intact for excavation at a later date with, perhaps, more advanced techniques. *Selective excavation* is much more common. Many prehistoric sites are simply too large for total excavation and can only be tested selectively, using sampling methods or carefully placed trenches. Selective excavation is used to obtain stratigraphic and chronological data as well as samples of pottery, stone tools, and animal bones. From this evidence, the archaeologist can decide whether or not to undertake further excavation. Some of the world's most important archaeological sites have been excavated selectively.

Vertical and Horizontal Excavation

Invariably, vertical excavation is selective digging, uncovering a limited area on a site for the purpose of recovering specific information. Most vertical excavations are probes of deep archaeological deposits, their real objective being to reveal the chronological sequence at a site. Horizontal excavation is used to expose contemporaneous settlement over a larger area.

Vertical Excavation   *Test pits,* sometimes given the French name *sondages,* are a frequently used form of vertical excavation. They consist of small trenches just large enough to accommodate one or two diggers and are designed to penetrate to the lower strata of a site to establish the extent of archaeological deposits (Figure 10.4). Test pits are dug to obtain samples of artifacts from lower layers, and this method may be supplemented by augers or borers.

Test pits are a preliminary to large-scale excavation, for the information they reveal is limited, at best. Some archaeologists will use them only outside the main area of a site, on the grounds that they will destroy critical strata. But carefully placed test pits can provide valuable insights into the stratigraphy and artifact content of a site before larger-scale excavation begins.

Test pits are also used to obtain samples from different areas of sites, such as shell middens, where dense concentrations of artifacts are found throughout the deposits. In such cases, test pits are excavated on a grid pattern, positioning of the pits being determined by probabilistic sampling or by a regular pattern such as alternate squares.

Vertical trenches are much larger, deeper cuttings used to establish such phenomena as sequences of building operations, histories of complex earthworks, and long cultural sequences in deep caves (Figure 10.5). Vertical trenches have been widely used to excavate Near Eastern mounds, such as the Tepe Yahya site in Iran (Lamberg-Karlovsky, 1970). They may also be used to obtain a cross-section across a site threatened by destruc-

Figure 10.4 A line of test pits at Quirigua, a Mesoamerican site, laid out at fifteen-meter intervals and aligned with the site grid.

tion or to examine outlying structures near a village or a cemetery that has been dug on a large scale. Vertical excavations of this kind are almost always dug in the expectation that the most important information to come from them will be the record of layers in the walls of the trenches and the finds from them. But clearly, the amount of information to be obtained from such cuttings is of limited value compared to that from a larger excavation.

Tunneling is a form of vertical excavation done in a horizontal plane. Austen Henry Layard made use of tunneling to penetrate into the deep horizons of the Kuyunjik mound at the ancient city of Nineveh on the Tigris. Today, tunneling operations are confined to specialized excavations investigating the center of huge earthworks and other deep structures.

Horizontal (Area) Excavation   Horizontal, or area, excavation is done on a much larger scale than vertical excavation and is as close to total excavation as archaeology can get. An area dig implies covering wide areas to recover building plans or the layout of entire settlements (Figure 10.6). The only sites that almost invariably are totally excavated are very small hunting camps, isolated huts, and burial mounds.

A good example of horizontal excavation comes from St. Augustine, Florida (Deagan, 1983; Milanich and Milbralta, 1989). St. Augustine was

Figure 10.5 A classic example of vertical excavation from Sir Mortimer Wheeler's excavations at Maiden Castle, Dorset, England. The recording posts on either side of the cutting and the workers give an idea of the scale of the dig.

founded on the east coast of Florida by the Spanish conquistador Pedro Menéndez de Avilés in 1566. Sixteenth-century St. Augustine was plagued with floods, fire, and hurricanes and was plundered by Sir Francis Drake in 1586. He destroyed the town, which was a military presidio and mission designed to protect Spanish treasure fleets passing through the Florida Straits. In 1702, St. Augustine was attacked by the British. The inhabitants

Figure 10.6 Horizontal excavation at St. Augustine, Florida, showing oyster-shell house footings from an early eighteenth-century building.

took refuge in the Castillo de San Marcos (which still stands). The siege lasted six weeks before the besiegers retreated, after burning the wooden buildings of the town to the ground. This time the colonists replaced them with masonry buildings, as the town expanded in the first half of the eighteenth century.

Kathleen Deagan and a team of archaeologists have investigated eighteenth-century and earlier St. Augustine on a systematic basis since 1977, combining historic preservation with archaeological excavation. Excavating the eighteenth-century town is a difficult process on many accounts, partly because the entire archaeological deposit for three centuries is only about three feet deep at the most, and it has been much disturbed. The excavators have cleared and recorded dozens of barrel-lined trash pits. They have also used horizontal excavations to uncover the foundations of eighteenth-century houses built of tabby, a cementlike substance of oyster shells, lime, and sand. The foundations of oyster shell or tabby were laid in footing trenches in the shape of the intended house (Figure 10.7). Then the walls were added. The tabby floor soon wore out, so another layer of

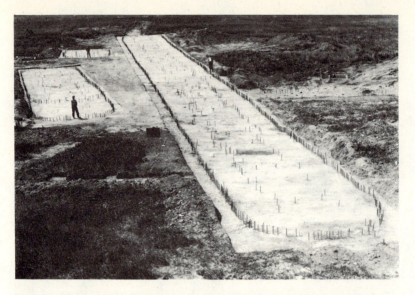

Figure 10.7 Horizontal excavation of an open area: an Iroquois longhouse at the Howlett Hill site, Onondaga, New York. The small stakes mark the house's wall posts; hearths and roof supports are found inside the house.

earth was added and a new floor poured on top. Since the deposits outside the house had been disturbed, the artifacts from the foundations and floors were of great importance. And selective, horizontal excavation was the best way to uncover them.

The problems with horizontal digs are exactly the same as those with any excavation: stratigraphic control and accurate measurement. Area excavations imply exposure of large, open areas of ground to a depth of several meters. A complex network of walls or post holes may lie within the area to be investigated. Each feature relates to other structures, a relationship that must be carefully recorded so that the site can be interpreted correctly, especially if several periods of occupation are involved. If the entire area is uncovered, obviously it is difficult to measure the position of the structures in the middle of the trench, far from the walls at the excavation's edge. To achieve better control of measurement and recording, it is better to use a system that gives a network of vertical stratigraphic sections across the area to be excavated. This work is often done by laying out a grid of square or rectangular excavation units, with walls several yards thick between each square (see Figure 10.8). Such areas may average twelve feet square or larger. As the figure shows, this system allows stratigraphic control of large areas. Large-scale excavation with grids is extremely expensive and time-consuming and is difficult to use where the ground is irregular, but it has been employed with great success at many excavations, being used to uncover structures, town plans, and

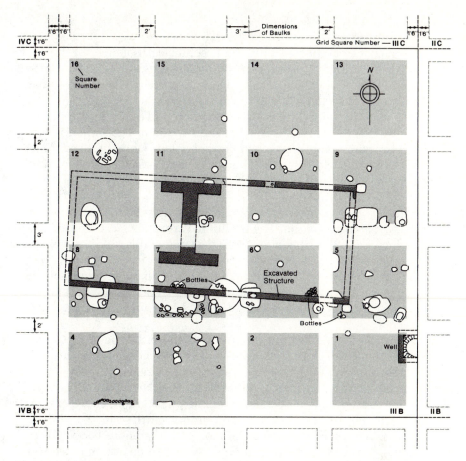

Figure 10.8 A horizontal-grid excavation showing the layout of squares relative to an excavated structure at Colonial Williamsburg.

fortifications. Many area digs are "open excavations," in which large tracts of a site are exposed layer by layer without a grid.

Stripping off overlying areas with no archaeological significance to expose buried subsurface features is another type of large-scale excavation. Stripping is especially useful when a site is buried only a short distance below the surface and the structures are preserved in the form of post holes and other discolorations in the soil.

Horizontal excavation depends, of course, on precise stratigraphic control. It is normally combined with vertical trenches, which provide the information necessary for accurately peeling off successive horizontal layers. Many excavations involve using both vertical and horizontal excavations, with horizontal digging being the result of initial vertical trenches that reveal structures to be uncovered.

TOOLS OF THE TRADE

Every archaeological site poses different technical problems, not the least of which is deciding what types of tools will be used to excavate them (Atkinson, 1953). The choice of digging tools radically affects the excavation as a whole. The following are some of the options.

Earth-moving equipment is often used to remove the sterile overburden covering large areas of a site or when speed of excavation is vital. Backhoes are sometimes used to cut crude test pits when sites are threatened by immediate destruction. The use of mechanical equipment is always limited, however, for such devices are highly destructive of fragile archaeological remains.

Spades, shovels, mattocks, picks, and forks are used for loosening and moving large amounts of soil. The traditional archaeological symbol is the spade, which has a flat back and a straight edge and is used for cleaning walls. Shovels, with their scooplike shape, are used for piling up earth in a trench preparatory to its being examined; they have innumerable applications in cleaning straight edges and tidying trenches, and they are the principal working tool of the archaeologist where much ground has to be uncovered.

Tools for loosening soil are the mattock, the pick, and the fork. The mattock and the pick may be considered together because they are variants on the same type of tool; when used with care, they are a delicate gauge of soil texture, an indication used often in larger sites. The traditional Near Eastern excavation used teams of pickmen, shovelers, and basket carriers to remove the soil and dump it off the site.

The most common archaeological tool is the diamond-shaped trowel, its straight edges and tip having innumerable uses: soil can be eased from a delicate specimen; the edges can scrape a feature in sandy soil into higher relief; and as a weapon of stratigraphic recording, it can trace a scarcely visible stratum line or barely discernible feature. It is also used for clearing post holes and other minor work, so much so that it is rarely out of a digger's hand on smaller sites.

Brushes are among the most useful tools, especially for dry sites. The most commonly used is the household brush with fairly coarse bristles that can be held by the handle or the bristles. Wielded with short strokes, it effectively cleans objects found in dry and preferably hard soil. The excavator uses various paintbrushes for more delicate jobs. The one-inch or half-inch domestic paintbrush has wide application in cleaning animal bones and coarser specimens. Fine camel's-hair artists' brushes are best for most delicate bones, beads, and fragile ironwork.

Small tools, some improvised on the site, aid in clearing delicate finds. Six-inch nails may be filed to a point and used for delicate cleaning jobs on bones and other fragile artifacts. The needle is another tool used to clear soil from such delicate parts of skeletons as the eye sockets and cheekbones. One of the most useful digging tools is the dental pick, available in a bewildering variety of shapes. Often, dental picks can be obtained without charge from dentists, who discard them as soon as they show signs of wear. Continental European archaeologists have used a small, hooked digging tool, a *crochet,* for many years; it is widely used for excavations in which a trowel is too big but smaller tools are too slow and inefficient.

Screens are essential tools because many finds, such as coins, glass beads, shells, small tacks, nails, and other artifacts, are minuscule. Most deposits from sites where small artifacts are likely to occur are laboriously sifted through fine screens with openings of one-quarter to one-eighth inch or smaller. Flotation techniques are also widely used (see Chapter 13).

Surveying tools normally include lines or metal tapes, plumb bobs, string, spirit levels, drawing boards, drawing instruments, a plane table, and a surveyor's level and compass—all essential for accurate recording of site plans and sections for setting up the archaeological archive.

Storage containers are vital on any excavation to pack and transport the finds to the laboratory, as well as to store them permanently. Paper and plastic bags are essential for pottery, animal bones, and other small finds; vegetal remains and other special items may require much more delicate packaging. Cardboard cartons, supermarket bags, even large oil drums can be used for storing finds. One of the disappointments of archaeology is the gradual disappearance of the metal tobacco can, which served generations of archaeologists faithfully.

This by no means exhausts the list of equipment at the archaeologist's disposal, for much depends on conditions in the field and the type of finds encountered.

THE PROCESS OF ARCHAEOLOGICAL EXCAVATION

There is only one way to learn how to excavate and fully understand archaeological excavation, and that is to go to a field school or on a dig and learn by doing it. *In the Beginning* is not a how-to-manual and can give you only an outline summary of the process of excavation, couched in the most general terms. The interested reader is urged to consult the specialist literature (Alexander, 1970; Atkinson, 1953; Barker, 1986; Dancey, 1981).

The description of excavation that follows can be applied, generally, to any archaeological site. Realize, however, that very few digs are conducted under ideal conditions, with unlimited time, adequate funds, and superb facilities. As Philip Barker puts it: "Just as 'all art constantly aspires toward the condition of music,' all excavations should aspire to the condition of total excavation." In other words, the ideal should always be kept in mind (Barker, 1983).

The excavator's aim should be to explain the origin of every layer and feature encountered in the site, whether natural or humanly made. It is not enough just to excavate and describe the site; one must also explain how the site was formed. This process is achieved by removing the superimposed layers of the site one by one. In so doing, the archaeologist records the full details of each layer and its contents as they are excavated. The process of archaeological excavation involves deciding where to dig, the actual digging, recording of the evidence contained in the excavation, and interpretation of the site and the processes by which it was formed.

Deciding Where to Dig

All archaeological excavation begins with making a precise surface survey and an accurate contour map of the site. A grid is then laid out over the site (see Chapter 9). The surface survey and the collections of artifacts made as part of it determine the working hypotheses that the archaeologist uses as a basis for deciding where to dig.

The first decision to be made is whether to carry out a total or a selective excavation. This decision depends on the size of the site, its possible imminent destruction, the hypotheses to be tested, and the time and money available. Most excavations are selective. Anyone contemplating a selective dig is faced with choosing the areas of the site to be dug. The choice can be clear-cut and nonprobabilistic, or it can be based on complex sampling approaches. A selective excavation to determine the age of one of the stone uprights at Stonehenge obviously will be at the foot of the stones. But excavation of a shell midden with no surface features may be determined by probabilistic sampling and selection of random grid squares that are excavated to obtain artifact samples.

In many cases, an excavation can involve both probabilistic and nonprobabilistic choices. For the Maya ceremonial center at Tikal in Guatemala, the archaeologists were eager to learn something about the hundreds of mounds that lay in the hinterland around the main ceremonial precincts (Coe, 1982). These extended at least ten kilometers from the center of the site and were identified along four strips of carefully surveyed ground, extending out from Tikal. Because, obviously, excavation of every mound and structure identified on the surface was impossible, a test-pit program was designed to collect random samples of datable pottery so that the chronological span of the occupation could be established. By using a proportional, stratified random sampling scheme, the investigators were able to select about one hundred mound structures for testing and obtain the data they sought.

The choice of where to dig can also be determined by logistical considerations, such as access to the trench, which can present problems in small caves; by the time and funds available; or, regrettably often, by the imminent destruction of part of a site that is close to industrial activity or road construction. Ideally, though, the archaeologist will dig where the results will be maximal and the chances of acquiring data to test working hypotheses are best.

The location of some excavations may be established by test digging.

When Richard MacNeish (1978) surveyed the Tehuacán Valley in Mexico, he tested thirty-nine sites with vertical trenches and selected eleven of them for more extensive excavation (see Figure 10.17). The sites chosen were those from which MacNeish felt he could obtain maximal information on different chronological periods. This strategy was successful. The excavations enabled him to trace the early history of domesticated maize (see Chapter 19).

Stratigraphy and Sections

The actual mechanics of archaeological excavation are best learned in the field. There is an art in the skillful use of the trowel, brush, and other implements to clear archaeological deposits (Atkinson, 1953; Barker, 1986). Stripping off layers exposed in a trench requires a sensitive eye for changing soil colors and textures, especially when excavating post holes and other features, and a few hours of practical experience are worth thousands of words of instructional text. Figures 10.16 through 10.20 will give some idea of the practical problems (Harris, 1989).

We touched briefly on archaeological stratigraphy in Chapter 5, where we said that the basis of all excavation is the properly recorded and interpreted stratigraphic profile (Wheeler, 1954). A section through a site gives a picture of the accumulated soils and occupation levels that constitute the ancient and modern history of the locality. Obviously, anyone recording stratigraphy needs to know as much about the history of the natural processes that the site has undergone since abandonment as about the formation of the ancient site itself (Stein, 1987). The soils that cover the archaeological finds have undergone transformations that radically affect the ways in which artifacts are preserved or moved around in the soil. Burrowing animals, later human activity, erosion, wind action, grazing cattle—all can modify superimposed layers in drastic ways. Charles Darwin pointed out that even the common earthworm's activities affect the world's soils (Darwin, 1881; Stein, 1983; Schiffer, 1987).

Archaeological stratigraphy is usually much more complicated than geological layering, for the phenomena observed are much more localized and the effects of human behavior tend to be intensive and often involve constant reuse of the same location (Adams, 1975; Drucker, 1972; Villa and Courtin, 1983). Subsequent activity can radically alter the context of artifacts, structures, and other finds. A village site can be leveled and then reoccupied by a new community that digs the foundations of its structures into the lower levels and sometimes even reuses the building materials of earlier generations. Post holes and storage pits, as well as burials, are sunk deep into older strata; their presence can be detected only by changes in soil color or the artifact content.

Anyone attempting to interpret archaeological stratigraphy has to take these points into account (Harris, 1989):

1. Human activities at the times in prehistory when the site was occupied and the effects, if any, on earlier occupations.
2. Human activities, such as plowing and industrial activity, *subsequent* to final abandonment of the site (Wood and Johnson, 1978).
3. Natural processes of deposition and erosion at the time of prehistoric occupation. Cave sites were often abandoned at times when the walls were shattered by frost and fragments of the rock face were showering down on the interior (Butzer, 1982). Such phenomena appear as dense layers of rock fragments that can separate different prehistoric occupations (Wood and Johnson, 1978).
4. Natural phenomena that have modified the stratigraphy *after* abandonment of the site (floods, tree uprooting, animal burrowing).

Interpreting archaeological stratigraphy involves reconstructing the depositional history of the site and then interpreting the significance of the natural and occupation levels that are observed. This analysis means distinguishing between types of human activity; between deposits that result from rubbish accumulation, architectural remains, and storage pits; and between activity areas and other artifact patterns.

Vertical trenches and sections are by no means the only way of recording archaeological stratigraphy. Often—and Koster is a good example—safety considerations make it impossible to maintain vertical sections to any great depth, and the sides of the trenches are stepped (Figure 10.2). The only essential is that the section be absolutely clean when the time comes to record it with camera and pencil.

Philip Barker, English archaeologist and expert excavator, advocates a combined horizontal and vertical excavation for recording archaeological stratigraphy. He points out that a vertical profile gives a view of stratigraphy in the vertical plane only (Barker, 1986). Many important features appear in the section as a fine line and are decipherable only in the horizontal plane. The principal purpose of a stratigraphic profile is to record the information for posterity so that later observers have an accurate impression of how it was formed. Because stratigraphy demonstrates relationships—among sites and structures, artifacts, and natural layers—Barker advocates cumulative recording of stratigraphy, which would enable the archaeologist to record layers in section and in plan at the same time. Such recording requires extremely skillful excavation. Various modifications of this technique are used in both Europe and North America. The Scandinavians have developed fine-tuned stratigraphic observations in which each layer is removed entirely and its surface is surveyed with great accuracy. As a result, theoretically, one can reconstruct the stratigraphy at any point on the site (Biddle and Kjølbye-Biddle, 1969).

All archaeological stratigraphy is three-dimensional; that is to say, it involves observations in both the vertical and horizontal planes. The ultimate objective of archaeological excavation is to record the three-dimensional relationships throughout a site, for these are the relationships that provide the provenience.

Archaeological Recording

Notebooks are an important part of record keeping. An archaeologist maintains a number of notebooks throughout the excavation, including the site diary or daybook. In this large notebook he or she records all events at the site—the amount of work done, the daily schedule, the number of people on the digging team, and any labor problems that may arise. Dimensions of all sites and trenches are recorded. Any interpretations or ideas on the interpretations, even those considered and then discarded, are meticulously recorded in this book. Important finds and significant stratigraphic details are also noted carefully, as is much apparently insignificant information that may later prove to be vital in the laboratory. The site diary purports to be a complete record of the procedures and proceedings of the excavation. It is more than just an aid to the fallible memory of the excavator; it is a permanent record of the dig for future generations of scientists who may return to the site to amplify the original findings. Site diaries can be a most important tool in the hands of later researchers. The Knossos site diaries kept by Sir Arthur Evans as he uncovered Minoan civilization for the first time have been used again and again by later investigators in Crete (Boardman and Palmer, 1963).

A small-finds register is also important in the records on any dig. Although some artifacts, such as pottery or stone implements, may be very common, others, such as iron tools or beads, will turn out to be extremely rare and have special significance. A small-finds notebook will help in assessing their significance.

Site plans may vary from a simple contour plan for a burial mound or occupation midden to a complex plan of an entire prehistoric town or of a complicated series of structures (Barker, 1986). Accurate plans are important, for they provide a record not only of the site's features but also of the measurement recording grid set up prior to excavation to provide a framework for the trenching.

Stratigraphic records can be drawn in a vertical plane, or they can be drawn axonometrically. Any form of stratigraphic record is complex and requires not only skill in drawing but also considerable interpretative ability. The difficulty of recording varies with the site's complexity and with its stratigraphic conditions. Often, the different occupation levels, or geological events, are clearly delineated in the stratigraphic sections. On other sites, the layers may be much more complex and less visible, especially in drier climates where the soil's aridity has leached out colors.

Sections can be recorded with a horizontal datum string set up on the wall, with ends related to the site grid. All features on the profile are then carefully recorded with reference to the datum line. Some archaeologists have also used scaled photographs or surveying instruments to record sections, the latter being essential with large sections, like those through city ramparts.

Three-dimensional recording is the recording of artifacts and structures in time and space. The provenience of archaeological finds is recorded with reference to the site grid (see Figure 10.9). Three-dimensional recording is carried out with a surveyor's level or with tapes and plumb bobs. It assumes particular importance on sites where artifacts are recorded in their original positions or on those where different periods in the construction of a building are being sorted out.

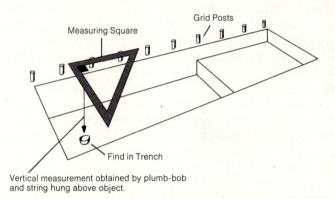

Measuring Square

Grid Posts

Find in Trench

Vertical measurement obtained by plumb-bob and string hung above object.

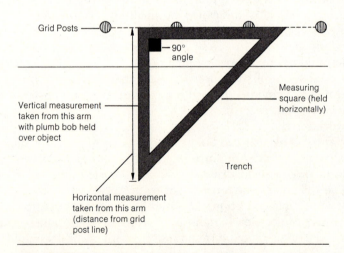

Grid Posts

90° angle

Measuring square (held horizontally)

Vertical measurement taken from this arm with plumb bob held over object

Trench

Horizontal measurement taken from this arm (distance from grid post line)

Figure 10.9 Three-dimensional recording. Top: Using a measuring square. Bottom: A close view of the square from above. The horizontal measurement is taken along the edge, perpendicular to the grid post line; the vertical measurement, from that arm with a plumb tool.

High technology is adding new accuracy to three-dimensional recording. By using theodolites equipped with laser beams, an excavation team can cut recording times dramatically. Harold Dibble has used the laser surveying device with great success at the La Quina Middle Paleolithic rockshelter in southwestern France. He estimates that the device cuts recording time by 50 percent and increases accuracy by 300 to 500 percent. A small microprocessor wired to the surveyor's tool records the measurement data, eliminating handwriting. Later, back in camp, the small field computer unloads its data into a personal computer that processes the measurements and produces a color-coded diagram of the day's work. The resulting map can be analyzed in a few minutes. Dibble is also experimenting with digitized graphics to analyze and record actual artifacts (Dibble, 1987).

Grids, units, forms, and labels are the backbone of all recording efforts. Site grids are normally laid out with painted pegs and strings stretched over the trenches when recording is necessary. Small-scale recording of complex features may involve using an even smaller grid that covers but one square of the entire site grid.

In an interesting variant on the grid, Hallam Movius erected a permanent site grid *over* the deep deposits in the Abri Pataud rockshelter at Les Eyzies, France (Figure 10.10) (Movius, 1977). Using plumb bobs, a grid of two-meter squares of metal pipe provided a framework for vertical and horizontal measurements on the surface of the deposits. Similar grids have been erected over underwater wrecks in the Mediterranean (Bass, 1966), although laser recording is gradually replacing this technique.

The various squares in the grid and the levels of the site are designated by grid numbers (Figure 10.10, bottom), which provide the means for identifying the location of finds, as well as a basis for recording them. The labels attached to each bag or marked on the find bear the grid square numbers, which are then recorded in the site notebook. A great deal of time is saved if standardized forms are used to record site data. The forms relating to, say, radiocarbon samples can then be assembled in order in a looseleaf notebook for later reference in the laboratory and museum.

Analysis, Interpretation, and Publication

The process of archaeological excavation itself ends with filling in the trenches and transporting the finds and site records to the laboratory. The archaeologist retires from the field with a complete record of the excavations and with the data needed to test the hypotheses that were formulated before going into the field. But with this step, the job is far from finished; in fact, the work has hardly begun. The next stage in the research process is analyzing the finds, a topic covered in Chapters 13–15. Once the analysis is completed, interpretation of the site can begin (see Chapters 17–18).

In these days of high printing costs, it is impossible to publish the finds from any but the smallest sites in complete detail. Fortunately, many data

retrieval systems enable us to store data on computer tape and microfilm so that they will be available to the specialists who need them.

Beyond publication, the archaeologist has one final obligation—to place the finds and site records in a convenient repository where they will be safe and readily accessible to later generations.

SPECIAL EXCAVATION PROBLEMS

Not all excavation consists of sifting through shell mounds or uncovering huge palaces. A great deal of archaeological fieldwork is dull and monotonous, but occasionally archaeologists face unexpected and exciting challenges that require special excavation techniques. Imagine being confronted with a royal grave, such as that of Tutankhamun, which took Howard Carter nearly ten years to excavate, or with the mass of waterlogged artifacts that came from the trenches at Ozette, Washington. In both sites, the excavators had to find special techniques for dealing with these fragile discoveries.

Let us examine some of the most common problems in excavation.

Fragile Objects

Narratives of nineteenth-century excavation abound with accounts of spectacular and delicate discoveries that crumbled to dust on exposure to the air. Regrettably, similar discoveries are still made today, but many spectacular recoveries of fragile artifacts have been made. In almost every find, the archaeologist responsible has had to use great ingenuity, often with limited preservation materials on hand.

Leonard Woolley faced very difficult recovery problems when he excavated the Royal Cemetery at Ur-of-the-Chaldees in the 1920s (Woolley, 1954). In one place, he recovered an offering stand of wood, gold, and silver, portraying a he-goat with his front legs on the branches of a thicket, by pouring paraffin wax over the scattered remains. Later, he rebuilt the stand in the laboratory and restored it to a close approximation of the original.

Arthur Evans, who discovered the Palace of Minos in Crete, realized that the walls of the palace were covered with fine frescoes, of which nothing but tiny fragments still remained. Painstakingly, he recovered the fragments and then pieced together the original frescoes. Unfortunately, there was little evidence of the original, and some of his reconstructions are regarded as somewhat fanciful.

Figure 10.10 The site grid at the Abri Pataud rockshelter in France. Top: The two-meter grid recording system. This permanent grid was used over many seasons of excavation. Bottom: Measuring the horizontal coordinates of a find. Notice the small board recording the grid square number and level.

Conservation of archaeological finds has become a highly specialized field of endeavor (Dowman, 1970; Organ, 1968; Plenderleith and Werner, 1973), which covers every form of find, from textiles to leather, human skin, and basketry. Many conservation efforts, like those used to preserve the Danish bog corpses, can take years to complete (Glob, 1969).

One of the largest conservation efforts was mounted at Ozette, Washington, where the sheer volume of waterlogged wooden artifacts threatened to overwhelm the excavators. The finds that needed treatment ranged from tiny fishhooks to entire planks. A large conservation laboratory was set up in Neah Bay, where the finds were processed after transportation from the site. Many objects were left to soak in polyethylene glycol to replace the water that had penetrated into the wood cells, a treatment that takes years for large objects. (A similar technique, incidentally, was used with the seventeenth-century Swedish warship *Vasa*, which was raised from the bottom of Stockholm harbor.) The results of this major conservation effort can be seen in the Neah Bay Museum, where many of the artifacts are preserved (Kirk, 1974).

Burials

Human remains have been encountered either as isolated finds or in the midst of a settlement site. Some projects are devoted to excavating an entire cemetery. In all cases where graves are excavated, the burial and its associated grave, funerary furniture, and ornamentation are considered as a single excavation unit or grave lot.

The public considers the unearthing and recording of human burials one of the most romantic aspects of the archaeologist's job. No doubt this is true when the skeletons are adorned with an array of rich grave goods. But in fact excavation of burials is a difficult and routine task that must be performed with care because of the delicacy and often bad state of the bones. The record of the bones' position and the placement of the grave goods and body ornaments is as important as the association of the burial, for the archaeological objective is reconstructing burial customs as much as establishing chronology (Anderson, 1969).

Although the pharaohs of Egypt were sometimes buried under great pyramids, and at Palenque, Mexico, a great burial chamber was covered by the Temple of the Inscriptions, most burials are normally located by means of a simple surface feature, such as a gravestone or a pile of stones, or by an accidental discovery during excavation. Once the grave outline has been found, the skeleton is carefully exposed from above. The first part of the skeleton to be identified will probably be the skull or one of the limb bones. The main outline of the burial is then traced before the delicate backbone, feet, and finger bones are uncovered. The greatest care is taken not to displace the bones or any of the ornaments or grave goods that surround them. In many cases the burial is in a delicate state, and the bones may be soft; therefore, they are exposed gradually, giving them time to dry before they are coated with a suitable chemical, such as polyvinyl acetate or Bedacryl. The hardened bones can then be removed to the safety of the laboratory (Brothwell, 1982; Stirland, 1987). Normally, the undersurfaces of the bones are left in the soil so that the skeleton may be recorded photographically before removal (Fig. 10.11). Photographing skeletons requires careful use of the camera to avoid parallax errors. Either the burial is removed bone by bone, or it is surrounded with a cocoon of plaster of paris and metal strips, the inside of which is packed with earth, and the whole structure is then transported to the laboratory, where it is cleaned at leisure. This cast technique is expensive and is generally used only when a skeleton is of outstanding scientific importance or when it is to be displayed in a museum. Usually, however, the bones are carefully

Figure 10.11 A classic Mayan collective tomb at Gualán in the Motagua Valley of Guatemala. Note the clean excavation, the carefully cleaned-up skeletons, and the stone lining of the tomb.

removed, one by one, hardened with chemicals, and then packed in cardboard cartons or wooden boxes with cotton, wool, and straw for transport to the laboratory. Bones to be tested for trace elements should not, of course, be treated with chemicals.

Some burials are deposited in funerary chambers so elaborate that the contents of the tomb may reveal information not only on the funeral rites but also, as in the Ur-of-the-Chaldees royal burials, on the social order of the royal court.

The great royal tombs of the Shang civilization of northern China are an example of complex tombs, where careful excavation made possible recording of many chariot features that otherwise would have been lost (Chang, 1978). The shaft, axle, and lower parts of the chariot wheels are visible as discolored areas in the ground. The area was dug to recover the dimensions and character of the chariots, which were found at the entrance ramps of the great Shang tombs. The charioteers were buried so as to accompany their masters.

Excavation of American Indian burials has generated furious political controversy in recent years, with Indian groups arguing that it is both illegal and unethical to dig up even the prehistoric dead. Some tribes have demanded back skeletal collections kept in such major museums as the Smithsonian Institution, and a flurry of reburial legislation is being enacted or developed at the federal and state levels (Chapter 19). In some states, like California, it is now illegal to disturb ancient Indian burial grounds (Anderson, 1985).

Human skeletons are a valuable source of information on prehistoric populations. The bones can be used to identify the sex and age of a burial, as well as to study ancient diseases. A whole series of new techniques are revolutionizing studies of prehistoric diet, even DNA (Chapman and others, 1981; Brothwell, 1982; Stirland, 1987).

Structures and Pits

Excavation of houses and household clusters involves careful uncovering of the structures themselves and also of the artifacts associated with them. Humans have constructed every type of dwelling, from simple brush shelters to elaborate palaces. Recovering the floor plans of such dwellings requires extremely sensitive methods of excavation.

Open excavations are normally used to uncover structures of considerable size (Barker, 1983). Grids allow stratigraphic control over the building site, especially over the study of successive occupation stages. Many such structures may have been built of perishable materials like wood or matting. Wooden houses are normally recognized by the post holes of the wall timbers and, sometimes, foundation trenches. Clay walls collapse into a pile when a hut is burned or falls down; thus the wall clay may bear impressions of matting, sticks, or thatch. Stone structures are often better preserved, especially if mortar was used, although sometimes the stone has been removed by later builders, and only foundation trenches remain (Figure 10.12). Stratigraphic cross-sections across walls give an insight into the structure's history. The dating of most stone structures is complicated, especially when successive rebuilding or occupation of the building is involved (Figure 10.13).

Some of the most spectacular buildings in the archaeological record leave few traces on the surface. Figure 10.6 shows an Iroquois longhouse that was identified purely from subsurface markings in the soil. Numerous longhouses have been identified in the same way from early farming sites in Europe (Champion and others, 1984).

The pueblos of the American Southwest offer another type of problem in excavation. The many rooms of the pueblos contain complicated deposits full of occupation debris and many artifacts (Figure 10.14). Efforts have been made to record the artifact patterns in these rooms in order to establish both the activities carried out in them and possible residential arrangements (Hill, 1970).

Storage and rubbish pits are commonly found on archaeological sites and may reach several meters in depth (Figure 10.15). Their contents furnish important information on dietary habits gleaned from food residues or caches of seeds. Trash pits are even more informative. Garbage pits and privies at Colonial Williamsburg have yielded a host of esoteric finds, including wax seals from documents that were used as toilet tissue (Nöel Hume, 1969). Some historic pits can be dated from military buttons and other finds.

Figure 10.12 The Bronze Age palace of Nestor of Mycenaean Greece.

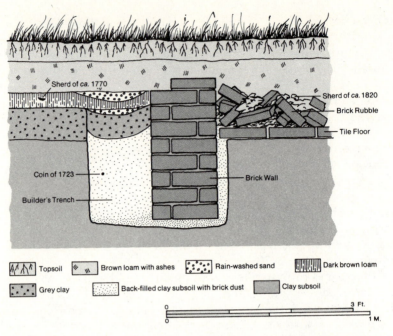

Figure 10.13 Dating construction of a building by its associated artifacts. The brick wall was built in a foundation trench that was filled with brick dust and clay. Someone dropped a coin dated 1723 into the clay as the trench was being filled. Obviously, then, the building of which the wall forms a part dates to no earlier than 1723.

Figure 10.14 The Cliff Palace at Mesa Verde, a southwestern pueblo in Colorado.

Figure 10.15 A double storage pit at Maiden Castle, Dorset, England, that was cut into the chalk subsoil.

Storage and trash pits are normally identified by circular discolorations in the soil. The contents are then cross-sectioned, and the associated finds are analyzed as an associated unit (Figure 10.15). Large pits, which may contain thousands of seeds and other informative materials, are excavated with particular care.

Post holes are normally associated with houses and other such structures. The posts they once contained were buried in holes that were dug larger than the base of the post itself. Once the structure was abandoned, the post might be left to rot, might be removed, or might be cut off. The traces each of these outcomes leaves in the ground differ sharply and can be identified with careful excavation. Sometimes it is possible to find fragments of the post or of the charcoal from its burning, which enable one to identify the type of wood used. Some interesting experiments in Britain have shown that most small posts will last about fifteen years in damp ground (Morgan, 1975), but much depends on soil conditions.

These are but a few of the many unusual excavation problems that archaeologists may confront in the field. Each archaeological site offers challenges to the investigator, including preservation, recording, or interpretation. But whatever the nature of the site, we always return again and again to stratigraphy and settlement patterns, to chronologies and cultural sequences, and to research designs, sampling, and careful surveys—principles of excavation that originated with the nineteenth-century archaeologists and have been refined progressively over the years. Though individual methods may vary from site to site and from area to area, no one denies the fundamental objective of archaeological excavation: recovering and recording data from below the ground as systematically and scientifically as possible.

Figures 10.16 through 10.20 constitute a picture essay on archaeological excavation. The pictures illustrate the great variety of excavation problems encountered by archaeologists around the world.

Figure 10.16 Excavation at site FxJj50, Koobi Fora, Kenya. It is an early hominid site, a scatter of broken animal bones and stone tools over two million years old.

Figure 10.17 Coxcatlán, Tehuacán Valley, Mexico. Excavation of a dry cave that yielded vital information on early maize civilization. Caves and rockshelters suffer from the disadvantage that their deposits are often much disturbed by natural phenomena, burrowing animals, and later human activity.

SUMMARY

- Excavation is a primary way in which archaeologists acquire subsurface data about the past. Modern archaeologists tend to carry out as little excavation as possible, however, because digging archaeological sites destroys a finite resource—the archaeological record.
- Modern excavations are often conducted by multidisciplinary research teams made up of specialists from several disciplines, who work together on a carefully formulated research design.
- All archaeological excavation is destruction of a finite resource. Accurate methods for planning, recording, and observation are essential.
- The Koster site in Illinois, where the excavators devised a sophisticated data flow system to keep their research design up to date, illustrated the essential research design.

Figure 10.18 Galatea Bay shell midden, North Island, New Zealand. An exemplary excavation through a midden (a dump of remains and occupation debris, including shells, fish bones, ash, and occasional artifacts). Sampling is often used to dig such sites (Shawcross, 1967; Terrell, 1967).

- Sites can be excavated totally or, as is more common, selectively. Vertical excavation is used to test stratigraphy and to make deep probes of archaeological deposits. Test pits, often combined with various sampling methods, are dug to give an overall impression of an unexcavated site before major digging begins. Horizontal or area excavation is used to uncover far wider areas and especially to excavate site layouts and buildings.
- The process of archaeological excavation begins with a precise site survey and establishment of a site recording grid. A research design is formulated, and hypotheses are developed for testing. Placement of trenches is determined by locating likely areas or by sampling methods. Excavation involves not only digging but also recording of stratigraphy and the proveniences of finds, as well as observations of the processes that led to the site's formation.

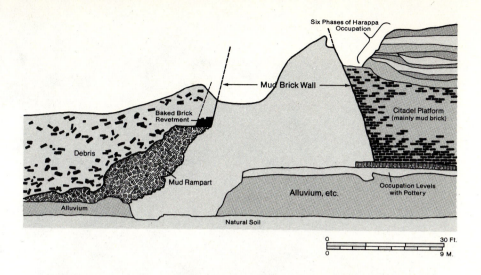

Figure 10.19 City mounds and other mound sites (Rosen, 1986). Top: Stratigraphic profile through the ramparts of the ancient city of Harappa in the Indus Valley, Pakistan. Bottom: Photograph of the actual excavation, a deep probe into the depths of the city's citadel. Vertical excavation provided the history of the defenses (Wheeler, 1967). The right of the top illustration is the back of this picture.

Figure 10.20 A quadrant excavation on a round barrow in Wiltshire, England, photographed from above.

- Careful stratigraphic observation in three dimensions is the basis of all good excavation and is used to demonstrate relationships among layers and between layers and artifacts.
- Three-dimensional recording methods are used to establish the provenience of artifacts and features.
- Excavation is followed by analysis and interpretation and, finally, publication of the finds to provide a permanent record of the work carried out.
- Among the special excavation problems we discussed were the recovery of fragile objects and human skeletons and the digging of post holes and structures.

GUIDE TO FURTHER READING

Some of the best excavation manuals are from Britain, which is no surprise because of the long tradition of fieldwork and excavation there. The British are lucky in having a wide range of very challenging excavation problems to confront, and the literature reflects this breadth. These are the major publications on excavation.

Alexander, John. *The Directing of Archaeological Excavations.* New York: Humanities Press, 1970. Provides very wide coverage of different site problems.

Atkinson, R.J.C. *Field Archaeology.* London: Methuen, 1953. An older manual, but superb in its clear exposition of basic approaches.

Barker, Philip. *Understanding Archaeological Excavation.* London: Batsford, 1986. An expert guide to excavation that can be used in conjunction with Alexander and Atkinson. Strong British orientation.

Dancey, H. S. *Archaeological Field Methods: An Introduction.* Minneapolis: Burgess, 1981. An excellent brief survey of American fieldwork approaches.

Joukowsky, Martha. *Complete Manual of Field Archaeology.* Englewood Cliffs, N.J.: Prentice-Hall, 1981. A comprehensive survey of excavation methods in both New and Old World contexts. Recommended for general reading.

Wheeler, R. E. M. *Archaeology from the Earth.* Oxford: Clarendon Press, 1954. An archaeological classic that describes excavation on a grand scale with verve and elegance. A must for every archaeologist's bookshelf, if only for its commonsense information.

PART Five

ANALYZING THE PAST

Artifacts and Technology

Intelligence . . . is the faculty of making artificial objects, especially tools to make tools.

Henri Bergson
L'Évolution Créatrice, 1907

*P*art Five begins our exploration of archaeology's ultimate objectives: constructing culture history, reconstructing past lifeways, and studying cultural process. Upon returning from the field, we begin by sorting the data that comes from the excavation into categories. From there we concentrate on artifacts and prehistoric technology. We outline the basic principles of archaeological classification and examine the ways in which ancient peoples used organic and inorganic raw materials. Proper understanding of technology, its uses, and its limitations is an essential preliminary to any discussion of prehistoric lifeways and culture change in the past.

Chapter
11

Identifying and Classifying Data

Once the excavations and surveys are completed, the archaeologist is confronted with the enormous task of organizing, analyzing, and interpreting the data. This chapter describes the first stage in the long work of identifying and classifying artifacts.

PROCESSING ARCHAEOLOGICAL DATA

The first stage in any laboratory analysis starts in the field—processing and organizing the finds so that they can be analyzed and interpreted. The basic processing of archaeological data goes on simultaneously with excavation, for the excavator needs to know where the data are weak and where they are strong. The objective of data collection is to test working hypotheses, and the data acquired for these purposes are normally highly specific. It would be nothing less than stupid to discover in the laboratory that you had failed to collect data needed to verify part of your hypothesis simply because you did not monitor it. The wise excavator keeps an eye on the data flowing from the trenches and plans further excavation to obtain larger samples, if they are required.

Preliminary Processing

An essential part of preliminary data processing is the packing, conservation, and marking of the artifacts and other finds. As we stressed in Chapter 4, the provenience of archaeological finds is a major key to understanding their significance. It is no coincidence, then, that most archaeologists develop a careful sequence of stages for processing artifacts and other small finds.

The Field Laboratory   The first stages in processing newly excavated archaeological data are entirely routine and are common to all finds (Figure 11.1). Most excavations maintain some form of field laboratory, where the finds are taken for preliminary examination. It is here that the major site records are kept and developed, stratigraphic profile drawings are kept up to date, and radiocarbon samples and other special finds are packed for examination by specialists. The field laboratory is staffed by a small group of people whose job is to ensure that all finds are processed promptly, packed carefully, and labeled and recorded precisely. The successful laboratory is organized to cope with a steady flow of finds, all of which are handled promptly, thus enabling the director of the excavation to evaluate the available data daily, even hourly.

Cleaning   The laboratory staff's first task is to clean the newly excavated finds. For stone implements or potsherds, water is used for cleaning. More delicate artifacts may have to wait for special laboratory treatment, or they may simply be brushed clean with a fine brush. Cleaning the artifacts is essential, for it permits at least a superficial examination of the find a short time after its discovery, which is part of the process of evaluating the data.

Figure 11.1 Preliminary data processing: archaeologists sorting pottery finds at a site.

Labeling "Never let the sun set on an unmarked artifact," one of my professors used to say. He was right, for an artifact without provenience is almost useless. The finds should arrive in the laboratory in a bag or other container with a label attached, and they should never be separated from this label throughout cleaning and conservation. Sometimes special drying trays are used, with an individual compartment for each batch of finds. With these, the label is pinned to the side of the compartment while the finds dry out. Large or especially important artifacts are normally marked with black ink, and the mark is covered with clear lacquer. A large number of potsherds or stone waste flakes are placed in labeled bags, with labels inside and outside the bag. Many excavators are now using computer code bars, like those found in groceries, to label bags and artifact lots.

Conservation Fragile artifacts, animal or human bones, or very small finds may need special conservation work, which begins as soon as the find reaches the laboratory—sometimes even in the trench itself. Entire burials can be lifted out of a trench in their original matrix if they are encased in plaster of pairs. But most conservation work is carried out in the laboratory. Some sites, such as Ozette, Washington, require a special laboratory for treating thousands of waterlogged wooden finds, often for months on end. Much of the wood from the Ozette site was lifted in a waterlogged state and slowly dried out in the laboratory.

Conservation can involve many activities: reassembling fragmented pots, a time-consuming and delicate process; hardening bones, using such chemicals as polyvinyl acetate; or treatment of iron objects. Most field conservation measures are designed to transport the find to the laboratory safely, where it will be examined and preserved at leisure.

Sorting and Inventorying These procedures begin with a rough sorting of the finds, which is usually based on the raw material involved.

Finds are counted and recorded in broad categories—bone, stone tools, and so on—to give a general impression of the data and to record the numbers in each category and within each level. These count data are carefully related to provenience and context. Subsequently, the artifact counts may be refined by cataloging each specimen individually. Some excavations maintain loose-leaf catalog books. Most, such as the Koster dig in Illinois, record their artifact data on computer terminals (Struever and Holton, 1979). Cataloging is very time-consuming, and therefore it is ordinarily reserved for highly significant artifacts and for special lots, such as the contents of storage pits or inventories from house floors. Data of this type are vital for studies of household and other activities.

Packing and Storage These make up the final stage of preliminary data processing. Potsherds, animal bones, and stone tools are placed in bags and taken to the laboratory in cartons. Radiocarbon samples, soil specimens, vegetable remains, and other such materials are packed separately, ready for shipment to specialists. Such delicate finds as burials are packed with great care, using tissue paper and special packing materials to prevent breakage in transit. Packing, like all preliminary processing, requires great skill and patience, far more than that accorded your china by a moving company! A complex site can devour huge quantities of packing materials. Howard Carter used several miles of wadding to pack the wooden finds from Tutankhamun's tomb (Carter and others, 1923–1933).

The preliminary data processing ends with storing the finds in the permanent laboratory. Days, months, and sometimes even years later the long tasks of classification and analysis begin. In the remainder of this chapter we will discuss objectives and methods of classifying and ordering artifacts.

CLASSIFYING ARTIFACTS

Our attitude toward life and our surroundings involves constant classification and sorting of massive quantities of data. We classify types of eating utensils: knives, forks, and spoons—each type has a different use and is kept in a separate compartment in the drawer. We group roads according to their surface, finish, and size. A station wagon is classified separately from a truck. In addition to classifying artifacts, life-styles, and cultures, we make choices among them. If we are eating soup, we choose to use a spoon. Some people eat rice with a fork, some use chopsticks or their fingers, and others have decided that a spoon is more suitable. A variety of choices are available, the final decision often being dictated by cultural custom rather than functional pragmatism.

All people classify, because doing so is a requirement for abstract thought and language. But everyday classes are not often best for archaeological purposes. In our daily life we habitually use classification as a tool for our life-style. Like the computer, however, it should be a servant rather than a master. Sometimes our classifications of good and bad—those based on color of skin or on our definitions of what is moral or immoral—are made and then adhered to as binding principles of life without ever being questioned or modified, no matter how much our circumstances may change. The dogmatism and rigidity that result from these attitudes are as dangerous in archaeology as they are in daily life. In archaeology, classification is a research tool, a means for ordering data. All classifications used by archaeologists follow directly from the problems that they are studying. Let us say that our prehistorian is studying changes in pottery designs over a 500-year period in the Southwest. The classification he or she uses will follow not only from what other people have done but also from the problems being studied. How and even what you classify stems directly from the research questions asked of the data. Because the objectives of classifications may change according to the problems being investigated, archaeologists must be sensitive to the need for revising their classifications when circumstances require it.

Taxonomy and Systematics

Taxonomy is the name given to the system of classifying concepts, materials, objects, and phenomena used in many sciences, including archaeology. The taxonomies of biology, botany, geology, and some other disciplines are highly sophisticated and often very rigid systems that were created in the nineteenth and early twentieth centuries, and many are now outgrown. In contrast, archaeology has built its own taxonomy of specialist terminologies and concepts quite haphazardly. Universal comparisons and classifications have been a virtual impossibility. British archaeologists refer to *cultures,* North American scholars refer to *phases,* and the French to *civilizations.* Each term has basically the same meaning, but the subtle differences stem from cultural traditions and from different field situations (Dunnell, 1986b; McKern, 1939; Rouse, 1939).

Systematics is essentially a way of creating units that can be used to *categorize* things as a basis for explaining archaeological or other phenomena (Dunnell, 1971). It is a means of creating units of classification within a scientific discipline. Biologists classify human beings within a hierarchy of classification developed by Carl Linnaeus in the eighteenth century. It begins with the kingdom *Animalia,* the phylum *Chordata* (animals with notochords and gill slits), the subphylum *Vertebrata* (animals with backbones), the class *Mammalia,* the subclass *Eutheria,* the order *Primates,* the suborder *Hominoidea* (apes and hominidae), the family *Hominidae,* the genus *Homo,* the species *sapiens,* and, finally, the subspecies *sapiens.* This hierarchy is gradually refined down until only *Homo sapiens sapiens* remains in its own taxonomic niche. The biological classification just described is based on each form having common progenitors. It consists of empirically defined units arranged in the form of a hierarchy. Each element in the hierarchy is precisely defined and related to the others. Again, classification in archaeology is a matter of using a classification closely related to the problem being studied.

Objectives of Classification

As we have stated, classification in archaeology depends on the problem being studied. Four major objectives can be identified, however:

1. *Organizing data into manageable units.* This step is part of the preliminary data-processing operation, and it commonly involves separating finds on the basis of raw material (stone, bone, and so on) or artifacts from food remains. This preliminary ordering allows much more detailed classification later on.

2. *Describing types.* By identifying the individual features (attributes) of hundreds of artifacts, or clusters of artifacts, the archaeologist can group them, by common attributes, into relatively few types. These types represent patterns of separate associations of attributes. Such types are economical ways of describing large numbers of artifacts. Which attributes are chosen depends on the purpose of the typology.

Artifact types (sometimes called archaeological types) are based on criteria set up by archaeologists as a convenient way of studying ancient toolkits and technology. They are a useful scientific device that provide a manageable way of classifying small and large collections of prehistoric tools and the by-products from manufacturing them.

3. *Identifying relationships between types.* Describing types provides a hierarchy, which orders the relationships between artifacts. These stem, in part, from the use of a variety of raw materials, manufacturing techniques, and functions.

These three objectives are much used in culture-historical research. Processual archaeologists may use classification for a fourth:

4. *Studying assemblage variability in the archaeological record.* These studies are often combined with middle-range research on dynamic, living cultural systems (See Chapter 14).

Archaeological classifications are artificial formulations that are based on criteria set up by archaeologists. These classificatory systems, however, do not necessarily coincide with those developed by the people who made the original artifacts (Willey and Phillips, 1958; Dunnell, 1986b).

Typology

The system of classification that is based on the construction of types is *typology.* It is a search for structure among either objects or the variables that define these objects, a search that has taken on added meaning and complexity as archaeologists have begun to use computer technology and sophisticated statistical methods. This kind of typology is totally different from arbitrarily dividing up the objects and variables. I remember sitting in a Cambridge archaeological laboratory many years ago and learning the basics of stone tool classification. Our instructor laid out a series of Acheulian hand axes in front of us, magnificent specimens from the gravels of the Thames River (Figure 6.1). He divided them into different categories. "These are pointed axes, these ovates (oval-shaped), these ovates with twisted edges, these linguate, with tongue-shaped ends," he declared. One of us pointed out that some of the axes in the pointed category were far from ideal examples of the form, in fact one or two were distinctly oval. "They are pointed handaxes," pronounced our instructor firmly, brooking no disagreement. The arbitrariness of his classifications was just like that used by a stamp collector classifying postage stamps. It was as if prehistoric handaxes were all standardized productions turned out by an impersonal stone flaking machine. One lost the opportunity to examine the underlying patterns of human design and behavior, which is what interests archaeologists more than mere classification.

Typology enables one to construct objectively defined units of analysis that apply to two or more samples of artifacts, so that these samples can be compared objectively. These samples can come from different sites, or from separate levels of the same site. Typology is classification to permit comparison, an opportunity to examine underlying patterns of human design and behavior (Brown, 1982). The value of typology is that it enables one to *compare* what has been found at two sites or in different levels of the same site. Typology, as James Deetz (1967) puts it, has one main aim: "classification which permits comparison. . . . Such a comparison allows the archaeologist to align his assemblage with others in time and space." Let's look over a group of archaeologists' shoulders as they sort through a large pile of potsherds, from one occupation level, on the laboratory table.

First the sherds are separated by decoration or lack of it, paste, temper, firing methods, and vessel shape. Once the undecorated or shapeless potsherds have been counted and weighed, they are put to one side, unless they have some special significance. Then the remaining sherds are examined individually and divided into types, according to the features they display. Soon a number of piles are on the table: one consists of sherds painted with black designs; a second, red-painted fragments; a third, a group of plain sherds that come from shallow platters. Once the preliminary sort is completed, the archaeologists look over each pile in turn. They have already identified three broad types in the pottery collection. But when they examine the first pile more closely, they find that the black-painted sherds can be divided into several smaller groupings: one with square, black panels; another with diamond designs; and a third with black-dotted decoration. The other two major piles also yield several subtypes. Eventually, the original three types become nine as the archaeologists study the collection in minute detail, identifying dozens, if not hundreds of attributes, conspicuous and inconspicuous, stylistic or dimensional, even some based on chemical analyses. These data are programmed into a computer in preparing for the quantitative analyses that will help sort out discrete types and variations among them. This is the process of typology, classifying artifacts so that one type can be compared with another. Obviously, the nine types from this one site can be compared with other arbitrary types found during laboratory sorting of collections from nearby sites.

For accurate and meaningful comparisons to be made, rigorous definitions of analytical types are needed, to define not only the "norm" of the artifact type but also its approximate range of variation, at either end of which one type becomes one of two others. Conventional analytical definitions are usually couched in terms of one or more attributes that indicate how the artifact was made, the shape, the decoration, or some other feature that the maker wanted the finished product to display. These definitions are set up following carefully defined technological differences, often bolstered by measurements or statistical clusterings of attributes. Most often, the average artifact, rather than the variation between individual examples, is the ultimate objective of the definition. A classifier who finds a group, or even an individual artifact, that deviates at all conspicuously from the norm often erects a new analytical type. Splitters tend to proliferate types, and lumpers do the opposite. The whole operation is more or less intuitive (Dunnell, 1971).

Types

All of us have feelings and reactions about any artifact, whether it is a magnificent wooden helmet from the Pacific Northwest coast (Figure 11.2), or a simple acorn pounder from the southern California interior. Our immediate instinct is to look at and classify these and other prehistoric artifacts from our own cultural standpoint. That is, of course, what prehistoric peoples did as well. The owners of the tools archaeologists study classified them into groups for themselves, each one having a definite role

Figure 11.2 Tlingit carved wood helmet from the Pacific Northwest coast, a "natural" type, classified as such when found in an archaeological context. This artifact would obviously be classified as a helmet from the perspective of our cultural experience. (Height, 9 inches; width, 10 inches)

in their society. We assign different roles in eating to a knife, a fork, and a spoon. Knives cut meat; steak knives are used in eating steaks. The prehistoric arrowhead is employed in the chase; one type of missile head is used to hunt deer, another to shoot birds, and so on. The use of an artifact may be determined not only by convenience and practical considerations but also by custom or regulation. The light-barbed spearheads used by some Australian hunting bands to catch fish are too fragile for dispatching a kangaroo; the special barbs permit the impaled fish to be lifted out of the water. Pots are made by women in most African and American Indian societies, which have division of labor by sex; each has formed complicated customs, regulations, or taboos, which, functional considerations apart, categorize clay pots into different types with varying uses and rules in the culture (Figure 11.3).

Furthermore, each society has its own conception of what a particular artifact should look like. Americans have generally preferred larger cars, Europeans small ones. These preferences reflect not only pragmatic considerations of road width and longer distances in the New World but also differing attitudes toward traveling and, for many Americans, a preoccupation with prestige and driveway display manifested in chromium plating, wheel covers, and style. We think that a car should have a color-coordinated interior and a long hood to look "right." The steering wheel is on the left, and the car is equipped with turn signals and seat belts by law. In other words, we know what we want and expect an automobile to look like, even though minor design details change—as do the length of women's skirts and the width of men's ties.

The problem that confronts the archaeologist is to devise archaeological types that are appropriate to the research problems they are tackling, an extremely difficult task. In archaeology, a type is a grouping of artifacts created for comparison with other groups. This grouping may or may not coincide with the actual tool types designated by the original makers. A good example comes from the world-famous Olduvai Gorge site in East Africa, where Louis and Mary Leakey excavated a series of cache sites used by very early humans, *Homo habilis*. Mary Leakey studied the stone tools and grouped them in the "Oldowan tradition," a tradition characterized by jagged-edged chopping tools and flakes. Her classifications were based on close examination of the artifacts, and the idea that the first human toolkit was based on crude stone choppers soon became archaeological dogma. Recently, Nicholas Toth of Indiana University has taken a radically different approach to classifying Oldowan artifacts. He has spent many hours not only studying and classifying the original artifacts, but also learning Oldowan technology for himself, fabricating hundreds of artifacts identical to those made by *Homo habilis* nearly 2 million years ago. His controlled experiments have shown that *Homo habilis* was not using chopping tools at all. The primeval stone workers were more interested in the sharp-edged flakes they knocked off lumps of lava, for cutting and butchering the game meat they scavenged from predator kills. The "chop-

Figure 11.3 A Chumash parching tray. A good example of the difficulties in archaeological classification. This finely crafted basket was made by the Chumash Indians of southern California (Deetz, 1967). It was made by weaving plant fibers. The design was formed in the maker's mind by several factors, most important of which is the tremendous reservoir of inherited cultural experience that the Chumash have learned, generation by generation, over the several thousand years that they have lived in southern California. The designs of their baskets are almost unconscious and relate to the feeling that such and such a form and color are "correct" and traditionally acceptable. But there are more pragmatic and complex reasons, too, including the flat, circular shape that enables the user to roast seeds by tossing them with red embers.

Each attribute of the basket has a good reason for its presence—whether traditional, innovative, functional, or imposed by the technology used to make it. The band of decoration around the rim is a feature of the decorative tradition of the Chumash and occurs on most of their baskets. It has a rich red-brown color from the species of reed used to make it. The steplike decoration was dictated by the sewing and weaving techniques, but the diamond pattern is unique, the innovative stamp of one weaver, which might or might not be adopted by other craftspeople in later generations. The problem for the archaeologist is to measure the variations in human artifacts and to establish the causes behind and directions of change and to find what these variations can be used to measure. This fine parching tray is a warning that variations in human artifacts are both complex and subtle.

ping tools" were, in fact, just the end product of knocking flakes off convenient lumps of lava and not artifacts at all. Controlled experiments like Toth's provide useful insights into how prehistoric peoples thought of the raw materials they used, and how they used them to manufacture the tools they needed. Toth and other experts are now trying to study the tell-tale patterns of edge wear on the cutting edges of Oldowan flakes, for the scars left by working, for example, fresh bone as opposed to hide or wood are highly distinctive. With controlled experimentation and careful examination of edge wear, they hope to achieve a closer marriage between the ways in which the first humans used stone tools and the classifications devised by the archaeologist hundreds of thousands of years later.

Everyone agrees that a type is based on clusters of attributes or on clusters of objects. Although patterns of attributes may be fairly easy to identify, how do archaeologists know what is a type and what is not? Should they try to reproduce the categories of pot that the makers themselves conceived? Or should they just go ahead and create "archaeological" types designed purely for analytical purposes? This is the hub of the controversy about types in archaeology.

The archaeologist constructs typologies based on the reoccurrence of formal patterns of physical features of artifacts. Many of these formal types have restricted distributions in space and time, which suggest they represent distinctive "styles" of construction and/or tasks that were carried out in the culture to which they belong. For example, the so-called Chavín art style was widespread over much of coastal and highland Peru after 900 B.C. The characteristic jaguar, snake, and human forms of this art are highly characteristic, and mark the spread of a distinctive iconography over an enormous area that flourished until 200 B.C. Chavín art, and the characteristic styles associated with it, had a specific role in Peruvian society of the time (Figure 8.8).

Archaeologists tend to use four "types of types," which we describe briefly here, which, in practice, are rarely separated one from another, for experts tend to draw this kind of information from more general classifications of artifacts (Steward, 1955) (Figure 11.4).

Descriptive Descriptive types are the most elementary, descriptions based solely on the form of the artifact-physical or external properties. The descriptive type is used when the use or cultural significance of the object or practice is unknown. For example, the excavations at Snaketown in Arizona revealed a "large basin-like depression," a mysterious feature that turned up, also, at other Hohokam sites in the Southwest. This descriptive type was subsequently proven to be a ball court, and so the noncommittal descriptive classification was abandoned in favor of a functional one that defined the structure's role in Hohokam culture. Descriptive types are commonly used for artifacts from early prehistory, when functional interpretations are much harder to reach (Figure 8.4). For instance, the famous prehistoric stone circles found throughout Britain are usually classified as just that, because we have no idea what their purpose was, except for a general impression that they had a ritual and symbolic function.

Chronological Chronological types are defined by form, but are time markers. They are types with chronological significance. Like descriptive types, they are part of a culture's inventory as reflected in the archaeological record, but are widely used to distinguish chronological differences. For example, on the Great Plains of North America, Clovis and Folsom points were used for short periods of prehistoric time, the former for about

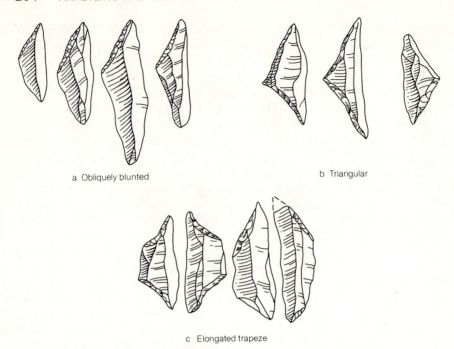

a Obliquely blunted   b Triangular

c Elongated trapeze

Figure 11.4 Some 9000-year-old Mesolithic artifacts from Star Carr, England (actual size). You can classify these by descriptive type as geometric stone tools; by chronological type as Mesolithic microliths, Star Carr forms; and by functional type as microlithic arrowhead barbs.

five centuries from about 9500 to 9000 B.C. Projectile points have long been used as chronological markers in North American archaeology. Pottery is probably the most common form of chronological type, for the clay, decoration, and so on change, and are shown to have noncultural significance and to be significant and historical indexes. Chronological types are defined in terms of attributes that do show change over time. The archaeologist compares artifacts known to be of different ages. Certain attributes are observed to be different, so he or she uses them to define the types.

The great Egyptologist Flinders Petrie used chronological types when he studied the pre-Dynastic jars from Diospolis Parva on the Nile. He based his chronological indices on the changing handle designs, which degenerated from a fully functional handle for lifting the vessel down to a meaningless squiggle painted on the pot (Petrie, 1889). Chronological types figure prominently in southwestern archaeology and were used by Alfred Kidder (1924) in his classic excavations at Pecos. Chronological types have the disadvantage that they are often hard for an archaeologist other than their originator to duplicate, except under favorable conditions or by archaeologists who have received identical extensive training (Sackett, 1977).

Functional   Functional types are based on cultural use or role in their user's culture rather than on outward form or chronological position. The same artifacts can be treated as of the functional type or the descriptive one. You can classify an assemblage in broad categories: "wood," "bone," "stone," and so on. But equally well, you may adopt a functional classification: "weapons," "clothing," "food preparation," and so on.

Ideally, functional types should reflect the precise roles and functional classifications made by the members of the society from which they came. Needless to say, such an objective is very difficult to achieve because of incomplete preservation and lack of written records. We have no means of visualizing the complex roles that some artifacts achieved in prehistoric society. Although in some cases obvious functional roles, such as that of an arrowhead for hunting or warfare or of a pot for carrying water, can be correctly established in the laboratory, functional classifications are necessarily restricted and limited. Let us consider a Scandinavian flint dagger (Figure 11.5)—a beautifully made, pressure-flaked tool, a copy of the bronze daggers so fashionable at the time in central Europe. This tool has been classified by generations of

Figure 11.5 A pressure-flaked Scandinavian flint dagger. (After Oakley; one-half actual size)

archaeologists as a dagger, by implication a weapon of war and defense, worn by Scandinavian farmers who still had no metal and made a slavish imitation of a more advanced metal tool. This instinctive designation may seem obvious, but we really do not know if our functional classification is correct. Was the dagger actually used in warfare and for personal defense? Was it a weapon, or was it purely an object of prestige for the owner, perhaps with some religious function?

It is in cases like this that we are confronted with the truth that the archaeological record is static and that it is very difficult to make analogies between the material culture of modern times and that of the past (Chapter 14). Middle-range research and theory, also described in Chapter 14, offer some opportunities for making more meaningful artifact and assemblage classifications.

Stylistic   Stylistic types are best exemplified by items such as clothing because style is often used to convey information through public display. The Aztecs of central Mexico lived in a ranked society where everyone's dress was carefully regulated by sumptuary laws (Anawalt, 1981). Thus a glance at the noble in the marketplace could reveal not only his rank but also the number of prisoners he had taken in battle and many other subtle distinctions. Even the gods had their own regalia and costumes that reflected their roles in the pantheon (Figure 11.6) (Fagan, 1984a). Stylistic types can be expected, theoretically at any rate, to have a structure entirely different from that of functional ones. They are not used often in archaeological classification, except when historical records are available. (For discussion of the style controversy, see Plog, 1983.)

PROCESSES OF ARCHAEOLOGICAL CLASSIFICATION

As we have emphasized, archaeological classification is the ordering of data on the basis of shared characteristics. But how do archaeologists go about this process, and what procedures do they use to do so (Rouse, 1972; Dunnell, 1986b)?

Traditionally, classification has been based on the archaeologist's "concept of types," subject of one of the great controversies in archaeology. On a formal level, a type can be defined as "a group or class of items that is internally cohesive and separated from other groups by one or more discontinuities" (Whallon and Brown, 1982). Until the late 1950s, almost all archaeological classification was qualitative, based to a great extent on instinct and experience rather than numerical methods or empirical testing. The new perspectives on the archaeological record that emerged in the 1960s coincided with a new generation of quantitative techniques that

Figure 11.6 Aztec warriors in their elaborate uniforms with their captives. The Aztecs had strict sumptuary laws, which governed the uniform of each grade of warrior (From the Codex Mendoza).

bear on the traditional problem of archaeological classification, techniques that are revolutionizing typology.

Quantitative Methods

The concept of quantitative methods has great breadth in archaeology. It refers not only to the standard techniques of statistical analysis and inference that readily come to mind but also to various techniques of numerical analysis, numerical manipulation, and graphical techniques for displaying data so that the patterns in the data are more readily apparent. Modern archaeology relies heavily on all manner of quantitative methods. In fact, quantitative methods are now central to archaeology in that the descriptive and explanatory power inherent in those methods and the carefully structured reasoning behind the methods provide us with very powerful tools for answering such fundamental questions as "How old is it?" "Where does it come from?" and "What was it used for?"

An understanding of the process of applying quantitative methods to archaeological problems and a basic level of computer literacy are fundamental skills for all modern archaeologists. Quantitative methods are no longer the sole province of the specialist but rather are fundamental tools employed by all archaeologists at some level. There are certainly some cases where very specialized data require arcane analyses and approaches requiring specialist expertise (Shennan, 1988). In general, however, some very sophisticated techniques are performed almost routinely by most practicing archaeologists today. There are three fundamental issues in applying quantitative methods to archaeological problems. The first is realizing *when* quantitative methods can aid in resolving a problem. The second is being familiar enough with various techniques and their under-lying assumptions to know which techniques are appropriate to specific kinds of archaeological problems. Finally, the third issue revolves around being familiar enough with the data, the methods, and general anthropo-logical theory to formulate a reasonable interpretation of the analytical results that has meaning in terms of the ultimate topic of archaeology, human behavior.

Quantitative methods are valuable in archaeology in three broad areas: data exploration and characterization, data description, and hypoth-esis testing or confirmation. All three will be discussed at length. In this discussion it is important to keep in mind the distinction between descrip-tive techniques and confirmatory or inferential techniques. The former term applies to economical methods of describing sets of data in ways that are useful to other researchers and preserve the inherent structure of the data. The latter refers to methods aimed at inferring the characteristics of an unobservable population of phenomena on the basis of the characteris-tics of a sample taken from that population and providing some guide as to the reliability of the inference.

Exploration   In recent years, a new suite of analytical tools have been added to the archaeologist's repertoire. These tools rely on a slightly diffe-rent way of thinking about archaeological data, as well as new ways of looking at the data. Collectively known as exploratory data analysis (EDA), these techniques have been specifically designed to aid in detecting pat-terns and deviations in sets of data by relying heavily on visual displays of data rather than on summary statistics and statistical significance tests. Two basic principles are behind these techniques. The first is that the fastest, most sophisticated pattern recognition hardware and software known are the human eye and brain. To the extent that large quantities of data can be reorganized and presented in a graphical rather than numerical form, the researcher can more readily detect patterns and deviations in the data that may have important implications for the prob-lem at hand. The proliferation of microcomputers and minicomputers with graphics capabilities in the 1980s dramatically speeded the develop-ment and acceptance of these techniques among archaeologists and other scientists. The second principle is a basic assumption about the structure of data sets. In EDA parlance, a set of observations can be divided into a general pattern, sometimes called the "smooth," and deviations from that pattern, the "rough." The smooth is important for understanding the general distribution of the data and the phenomena responsible for the observed regularity. The rough is important for potentially pointing out either unique events or perturbations in the normal operation of the system. These techniques for analyzing data have a very compelling application in archaeology, particularly in the area of typology, where the ultimate goal of the analysis is to identify regular patterns in the artifactual data that may reveal patterning in the human behavior that produced or distributed the artifacts. EDA is useful for reducing masses of data to some kind of observable order, usually in the form of frequency distributions, to obtain an initial impression of the rough and the smooth. This may be achieved through any number of graphical devices including bar charts, histograms, frequency curves, box plots, and stem-and-leaf plots. These can give the researcher valuable insights into the structure of the data, point up possible relationships between variables, and serve to suggest appropriate techniques for later descriptive or confirmatory analysis (for an excellent discussion of EDA, see Shennan, 1988).

Description   Descriptive statistics aid in the economical presentation of facets of the archaeological record. These techniques provide a means for organizing and quantifying archaeological data in a manner that facilitates objective comparison while preserving the inherent structure of the data. Descriptive statistics provide archaeologists with an economical way of indicating the numbers and kinds of artifacts found at a site or the dimensions of artifacts and the degree of variation in those dimensions. It provides a means of taking masses of data stored in computer databases and summarizing them into a readily digestible form. Today, descriptive statistics are often employed on-site as an aid to excavation or survey. The basic data are often collected and entered into a computer database in the field laboratory on a daily basis. Those data can then be quickly summarized using basic descriptive techniques to indicate differences in the frequency of artifacts between excavation areas or levels or to indicate emergent patterns in survey data that can then be used to refine field techniques and strategies. Descriptive statistics generally involve summarizing sets of data using very straightforward measures of the structure of the data. These include such things as measures of central tendency (mean, median, mode) and measures of dispersion (standard deviation, spread, range), as well as basic graphical devices such as bar graphs, histograms, and line graphs. In archaeology, the ultimate goal of descriptive statistics is to organize data into a more manageable form in order to facilitate comparison and indicate patterning. It is one of the oldest and simplest sets of techniques of quantitative analysis for archaeologists and remains one of the most frequently used because of its simplicity and its power. In innumerable archaeological problems, basic descriptive statistics are all that is required to characterize the data adequately and to provide meaningful interpretive information on the problem.

Hypothesis Testing (Confirmation)   Confirmatory or inferential statistics are designed to allow the researcher to make informed inferences about the characteristics of a population or the relationship between variables on the basis of data collected from a sample of the population of interest. The most important point to remember about true confirmatory statistics is that all of the various techniques provide a summary statistic that indicates how reliable the inference is likely to be. Archaeologists are concerned with making inferences about the past on the basis of patterns and relationships evident in the archaeological record. However, because the relationship between the observable phenomena (the archaeological record) and the unobservable phenomena of real interest (past human behavior) is often a very imperfect one, archaeologists need to know how reliable their inferences are. Since we cannot go back in a time machine to see for ourselves whether or not our inferences are good, we must rely on mathematics and the known laws of probability to give us an indication of the reliability of our inferences. As Stephen Shennan (1988) puts it, "The area where mathematics meets the messier parts of the real world is usually statistics." The tricky part about employing any of the various univariate and multivariate techniques of inferential statistics is that the test statistic (Student's t, F test, chi square, etc.) is only measuring the reliability of the *mathematical relationship* between variables in a data set, between a sample and its presumed population, or between data sets. How inferences about these mathematical relationships are interpreted in terms of the actualities of the archaeological record or human behavior depends on the archaeologist. Those interpretations can only be judged with reference to the archaeologist's understanding of the data, the technique employed and its assumptions and limitations, a coherent body of theory about the archaeological record and human behavior, and common sense.

Quantitative approaches to artifact classification, and indeed archaeology in general, have been associated with the scientific, overtly explicit, objective, hypothetico-deductive approach of processual archaeology, the so-called new archaeology of the 1960s and 1970s. Aspects of all three previously discussed areas of quantitative methods have been used with widely differing degrees of success in archaeology (Thomas, 1989). Furthermore, the systemic approach of processual archaeology entails investigating relationships between a wide range of variables affecting cultural change, and quantitative methods lend themselves to such research.

A discussion of all of the various applications of quantitative methods in archaeology is beyond the scope of this book, and the interested reader is referred to Stephen Shennan's (1988) admirable account of these approaches for information on widely used statistical and numerical procedures. Clearly, quantitative methods and computerized data manipulation and storage have become, and will remain, a central component of modern archaeology. Although almost all of these techniques have been borrowed from other disciplines, increasingly archaeological knowledge and information are being integrated into new techniques of quantitative analysis tailored to the kinds of data with which archaeologists deal. For most archaeologists, a basic familiarity with standard EDA, descriptive and confirmatory techniques, such as correlation and regression analysis, will be sufficient. A significant number of scholars, however, are forging past the frontiers of intelligent, knowledge-based, expert systems for computers and other approaches to determine their potential for archaeology.

In the final analysis, quantitative methods enable archaeologists to organize their artifact and other data in intelligent, efficient and replicable ways, allowing them to view the data more clearly and objectively toward the goal of discerning patterns that relate to past human behavior. These techniques also allow archaeologists to evaluate objectively the reliability of their inferences from small samples to larger populations of archaeological entities, as well as inferences about the interrelations between variables. To the extent that these techniques are applied to attribute and object pattern recognition, they are extremely valuable aids to artifact classification.

Quantitative methods have been applied to two contrasting approaches to artifact classification, both of which were in use before the advent of computers and statistical methods in archaeology: attribute analysis and object clustering.

Attribute Analysis   Attribute analysis emphasizes combinations of attributes that distinguish and isolate one artifact type from another. The physical characters or features of significance used to distinguish one artifact from another are known as *attributes* (for a detailed discussion, see Whallon and Brown, 1982). As archaeologists work out their typologies, they find themselves examining hundreds of individual fragments, each of which bears several distinctive attributes (Figure 11.7). Every commonplace artifact we use can be examined by its attributes. The familiar glass beer mug has a curved handle that extends from near the lip to the base, often fluted sides, a straight, rounded rim, and dimensions that are set by the amount of beer it is intended to contain. It is manufactured of clear, relatively thick glass (the thickness can be defined by precise measurement). You can find numerous attributes on any human artifact, be it a diamond ring or a prehistoric pot. For example, a collection of 50 potsherds lying on a laboratory table may bear black-painted designs, while eight have red panels on the neck, 10 are shallow bowls, and so on. An individual potsherd may come from a vessel made of bright red clay that was mixed with powdered sea shells so that the clay would fire better. It may come from a pot with a thick rim made by applying a rolled circle of clay before firing, and a criss-cross design cut into the wet clay with a sharp knife during manufacture. Each of the many individual features is an attribute, most of which are obvious enough. Only a critically selected few of these attributes, however, will be used in classifying the artifacts. (If all were used, then no classification would be possible: each artifact

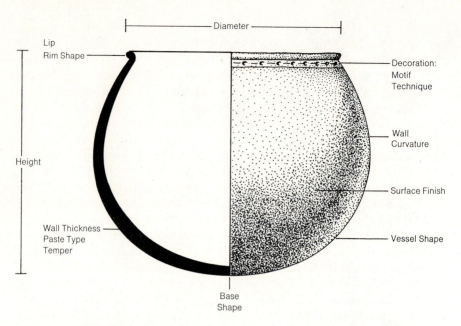

Figure 11.7 Some common attributes of a clay vessel. Specific attributes that could be listed for this pot are concave shoulder, dot-and-drag decoration, mica temper, round base, and thickness of wall at base.

would be an individual object identified by an infinite number of attributes.) Thus, the archaeologist works with only those attributes considered most appropriate for the classificatory task at hand.

A number of broad groups of attributes are in common use:

Formal attributes are such features as the shape of the artifact, its measurable dimensions, and its components. Usually, they are fairly obvious.

Stylistic attributes involve decoration, color, surface finish, and so on (Sackett, 1977, 1982).

Technological attributes cover the material used to make an artifact and the way it was made.

The selection of attributes normally proceeds through a close examination of a collection of artifacts. EDA techniques can be very useful in helping to determine which attributes provide the most diagnostic discrimination. A group of potsherds can be divided into different decorative styles based on shapes, surfaces, and colors. The selected attributes are then hand-recorded, and a series of artifact types is erected from them. The definition of the type here can depend on the order in which the attributes are examined (see Figure 11.7) and on the researcher's decision as to which are important.

Statistical typologies are derived from attribute clusters, usually coded on a computer, which are then used to divide the artifact collection into categories defined by statistically derived attribute clusters. James Sackett (1966) used this approach on 32,000-year-old Aurignacian end scrapers from Upper Paleolithic sites in southwestern France and found that the extent and location of trimming on the edges and the angle between the two longer sides were important variables that may have defined classes of artifacts used for different purposes.

Object Clustering The object clustering approach to classification begins with a series of so-called operational taxonomic units (OTUs), usually artifacts (Cowgill, 1982). The archaeologist calculates the similarities between all possible pairs of objects, using similarity coefficients. On the basis of similarity scores, the analyst can then link the OTUs into a hierarchical structure, which ranges all the way from the complete uniqueness of all artifacts (an unanalyzed collection) to complete unity, when all OTUs are in the same cluster. In contrast to attribute approaches, object clustering uses attributes to assess the *similarity* between objects, not associations (Cowgill, 1982, describes the differences between the two approaches). Object clustering classifications are based on a quantitative approach known as cluster analysis, a form of numerical taxonomy. It has, of course, a long nonnumerical history in archaeology, for the Midwestern taxonomic system was also based to a considerable degree on similarities between artifacts and assemblages.

Each approach to classification supplies different information about the very structure of archaeological data, all of which are valuable. In a sense, the approaches are descriptions of the structure in archaeological data, based, in their quantitative guises, on a greater concern for techniques for discovering variations in artifacts than on the actual selection of attributes for comparison. At present there is still little theoretical justification for selecting the attributes that are used to classify artifacts or to cluster them. Certainly as far as stone tools are concerned, it is likely that classifications based on function and technology will become more widespread as a result of highly precise inductive research into such phenomena as edge wear on modern artifacts. This provides a basis for testing hypotheses about tool use in the past and a firm foundation for classifications based on actual human behavior.

Assemblages and Patterns

Culture history in archaeology is based on classification of artifacts and assemblages, defined as associations of artifacts that are thought to be contemporary. This was the approach espoused by V. Gordon Childe in the 1930s and 1940s and was also popular in North America. "We find certain types of remains . . . constantly recurring together," Childe (1925) wrote: "Such a complex of regularly associated traits we shall term . . . a 'culture.' We may assume that such a complex is the material expression of what would today be called a 'people.' " This assumption was virtually archaeological law until the 1950s, when a number of prehistorians began using statistical methods to look at assemblages of artifacts.

These earlier archaeologists had assumed a steady, almost inevitable progression of human culture through the ages. They assumed that artifact assemblages with recurring patterns were merely traces of contemporary cultural "species" that extended far back into antiquity. This "organic" view of culture history regarded assemblages of artifacts as distinct categories like organic species that did not modify their form from one context to the next (Sackett, 1981). The argument went on to assume that a specific cultural tradition leads to only one characteristic type of industry in the archaeological record that is circumscribed in time and space.

What Do Assemblages and Patternings Mean?

For generations archaeologists studying culture history classified artifacts into assemblages, associations of tools that were thought to be contemporary. This approach assumed that human culture had evolved through the millennia. Thus artifact assemblages were merely traces of contemporary cultural "species" that extended far back into prehistory. This "organic" view of culture history saw assemblages of artifacts as distinct categories, like organic species, which did not modify their form from one context to the next. It was assumed in the organic approach that a specific cultural tradition leads to only one characteristic type of industry in the archaeological record, an industry circumscribed in time and space.

The organic view of the past is a highly organized scheme, rather like the Medieval "Chain of Being" in early biology, where every living thing had its place in the general scheme of things.

American archaeologists have generally preferred a more "cultural" perspective, making considerable use of data on artifacts and other cultural traits known to have been used by living societies in North America. The observation of these data have shown that there is a strong correlation between the distributions of distinctive cultural forms and different environments. For example, plank houses and an elaborate canoe technology are characteristic of the peoples of the Pacific Northwest coast, where readily split cedar and other trees flourished in abundance. In contrast, desert peoples in the Great Basin lived in much more transitory settlements of brush shelters and houses, using a highly portable toolkit that was adapted to a mobile desert lifeway. It is all very well to say that such correlations were true of historic times, but what about earlier prehistory? Can one say that artifact assemblages from the Great Basin dating to 5000 years ago reflect similar adaptations, similar social groups? Were conditions different in the past from today—can one use modern artifact patternings as a basis for interpreting ancient behavior?

Observations of living societies, such as Lewis Binford's research on the Nunamiut caribou hunters in Alaska, have shown that it is almost impossible to distinguish among ethnic and cultural groups from artifact assemblages alone (Binford, 1978, 1983a). Thus the role of classification in archaeology is shifting away from organic viewpoints that view artifacts and cultures as finite in time and space to new means of problem-oriented classification that concentrate not just on individual tools but on entire assemblages and their patterns in archaeological sites. In other words, classification alone is meaningless, unless the classifications are interpreted in terms of other data. This is where middle-range theory comes in (Chapter 14).

Artifact classifications are still carried out, for the most part, using approaches meant for reconstructing culture history, formulations of time and space that owed much to functional classifications of artifacts based on common sense. Robert Dunnell (1978) points out that relatively few new classificatory concepts are relevant to the new interest in processual archaeology. In classifying artifacts, archaeologists have usually made use of functional units or stylistic types on the basis of their historical significance through time. Recently, archaeologists have adopted inductive, statistical procedures (Spaulding, 1953; Doran and Hodson, 1975) that are technically more rigorous and of great use within an assemblage but less applicable on a wider canvas. Thus the same classificatory units have remained in use, while archaeologists pay lip service to newer approaches. As Dunnell (1986b) points out, the question of questions is a simple one: Can style be explained within a scientific and evolutionary framework, using laws of cultural change? So far, such a theoretical framework does not exist.

SUMMARY

- The first stage in laboratory analysis is processing field data into a form that will enable one to analyze and interpret them. The basic processing of data takes place as excavation proceeds: finds are washed, conserved, labeled, and sorted into basic categories, such as bone (animal and human), stone, shell, or wood. The finds are also inventoried during this stage.
- Classifying artifacts in archaeology is somewhat different from our day-to-day classifying of the objects around us.
- Two systems of classification are taxonomy and systematics. Taxonomy is a classification system of concepts and terms used by many sciences, archaeology among them. Systematics is a way of creating units that can be used to categorize things as a basis for explaining archaeological or other phenomena. It is a means of creating units of classification within a scientific discipline.
- The objectives of archaeological classification are to organize data into manageable units, to describe types, and to identify relationships among types.

- Archaeological types are groupings of artifacts created for comparisons with other groups. These groupings may or may not coincide with the actual tool types designed by the manufacturers.
- Types are based on clusters of attributes. There are four "types of types" commonly used today:

  Descriptive types are based on the form of the artifacts, using physical or external properties.
  Chronological types are defined by form but are time markers.
  Functional types are based on cultural use or role rather than outward form or chronological position.
  Stylistic types use changing styles for classification purposes.

- Archaeological classification begins with identifying artifact attributes, the characteristics that distinguish one artifact from another. Formal attributes are such features as the shape of an artifact, and technological attributes include the materials used to make an artifact and manufacturing methods. Attributes can be selected by closely examining a collection of artifacts, or they can be derived statistically.
- Statistically based classifications are now in common use, based on quantitative analyses, including the use of exploratory data analysis (EDA). Attribute-based and object cluster classifications are two major approaches now based on quantitative methods.
- Culture history in archaeology is based on classification of artifacts and assemblages, defined as associations of artifacts that are thought to be contemporary. This "organic" view of culture history has been ·replaced by a more "cultural" viewpoint in which environment and culture play important roles. This approach uses living societies and middle-range theory (Chapter 14) to interpret artifact classifications.

GUIDE TO FURTHER READING

The literature on archaeological classification is both complex and enormous. I strongly advise you to obtain expert advice before delving into even key references. Here, however, are some useful starting points.

Cowgill, George L. "Clusters of Objects and Associations between Variables: Two Approaches to Archaeological Classification," in Robert A. Whallon and James A. Brown, eds., *Essays in Archaeological Typology*, pp. 30–55. Evanston, Ill.: Center for American Archaeology, 1982. An excellent comparison of attribute-based and object cluster–based classifications in archaeology.

Dunnell, R. G. "Methodological Issues in Americanist Artifact Classification," *Advances in Archaeological Method and Theory* 9 (1986): 149–208. A specialist essay on artifact classification that summarizes the major controversies surrounding the subject.

Dunnell, Robert C. *Systematics in Prehistory.* New York: Free Press, 1971. A highly technical introduction to systematic classification in archaeology.

Shennan, Stephen. *Quantifying Archaeology.* Orlando, Fla.: Academic Press, 1988. A superb introduction to quantitative archaeology for the advanced student. Includes simple exercises.

Thomas, David Hurst. *Refiguring Anthropology.* Prospect Heights, Ill.: Waveland Press, 1989. A widely used basic text on quantitative approaches.

Chapter
12

Technology and Artifacts

"*W*hatever the ultimate inspiration or the intermediate cause, it was by their hands that the early Europeans dragged themselves out of the primeval mist of savagery, struggled up the long slopes of barbarism and ultimately attained to some kind of civilized existence," wrote Grahame Clark (1952) about prehistoric Europe. His words provide us with ample justification for studying the technology of the ancients.

The tools that people have manufactured throughout their long history have been the means by which they augmented their limbs and extended the use of their environment. The technological achievements of humanity over the past three million years of cultural evolution have been both impressive and terrifying. Today we can land an astronaut on the moon, transplant human hearts, and build sophisticated computers. Yet in the final analysis, our contemporary armory of lasers, atomic bombs, household appliances, and every conceivable artifact designed for a multitude of specialized needs has evolved in a direct, albeit branching, way from the first simple tools made by the earliest human beings. In this chapter we examine some of the main technologies used by prehistoric people to adapt to their natural environments and look at some of the ways in which archaeologists study them. We emphasize, however, that the study of artifacts and technologies is only a small part of the total archaeological process. The data that come from these studies are designed to verify specific research hypotheses formulated before collection of data began.

STONE

Certain categories of rock have, with bone and wood, been the primary raw materials for human technology for most of human existence. Metallurgy is but a recent development, and stone tools have provided the foundation for classification of many prehistoric cultures since scientific archaeology began. The raw material itself has set severe limits on people's technological achievements for much of their history, and the evolution of stoneworking over the millions of years during which it has been practiced has been infinitely slow. Nonetheless, people eventually exploited almost every possibility afforded by suitable rocks for making implements.

Working Stone

The manufacture of stone tools is what is called a "reductive technology," for stone is acquired, then shaped by removing flakes until the desired form is achieved. Obviously, the more complex the artifact, the more reduction is required (Swanson, 1975). Basically, the process of tool manufacture is linear. The stoneworker acquires the raw material, prepares a lump of stone (the core), then carries out the initial reduction by removing a series of flakes. These flakes are then trimmed and shaped further, depending on the artifact required. Later, after use, a tool may be resharpened or modified for further use.

Flaked stone tools are dependent on the property of conchoidal fracture, which is characteristic of many crystalline rocks, such as flint or obsidian (volcanic glass). The simplest way of producing a stone that will cut or chop, surely the basic tool produced by prehistoric people, is simply to break off a piece and use the resulting sharp edge (Figure 12.1). But to produce a tool that has a more specialized use or can be employed for several purposes requires a slightly more sophisticated flaking technique. First, an angular fragment or smooth pebble of suitable rock can be brought to the desired shape by systematically flaking it with another stone. The flakes removed from this core, or lump, are then primarily waste products, whereas the core becomes the implement that is the intentional end product of the toolmaker. Furthermore, the flakes struck from the core can themselves be used as sharp-edged knives, or they can be further modified to make other artifacts. From this simple beginning, many complex stone industries have evolved, the earliest tools being simple—many of them virtually indistinguishable from naturally fractured rock.

Principles of Manufacture   Identifying human-made implements as distinct from naturally broken rocks can be learned only by experience

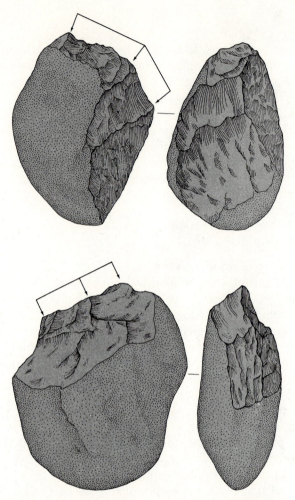

Figure 12.1 These cores from Olduvai Gorge, Tanzania, are some of the earliest human tool forms.
Arrows show the working edges. (Three-fifths actual size)

in handling many artifacts. Here is a generalized description of the
principles of stone implement manufacture (Crabtree, 1972). Generally,
Stone Age people and other makers of stone tools chose flint, obsidian,
and other hard homogeneous rocks to fashion their artifacts. All these
rocks break in a systematic way, like glass. The effect is similar to that
of a hole in a window produced by a BB gun. A sharp blow directed
vertically at a point on the surface of a suitable stone dislodges a flake,
with its apex at the point where the hammer hit the stone. This blow
effects a *conchoidal fracture* (Figure 12.2). When a blow is directed at a
stone slab obliquely from the edge, however, and the break occurs con-

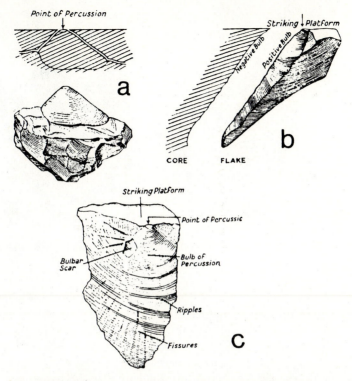

Figure 12.2 How stone fractures when a blow is struck on homogeneous types of rock: (a) When a blow is struck, a cone of percussion is formed by the shock waves rippling through the stone. (b) A flake is formed when the block (or core) is hit at the edge and the stone fractures along the edge of the ripple. (c) Features of a struck flake.

choidally, a flake is detached. The fractured face of the flake has a characteristic shape, with a bulge extending from the surface of the piece outward down the side. This is known as the *bulb of percussion* (or force); there is a corresponding hollow or flake scar on the core from which the flake has been struck. The bulb of percussion is readily recognized, as Figure 12.3 shows, not only by the bulge itself but also from the concentric rings that radiate from the center of the impact point, widening gradually away from it. Such deliberate human-made fractures are quite different from those produced by such natural means as frost, extreme heat or cold, water action, or stones falling from a cliff and fracturing boulders below (Crabtree, 1972). In these types the rock sometimes breaks in a similar manner, but most of the flake scars are irregular, and instead of concentric rings and a bulb of percussion, often a rough depressed area is left on the surface with concentric rings formed around it.

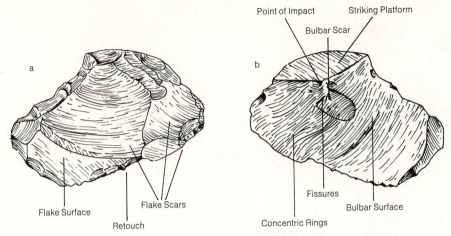

Figure 12.3 The components of a flake tool: (a) flake surface; (b) bulbar surface.

Careful examination is needed to distinguish human-worked from naturally fractured stones, a particularly acute problem with tools of the earliest human beings. Many of their artifacts were made by the simplest of hammerstone techniques, removing two or three flakes from the pebble (Figure 12.3). This work produced a jagged edge that was effective, so experiment shows, in dismembering carcasses of game. Several famous controversies have raged over alleged "artifacts" found in Lower Pleistocene deposits in Europe and Africa that are contemporary with periods when hominids were already flourishing elsewhere. A celebrated furor arose over alleged tools, named "eoliths," found early in this century in Lower Pleistocene horizons in eastern England (Grayson, 1986). These were championed for many years as early evidence of human occupation until reexamination of the geological contexts and accurate measurements of the flaking angles on the eoliths demonstrated that they were probably of natural origin. Under such circumstances, the only sure identification of human-fractured stone implements is to find them in association with fossil human remains and broken animal bones, preferably on living sites.

Methods Figures 12.4 through 12.7 show some of the major stone-flaking methods prehistoric peoples used (Crabtree, 1972). The simplest and earliest was direct fracturing of the stone with a hammerstone (Figure 12.4). After thousands of years, people began to make tools flaked on both surfaces, such as Acheulian hand axes (Figure 12.5). As time went on, the stoneworkers began to use bone hammers to trim the edges of their hand axes. The hand axe of 150,000 years ago had a symmetrical shape, sharp, tough working edges, and a beautiful finish.

As people became more skillful and specialized, such as the hunter-gatherers of about 100,000 years ago, they began to develop stone tech-

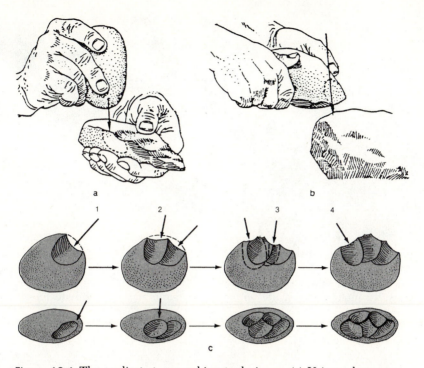

Figure 12.4 The earliest stoneworking techniques: (a) Using a hammer-stone. (b) A variant on the hammerstone, striking a core against a stone block, the so-called anvil technique. (c) The earliest stone tools were made by a simple method. The top row shows the side view: First, two flakes were struck off (1 and 2); second, the stone was turned over, and two more flakes were removed (3); third, a fifth flake completed the useful life of the core (4). The bottom row shows the process from above.

nologies producing artifacts for highly specific purposes. They shaped special cores that were carefully prepared to provide one flake or two of a standard size and shape (Figure 12.6). About 35,000 years ago, some stoneworkers developed a new technology based on preparing cylindrical cores from which long, parallel-sided blades were removed with a punch and hammerstone (Figure 12.7) (Holmes, 1919). These regular blanks were then trimmed into knives, scraping tools, and other specialized artifacts (Figure 12.8). Blade technology was so successful that it spread all over the world. It was the first stone technology introduced into the Americas (Fagan, 1987) and has been shown to be highly efficient. Controlled experiments resulted in 6 percent of the raw material being left on one exhausted blade core; 91 percent of it formed 83 usable blades (Sheets and Muto, 1972).

Once blades had been removed from their cores, they were trimmed into shape using a variety of techniques. In some, the blade's side was flaked with an antler or a piece of wood to sharpen or blunt it. Sometimes the flake would be pressed against another stone, a bone, or a

Figure 12.5 An Acheulian hand axe from Wolvercote, Oxford, England, with finely trimmed edges made with a bone hammer. (Approximate length, 5 inches)

piece of wood to produce a steep, stepped edge or a notch (Figure 12.8a and b).

The best-known and most common technique used in the later periods of prehistory, especially in the New World, was pressure flaking (Figure 12.8c and d). The stoneworker used a small billet of wood or antler pressed against the working edge so as to exert pressure in a limited direction and remove a fine, shallow, parallel-sided flake. This formed one of many flake scars that eventually covered most of the implement's surfaces. The advantage of pressure flaking is that it facilitates production of many standardized tools with extremely effective working edges in a comparatively short time (Sheets and Muto, 1972).

In southwestern Asia, Europe, and many parts of Africa and southern and eastern Asia, small blades were fashioned into minute arrowheads, barbs, and adzes, known as *microliths,* often made by a characteristic notching technique (Clark, 1932). These also evolved in arctic America and Australia.

The blade technologies of later times could produce far more tools per pound of material than earlier methods. Even tougher working edges were developed by later Stone Age peoples, who began to grind and polish stone when they needed a sharp and highly durable blade. The edges were shaped by rough flaking and then laboriously polished and ground against a coarser rock, such as sandstone, to produce a sharp, tough working edge. Modern experiments have demonstrated the greater effectiveness of polished stone axes in felling forest trees, the

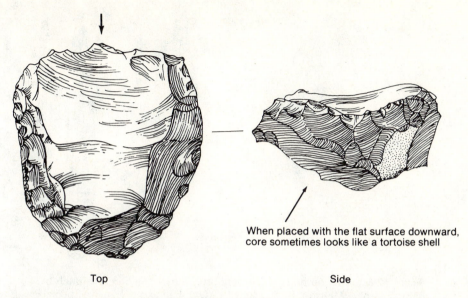

When placed with the flat surface downward, core sometimes looks like a tortoise shell

Top   Side

Figure 12.6 A special core shaped to produce one thin flake. Arrow indicates where flake was removed. (One-half actual size)

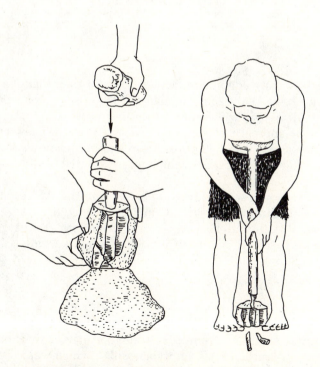

Figure 12.7 Two uses of the blade technique, employing a punch.

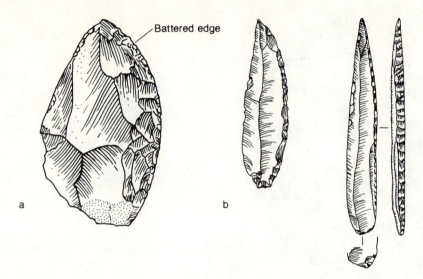

Figure 12.8 Some methods of trimming stone tools: (a) Steep retouch by battering, on a Mousterian side scraper. (One-half actual size) (b) Specialized blade tools made by pressing and sharpening the edges. These are backed blades used as spearpoints about 22,000 years ago. (Actual size) (c) The pressure-flaking technique. (d) Paleo-Indian pressure-flaked points: (1) Clovis point, (2) Folsom point, (3) Scotts Bluff point, (4) Eden point. (All actual size; used with permission of McGraw-Hill Book Company and Thames and Hudson, Ltd.)

toughened working edge taking longer to blunt than that of a flaked axe (Townsend, 1969; White and Thomas, 1972). Polished stone axes became important in many early farming societies, especially in Europe, Asia, Mesoamerica, and parts of temperate North America. They were used in New Guinea as early as 28,000 years ago and in Melanesia and Polynesia for the manufacture of canoes, which were essential for fishing and trade (White and O'Connell, 1982).

Expert stoneworkers still fashion artifacts to this day, especially gunflints for use in flintlock muskets. Gunflint manufacture was a flourishing industry in Britain and France into the twentieth century and is still practiced in Angola, in Africa, where flintlock muskets are still in use for hunting (Phillipson, 1969).

Stone Tool Analysis

Lithic Analysis   Early attempts at stone tool analysis were based on the classification of finished tools, or "type fossils," which were thought to be representative of different human cultures. This type fossil approach was abandoned gradually as more sophisticated typological methods came into use, methods that named well-defined artifact types according to their

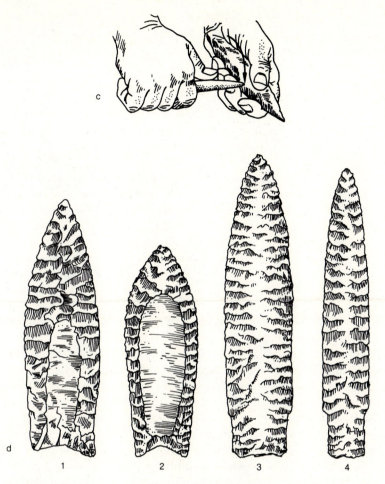

Figure 12.8 *(Continued)*

shape, dimensions, and assumed use, such as the Acheulian hand ax (Figure 12.5) and the Mousterian side scraper (Figure 12.8a). This approach led, like the type fossil concept before it, to searches for perfect "typical" artifacts. Many functional labels such as "projectile point" remain in use in modern stone tool studies, but they are no longer thought of as anything more than a generalized description of the form of an artifact. Functional analyses of this type have achieved great refinement in western Europe, where many varieties of Stone Age tools are to be found (Bordaz, 1970; Bordes, 1968; Sackett, 1977). As with other artifact forms, recent classifications have a sophisticated concern with attribute analyses based on attributes chosen for their ability to throw light on manufacturing technology or function.

In recent years, the focus of lithic analysis has shifted dramatically away from a preoccupation with finished tools to a broader concern with prehistoric lithic technology in a context of human behavior. Modern studies of stone technology rely on a combination of several approaches, which focus as much on the processes of manufacture of artifacts as they do on the artifacts themselves.

Debitage Analysis   The making of any stone artifact is the result of a *reduction sequence,* a series of steps that begin with the selection of a core of fine-grained rock and end with the completion of a finished artifact. Reconstructing these reduction sequences is one way in which archaeologists achieve an understanding of artifact manufacturing processes in prehistory.

Prehistoric stone tool manufacture can be reconstructed in several ways, for the clues lie in surviving abandoned cores, in flake scars, in striking platforms, in the dimensions of flakes and blades, even in the obvious and not-so-obvious mistakes made by ancient artisans. For example, a blow struck at the wrong point on a Levallois core can shatter the core in distinctive ways, easily recognized by someone familiar with lithic technology as the result of a mistake. Most steps in stone tool manufacture can be recognized by studying finished artifacts, cores, and, above all, the debris, often called debitage, left behind by the stoneworker. By close examination of debitage, an expert lithic technologist can separate primary flakes, flakes resulting from the rough blocking out of the core, from the finer flakes that were removed as the artisan prepared the striking platform on the top or sides of the core. Then there are the flakes that all this preparatory work was aimed at—the artifact blanks struck from the core. Finally, there are the fine retouching flakes that turn the blank into the finished projectile point, scraper, or whatever other implement was needed (Collins, 1975; Sullivan and Rozen, 1985).

Some of the most productive analyses of artifact manufacturing processes have come from meticulous combinations of debitage analysis with experimental replications of early technology. Nicholas Toth spent months replicating very early hominid technology as used at Olduvai Gorge, Tanzania, more than 1.75 million years ago. He compared his own cores and debitage with the originals and was not only able to show that the flakes removed from the cores were more important than the cores themselves, often called chopping tools, but that some of the world's very early stone toolmakers were left-handed as well (Toth, 1985).

Lithic Experimentation   Archaeologists have experimented with the making of stone tools since the mid-nineteenth century, and today many archaeological laboratories ring to the sound of people trying to make stone tools and replicate ancient technology—and cutting their fingers in the process (Flenniken, 1984). Experimental work began with general attempts to compare the stone toolmaking methods of living peoples like the Australian Aborigines with those of prehistoric cultures (Figure 12.9). Modern experimenters have drawn on both experimentation and ethnographic observation to work out prehistoric techniques (Swanson, 1975). Recent research has focused not only on reconstructing reduction se-

Figure 12.9 Australian Aborigines making stone tools.

quences but also on quarry sites, both as part of efforts to reconstruct prehistoric trade in obsidian and other rocks that can be traced back to source (Chapter 16) (Torrence, 1986) and also in attempts to achieve closer understanding of the relationships between human behavior and lithic technology (Ericson and Purdy, 1984). There is another side to experimental lithic technology as well. Obsidian flake and blade edges are so sharp that they are widely used by modern eye surgeons, on the grounds that such cutting tools are superior to modern steel!

Petrological Analyses   Petrological analyses have been applied with great success to the rocks from which stone tools are made, especially ground stone axes in Europe. Petrology is the study of rocks (Greek, *petros* = "stone"). A thin section of the ax is prepared and examined under a microscope. The minerals in the rock can then be identified and compared with samples from quarry sites (Ericson and Purdy, 1984). British archaeologists have had remarkable success with this approach and have identified more than twenty sources of ax blade stone (Champion and others, 1984; Clark, 1952). Such research can lead to vital information on prehistoric trade (see Chapter 17). Spectrographic analysis of distinctive trace elements in obsidian has yielded remarkable results in the Near East and Mesoamerica, where this distinctive volcanic rock was traded widely from several quarry centers (Torrence, 1986).

Refitting   Watch someone making stone tools and you will find that they are sitting in the middle of a pile of ever-accumulating debris—chips, flakes, abandoned cores, and discarded hammerstones. Prehistoric stoneworkers produced the same sort of debris—hundreds, if not thousands, of small waste fragments, by-products of toolmaking that are buried on archaeological sites of all ages. Vital information on prehistoric lithic technology comes from careful excavation of all the debitage from a place where a prehistoric artisan worked, then trying to fit the pieces together one by one, to reconstruct the procedures used. Refitting taxes the patience of even the most even-tempered archaeologist but can yield remarkable results. At the 9,000-year-old Meer II site in northern Belgium, David Cahen and Lawrence Keeley (1980) combined edge-wear analysis with refitting to reconstruct a fascinating scenario. They used the evidence from three borers that were turned counterclockwise to show that a right-handed artisan walked away from the settlement and made some tools, using some prepared blanks and cores he brought with him. Later a *left-handed* artisan came and sat next to him, bringing a previously prepared core, from which he proceeded to strike some blanks that he turned into tools. Reconstruction in this sort of fine detail is often impossible but has the advantage that the artifact pattern revealed in the archaeological record can be interpreted with extreme precision because the refitting shows that no modification has affected the evidence displayed in the archaeological record.

Another twist on refitting is to trace the movement of individual fragments or cores horizontally across a site, a process that requires even more patience than simple refitting. This procedure is of great value in reconstructing the functions of different locations in, say, a rockshelter site, where a stoneworker might make tools in one place, then carry a core over to a nearby hearth and fashion another blade for a quite different process. This approach has been used with great effectiveness on Folsom Paleo-Indian sites on the Great Plains, where individual flakes have been refitted to their cores having been excavated from locations as much as twelve feet away.

Use-Wear Analysis   Use-wear analysis involves both microscopic examination of artifact working edges and actual experiments with using stone tools (Hayden, 1979; Keeley, 1980). Soviet archaeologist S. A. Semenov (1964) used a high-magnification microscope to study the working edges of hundreds of Upper Paleolithic tools. He found that the scraping edges of so-called end scrapers bore clear signs not only of scratches but of luster from wear as well. He experimented with such scrapers and found that identical marks could be obtained by using the scraper as both a graver and a scraping tool. Many researchers have experimented with both low- and high-power magnification in recent years and are now able to distinguish with considerable confidence between the wear polishes associated with different materials like wood, bone, and hide (Keeley, 1980; Phillips, 1988). The approach is now reliable enough to allow one to state whether a tool was used to slice wood, cut up vegetables, or strip meat from bones, but relatively few archaeologists are trained in using the microscopes and photographic techniques required for analyzing wear. In Cahen and Keeley's study (1980) of stone tools from the 9,000-year-old Meer II site in Belgium, by reassembling some of the stone flakes and cores, studying the wear patterns on working edges, and examining distribution of the stone fragments throughout the site, they were able to show that two people, one of them left-handed, had made some tools that they then used to bore and grave fragments of bone. In instances like this, tool-wear analysis offers exciting opportunities for studying the behavior of individual stoneworkers thousands of years ago. There are many examples of distinctive microwear patterns, among them polishes that can be identified with high-powered microscopes. One instance is the flint sickle blade used for harvesting wild or domesticated grasses, which often shows a gloss caused by the silica in the grass stems (Garrod and Bate, 1937).

Patrick Vaughan (1985) has recently completed a use-wear analysis on an 18,000-year-old Magdalenian "O" stone tool assemblage from Cassegros in southwestern France. Cassegros was chosen because of the meticulous excavation methods used at the site and because the spatial and temporal distributions of the relatively small numbers of stone artifacts were well established, an essential preliminary for painstaking use-wear analysis. Vaughan analyzed the Magdalenian artifacts' use wear by relying on information on use-wear polishes, striations, and edge rounding, which had been produced by controlled experiments. These experiments had shown that minute abrasion chips on the edges of artifacts are much less significant as an indicator of use than polishes, striation, and rounding. The Cassegros analysis was designed to document patterns of tool usage and to locate activity areas within the cave levels.

The edges of a 532-item sample of the stone artifacts were cleaned with medicinal alcohol or other chemicals, then examined under a 280-power metallurgical microscope. Higher or lower powers were used when needed. Twenty-five variables relating to use wear were coded on a computer and analyzed statistically—with fascinating results. Tools displaying the characteristic use-wear patterns associated with working *dry hide* were common inside the cave. So were stone artifacts whose edges had worked harder materials like wood; Vaughan believes they were used to make wooden racks, frames, pegs, and other devices used to stretch and deflesh or dehair skins. Stone tools may also have been used to fashion antler, bone, and wood implements used to prepare *fresh hides,* for, interestingly enough, the Cassegros stone tools show few signs of fresh-hide as opposed to dry-hide use wear. Vaughan speculates that Cassegros was a hide-processing station used in the fall, when reindeer hunters pursue their quarry for hides.

The Cassegros research demonstrates the great potential of use-wear analysis for providing highly specific information on ancient tool use. (For detailed information, see Vaughan, 1985.)

The important thing about lithic analysis is not just the study of the implements themselves; it is understanding what the implements mean in terms of human behavior. And the new, multifaceted approaches to lithic analysis offer a real chance that methods like edge-wear analysis will provide definitive ways of classifying stone tools in terms of their original functions.

CLAY (CERAMICS)

Objects made of clay are among the most imperishable of all archaeological finds, but pottery is a relatively recent innovation. From the very earliest times, people used animal skins, bark trays, ostrich eggshells, and wild gourds for carrying loads beyond the immediate surroundings of their settlements. Such informal vessels were ideal for hunter-gatherers, who were constantly on the move. At one time it was thought that pottery's beginnings coincided with the origins of food production. We now know, however, that both agriculture and domesticated animals existed in the Near East from the eighth millennium B.C. if not earlier. Pottery did not appear until slightly before 6000 B.C. at such early agricultural settlements in the Near East as Jarmo and Jericho (Braidwood and Braidwood, 1983). In contrast, in Japan pottery was made by hunter-gatherers as early as 8000 B.C. (Akazawa and Aikens, 1986). The inhabitants of the Tehuacán Valley in highland Mexico began cultivating crops several thousand years before the first pottery appeared in North America in about 2500 B.C. (MacNeish, 1978).

The invention of pottery seems to have coincided with the beginnings of more lasting settlement. Clay receptacles have the advantage of being both durable and long-lived. We can assume that the first clay vessels were used for domestic purposes: for cooking, carrying water, and storing food. They soon assumed more specialized roles in salt making, in ceremonial activities, and as oil lamps and burial urns. Broken ceramic vessels are among the most common archaeological finds. Their shape, style, and form have provided the foundations for thousands of archaeological analyses (Olin and Franklin, 1982; Rice, 1989).

Pottery Technology

Modern industrial potters turn out dinnerware pieces by the millions, using mass-production methods and automated technology. Prehistoric artisans created each of their pieces individually, using the simplest of technology but attaining astonishing skill in shaping and adorning their vessels (Rice, 1987).

The clay used in potmaking was invariably selected with the utmost care; often it was even traded over considerable distances. The consistency of the clay is critical; it is pounded meticulously and mixed with water to make it entirely even in texture. By careful kneading, the potter removes the air bubbles and makes the clay as plastic as possible, allowing it to be molded into shape as the pot is built up. When the clay is fired, it loses its water content and can crack, so the potter adds a *temper* to the clay, a substance that helps reduce shrinkage and cracking. Although some pot clays contain a suitable temper in their natural state, potmakers commonly add fine sand, powdered shell, or even mica as artificial temper.

Potmaking (ceramics) is a highly skilled art, with three major methods:

1. *Coil.* The vessel is built up with long coils or wedges of clay that are shaped and joined together with a mixture of clay and water (Figure 12.10). Sometimes the pot is built up from a lump of clay. Hand methods were common wherever potmaking was a part-time activity satisfying local needs.

2. *Mold.* The vessel is made from a lump of clay that is either pressed into a concave mold or placed over the top of a convex shape. Molding techniques were used to make large numbers of vessels of the same size and shape, as well as figurines, fishing net weights, and spindle whorls. Sometimes several molds were used to make the different parts of a vessel.

3. *Potter's wheel.* Wheel-made pots came into wide use after the invention of the potter's wheel in Mesopotamia about five thousand years ago. The vessel is formed from a lump of clay rotating on a

Figure 12.10 Pueblo Indian woman making pots by the coil method.

platform turned by the potter's hands or feet. The wheel method has the advantage of speed and standardization and was used to mass-produce thousands of similar vessels, such as the bright red Roman Samian ware (Shepard, 1971). Wheel-made pots can sometimes be identified by the parallel rotation marks on their interior surface.

Surface finishes provided a pleasing appearance and also improved the durability of the vessel in day-to-day use. The potter smoothed the exterior surface of the pot with wet hands. Often a wet clay solution, known as a *slip,* was applied to the smooth surface. Brightly colored slips were often used and formed painted decorations on the vessel (Figure 12.11). In later times, *glazes* came into use in some areas. A glaze is a form of slip that turns to a glasslike finish during high-temperature firing. When a slip was not applied, the vessel was allowed to dry slowly until the external surface was almost like leather in texture. It was then burnished with a round stone or similar object to give it a shiny, hard surface. Some pots were decorated with incised or stamped decorations, using shells, combs, stamps, and other tools. Some were even modeled into human effigies or given decorations imitating the cords used to suspend the pot from the roof (Figure 12.12).

The firing of clay objects requires careful judgment on the part of the

Figure 12.11 A painted Zuñi pot of the 1880s. (Height, 9¾ inches)

Figure 12.12 A spouted Mochica bottle from Peru.

potter. Most early pottery was fired over open hearths. The vessels were covered with fast-burning wood, whose ash would fall around the vessels and bake them evenly over a few hours. Far higher temperatures were attained in special ovens, known as *kilns,* which would not only bake the clay and remove its plasticity but also dissolve carbons and iron compounds. Kilns were used for firing vessels at high temperatures and also for glazing, when two firings were needed. Once fired, the pots were allowed to cool slowly, and small cracks were repaired before they were ready for use.

The making of clay vessels was circumscribed by all manner of social and other variables. Archaeological literature is rich in descriptions of potmaking techniques among people all over the world. Unfortunately, however, few of these studies go beyond technology and processes of manufacture. They may tell us something about the division of labor in making pots, but they reveal little about the potters' status in their own society, their artistic attitudes, or changing ceramic fashions. In many societies, pottery has a well-defined economic role, and the training of potters is long and elaborate. The analysis of ceramics in archaeology must, however, depend on an understanding of the cultural influences that lie behind the variations in pottery in the archaeological record (Fontana and others, 1962; Matson, 1965; Rice, 1984, 1987). Although recent research has focused on the significance of the variations, it also deals with the role of the individual potter (Hardin, 1977; Krause, 1985).

Ceramic Analysis

Serious potsherd archaeology began in the New World with N. C. Nelson in 1914 and A. V. Kidder a few years later. Within a generation, regional pottery sequences were available for most parts of North America. An enormous expenditure of archaeological energy has gone into ceramic analysis since these pioneer studies, and a sophisticated literature covers the common analytical methods (Bennett, 1974; Bishop and others, 1982; Olin and Franklin, 1982; Rice, 1987; Shepard, 1971).

Analogy and Experiment   Controlled experiments to replicate prehistoric ceramic technology have been undertaken to acquire data on firing temperatures, properties of tempers, and glazing techniques (Coles, 1973; Shepard, 1971). Ethnographic analogy has been a fruitful source of basic information on potters and their techniques, and the direct historical approach traces modern pottery styles back to the prehistoric past.

Form and Function Analysis   Two features of prehistoric pottery are immediately obvious when we examine a collection of vessels: shape and decoration. Generations of archaeologists have used ethnographic analogy to assign specific functions to different vessel forms. Bowls are commonly used for cooking and eating, but globular vessels are most suitable for storing liquids. Sometimes associations of clay vessels and other artifacts, such as cooking utensils, leave no doubt as to their function. But such instances are rare, and one usually has to rely on analysis of the vessel's form to infer its function.

Form analysis depends on the common assumption that the shape of a vessel directly reflects its function. This assumption, which is based on ethnographic analogies, can be dangerous, for many intangibles affect the function of pottery. Intangibles include the properties of the clay used, the technological devices available, and perhaps most important, the cultural values that constrain not only the technology but also the uses and fashions of the vessels. Changes in vessel form can sometimes reflect a change in economic activities, but the economic evidence must be complete before such conclusions can be drawn. At the Isamu Pati mound village in Zambia, occupied intermittently from the seventh to the thirteenth centuries A.D., the uppermost levels contained a much higher proportion of cattle bones than the lower horizons (Fagan, 1967). At the same time, the pottery changed dramatically from a preponderance of simple bag-shaped vessels (Figure 12.13) to an overwhelming dominance of spherical pots with out-turned lips. These could only have contained liquid and were interpreted tentatively as reflecting a change in dietary habits, perhaps an increase in the consumption of milk. The functional distinction between utilitarian and ceremonial vessels is one of the most evident, but it must be supported not only by vessel form but also by direct association. For example, ceremonial pots were commonly buried with important people in many parts of the world, especially Mesoamerica.

Form analysis is based on careful classification of clusters of different vessel shapes. These shapes can be derived from complete vessels or from potsherds that preserve the rim and shoulder profiles of the vessel. It is possible to reconstruct the pot form from these pieces by projecting measurements of diameter and vessel height. Such analyses produce broad categories of vessel form that are capable of considerable refinement. (For an excellent example, see Sabloff, 1975).

Stylistic Analysis   This form of analysis is much more commonly used, for it concentrates not on the form and function of the vessel but on the decorative styles used by the potters. These are assumed to be independent of functional considerations and so to reflect more accurately the cultural choices made by the makers. In areas like the American Southwest, pottery styles have been used to trace cultural variations over thousands of years.

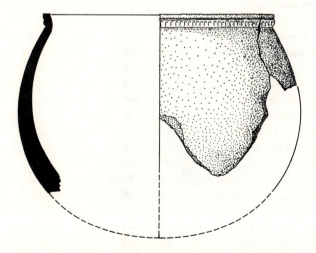

Figure 12.13 A utilitarian clay vessel: an Iron Age pot from the Kalomo culture of Zambia. (One-third actual size)

Even a cursory glance at pottery reports from different parts of the world will show you that archaeologists have used dozens of different stylistic classifications to study their potsherds. Only in recent years have people tried to standardize stylistic classifications, using clusters of easily recognized attributes to produce hierarchies of types, varieties, and modes.

With this approach, small numbers of distinctive attributes from different pottery assemblages are recorded. These attributes commonly appear in associated sets of features that provide the basis for erecting types and varieties of pottery styles, which are assumed to represent the social system behind the pots studied. Although a *variety* may represent only the activities of one family of potters, a *type* can represent the work of several villages or an entire community. Thus, goes the argument, standardized pottery types reflect a fairly rigid social system that prescribes what pottery styles are used, but less formal designs are characteristic of a less restrictive society. James Gifford studied the ceramics from Barton Ramie in the Belize Valley and traced the development of Maya pottery from 800 B.C. onward. He argued that the highly localized styles of earlier times reflected a much more flexible social system than in the Late Preclassic period, after 300 B.C., when pottery designs were standardized over large areas and were controlled, perhaps by rigid cultural values (Gifford, 1976).

Gifford's analysis is based on behavioral assumptions that have yet to be tested. Can one really assume that pottery styles reflect social behavior? The answer must await the day when many more standardized typologies from different areas of the world are available.

Technological Analysis Traditional classifications of prehistoric pottery are commonly used to order archaeological data, to establish relationships between different sites and occupation levels in space and time. These classifications differ little in basic conception from those employed for many generations, except that the means of classification have become ever more sophisticated. Today's archaeologists are concerned, however, with far more sophisticated problems than those of time and space relationships in attempts to study actual prehistoric behavior. The more elaborate, computer-generated classifications of today reveal that many of the archaeologist's classificatory cornerstones, such as pottery temper, are in fact subject to complex behavioral and environmental factors rather than being the simple barometers of human behavior they were once thought to be. For example, Marian Saffer (1979) found that pottery classifications developed for pottery from the Georgia coast in the southeastern United States were based on simple criteria, among them sand, grit, and ground-up potsherds. There appeared to be little variation in the style and decoration in Georgia coastal pottery for two thousand years. As a result, archaeologists used variations in temper as criteria for distinguishing new cultures and phases. Saffer used clay samples from the islands and the mainland, as well as many decorative and stylistic attributes, together with a sophisticated computer analysis to show that variations in temper could be correlated with the qualities of different potting clays. Thus variations in temper are due not only to cultural factors but to environmental conditions as well (Rice, 1982).

Technological analyses of pottery focus on the fabric and paste in potting clays, relate ceramic vessels to locally available resources (Bronitsky, 1986). These also provide useful, statistically based yardsticks for interpreting variability between different pottery forms and for developing much more sophisticated pottery classifications. Furthermore, the current interest in regional studies of prehistoric cultures and in trade and exchange encourages the analysis of pottery clays as a means of tracing centers of ceramic manufacture. Throughout later prehistory, clay vessels were major trade commodities, not only for their own qualities but also because they were convenient receptacles for such products as olive oil, wine, or salt.

Trace element analyses of mineral elements in clays and other temper studies can relate prehistoric pottery industries to local clay resources, establishing whether vessels were manufactured locally or traded in from a distance, as was the case, for example, across Lake Malawi in Central Africa (Asaro and Perlman, 1967).

Numerous other procedures yield valuable information on ancient ceramics, including neutron activation analysis, X-ray diffraction studies, and ceramic petrology. All these approaches can be used in combination to study what can be called "ceramic ecology," the interaction of resources, local knowledge, and style that ultimately leads to a finished clay vessel (Stimmell and others, 1982). For example, Mississippian pottery, manufactured in the southern and southeastern United States between A.D. 800 and 1500, was fired to a temperature between 800°C and 900°C. The Mississippians used crushed shell to temper their pots, so their vessels should not vitrify at these temperatures. But they did, and scanning electron microscope photographs revealed that the potters may have added salt to their raw clay, perhaps even tasting the clay during manufacture to see if it was correctly mixed. During the Mississippian, human settlement was concentrated in valley bottoms, where the potters used clays heavy in montmorillonite, adding crushed shell to it, so that they could work it more easily. This created another problem, that of poor firing. So the potters added salt to improve the firing qualities. However, salt was available in only a relatively few locations, so a complex trading system in this newly vital commodity developed. This stimulated development at major centers like Cahokia near St. Louis, since salt was nearby (Stimmell and others, 1982).

Technological analyses of pottery offer useful ways to amplify manufacturing data obtained from archaeological sources and ethnographic analogy (Arnold, 1985; Stark, 1984).

METALS AND METALLURGY

The study of metallurgy and metals found in archaeological sites is limited both by the state of preservation and by our knowledge of prehistoric metallurgy as a whole (Muhly and Wertime, 1980; Tylecote, 1972). Preservation of metal tools in archaeological horizons depends entirely on the soil's acidity. In some circumstances, iron tools are preserved perfectly and can be studied in great detail; in other cases, soil acids have reduced the iron to a rusty mass that is almost entirely useless. Copper, silver, and gold normally survive somewhat better.

Metals first became familiar to people in the form of rocks in their environment. Properties of metal-bearing rocks—color, luster, and weight—made them attractive for use in the natural state. Eventually, people realized that heat made such stone as flint and chert easier to work. When this knowledge was applied to metallic rocks, stoneworkers discovered that native copper and other rocks could be formed into tools by a sequence of hammering and heating (Wheeler and Madden, 1980). Of the seventy or so metallic elements on earth, only eight—iron, copper, arsenic, tin, silver, gold, lead, and mercury—were worked before the eighteenth century A.D. Properties of these metals that were important to ancient metalworkers were, among others, color, luster, reflecting abilities (for mirrors), acoustic quality, ease of casting and welding, and degrees of hardness, strength, and malleability. Metal that was easily recycled had obvious advantages. Almost every prehistoric metal was prized initially for its decorative qualities.

We know much about ancient metallurgy because prehistoric artifacts preserve traces of their thermal and mechanical history in their metallic microstructure. This structure can be studied under an optical microscope. Each grain of the metal is a crystal that forms as the metal solidifies. The shape and size of the grains can reveal whether alloys were used and indicate the cooling conditions and the type of mold used. At first, prehistoric metallurgists used "pure" metals, which could be easily worked but produced only soft tools. Then they discovered how to alloy each of these metals with a second one to produce stronger, harder objects with lower melting points. The basic data for studying prehistoric alloys come from *phase diagrams,* which relate temperature and alloy composition, showing the relative solubility of metals when combined with other metals. Phase diagrams were developed under controlled conditions in a laboratory and tend to reflect ideal conditions. By examining the object under an optical microscope, one can often spot differences in chemical composition, such as the cored, treelike structure that is characteristic of cast copper-tin alloys. Metals contain insoluble particles that can give clues to the smelting procedures and types of ores used. An energy-dispersive X-ray spectrometer and a scanning electron microscope are used to identify the particles. This impressive battery of analytical techniques has enabled archaeologists to study how six thousand years of experimentation took humanity from simple manipulation of rocks to the production of steel in about 1000 B.C. The record of these millennia is read in the lenses of the microscope, which reveals the triumphs and frustrations of the ancient smith. (Tylecote, 1980, is an excellent review of our knowledge of prehistoric smelting techniques.)

Copper

The earliest metal tools were made by cold-hammering copper into simple artifacts. Such objects were fairly common in Near Eastern villages by 6000 B.C. Eventually, some people began to melt the copper. They may have achieved sufficiently high temperatures with established methods used to fire pottery in clay kilns. The copper was usually melted or smelted into shapes and ingots within the furnace hearth itself. Copper metallurgy was widespread about 4000 B.C. (Muhly, 1980). European smiths were working copper in the Balkans as early as 3500 B.C. (Cernych, 1978; Coles and Harding, 1979; Tringham, 1971). In contrast to high-quality stone and iron, copper ores are rare and concentrated in well-defined regions. The metal was normally, but not invariably, alloyed with tin, which is even rarer. In the New World, copperworking was well developed among the Aztecs and the Inca. The Hopewell Indians of Lake Superior exploited the native deposits of copper ore on the southern shores of the lake, and the metal was widely traded and cold-hammered into artifacts from Archaic to Woodland times (Figure 12.14).

Bronze

But the real explosion—it was nothing less—in copper metallurgy took place midway through the fourth millennium B.C., when the smiths of both the Near East and Southeast Asia discovered that they could improve the properties of copper by alloying it with a second metal such as arsenic, lead, or tin (Coles and Harding, 1979; Bayard, 1972). Perhaps the first

Figure 12.14 Hopewell hammered-copper ornaments, found in 1920 in Ross County, Ohio: a bird and a cutout breastplate.

alloys came about when smiths tried to produce different colors and textures in ornaments. But they soon realized the advantages of tin, zinc, and other alloys that led to stronger, harder, and more easily worked artifacts. There is reason to believe that they experimented with the proportions of tin for some time, but most early bronzes contain about 5 to 10 percent (10 percent is the optimum for hardness). An extraordinary development of metallurgical technology occurred during the third millennium B.C., perhaps in part resulting from the evolution of writing (Muhly, 1980). By 2500 B.C., practically every type of metallurgical phenomenon except hardening of steel was known and used regularly. The use of tin alloying may have stimulated much trading activity, for the metal is relatively rare, especially in the Near East.

Chinese workers in bronze, laboring for the rulers of Shang urban centers in the Huangho Valley, were responsible for some of the most sophisticated bronze vessels of prehistoric times. Clay molds were used to cast elaborate legged cauldrons and smaller vessels with distinctive shapes and decoration. Casting was used to produce not only weapons but also elaborate works of art that were valued by early Chinese antiquarians as well as modern collectors (Chang, 1984).

Gold

Gold-decked burials fascinate many people, but in fact they are rare finds in archaeological excavations. Gold did, however, have a vital part in prestige and ornament in many prehistoric societies. It is not without reason that Tutankhamun is sometimes described as the "Golden Pharaoh": his grave was rich in spectacular gold finds. The recent discovery of the burial of a Moche lord of A.D. 200 under an adobe platform at Sipan, on the northern coast of Peru, revealed the remarkable wealth of this desert civilization. The richly adorned skeleton lay in a wooden coffin and was that of an adult male warrior-priest about thirty-five years of age. The shroud-wrapped nobleman wore a pair of gold eyes, a gold nose, and a gold chin-and-neck visor; his head lying on a gold, saucerlike headrest. Hundreds of minute gold and turquoise beads adorned the Lord of Sipan, who wore sixteen gold disks as large as silver dollars on his chest. There were gold-and-feather headdresses and intricate ear ornaments, one of a warrior with a movable club (Alva, 1988). The Chimú peoples of coastal Peru were master goldsmiths of pre-Columbian Latin America (Figure 12.15). The Aztecs and the Inca also were talented goldsmiths, whose magnificent products were shipped off to Europe and melted down for royal treasuries in the sixteenth century.

Gold is a metal that rarely forms compounds in its natural state. It was collected in this form, or in grains gathered by crushing quartz and concentrating the fine gold by washing. The melting point of gold is about the same as that of copper, so no elaborate technology was needed. Gold is easily hammered into thin sheets without annealing. Prehistoric smiths frequently used such sheets to sheath wooden objects such as statuettes.

Figure 12.15 Gold beaker with repoussé (hammered into relief from reverse side) decoration and turquoise inlay, attributed to Chimu goldsmiths of Peru. (About two-thirds actual size)

They also cast gold and used appliqué techniques, as well as alloying it with silver and other ones. Gold was worked in the Near East almost as early as copper, and it was soon associated with royal prestige. The metal was widely traded in dust, ornament, and bead form in many parts of the New World and the Old (Champion and others, 1984; Fagan, 1984).

Iron

Bronze Age smiths certainly knew about iron. It was a curiosity, of little apparent use. They knew where to find the ore and how to fashion iron objects by hammering and heating. But the crucial process in iron production is carburization, in which iron is converted into steel. The result is a much harder object, far tougher than bronze tools. To carburize an iron object, it is heated in close contact with charcoal for a considerable period of time. The solubility of carbon in iron is very low at room temperature but increases dramatically at temperatures above 910°C, which could easily be achieved with charcoal and a good Bronze Age bellows. It was this technological development that led to the widespread adoption of iron technologies in the eastern Mediterranean area at least by 1000 B.C. (Muhly and Wertime, 1980).

Iron tools are found occasionally in some sites as early as 3000 B.C., but widespread smelting does not seem to have begun until the second millennium B.C. Use of iron was sporadic at first, for objects made of the metal were still curiosities. Iron tools were not common until around 1200 B.C., when the first weapons made of it appear in eastern Mediterranean tombs. The new metal was slow to catch on, partly because of the difficulty of smelting it. Its widespread adoption may coincide with a period of disruption in eastern Mediterranean trade routes as a result of the collapse of several major kingdoms, among them that of the Hittites, after 1200 B.C. Deprived of tin, the smiths turned to a much more readily available substitute—iron. It was soon in use even for utilitarian tools and was first established on a large scale in continental Europe in the seventh century B.C. by the Hallstatt peoples (Collis, 1984). In earlier times iron had a comparatively limited economic role, most artifacts being slavish copies of bronze tools before the metal's full potentials were realized. Weapons such as swords and spears were the first artifacts to be modified to make use of the new material. Specialized ironworking tools, such as tongs, as well as woodworking artifacts, began to be used as soon as the qualities of iron were recognized.

Iron ore is much more abundant in the natural state than copper ore. It is readily obtainable from surface outcrops and bog deposits. Once its potential was realized, it became much more widely used, and stone and bronze were relegated to subsidiary, often ornamental uses.

The influence of iron was immense, for it made available abundant supplies of tough cutting edges for agriculture. With iron tools, clearing forests became easier, and people achieved even greater mastery over their environment. Ironworking profoundly influenced the development of literate civilizations. Some people, such as the Australian aborigines and the pre-Columbian Americans, never developed iron metallurgy.

Metal Technologies

Copper technology began with the cold hammering of the ore into simple artifacts. Copper smelting may have originated in the accidental melting of some copper ore in a domestic hearth or oven. In smelting, the ore is melted at a high temperature in a small kiln and the molten metal is allowed to trickle down through the charcoal fuel into a vessel at the base of the furnace. The copper is further reduced at a high temperature and then cooled slowly and hammered into shape. This *annealing* (heating, cooling, and hammering) adds strength to the metal. Molten copper was poured into molds and cast into widely varied shapes.

Copper ores were obtained from weathered surface outcrops, but the best material came from subsurface ores, which were mined by expert diggers. Copper mines were in many parts of the Old World and provide a fruitful field for the student of metallurgy to investigate. The most elaborate European workings were in the Tyrol and Salzburg areas, where many oval workings were entered by a shaft from above (Champion and others, 1984). At Mitterburg, Austria, the miners drove shafts into the hillside with bronze picks and extracted the copper by elaborate fire-setting techniques. Many early copper workings have been found in southern Africa, where the miners followed surface lodes under the ground (Figure 12.16) (Bisson, 1977; Summers, 1969). Fortunately, the traditional

Figure 12.16 Excavation in a prehistoric copper mine at Kansanshi, Zambia. The miners followed outcrops of copper ore deep into the ground with narrow shafts, the earth fillings of which yield both radiocarbon samples and artifacts abandoned by the miners.

Central African processes of copper smelting have been recorded. The ore was placed in a small furnace with alternating layers of charcoal and smelted for several hours at high heat maintained with goatskin bellows (Figure 12.17). After each firing, the furnace was destroyed and the molten copper dripped onto the top of a sand-filled pot buried under the fire (Bisson, 1977).

Bronze technology depended on alloying, the mingling of small quantities of such substances as arsenic and tin with copper. With its lower melting point, bronze soon superseded copper for much metalwork. Some of the most sophisticated bronzeworking was created by Chinese smiths, who cast elaborate vessels in clay molds (Figure 12.18).

Ironworking is a much more elaborate technology that requires a

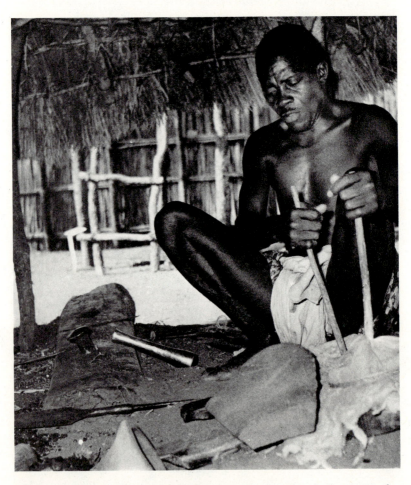

Figure 12.17 An African ironworker using a goatskin bellows. Similar bellows were used for copper smelting.

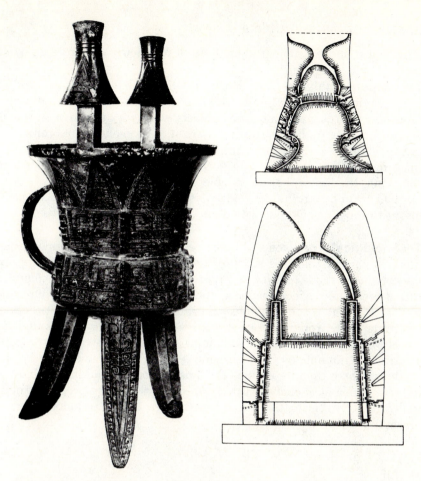

Figure 12.18 Shang ceremonial bronze vessel from about the twelfth century B.C. and diagrams of clay molds for casting such vessels.

melting temperature of at least 1,537°C. Prehistoric smiths normally used an elaborate furnace filled with alternating layers of charcoal and iron ore that was maintained at a high temperature for many hours with a bellows. A single firing often yielded only a spongy lump of iron, called a bloom, which then had to be forged and hammered into artifacts. It took some time for the metallurgists to learn that they could strengthen working edges by quenching the tool in cold water. This process gave greater strength, but it also made the tool brittle. The tempering process, reheating the blade to a temperature below 727°C, restored the strength. Iron technology was so slow in developing that it remained basically unchanged from about 600 B.C. until Medieval times (Piggott, 1965).

Analysis of Metal Artifacts

Typological and technological analyses of metal artifacts are employed.

Typological Analyses In Europe, metal tools have been analyzed for typology since the early nineteenth century. Stylistic changes in bronze brooches, swords, axes, and iron artifacts were very sensitive to fashion and to changing trading patterns. As a result, the evolution of bronze pins or iron slashing swords, for example, can be traced across Europe, with small design changes providing both relative dating and occasional insights into the lifeways of the people using them (Champion and others, 1984; Coles and Harding, 1979). In many ways, such studies are similar in intent to those carried out with stone implements or potsherds.

Technological Analyses In many respects, technological analyses are more important than the study of finished artifacts. Many of the most important questions relating to prehistoric metallurgy involve manufacturing techniques. Technological studies start with ethnographic analogies and actual reconstructions of prehistoric metallurgical processes. Chemists study iron and copper slag and residues from excavated furnaces. Microscopic examination of metal structure and ores yields valuable information not only on the metal and its constituents and alloys but also on the methods used to produce the finished tool. The ultimate objective of the technological analyses is to reconstruct the entire process of metal tool production, from the mining of the ore to the production of the finished artifact.

BONE

Bone as a material for toolmaking probably dates to the very beginnings of human history, but the earliest artifacts apparently consisted of little more than fragments of fractured animal bone used for purposes that could not be fulfilled by wood or stone implements (Leakey, 1973).

The earliest standardized bone tools date from later prehistoric times. Splinters of bone were sharpened and used as points in many societies, but bone and antler artifacts were especially favored by the Upper Paleolithic peoples of southwestern France from 30,000 to 12,000 years ago and by postglacial hunter-gatherers in Scandinavia (Bordes, 1968). In both the Old World and the New, later bone implements were ground and scraped from long bones, hardened in the fire, and polished with beeswax, to produce arrowheads, spearpoints, needles, and other artifacts. Bone was also carved and engraved, especially during Upper Paleolithic times in western Europe, as was reindeer antler (Leroi-Gourhan, 1967).

Deer antler was an even more important material than bone for some later hunter-gatherers. Fully grown deer antler is particularly suitable for making barbed or simple harpoons and spearpoints. Bone and antler were much used in prehistoric times for harpoons for fishing and for conventional hunting. Numerous harpoons are found in Magdalenian sites in western Europe (Figure 12.19) and also in Eskimo settlements in the Arctic, where they form a valuable index of cultural development, analogous to that of pottery in the American Southwest (Dumond, 1987).

The humble bone or ivory needle may have been a revolutionary artifact in prehistory, for it enabled humans to manufacture layered, tailored clothing. Such garments were essential for colonizing Arctic latitudes of the Old World, an event that occurred at least 25,000 years ago (Fagan, 1991b).

Bone Tool Analysis

In the Arctic, where bone and ivory are critical materials, elaborate typological studies have been made of the stylistic and functional changes in such diverse items as harpoons and the winged ivory objects fastened to the butts of harpoons (Figure 12.20). Other artifacts include picks made of walrus tusk and snow shovels and wedges of ivory and bone, as well as drills and domestic utensils. Studying such a range of bone artifacts is complicated by the elaborate and variable engraved designs applied to some, but H. B. Collins and others have been able to trace the develop-

Figure 12.19 Magdalenian harpoons from France, around 15,000 years ago. (About two-thirds actual size)

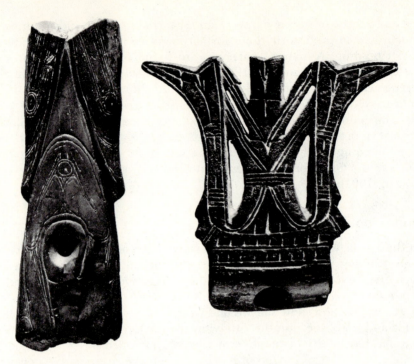

Figure 12.20 Bone and ivory artifacts. Left: Harpoon socket piece, Old Bering Sea style (9.5 cm long). Right: Turreted ivory object of the Punuk phase (7 cm wide). (From the University of Alaska Museum; used by permission)

ment of the harpoon of the Northern Maritime Eskimo, from the elaborate types of the Okvik and Old Bering Sea phases to the simpler forms characteristic of the Punuk phase and the modern Eskimo weapons (Collins, 1937; Fitzhugh, 1988).

Functional Analysis   In some areas, such as the Arctic and southern Africa, contemporary ethnographic accounts can be used for fruitful analogies with prehistoric tools. There are, however, dangers to this approach. Although no one can seriously doubt the functional classification of the Old Bering Sea harpoon socket in Figure 12.20, a classification based firmly in analogies, the situation is more complex for the remote past. The Magdalenian peoples who lived in southwestern France 15,000 years ago made extensive use of bone and antler to produce a wide range of artifacts, ranging from spear throwers to harpoons and thong straighteners.

Technological Analysis   The way in which the tool was made is the subject of technological analysis. The simplest bone technologies involved splitting and flaking bones. Fine points were produced by polishing slivers of bone against grinding surfaces. The Magdalenians used fine lengths of reindeer antler, which they removed from the beam by grooving through the hard outer core of the antler with stone burins or engraving tools. It is no coincidence that their material culture includes a wide range of scraping and graving tools (White, 1986).

As with all technological analyses, ethnographic analogy and experimentation with prehistoric boneworking methods under controlled modern conditions provide the best insights into early toolmaking (Coles, 1973).

WOOD

Nonhuman primates sometimes use sticks to obtain grubs, or for other purposes, so it is logical to assume that since the earliest times, humans may have used sticks also. Wood implements form a major part of many modern hunter-gatherer tool kits; occasional tantalizing glimpses of prehistoric wood artifacts have come down to us where preservation conditions have been favorable. One of the earliest is a fire-hardened spearpoint found in the Clacton Channel, England, which dates to the Holstein interglacial, thought to be around 150,000 B.P. (Clark, 1970). Numerous wood artifacts, as well as basketry, have come from dry sites in western North America (Fagan, 1990).

The Ozette prehistoric village on the Olympia Peninsula in Washington was buried by a prehistoric landslide that covered up not only several wood longhouses but also many domestic artifacts, baskets, boxes, and other fine wooden tools. The waterlogged conditions preserved fibers and delicate halibut fishhooks complete with their bindings. Richard Daugherty's most important wooden find was a ritual whale fin carved in cedar wood, decorated with seven hundred sea otter teeth (Figure 12.21). One of Captain Cook's artists drew a similar artifact during his voyage of exploration to the Pacific Northwest coast in 1778, but no modern examples survive (Kirk, 1974).

Wood Technology and Analysis

The manufacture of wood tools involves such well-understood mechanical processes as cutting, whittling, scraping, planing, carving, and polishing. Fire was often used to harden sharpened spearpoints, and oil and paint imparted a fine sheen and appearance to all kinds of wood artifacts. On the rare occasions when wood artifacts are preserved, important clues to their manufacture can be obtained by closely examining the objects themselves. Unfinished tools are very useful, especially handles and weapons that have been blocked out but not finished (Coles and others, 1978; Coles and Coles, 1986). Even more revealing are wood fragments from abandoned buildings, fortifications, and even track walkways. Microscopic

Figure 12.21 A whale fin carved from cedar wood and inlaid with more than seven hundred sea otter teeth, found at Ozette, Washington. The teeth at the base are set in the design of a mythical bird with a whale in its talons.

analysis of wood fragments and charcoal can provide information on the woods used to build houses, canoes, and other such objects. On very rare occasions, stone projectile heads and axes have been recovered in both waterlogged and dry conditions where their wood handles and shafts have survived, together with the thongs used to bind stone to wood. The Ozette excavations yielded complete house planks and even some wood boxes that had been assembled by skillful grooving and bending of planks (Kirk, 1974).

In many instances, the only clues to the use of wood come from stone artifacts, such as spokeshaves and scrapers used to work it, or from stone ax blades and other tools that were once mounted in wood handles (Figure 12.22). Only the form of the artifact and occasional ethnographic analogies allow one to reconstruct the nature of the perishable mount that once made the artifact an effective tool.

One often forgets just how important wood was to prehistoric societies. The thousands upon thousands of ground stone axes in the archaeo-

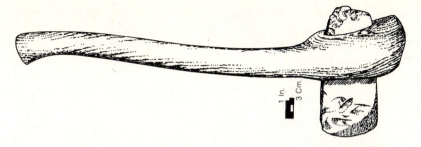

Figure 12.22 Artifacts as evidence for subsistence: a reconstructed Neolithic stone ax with a handle of ash wood. The handle is a copy of an example found in a Danish bog; only the stone is original, which illustrates how little of an artifact survives under normal conditions. (Approximate length, 30 inches)

logical record all once had wood handles. Wood was used for house building, fortifications, fuel, canoes, and containers. Most skilled woodworking societies used the simplest technology to produce both utilitarian and ceremonial objects. They used fire and the ringing of bark to fell trees, stone wedges to split logs, and shells and stones to scrape spear shafts (Drucker, 1966). Wood was probably the most important raw material available to our ancestors. It is a tragedy that it rarely survives in the archaeological record. But as John Coles and colleagues (1978) point out, wooden artifacts do occur, with greater frequency than has been believed, and very often finding them is simply a matter of investigating the localities where they are likely to occur.

BASKETRY AND TEXTILES

We do not have the space to discuss basketry in detail, but production of baskets is estimated to be one of the oldest crafts (Adovasio and Gunn, 1977). Basketry includes such items as containers, matting, bags, and a wide range of fiber objects. Textiles are found in many later, dry sites, and they are especially evident among prehistoric Peruvian artifacts (King, 1978).

Some scholars believe that basketry and textiles are among the most sensitive artifacts for the archaeologist to work with, culturally speaking, on the grounds that people lived in much more intimate association with baskets and textiles than with clay vessels, stone tools, or houses. Furthermore, even small fragments of basketry and textiles display remarkable idiosyncrasies of individual manufacture. Much research has concentrated on methods of manufacture and on raw materials, and it is only in recent years that people have realized the great value of basketry and textiles as time markers and as potential sources of information on social organization, subsistence activities, and technology.

In a remarkable experiment, Dale Croes and Jonathan Davis (1977) used a computer mapping program to study the baskets made by several families occupying a large house at the waterlogged Ozette site in Washington. They compiled a computer plot of the distribution of basket types and found that basketry activities were concentrated near the walls of the house. Using the computer, they then plotted and compared different attributes throughout the structure. The clusters that resulted from these analyses were used to show that basketry styles differed from family to family within the group who lived in the house. This is highly experimental research, but it does show the great potential for computer-aided studies of basketry and other artifacts. When preserved, baskets are amenable to the same kinds of functional and stylistic analyses as other artifacts.

Patricia Anawalt is a textile expert who has spent many years studying pre-Columbian garments depicted on Mexican Indian codices. This research has enabled her to work out some of the complicated sumptuary rules that governed military uniforms and other clothing. For example, the lengths, material, and decoration of Aztec men's cloaks were regulated precisely by the state. Even the type of knot was specified (Anawalt, 1981). Unfortunately, almost no pre-Columbian textiles survive in the archaeological record.

The dry climate of the Peruvian coast has preserved the wardrobes of Paracas nobles buried between 600 and 150 B.C. Paracas rulers wore mantles, tunics, ponchos, skirts, loincloths, and headpieces. These garments were embroidered with rows of brightly colored anthropomorphic, zoomorphic, and composite figures. Interpreting the iconographic patterns that appear on these ancient garments tells us something of Paracas religious and social customs (Paul and Turpin, 1986). One of the important functions of a Paracas ruler was to mediate between people and the supernatural forces that influenced and determined life's events. Many of the ruler's garments were adorned with shaman figures, showing that the wearer had a special relationship to the supernatural (Anton, 1988).

It is easy for archaeologists to become preoccupied with technology and artifacts, but as the Ozette experiment and other recent studies have emphasized, the potential is great for insights into prehistoric society and subsistence from such research, provided that the ultimate objective is to study people rather than inanimate objects.

SUMMARY

- One of the main inorganic materials used by prehistoric people was stone, especially hard, homogeneous rock, which fractures according to the conchoidal principle.

- We describe the basic techniques for manufacturing stone tools, starting with the stone-on-stone technique, the cylinder-hammer method, and the prepared cores used to produce blanks for Middle Paleolithic artifacts. Blade technology came into use about 35,000 years ago.
- Stone technology and artifacts were first studied by means of rigid "type fossil" concepts, which were superseded by functional analyses: artifacts were classified according to shape, dimensions, and assumed use. The functional approaches have in turn been replaced by attribute analysis, which involves the study of finished artifacts and also of the by-products of their manufacture.
- Lithic experimentation and ethnoarchaeology have leading roles in the study of stone technologies; edge-wear and petrological studies throw light on the trade in raw materials and the uses to which tools were put.
- Ceramics (clay objects) are a major preoccupation of archaeologists and date to the last 10,000 years of prehistory. We described the process of pottery manufacture, the various methods used, and the surface finishes employed.
- Ceramic analysis proceeds by analogy and experiment, research in which controlled experiments with firing and the properties of clay have had leading parts. The vessels themselves are studied by form and functional analyses, on the assumption that the shape of a vessel directly reflects its function. This assumption can be a dangerous one, however, and many archaeologists prefer to use stylistic analyses. Clusters of attributes are used now, also, in attempts to standardize stylistic classifications.
- Prehistoric metallurgy is a phenomenon of the past six thousand years. We described the basic properties of copper, bronze, gold, and iron and some of the cultural contexts in which metallurgy developed. Typological and technological analyses are used to study prehistoric metallurgy, with European archaeologists emphasizing typological comparisons based on minute stylistic variations.
- Bone tools are thought to be among the earliest of all artifacts. They are important in some areas, particularly the Arctic, as indicators of typological change. The functional analysis of bone tools is somewhat easier than that of stone tools or ceramics, for the uses of bone objects are often easier to determine. Technological analyses of bone artifacts have concentrated on the ways in which the tools were made. Ethnographic analogy also is important in bone studies.
- Wood artifacts are a mine of information on prehistoric life. The manufacture of wood tools involves well-understood mechanical processes, such as cutting and whittling, and these can often be identified even from unfinished artifacts. Stone artifacts and other materials have been found mounted in wood handles, and this provides insights into the uses of composite artifacts.

- Basketry and textiles are among the least understood of prehistoric technologies, but they offer unique opportunities for studying individual idiosyncrasies in the archaeological record, as well as providing useful chronological markers.

GUIDE TO FURTHER READING

Arnold, Dean E. *Ceramic Theory and Cultural Process.* Cambridge: Cambridge University Press, 1985. A well-written and closely argued discourse on ceramic ecology.

Binford, Lewis R. *Bones: Ancient Men and Modern Myths.* Orlando, Fla.: Academic Press, 1981. A provocative and far-ranging discussion of faunal analysis and bone technology in prehistoric times that draws on ethnographic analogy.

Clark, J. G. D. *Prehistoric Europe: The Economic Basis.* Stanford, Calif.: Stanford University Press, 1952. A classic essay on European prehistory that covers the relationship between technology and economic life.

Crabtree, Don E. *An Introduction to Flintworking.* Pocatello: Idaho State Museum, 1972. The best simple account of basic lithic technology ever written, by an expert with a lifetime of experience. Valuable glossary and clear illustrations.

Hill, James N., and Joel D. Gunn, eds. *The Individual in Prehistory.* Orlando, Fla.: Academic Press, 1977. Essays on ways in which one might identify the work of one human being in the archaeological record. Especially strong on pottery and basketry. For the more advanced reader.

Keeley, Lawrence H. *Experimental Determination of Stone Tool Uses.* Chicago: University of Chicago Press, 1980. An especially valuable monograph on use wear and stone tools.

Muhly, James D., and Theodore Wertime, eds. *The Coming of the Age of Iron.* New Haven, Conn.: Yale University Press, 1980. Essays on early metallurgy, ranging more widely than just ironworking.

Rice, Prudence M. *Pottery Analysis: A Sourcebook.* Chicago: University of Chicago Press, 1987. An excellent reference book for anyone interested in ceramics.

Shepard, Anna O. *Ceramics for the Archaeologist,* 2d ed. Washington, D.C.: Smithsonian Institution, 1971. The definitive work on ceramics in the New World. Technical and informative.

PART
Six

RECONSTRUCTING PAST LIFEWAYS

And I prophesied as I was commanded; and as I prophesied, there was a noise, and behold, a rattling; and the bones came together, bone to its bone. And as I looked, there were sinews on them, and flesh had come upon them, and skin had covered them.

Ezekiel 37:10

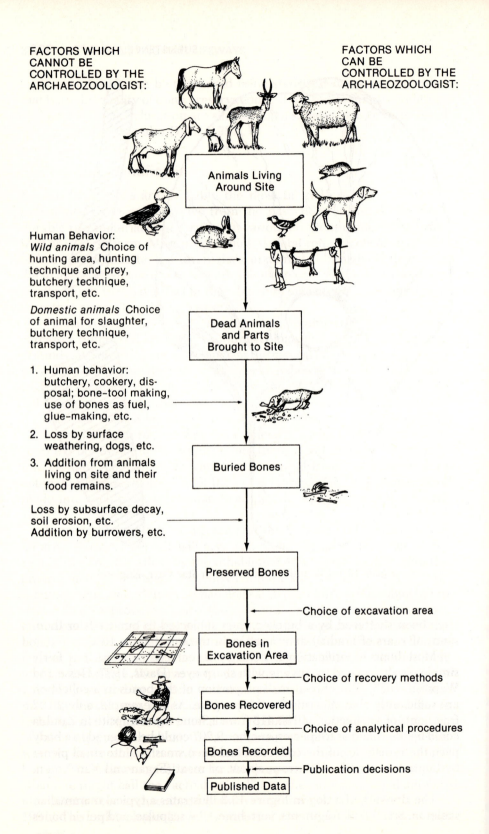

FACTORS WHICH
CANNOT BE
CONTROLLED BY THE
ARCHAEOZOOLOGIST:

FACTORS WHICH
CAN BE
CONTROLLED BY THE
ARCHAEOZOOLOGIST:

Animals Living
Around Site

Human Behavior:
Wild animals Choice of
hunting area, hunting
technique and prey,
butchery technique,
transport, etc.

Domestic animals Choice
of animal for slaughter,
butchery technique,
transport, etc.

Dead Animals
and Parts
Brought to Site

1. Human behavior:
   butchery, cookery, disposal; bone-tool making,
   use of bones as fuel,
   glue-making, etc.

2. Loss by surface
   weathering, dogs, etc.

3. Addition from animals
   living on site and their
   food remains.

Loss by subsurface decay,
soil erosion, etc.
Addition by burrowers, etc.

Buried Bones

Preserved Bones

Choice of excavation area

Bones in
Excavation Area

Choice of recovery methods

Bones Recovered

Choice of analytical procedures

Bones Recorded

Publication decisions

Published Data

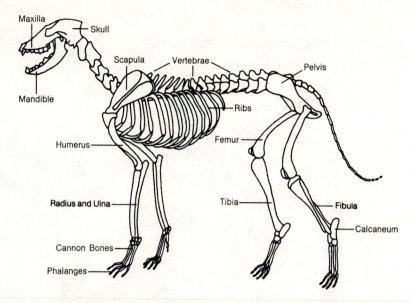

Figure 13.3 Skeleton of a dog, showing the most important body parts from the osteological viewpoint.

are normally of little use in differentiating a domestic from a wild animal or one species of antelope from another. Upper and lower jaws and their dentition, individual teeth, the bony cores of horns, and sometimes the articular surfaces of long bones are easy to identify (Davis, 1987). Teeth are identified by comparing the cusp patterns on their surfaces with those on comparative collections carefully taken from the site area (Figure 13.4). In some parts of the world, the articular ends of long bones can be used as well, especially in such regions as the Near East or parts of North America, where the indigenous mammalian fauna is somewhat restricted (Hole and others, 1969). It is even possible to distinguish the fragmentary long bones of domestic stock from those of wild animals of the same size in the Near East, provided that the collections are large enough and the comparative material is sufficiently complete and representative of all ages of individuals and of variations in size from male to female. But in other areas, such as sub-Saharan Africa, the indigenous fauna is so rich and varied, with such small variations in skeletal geography, that only horn cores or teeth can help distinguish between species of antelope and separate domestic stock from game animals. Even the dentition is confusing, for the cusp patterns of buffalo and domestic cattle are remarkably similar,

---

Figure 13.2 Analysis of bones from the archaeological record. The figure on the facing page shows some of the factors that affect the data. Factors that the archaeologist cannot control are on the left; those that the archaeologist can control are on the right.

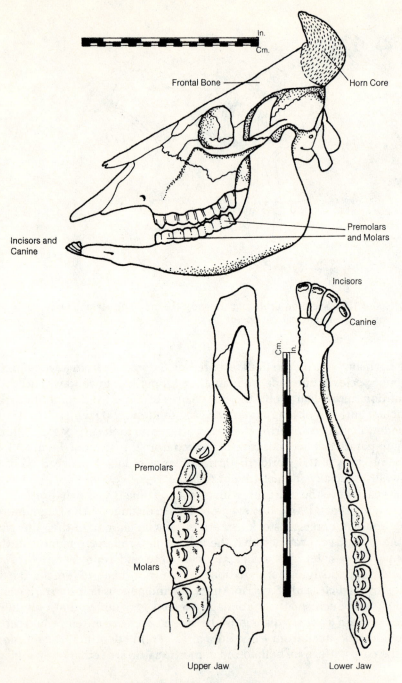

Figure 13.4 The skull and mandible of a domestic ox, showing important osteological features. (One-fourth actual size)

often distinguishable only by the smaller size of the latter. There is considerable disagreement among experts as to what constitutes identifiability of bone, so it is best to think in terms of levels of identifiability rather than simply to reject many fragments out of hand (Davis, 1987; Klein and Cruz-Uribe, 1984). For example, you can sometimes identify a fragment as coming from a medium-sized carnivore even if you have no way of telling that it is from a wolf.

The identification stage of a bone analysis is the most important, for several fundamental questions need answering: Are domestic and wild species present? If so, what are the proportions of each group? What types of domestic stock did the inhabitants keep? Did they have any hunting preferences that are reflected in the proportions of game animals found in the occupation levels? Are any wild species characteristic of vegetational associations no longer found in the area today?

Comparing Bone Assemblages

In the early days of faunal analysis, experts simply compared different bone collections by comparing the animals represented in each and the relative proportions of each form present. As Donald Grayson points out (1979), such figures have little value, for it is almost impossible to infer the living population from them. But zooarchaeologists Richard Klein and Kathryn Cruz-Uribe (1984) have developed measures of taxonomic abundance for assessing whether differences between assemblages are real or the result of biased collecting or other factors. They also use the same measures to make estimates of the relative abundance of different species.

The *number of identified specimens* (NISP) is a count of the number of bones or bone fragments from each species in a bone sample. This measure has obvious disadvantages, especially since it can overemphasize the importance of one species that has more bones than another or has carcasses that were butchered more thoroughly than those of other species. Both human activities like butchering and natural processes like weathering can affect the NISP as well. The NISP does have a certain value, especially when used in conjunction with an estimate of the minimum number of individuals from which the identified bones have come.

The *minimum number of individuals* (MNI) is a count of the number of individuals necessary to account for all the identifiable bones. This count is usually smaller than the NISP and is often based on careful counts of such individual body parts as heel bones. The MNI overcomes many limitations of the NISP in that it is a more accurate estimate of the actual number of animals present. However, everything depends on the experts using the same method of calculating the MNI—which they often do not.

The NISP and MNI together permit us to estimate the number of animals present in a bone sample, but they are highly imperfect ways of measuring abundance of animals in an archaeological sample, let alone of providing a means for relating the bone materials to a living animal population in the past. Klein and Cruz-Uribe (1984) have developed sophisticated computer programs to overcome some of the limitations of NISP and MNI, programs that lay out the basic information that is vital for intersample comparisons.

Species Abundance and Cultural Change

Climatic rather than cultural change was probably responsible for most long-term shifts in animal species abundance in the Ice Age. Some shifts must reflect human activity, changes in the way in which people exploited other animals (Klein and Cruz-Uribe, 1984). These changes are, however, very difficult to distinguish from environmental changes.

One of the few places where it has been possible to document such changes is in South Africa. Richard Klein has studied large faunal samples from two coastal caves in the Cape Province. The Klasies River cave was occupied by Middle Stone Age hunter-gatherers between about 130,000 and 95,000 years ago, during a period of warmer climate, and thereafter until about 70,000 years ago, when the weather had become much cooler. The seashore was close to the cave during the earlier, warmer millennia. Numerous mollusks, seal bones, and penguin remains tell us much about Middle Stone Age diet in the cave. Seabirds and fish are rare. Eland, a large antelope, is the most common large mammal, more than twice as common as the Cape buffalo. The rest of the land mammals are species common in the area during modern historic times.

In contrast, the Nelson's Bay cave nearby contains evidence of later Stone Age occupation, dating to after 20,000 years ago, much of it at a time when the sea was some miles from the cave, during the coldest part of the last Ice Age glaciation (Figure 13.5). Bones of flying seabirds and fish are abundant in this cave, whereas eland are only a third as common as buffalo.

Klein points out that tool kits are quite different in the two caves. The Middle Stone Age people of the Klasies River cave used large flake tools and spears. In contrast, the later Nelson's Bay hunters had bows and arrows and a rich tool kit of small stone tools and bone artifacts, many of them for specialized purposes such as fowling and fishing. These innovations allowed Late Stone Age hunters to kill dangerous or more elusive species with greater frequency. So the reason that the Middle Stone Age people took more eland was not that eland were more abundant in earlier times but that more elusive creatures were captured less frequently. There is every indication that the Klasies people were less advanced behaviorally (Klein and Cruz-Uribe, 1984).

Klein combines some other faunal evidence with his mammalian and climatic data. The Klasies River site contains larger tortoise and limpet remains, as if these creatures were permitted to grow to a larger size than in later times. This implies less pressure on the tortoise and shellfish population from a smaller human population before technologically more advanced people arrived.

Figure 13.5 Nelson's Bay cave, South Africa.

Game Animals

Though the listing of game animals and their habits gives an insight into hunting practices, in many cases the content of the faunal list gains particular significance when we seek to explain why the hunters concentrated on certain species and apparently ignored others.

Taboos   Dominance by one game species can result from economic necessity or convenience, or it can simply be a matter of cultural preference. Many societies restrict hunting of particular animals or consumption of certain game meat to one or the other sex. The !Kung San of the Dobe area of Botswana have complicated personal and age- and sex-specific taboos on eating mammals (Lee, 1979). No one can eat all twenty-nine game animals regularly taken by the San; indeed, no two individuals will have the same set of taboos. Some mammals can be eaten by everyone but with restrictions on what part they may eat. Ritual curers will set personal dietary restrictions on other animals; no one eats primates and certain carnivores. Such complicated taboos are repeated with innumerable variations in other hunter-gatherer and agricultural societies and have undoubtedly affected the proportions of game animals found in archaeological sites.

Examples of specialized hunting are common, even if the reasons for the attention given to one or more species are rarely explained. Upper Paleolithic hunters of Solutré in southwestern France concentrated on wild horses, apparently driving them over cliffs in large herds (Smith, 1966). The Archaic Riverton culture peoples of the central Wabash Valley of Illinois hunted the white-tailed deer as the basic meat staple in their diet to such an extent that the remains of this mammal were more numerous than those of any other species in the sites, except, in most cases, birds, fish, and turtles (Winters, 1969). The specialized big-game hunting economies of the Plains Indians are well known (Frison, 1978).

Overhunting   Another factor is overhunting, or the gradual extinction of a favorite species (Grayson, 1980). One well-known example is *Bos primigenius* (Figure 13.6), the European aurochs or wild ox, which was a major quarry of Upper Paleolithic hunters in western Europe and was still hunted in postglacial times and after food production began (Kurten, 1968). The last aurochs died in a Polish park in 1627. We know from illustrations and contemporary descriptions what these massive animals looked like. The bulls were large, up to 6½ feet at the shoulder, and often had very long horns. The male coat was black with a white stripe along the back and white curly hair between the horns. Professor Lutz Heck of Berlin has tried to reconstitute the aurochs by crossing breeds of cattle that exhibit characteristics of the wild ancestor. Heck's experiments were successful—forty "reconstituted" aurochs were living by 1951. The mental characteristics of the aurochs reappeared along with the physical ap-

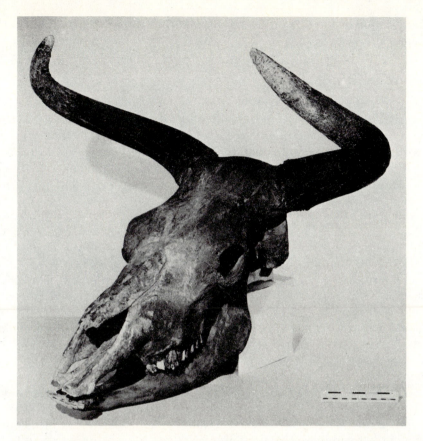

Figure 13.6 A *Bos primigenius* skull from Cambridgeshire, England.

pearance. Reconstituted aurochs are fierce, temperamental, and extremely agile if allowed to run wild. The German experiments have provided a far more convincing reconstruction of a most formidable Pleistocene mammal than could any number of skeletal reconstructions or artists' impressions.

Changes in Hunting Activities   Hunting activities have changed drastically in recent times. Richard Lee (1979) records how the older members of the San state that in earlier times there were more game animals and a bigger hunting population in the central interior of Botswana. Their forefathers used to hunt in large groups, killing buffalo, giraffe, and elephants. Today, their descendants have a predominantly gathering economy, supplemented by the meat of twenty-nine mammals, mostly those whose carcasses have a relatively high meat yield. Hunting is a common pursuit, the warthog being the most important source of meat, together with small game. This change in hunting habits results directly from the importation of Victorian rifles and from early hunting safaris, which decimated the wonderful African fauna within three generations.

Seasonal Occupation

Many prehistoric hunter-gatherers and farmers, like their modern counterparts, lived their lives in regular, seasonal cycles in which subsistence activities change according to the seasons of the year. The Pacific Northwest Indians congregated near salmon rivers when the seasonal runs upstream took place. They would catch thousands of salmon and dry them for consumption during the winter months. The early dry season in Central Africa brings into season an abundance of wild fruit, which formed an important part of early farmers' diet 1,500 years ago. How do archaeologists study seasonal activities and reconstruct the "economic seasons" of the year (Jochim, 1979)? Every aspect of prehistoric life was affected by seasonal movements. The Northwest Indians enjoyed a complex ceremonial life during the sedentary winter months. The settlement pattern of the Khoi Khoi pastoralists of the Cape of Good Hope changed radically between dry and wet seasons (Elphick, 1977). During the dry months they would congregate at the few permanent water holes and near perennial rivers. When the rains came, the cattle herders spread out over the neighboring arid lands, watering their herds in the standing waters left by rainstorms.

How do archaeologists study seasonality? A variety of approaches have been used with some success (Monks, 1981). The simplest method uses bones or plant remains. To illustrate this technique, in one case bird bones were used to establish that a San Francisco Bay site was visited about June 28, when cormorants were young (Howard, 1929). Grahame Clark has argued that the presence of cod bones in Norwegian sites indicates that they were occupied during the winter and early spring (Clark, 1952). This type of analysis is fine, provided that the habits of the animals or of the plants being examined are well known or have not changed through time. Some plants are available for much of the year but are edible only during a few short weeks. Knowledge about the ecology of both animals and plants is essential, for the "scheduling" of resource exploitation, though perhaps not explicit, was certainly a major factor in the evolution of cultural systems. Some species such as deer are relatively insensitive to seasonal changes, but people sometimes exploited them in different ways at different times of the year. The Coast Salish of the Pacific Northwest took bucks in the spring and does in the fall (Monks, 1981).

Then there are physiological events in an animal's life that an archaeologist can use to establish seasonal occupation. During the fifteenth century A.D., a group of Plains hunters regularly took bison near a waterhole at Garnsey, New Mexico (Speth, 1983). John Speth analyzed the body parts at the kill site and discovered that the hunters had a strong preference for

out, however, the problem is
alone but to establish what t
studies of caribou hunting ar
Alaska have provided a mass
exploit animals and are direc
mains (see Chapter 14).

Sex, Age, and Slaughter Pa
animal and the age at which
the hunting or stock-raising h
Archaeologists have used a va
from fragmentary bones (Da

In many mammal species
and build. For example, male
ally lack them. In humans, th
the male in order to accomm
proportions of males and fer
comparing the ratio of male
ences between male and fema
harder when less is known
fragmentary. Zooarchaeolog
distinguish sex, but such appr
cal difficulties; they work bes
be possible to identify differ
may not reflect differences k

How old were these cat
inhabitants concentrate on in
ones? These are the kinds of
sites. To answer them, one h
faunal sample at death. The
mine the age of an animal at
of limb bones. In almost all
unfused come from younger
classes: immature and fully gi
fuse, as is sometimes the case
additional classes. Unfortuna
to provide the kind of data

Fortunately, teeth and u
way of establishing animal ag
to the age of an individual
lower jaws allow us to study
we can identify not only the
animals as well.

Individual teeth can als
Some biologists are using gr
highly experimental. A far m

male beasts during the spring, the season at which the hunts took place. The butchers had abandoned body parts with a low meat yield like skulls and upper neck bones. In contrast, bones that yielded a great deal of meat, marrow, or grease were underrepresented at Garnsey. Many more high-utility bones like these were taken from males than females. Speth believes that the hunters concentrated on males because their meat had a higher fat content and they were in better condition than females after the winter months.

Growth patterns in animal bones can sometimes yield clues on seasonal occupation. The epiphyses at the ends of limb bones are slowly joined to the main bones by ossification as an animal ages. This approach can certainly give some clues as to the general age of an animal population in, say, a hunting camp, but such variables as nutrition, even castration in domesticated animals, can affect the rate of fusion. Some species, such as ducks, mature much faster than others, such as deer. Clearly, knowledge of the different ages at which epiphyses fuse is essential to this approach.

Everyone knows that teeth erupt from upper and lower jaws as one grows into adulthood, often causing problems with wisdom teeth in people. Teeth are such durable animal remains that many archaeologists have tried to use them to age game and domestic animal populations. It is easy enough to study tooth eruption from complete or even fragmentary upper and lower jaws, and it has been done with domesticated sheep, goats, and wild deer. Again, factors of nutrition, even domestication, can affect eruption rates, and the rate at which teeth wear can vary dramatically between one population and another (Monks, 1981).

In some cases, too, archaeologists have used reindeer and deer antlers to study seasonal occupations. The males of the deer family shed their antlers after the fall breeding season. By studying the antlers in a site, it is sometimes possible to establish the general season at which the settlement was in use (Clark, 1954).

Interpretation of seasonal occupation depends heavily on ethnographic analogies. One classic example is wild wheat. Botanist Jack Harlan (1967) has studied the gathering of wild wheat in the Near East and has shown that the collectors have to schedule their collecting activities very precisely if they are to gather the harvest before the ears fall off the stems or the grain is consumed by birds and other animals. It is reasonable to assume that the same precise scheduling was essential during prehistoric times, an analogy that has enabled Near Eastern archaeologists to interpret seasonal occupations on sites in Syria and elsewhere.

Seasonality is still a surprisingly neglected subject in the archaeological literature, but it has great potential. By studying not only large mammals and obvious plant remains but also tiny mollusks and even fish bones and fish scales, it may be possible to narrow the window of seasonal occupation at many sites to surprisingly tight limits. (Interested readers should consult Monks, 1981, for an extended discussion of various approaches.)

Domestic Animals

Nearly all domestic ani
tion to be sociable, facil
1981). Domestic anima
they were domesticate
Scholars have assumec
when a certain level c
everywhere seems to
regular food supply to
pendent on such cond
growth.

Wild animals lack
mestic counterparts. T
not the type produced
aurochs, ancestors of t
milk for their young, bi
erable changes have ta
characteristics in their
in the wild (Olsen, 19

The history of the
bones found in the de|
sites (Clutton-Brock ar
of wild and domestica
the bones in most sit
growth variation in dc
ertheless, a number of
cal change toward dor
the wild species of sor
with those of the dor
variations first increas
mals and less variatio:
and it is difficult to ide
or small collections.

The bones of dor
adaptability is inherer
change the size and |
corresponding effects
sheep, and other dom
ning of domestication

Slaughtering and |

Some insights into pe
be obtained by studyi
frequency and distrib

tools used by the skinners are found in direct association with the bones, so that the excavations preserve the moment of butchery for posterity (Wheat, 1972).

Interpreting butchery techniques is a complicated matter, for many variables affect the way in which carcasses were dismembered. The Nunamiut relied heavily on stored meat, and the way they dismembered a caribou varied according to storage needs, meat yield of different body parts, and proximity of the base camp. The animal's size may affect the number of bones found at a base site: goats, chickens, or small deer could have been carried to the village as complete carcasses, but of larger beasts often only small portions were brought in. Sometimes animals with high meat yield were consumed where they were killed and every scrap of flesh and entrails utilized. Even using the NISP and MNI indices, interpretation is difficult. Once again, the problem is to establish the meaning of archaeological distributions in terms of human behavior. Just how complicated this is in the context of butchery can be appreciated from Binford's comment (1978) that the Nunamiut criteria for selecting meat for consumption are the amount of usable meat, the time required to process it, and the quality of the flesh. The only way to interpret archaeological distributions is with a detailed understanding of the cultural systems that generated them (see Chapter 14).

VEGETAL REMAINS

Foraging, the gathering of wild vegetable foods, was a staple of the prehistoric world from the earliest times up to the moment when people first began to cultivate the soil some 10,000 years ago. Unfortunately, the foods that were collected or cultivated are very hard to find in the archaeological record, so our knowledge of prehistoric foraging and the early history of food crops is very incomplete (Hawkes, 1983; Rindos, 1983). Seeds, fruits, grasses, and leaves are among the most fragile of organic materials and did not survive long unless they are carbonized or preserved under very wet or arid conditions.

Carbonized and Unburned Seeds

These are normally found in cooking pots, in midden deposits, or among the ashes of hearths, where they were dropped by accident. Though the preservation conditions are not ideal, one can identify domestic and wild plant species from such discoveries (Ford, 1985; Hudson, 1979; Renfrew, 1973; Zeist and Casparie, 1983; Pearsall, 1989). Much early evidence for cereal cultivation in the Near East comes from carbonized seeds. Many more unburned vegetable remains occur in waterlogged sites and in dry caves. The Star Carr site in northeastern England yielded a range of fungi and wild seeds, some of which were eaten recently by European peasants

(Clark, 1954). A Stone Age campsite at Gwisho hot springs in central Zambia, on the edge of a tract of savannah woodland rich in vegetal foods, contained quantities of seeds and fruit preserved by the high water table in the spring (Fagan and Van Noten, 1971). Ten thousand identifiable vegetal fragments came from the occupation levels at Gwisho, many of them from six species eaten by southern African hunters, a remarkable continuity of subsistence patterns over more than four thousand years.

The extremely dry conditions of the North American desert West and of the Peruvian coast have preserved thousands of seeds, as well as human coprolites that contain a wealth of vegetal material. Hogup Cave in Utah was occupied as early as 7000 B.C. From about 6400 to 1200 B.C., the inhabitants relied so heavily on pickleweed seeds in their diet that the early deposits are literally golden with the chaff threshed from them (Aikens, 1970; Madsen and O'Connell, 1982). After 1200 B.C., deposits of pickleweed and the milling stones used to process it decline rapidly. An abrupt rise in the nearby Great Salt Lake may have drowned the marsh where the seed was collected, so the cave was only visited by hunting parties.

Tehuacán

The Tehuacán Valley in the state of Puebla, Mexico, has provided a record of continuous human occupation from the earliest times to the Spanish conquest (Byers, 1967; MacNeish, 1970). Early inhabitants of the valley lived mainly by hunting rabbits, birds, and turtles. Later, about 6700–5000 B.C., their successors subsisted mostly on wild plants such as beans and amaranth. These people, who lived in caves during the dry season, began to cultivate squashes and avocados; pollen from a plant that some botanists believe is transitional between wild teosinte and corn, through human selection, occurs in the cave deposits. Grinding stones, pestles, and mortars were in use for the first time, indicating that seeds were being ground for food.

Richard MacNeish has excavated more than a dozen sites in Tehuacán, five of which contained the remains of ancient corn; 80,000 wild plant remains and 25,000 specimens of corn came from the sites, providing a detailed picture of agriculture's origins in highland Mexico. The transitional pollens and cobs came from the lowest occupation level in San Marcos Cave, and the cobs were no more than 20 millimeters (0.78 inch) long. Coxcatlán Cave contained important botanical evidence, too, for by 5000 B.C., although the inhabitants of this and other sites were still gathering most of their vegetal food, 10 percent of the diet came from domestic cultivation—gourds, squashes, beans, chili peppers, and corn. One-third of Tehuacán's subsistence was based on agriculture by 3400 B.C., a period when the domestic dog first appeared; permanent settlement began soon after that. Pottery was being manufactured by 2300 B.C., and more hybrid types of corn came into use.

So many vegetal remains were found in the settlements of Tehuacán that the history of domestic corn in this area can be written in quite astonishing detail (Figure 13.8). Much controversy surrounds the ultimate ancestry of the maize. One school of thought regards teosinte, a native annual grass, as the ancestor (Beadle, 1981). Another, a long-lived theory, contends that the wild ancestor of maize became extinct some two thousand years ago, as did the early cultivated varieties, which were superseded by more modern forms (Mangelsdorf, 1974). Botanical evidence of this completeness is unique in the archaeological record.

Flotation Recovery

Flotation techniques have been employed systemically to recover seeds in central Illinois and also at Ali Kosh in Iran. The method uses water or chemicals to free the seeds, which are often of microscopic size, from the fine earth or occupation residue that masks them: the vegetal remains usually float and the residue sinks. Although this technique enables us to recover seeds from many sites where it was impossible before, by no means can it be applied universally, for its effectiveness depends on soil conditions. By flotation, Stuart Struever and his colleagues recovered more than 36,000 fragments of carbonized hickory nut shell from ovens, hearths, and storage-refuse pits in the Apple Creek site in the lower Illinois Valley (Struever, 1968). This settlement also yielded 4,200 fragments of acorn shell, as well as more than two thousand other seeds from at least three species. Few cultivated seeds were found, indicating that the inhabitants relied on hickory nuts and acorns for much of their vegetable diet (Asch and others, 1972; Smith, 1986).

Kent Flannery's experiments with flotation at the Ali Kosh site in Iran were also successful—indeed, the results were dramatic (Hole and others, 1969). After the first season of excavations, Flannery and his colleagues stated confidently that "plant remains were scarce at Ali Kosh." Two years later they used a modified version of Struever's flotation technique and recovered more than 40,000 seeds stratified throughout the cultural sequence at the Ali Kosh mound. The data gave a startlingly complete botanical history for the site, showing the increasing importance of emmer wheat and two-row hulled barley and the effects of irrigation (Figure 13.9).

Flotation has revolutionized the study of prehistoric vegetal remains. The methods used are being refined as more experience is gained with them under varied field conditions. Simple hand flotation systems were used at Ali Kosh and Apple Creek, where the deposit was hand-sorted and passed through fine meshes immersed in water. A variation on this method was used in dry areas. The samples were poured into mesh-lined sieves suspended in water-filled oil drums, and fine seeds were carefully removed and dried in newspaper before study.

A major goal of excavators has been speed, to recover large quantities of seeds in a relatively short time (Watson, 1976). A number of ingenious

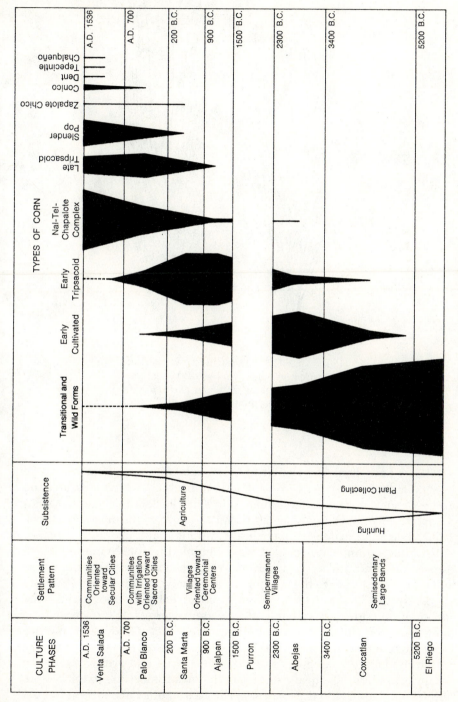

Figure 13.8 Evolution of maize in the Tehuacán Valley of Mexico.

Figure 13.9 Differences between wild and domesticated wheat: (a) the wild ancestor of one-grained wheat (einkorn, *Triticum boeoticum*); (b) cultivated einkorn *(T. monococcum).*

machines have been developed to carry out large-scale flotation; these include a device known as a froth flotation machine, which separates the archaeological material from its matrix in a special flotation chamber, with a mixture of water and chemicals to aid the process (Jarman and others, 1972). This is an expensive machine to assemble and operate compared with a much simpler device that was assembled for the Mammoth Cave excavations in Kentucky, in which water is forced through a pressure hose and a shower head onto the bottom of a screened container that sits inside an oil drum (Figure 13.10). The sample of earth is poured into the screened container and agitated by the water pouring into the screen. The light plant remains and other fine materials float on the water and are carried out of the container by a sluiceway that leads to fine mesh screens, where the finds are caught, wrapped in fine cloth, and preserved for the botanists to study. The heavy sludge, in the meantime, sinks to the bottom of the container inside the oil drum. This Mammoth Cave system has the

Figure 13.10 A simple flotation device used at Mammoth Cave in western Kentucky.

advantage of being cheap to make and easy to operate. It is estimated to process about 0.50 cubic meter of deposit per working day. To work most effectively, the system has to be close to a source of running water, whether a river or a faucet.

Flotation is rewriting the early history of farming in all parts of the world (Zeist and Casparie, 1983), partly because it yields much larger samples of domestic and wild seeds to work with. In the southeastern United States, flotation samples have revealed that maize and bean cultivation were widespread in fertile river valleys by the early second millennium A.D. (Smith, 1986). (Archaeologists sometimes distinguish between horticulture, cultivation using simple hoe and digging stick techniques, and agriculture, more intensified cultivation often using plows, irrigation, and sometimes animals.)

Andrew Moore excavated a Stone Age farming village at Abu Hureyra on the Euphrates River in Syria and obtained large samples of emmer, einkorn, and barley, staple cereal crops that were rotated with pulses like lentils, vetches, and chickpeas. Between about 7500 and 5500 B.C., the people developed more productive strains of food crops. But they still supplemented their diet by collecting significant quantities of wild vegetable foods (Moore, 1983, 1985). They lived in the same place for a long period of time because they rotated their crops and used a simple fallow system that allowed exhausted fields to recover before being replanted.

Grain Impressions

Apart from the seeds themselves, which reveal what the food plants were, grain impressions in the walls of clay vessels or adobe brick help to uncover the history of agriculture or gathering. The microscopic casts of grains that adhered to the wet clay of a pot while it was being made are preserved in the firing and can be identified with a microscope. Numerous grain impressions have been found in European handmade pottery from the end of the Stone Age (Figure 13.11). Indeed, a remarkably complete crop history of prehistoric Europe has been pieced together from grain impressions. The most abundantly cultivated cereal in prehistoric Europe was emmer wheat *(Triticum dicoccum);* wheat was the most important grain during early farming times, but barley rose into prominence during the Bronze Age (Renfrew, 1973; Champion and others, 1984). Grain impressions have been studied in the Near East and the western Sahara; some related work on adobe bricks has been carried out in the western United States (Darrah, 1938).

Palynology

The study of pollen has been an extremely valuable tool for studying European forest clearance (Figure 13.12). Many years ago, Danish botanist Johannes Iversen was studying pollen diagrams from Scandinavian peat sequences when he noticed a remarkably sudden change in the composition of the forests at the beginning of the sub-Boreal period (Iversen, 1941). The components of high forest—oak, ash, beech, and elm—simultaneously declined, while the pollens of grasses increased sharply. At one locality Iversen found a charcoal layer immediately underlying the zone where forest trees declined. The increase in grass pollens was also associated with the appearance of several cultivation weeds, including *plantago,* which is characteristically associated with cereal agriculture in Europe and went with European farmers throughout the world, even to North America. Iversen concluded that the tree cover vanished as a direct

Figure 13.11 A grain impression from a Neolithic pot at Hurst Fen, Cambridgeshire, England.

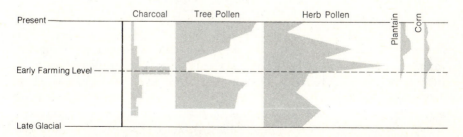

Figure 13.12 Fluctuation in frequencies of charcoal and fossil pollen brought by Neolithic colonization, Ordrup Mose, Denmark. The amount of grass pollen rises sharply as the forest decreases. (After Iversen)

result of farming activity—humanity's first major imprint on the environment. Similar pollen curves have been plotted from data gathered elsewhere in Europe.

Plant Phytolith Analysis

Opal phytoliths are created from hydrated silica dissolved in groundwater that is absorbed through a plant's roots and carried through its vascular system (Dunn, 1983; Rovner, 1983; Piperno, 1988). Silica production is continuous throughout the growth of a plant. Phytolith samples are collected in much the same way as pollen samples, then studied by identifying individual species. Most research in the field has been with grasses, and so the archaeological applications are obvious, especially in the study of prehistoric agriculture.

Archaeological applications of phytolith research have hardly begun, but the method shows great promise. A study of phytoliths from two sites in north-central Wyoming, one dating to about 9000 B.C., the other occupied from 5000 B.C. to the present, revealed that the earlier location was occupied during a warmer climatic period. The earliest inhabitants of the later site also lived in a warmer climate, but the weather cooled off around 1000 B.C. Other studies of this type have been conducted, but the research is still isolated. More has been attempted with prehistoric agriculture. Anna Roosevelt used phytolith analysis on sites in the Orinoco River Valley of Venezuela. She found that the percentages of grass phytoliths increased dramatically at the very moment when maize was introduced to the area, as indicated by carbon 13 and carbon 12 analysis of skeletal material and actual seeds. A similar result was obtained at the Early Preclassic site of Cuello in Belize, where carbonized seeds came from a level where phytolith quantities also suggested the presence of maize (Hammond and Miksicek, 1981).

Phytolith analysis has many potential applications in archaeology in the study of diet, by using coprolites and even phytoliths embedded in jawbones, but research is still in its infancy. It is likely to become as important as palynology in the years to come.

Interpreting Evidence

No matter how effective the recovery techniques used for vegetal remains, the picture of either food gathering or agriculture is bound to be incomplete. A look at modern hunter-gatherers reveals the problem (Lee, 1979). The !Kung San of the Kalahari in southern Africa are classic hunter-gatherers who appear in every book on ethnography, yet until comparatively recently, little was known of their ecology or subsistence patterns. Many early writers on hunter-gatherers assumed that the !Kung relied on game alone and lived in perennial starvation that was relieved periodically by meat-eating orgies. In fact, nothing could be further from the truth.

Much subsistence activity of the San and other hunter-gatherers is conducted by the women, who gather wild vegetable foods that comprise a substantial part of their diet. Many early observers were naturally preoccupied with hunting techniques and more spectacular subsistence activities, for in former times many people pursued larger game, often cooperating with other bands in the chase.

Today, vegetable foods have a leading part in the San diet and have presumably increased in importance as the large game herds have diminished. The San know of at least eighty-five species of edible fruit, seeds, and plants; of this enormous subsistence base, they eat regularly only some nine species, especially the *bauhinia.* In a famine year or when prime vegetable food sources are exhausted, they turn to other species, having an excellent cushion of edible food to fall back on when their conventional diet staple is scarce. Theoretically, therefore, the San can never starve, even if food is scarce at times. Their territory, of course, is delineated in part by available sources of vegetable foods as well as by water supplies; its frontiers in many cases represent a day's walking distance out to the gathering grounds and back to the base camp.

AGRICULTURE AND DOMESTIC AND WILD ANIMALS

Very few subsistence-farming peoples have ever relied on agricultural products or their herds alone to provide them with food the year around. Hunting, fishing, and gathering have always supplemented the diet, and in famine years or times of epidemic the people have fallen back on the natural resources of their environment for survival.

Since food production has led to increased population densities, however, famine often ensues because the resource base of wild foods for farmers is smaller than that which may have supported a smaller hunter-gatherer population in comfort (Scudder, 1962). Even in times of plenty, most food producers rely on game for some of their meat, as evidenced by the bones of wild animals in faunal collections where cattle and small stock are also present. The proportions of domestic and wild species in such a collection are important in assessing the roles of hunting and pastoralism in the economy. If such figures are based on how many individuals are represented in the collection or on some sound formulas, the results can be revealing, especially when a series of collections is available from a cultural sequence extending over several hundred years.

The changeover from hunting and gathering to full-fledged agriculture and animal domestication took place remarkably rapidly in many places. At Abu Hureyra by the Euphrates River in Syria, a tiny hunter-gatherer settlement was occupied just before 8000 B.C. by people exploiting a wide range of wild plants and game animals. Less than five hundred years later, the same location was the site of a sedentary farming village with far more elaborate dwellings and an economy based on farming of no less than seven species of cereals and pulses. Both the settlements relied heavily on gazelle hunting, until about 7000 B.C., when the Abu Hureyra people abruptly switched to the intensive herding of sheep and goats (Legge and Rowley-Conwy, 1987; Moore, 1989).

Deh Luran

Just how important an influence domesticated animals had on prehistoric horticulture and agriculture is well documented on the Deh Luran Plain in Iran (Hole and others, 1969). The inhabitants first cultivated cereal crops and kept goats sometime before 7000 B.C. Their first food production involved plants and animals introduced from the mountains to the rolling steppe of the plain. As the excavators point out, "What man did, before 7000 B.C., was to domesticate the annuals he could eat, and then domesticate the animals who lived on the perennials." The cultivation system was expanded so that domestic grains increased from 5 percent of the vegetal remains to about 40 percent between 7000 and 6000 B.C. But this early domestic plant and animal complex, based as it was on upland-mountain environmental adaptations, inhibited rapid population growth. Even so, the vegetational pattern of the steppe was altered as field weeds were established and land clearance and grazing removed the natural grass covering.

Between 5500 and 5000 B.C., some simple irrigation techniques were introduced that took advantage of the local drainage pattern. Barley cultivation became of prime importance, and the cultivation areas expanded. Sheep increased in importance, and cattle were introduced, the latter assuming a vital role in the economy only when plows began to be used around 2000 B.C. Each gradual or rapid change in the subsistence pattern or environment of Deh Luran instituted by humans led to a complicated chain reaction affecting every sector of the inhabitants' culture.

The rate of herd growth is affected by many factors, among them endemic stock disease, nutrient qualities of grazing grass, availability of water supplies, and in some areas, distribution of the dreaded tsetse fly, carrier of trypanosomiasis, which is fatal to cattle and harmful to humans (Lambrecht, 1964). Similar factors also affect the growth rate of domestic stock because the size of cattle or smaller stock can vary widely from one environment to another.

BIRDS, FISH, AND MOLLUSKS

Birds

Bird bones have been sadly neglected in archaeology, although some early investigators did realize their significance. Japetus Steenstrup and other early investigators of Danish shell middens took care to identify bird bones, including those of migrant birds (Lubbock, 1865). In 1902 the famous Peruvianist Max Uhle dug a large Indian mound at Emeryville on the eastern shores of San Francisco Bay. The site was excavated again in 1926, and Hildegaard Howard studied a large collection of bird remains from the dig. Her (1929) report illustrates the potential importance of bird faunas in archaeology. She found that water birds were the predominant species, especially ducks, geese, and cormorants, and that land birds distinctive of hill country were absent. All the geese were winter visitors, mostly found in the bay area between January and April of each year. The cormorant bones were nearly all immature, suggesting that the Indians had been robbing cormorant rookeries; most of the cormorant bones equaled an adult bird's in size, but ossification was less complete, equivalent to that in modern birds about five to six weeks old. Howard examined rookery records and estimated that a date of June 28 each year would be the approximate time when the rookeries could be raided. Thus from the evidence she concluded that the Emeryville mound was occupied during both the winter and the early summer, and probably all year.

Bird hunting has often been a sideline in the struggle for subsistence. In many societies, boys have hunted winged prey with bow and arrows while training for hunting larger game. A specialized bird-hunting kit is found in several cultures, among them the postglacial hunter-gatherer cultures of northern Europe. Though bows and spears were used in the chase, snaring was obviously practiced regularly. The birds found in some African hunting and farming sites are almost invariably species like guinea fowl, which fly rarely and are easily snared (Dawson, 1969; Fagan, 1967). No traces of the snares have been found in excavations, for they would have been made of perishable materials. Surprisingly little has been written on prehistoric fowling, perhaps because bird bones are fragile and present tricky identification problems (Avery and Underhill, 1986; Gilbert and others, 1985; Klein and Cruz-Uribe, 1984).

Fish

Fishing, like fowling, became increasingly important as people began to specialize in different and distinctive economies and as their environmental adaptations became more sophisticated and their technological abilities improved. Evidence for this activity comes from both artifacts and fish bones (Wheeler and Jones, 1989).

Freshwater and ocean fish can be caught in various ways. Nets, basket traps, and dams were methods in wide use from 10,000 years ago on, but their remains rarely survive in the archaeological record except in dry sites or waterlogged deposits (Petersen and others, 1984). Basket fish traps have been found in Danish peat bogs, dating to the Atlantic vegetational period (J. G. D. Clark, 1975). The ancient Egyptians employed somewhat similar traps, depicted in Old Kingdom tomb paintings (2600–2180 B.C.).

Nets remain the most popular fishing device and were used in northern Europe in postglacial times, too. A larger fish weir, constructed of vertical sticks four to sixteen feet long and sharpened at one end with a stone ax, enclosed an area of two acres at Boylston Street, Boston (Johnson and others, 1942). The weir was built about 2500 B.C. and was probably the work of coastal Archaic people. Such traps were evidently widely used along the Atlantic Coast, built in estuary areas where tidal currents were strong. In the Boston weir, brush and flexible withes were placed between the stakes; fish were diverted into the enclosure by "leaders," also made of brush, leading to the trap mouth. Some days' work must have been necessary to build this weir, which provided an almost inexhaustible food supply for its designers.

Fishhooks, harpoons, and barbed spearheads are frequent finds in lakeside or riverside encampments. The earliest fishhooks had no barbs, but they did have a U-shaped profile (Figure 13.13). Postglacial hunting peoples, such as the Maglemose folk of Denmark, used such artifacts in the seventh millennium B.C., in all probability to hunt the pike, a prized freshwater fish in prehistoric times (Clark, 1952).

Artifacts alone tell us little about the role of fish in the prehistoric economy or about the fishing techniques of prehistoric peoples. Did they fish all year or only when salmon were running? Did they concentrate on bottom fish or rely on stranded whales for protein? Such questions can be answered only by examining the fish bones themselves—or if they survive, which is unusual, actual fish scales. Perhaps the most effective method of collecting fish remains is by taking samples from each level, an approach advocated by Richard Casteel, who found that it was one-ninth as time-consuming as normal collection methods. Furthermore, he succeeded in identifying 30 percent more fish types from his column samples. This type of approach is particularly important on sites like the Glen Cannery site

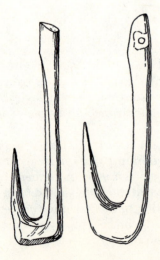

Figure 13.13 Bone fishhooks of the Maglemose culture in northern Europe. (After J. G. D. Clark; two-thirds actual size)

in British Columbia, where fishing was the major economic activity (Casteel, 1976).

The Chumash Indians of southern California were remarkably skillful fishermen, venturing far offshore in frameless plank canoes and fishing with hook and line, basket, net, and harpoon. Their piscatory skill is reflected in the archaeological sites of Century Ranch, Los Angeles, where the bones of such deep-sea fish as the albacore and oceanic skipjack were found, together with the remains of large deep-water rockfish that live near the sea bottom in water too deep to be fished from the shore (King and others, 1968). Five other species normally occurring offshore, including the barracuda, were found in the same midden. The bones of shallow-water fish, among them the leopard shark and the California halibut, were discovered in the same sites, indicating that both surf fishing and canoe fishing in estuaries with hook and line, basket, or net were also practiced.

The degree to which a community depends on fishing can be impressive. Lakeside or seaside fishing encampments tend to be occupied longer than hunting camps, for the food supply, especially when combined with collection of shellfish, is both reliable and nourishing.

Mollusks

Shellfish from seashore, lake, or river formed an important part of the prehistoric diet for many thousands of years (Waselkov, 1987). Augustin de Beaulieu, who visited the Cape of Good Hope in 1620 with a fleet of ships from Honfleur, France, was a curious and perceptive observer whose wanderings over the Cape Peninsula enabled him to describe the Khoi Khoi, the indigenous cattle herders and gatherers: "Also they go along the seashore where they find certain shell fish, or some dead whale or other fish, however putrefied it may be, and this they put on the fire for a little and make a good meal of it" (Raven-Hart, 1967). The identification of the mollusks in shell middens is a matter for expert conchologists, who possess a mine of information on the edibility and seasons of shellfish. With such data it was determined that the Khoi Khoi seem to have depended on shellfish at dry times of the year, when inland pastures were parched and vegetable foods scarce.

Freshwater mollusks were important to many Archaic bands living in the southeastern United States, but because each mollusk in itself has limited food value, the amount of mollusks needed to feed even a small band of about twenty-five people must have been enormous. It has been calculated that such a band would need between 1,900 and 2,250 mussels from the Meramec River each day, and a colossal accumulation of between 57,000 and 67,000 each month (Parmalee and Klippel, 1974). A group of one hundred persons would need at least three tons of mussels each month. Confronted with such figures, no one can believe that mollusks were the staple diet of any prehistoric peoples. Rather, they were a valuable supplemental food at times of scarcity during the year or a source of variety in a staple diet of fish, game, or vegetable foods (Bobrowsky, 1984; Waselkov, 1987).

When freshwater or seawater mollusks were collected, the collectors soon accumulated huge piles of shells at strategic places on the coast or on the shores of lakes, near rocky outcrops or tidal pools where mollusks were commonly found (Meehan, 1982). Modern midden analysis involves systematic sampling of the deposits and counting and weighing of the various constituents of the soil. The proportions of different shells are readily calculated, and their size, which sometimes changes through time, is easily measured. California shell middens have long been the subject of intensive research, with the changes in frequency of mollusks projected against ecological changes in the site areas.

The La Jolla culture middens of La Batiquitos Lagoon in San Diego are a notable example of such analysis. Claude N. Warren (Crabtree, 1963) took column samples from one shell mound and found that the remains of five species of shellfish were the dominant elements in the molluscan diet of the inhabitants. The changes in the major species of shellfish were then calculated for each excavated level. They found that *Mytilus,* the bay mussel, was the most common in the lower levels, gradually being replaced by *Chione,* the Venus shell, and *Pecten,* the scallop, both of which assumed greater importance in the later phases of the site's occupation, which has been radiocarbon-dated from the fifth to the second millennia B.C. Warren found that *Ostrea,* the oyster, a species characteristic of a rocky coast, was also most common in the lower levels, indicating that the San Diego shore was rocky beach at that time, with extensive colonies of shellfish. By about 6,300 years ago La Batiquitos Lagoon was silted to the extent that it was ecologically more suitable for *Pecten* than the rock-loving *Mytilus.* Soon afterward, however, the lagoons became so silted that even *Pecten* and *Chione* could no longer support a large population dependent on shellfish. The inhabitants then had to move elsewhere. Similar investigations elsewhere in California have also shown the great potential of mollusks in the study of prehistoric ecology.

Many peoples collected mollusks seasonally, but it is difficult to identify such practices from the archaeological record. Growth bands in mollusk shells have been used to measure seasonality, but the most promising approach is to measure the oxygen isotopic ratio of its shell carbonate, which is a function of the water temperature from which precipitation occurred (Lightfoot and Cerrato, 1988). Using a mass spectrometer, you can measure the oxygen 18 composition at the edge of a shell, obtaining the temperature of the water at the time of the mollusk's death. It is difficult to obtain actual temperature readings, but you can gain an idea of seasonal fluctuations, thereby establishing whether a mollusk was taken in winter or summer (Deith, 1983; Killingley, 1981).

Both freshwater and seawater shells had ornamental roles as well. Favored species were traded over great distances in North America. Millions of *Mercenaria* and *Busycon* shells were turned into wampum belts in New England in early Colonial times. *Spondylus gaederopus,* a mussel native to the Black Sea, the Sea of Marmora, and the Aegean, was widely distributed as far north and west as Poland and the Rhineland by European farmers in the fifth millennium B.C. The *Conus* shell, common on the East African coast, was widely traded, finding its way into the African interior and becoming a traditional perquisite of chieftainly prestige. The nineteenth-century missionary and explorer David Livingstone records his visit to Chief Shinte in western Zambia in 1855: the going price for two *Conus* shells at that time was a slave; for five, a tusk of elephant ivory. Archaeological digs have indicated that *Conus* shells were used in the Zambezi Valley seven hundred years earlier, reflecting a long history of trade in such prestigious ornaments (Figure 13.14) (Fagan, 1969). Indeed, as late as 1910, enterprising merchants were trading china replicas of *Conus* shells to the tribes of Central Africa.

Subsistence Data from Rock Art

Rock art is a major source of information on economic activities. Upper Paleolithic cave art in southwestern France depicts dozens of mammal species, perhaps meant to represent large, meaty animals that were economically (and symbolically) valuable (Rice and Peterson, 1985; Bahn and Vertut, 1988).

Much more detailed information comes from southern Africa. Some years ago, African archaeologist J. Desmond Clark published an account of Late Stone Age hunting and gathering practices in southern Africa in which he drew heavily on the rock art of Zimbabwe and South Africa. The paintings depict the chase, weapons, collecting, and camp life. Clark remarked, "In the rock art there is preserved an invaluable record of the people's hunting methods, the different kinds of weapons and domestic equipment they used, their customs and ceremonies" (Clark, 1959).

The rock paintings of Natal, South Africa, provide fascinating information on fishing practices and the boats associated with them. Patricia Vinnecombe (1960) recorded a fishing scene in the Tsoelike River rockshelter in Lesotho, southern Africa (Figure 13.15). The fishermen, armed with long spears, are massed in boats, apparently cornering a shoal of fish that are swimming around in confusion. Some boats have lines under their hulls that may represent anchors; the fish cannot be identified with certainty, but they may be freshwater catfish or yellowfish. Vinnecombe's paper generated much discussion—some authorities argued that the boats in the painting were probably made of bark (Clark, 1960). Another famous scene from the Cape Province of South Africa depicts a group of ostriches feeding peacefully; among them lurks a hunter wearing an ostrich skin, his legs and bow protruding beneath the belly of an apparently harmless bird. Such vignettes of prehistoric hunting life add insight into data obtained from the food residues recovered from caves and rockshelters, but the

Figure 13.14 Ingombe Ilede, Zambia, Central Africa: burial with *Conus* shells, around the fifteenth century A.D. The shells are the circular objects around the neck numbered 1–4.

actual interpretation of the art is subject to many sophisticated variables, among them the symbolic meaning of the paintings (see Lewis-Williams, 1981; Lewis-Williams and Loubser, 1986).

Not only rock art but even pottery can throw light on prehistoric subsistence. The Mimbres culture developed in southwestern New Mexico in the late first millennium A.D. and is famous for its black-on-white painted pottery that was produced mainly between A.D. 950 and 1150 in some twenty villages along the Mimbres River. The potters depicted humans, other mammals, birds, reptiles, fish, insects, and mythical creatures. About 11 percent of the images are fish, many of them species that can be identified as being native to the Gulf of California, over 450 miles away.

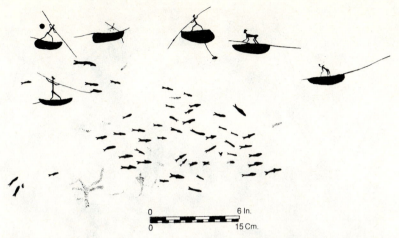

Figure 13.15 A rock drawing depicting a fishing scene from Lesotho, southern Africa.

Both the distribution of modern fish species and the marine mollusks found in Mimbres villages strongly suggest that the people were visiting the ocean, perhaps to collect marine shells for making beads (Figure 13.16) (Jett and Moyle, 1986).

PREHISTORIC DIET

The ultimate objective of economic archaeology is not only to establish how people obtained their food but also to reconstruct their actual diet. Dietary reconstruction is difficult, mainly because of incomplete economic information. Yet the problems involved are fundamental. What proportion of the diet was meat? How diverse were dietary sources? Did the principal sources of diet change from season to season? To what extent did the people rely on food from neighboring areas? Was food stored? What limitations or restrictions did technology or society place on diet? All these questions lie behind any inquiry into prehistoric subsistence (Gilbert and others, 1985; Sheridan and Bailey, 1981).

    Diet (what is eaten) and *nutrition* (the ability of a diet to maintain the body in its environment) have to be studied in close conjunction, for they are quite distinct from subsistence, the actual process of obtaining resources. The baseline for any study of prehistoric diet and nutrition must be surveys of modern hunter-gatherers, subsistence cultivators, and pastoralists. Unfortunately, however, lack of agreement among dietary experts is so widespread that it is difficult to estimate the caloric needs of prehistoric peoples (Dennell, 1979). So many cultural, medical, and physiological factors have to be weighed, even in modern situations, that re-

Figure 13.16 Mimbres painted bowl depicting a man spearing a large fish, sometimes interpreted as a whale.

search into prehistoric nutrition and food consumption will often be little more than inspired guesswork. Despite such recovery methods as flotation, it is still impossible to assess the intake of vitamins, minerals, and milk products in prehistoric diets. Nor do we have adequate data on the waste of food in preparation and storage or on the effects of different cooking techniques. Archaeological data can only indicate some of the foods eaten by prehistoric communities and show, at least qualitatively, how important some of them were generally. We are far from being able to ascribe precise food value to animal and plant remains, as would be demanded for precise studies of diet and nutrition.

Sources of Data on Diet and Nutrition

There are only a few sources of data on prehistoric diet and nutrition, and these are subject to serious limitations (Begler and Keatinge, 1979; Dennell, 1979). *Human skeletal remains* can sometimes provide evidence of ancient malnutrition and other dietary conditions (Huss-Ashmore and others, 1982; Larsen, 1987). For example, the parish church of Rothwell in Britain's Midlands has a massive bone crypt that houses the remains of more than 20,000 people disinterred from the graveyard when the church was expanded in the thirteenth century A.D., as well as skeletons from a nearby sixteenth-century hospice. A preliminary study of some of the bones has shown that many of these Medieval and later people suffered from malnutrition, as well as arthritis, tuberculosis, and other infections. Fractures were also common (Shackley, 1985).

Physical anthropologist Jane Buikstra has studied diet and health among the prehistoric populations of the lower Illinois Valley. As early as 5500 B.C., the inhabitants of this area began harvesting hickory and other nuts on an ever-larger scale. Nuts provided a high-quality food resource, but to support large numbers of people, they had to be harvested over large areas. As time went on, the growing population of the valley turned more and more to wild seeds, especially oily ones like marsh elder that were high in protein and a concentrated source of food energy. In time, they actually cultivated marsh elder as well as sunflowers, whose seeds had equivalent food value. They supplemented the oily species with starchy seeds like knotweed that were highly dependable and easily stored. In the last half of the first millennium A.D., the starchy seeds gave way to cultivated maize. By this time there was considerable competition for game and other wild-animal foods, and Illinois Valley populations may have ranged as high as 40,000 people. As much more complex social organization and regional trade evolved, Buikstra observes that dental diseases became much more common and tuberculosis spread among the dense village populations. The introduction of maize appears to have coincided with a deterioration in child health, too. However, the effects of intensification of food production on prehistoric diet and health are still little understood (Buikstra, 1984; Cook, 1984).

One promising technique involves identifying types of plant foods from the isotopic analysis of prehistoric bone and hair. By using the ratio between two stable carbon isotopes—carbon 12 and carbon 13 in animal tissue—one can establish the diet of the organism. Research on controlled animal populations has shown that as carbon is passed along the food chain, the carbon composition of animals continues to reflect the relative isotopic composition of their diet (Huss-Ashmore and others, 1982). Carbon is metabolized in plants through three major pathways: C_3, C_4, and Crassulacean acid metabolism. The plants that make up the diet of animals have distinct carbon 13 values. Maize, for example, is a C_4 plant. In contrast, most indigenous temperate flora in North America is composed of C_3 varieties. Thus a population that shifts its diet from wild vegetable foods to maize will also experience a shift in dietary isotopic values. Because carbon 13 and carbon 12 values do not change after death, you can study archaeological carbon from food remains, soil humus, and skeletal remains to gain insight into ancient diet.

This approach is of great importance to archaeologists studying the introduction of agriculture in different areas. Van der Merwe (1982) and

Valliant and Vogel (1978) studied fifty-two skeletons from ten midwestern sites dating from 300 B.C. to A.D. 1300. The delta carbon 13 value (reflecting the immediate carbon source of the skeleton) for premaize skeletons averaged -21.4 ± 0.78 percent, whereas those from agricultural settlements averaged -11.8 ± 1.3 percent. Another study of prehistoric populations in southeastern Missouri and northeastern Arkansas showed a dramatic shift in the delta carbon 13 value after A.D. 1000, when intensive maize cultivation took hold in the area. The researchers concluded that the maize was introduced several centuries after the Mississippian period began in this part of the Midwest, the period associated with intensive maize cultivation (Boulton and others, 1984).

The stable carbon isotope method is not restricted to use with agriculture; it has been applied with success to measure the reliance on marine species of prehistoric Northwest Coast populations in British Columbia (Chisholm and others, 1983). Forty-eight samples from prehistoric human skeletons from fifteen sites along the coast revealed a dietary reliance of about 90 percent on marine sources, a figure much higher than crude ethnographic estimates. The same data suggest that there has been little dietary change along the British Columbia coast for the past five thousand years, which is hardly surprising, given the rich maritime resources of the shoreline.

Isotopic and elemental analyses of prehistoric skeletons have provided a useful way of studying the origin and spread of maize in the New World by using stable carbon isotopes of skeletal collagen and a way of detecting the consumption of marine foods. There remain important potential avenues of inquiry. Can one, for example, establish the importance of meat in early hominid diets? The debate about the uses and limitations of the technique continue, but research proceeds slowly owing to the complex, multidisciplinary nature of the inquiry (Sillen and others, 1989).

Stomach contents and feces provide unrivaled momentary insights into meals eaten by individual members of a prehistoric society. Dietary reconstructions based on these sources, however, suffer from the disadvantage that they are rare and represent but one person's food intake. Furthermore, some foods are more rapidly digested than others. But even these insights are better than no data at all. The stomach of Tollund man, who was executed around the time of Christ, contained the remains of a finely ground meal made from barley, linseed, and several wild grasses; no meat was found in the stomach contents (Glob, 1969).

Many American scholars have studied coprolites (human droppings) from dry caves in the United States and Mexico. Most analyses have consisted of dry sorting and microscopic analysis, but more advanced techniques are being developed. Robert Heizer and his colleagues analyzed numerous coprolites from the Lovelock Cave in central Nevada (Heizer, 1969). Most of the 101 coprolites analyzed contained bulrush and cattail seeds; they also showed that Lahontan chub from the waters of nearby Humboldt Lake were regularly eaten (Figure 13.17). Undoubtedly caught with fiber dip nets found in the cave, they were eaten raw or roasted. One

Figure 13.17 Fish scale found in a human coprolite.

coprolite contained the remains of at least fifty-one chub, calculated by a fish expert to represent a total fish weight of 3.65 pounds. Adult and baby birds, the water tiger beetle, and possibly freshwater gastropods were also eaten. Collecting vegetable foods seems to have been done casually. The remains of large mammals were not found in the feces. Identifying large mammals is particularly difficult, except from hairs or splinters of heavy mammal bones.

Coprolites have been analyzed from stratified cave sequences in the Tehuacán Valley also. A diet of grass seeds and a starchy root known as *ceiba*, eaten as a starvation food, became common at the beginning of the incipient agriculture stage; this diet continued in sporadic use almost up to the time of the Spanish conquest (Bryant and Williams-Dean, 1975). Maize is conspicuously absent from the Tehuacán Valley cave coprolites, as though the crop was grown for tribute purposes and not eaten by the inhabitants—or ground so finely that the meal was digested without a trace. There is always the possibility, too, that the cave dwellers were living in a marginal area where maize cultivation was impossible.

Recent coprolite studies in North America have analyzed pollen grains found in human feces. Fifty-four samples from Glen Canyon in Utah showed that the pollen ingested by their owners could yield valuable information on plants eaten, seasonal occupation, and even the medicinal use of juniper stem tea (Bryant, 1974). Vaughn Bryant analyzed coprolite pollen from a site near the mouth of the Pecos River in southwestern Texas. He found that the inhabitants of the site between 800 B.C. and A.D. 500 spent the spring and summer months at this locality. During their stay they ate many vegetable foods, including several flowers. One danger of using pollen grains is that of contamination from the background pollen "rain" that is always with us. But Bryant was able to show that all but two of the species represented in the pollen were local plants. French archaeologist Henry de Lumley (1969) used pollen data from 400,000-year-old coprolites to determine that the Terra Amata Stone Age campsite near Nice was occupied in spring and summer. In all these instances, too, valuable insights were obtained into minor details of prehistoric diet, as well as into intestinal parasites such as were commonplace among peoples living on a diet of game meat that was often "high" (Horne, 1985).

Basically, information on prehistoric diets comes from the analysis and the identification procedures described in this chapter. Because the ultimate objective is explaining how people lived in the past, new theoretical frameworks, systematic use of ethnographic analogy, and quantitative methods will, it is hoped, intensify research on the dietary requirements of prehistoric peoples.

In this chapter we have focused on food remains and subsistence and not on the manufactured artifacts that also reflect the economic practices of prehistoric peoples. The next chapters deal almost exclusively with artifacts and artifact patterns. These often reflect specific human activities in the past, including ancient subsistence activities, and we will provide examples of those from time to time in the text as appropriate.

SUMMARY

- Archaeologists rely on many sources to reconstruct prehistoric subsistence methods. These include environmental data, animal bones, vegetal remains, human feces, artifacts, and prehistoric art.
- Zooarchaeology involves the study of animal bones. We described the sorting of teeth, horns, and some limb bones. Bone identification is carried out by direct comparison between modern and ancient bones.
- Game animal remains can give insights into prehistoric hunting practices. The proportions of animals present can be affected by cultural taboos, the relative meat yields of different species, and hunting preferences. Overhunting and extinction can also affect the numbers of animals in a site.

- Early domesticated animals are very difficult to distinguish from their wild ancestors. Domestication alters both the characteristics of an animal and its bone structure.
- Slaughtering and butchery practices can be derived from the frequency and distribution of animal bones in the ground. Teeth can be used to establish the age of animals slaughtered, but hunting and slaughter patterns are subject to all manner of subtle variables, including convenience and season of the year. Understanding the cultural systems of which the food remains are a part is essential for interpreting slaughter and butchery patterns.
- Carbonized and unburned vegetable remains are recovered from hearths and pits, often using a flotation method with water to separate seeds from the matrix around them. Dry sites, such as the rockshelters and camps in the Tehuacán Valley of Mexico, provide abundant evidence for early crop domestication; grain impressions on European pots are studied to reconstruct prehistoric agriculture in the Old World. Danish archaeologists have used pollen analysis to study forest clearance in temperate zones during early farming times.
- Bird bones have been much neglected, but they provide valuable information on seasonal occupation; fish remains reflect specialized coastal adaptations that became common in later prehistoric times. Hooks, nets, and other artifacts, as well as fish remains themselves, provide insights into both coastal and offshore fishing practices.
- Freshwater and saltwater mollusks were both consumed as food and traded over enormous distances as prestigious luxuries or ornaments. We cited the African *Conus* shell, which was an important trade commodity in southern Africa.
- Prehistoric diet and nutrition must be studied together, for they are distinct from subsistence, which is the actual process of obtaining food. It is difficult to estimate the caloric needs of modern peoples, let alone those of prehistoric groups. Despite such recovery methods as flotation, archaeological data can indicate only some of the foods eaten by prehistoric communities and show their importance in general. But this is far from ascribing their true caloric importance to prehistoric peoples.
- Human skeletal remains, stomach contents, and feces are the few direct sources available to us of information on prehistoric diet. The information they yield is limited, at best.

GUIDE TO FURTHER READING

Alas, no one has yet written a comprehensive book on subsistence studies in archaeology. Here are some volumes that cover aspects of this vast subject.

Binford, Lewis R. *Bones: Ancient Men and Modern Myths.* Orlando, Fla.: Academic Press, 1981. A provocative essay on animal bones concentrating both on ethnographic analogy and faunal analysis.

Davis, Simon J. M. *The Archaeology of Animals.* London: Batsford, 1987. A superbly illustrated, definitive book on zooarchaeology for beginners. Strongly recommended; comprehensive.

Hesse, Brian, and Paula Wapnish. *Animal Bone Archaeology.* Washington, D.C.: Taraxacum, 1985. A basic manual on zooarchaeology for working archaeologists.

Klein, Richard G., and Kathryn Cruz-Uribe. *The Analysis of Animal Bones from Archaeological Sites.* Chicago: University of Chicago Press, 1984. The authors describe statistical approaches to faunal analysis. A book for more advanced readers.

Olsen, Stanley J. *Osteology for the Archaeologist,* rev. ed. Cambridge: Peabody Museum, 1979. A primer for archaeologists on bone identification and analysis, oriented toward the New World.

Renfrew, Jane. *Paleoethnobotany.* London: Methuen, 1973. A primer on prehistoric vegetal remains that is oriented toward the Old World but has wide implications. A useful introduction to this complex subject.

Chapter
14

Analogy, Middle-Range Theory, and the Living Past

*I*n Chapter 1 we described a new and exciting goal of archaeology: decoding the archaeological record, using the present in the service of the past, as Lewis Binford (1983a) puts it. So far, we have considered the processes of archaeological research—data acquisition, analysis, and interpretation. It is now time to look more closely at the relationship between past and present, at what Binford calls middle-range theory, at analogy, ethnoarchaeology, and experimental archaeology. These are the tools that archaeologists use to bridge the gap between the world of the past and the archaeological record of the present.

EARLY COMPARISONS

For well over a century anthropologists have been working among non-Western peoples. They have recovered a mass of information of great interpretative value, much of it still buried in museum storerooms and archives. For their part, archaeologists have long recognized the value of comparisons between prehistoric and modern cultures. In Part One we discussed the evolutionists of the late nineteenth century, who considered living tribes to be good examples of successive stages of development in culture history. Each stage of cultural development was correlated with a stage of technology, a form of the family, a kind of religious belief, and a type of political control that could be observed in some living group of people. Thus the Australian Aborigines, the Eskimo, and the San, who retained a hunter-gatherer way of life, manufactured stone tools, and had no knowledge of metallurgy, were considered to be living representatives of Paleolithic peoples. British geologist W. J. Sollas wrote a bestseller titled *Ancient Hunters* in 1911. In this famed work, he went so far as to equate the living Eskimo with the Magdalenians of Upper Paleolithic France, who had lived more than 14,000 years earlier. Many early investigators thought that the most primitive Stone Age peoples were matriarchal, had no government, and believed in numerous spirits. They believed it was perfectly in order to turn to the literature on Eskimo, or other living gatherers, for the "correct" interpretation of artifacts in the archaeological record.

This kind of simplistic comparison has been abandoned by Western archaeologists, who no longer believe in unilineal evolution. In the Soviet Union, however, unilineal schemes of evolution formed an important part of Marxist-Leninist doctrine until recently. Older Soviet archaeological monographs referred to the "correct stage of development" in order to interpret the social structure of archaeologically known peoples (Rudenko, 1961). For them, the first stage of prehistoric Eskimo culture was characterized by primitive communism and a matriarchal form of the family, when in fact modern anthropological observations record all known Eskimo groups as patrilocal. American sailors traded with the Eskimo, argues Rudenko, and so they became patrilocal!

ANALOGY

Analogy is a process of reasoning that assumes that if objects have some similar attributes, they will share other similarities as well. It involves using a known, identifiable phenomenon to identify unknown ones of broadly similar type. It implies that a particular relationship exists between two or more phenomena because the same relationship may be observed in a similar situation. Our abilities to reason by analogy are often tested in aptitude examinations by such questions as this: "A fish is to water as a bird is to: (a) a tree, (b) a house, (c) air, (d) grass seed." Obviously, if we grasp the relationship between fish and water, we will have no trouble completing the question. Analogy in archaeology involves inferring that the relationships among various traces of human activity in the archaeological record are the same as or similar to those of similar phenomena found among modern "primitive" peoples. Analogies in archaeology only suggest what modern human behavior is capable of and what the boundaries of prehistoric behavior *might* have been. One can use them to generate hypotheses that can then be tested by real archaeological data.

Archaeologists use analogy on many levels. In a simple one, someone infers that small, pointed pieces of stone are projectile points because there are ethnographic records of peoples making small, pointed pieces of stone for the tips of lances or arrows. People often make use of an ethnographic name, such as *arrowhead,* as a label for an artifact. In doing so, they are assuming that their artifact type, which they recognize by attributes whose presence cannot be explained by natural processes, is identical in form to other, known arrowheads used by the people who made the artifact in question (Figure 14.1). But this simple analogy is a far cry from claiming similarities—or analogies—between the ways in which the prehistoric culture referred to used the arrowhead and the ways in which a living society uses it. To do the latter is to assume that the relation-

Figure 14.1 Eskimo demonstrating a sinew-backed bow and an ivory-tipped arrow at Chicago's Columbian Exposition in 1893. Archaeologists often make use of an ethnographic name, such as *arrowhead*, assuming that their artifact is identical to arrowheads used by the people who made the artifact. This is a simple example of an archaeological analogy.

ship between the form and the function of the artifact has remained static through the ages. If you explain the past simply by analogy with the present, you are assuming that nothing new has been learned.

Many archaeologists make use of analogies based on the technology, style, and function of cultures as they are defined archaeologically. Grahame Clark (1952) wrote an economic prehistory of Europe in which he made systematic and judicious use of analogy to interpret such artifacts as freshwater fish spears that were still common in historical European folk culture. This type of analogy is secure enough, as are those about small, pointed pieces of stone claimed to be arrowheads (for discussion, see Wylie, 1985). Enough of these have been found embedded in the bones of animals and people for us safely to acknowledge that such tools were most likely to be projectile points. Still, we have no way of knowing if the points were part of ritual activity as well as the hunt. Similarly, the archaeologist will have information about how houses were constructed and what they looked like, what plants were grown and how these were prepared for food, and perhaps some facts on grave furniture. But the archaeologist will not know what the people who lived at this site *thought* a proper house should look like or which relatives would be invited to help build a house or what spirits were responsible for making crops grow or who in the house customarily prepared the food or whether or not the people believed in life after death. Most analogies drawn from the ideas and beliefs of present-day people are probably inadequate (Asher, 1961; Thompson, 1956).

Archaeologists develop analogies in many ways. One approach is *direct historical analogy,* using the simple principle of working from the known to the unknown. In archaeological problems, the known is the living people with written records of their way of life, and the unknown is their ancestors for whom we have no written records. Text-aided analogies involve using written records to interpret archaeological data. Ivor Noël Hume, working at the Colonial settlement on Martin's Hundred, Virginia, found some short strands of gold and silver wire in the cellar filling of one of the houses. Each was as thick as a sewing thread, the kind of wire used in the early seventeenth century for decorating clothing. Noël Hume turned to historical records for analogies. He found European paintings showing military captains wearing clothes adorned with gold and silver wire and a resolution of the Virginia governor and his council in 1621 forbidding "any but ye Council & heads of hundreds to wear gold in their cloaths" (Noël Hume, 1982). Using this and other historical analogies, he was able to identify the owner of the house as William Harewood, a member of the council and the head of Martin's Hundred.

Then there are analogies for settlements occupied by peoples who had no knowledge of writing themselves but who were contemporary with literate societies. Their customs or affiliations may be mentioned in the written records of their literate neighbors. The Iron Age inhabitants of Maiden Castle in Dorset, England, though illiterate themselves, were subdued by the legions of a thoroughly literate Roman Empire; the conquerors left numerous traces of their campaigns, both in documentary records and in the archaeological record. Sir Mortimer Wheeler's classic 1943 account of the investment of Maiden Castle in the first century A.D. owes much to the Roman records of the conquest (Figure 14.2).

According to the proponents of the direct historical approach, confidence in interpretation of past lifeways diminishes as we move from historic to prehistoric times. Analogies to living peoples become less and less secure as we grow remote from written records. Furthermore, the earlier the site, the more likely it is that site formation processes and other variables have affected the patterns of artifacts, food remains, and structures in the ground. Nevertheless, many archaeologists have taken a *functionalist* approach to analogy.

Functionalist ethnographies integrate various aspects of culture with one another and with the adaptation of the culture as a whole to its environment. Functionalism stresses the notion that cultures are not made up of random selections of traits but that cultural traits are integrated in

Figure 14.2 Aerial photograph of Maiden Castle, Dorset, England, stormed by the Romans in A.D. 43, an event described through excavation and analogy by Sir Mortimer Wheeler.

various ways and influence each other in fairly predictable ways. Much of processual archaeology, with its emphasis on adaptation and cultural systems, falls under the general title of functionalist archaeology. Functionalist thinking is evident in the way in which many archaeologists select analogies from the ethnographic data to help them interpret their archaeological finds. Because several ethnologically known cultures might provide reasonable analogies, functionally oriented scholars suggest selecting the ones that most resemble the archaeological culture in subsistence, technology, and environment—and are least removed from the archaeological culture in time and space.

We might want to know about the role of sandalmaking among the Great Basin Indians of six thousand years ago. Were sandals produced by men, women, individuals on their own initiative, or formal groups working together? If we consider sandalmaking an aspect of technology, we might turn to the ethnographic literature on Australian and San material culture, in which sandals are sometimes featured. Among both the San and the Australian Aborigines, domestic tasks are generally done by women working alone or with one or two helpers. The analogy might lead us to argue that sandalmaking was regarded as a domestic task by Great Basin people and carried out by women who usually worked alone. Conversely, weaving is men's work among the Pueblo Indians and is carried out in special ceremonial rooms; because much ritual performed there today reflects very ancient Pueblo Indian practices, we might be led to infer by analogy that the Great Basin people of six thousand years ago did not regard weaving as domestic work, and so it was carried out by men. No matter what alternative we chose, we would probably not have much confidence in our choice.

The selection of possibly appropriate analogies from the ethnographic literature is increasingly being seen as only the first step toward interpretation. Once several analogies are chosen, the implications of each are explicitly stated and then are tested against the archaeological data. In our example of sandalmaking among Great Basin peoples, the ethnographic literature provided conflicting analogies. If we want to gain confidence in selecting one analogy or the other, we must state explicitly the implications each would have for the archaeological data and then examine the latter again in the light of each implication. If sandalmaking were a domestic task done by women working alone, we might expect to find the raw materials for sandal manufacture associated with tools that more surely represent women's work, such as grinding stones for food preparation. We might also expect to find tools for sandalmaking (such as awls and scrapers for preparing fiber) among the debris of more domestic sites. We could anticipate that women working alone might introduce more variation into the finished product than might be done in products made by group effort or by individuals working in the company of other specialists. A contrasting list of implications for the possibility that men produced sandals could also be made, and both sets could be tested against the archaeological data.

Devising test implications is not an easy task. To find a measure for the amount of variation in a finished product that one would expect under specific production conditions requires sophisticated measurements, various statistical tests, and often experimentation among groups of people. Archaeologists willing to make the effort entailed in this approach, however, have found that they are able to discover more about ancient societies than was previously thought possible. Reasoning by analogy is, of course, an important part of this process, but it is only one step in the archaeologist's task. Analogies provide the material from which test implications are drawn; they are no longer ends in themselves. James Hill (1970) used this approach at Broken K Pueblo in Hay Hollow Valley, Arizona. He analyzed the functions of the ninety-five rooms of the pueblo using sampling techniques and artifact patterning for the purpose. Then he turned to the ethnography of living Pueblo peoples, identified three room functions, and hypothesized that the different artifact patternings in Broken K reflected the same three room functions. Hill then listed sixteen test implications based on the ethnographic data that could be tested against the excavated material. Testing suggested that most of his implications were confirmed. Or were they? Did the artifact patternings at Broken K Pueblo actually reflect functions similar to those of modern pueblos? More recent research has hinted that a more durable phenomenon, pueblo architecture, may in fact be a more accurate source of analogy for the function of prehistoric rooms (Adams, 1983). Another approach uses statistical analyses of human debris from different rooms (Ciolek-Torrello, 1984).

Recently, many archaeologists have questioned the validity of ethnographic comparisons for the remote past. Some argue that archaeologists should interpret their data through ecological connections, by invoking universal principles of evolutionary biology and ecology that operated in the past as they do today (Gould, 1980; Gould and Watson, 1982). Most scholars would not go so far, however. Analogy is not necessarily misleading, provided that the right criteria and research strategies are used to strengthen and evaluate inferences made from ethnographic and other analogies. (This is a complicated debate; see Wylie, 1985, for a recent summary.)

A great deal of archaeological analogy is based on guesswork, on the assumption that because an artifact is used in a specific way today, it was used in that way millennia earlier. The great contribution of the processual archaeologists has been not in their search for general laws but in their insistence that independent data should be used to test and verify conclusions from surveys, excavations, and laboratory analyses. The basic objective in using hypotheses and deductions—the scientific method, if you will—is not to formulate laws but to explore the relationship between past and present. This relationship is assumed to have two parts. The first is that the past is dead and knowable only through the present. The second is that accurate knowledge of the past is essential to understanding the present

(Leone, 1982). Lewis Binford (1977, 1978, 1981b, 1983a) has argued that conventional analogy based on guesses or hunches constitutes projection of the present into the past. By turning these guesses into testable hypotheses associated with theory, the projections into the past could be sorted out, according to their match against evidence that might represent their presence in the past. In other words, how do the image or images of the past we create match up against reality?

Whatever one's approach to archaeology, the leading problem in archaeological analogy is to let the present serve the past. Processual archaeologists try to achieve this end by three interlocking approaches, whereby they study the past by using the present:

Middle-range theory: methods, theories, and ideas from the present that can be applied to any time period and anywhere in the world to explain what we have discovered, excavated, or analyzed from the past.

Ethnoarchaeology: the study of living societies to aid in the understanding and interpreting of the archaeological record.

Experimental archaeology: controlled, modern experiments with ancient technologies and material culture that can serve as a basis for interpreting the past.

MIDDLE-RANGE THEORY

Lewis Binford (1977) was the first archaeologist to use the sociological term *middle-range theory* to characterize the body of theory that is emerging as archaeologists develop methods of inference that bridge the gap between what actually happened in the past and the archaeological record of today, which is our chronicle of ancient times.

Middle-range theory is based on the notion that the archaeological record is a static and contemporary phenomenon—what survives today of the once-dynamic past. As Binford (1983b) wrote in one of his notebooks: "The archaeological record is contemporary; it exists with me today and any observation I make about it is a contemporary observation." How can one make inferences about the past unless one knows "the necessary and determinant linkages between dynamic causes and static consequences"? The dynamic elements of the past are long gone. Binford (1981b) and others have been searching for " 'Rosetta stones' that permit the accurate conversion from observation on statics to statement about dynamics."

Middle-range theory begins with three fundamental assumptions:

1. The archaeological record is a static contemporary phenomenon—static information preserved in structured arrangements of matter.
2. Once energy ceased to power the cultural system preserved in the archaeological record, a static condition was achieved. Thus the

contents of the archaeological record are a complex mechanical system, created both by long-dead human interaction and by subsequent mechanical forces and formation processes (Chapter 7) (Schiffer, 1987).

3. To understand and explain the past, we must comprehend the relationship between static, material properties common to both past and present and the long-extinct dynamic properties of the past.

This new body of theory is often described as "actualistic" and is designed to treat the relationship between statics and dynamics, between behavior and material derivatives. It is actualistic because it studies the coincidence of both the static and the dynamic in cultural systems in the only time frame in which it can be achieved—the present. Archaeologists have long wrestled with a body of general theory for observing and conveying meaning to the archaeological record. Middle-range theory is quite distinct from this body of theory, for it is tested with living cultural systems and provides the instruments for testing the variables identified in archaeological theory. In other words, middle-range theory provides the conceptual tools for explaining artifact patterns and other material phenomena from the archaeological record. Michael Schiffer (1987) argues, in contrast, that the subject matter of archaeology is the relationship between human behavior and material culture in all times and places. Binford (1981a, 1981b) considers that the archaeological record is static and material, containing no *direct* information on the subject whatsoever. (For a critique, see Raab and Goodyear, 1984.)

ETHNOARCHAEOLOGY

Middle-range research is crucial to archaeology, whether one believes that this research is meant to specify the relationships between behavior and material remains or to understand the determinants of patterning and structural properties of the archaeological record. It is conducted by studying living systems (ethnoarchaeology) and/or by using historical documents or controlled experiments.

Ethnoarchaeology is the study of living societies to aid in the understanding and interpreting of the archaeological record. By living in, say, an Eskimo hunting camp and observing the activities of its occupants, the archaeologist hopes to record archaeologically observable patterns, knowing what activities brought them into existence. Sometimes historical documents can be used to amplify observations in the field. Archaeologists have actually lived on San campsites, then gone back later and recorded the scatter of artifacts on them or excavated them (Yellen, 1977). The earliest ethnoarchaeological work focused on specific artifact patternings and on studies of hunter-gatherer encampments that might provide ways of interpreting the very earliest human encampments of Olduvai Gorge and elsewhere. But a major focus of later work has been to develop archaeological methods of inference that bridge the gap between past and present.

Ethnoarchaeology is a form of ethnography that has a strongly materialist bias (Gould, 1978). Many archaeologists regard it as simply a mass of observed data on human behavior from which they can draw up suitable hypotheses to compare with the finds from their excavations and laboratory analyses. This interpretation is totally wrong, for in fact ethnoarchaeological research deals with dynamic processes in the modern world.

Ethnoarchaeology Among the San and the Australian Aborigines

Most, but by no means all, ethnoarchaeological research has been among hunter-gatherers, especially those perceived as having ancestry among earlier, prehistoric peoples. Both the San of southern Africa's Kalahari desert and the Australian aborigines fall into this category.

Anthropologist Richard Lee (1979) has spent many years studying the human ecology of the !Kung San of the Kalahari and has accumulated a mass of information that is of use to archaeologists. Archaeologist John Yellen (1977) worked with Lee, collecting data on house and camp arrangements, hearth locations, census information, and bone refuse. Yellen pointed out that a !Kung camp develops through conscious acts, such as the construction of windbreaks and hearths, as well as through such incidental deeds as the discarding of refuse and manufacturing debris (Figure 14.3). He recognized communal areas in the campsites, often in the middle of the settlement, which belonged to no one in particular, and family areas focused on hearths that belonged to individual families. The communal activities of the camp members, such as dancing and the first distribution of meat, take place in the open spaces that belong to no one family. Such activities leave few traces in the archaeological record. Cooking and food processing as well as manufacturing of artifacts normally take place around family hearths. Yellen points out some interesting variations on this pattern: manufacturing activities taking place at one hearth will sometimes involve people from other families; large skins will normally be pegged out for treatment away from main living areas because of vermin and carnivores. The !Kung study showed that it is dangerous to assume that activities with the greatest archaeological visibility, such as meat preparation or cracking of nuts, take place in special places. The activity patterning at !Kung campsites relates, for the most part, directly to family groups. Hypothetically, argues Yellen, it should be possible to use artifact clusters through time to study the development and evolution of such social structures.

Richard Gould (1978) combined archaeology and ethnoarchaeology in the Western Desert of Australia. He excavated the Puntutjarpa rockshel-

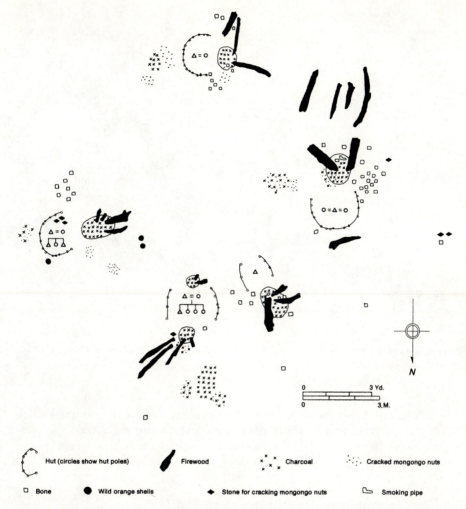

Figure 14.3 A San camp in Botswana, southern Africa, as plotted by John Yellen to show the layout of activity areas and artifacts. (After Lee and De Vore, 1976)

ter, where he found human occupation going back to about 6,800 years ago (Gould, 1977). The site is still visited by the local people, although they no longer live there. The later stone tools found at Puntutjarpa consisted of cores, flake tools, and smaller artifacts identical to modern Ngatatjara implements still in use today. By examining traces of edge wear on Ngatatjara tools and on prehistoric implements from the shelter, Gould was able to demonstrate remarkable continuity between past and present to the point where he could establish that some stone tools more than five thousand years old were hafted, even though no trace of the wooden handle survived. He also compared modern living surfaces with equivalent features found in the rockshelter (Figure 14.4).

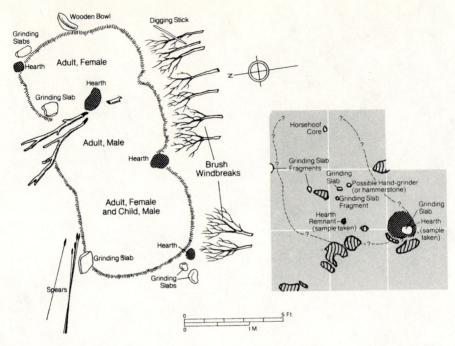

Figure 14.4 Comparison of a prehistoric camp site at Puntutjarpa Rockshelter, Australia, at the right, with a modern aborigine campsite.

Incidentally, it is of interest to note that San camps are compactly laid out, whereas Australian settlements tend to be more scattered. This may be a reflection of the danger to women and children at camp from predators, including lions, in the African environment.

Lithic Technology Among the Highland Maya

Although ethnoarchaeological investigations have tended to focus on hunter-gatherers, there are numerous instances of fascinating research on more complex societies, even our own. A major long-term study of modern urban garbage in Tucson, Arizona, for example, is based on the latest archaeological methods and research designs (Rathje and Ritenbaugh, 1984a, 1984b). The project is designed to investigate the relationships between resource management, urban demography, and social and economic stratification in a modern context, where some control data from interviews and other perspectives are available to amplify an archaeological study of a type that might be conducted at an ancient urban center. The Tucson garbage study has produced remarkable results, showing widely different patterns of resource management from one segment of the city's population to another, with the middle class being the most wasteful.

In an example of immediate relevance to archaeology, when Brian Hayden was examining Maya stone tools of the postconquest Colonial period from sites once occupied by a minor Mayan group known as the Coxoh, near the Mexico-Guatemala border, he discovered that some present-day Mayan-speaking communities in the area still made and used stone artifacts. Even after four and a half centuries of European contact, a few people were making *metates* in the traditional way, and simple stone tools still fulfilled many basic functions. There were no living Coxoh populations for direct historic versus modern comparisons, so the archaeologists studied stone tool technology among the most closely related groups they could find (Hayden, 1987).

The objectives of the project were to "record and understand the conception, life, death, and discard of lithic artifacts (or their substitutes)." The investigators combined descriptive research with highly exploratory, new theoretical approaches based on design analysis theory, among other things. The research was broad-based, concerned with the properties of the stone collected for tool manufacture, the efficiency of stone technology, and the evolution of the forms of stone tools as they were used and reused. The researchers looked closely at patterns of waste deposition and site formation processes and at the social and economic positions of stone-working artisans. They were able to work closely with a fifty-year-old specialist *metate* maker named Ramon Ramos Rosario, one of the few full-time specialists still working. Since his lands cannot support his family, Ramon makes his living manufacturing and selling *manos* and *metates,* selling them over a wide area of western Guatemala. He can sell more widely today because of improved public transport. In earlier years, he and other specialists would sell locally. Hayden followed Ramon through the entire manufacturing process, from the selection of the material to the final surface smoothing of the artifact. Time and motion studies showed that it took this expert two and a half days to rough out and smooth a *metate* blank using only stone tools and four and a half to five and a half days to finish both a *metate* and a *mano.* Finally, Hayden examined the characteristics of the picks used to chip and peck the rock as if they were archaeological finds, combining these studies with use-wear analysis. Hayden seriated the picks on the basis of the intensity of edge-wear development and as a way of estimating the relative length of use of comparable tools. He compared his results to prehistoric artifacts and was able to show that many blunt-edged Mayan celts in archaeological sites, tools that were of no use for woodworking, were probably used by women to repeck (roughen) used *manos* and *metates.*

The study also threw interesting light on site formation processes. For example, the stoneworker removes as much waste material from the *metate* blank at the quarry as possible to save weight. At the same time, he carefully conserves the stone tools used in roughing out blanks, caching them at the quarry and resharpening them to prolong their life. Observations like this, combined with specific environmental conditions, could one day provide a body of what Hayden calls "robust" middle-range theory.

The Mayan project also involved studies of stoneworking with bottle glass, studies that focused not only on manufacture and use but also on discard patterns and work areas. For instance, the Mayan stoneworkers of today discard their glass debris away from the homestead and often do their work outside domestic areas to avoid injury. Thus even a lithic specialist's house may not contain the higher proportions of stone debris that one might reasonably expect in the archaeological record.

The importance of the Mayan lithic study is that it demonstrates the power and potential of a many-sided approach to ethnoarchaeology, using data from the dynamic present to evaluate archaeological evidence from the static archaeological record (for extended discussion of this important project, see Hayden, 1987).

Nunamiut Eskimo

Lewis Binford and his students undertook ethnoarchaeological studies to help begin construction of middle-range theory. He decided to study the Nunamiut Eskimo of Alaska, 80 percent of whose subsistence comes from hunting caribou. His aims were to find out as much as he could about "all aspects of the procurement, processing, and consumption strategies of the Nunamiut Eskimo and relate these behaviors directly to their faunal consequences" (Binford, 1978). He chose to concentrate on animal bones rather than artifacts because although the bones were not human-manufactured, the patterns of their use were the result of cultural activity.

The Nunamiut depend more heavily on meat than any other hunter-gatherers known. Indeed, Binford estimates that each adult eats around a cup and a half of vegetable foods a year, supplemented by the partially digested stomach contents of caribou. In an environment that has a growing season of only twenty-two days, the Eskimo relies on stored food entirely for eight and a half months a year and partly for an additional month and a half. Fresh meat is freely available for only two months a year. Binford soon realized that the strategies the Eskimo used to feed themselves were based not only on game distributions but on other considerations as well. With such a heavy reliance on stored food, the problem of bulk was always important. Was it easier to move people to where fresh meat was available or to carry the meat back to a base camp where precious stored food was kept? It is no coincidence that the Nunamiut move around most in late summer and early fall, when stored foods are at their lowest levels. The Nunamiut's way of life involved complicated and interacting decisions related to the distribution of food resources at different seasons, the storage potential of different animals and of different parts of an animal, and also the logistics of procuring, carrying, and storing meat.

By close study, not only of the Nunamiut's annual round of activities but also of their butchery and storage strategies, Binford was able to develop indices that measured, in exhaustive detail, the utility of different body parts of caribou and to describe the butchering techniques, distribution of body parts, and methods of food preparation used. He showed that the people have an intimate knowledge of caribou anatomy, which is related to meat yield, storage potential, and consumption needs relative to the logistical, storage, and social needs of the moment. The field study also included analysis of forty-two archaeologically known locations that dated to earlier times.

The Nunamiut adaptation depended on long-term storage strategies that were keyed to two aggressive periods of caribou hunting, in spring and fall. That the Nunamiut were able to hunt the caribou twice a year was a factor of the topography in their homeland, which lies close to the borders of both summer and winter caribou feeding ranges (Figure 14.5). The movement of the people was keyed to seasonal game movements and to storage and other needs. Fall hunting was directed toward calves, whose skins were used to make winter clothing. Small, mobile parties of Nunamiut would pursue them, knowing that their prey would yield not only skins but also the added bonus of heads and tongues to feed the people who processed the skins. Without taking account of this fact, the Nunamiut would have been unable to maintain a viable cultural system.

What is the importance of the Nunamiut research? First, it provides a mass of empirical data on human exploitation of animals that is applicable not only to the Nunamiut and other caribou hunters but also to the interpretation of different types of archaeological sites in many parts of the world. Binford showed how local any cultural adaptation is, that of the Nunamiut depending on interacting topographic, climatic, logistical, and other realities. These adaptations are so local that he was able to draw a number of important conclusions:

1. The continuing dynamics of a local adaptation can result in considerable variation in archaeological sites.
2. There may be considerable interregional variations within a culture, which are reflected in different archaeological remains. Yet the inhabitants of one site were well aware of the general cultural variations displayed at other sites nearby.
3. The adaptive strategies and the factors affecting the people's decision making may remain constant, even if the archaeological remains show great variability.
4. Perhaps most important, changes in stone tool frequencies or pottery forms may reflect no significant change in adaptation at all. This can be determined only from sites where food remains and other such data are found.

"There is an unrelenting demonstration that the Nunamiut behave rationally in their treatment of animal foods," Binford (1978) writes. "This rationality is facilitated by a truly remarkable knowledge of animal anat-

Figure 14.5 The Mask site, a Nunamiut Eskimo hunting stand: (top) the hunting stand in its environmental setting; (bottom) caribou remains at the stand.

omy. It is facilitated by an outlook that is future-oriented. . . . The Eskimo are pragmatic, they are empiricists, and they are very skeptical of statements as to the 'right' way to do something."

Such ethnoarchaeological studies show that archaeologists can no longer assume that all variability in the archaeological record is directly related to cultural similarity and difference. They have profoundly affected archaeological studies of prehistoric hunter-gatherers, both on the earliest hominids and in more recently occupied areas such as the Great Basin (O'Connell, 1975). It has led to such fundamental cross-cultural statements of possible predictive value as "optimal foraging strategy"

(Chapter 15). So far, the main influence of middle-range theory and ethnoarchaeology has been on the archaeology of hunter-gatherers (but see Kramer, 1983; Krause, 1985).

Structures and Symbols

Ian Hodder (1982b, 1985) has taken a somewhat different structural and symbolic tack in ethnoarchaeological studies of farming and hunter-gatherer societies in tropical Africa. He studied the Nuba farmers of the Sudan and the Lozi of western Zambia, among other peoples. "Symbols are actively involved in social strategies," he writes. Every society, he believes, has a set of general conceptual principles that form a "structure" that runs through each society. Structuralism has long been debated in anthropology but is new to archaeology. Under this approach, Hodder would have archaeologists looking for the principles and concepts that played a part in all social and ecological actions in individual ancient societies, a structure that affected the patterning of the material culture found in the archaeological record. It is still too early to say what effect structural and symbolic approaches will have on archaeological research and the search for middle-range theory (for tentative examples, see Miller and Tilley, 1983), but it is certainly a healthy reaction away from the functional approach that dominated thinking in the late 1970s.

EXPERIMENTAL ARCHAEOLOGY

Controlled experiments with the dynamics of material culture can be a fruitful source of data to test middle-range theory. Experimental archaeology began in Europe during the eighteenth century, when people tried to blow the spectacular bronze horns recovered from peat bogs in Scandinavia and Britain. The exaggerated claims for the qualities of the horns fascinated the gullible public. One ardent experimenter, Dr. Robert Ball of Dublin, Ireland, blew an Irish horn so hard that he was able to produce "a deep bass note, resembling the bellowing of a bull." Sadly, a subsequent experiment with a trumpet caused him to burst a blood vessel, and he died several days later. Dr. Ball is the only recorded casualty of experimental archaeology, for most modern experiments have been conducted with greater precision and perhaps less gusto (Coles, 1973).

Scientific archaeologists have been interested in experimenting with prehistoric technologies and lifeways ever since the early days of anthropology. Much early experimental effort went into stone toolmaking and the study of prehistoric stone technology by replication. One French archaeologist even went so far as to make stone tools by casting pebbles into a cement mixer! In a sense, the early stoneworking experiments were the product of academic curiosity, and it was not until the early years of this century that experimental archaeology involving stone tools took on more immediate relevance. One reason that it did was the capture and observation of Ishi, one of the last California Indians to follow a traditional way of life.

Ishi

Ishi, the last "wild" Yahi Indian, was captured near Oroville, California, in 1913 (Kroeber, 1965). Fortunately, the story of his capture came to the notice of University of California anthropologists Alfred Kroeber and Thomas Waterman. They managed to assume responsibility for Ishi, who resided at the University Museum at Berkeley for four and a half years before he died of tuberculosis. Ishi became a local attraction, a living museum exhibit that brought hundreds of visitors to the campus. But he was far more than an exhibit; he proved to be a mine of information about the hunter-gatherer way of life and about the simple technology that the Yahi had enjoyed. Kroeber, Waterman, and a doctor named Saxon Pope from the University of California Medical School accompanied Ishi to his homeland and observed him as he stalked game and used his bow and snares. They acquired a mass of vital anthropological and linguistic information that would otherwise have been lost forever. Pope, an archery expert, not only apprenticed himself to Ishi but also spent years studying bows and arrows in the museum collections. He subsequently published a monograph on the subject, which did much to make archery the popular sport it is today (Pope, 1923).

Stone Technology

Ishi left a wonderful legacy to archaeologists, a mass of data that made people realize just how ignorant we were about prehistoric technologies. Only the sketchiest historical accounts of stoneworking and other craft activities survived in the records of early explorers. Some of the Spanish friars, notably Juan de Torquemada, saw Indian stoneworkers flaking obsidian knives. In 1615 he described how the Indians would take a stick and press it against a stone core with their "breast." "With the force of the knife there flies off a knife," he wrote. But until recently, no one knew just how pressure flaking, as it is called, was done.

It was an Idaho rancher named Don Crabtree who worked out some of the ways in which the Paleo-Indians had made the beautiful Folsom projectile points found on the Plains. He experimented for more than forty years and was able to describe no fewer than eleven methods of reproducing the "flute" at the base of the artifact (Crabtree, 1966, 1972b). Eventually, he came across Torquemada's account of pressure flaking and used a chest punch to remove flakes from the base of unfinished points gripped in a vise on the ground. The result was points that were almost indistinguishable from the prehistoric artifacts. Many others have followed in Crabtree's footsteps and have successfully replicated almost every kind of stone artifact made by pre-Columbian Indians. Stone tool edges can be so sharp that they are better than steel for delicate surgery.

Some eye surgeons use commercially produced obsidian blades for this purpose, made under the quality-control supervision of an archaeologist!

Crabtree's long-term experiments raise a basic question: Does the production of an exact replica mean, in fact, that modern experimentation has recovered the original technique? The answer, of course, is that we can never be certain. Lithic expert Jeff Flenniken has replicated dozens of Paleo-Indian projectile points and argues that many of the different "types" identified by Plains archaeologists are in fact simply heads that have been modified for reuse after they have broken in use. By reducing an existing head, he argues, the Paleo-Indian artisan produced a different but convenient shape that did the job to be done just as well as the original. The same reduction process might lead the worker to the same shape again and again, but he certainly did not design it that way (Flenniken, 1984). David Hurst Thomas (1986), a Great Basin specialist, disagrees. He argues that modern stoneworkers must not interpret prehistoric artifacts in terms of their own experience, for to do so ignores the vast chronological gap that separates us from prehistoric times. Thomas believes that a strictly technological approach to stone tool experimentation restricts the questions to be asked about lithic technology. Lithic experimentation is a valuable approach to the past, but only if combined with other approaches, such as retrofitting or edge wear analysis.

Criteria for Experimental Archaeology

Experimental archaeology can rarely provide conclusive answers. It can merely provide some possible insights into the methods and techniques used in prehistory, for many of the behaviors involved in, say, prehistoric agriculture have left no tangible traces in the archaeological record. But some general rules must be applied to all experimental archaeology. First, the materials used in the experiment must be those available locally to the prehistoric society one is studying. Second, the methods must conform with the society's technological abilities. Obviously, modern technology must not be allowed to interfere with the experiment. Experiments with a prehistoric plow must be conducted with a plowshare made correctly, with careful reference to the direction of wood grain, the shape and method of manufacture of working edges, and all other specifications. If the plow is drawn by a tractor, the experiment's efficiency will be radically affected; thus, for accuracy, you will need a pair of trained oxen. The results of the experiment must be replicable and consist of tests that lead to suggested conclusions.

Some Examples of Experimental Archaeology

One of the best-known instances of experimental archaeology is the *Kon-Tiki* expedition, on which Thor Heyerdahl attempted to prove that Polynesia had been settled by adventurous Peruvians who sailed rafts across thousands of miles of ocean (Heyerdahl, 1950). He did succeed in reaching Polynesia, but his expedition showed that long ocean voyages in rafts were possible; he did not prove that the Peruvians settled Polynesia.

Most experimental archaeology is far more limited in scope, often involving experiments with spears or bows against animal targets and the like (Odell and Cowan, 1986). Many experiments have been done on clearance of forests in Europe and elsewhere. Stone axes have been surprisingly effective at clearing woodland, one Danish experiment yielding estimates that a man could clear one-half acre of forest in a week. Tree ringing and fire have been shown to be effective tree-felling techniques in West Africa and Mesoamerica (Shaw, 1969). Experiments with agriculture over eight or more years have been conducted in the southern Mayan lowlands and the Mesa Verde National Park. The latter experiment lasted seventeen years. Two and one-half acres of heavy red clay soil was cultivated and planted with maize, beans, and other small crops. Good crop yields were obtained in all but two of the seventeen years, when drought killed the young crop. The test revealed how important careful crop rotation is to preserving the land's carrying capacity.

Housing Experiments   Houses of poles and thatch, logs, or hut clay normally survive in the form of post holes, foundation trenches, or collapsed rubble. Unfortunately, traces of the roof and information on wall and roof heights are usually lacking. But this absence has not deterred experimenters from building replicas of Mississippian houses in Tennessee, using excavated floor plans associated with charred poles, thatching grass, and wall-clay fragments (Figure 14.6) (Nash, 1968). Two types of house, dating to A.D. 1000–1600, were rebuilt. One of these was a "small pole" type with slender poles bent over to form an inverted basketlike rectangular structure with clay plaster on the exterior. Later houses were given long walls, which supported a steep, peaked roof. In this, as in many other instances, many details of the rafter and roof design are probably lost forever.

Butser Hill   An ambitious long-term experimental archaeology project flourishes at Butser Hill in southern England, where Peter Reynolds has reconstructed a communal Iron Age round house dating to about 300 B.C. The house is built of hazel rods and a binding mixture of clay, earth, animal hair, and hay. This is part of a much larger experimental project that is exploring every aspect of Iron Age life. Reynolds and other members of the Butser team have grown prehistoric cereals using Iron Age technology, kept a selection of livestock that resembled prehistoric breeds, and even stored grain in subterranean storage pits. The project is concerned not only with how individual aspects of Iron Age subsistence operated but also with how they fitted together. Some fascinating results have come from the Butser experiment; for instance, Reynolds found that wheat yields were far higher than had been expected and that grain could be

Figure 14.6 Reconstruction of a Mississippian house.

stored underground for long periods without rotting. The Butser experiment provides valuable data for interpreting Iron Age sites and also information that can be used for calculating prehistoric crop yields and land carrying capacities (Reynolds, 1979).

Overton Down   One of the longest experiments in archaeological interpretation is that of the Overton Down earthwork in England, which will last as long as 128 years. In 1960 the British Association for the Advancement of Science built an experimental earthwork at Overton Down, Wiltshire (Jewell and Dimbleby, 1966). The earthwork and its associated ditch were built on chalk subsoil, with profiles approximating those of prehistoric monuments. Archaeological materials including textiles, leather, wood, animal and human bones, and pottery were buried within and on the earthwork. The Overton Down earthwork was partly built with modern picks, shovels, and hatchets and partly with red deer antlers and ox shoulder blades in an attempt to establish relative work rates for different technologies. The difference was about 1.3:1.0 in favor of modern tools, mostly because modern shovels were more efficient. Overton Down was then abandoned, but small and very precise excavations of the ditch and bank were to take place at intervals of 2, 4, 8, 16, 32, 64, and 128 years. The digs were to be used to check the decay and attrition of the earthwork and the silting of the ditch over a lengthening period. The project will yield priceless information of great use for interpreting archaeological sites of a similar type on chalk soils.

These are but a few of the classic examples of experimental archaeology, many of them long-term efforts that will yield valuable interpretative data for archaeologists well into the twenty-first century. Such types of controlled experiments will give archaeologists the objective data they need to understand the static archaeological record as studied in the dynamic present.

In this chapter we have described "living archaeology," a new and accelerating search for reliable methods of inferring past conditions from the archaeological record. Middle-range research is a quest for a scientifically built language that gives meaning to the archaeological observations, for methods that will enable us to evaluate our ideas about the past, and one day to make progress in answering the question of questions, not "what happened?" but "why?"

SUMMARY

- The diversity of modern human societies provides us with a unique source of interpretative information about the past. For this reason, archaeologists have been studying living cultures as a means for better interpreting the archaeological record.
- Ethnographic analogy helps in ascribing meaning to the prehistoric past. Analogy itself is a form of reasoning that assumes that if objects have some similar attributes, they will share other similarities as well. It involves using a known, identifiable phenomenon to identify unknown ones of a broadly similar type.
- Early analogies were based on unilinear evolutionary schemes and involved direct comparisons between entire living and prehistoric societies. Today, most simple analogies are based on technology, style, and function of artifacts, as they are defined archaeologically. Such analogies, however, based as they are on people's beliefs, can be unreliable.
- Direct historical analogies and comparisons made with the aid of texts are common, but meaningful analogies for American and Paleolithic sites are much harder to achieve. One approach has been to devise test implications, using several analogies. This technique is based on the functional approach assuming that cultures are not made up of random traits but are integrated in various ways. Thus analogies are made between recent and prehistoric societies with closely similar general characteristics.
- Middle-range research is carried out on living societies, using ethnoarchaeology, experimental archaeology, and historical documents. It is designed to create a body of middle-range theory, objective theoretical devices for forging a link between the dynamic living systems of today and the static archaeological record of the past.

- Ethnoarchaeology is ethnographic archaeology with a strongly materialist bias. Archaeologists engage in ethnoarchaeology as part of middle-range research in attempts to make meaningful interpretations of artifact patterns in the archaeological record. We examined examples of this research among the San, Australian Aborigines, and Nunamiut Eskimo.
- Experimental archaeology seeks to replicate prehistoric technology and lifeways under carefully controlled conditions. As such, it is a form of archaeological analogy. Experiments have been conducted on every aspect of prehistoric culture, from lithics to housing. Archaeology by experiment rarely produces conclusive answers but does provide insights into the methods and techniques used by prehistoric cultures.

GUIDE TO FURTHER READING

Binford, Lewis R. *In Pursuit of the Past.* New York: Thames and Hudson, 1983. An account of living archaeology and middle-range theory for a more general audience. Strongly recommended for beginners.

Binford, Lewis R. *Nunamiut Ethnoarchaeology.* Orlando, Fla.: Academic Press, 1978. A descriptive monograph about ethnoarchaeology among caribou hunters. A must for the serious student.

Coles, John M. *Archaeology by Experiment.* London: Heinemann, 1973. An introduction to experimental archaeology with numerous examples, mainly from the Old World.

Gould, Richard H. *Living Archaeology.* Cambridge: Cambridge University Press, 1980. A wide-ranging discussion of ethnoarchaeology that covers both method and theory.

Hodder, Ian, ed. *Symbols in Action.* Cambridge: Cambridge University Press, 1982. Ethnoarchaeological studies in tropical Africa that are used to support a structural and symbolic approach to archaeology.

Yellen, John E. *Archaeological Approaches to the Present: Models for Predicting the Past.* Orlando, Fla.: Academic Press, 1977. Ethnoarchaeology among the San of the Kalahari. A technical work with broad implications.

Chapter
15

Settlement Archaeology and Spatial Analysis

So far we have examined the ways in which archaeologists study artifacts and prehistoric subsistence and the various technologies that people developed to adapt to their environments. We also glanced briefly at some methods used to reconstruct the prehistoric environment itself. But what about the relationships between different prehistoric settlements and the environment? In this chapter we examine some of the ways in which archaeologists have studied changing settlement patterns in prehistoric times.

One of the pervasive theoretical frameworks for archaeology is that of cultural ecology, the study of the interrelationships between people and their environment. But environment covers not only the natural environment but the social environment as well (Jochim, 1979). Technology and subsistence have leading roles in the study of prehistoric settlement patterns, and the research methods used rely heavily on both systems models and cultural ecology, as well as on large bodies of information manipulated by computers and quantitative methods.

SETTLEMENT ARCHAEOLOGY AND SETTLEMENT PATTERNS

Settlement archaeology, the study of changing human settlement patterns, is part of the analysis of adaptive interactions between people and their external environment, both natural and cultural (Chang, 1968).

Settlement patterns, the layout of human settlements on the land-

386

scape, are the result of relationships between people who decided, on the basis of practical, political, economic, and social considerations, to place their houses, settlements, and religious structures where they did (Nir, 1983). Thus settlement archaeology offers the archaeologist a chance to examine not only relationships between different communities but trading networks, exploitation, and social organization as well. The study of settlement patterns involves examining the degree to which human settlement reflects a society and its technology's adaptation to a specific environment.

Determinants of Settlement Patterns

Settlement patterns are determined by many factors related to the environment, economic practices, and technological skills. Inherited cultural patterns and established networks of human behavior have an impelling influence on settlement patterns in some societies. The distribution of San camps in the Kalahari desert depends on the availability of water supplies and vegetable foods, and ancient Mayan centers in Mexico were laid out in segments dictated by political and religious considerations.

Village layout may be determined by the need to protect one's herds against animal predators or war parties. Other settlements may be strung out at regular intervals along an important trade artery, such as a river. Even the positioning of individual houses is dictated by a complex variety of social, economic, and even personal factors that can defy explanation.

The determinants of settlement patterns operate on at least three levels, each formed by factors that differ in quality or degree from the ones that shape other levels (Trigger, 1968b).

1. *Building or structure.* Houses, household clusters, and activity areas are minimal units of archaeological analysis.
2. *Communities.* The arrangement of structures within a single group constitutes a community. The term *community* is defined as a "maximal group of persons who normally reside in face-to-face association" (Murdock, 1949).
3. *Distribution of communities.* The density and distribution of communities, whatever their size, is determined to a considerable extent by the natural resources in their environment and by the economy, nutritional requirements, and technological level of the population, as well as by social and religious constraints.

A critical part of settlement archaeology is understanding the factors that interact to determine a settlement pattern at any of these three levels. These factors can best be understood by referring to anthropological analogy with modern societies (see Chapter 14). And the ultimate objective of the exercise is to study prehistoric settlement systems as an aspect of the whole picture of a prehistoric society.

STRUCTURES AND COMMUNITIES

Structures

Human dwelling places occur in an infinite range of sizes and types, from the crude windbreak of the Tasmanian aborigine to the magnificent palaces of King Henry VIII. Temples, fortifications, and even cattle pens are all forms of standardized structures. Domestic architecture may be standardized, or it may vary according to strict guidelines dictated by a number of factors. The study of individual structures can be approached from several standpoints.

Form and material are among the major determinants of house design. For example, 15,000 years ago the mammoth hunters of the western Russian plains lived in semisubterranean dwellings with roofs made of skins and mammoth bones and with interior hearths (Soffer, 1985). Theirs was a treeless, arctic environment, where protection from icy cold winds was vital. The people made use of the only abundant raw materials available to them, the bones and skins of the huge mammoths they hunted. In contrast, the Tonga peoples of the Middle Zambezi Valley in Central Africa, where the midday temperature is often over 100°F, and the nights are hot most of the year, spend more of their lives in the shade of their pole-and-mud huts than they do inside them. Their dwellings therefore have thatched roofs that project far from the walls to form large and shady verandas (Figure 15.1) (Reynolds, 1967).

The raw materials used to build a structure affect not only its form but also its preservation in the archaeological record. Unfired mud brick was used throughout the Near East for house building, and it is still employed today. Once a house is abandoned, the unmaintained brick melts and reverts to clay. It took archaeologists generations to learn how to recover traces of mud-brick houses from their matrix (Lloyd, 1963). As we saw in Chapter 10, wooden structures often leave no trace in the soil except, perhaps, post holes or foundation trenches.

Function radically affects house design, too. The earliest human beings lived in temporary brush shelters that reflected their mobile life-style and the fact that the nights were rarely cold. More sedentary communities, such as subsistence farmers in the Near East, built houses that combined a need for shelter with a need for storage and cooking facilities for each family.

Social and political organization can affect the design of structures also, for the size and layout of a dwelling can reflect the family organization of the occupants, as well as their social standing. A polygamous family may live in a house with several kitchen areas, each owned by a different wife. Sometimes, with controlled use of anthropological data, particular house types in the archaeological record can be related to specific forms of family organization. Within one house, a family unit can be distin-

Figure 15.1 Tonga hut from the Middle Zambezi Valley, Central Africa.

guished only by interpreting the use of the artifacts found in it, in order to identify different rooms, especially cooking areas.

Many societies developed special architectural styles and structures that were associated with political or religious activities or with leadership. Classic Mayan temples, exemplified by the pyramids at Tikal (Figure 15.2), provide an excellent instance of such structures (Sabloff, 1989). The plazas and pyramids were designed to create a sense of awe. Artisans' houses can be identified by distinctive artifact clusters, such as the potters' workshops found by James Mellaart (1975) at the early town of Hacilar in Turkey, dating to about 5300 B.C.

Recovering Houses and Households

Evidence for individual houses and households is obtained by carefully excavating features, household clusters, and activity sets in the archaeological record. In many societies, limited economic opportunities and even distribution of wealth resulted in standardized floor plans (Netting and others, 1984). Such houses, which served as shelters for their occupants, provide the archaeologist, centuries afterward, with convenient analytic units, as long as the house remains isolated from surrounding occupation debris. The variations between houses may reflect a variation between families in subsistence activities, social status, manufacturing activity,

Figure 15.2 Temple I at Tikal, Guatemala, which dates to about A.D. 700, an example of a ceremonial structure.

wealth, and so on. (For an example of commoners' housing among the Maya, see Webster and Gordon, 1988).

Early Mesoamerican Houses   Between 1350 and 850 B.C. the one-room, thatched wattle-and-daub house became the most common dwelling type in Early Formative Mesoamerican villages. In the Valley of Oaxaca, Early Formative houses were generally rectangular. The floors were sand-covered and dug out from the subsoil, and the thatched roof was supported by pine posts. The puddled clay walls were smoothed and sometimes whitewashed (Flannery, 1976; Flannery and Marcus, 1983).

House Contents   In studying such houses, Kent Flannery and his colleagues distinguished carefully between the households themselves, the household unit of associated features, such as storage pits and graves, and the various activity areas sometimes associated with them (Figure 15.3) (Flannery and Marcus, 1983; Winter, 1976). Many of the houses were swept clean before abandonment, but several contained accumulations of debris that included not only potsherds and bone tools but food remains

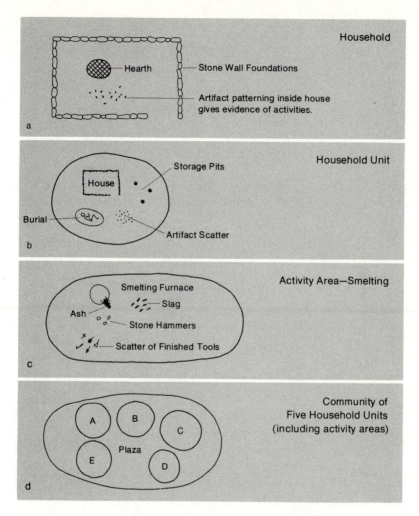

Figure 15.3 Various spatial units used by archaeologists in studying human settlement: (a) household; (b) household unit; (c) activity area; (d) community.

as well. Marcus Winter broke down the house contents into at least five possible activities, including sewing and basketry (needles), cooking and food consumption (pots and food remains), and cutting and scraping (stone tools). He plotted the house contents (Figure 15.3) in an attempt to distinguish the craft activities of the family who occupied each dwelling.

Household Unit   It was possible for the archaeologists to isolate the household units in Oaxaca. These included bell-shaped storage pits large enough to hold a metric ton of maize; and some of them contained maize pollen and grinders. Human burials were associated with some houses, perhaps those of the family, but archaeologists were unable to prove this. The Oaxaca household units also included various types of ovens, refuse middens, and drainage ditches (Figures 15.4 and 15.5).

Activity Sets   Activity sets are sets of artifacts associated with specific activities, such as a bow and arrow with hunting. Twenty-two household clusters were analyzed for traces of activity sets that would indicate specialist activities. Food procurement, preparation, and food storage activities were common to all households; these were identified by grindstone fragments, storage pits, jars, and food remains. Every household chipped local stone and made baskets; but there were also signs of specialist activities. One large pit at Tierras Largas contained large quantities of pressure-

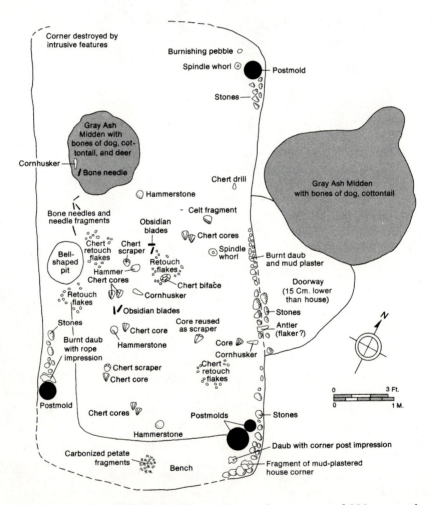

Figure 15.4 Plan of a house at Tierras Largas, Oaxaca, around 900 B.C., with selected artifacts plotted on the floor.

Figure 15.5 Features near houses at San José Mogote: storage pits, drainage canals, and a large cistern.

flaking debris, while other household clusters yielded no such fine debitage. Perhaps this household boasted a part-time specialist who made fine stone artifacts for others.

The Oaxacan study offered some potential for identifying division of labor within a household and artifacts used by children rather than adults. Unfortunately, the excavated samples were too small for definitive study, but Figure 15.6, from Evon Vogt's classic study of the Maya of Zinacantán in Chiapas, shows some of the long-term possibilities (see Kent, 1984; Vogt, 1967).

Communities

Many variables act to determine the layout of communities, both large and small (Figure 15.7).

Environment and Economy   These two factors limit the size and permanence of a settlement because the ability to gather and store food is as important as the technology necessary to transport and process it into edible form. Environment and economy are vital because they determine whether a community lives in one place permanently or must shift camp

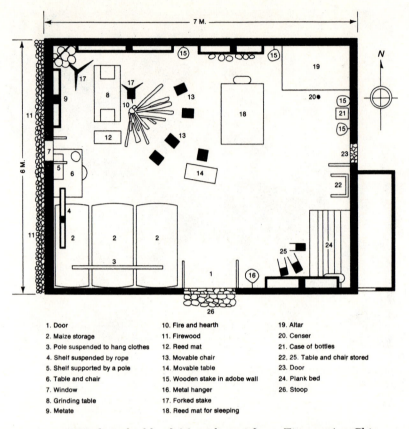

1. Door	10. Fire and hearth	19. Altar
2. Maize storage	11. Firewood	20. Censer
3. Pole suspended to hang clothes	12. Reed mat	21. Case of bottles
4. Shelf suspended by rope	13. Movable chair	22, 25. Table and chair stored
5. Shelf supported by a pole	14. Movable table	23. Door
6. Table and chair	15. Wooden stake in adobe wall	24. Plank bed
7. Window	16. Metal hanger	26. Stoop
8. Grinding table	17. Forked stake	
9. Metate	18. Reed mat for sleeping	

Figure 15.6 Modern highland Maya house from Zinacantán, Chiapas, Mexico, conceptually divided into male and female workspaces.

at regular intervals during the year. Preliterate 'Ubaid farmers in Mesopotamia (c. 4500 B.C.) relied on simple irrigation agriculture. Because they had no need to move in order to achieve a stable subsistence cycle, they lived at the same location for centuries, forming large tells (Redman, 1978a).

Social and Political Factors These are also strong determinants, even in simple societies. Family and kinship considerations are important in camps and small villages. State-organized societies reserved special precincts for ceremonial centers, palaces, and official buildings where the business of the state was conducted (see Figure 15.2). Whole sectors of towns were sometimes reserved for minority religious groups or foreign traders living under the protection of the local ruler. These quarters may be reflected in the archaeological record by exotic objects, unusual architecture, or religious objects. At the trading port of Kilwa on the Tanzanian

Figure 15.7 Examples of communities. Top: !Kung San winter camp at a water hole. Bottom: Algonquin village in North Carolina, painted by John White in 1585.

coast, the sultan lived in a magnificent palace, a special precinct with its own mosque. The fine artifacts in the palace are not duplicated in any numbers elsewhere in the site, where a cosmopolitan population of Arabs and Africans lived and traded (Chittick, 1974).

Studying a Community: Teotihuacán

The behavior of a complete community, insofar as it can be discerned as having a pattern, is reflected in its artifact grouping and in the characteristic settlement pattern of the location as a whole—house design and layout and the distribution of household clusters and activity areas. The archaeologist uses site survey and selective excavation, as well as sampling techniques, to look for systematic and statistical associations of settlement attributes—in the same way as for artifact attributes—that may reflect a grouping of social units.

The most ambitious settlement pattern study of a community ever undertaken was really a study of many communities, George Cowgill and René Millon's survey of the Classic city of Teotihuacán in the Valley of Mexico, which flourished from around 250 B.C. to A.D. 700 (Millon, 1973, 1981). Their objective was to examine the changing settlement pattern of the urban complex during the vital period when the city was growing rapidly. How large was the population? How did it come into being? What was the social composition of the city, and how was it organized?

Cowgill and Millon spent years mapping and sampling the city (see Chapter 9). They found that it was built in four quadrants, following a master plan that was adhered to for centuries. The basic cruciform layout was established very early, when the great Street of the Dead (Figure 15.8) was laid out. The oldest part of the city lies in the northern quadrant, where most of the city's craftspeople lived. It contains many more structures than the southern quadrants, where exceptionally fertile soils, ideal

Figure 15.8 Teotihuacán, Mexico, Pyramid of the Sun.

for irrigation agriculture, are located. The archaeologists found that the city spread southward from the northern quadrant and that it was organized into neighborhoods, or *barrios,* groups of apartment compounds separated from one another. Teotihuacán's population may have reached a peak of more than 150,000 people in A.D. 600. More than two thousand compounds contained thousands of standardized, one-story apartments sharing courtyards and temples with their neighbors. Some of these compounds contained large concentrations of obsidian flakes or potters' artifacts and were identified as specialist precincts or groups of workshops.

There were foreign traders' quarters, too. One Oaxacan *barrio* seems to have flourished in the western part of the city, a compound where Oaxacan pottery and artifacts were common. The percentage of Oaxacan wares was very high in this area compared with other precincts, and Millon hypothesizes that there may have been an Oaxacan quarter in Teotihuacán for centuries.

A major objective of the Teotihuacán research is to understand the diverse internal workings of this remarkable city as a going organization throughout its long history. This result can be won only by comprehensive surveys that rely heavily on samples of artifact patterns and analyses of house contents and entire neighborhoods conducted all over this enormous site. (For more details and statistical information, see Cowgill and others, 1984.)

Analysis of Smaller Communities

Communities much smaller than Teotihuacán can be investigated somewhat more easily, but large amounts of archaeological data are still involved. Early Formative villages in the Valley of Oaxaca were investigated to test a number of hypotheses about the relationships between parts of the settlement. Were the villages subdivided into a number of *barrios,* which are still an organizational unit in modern Indian communities that have well-defined communal and ceremonial responsibilities (Flannery, 1976; Flannery and Marcus, 1983)? By studying artifact patterns and inventories, the archaeologists found traces of at least four residential wards at San José Mogote, each separated from its neighbors by an erosion gully where the trash was dumped. This larger village displayed some different craft specializations among the wards.

In many smaller communities, the distinctions between zones of the settlement may be inconspicuous. At Santo Domingo Tomaltepec in Oaxaca, Michael Whalen (1981) managed to isolate three distinct zones in the village of four or five households, occupied between 1150 and 1000 B.C. He found a cemetery, a zone with two houses containing more trade goods, perhaps a "higher-status residential area," and another zone with almost no imports. There was, however, little separation between the zones. Unlike Teotihuacán, the village had no formal layout, nor were any public buildings discernible.

Population Estimates for Communities

How does one estimate community populations? Obviously, as in the Algonquin historical villages (see Figure 15.7), written records can sometimes provide a fairly accurate estimate. Modern censuses of villages and towns, however, are of only marginal use, for many variables affect even nineteenth-century population densities relative to those of prehistoric times. Some investigators have attempted to estimate population sizes with mathematical formulas that allocate so much living space to each individual and each family. But again, one is dealing with so many intangible variables, such as social restrictions, that it is difficult to be accurate. Estimates of the rates at which people accumulate refuse middens over long periods have also been used to calculate population size (Cook, 1972; Zubrow, 1976), but this method has the same serious disadvantages as the others mentioned.

About the only reliable estimates of population are based on the number of households at any one moment in a community's history. Millon's guesses about Teotihuacán's population are based on such house counts. Using samples of early Mesoamerican village households, Joyce Marcus (1976) showed that perhaps 90 percent were small hamlets with from one to ten or twelve households and up to sixty people. But some villages were much larger than this average. The contemporary Olmec site of San Lorenzo in Veracruz may have housed as many as 1,200 people. Thus you can see that this method, too, is far from accurate (see De Roche, 1983).

Community population estimates are important because they can give insights into the maximum size that a settlement can achieve. What, for example, was the maximum size that early Mesoamerican hamlets and villages could reach before further growth was impossible? Characteristically, societies that were not organized into large states tended to live in small villages, which frequently split off from one another as further growth at the mother settlement was cut off. This process is straightforward enough, and in Formative Mesoamerica many villages split off in just this manner. But others, such as the Olmec settlement at San Lorenzo, were able to grow larger and still remain viable settlements. Why was this growth possible? The search for explanations of evolving settlement patterns takes us on to a broader area of research, the layout of communities against the background of their natural environment (Flannery and Marcus, 1983). (For highly technical essays on intersite spatial analysis, see Hietala, 1984.)

RECONSTRUCTING THE NATURAL ENVIRONMENT

The density and distribution of communities, whatever their size, are determined to a considerable extent by the natural resources of the region in which they flourish and by cultural factors. The requirements of hunter-gatherers, for example, differ from those of agriculturalists, and those of cattle herders are different from both. In Africa, the distribution of cattle is determined by zones of tsetse fly–infested country, for the insect's bite is fatal to stock and dangerous to humans. Pastoral populations tend to concentrate their settlements in grassland areas that are free from these flies and where good fodder and abundant standing water are available (Clark and Brandt, 1984).

By the same token, the settlement patterns of agricultural populations are determined by equally critical factors. Such shifting cultivators as the Bemba farmers of northern Zambia have an understanding of their environment that is astonishingly detailed. They can rate a garden's fertility and its suitability for different crops by examining the vegetational cover and the soil's physical characteristics. Critical factors are the land's staying power, the number of seasons during which it can be cropped with satisfactory results, and the fallow period required before it can be reused. As land is exhausted, the Bemba use new or regenerated plots and move their settlements accordingly (Allan, 1965). Like the Bemba, the archaeologist has to achieve a detailed understanding of the environmental variables that affected prehistoric settlement patterns.

The dynamics of human behavior are closely tied to those of the natural environment, the dynamics of such resources as soils, plants, and animals. The changes and patterns of behavior in these resources are just as variable as those of human populations, and they condition the way in which people plan their hunting and gathering activities and plant their crops. Increasingly, archaeologists are becoming involved not only with cultural ecology but also with modern ecological research on feeding activities, energy inputs and outputs, and data on the ways in which modern populations use natural resources (Hardesty, 1977; Jochim, 1979).

By way of illustration, the hunter-gatherers of the Tehuacán Valley in Mexico are known to have concentrated in larger camps during the wet season and to have dispersed over a much wider area in smaller settlements during the months of the dry season. Their food procurement activities were scheduled carefully from season to season (MacNeish, 1970). These activities, in terms of energy maximization and specialization and clustering of population, are much better understood now that archaeologists are beginning to use the concepts of modern ecology.

A viable concept of environment that an archaeologist can adopt is that it must be considered a dynamic factor in the analysis of archaeological context (Butzer, 1982). Archaeology has a four-dimensional spatial and temporal context that consists of both a cultural and a noncultural environment. The ultimate goal of environmental archaeology is to understand the relationship between culture and environment. The immediate goal of environmental archaeology is to define the characteristics and processes of the biophysical environment. This environment is the matrix for the interaction that occurs between socioeconomic systems and the natural environment. Another objective is to understand the human ecosystem that is defined by the interaction between the environmental and human systems. Archaeological sites, or distributions of them, are part of the human ecosystem, a useful conceptual framework for examining such interactions.

Butzer (1982) considers that environmental archaeology has five major themes, which are common to geography and biology as well but are especially important in the study of prehistoric human ecology:

1. *Spatial patterning,* both of natural and human phenomena, is amenable to spatial analysis.
2. The *size* and *scale* of both environmental and human phenomena can be measured, also through spatial analysis.
3. The *complexity* of both environments and human communities can vary greatly and must be defined and delimited.
4. The *interaction of human* and *nonhuman communities* is unavoidable in any complex environment where the distribution of resources is uneven. These communities interact internally and with one another as well as with the nonliving environment, and interaction takes place on many levels and at changing or unequal rates.
5. *Equilibrium* between human societies and their environments is an ideal that is almost never achieved. Thanks to constant negative feedback resulting from both internal and external processes and inputs, they are in a continual state of environmental readjustment.

Environmental Systems

Environmental systems provide the spatial and temporal frameworks within which human societies flourish. These are some key ecological concepts.

Human societies are part of the *biosphere,* which encompasses all the earth's living organisms interacting with the physical environment. The biosphere is organized both vertically and horizontally, with genes and cells at the base and organisms, populations, and communities above them. The community, all the biological populations in an area, functions together with the nonliving environment in an ecosystem.

Every ecosystem is maintained by the regulation of trophic levels (vertical food chains) and by patterns of energy flow (Figure 15.9). The complexities of even modern ecosystems make them difficult to study empirically; prehistoric ones are impossible to reconstruct. But the broad conceptual framework of the ecosystem serves as a very useful research tool for archaeologists.

Human ecosystems differ from biological ecosystems in many ways. Information, technology, and social organization all have much greater roles. Human beings, both as individuals and as groups, have unique capacities for matching resources with specific objectives. They not only think objectively about such matching but also transform the natural envi-

Perspectives

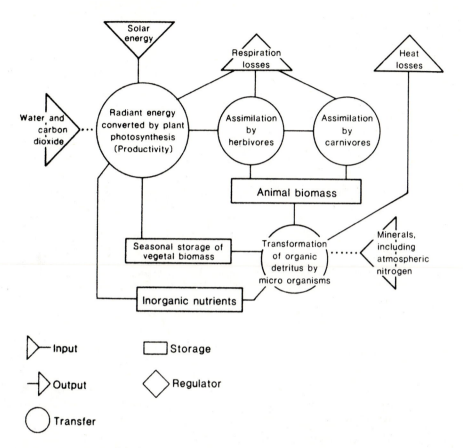

Figure 15.9 A simplified energy cycle for an environmental system. (After Butzer, 1982)

ronment to meet their objectives. As Figure 15.10 shows, value systems and goal orientation are important to human ecosystems, as are group attitudes and decision-making institutions, especially in more complex societies. Any attempt to reconstruct prehistoric environments must take account not only of environmental resources and constraints but also of the ways in which human beings used resources and intervened in the environment and changed it.

Geoarchaeology and Other Approaches

Archaeological research using the methods and concepts of the early sciences, or *geoarchaeology,* is a cornerstone of environmental reconstruction (Butzer, 1982). This is a far wider enterprise than merely geology; it

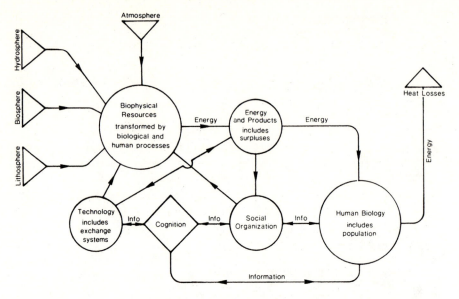

Figure 15.10 A much-simplified energy cycle for a human ecosystem. This chart does not include provisions for storage of food and other resources. (After Butzer, 1982)

is deeply enmeshed in the planning and execution of both surveys and excavations and encompasses at least five major approaches:

1. Geochemical, electromagnetic, and other remote-sensing techniques to locate sites and features (Chapter 9).
2. Studies of site formation processes and of the spatial context of a site within its habitat (Chapter 7).
3. Development of methods for differentiating cultural from natural features. This distinction includes disturbances due to biological, geological, and pedological processes since sites were occupied.
4. Relative and chronometric dating to establish chronological contexts both in and outside a site (Chapters 5 and 6).
5. Reconstructing the ancient landscape by a variety of paleogeographic and biological methods. These include pollen analysis and phytolith studies (Chapters 5 and 13).

Until recently, geoarchaeology was little more than a battery of techniques, many of them either developed and used by nonarchaeologists or used as a sideline. This was an ineffective approach, for nonarchaeologists have little appreciation of prehistoric human activities. People are geomorphic agents, just like the wind. Accidentally or deliberately, they carry inorganic and organic materials to their homes. They remove rubbish, make tools, build houses, abandon tools. All these mineral and organic materials are subjected to all manner of mechanical and biochemical processes during occupation and after the site is occupied. The controlling geomorphic system at a site, whatever its size, is made up not only of natural elements but of a vital cultural component as well. And the geoarchaeologist is involved with archaeological investigations from the very beginning and deals not only with formation of sites and with the changes they underwent during occupation but also with what happened to them after abandonment.

In the field, the geoarchaeologist is part of the multidisciplinary research team, recording vertical profiles within the excavation and in special pits close by, to obtain information on soil sediment sequences (Butzer, 1982). At the same time, he or she takes soil samples for pollen and sediment analyses and relates the site to its landscape by topographic survey. Working closely with survey archaeologists, geoarchaeologists locate sites and other cultural features on the natural landscape using aerial photographs, satellite images, and even geophysical prospecting on individual sites. As part of this process, they examine dozens of natural geological exposures, where they study the stratigraphic and sedimentary history of the entire region as a wider context for the sites found within it. Back in the laboratory, maps and soil samples are analyzed. Studying the sediments in the site, they work out the microstratigraphy of the site relative to that of the surrounding area (Figure 15.11) and analyze the deposits for such properties as pH and organic content to establish the effects of human activity on the sedimentary sequence at the site. The ultimate objective is to identify not only the microenvironment of the site but also that of the region as a whole—to establish ecological and spatial frameworks for the socioeconomic and settlement patterns that are revealed by archaeological excavations and surveys.

Geoarchaeology is a highly technical field, requiring expert skill in many procedures ranging from palynology to isotopic analysis. But it is far more than geology in the service of archaeology, or merely a collection of scientific methods used to study prehistoric remains. It is an integral part of the settlement archaeology process, even if many of its research procedures are the province of specialists.

In addition to geoarchaeology, both animal bones and paleobotanical finds can yield important information on prehistoric environments, especially if combined with other approaches. Pollen analysis has proved useful for this purpose and has sometimes provided reconstructions of the surroundings of prehistoric sites, as well as measures of the effects of human activities such as agriculture on the natural vegetation (Dimbleby, 1985). Thousands of tiny pollen grains and waterlogged wood fragments found in the deposits of the 10,000-year-old hunter-gatherer site at Star Carr, England, showed that the occupants had thrown down a tiny birch platform in some lakeside reeds. The site was surrounded by birch trees that came down to the water's edge. Some pine and willow trees grew nearby, and water plants and fungi were common (Figure 15.12) (Clark, 1954, 1972).

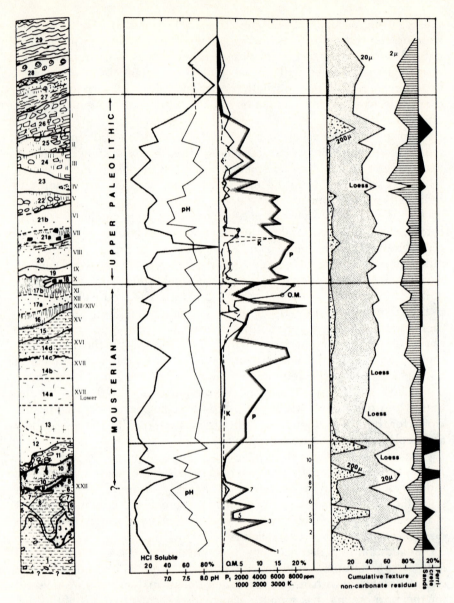

Figure 15.11 The complexities of microstratigraphy. A composite archaeosedimentary profile for Cueva Morín, a Paleolithic cave in northern Spain. The different sedimentary classes form the vertical columns; the actual stratigraphic layers appear at the left. (After Butzer, 1982)

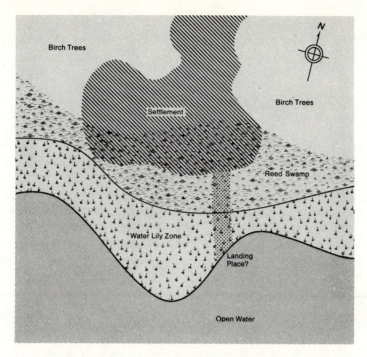

Figure 15.12 Reconstruction of the vegetational surroundings of the Star Carr site in England.

(Readers interested in a detailed summary of geoarchaeology should read Butzer, 1982.)

Inventorying Environmental Resources

Cultural adaptation to any environment can be understood only in the context of two categories of data: the ancient environment and resources available therein, and the technology of the culture being studied. Once these data are on hand, the archaeologist can proceed to establish which subsistence and economic options the people chose, given the available resources and their technological ability to exploit them.

It is easy enough to make an inventory of the natural resources available in any area, but it is not sufficient merely to list them, for it is the ways in which they can be exploited—the seasons of availability of vegetable foods, the migration patterns of game, the months when salmon runs take place—and not just the resources themselves that are significant. These many variables, to say nothing of soil distributions, rainfall patterns, and distributions of valuable raw materials, determine the critical element of a settlement pattern—the carrying capacity of the land.

Carrying capacity is the number and density of people that any tract of land can support. It is a flexible statistic that can be affected by factors other than those of the available resources in an area. People can alter the carrying capacity of their land by taking up agriculture or by cultivating a new crop that needs deeper plowing and thus exhausts the land faster. The introduction of fertilizer can enable people to settle permanently in one village because their lands are kept fertile by artificial means.

Prehistoric carrying capacities are very difficult to establish, except with carefully controlled experimental data, such as those obtained for southwestern agriculture and Mayan cultivation (see Chapter 14). Attempts have been made to measure the amount of meat available to prehistoric hunters in the Mississippi Valley (Smith, 1974), and it has been clear for some time that Classic Maya populations were much larger than those that could be supported from the felling and burning of trees to make forest gardens (Hammond, 1982). One problem has been that earlier settlement models were far too simple to accommodate the complexity of the data. Recent research has concentrated on resource inventories, systems models, and even computer simulation of the variables that affect carrying capacity (Hodder, 1978).

One approach that has been tried is *site catchment analysis,* which is difficult to apply under modern conditions when the environment is greatly modified. It is based on the assumption that every human settlement has a *catchment area* around it. This is a zone of domestic and wild resources within easy walking distance of the settlement. The !Kung San of the Kalahari in southern Africa are unlikely to forage much farther from their base camps than ten kilometers, a comfortable day's walking distance. The fundamental assumption then is simple: the farther the resources in an area are from a site, the less likely they are to be exploited.

Most site catchment studies, like those done in the Mount Carmel area of Israel in the 1960s, were rather generalized, little more than broad statements about resource availability (Vita-Finzi and Higgs, 1970). The approach has been much refined since then (Bailey, 1981) and is used as a way of making empirical statements about the sources of origin of materials recovered in archaeological sites. Two key concepts are important.

The *economic catchment area* of a site is the area from which the food resources consumed by the inhabitants are obtained. Such areas vary in size and shape according to the resources exploited, the site function, and the lifeway of its inhabitants. Clearly, the accuracy with which the economic catchment area can be defined will depend on the precision with which one can identify food remains in the site itself.

The *site exploitation territory* is quite different; it is the potential rather than the actual territory from which food resources may be obtained. This theoretical territory is *assumed* to have been used regularly for subsistence by the site inhabitants. Its boundaries are defined by "least cost" principles, by the maximum radii of the distances that people are willing to cover on foot. Much depends on the nature of the resources and how they are exploited. For example, in two hours' walking time a person can cover about ten kilometers—a reasonable distance to travel for some purposes. But a much smaller radius of one kilometer is useful when analyzing farming economies where land is exploited very intensively, for it is most economical of labor to use land close to the village. The boundaries of such radii are based on assumptions about normal human behavior and on examination of the economic potential of resources lying with them. Thus this type of site catchment analysis is little more than a statement of what was potentially available to the site inhabitants.

Site catchment analysis involves examining both the economic catchment area and the site exploitation territory as a way of assessing the relationship between what was *potentially* available in the environment and what was *actually* exploited. Typically, variations in the economic potential of a site catchment area are compared with variations in patterns of data from the site itself.

This approach helps with a major problem in settlement archaeology—defining variations in activities at different sites and testing hypotheses about how sites were linked. An interesting example of this approach comes from work by Kent Flannery and others in the Valley of Oaxaca, Mexico. They focused on individual sites where rigorously analyzed data from households and communities were available for comparison (Flannery, 1976; Flannery and Marcus, 1983). At San José Mogote, a village occupied between 1150 and 850 B.C., Flannery wanted to know from how far away the villagers obtained their animal and plant resources. He tested the various resources: those from within the village (turkeys, stored maize, edible fruit); those from the river, one kilometer away (reeds, sand, mud turtles); those on the high alluvium, within two to five kilometers (maize and other crops); those on the piedmont, up to five kilometers away (seasonal vegetable foods); and those in the mountains, five to fifteen kilometers distant (hut timbers, game, and firewood). Mineral resources—essentials such as salt, chert, and pottery clay—were obtained from three to fifty kilometers away. Pacific marine shells, freshwater mussels, jadeite, and other exotic substances and objects came from distant regions, perhaps as far as two hundred kilometers away.

San José Mogote thus needed a circle with a radius of under five kilometers to satisfy its basic agricultural needs, five kilometers to supply basic minerals and seasonal wild vegetable foods, and fifteen kilometers for game meat and construction materials. Exotic trade materials and ceremonial life required occasional collecting trips of up to fifty kilometers from the settlement and some of even greater distances. When Flannery plotted San José Mogote catchment areas relative to those of the neighboring Early Formative villages, he found that the innermost circles (two to five kilometers) of one village did not overlap those of any other village but that wider circles did, as the exclusive possession of catchment areas was progressively reduced. Once the fifty-kilometer ring was reached, all the villages of Oaxaca shared a common catchment area. Seasonal campsites were placed at strategic points on the outer rings, places where hut timbers, game, and trade materials were collected, perhaps by three or four villages sharing the same area. Such temporary camps were annexes to the main villages, providing more ready access to resources, which were, in their way, as important as those in the inner rings.

Site catchment analysis is a very general way of assessing resources, but not one that can provide fine-tuned data, except where the environment has been unchanged for many centuries (Roper, 1979).

SITE DISTRIBUTIONS AND INTERACTIONS

The distribution of natural resources in the environment was but one determinant of settlement patterns. As human societies became more complex, so too did the interactions between them, and these interactions were reflected in evolving settlement patterns. The study of entire settlement patterns brings into play a number of basic research methods that require large quantities of archaeological data.

Distribution Maps

The distribution map, which plots site distributions against the environmental background, has been used by archaeologists for a long time. One of the early pioneers in this field was the Englishman Sir Cyril Fox, whose classic monograph *The Personality of Britain* (1932) plotted archaeological sites against base maps of reconstructed prehistoric vegetation and modern topography. Other studies soon followed, as people found that prehistoric settlement patterns did tend to coincide with many environmental zones.

Distribution maps, and the settlement pattern plotted on them, are normally derived from aerial photographs and ground reconnaissance. As such, they are subject to several obvious sources of error, among them the location of archaeologists in the field, site destruction by modern construction, and the difficulties of dating sites without excavation. Most early interpretations of distribution maps were based on "eyeballing" distributions to show, using radiocarbon dates, the direction of spread of a culture trait, such as a sword type, or to explain how a scatter of site clusters came to take shape on the landscape. Obviously, however, such impressionistic interpretations are far too superficial.

Ultimately, the objective is not only to describe the distribution or settlement pattern itself but to look as well at the factors that generated the settlement pattern in the first place. These factors cannot be deduced from archaeological evidence alone, but they can be deduced by computer simulations or statistical techniques of probability.

SPATIAL ANALYSIS

Any attempt to analyze a settlement pattern must begin with development of a site typology. Such a classification should provide objective criteria for separating sites on the basis of size, function, and other features. Archaeologists in the Valley of Mexico, for example, use a local classification that distinguishes between primary and secondary regional centers, nucleated and dispersed villages, hamlets, camps, and residences, on the basis of population size, architecture, and other specific criteria. Each of these site types has a relationship to the others; the sites form a constellation that makes up a settlement pattern on a local, regional, and even continental level. And the precise definitions of site types—ceremonial centers, villages, and so on—supply us with an explicit administrative hierarchy, a series of successive levels of settlement that organizes our patterns of dots on the map hierarchically (Figure 15.13). This hierarchy raises a fundamental question: What were the rules that shaped it on the landscape?

Site Distribution Analyses

Our thinking about site hierarchies, settlement spacing, and hypothetical rules of settlement patterning depends on accurate distribution information and, even more important, on our evaluation of the significance of the various clusters of sites that can be discerned on the map. Are these

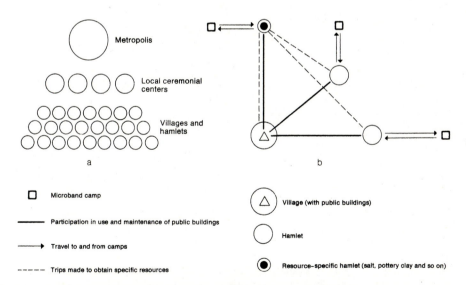

Figure 15.13 (a) A hypothetical population pyramid of archaeological site types. (b) A simplified diagram showing possible and hypothetical interactions between various Early Formative settlement types in the Valley of Oaxaca.

clusterings accidental, the result of deliberate human planning, or due to modern factors?

A number of statistical techniques can be used to analyze site distributions, most of them borrowed from geographers. David Thomas used a method called *cluster analysis* to study socioeconomic patterns in the Great Basin, where he found striking differences in site distributions. He discovered that "harvesting village and rabbit-driving implements are in a clumped distribution, while hunting artifacts tend to be distributed over piñon-juniper and upper sagebrush-grass zones." He was able to compare the theoretical distributions of the artifacts with his observed patterns (Thomas, 1983a).

Other approaches include *point-pattern analysis,* in which site distributions are plotted on a grid and tested for nonrandom patterning (Figure 15.14). The *nearest-neighbor statistic* of the geographers is another. It has been used experimentally on Olmec sites as a test for measuring the intensity of a settlement pattern (Earle, 1976; Earle and Ericson, 1977). Timothy Earle found that Olmec ceremonial centers were spaced at regular intervals in territories that were forty-four kilometers in diameter, with lesser centers within each territory. He tried to use that statistic to examine the intensity of interaction between major and minor centers. All these techniques are still in an experimental stage, and all require sophisticated statistical manipulations and data of meticulous quality to be effective (Stark and Young, 1981).

One essential ingredient for understanding settlement patterns—which Earle attempted to find in studying the Olmec—is knowledge of

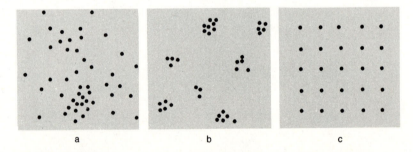

Figure 15.14 Three possible models for archaeological distributions: (a) A random distribution, with the points scattered at random. All points have an equal probability of being located at any given place on what is assumed to be a featureless landscape. (b) Clusters of points, representing artifacts or sites grouped in clumps. Distribution in clumps can occur when people are attracted toward a valuable resource or when a village, for example, generates new settlements that are located nearby. An extreme example is, of course, a distribution in which everyone is located at the same point. (c) A spaced distribution, which has the sites or artifacts at more or less regular intervals. Here, people are spaced at regular intervals because they are competing with one another for resources or in some other way.

how site hierarchies came into being and of the intensity of interaction between the inhabitants of each site type. One useful concept for this end is that of *central-place theory.*

Central-Place Theory

Central-place theory, which was first developed by the German geographer Walter Christaller (1933) in a study of southern German communities, is a series of statements about the relationship between settlement systems. Christaller stated that "if the population distribution and its purchasing power, as well as the topography, its resources, and transport facilities, are all uniform, then all central places providing similar services, performing similar functions, and serving areas of equal size, will be spaced at an equal distance from one another."

After this general definition, Christaller went on to develop a hierarchy of central places, which divided groups of centers of decreasing size and facilities into various hierarchical groups. In these hierarchies it was assumed that there were fewer large places than small ones, which provided the widest range of services possible. Not only did the largest places perform the services of the smaller ones, but they also performed central functions that distinguish them from their lesser neighbors.

The simple Christaller model has been modified by later research to allow the size of a service area to vary with the size of the central place that services it. Under this arrangement, the central-place function of Teotihuacán, for example, affects a much larger area than that serviced by smaller centers lying within, say, twenty miles of the city. The latter merely duplicate services available at Teotihuacán and are less likely to develop close to the city than they are to develop close to one another. Behind these modifications is the assumption that the location of any form of center will be determined, at least in part, by convenience to its clients. It will be located where it can be reached with minimal effort.

Ideally, a single service center that provides multiple services to a surrounding population situated on a flat plain will service a circular area, with the center located in the middle. But when there are several types of central place, each fulfilling different functions within a region, the most logical shape of the service territory would be a hexagon.

The hexagon is a theoretical configuration, to be sure, but it does reflect the essential regularity of service areas. This shape of territory minimizes the distance to the centers from the boundaries of the area and keeps population movement to a minimum (Figure 15.15). This model has been tested using southern English market towns, which were spaced four to six miles apart in Medieval times, a convenient day's journey by cart from the surrounding rural villages. Indeed, a twelfth-century law expressly forbade placement of markets closer than six miles apart. Although Ian Hodder and Mark Hassell (1972) have shown that a hexagonal model works relatively well when applied to Romano-British towns, this spacing

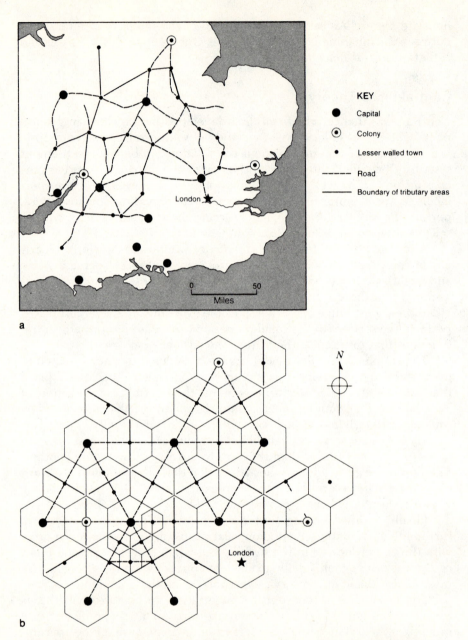

a

b

Figure 15.15 Map of Romano-British settlement in southern Britain during the third century A.D.: (a) The site hierarchy plotted on a conventional map; (b) the hexagonal lattice erected over the hierarchy. (Hodder and Hassell, 1972)

cannot be claimed as a universal law, for many factors, such as terrain or population density, can still act on even the most seemingly regular patterns.

Central-place theory's main use to archaeologists is as a descriptive device for regional settlement patterns. Richard Blanton (1978) has used it to document the rise of Teotihuacán, showing how this rapidly burgeoning central place took over the functions of nearby secondary centers and affected the entire settlement hierarchy at the same time. The central-place model provides a means of suggesting hypotheses as to what economic moves and organizational decisions were needed. These can then be tested against field data. In addition, the notion of a hierarchy of central places serving areas of different sizes—that is, in an interlocking relationship in space—is vital to archaeology. A number of attempts have been made to show that the distribution of specific prehistoric sites was patterned on a centralized or hierarchical system. The Hopewell people of the Midwest are an example. Famous traders, their cult objects were traded over the length and breadth of Ohio, Illinois, Michigan, and Wisconsin, as well as wider afield. Stuart Struever and Gail Houart (1972) examined the relationships between Hopewell sites in the Midwest and were able to suggest that the large mound sites were regional centers, where important trading was focused. They assembled a picture of the hierarchy of sites through which the Hopewell trade objects were handled, the levels of the hierarchy being defined by site size, similarity of construction, location, and distance apart.

SOCIOECOLOGICAL MODELS

The formal methods of spatial analysis archaeologists use are little more than general perspectives, part of a wider examination of archaeological sites considering the spaced resources available to their inhabitants and the constraints placed on them by such variables as perception, information, and technology (Butzer, 1982).

Hunter-Gatherer Sites

A large and complex literature surrounds living and prehistoric hunter-gatherers (Bettinger, 1986). The implicit models used by archaeologists to describe the spatial behavior of hunter-gatherers have a distinct evolutionary undertone. The assumption seems to be that human beings progressed from a simple, unspecialized, freewheeling way of life to a more and more specialized existence circumscribed within a scheduled annual round. This led, eventually, to a farming life with more lasting settlement. The chronicle of North American prehistory seems to bear out this general scenario, for the earliest Paleo-Indian and Archaic societies were adapted to a highly mobile lifeway. During Middle and Late Archaic times, and certainly after 2000 B.C., hunter-gatherer societies living in areas of rela-tively abundant and seasonally predictable food resources such as the Bottomlands of the Midwest and some coastal areas such as the Pacific Northwest evolved a more sedentary settlement pattern. This had them residing at one location for many months of the year, sometimes even year round. In the Midwest, rising population densities and resource shortages apparently led to the deliberate cultivation of some native plants such as goosefoot to amplify wild sources. Maize agriculture did not take hold in the Eastern Woodlands of North America until the first millennium A.D. (Fagan, 1990).

Karl Butzer (1974, 1982) made another assumption when he studied the Lower Paleolithic Acheulian sites of Ambrona and Torralba in central Spain. He argued that early hunter-gatherers shared the ability of large grazing animals like elephants to adopt different feeding habits and sea-sonal movements according to the abundance of resources through the year. Ambrona and Torralba lie along the only low-altitude mountain pass dividing the plains of Castile. This was the route through which large mammals migrated in spring and fall from winter to summer pastures and back again. The Acheulians preyed on these migrating beasts. During other seasons of the year, they spread over the neighboring country in temporary camps near water and constantly moving herds (Figure 15.16). This settlement pattern is suggested not only by site distributions but also by such phenomena as migratory bird bones in the archaeological depos-its. It is, of course, possible that the Acheulians were scavenging elephants that died after becoming enmired in swampy ground.

These Mexican and Spanish examples suggest that the movements of hunter-gatherers were related to different ways of exploiting local re-sources that can be detected in the archaeological record. The first re-quirement in establishing spatial and temporal variables is to find the span of time during which individual sites were used (Binford, 1978; Butzer, 1982). They can be ephemeral, occupied for a few hours or days; tempo-rary, used for several days or weeks; seasonal; or semipermanent. Func-tional and social considerations affect the duration of occupation, too, but these cannot always be inferred from the archaeological record. Armed with these data, you can prepare "mobility models" for hunter-gatherers, samples of which are shown in Figure 15.17.

Early Archaic Settlement on the Atlantic Slope   The large-scale cul-tural resource management surveys and test excavations of recent years have led to many important regional studies of prehistoric culture, not just in North America but throughout the world. Many of these describe rela-tively small hunter-gatherer populations using models derived from gen-eral ecological and anthropological theory derived by ethnoarchaeological research.

David Anderson and Glen Hanson's (1988) study of Early Archaic settlement in the Savannah River Valley of the southeastern United States

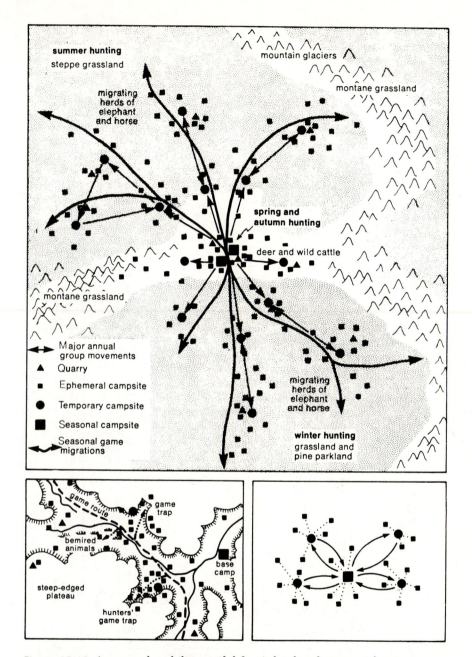

Figure 15.16 A seasonal mobility model for Acheulian hunter-gatherers in central Spain, based in part on data from Ambrona and Torralba. During spring and fall, the hunters preyed on herds migrating through the mountain passes (map at lower left). In summer and winter, the hunters divided into smaller groups and lived in temporary sites near water, animal herds, and stone outcrops. (After Butzer, 1982)

Synthesis

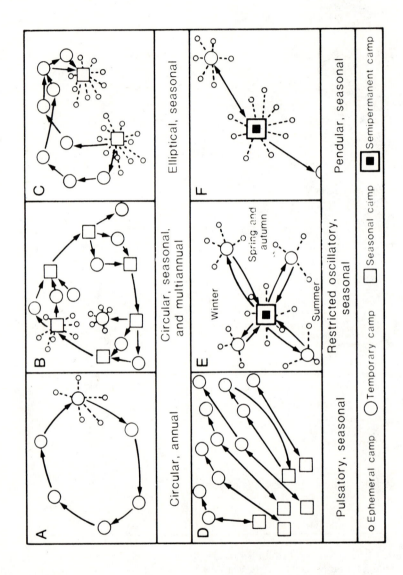

A Circular, annual

B Circular, seasonal,
   and multiannual

C Elliptical, seasonal

D Pulsatory, seasonal

E Restricted oscillatory,
   seasonal

F Pendular, seasonal

o Ephemeral camp   ○ Temporary camp   □ Seasonal camp   ■ Semipermanent camp

416

is an excellent example of a regional research project carried out with a sophisticated theoretical underpinning combined with widespread surveying and careful excavation.

Modern ecological research has established that clear relations exist between the distribution of resources within an environment and the foraging strategies of the animals that live in it. In ecosystems with patchily distributed resources, animals tend to forage for specific resources, whereas they tend to be more eclectic in their foraging when resources are evenly distributed throughout the landscape. By the same token, hunter-gatherer populations tend to be less mobile, to collect and store food in environments with patchy resources, whereas in more uniform environments they tend to forage over the landscape, moving frequently. This phenomenon led Anderson and Hanson to predict that as homogeneous hardwood forest spread over the southeastern Atlantic slope at the very end of the Ice Age some 10,000 years ago, Early Archaic human populations would tend to adopt increasingly mobile foraging adaptations over the same region.

Ecological theory, based, among other things, on research into blackbird nesting behavior, also suggested that during the winters, when plant foods were relatively scarce in this woodland environment and deer concentrated in larger groups, Early Archaic populations would tend to live in more sedentary base camps, dispersing into more mobile, widely dispersed camps during the plentiful warmer months.

Anderson and Hanson developed a general biocultural model of Early Archaic settlement on the southern Atlantic Coast of North America that reflected both general ecological theory and the character of the regional archaeological record. They hypothesize that Early Archaic bands living in this area used warmer, well-provisioned base camps on the warmer coastal plain during the winter. These settlements were located within river drainages, close to raw material sources, and placed according to the availability of food resources, including deer, which tended to move in

Figure 15.17 Hypothetical mobility models for hunter-gatherers. (A) Seasonal camps on a semirandom annual circular movement. (B) Seasonal aggregation and dispersal to optimize use of scattered, less predictable resources. Over the years, the pattern will be roughly circular. (C) Elliptical nomadic pattern, such as one might find along a perennial river, with the inhabitants moving out into less well watered areas during the rainy season. (D) Pulsatory seasonal movement, as might occur when lowland herders venture into the highlands at certain seasons of the year. (E) Oscillatory pattern, where people use one base at certain times of the year, then disperse outward at other seasons. This is the Ambrona-Torralba model. (F) Pendular model, which might apply when people were experimenting with crops and were living in one place for much of the year, dispersing at others; can be likened to a seasonal pendulum effect. (After Butzer, 1982)

larger groups during the winter. In early spring the deer dispersed and edible plant resources appeared over much of the landscape, first at the warmer coast, then inland. The people now moved out into small, regularly spaced camps, their distribution reflecting the fairly even distribution of food resources. To some extent, the bands were "tethered" to raw material sources, which were irregularly distributed over the landscape. They foraged over the Upper Coastal Plain and the Piedmont (Figure 15.18) during the summer. Come fall, the bands moved downstream, probably choosing base camp locations that were different from the year before, for resources at those locations were probably still depleted. Anderson and Hanson use estimates derived from site surveys and excavations to argue that between 50 and 150 people lived in each neighboring drainage at the beginning of the Early Archaic, a figure that rose over the centuries, resulting in decreases in annual ranges as bands fissioned into new groups that occupied smaller territories.

The settlement pattern of Early Archaic bands over the South Atlantic Slope reflected the northwest-to-southeast flow of most major drainages there, from the Appalachian Mountains to the Atlantic. Anderson and Hanson believe that to maintain a viable equilibrium population, bands from three to five drainages had to be in regular contact. They maintained networks both through the movements of individuals and through regular gatherings, probably in the fall, reflected by major sites located midway between winter and summer foraging grounds. The two archaeologists argue that there was a South Atlantic Macroband of between five hundred and one thousand people, perhaps made up of as many as eight separate groups living in contiguous drainages. Other such macrobands may have lived on all sides of the region, those to the south and west separated from the South Atlantic Slope by natural geographic barriers. This important regional study argues that Early Archaic adaptations in this area, like many other prehistoric hunter-gatherer adaptations, were conditioned not only by the local environment but also by biological interaction between different groups, population spacing, and restraints of information exchange between neighboring groups.

Agricultural Settlements

The clustering and patterning of agricultural settlements are affected by cultural and environmental factors combined. The following are some key variables.

> *Distribution of economic resources* such as different types of land with separate uses for grazing, cultivation, and so on. Soil distributions are also vital, for different depths, textures, and subsoils can impose severe limitations for grazing and other uses. The earliest European farmers concentrated on well-drained, easily dug soils because they

lacked the heavy plows that enabled cultivators to turn over heavier clay soils. The distribution of game and vegetable food resources is also vital.

Available technology, land clearance techniques, available transport or draft animals, crop types exploited, and other such factors within the site itself are critical. So too is the socioeconomic organization that schedules planting and harvest, determines who works with whom, and copes with the obligations among members of the community. A wide range of symbolic and social values also place their imprint on settlement patterns, for they determine not only perceptions of resources but also attitudes toward the environment as well as toward one's neighbors.

Topography influences the placement of agricultural sites in relation to their neighbors, affects direction of trade routes, and encourages or inhibits communication. The Ancient Egyptians depended on the Nile for transportation and water; their modern successors do so still. The same topography can profoundly affect the ways in which agricultural settlement fills in areas that were not settled at first, for spacing of new communities will be affected by location of the original settlements with their continuing needs for land. Defense, too, can radically affect agricultural site distributions. Everyone may elect to live on hilltops, simply to guard against surprise attack.

Trade networks play a leading role in the emergence of central places, such as great cities like the Aztec capital of Tenochtitlán, which attracted trade from all over Mesoamerica (Fagan, 1984a). Originally a settlement pattern based on trade may be determined in part by environment or social considerations, but eventually a vertical hierarchy of sites may grow, as technological, demographic, social, and religious forces come into play. Eventually, as society becomes more complex, site networks may be modified by overriding religious or political considerations. This change happened in colonial Mexico, where the incoming Spanish authorities resettled thousands of Indians into small towns that were under the direct control of the central government.

Agricultural settlements on any scale are affected by so many environmental, economic, social, and other factors that simple propositions like those developed for hunter-gatherers are untenable. Any approach to the study of agricultural settlements has to emphasize not only the distribution patterns, so critical in interpreting hunter-gatherer subsistence patterns, but also the interactions between sites that made them occur, for agricultural settlements were far more dependent on one another than those of hunter-gatherers.

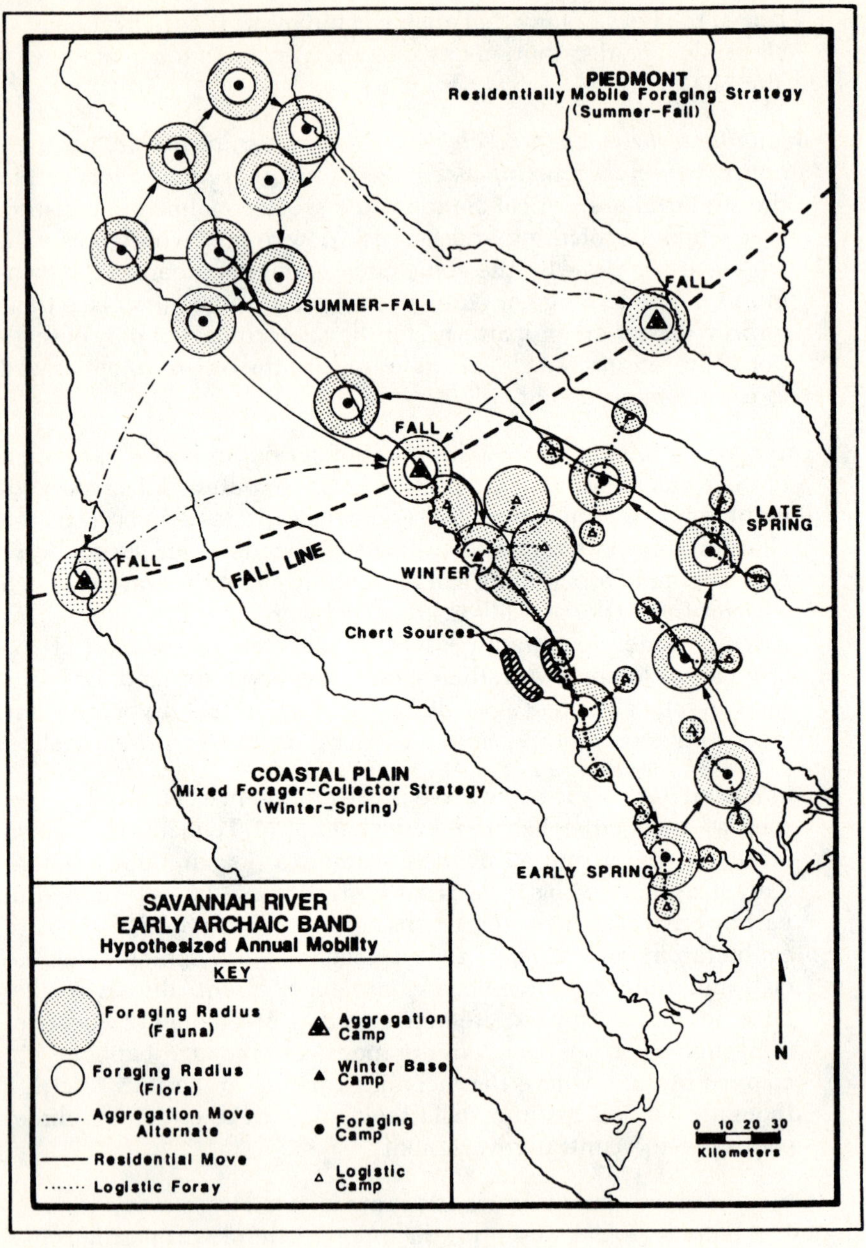
PIEDMONT
Residentially Mobile Foraging Strategy
(Summer-Fall)
SUMMER-FALL
FALL
FALL
FALL
FALL LINE
WINTER
LATE SPRING
Chert Sources
COASTAL PLAIN
Mixed Forager-Collector Strategy
(Winter-Spring)
EARLY SPRING
SAVANNAH RIVER
EARLY ARCHAIC BAND
Hypothesized Annual Mobility
KEY
Foraging Radius (Fauna)
Foraging Radius (Flora)
Aggregation Move Alternate
Residential Move
Logistic Foray
Aggregation Camp
Winter Base Camp
Foraging Camp
Logistic Camp
N
0 10 20 30
Kilometers

a

Figure 15.18 Anderson and Hanson's (1988) hypothesized model of Early Archaic settlement on the southern Atlantic Coast of North America: (a) model of seasonal mobility; (b) model of Early Archaic band-macroband distribution over the region.

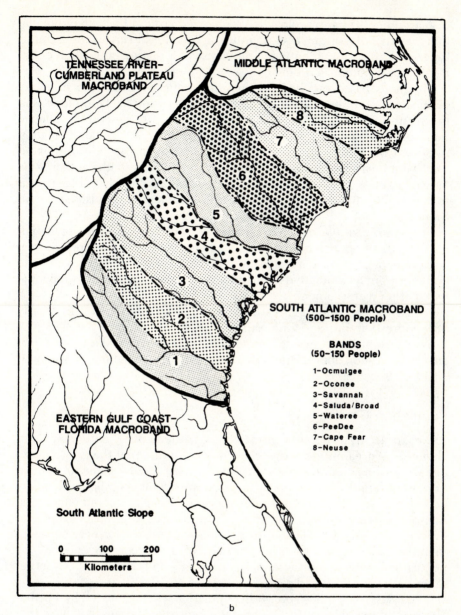

b

Figure 15.18 *(Continued)*

POPULATION

Settlement patterns evolve in response to three broad variables: environmental change, alterations in population density, and interaction among people. One major factor in the later cultural evolution of humanity has undoubtedly been rapidly growing population densities. Many of the classical arguments of archaeology have revolved around the role of population growth in the origins of agriculture, urban life, and civilization. Unfortunately, however, as mentioned previously, estimating population densities is a task fraught with difficulty.

Methods based on *food consumption* have been used to calculate populations of hunter-gatherer camps in Europe and of shell middens in the western United States. A clever though mainly theoretical calculation—but one that may give a reasonable estimate of general population size—was made by a group of California archaeologists, who estimated that about thirty people occupied the Scripps Estate in southern California between about 5500 and 3500 B.C. (Cook, 1972). They based their estimates on the amount of shell refuse and the number of grindstones found there.

Cemeteries and burial grounds have been used to estimate population also, but this evidence has the disadvantage that it is seldom representative of the population as a whole. Most cemeteries are used for a long time and represent a cumulative population rather than the number of people living at a given moment.

Most demographic figures from large geographic areas are clearly little more than guesses. One estimate places the average population of the early Sumerian states in Mesopotamia at about 17,000 souls (Sanders and Price, 1968); another puts the Late Glacial population of Britain at about 10,000 (Clark, 1952).

Population Growth

Although accurate population estimates, settlement by settlement, are obviously of great interest, especially if one assumes that the growing size of a village represents a growing population, the consequences of population growth and decline are even more important. Population is a key element in the cultural process, for there is a clear cause-and-effect relationship between population and the potential carrying capacity and productivity of agricultural land. Competition and cooperation between communities may result from a shortage of resources engendered by population growth, and these interactions may in turn affect both settlement patterns and population density (Hassan, 1981).

The classic hypothesis on world population was formulated by Thomas Henry Malthus late in the eighteenth century. Malthus believed that humankind's reproductive capacity far exceeds available food supplies; in other words, people must compete for the necessities of life. Competition causes famine, war, and misery. The Malthusian thesis has so dominated archaeological thinking for generations that many scholars believed that the capacity of land and other resources, as well as that of technology, places limits on population growth.

The Malthusian viewpoint has been challenged by economist Ester Boserup (1965), who stated the thesis that population growth should be treated as a quite independent variable when studying technological and cultural change. "As population grows," she argued,

> more people per unit of land are faced with the necessity of providing more food per unit of land, and they are able to do this by intensifying their relationship with the land—technology—moving from hunting and gathering through stages of cultivation with ever-shorter fallow periods up to the final stage of intensification, which is multicropping with no fallowing.

She went on to argue that people intensify their agricultural efforts only when forced by population pressure to do so. The implication is that more intensive land use is accompanied by parallel intensification of other aspects of culture and society (Spooner, 1972).

Boserup's theoretical viewpoint highlights population as another variable in settlement archaeology. Unfortunately, few regions have been surveyed in sufficient archaeological detail to enable population estimates or data on intensity of agriculture to be made with any statistical confidence. Elizabeth Brumfiel (1976) used site catchment analysis and modern agricultural data to study population growth in Formative villages in the Valley of Mexico. She recorded a slight increase in the settlement area at the end of the Formative, but the ratio of productive potential of the agricultural land to site size remained almost the same as before, and climatic conditions had also remained the same. But three of the larger sites had a much higher population-to-productivity ratio than the smaller settlements. From this difference she concluded that there were political and social reasons why this situation developed. Conceivably, she argued, the smaller villages had to pay taxes for services to larger settlements. Therefore, the smaller settlements boosted their agricultural production, while the larger centers enjoyed greater population densities but did not have to raise their own agricultural production.

The Brumfiel research, and that of other investigators, such as Jeffrey Parsons in the same region (Sanders and others, 1979), and Robert Adams (1974) on irrigation in Mesopotamia, clearly demonstrate the complex economic and social variables that could affect population growth in prehistory. Much of the time, settlement archaeology involves hypothesizing about intangibles, those aspects of human society that are never preserved in the archaeological record. But as Chapter 16 shows, much of our understanding of cultural evolution and changing settlement patterns comes from the insights we can obtain into the interactions between different communities reflected in their trading, social, and religious practices.

SUMMARY

- Settlement archaeology, the study of changing human settlement patterns, is part of the analysis of adaptive interactions between people and their environment.

- Settlement patterns are determined by many factors, among them the environment, economic practices, and technological skills. Learned cultural skills and established networks of human behavior also affect settlement, as do practical political considerations, population growth, and social organization. Settlement archaeology involves examining the complex relationships between parts of a cultural system and the natural environment.
- Bruce Trigger defines three levels of settlement: the building or structure, the arrangement of structures within individual communities, and the distribution of communities across the landscape.
- Single structures can be studied from the perspective of form and material or from a functional viewpoint. Social and political institutions also affect the design of individual houses.
- A community is a maximal group of people that normally resides in face-to-face associations. The layout of communities is much affected by political and social considerations. The archaeologist looks for clusters of settlement attributes that may indicate a grouping of social units. Estimates of population are very difficult to obtain from even comprehensive archaeological data—there simply are too many intangible variables that affect the archaeological record.
- Prehistoric environmental data are obtained both from Pleistocene geology and from animal bones, especially those of small mammals. Pollen analysis is one of the most effective methods of reconstructing ancient environments. We cited examples from Star Carr and Israel to show how people adapted to environments that were very different from those of today.
- Site catchment analysis is a method used to inventory resources within range of prehistoric sites. It is a study of the relationships between technology and available natural resources. We used examples from Israel and Oaxaca to demonstrate its applications.
- Site distribution maps are used to study prehistoric settlement patterns; these are analyzed using rigorous, objective criteria, which take into account sampling errors and other variables. The objective of such analyses is to establish the factors that governed human settlement in prehistoric times.
- Spatial analyses in archaeology make use of a variety of techniques that were developed by geographers. They include central-place theory and cluster analysis.
- Population estimates for prehistoric sites have been made by subjective guesswork, mathematical formulas, and sophisticated estimates of the carrying capacity of the land. Such estimates are rarely precise.
- Population growth was a major factor in later prehistory. Most archaeologists agree with Thomas Henry Malthus that humanity's reproductive capacity far exceeds available food supplies. But Ester Boserup and her colleagues disagree, arguing that people intensify

their food-gathering or production efforts in the face of rising population. This controversy highlights the necessity for archaeologists to examine the many intangible variables that affect cultural change over long periods of prehistoric time.

GUIDE TO FURTHER READING

Butzer, Karl W. *Archaeology as Human Ecology.* Cambridge: Cambridge University Press, 1982. An authoritative description of basic environmental and spatial concepts in archaeology. Strongly recommended as a starting point.

Flannery, Kent V., ed. *The Early Mesoamerican Village.* Orlando, Fla.: Academic Press, 1976. A modern classic, a study by a team of Michigan archaeologists of settlement patterns in the Valley of Oaxaca. Enlivened by some hypothetical but highly entertaining debates between fictitious archaeologists of different theoretical viewpoints.

Hietala, H., ed. *Intersite Spatial Analysis in Archaeology.* Cambridge: Cambridge University Press, 1984. Essays on relationships between sites in the archaeological record.

Sanders, William T., Jeffrey R. Parsons, and Robert S. Santley. *The Basin of Mexico: Ecological Processes in the Evolution of a Civilization,* 2 vols. Orlando, Fla.: Academic Press, 1979. A settlement-ecological study that gives an admirable impression of the state-of-the-art research in this field.

Winterhalder, Bruce, and Eric Alden Smith, eds. *Hunter-Gatherer Foraging Strategies.* Chicago: University of Chicago Press, 1981. Essays for the advanced reader that concentrate on analyses of hunter-gatherer societies. A strong emphasis on optimal foraging strategy.

Chapter
16

Trade, Social Organization, and Religious Life

*T*o this point we have discussed human cultures as more or less self-sufficient entities, each with its own territory and constellation of natural resources. Very few human societies have lived in complete isolation from their neighbors, however. One major theme of world prehistory is the increasing interdependence and competition between communities, the culmination of which is the highly interdependent, industrialized world we live in today. In this chapter we examine the ways in which archaeologists study these evolving interactions, which are reflected in the exchange of resources and trading and in kinship, marriage, and more complex social structures, as well as in shared religious beliefs.

TRADE AND EXCHANGE SYSTEMS (EXTERNAL TRADE)

Trade has been defined as the "mutually appropriative movement of goods between hands" (Renfrew, 1975). People make trade connections and the exchange systems that handle trade goods when they need to acquire goods and services that are not available to them within their own site catchment area. The movement of goods need not be over any great distance, and it can operate internally, within a society, or externally, across cultural boundaries—within interaction spheres. Trade always involves two elements: the goods and commodities being exchanged and the people doing the exchanging. Thus any form of trading activity implies both procurement and handling of tools and raw materials and some form of social system that provides the people-to-people relationships within which the trade flourishes. Not only raw materials and finished objects but also ideas and information passed along trade routes.

Conventionally, trade is recognized in the archaeological record by the discovery of objects exotic to the material culture or economy of the host society. For instance, glass was never manufactured in sub-Saharan Africa, yet imported glass beads are widespread in archaeological sites of the first millennium A.D. (Beck and Schofield, 1958). Until recently, such objects were recognized almost entirely on the basis of style and design— the appearance of distinctive pottery forms far from their known point of origin and so on. Sometimes exotics such as gold, amber, turquoise, or marine shells, commodities whose general area of origin was known, provided evidence of long-distance exchanges. Late Archaic and Woodland peoples in the North American Southeast used native copper from outcrops near Lake Superior and conch shells from the Gulf Coast, both commodities of known origin.

In the early days of archaeology, such exotica were deemed sufficient to identify trade, even what were loosely called "influences" or even "invasions." The assumptions made about the nature of human interactions were very limited and never precise (Torrence, 1986). Today, however, studies of prehistoric exchange are far more sophisticated, owing to two major developments. The first is a new focus throughout archaeology on the cultural process and on regional studies. The second is the development of a wide range of scientific techniques that are capable of describing the composition of certain types of raw material and even of identifying their sources with great precision. By far the most significant of these materials is obsidian, volcanic glass that is ideal for fabricating stone tools, ornaments, and in Mesoamerica, highly polished mirrors (Figure 16.1).

In the 1960s, Colin Renfrew and others used spectrographic analysis to identify no fewer than twelve early farming villages that had obtained obsidian from the Ciftlik area of central Turkey (Renfrew and others, 1966). This pioneer study showed that 80 percent of the chipped stone in villages within three hundred kilometers of Ciftlik was obsidian. Outside this "supply zone," the percentages of obsidian dropped away sharply with distance, to 5 percent in a Syrian village and 0.1 percent in the Jordan Valley. If these calculations were correct, each village was passing about half its imported obsidian further down the line (Figure 16.2).

The Ciftlik research provoked widespread interest and many new studies, not only in the Near East but in Mesoamerica, California, and other areas as well (Torrence, 1986). Obsidian has indeed proved an ideal raw material for monitoring prehistoric exchange and for developing new theoretical approaches to early trade, based not only on single sites but also on studies of entire regions. For example, Renfrew and his colleagues have identified no fewer than nine Neolithic and Early Bronze Age obsidian "interaction zones" between Sardinia and Mesopotamia, each of them linked to well-defined sources of supply. In Mesoamerica, many

Figure 16.1 An obsidian mirror from Mesoamerica, reflecting a figurine.

scholars have attempted to trace the exact trade routes over which obsidian traveled from highlands to lowlands. The use of source data enables one to conceive of exchange on a regional basis. Today, archaeologists regard exchange as "a form of interaction such that a *system of interrelations* operates on a regional level" (Torrence, 1986). Nowadays, the ultimate research goal is to identify the exchange mechanisms that distributed the obsidian within each interaction zone. Thus the data requirements have changed. No longer is it sufficient to know the approximate source of a raw material or an artifact. Sources must be pinpointed accurately, and distributions of traded goods or commodities must be quantified precisely. Such data provide the groundwork for studies of trade. However, as Robin Torrence points out (1986), it remains to translate these distributions and the source data into characterizations of human behavior.

Torrence has focused on obsidian, one of the few exchange commodities that was regularly traded in many parts of the prehistoric world, not

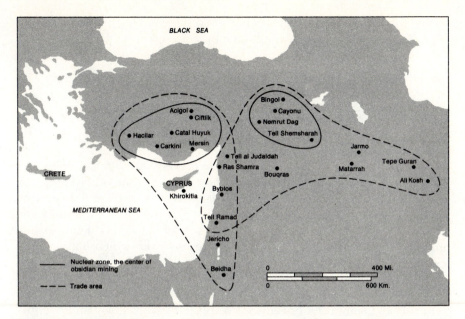

Figure 16.2 Obsidian trade routes in the neolithic Near East. The nuclear zone was the center of obsidian mining.

only by hunter-gatherers but by village farmers and much more complex societies as well. It has been the subject of numerous regional and single-site studies in the Mediterranean and in Mesoamerica, among other areas. Most of these studies have concentrated on the use of obsidian and the amount of it traded from settlement to settlement. Torrence believes that future studies will have to monitor exchange by taking analogies from ethnohistorical and historical studies of quarrying and trade and by developing new ways of inferring behavior from the archaeological record. Chipped stone is useful in this regard, for one can reconstruct the reduction strategies used to produce traded raw material and finished artifacts and thereby gain insights into efficiency of production and other such facets of human behavior. Prehistoric quarries, such as those in Greece, Mesoamerica, and Australia, are potentially valuable sources of information on the exchange of exotic materials. Torrence based his ideas on an innovative study of Aegean obsidian trade, finding that the exchange was noncommercial and noncompetitive: the prehistoric knappers visited quarries and prepared material for exchange with minimal concern for economical use of the raw material. On the island of Melos, for example, the visitors simply quarried what they wanted and left. There is no evidence of specialized production. During early farming times, obsidian mining may have been a seasonal occupation, but during the Bronze Age, it became a specialized occupation requiring special voyages to Melos and other quarries. The reason for the shift is unknown. Perhaps it was connected to a rising demand that outstripped the yield from seasonal visits. (For a full discussion of the methodology, see Torrence, 1986.)

Social Interaction and Organization (Internal Distribution)

Gift giving is a common medium of exchange and trade in societies that are relatively self-supporting. The exchange of gifts is designed primarily to reinforce a social relationship, both of an individual and of a group as a whole. This form of trade is common in New Guinea and the Pacific, widespread in Africa during the past two thousand years, and in the Americas as well. Much depends on the types of commodity being exchanged. The exchange of seashells may have involved individuals of higher status; that of foodstuffs and hut poles was a more common form of transaction involving many individuals and families. And of course, not only objects but also information can be exchanged, which may lead to technological innovation or social change. Gift giving and bartering formed a basic trading mechanism for millennia, a simple means of exchanging basic commodities. But this sporadic interaction between individuals and communities reduced people's self-sufficiency and eventually made them part of a larger society whose members were no longer so self-sufficient and who depended on one another not only for basic commodities but also for social purposes.

The decision to engage in trading—to acquire commodities from afar—depends both on how urgent the need for the goods is and on the difficulties in acquiring and transporting them. Clearly, such items as cattle or slaves are more easily transported than tons of iron ore or salt cakes. The former move on their own, but metals require human or animal carriers or wheeled carts. To ignore these differences is to oversimplify the study of prehistoric trade (Ericson and Earle, 1982).

Reciprocity, the mutual exchange of goods between two individuals or groups, is at the heart of much gift giving and barter trade. It can happen year after year at the same place, which can be as humble as someone's house. Such central places become the focus of gift giving and trade. When a village becomes involved in both the production of trade goods and their exchange with other communities, it will probably become an even more important center, a place to which people will travel to trade.

Redistribution of trade goods from a central place throughout a culture requires some form of organization to ensure that the redistribution is equitable. A redistributive mechanism may be controlled by a chief, a religious leader, or some form of management organization. Such an organization might control production of copper ornaments, or it might simply control distribution and delivery of trade objects. Considerable social organization is needed for the collection, storage, and redistribution of grain and other commodities. The chief, whose position is perhaps reinforced by religious power, has a serious responsibility to his community that can extend over several villages, as his lines of redistribution stretch out through people of lesser rank to the individual villager. A chief will negotiate exchanges with other chiefs, substituting the regulatory elements of reciprocal trading for a redistributive economy in which less trading in exotic materials is carried out by individual households.

Prehistoric trade was an important variable that developed in conjunction with sociopolitical organization. It has been assumed that trade proceeded from simple reciprocal exchange to the more complex redistribution of goods under a redistributor. In other words, trading is closely tied to growing complexity in social and political organization.

Markets (at a higher level than redistribution) are both places and particular styles of trading administration and organization that encourage people to set aside one place for trading and relatively stable, almost fixed prices for staple commodities. This stability does not mean regulated prices, but some regulation is needed in a network or markets in which commodities from an area of abundant supplies are sold to one with strong demand for the same materials. The mechanisms of the exchange relationship particularly require some regulation. Markets are normally associated with more complex societies. No literate civilization ever developed without strong central places, where trading activities were regulated and monopolies developed over both sources of materials and trade routes themselves.

Successful market trading required predictable supplies of basic commodities and adequate policing of trade routes. It is significant that most early Mesopotamian and Egyptian trade was riverine, where policing was easier. With the great caravan routes opened, the political and military issues—tribute, control of trade routes, and tolls—became paramount. The caravan, predating the great empires, was a form of organized trading that kept to carefully defined routes set up and maintained by state authorities. The travelers moved along these set routes, looking neither left nor right, bent only on delivering and exchanging imports and exports. These caravans were a far cry from the huge economic complex that accompanied Alexander the Great's army across Asia or the Grand Mogul's annual summer progress from the heat in Delhi to the mountains, which moved a half million people, including the entire Delhi bazaar.

Studying Market Networks

Emphasis on these mechanisms has led L. L. Johnson, C. C. Lamberg-Karlovsky, William Rathje, and others to study market networks and the mechanisms by which supplies are channeled down well-defined routes and by which profits are regulated and fed back to the source, providing further incentive for more supplies (Figure 16.3) (Sabloff and Lamberg-Karlovsky, 1975). There may or may not be a physical marketplace; it is the state of affairs surrounding the trade that forms the focus of the trading system and the mechanisms by means of which trade interacts with other

Figure 16.3 A ceremonial Mayan *metate*, a carved stone slab used for grinding corn and other foodstuffs, an artifact widely traded in the Mayan lowlands 1,500 years ago. ("Stela of the *Visor Paser*," 1303–1287 B.C.; limestone, 46.5 × 50.8 × 8.0 cm. Gift of Mrs. Frank E. Peabody. Courtesy, Museum of Fine Arts, Boston)

parts of the culture. Taking a systems approach to trading activity means emphasizing the role of archaeological finds as the material expressions of interdependent factors. These factors include the need for goods—which prompts a search for supplies. The supplies themselves represent production beyond local needs and are created to satisfy external demands. Other factors are the logistics of transportation and the extent of the trading network, as well as the social and political environment. With all these variables, no one aspect of trade can be viewed as an overriding cause of cultural change or of evolution in trading practices. Hitherto, archaeologists have concentrated on the objects of trade or on trade as an abstraction—trade as a cause of civilization; but they have had no profound knowledge about the workings of even one trading network from which to build more theoretical abstractions.

TEPE YAHYA: TRADE IN PREHISTORY

Trading was integral in early Sumerian civilization in the Near East, too, a many-faceted operation that absorbed the energies of thousands of people. Sumerian trade was much more tightly organized and controlled than, say, Hopewell trading. The redistribution systems of the cities combined many activities, all controlled by the central authority that ruled the settlements. Food surpluses were redistributed and raw materials were obtained from far away for the manufacture of ornaments, weapons, and prestigious luxuries. Demands for raw materials appear to have risen steadily, spreading market networks into territories remote from the home state. For these long-distance routes to succeed, political stability at both ends of the route was essential. An intricate system of political, financial, and logistical checks and balances had to be kept up, requiring an efficient and alert administrative organization.

The raw materials traded by the Sumerians included metals, timber, skins, ivory, and such precious stones as malachite. Many could be found only in the remote highlands to the north and east of Mesopotamia. The trade in steatite (soapstone, an easy-to-work material) shows how far-flung Mesopotamian trade became (Lamberg-Karlovsky, 1970, 1975). Steatite was used to make stone bowls as early as 10,000 B.C., but it suddenly became a fashionable material abound 2750 B.C. Steatite bowls are found in Early Dynastic Mesopotamian tells and also occur at Moenjo-daro in the Indus Valley, one of the great cities of the Indus civilization, and at contemporaneous sites on islands in the Persian Gulf. Objects of the same materials are also common in settlements near today's Iran-Pakistan border, the hinterland between Indus and Mesopotamian civilizations. Most of the steatite objects are stone bowls bearing intricate designs, the same designs being found all over the area where steatite is found.

Experiments with physicochemical analysis have identified at least a dozen sources of the stone, but so far only Tepe Yahya in Iran is known to have been a center of steatite bowl production (Figure 16.4). Abundant steatite deposits occur near the site. The bowls produced at Tepe Yahya and elsewhere were definitely items of luxury; they were so prized in Mesopotamia that they may have caused keen competition among people rich enough to afford them. The competition for luxury goods in general

Figure 16.4 The tell at Tepe Yahya, Iran, an important center of the steatite trade.

may have been intense enough to affect production rates in the source areas, with political vicissitudes in the Mesopotamian city-states constantly shifting production rates of steatite centers and making profits from the trade fluctuate. Interestingly, the demand for steatite around Tepe Yahya was minimal, and the occurrence of few finds in the Indus Valley contrasts sharply with the very large quantities found in Mesopotamia. Most of the trade was with the west, depending on the demand for luxuries among the increasingly wealthy elites of the Mesopotamian cities. Local artisans seem to have produced the steatite near Tepe Yahya, perhaps working part-time or at selected seasons. But the trade itself was not in the artisans' hands; it was run by middlemen and ultimately by the exploitative elite of Mesopotamia. C. C. Lamberg-Karlovsky (1975) calls this trade a form of economic imperialism: "Economic exploitation of foreign areas without political control."

The study of prehistoric trade is a vital source of information on social organization and the ways in which societies became more complex. Trade itself developed a great complexity, in both goods traded and the interactions of people involved. Colin Renfrew (1975) identified no fewer than ten types of interaction between people that can result from trading, ranging from simple contact between individuals to trading by professional traders, such as the *pochteca* of the Maya and the Aztec, who sometimes acted as spies (Figure 16.5) (Fagan, 1984a).

SOCIAL ORGANIZATION

"Data relevant to most, if not all, components of past sociocultural systems *are* preserved in the archaeological record," argued Lewis Binford (1968) some years ago. Traditionally, archaeologists had regarded the more intangible aspects of human society, such as religious and social organization, as particularly difficult to infer from archaeological data. Many minor differences between prehistoric peoples—speech, religion, and social organization among them—are, it is true, seldom obvious in the archaeological record, and traditional definitions of culture help us to recognize differences only when they are detectable in the data obtained by excavation, analysis, and induction. But Binford's approach sees human cultures in archaeology as sociocultural systems that enable one to think of social and religious factors as vital subsystems in regulating cultural change. These intangibles can be reconstructed, at least partially, he believes, by studying artifact patterns and stylistic changes in material culture, as well as by applying middle-range theory (Chapter 15). Other archaeologists have pointed out that material culture is extremely sensitive to changes in ideology, as reflected in stylistic changes in such items as New England Colonial tombstones (Deetz, 1967). As we saw in Chapter 15, other archaeologists disagree with this notion.

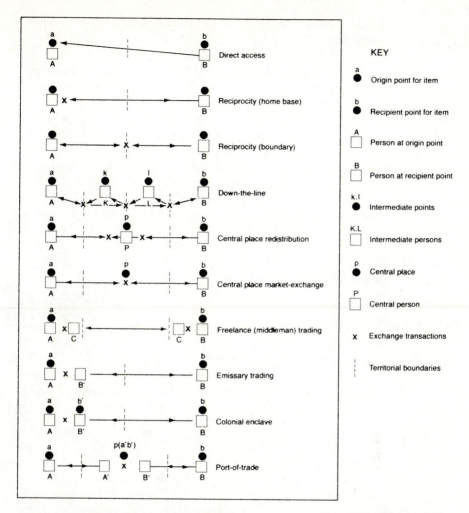

Figure 16.5 The ten ways in which prehistoric trade can operate, as determined by Colin Renfrew (1975). The diagram illustrates the wide variety of means by which trade goods are exchanged, each of which has specific implications for settlement patterns. The arrows show the direction of trading relationships.

Stages of Social Organization

Archaeologists look at social organization in prehistory with the aid of general conceptual schemes drawn up by anthropologists. Such schemes are particularly important when one is examining human cultural evolution. Edward Tylor, Lewis Morgan, and more recently, V. Gordon Childe and Leslie White were among those who realized that it was a mistake to consider human cultural evolution as divorced from social organization. Childe (1942) recognized this truth with his formulations of Neolithic and urban revolutions. Anthropologist Elman Service, in his classic *Primitive Social Organization* (1971), defined several broad levels of sociocultural evolution, which provided a general framework for tracing the evolution of human social organization from the first simple, primitive family structures of the earliest hunter-gatherers to the highly complex state-organized societies of the early civilizations.

All theories of cultural evolution are based on the premise that human societies have changed over long periods of time and that the general trend throughout prehistory has been toward a greater complexity of human culture and social institutions. Elman Service divided human societies into bands, tribes, chiefdoms, and states, a classification that has won wide acceptance but is much criticized for its arbitrary rigidity. Many archaeologists prefer a broader grouping, into which Service's categories fall.

Prestate Societies

Prestate societies are societies on a small scale, based on the community, band, or village. They vary greatly in their degree of political integration, and can be divided into three categories:

Bands are autonomous and self-sufficient groups that usually consist of only a few families. They are egalitarian, with leadership coming from the experience and personal qualities of particular individuals rather than from political power.

Tribes are egalitarian like bands, but with a greater level of social and cultural complexity. They have developed kin-based mechanisms to accommodate more sedentary living, to redistribute food, and to organize some communal services. Some more complex hunter-gatherer societies, including the Pacific Northwest groups, can be classified as tribal; most were associated with village farming. Being egalitarian, public opinion played a major role in decision making.

Chiefdoms are societies headed by individuals with unusual ritual, political, or entrepreneurial skills and are often hard to distinguish from tribes. Society is still kin-based, but more hierarchical, with power concentrated in the hands of powerful kin leaders, responsible for the redistribution of resources. Chiefdoms tend to have higher population densities and to display the first signs of social ranking, reflected in more elaborate material possessions. They vary greatly in their elaboration, the degree of elaboration depending on many factors, including the distribution of population over the landscape. Tahitian chiefs presided over powerful, constantly quarreling chiefdoms, frequently waging ferocious wars against their neighbors. The elaborate Mississippian chiefdoms of the American Midwest and South flourished during the early second millennium A.D., maintaining elaborate trade networks and ritual contacts over long distances.

State-organized Societies

State-organized societies operate on a large scale with centralized social and political organization, class stratification, and intensive agriculture. They have complex political structures, many permanent government institutions, and firm notions of social inequality.

A state-organized society is governed by a full-fledged ruling class, whose privileges and powers are bolstered by a hierarchic secular and religious bureaucracy, at least a rudimentary system of justice, and a system of ranked classes of nobility, warriors, traders, priests, bureaucrats, peasants, and perhaps slaves. The ruler enjoys great wealth and is often regarded as semidivine. Ancient Egyptian pharaohs were divine monarchs with absolute powers. Ownership of land and administration of state religion were vested in their hands (Figure 16.6). The pharaohs ruled by centuries of legal precedent, through an elaborate hierarchy of bureau-

Figure 16.6 Rameses II, seated on a cushioned chair, receives a foreign dignitary. ("Rameses II and Queen in Audience," stela from the eighteenth dynasty. Gift of Mrs. Frank E. Peabody. Courtesy, Museum of Fine Arts, Boston)

crats, whose principal officials represented practically hereditary dynasties (Kemp, 1989). Many state societies, such as those of the Maya and the Inca, were organized along rigid lines, with strict classes of nobles, craftsmen, and others. Only the most extraordinary act of military skill or religious devotion would allow a few lucky people entry into the highest classes of society. All the people knew exactly where they stood in society, even slaves. State-organized societies were the foundation of the early civilizations of the Near East, China, and the Americas; indeed, they were precursors of the Classical civilizations of Greece and Rome.

SOCIAL ORGANIZATION IN THE ARCHAEOLOGICAL RECORD

The archaeological evidence that bears directly on prehistoric social organization comes from several sources, each of which can give us insights into the general level of social organization of a prehistoric society and into much more specific social details as well.

Burials

Human burials are one important source of information about prehistoric social organization (Brown, 1971). The actual disposal of the corpse is really a minimal part of the sequence of mortuary practice in a society. Funerary rites are a ritual of passage and are usually reflected not only in the position of the body in the grave but also by the ornaments and grave furniture that accompany it. The contents of a grave, whether spectacular or extremely simple, are useful barometers of social ranking. In some, the differing status of burials may indicate that a society was rigidly ranked.

When C. Leonard Woolley excavated the Early Dynastic royal burials of Ur-of-the-Chaldees in Mesopotamia (Figure 16.7), he found a great cemetery containing 1,850 graves (Woolley, 1943). Sixteen of them stood out by virtue of their remarkable grave furniture. The royal tombs were sunk into the earlier levels of the mound, and a sepulcher consisting of several rooms was erected in the middle of a huge pit. The royal corpses were decked out in a cascade of gold and semiprecious stone ornaments, gold and silver ornaments were placed next to the biers, and several attendants were slaughtered to accompany the dead. Once the royal sepulcher was closed, the entire court filed into the grave pit, drank poison, and lay down to die in correct order of protocol. Woolley was able to identify the different rankings of the courtiers from their ornaments. In contrast to all this luxury, the average person was buried in a matting roll or a humble coffin.

In burials like this, pharaohs' graves, and even burials of Iron Age chieftains in Europe, the ranking of society is obvious. But what about less affluent societies in which differences in rank and social status are often more muted? It is very important for archaeologists to be able to recognize

Figure 16.7 The Royal Cemetery at Ur-of-the-Chaldees, excavated by Leonard Woolley.

such inequalities, for the degree of social ranking is often a measure of the size and complexity of a society. Very often, too, rank appears when centuries-old ties of kin and family are being replaced by rulers who preside over much more elaborate social systems. Brown (1981) points out that such variables as age, sex, personal ability, personality, and even circumstances of death can affect the way in which one is buried. The evidence for ranking comes not only from grave furniture and insignia of rank deposited with the deceased but also from the positions of graves in a settlement or cemetery and even from symbolic distinctions that are hard to find in the archaeological record (O'Shea, 1984). Generally, however, the greater and more secure a ruler's authority becomes, the more effort and wealth is expended on burial. This lavishness may also extend to immediate relatives and friends. (For essays on the archaeology of death, read Chapman and others, 1981.)

Physical anthropologists have just begun to look at groups of skeletons as another means of identifying the family relationships among groups of burials. The minute study of skeletal geography is an approach that is still in its infancy.

Structures

Evidence of social organization can sometimes be inferred from buildings. Teotihuacán shows every sign of having been an elaborately planned city, with special precincts for markets and craftspeople, and the houses of the leading priests and nobles were near the Street of the Dead, which bisected the city. In instances like this, it is easy enough to identify the houses belonging to each class in the society, both by their architecture and by the distinctive artifacts found in them.

Some civilizations seem to have regulated the houses occupied by the various classes of society with almost stultifying monotony. A classic example is the Harappan civilization of the Indus Valley. Both Harappa and Moenjo-daro were dominated by great citadels, with rectangular grids of monotonous workers' houses surrounding them. Special quarters of the city were reserved for craftspeople and for storage. In these and many other cases, one can study the relationships between different segments of society by examining the spacing between the structures in the site.

Artifact Patterns: Houses and Settlement

Theoretically, at any rate, distinctive artifact patterns within houses, other structures, household clusters, and communities should provide data on prehistoric social organization. Few archaeologists have ventured into this difficult research field, partly because no one has yet invented a battery of tested methods for studying and manipulating the many pottery-design elements that form the basis of most studies of prehistoric organization.

At issue, too, is the role of the individual potter and artifact user. Can one use artifact styles to identify individual fashions and social groupings in the archaeological record? Some stylistic attributes of basketry or pottery could be the result of individual effort, and others could be the work of a group of craftspeople or a social unit. The study of social organization from artifacts depends on making such distinctions (Hill and Gunn, 1977). Only recently, however, have archaeologists confronted the problem with rigorous methodology.

James Hill argues that it should sometimes be possible to identify the work of individual craftspeople and has experimented with assemblages of painted pottery from the Southwest. He suggests that there are five areas in which progress can be made (Hill and Gunn, 1977):

1. Studying artifact classes closely to see if one can identify the number of people making the objects and calculating the degree of craft specialization. Do we find fewer people making such artifacts throughout time? Does this shrinkage reflect increased craft specialization? And by studying the tools, can we identify the individual tasks assigned to specialists within the group?
2. Studying trade and identifying specific artifact classes that were exchanged outside the community. Can we identify objects made by an individual and establish their distribution in space and their maximum concentration at, presumably, the place of manufacture?
3. Examining residence units and pottery styles associated with them in minute detail, as has been done with southwestern pueblos (Longacre, 1970). If one could identify individual craftspeople, perhaps one could say something about social organization.

4. Examining burials, which are a potential source of information about relationships between individuals and groups of individuals. Graves may be clustered in different places and can be associated with artifacts found in nearby communities.
5. Finding artifacts made by the same individual in more than one community, we may be able to identify population movements.

This type of research is highly complex and involves methodologies that may not even exist yet. The problem is not only identifying the work of individuals but also controlling the many variables affecting, say, pottery making. As Margaret Ann Hardin (1977) points out, variables such as the choice of paintbrush and paint composition have to be controlled before individual variations can be identified.

RELIGION AND RITUAL

An anonymous archaeologist wrote cynically that "religion is the last resort of troubled excavators." At one time archaeologists ascribed any artifact or structure with even vaguely religious associations to a category broadly named "ritual." In many famous instances, the religious associations of an artifact or a structure can be determined readily enough. The Pyramid of the Sun at Teotihuacán is clearly a structure of religious significance; so too are the Temple of Amun at Karnak in Egypt and the famous stone circles at Stonehenge in England (Chippendale, 1983). The "Venus" figurines of the European Upper Paleolithic have been widely interpreted as fertility symbols or commemorations of womanhood, and later human figures have received similar interpretations, but the ritual associations of such objects are still in doubt (Figure 16.8) (Grasiozi, 1960; Rice, 1981). The cave art of Altamira and Lascaux has been called a manifestation of "sympathetic hunting magic" by many observers, and new investigative methods are dealing with this interpretation (Conkey, 1981; Leroi-Gourhan, 1967; Marshack, 1972). Burial mutilations, oral tradition, and even astronomy have been used to infer religious activities from archaeological data. Mother goddess cults, Baal-Astarte rituals, and earth worship are only a few of the fascinating manifestations of ritual found in archaeological literature—a delight to the eccentric and entertainment for the serious student of prehistory (Ucko, 1962).

Religion and Burials

The traditional archaeological evidence for religious rituals has come from burials. The first human beings to deliberately bury their dead were the Neanderthal peoples of 70,000 years ago. The bodies of Neanderthal families have been found in French caves, such as La Ferrassie, buried in shallow pits, the skeletons covered with the red ocher powder that was scattered over their corpses.

Figure 16.8 A Venus figurine from Dolní Věstonice, Czechoslovakia.

There are clear signs that highly organized religions were a feature of many of the more complex prehistoric societies. To verify this, we have only to mention the Chavín and Olmec art styles and religious beliefs that spread so widely in Peru and Mesoamerica just before the emergence of state-organized societies. Such organized religions can be detected by the patterning of characteristic art objects or other artifacts clearly associated with religious rituals or by the appearance of public temples or ceremonial centers in small villages and towns (Figure 16.9). The ceremonial centers of the Mesopotamians were towering ziggurats that gave rise to the legend of the Tower of Babel, and Mayan centers consisted of pyramids and other large structures grouped around huge open plazas. The ceremonial center became a focus for a group of independent settlements, "the sanctified terrain where were manifested those hierophanies that guaranteed the seasonal renewal of cyclic time, and where the splendor, potency, and wealth of their rulers symbolized the well being of the whole community" (Wheatley, 1971). According to Mircea Eliade (1954), the ceremonial center ensured the continuity of cultural traditions; the religious and moral models of society were laid down in sacred canons recited in temples in reassuring chants passed from generation to generation.

The distinctive religious art and architecture of Teotihuacán reflects such interest in cultural continuity and ritual; so too do the cult objects of the Hopewell and the endless religious friezes and inscriptions of the ancient Egyptians. Mayan calendars, too, are convincing evidence that the priests of one generation considered it their responsibility to ensure the continuity of religion for future generations.

Figure 16.9 A ceremonial Olmec ax head, depicting a god who combines the features of a man and a jaguar. His face is stylized, with flamelike eyelashes and a drooping mouth. (One-half actual size)

Religious Systems

Religious beliefs have often linked large areas of the world into gigantic spheres of common cosmology and ritual practices, even if the many peoples unified under a common religious banner enjoy widely disparate governmental, societal, and economic institutions. One has only to look at the distribution of Christianity and Islam to realize the importance of religion as an integrative force. Thousands of prehistoric societies were linked by common beliefs and cosmologies, which are reflected in the archaeological record by common artistic traditions, temple and ceremonial-center architecture, wall paintings, and even trade in cult objects. For example, in the Midwest the Hopewell religious cult with its preoccupations with ceremonial burial spread far beyond its Ohio heartland (Fagan,

1990). And in southern Africa, the ceremonial centers at Mapungubwe and Zimbabwe are associated with the rainmaking beliefs and ancestor cults of the Shona peoples (Garlake, 1973).

We can learn a great deal more about prehistoric cosmology and religion when ethnohistorical or written sources are available. David Friedel and Linda Schele's work on Mayan cosmology is a fine example of this type of research. They have studied Mayan images and hieroglyphs for years and have used changes in them to trace changes in the meaning of symbols associated with political power (Schele and Miller, 1986). For example, the religious symbolism of the late Preclassic was based on the passage of Venus as morning and evening star with the rising and setting of the sun. The people of any Mayan community could identify and verify their cosmos simply by observing the sky.

As time went on, Mayan cosmology was expanded and elaborated. The names of late Preclassic rulers were not recorded publicly. Perhaps such permanent verification on public monuments was not yet deemed necessary. Classic rulers followed a quite different strategy. They legitimized their rule through genealogies, public ceremonies, and monuments—much Classic Mayan art was erected as part of this process of legitimizing rulers, who claimed identity with gods in the Mayan cosmos.

Friedel and Schele (1987) believe that the metaphor of the twin ancestors—Venus and the sun—provided a potent image for lateral blood ties between lineages, communities, and everyone who believed in the same myths. Since twins are of the same womb and blood, so the Maya are all of common ancestry and blood, too.

This Mayan research shows that one should never think of religion and ritual in isolation but rather as integral to social organization, economic life, and political systems. The ideas and beliefs, the core of all religions, are reflected in many aspects of human life, especially in art and architecture. Ethnologist Roy Rappaport (1968, 1971) has examined this problem of integration. His conceptual framework ties religion to other aspects of human life (Figure 16.10). Every society has its own model of how the world is put together, its own ultimate beliefs. An origin myth and other sacred propositions can shape the entire world of a society.

Rappaport argues that these sacred propositions are interpreted for the faithful through a body of theology and rituals associated with it. The rituals are more or less standardized, religious acts often repeated at regular times of the year—harvests, plantings, and other key times. Others are performed when needed: marriages, funerals, and the like. Some societies, such as those of the ancient Egyptians and the Maya, made regular calendars to time religious events and astronomical cycles. These regular ceremonies performed important functions not only in integrating society but also in such activities as redistributing food, population control by infanticide, and dispersing of surplus male cattle in the form of ritually accumulated wealth. Any ritual, according to Rappaport, is designed to produce in the believer a religious experience that reinforces beliefs and

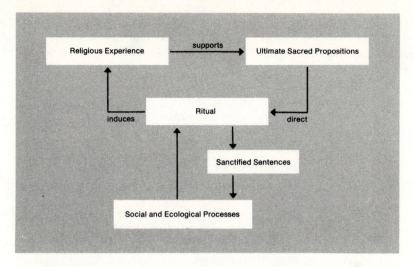

Figure 16.10 The circular relationship between Rappaport's (1968, 1971) ultimate sacred propositions, ritual, and religious experience. Ritual is also an articulation point between religion and socioenvironmental processes.

ensures maintenance of faith. Religious experiences are predominantly emotional, often supernatural and awe-inspiring. Each aspect of religion— sacred propositions, ritual, experience—supports the others. A religion will operate through sanctified attitudes, values, and messages, an ethic that adds a sacred blessing, derived from the ultimate sacred propositions of the society, to elicit predictable responses from the people. Such predictability, sparked by directives from some central religious authority, ensures orderly operation of society. In time, as in Mesopotamia, that authority can become secular as well. The institutions and individuals associated with these messages can become sanctified, for they are associated with the sacred propositions that lie at the heart of the society's beliefs. As societies became more complex, so too did the need for a stable framework to administer the needs of the many increasingly specialized subgroups that made up society as a whole.

There are signs that by 3000 B.C. in Egypt and Mesopotamia and between 1150 and 850 B.C. in Mesoamerica, administrative authority had become more institutionalized, dealing with all manner of social and economic problems, such as new rankings in society (reflected in burials), specialists' communities and households of specialists in each village, and an increased need for predictable social behavior and mutual interdependence. It is during these periods that the first of the more elaborate public buildings appear in the Near East and, independently, in Mexico, temples and monumental works that reflect not only the involvement of individual communities but also that of other villages without ceremonial structures of their own. The emergence of such ceremonial buildings and, presumably, administrative centers had, as we showed earlier, a major effect on the hierarchies and spacing of settlements. Thus, in a sense, a circular relationship links the ultimate sacred beliefs and rituals of a society with the processes of social and environmental change that act on them. And the link between administrative policy and belief is in ritual and the sanctified message.

To attempt to detect religion and ritual in the archaeological record without a careful research design is to invite disaster. As we have seen frequently, religious beliefs are intangible and survive only in the form of temples, ritual paraphernalia, and art. Viewed in isolation, the study of ancient religion seems a hopeless task, if archaeological finds are the only source of information available. But if one views religion and ritual as integral in a society closely tied to all other aspects of its activities, there is some hope that, armed with a theoretical framework, such as Rappaport's, we may be able to look at ritual and religious artifacts in the context of a society as a whole.

Formative Oaxaca

The presence or absence of distinctive ritual artifacts or buildings in a site or a society may be significant. In Formative Oaxaca, public buildings appear between 1400 and 1150 B.C., many of them oriented eight degrees west of north and built on adobe and earth platforms (Flannery, 1976). Rare conch-shell trumpets and turtle-shell drums traded from the coastal lowlands were apparently used in public ceremonies in such buildings. Clay figurines of dancers wearing costumes and masks that make them look like fantastic creatures and animals, as well as pottery masks, are also signs of communal ritual (Figure 16.11). The personal ritual of self-mutilation by bloodletting was widespread in early Mesoamerica. The Spanish described how the Aztec nobles would gash themselves with knives or with fish and stingray spines in acts of mutilation that were penances before the gods imposed by religion. A few stingray spines have come from Middle Formative villages, probably traded into the far interior for the specific use of community leaders. Marine fish spines have been found in public buildings, houses, and even refuse heaps of the Early Formative. Kent Flannery (1976) suggests that bloodletting fish spines were kept and used at home and that they were also used in public buildings. The ritual artifacts in the Oaxacan villages enabled Flannery and his colleagues to identify three levels of religious ceremony: personal bloodletting; dances run by sodalities, which cut across household lines; and public rituals in ceremonial buildings, involving a region wider than one village.

The Olmec Religion

Robert Drennan, in studying the Olmec religion, used Rappaport's scheme to look closely at the role of religion in social change in early

Figure 16.11 Four clay figurines grouped deliberately to form a scene, found buried beneath an Early Formative house at San José Mogote in Oaxaca, Mexico.

Mesoamerica. He argued that the sudden diffusion of the Olmec art style throughout Mesoamerica resulted from "the increased need for mechanisms of sanctification in various regions owing to internal social evolution" (Drennan, 1976). This diffusion occurred after the exchange networks for handling ritual objects, such as stingray spines, had been in operation for centuries. This interaction between lowlands and highlands was disrupted by the sudden collapse of Olmec society in the first millennium B.C. Drennan looked at the accumulated evidence on settlement patterns, population, and prehistoric agriculture in Olmec country. At the height of their prosperity, the two great Olmec centers of San Lorenzo and La Venta would have been strong magnets for increased human settlement, for drawing goods and services into the immediate vicinity of the ceremonial center (Coe and Diehl, 1980). However, the outlying villages were dependent on tropical rain forest agriculture, a shifting form of cultivation that tends to make people spread outward from their home base as their fields are exhausted and new forest is cleared. The land around San Lorenzo may have supported a peak population of 2,500 people living in those villages within two to eight kilometers of each other. This occupation would have left little margin of land to cover fluctuations in productivity caused by flooding and other environmental phenomena. And if the continued concentration of population and overuse of land continued, the resistance of society as a whole to environmental fluctuations would be drastically reduced. The result could be desanctification, the populace at large being unable to support the burden of a ritual system that regulated the checks and balances of their entire society. A social calamity ensued, resulting in the collapse not only of San Lorenzo and La Venta but also of the socioeconomic system and the beliefs behind it. Perhaps many of the large Olmec statues at both sites were mutilated because such disfigurement was the final defiant act of desanctification of the entire belief system upon which the Olmec once thought their very existence depended.

Drennan's desanctification hypothesis is highly tentative. It does, however, demonstrate the importance of considering religious beliefs and the rituals that go with them as a part of the many complex regulatory mechanisms affecting not only prehistoric societies but our own as well.

The study of prehistoric religion depends heavily on the study of sacred artifacts and temples and also on careful research design. The most effective way to study such intangibles as social organization or religious beliefs and rituals is to consider them as integral to a society, closely tied to all other aspects of its activities.

SUMMARY

- Human subsistence is based on natural resources and on exploitation of the environment, whether or not people produce food. Trade may have had its beginnings when people moved to a new territory where a previously available raw material was no longer abundant. Much early trade probably took the form of gift exchanges and the bartering of food and other commodities between neighboring settlements. The pattern of the trade was established by the distance between settlements and available sources of raw materials.
- Trade is normally recognized in the archaeological record by the discovery of objects exotic to the material culture of the economy of the host society. Prehistoric trade networks are studied by examining the distributions of such objects and of tool patterns in individual households and household clusters.
- Trading activity is closely tied to growing complexity in social and political organization among prehistoric peoples. It is not enough simply to identify trading activity in the archaeological record; one also has to understand the exchange processes that lay behind the trading.

- We cited two examples of prehistoric trading to show how trade cannot be studied except by referring to the cultural systems of which it was a part. Our first example was Mayan trade in the lowlands, where trade in *metates,* jadeite, and other raw materials was essential for survival. At Tepe Yahya in Iran, steatite trading assumed great importance, but it was controlled by middlemen and depended on a demand for luxury objects in Mesopotamia, hundreds of miles away.
- Redistribution of trade objects through a society is often controlled politically by chiefs and other leaders. We used obsidian trading in Mesoamerica to show how such redistribution mechanisms can be studied in the archaeological record.
- Social organization is difficult to study from archaeological evidence, although a systematic view of human culture makes it possible to examine it as one variable among the many that affect cultural change.
- Archaeologists distinguish between pre-state and state-organized societies, the latter characterized by social stratification, centralized political and social organization, and intensive agriculture.
- Social organization can be studied in the archaeological record by using burials and associated grave furniture, as at Ur-of-the-Chaldees, and by using structures or artifact patterns.
- The use of artifact patterns to study prehistoric social organization is still at an experimental stage.
- Religion has been studied traditionally through burials, burial rites, and sacred buildings. Organized religions were a feature of many of the more complex prehistoric societies, and they were often centers of elaborate ceremonial areas that were a focus for state-organized societies. The rituals that ensured the continuity of religious belief are reflected in architecture and art, and the presence or absence of sacred artifacts in the archaeological record may reveal valuable information on prehistoric religion, provided that research designs are carefully made.

GUIDE TO FURTHER READING

Chapman, Robert, Ian Kinnes, and Klavs Randsborg, eds. *The Archaeology of Death.* Cambridge: Cambridge University Press, 1981. A series of essays on the interpretation of mortuary practices. For the serious reader.

Earle, Timothy K., and Jonathan E. Ericson, eds. *Exchange Systems in Prehistory.* Orlando, Fla.: Academic Press, 1977. Articles dealing with method and theory in the study of prehistoric trade. For the more advanced reader.

Rappaport, Roy A. *Pigs for the Ancestors.* New Haven, Conn.: Yale University Press, 1968. A fascinating study of the role of ritual in the cultural ecology of a New Guinea tribe. Essential reading for anyone interested in ritual as integral to a cultural system.

Sabloff, Jeremy A., and C. C. Lamberg-Karlovsky, eds. *Early Civilization and Trade.* Albuquerque: University of New Mexico Press, 1975. Conference papers that cover a wide range of problems in the study of prehistoric trade. Strong on theory and actual case studies.

Woolley, C. Leonard. *Ur Excavations. Volume 2: The Royal Cemetery.* Philadelphia: University of Pennsylvania Museum, 1943. This detailed description of the pre-Dynastic royal cemetery is a classic of archaeology and provides fascinating insight into the study of prehistoric social organization.

Seven

INTERPRETING CULTURE CHANGE IN THE PAST

Is it too late for salvation? If not, please let me have the analytical expertise of the New Archaeology—and the humility and common sense of the Old.

Kent V. Flannery

The Early Mesoamerican Village, 1976

*O*nly in recent years have archaeologists become preoccupied with describing the past and also explaining it. In Part Seven we look at the explanation of the past from two perspectives: the culture-historical perspective, which is an inductive form of archaeological research, and the processual perspective, which is based on deductive research. Neither approach is mutually exclusive. Much processual archaeology, for example, is based on data derived from inductive research.

Part Seven shows what an amazing battery of powerful analytical tools is being brought to bear on archaeological interpretation. Archaeology is in the throes of a quantum jump in analytical sophistication, in which the work of mathematicians, statisticians, and scientists has a leading part. As Colin Renfrew (1979) observed, archaeologists are "replacing anecdote by analysis."

Chapter
17

Constructing Culture History

*I*n Part Two we discussed the fact that the reconstruction of culture history has been a major preoccupation of archaeologists from the early years of the twentieth century. Culture history itself describes human cultures in the past, and it is based on chronological and spatial ordering of archaeological data. This approach is a sound way of describing the past, but it is of minimal use for explaining variability in the archaeological record or cultural process. As we shall see, some of the mechanisms, like diffusion, which culture historians have used to explain the past are in fact not even explanations at all. In this chapter we describe the culture-historical approach and some of its limitations.

THE CULTURE-HISTORICAL METHOD

The study of culture history is based on two fundamental principles that were enumerated as long ago as the early years of the twentieth century by Franz Boas, N. C. Nelson, and A. V. Kidder (Willey and Sabloff, 1980). One is *inductive research methods,* the development of generalizations about a research problem that are based on numerous specific observations (see Chapter 8); the other is *a normative view of culture,* which is based on the notion that abstract rules govern what the culture considers normal behavior. The normative view is a descriptive approach to culture; it can be used to describe culture during one time period or throughout time. Archaeologists base it on the assumption that surviving artifacts, such as potsherds, display stylistic and other changes that represent the changing norms of human behavior over time.

Most archaeological interpretation in the New and Old Worlds has been based on normative models. The culture-historical approach has resulted in a descriptive outline of prehistory in time and space for much of the world. The interpretation of culture-historical data is based on simple analogies from historical and ethnographic data, far simpler than those envisaged by archaeologists studying living societies today (Chapter 14). Within its limitations, culture-historical reconstruction is a useful organizational tool that has added some descriptive order to world prehistory.

Constructing Culture History

All culture-history research is based on inductive methods, which acquire specific data from one or many archaeological sites that are not only accumulated but also subjected to a gradual synthesis that leads to generalizations based on the data.

The sequence of research begins with identifying a research area, with reconnaissance and surface surveys. These surveys yield a mass of surface collections, which allow the researcher to develop at least a tentative chronological sequence for the area, based on attributes and artifact types seriated according to the principles outlined in Chapter 12. The research continues with carefully selected excavations designed to test the validity of the sequence and to refine and expand it as well. Although the excavations may be meant, ultimately, to recover structures and village layouts, their primary goals are always stratigraphic—observing and recording occupation layers and developing relative and absolute chronologies. The data from the excavations are then analyzed and classified and used to refine the preliminary classifications and chronologies put together before digging began.

This database consists of artifacts and structures and of food remains and other information. The process of classification involves analyzing all these categories of data. Artifacts and structures are the primary interest of culture historians, for they provide a sensitive barometer for studying technological and cultural change throughout time and space. Often, artifacts and structures are divided into *complexes,* chronological subdivisions of artifact forms, such as stone tools, pottery, and bone objects, each of which can be used to chronicle an aspect of technological and cultural change. Some artifact complexes, such as pottery, are more sensitive than others, and these are the ones that are used for correlating cultural sequences with one another. Archaeologists have developed arbitrary time-space units to aid them in this process.

SYNTHESIS: ARCHAEOLOGICAL UNITS

The basis of all culture-historical reconstruction is the precise and carefully described site chronology. The synthesis of these chronologies beyond the confines of one site or local area involves not only repeating the same descriptive processes at other sites but also constantly refining the original cultural sequence from the original excavations. The synthesis is cumulative, for some new excavations may yield cultural materials that are not represented in the early digs. It is here that the techniques of seriation and cross-dating come into play. This is, of course, an entirely descriptive exercise, which yields no explanations whatsoever. It is a site-oriented procedure, too, very different from the regional surveys that have dominated archaeological research in recent years.

The archaeological units used to aid the synthesis form an arbitrary, hierarchic classification for this purpose. They represent the combining of the formal content of a site or sites with its distribution in time and space. Three occupation levels in a Utah cave each have distinctive artifact assemblages that have been sorted into types. Occupation levels at a dozen nearby sites contain examples of these three assemblages. What arbitrary units can we use to help us compare these various sites and occupation levels with their different contents? What arbitrary units will assist us to study cultural change as well? The archaeological units used most widely in the Americas are those developed by Gordon Willey and Philip Phillips (1958), and we describe some of these here.

Components and Phases

The basis of culture history is the local chronological sequence, whether at one site or many. Once chronological types are identified, they are studied closely to see how they cluster to reflect the cultural chronology of the site as a whole. It is here that you use the first in the hierarchy of archaeological units, components.

Components are the physically bounded positions of a site that contain a distinct assemblage, which serves to distinguish the culture of the inhabitants of a particular land. An occupation site like Martin's Hundred, Virginia, will consist of a single component, but a settlement occupied at three different times will contain three distinct components. Each may belong to a separate cultural phase. The Koster site in Illinois could be described as an excellent example of a multicomponent site, with its various layers representing different components separated by sterile layers of soil (Struever and Holton, 1979).

"Cultural homogeneity" is, of course, an intangible, so the definition of a component depends very much on stratigraphic observation and the archaeologist's observational skills. Some cave sites in southwestern France contain many occupation levels separated by sterile layers. These can, of course, be isolated stratigraphically and be grouped on the basis of shared chronological types like antler harpoons or side scrapers. In other sites, as in San Cristobal in the Great Basin, the midden deposits were so churned up that the various components had to be separated by quantitative artifact analysis rather than stratigraphic observation (Thomas, 1988).

Components occur at one location. To produce a regional chronology, one must synthesize them with components from other sites, using the next analytical step, phases.

Phases are cultural units represented by like components on different sites or at different levels of the same site, although always within a well-defined chronological bracket (Willey and Phillips, 1958). The characteristic assemblage of artifacts of the phase may be found over hundreds of miles within the area covered by a local sequence. Many archaeologists use the term "culture" in the same sense as phase. Both are concepts designed to assist in ordering artifacts in time and space. Phases or cultures usually are named after a key site where characteristic artifacts are found. The *Acheulian* culture, for example, is named after the northern French town of St. Acheul, where the stone hand axes so characteristic of this culture are found.

Thomas (1983a, 1988) uses the Gatecliff shelter in Nevada to show how components and phases mesh. He found five components at the site, each defined by chronological types. As long as he was excavating just one site, this procedure was fine. But he wanted to compare the Gatecliff findings with those from other excavated sites in central Nevada. He found that a number of these sites contained late components with artifacts like projectile points and Shoshone pottery similar to those found in equivalent stratigraphic contexts at Gatecliff. He brought together the components from Gatecliff and the other sites into a phase, which he named Yellow Blade. This period dates from about A.D. 1300 to 1850, the moment of European contact. The phase term applies not only to Gatecliff but to the entire region. It is the basic unit of area synthesis. Some phases are but a few years long; others span centuries, even millennia. All the phase really does is break up long, continuous periods of prehistoric time into discrete chronological and spatial units, each with its specific artifacts. The Gatecliff site was occupied for about eight thousand years, divided by chronological types into five components stacked one upon the other. Each of these components has its own dates and characteristic artifacts. The components can be compared to those from other sites and can be used to build up a regional chronology. The phase enables us to establish regional contemporaneity. At first a phase may embrace, as the Yellow Blade phase does, five hundred years or more. But as research proceeds, chronologies become more refined, and artifact classifications become finer, the original phase may be broken down even further into more and more chronologically precise subphases.

Regions and Culture Areas

Culture-historical synthesis involves working with much larger areas in time and space than those covered by phases or local sequences. The two major divisions are archaeological regions and culture areas.

Archaeological regions are normally defined by natural geographic boundaries. They may also be defined, however, by a heavy concentration of archaeological sites. Normally, a region will display some cultural homogeneity. Examples are the Santa Barbara Channel region and the Valley of Oaxaca in Mexico.

Culture areas define much larger tracts of land, and they often coincide with the broad ethnographic culture areas identified by early anthropologists. Many areas tend to coincide with the various physiographic divisions of the world. The southwestern United States is one such area, as it is defined in part by its history of research and in part by cultural and environmental associations that lasted more than two thousand years. Such large areas can be divided into subareas, where differences within the culture of an area are sufficiently distinctive to separate one subarea from another. Gordon Willey (1966) divided the Southwest into the Anasazi, Hohokam, and Mogollon subareas, among others (Figure 17.1). But *area* implies nothing more than a very general and widespread cultural homogeneity. Within any large area, societies will adapt to new circumstances, some evolving more quickly than others and enjoy quite different economies.

Stages, Periods, Horizons, and Traditions

In Chapter 5 we described the three-age system, an evolutionary framework of cultural stages that still provides a broad framework for Old World prehistory. This evolutionary scheme has no exact counterpart in the Americas, where the early archaeologists deliberately avoided evolutionary models. For generations, Old World archaeologists have been filling in details of the three-age framework. The Stone Age, the Bronze Age, and the Iron Age are the broadest of technological states. All are purely arbitrary technological labels, which in no way coincide exactly with any levels of social evolution. Periods, conversely, are units of time during which specific cultural phenomena are observed. The Stone Age is a technological stage; although it ended in Mesopotamia about six thousand years ago, it is still in progress in parts of the Amazon Basin. In contrast, the Inca period in Peru lasted from about A.D. 1200 to 1534 (Conrad and Demarast, 1984).

New World archaeologists have two units that synthesize archaeological data over wide areas: horizons and traditions.

Horizons link a number of phases in neighboring areas that have rather general cultural patterns in common. In some parts of the world, an all-embracing religious cult may transcend cultural boundaries and spread over an enormous area. Such cults are often associated with characteristic religious artifacts or art styles that can be identified in phases hundreds of miles apart—in well-defined chronological contexts. The Chavín art style of coastal Peru, for example, was associated with distinctive religious beliefs and rituals shared by many Peruvian societies in the highlands and lowlands between 900 and 200 B.C. (Keatinge, 1988). This

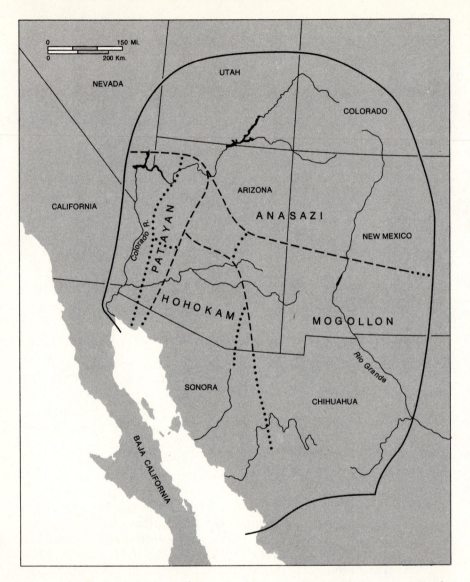

Figure 17.1 Archaeological regions and subareas in the North American Southwest. (After Willey)

commonality of belief is manifested in the archaeological record by Chavín art, a style that stresses savage, jaguarlike motifs; hence the use of the term *Chavín horizon* (Figure 17.2).

The term *tradition* has widespread application in archaeology. It is used to describe a lasting artifact type, assemblages of tools, architectural styles, economic practices, or art styles that last much longer than one phase or even the duration of a horizon. The toolmaking tradition, for

Figure 17.2 Chavín carving on a pillar in the temple interior at Chavín de Huantár, Peru. The Chavín art style formed one of the bases for identifying the Chavín horizon in Peruvian prehistory. Note that the reconstruction is somewhat stylized: the actual stonework is more irregular.

example, may continue in use while the many cultures that share it develop in entirely different ways. Tradition implies a degree of cultural continuity, even if shifts in cultural adaptation have taken place in the meantime. A good example of such a tradition is the so-called Arctic small tool tradition of Alaska, which originated at least as early as 4000 B.C. (Dumond, 1987). The small tools made by these hunter-gatherers were so effective that they continued in use until recent times and led to the modern Eskimo cultures of the Far North.

INTERPRETATION

The interpretation of culture history depends on analogy and descriptive cultural models, which are used to identify the variables that are in operation when culture change takes place. These models are used to account for changes in the archaeological record. This record, however, does not invariably show a smooth and orderly chronicle of culture change. A seriated pottery sequence from six sites may display the sudden arrival of a new ware that is radically different from others in the sequence. An entire new artifact inventory may suddenly appear in components at eight sites, while the tool kits of earlier centuries rapidly vanish. The economy of sites in a local sequence may change completely within fifty years as the plow comes into use in the locality. Such changes are readily observed in the thousands of local sequences found in the archaeological record. But how did these changes come about? What processes of cultural change were at work to cause major and minor alterations in the archaeological record? A number of descriptive models have been formulated to characterize culture change: some of these are cultural models, others noncultural; several involve internal change, others external influence.

Cultural Models

The widely used models of culture change in archaeology are inevitable variation, cultural selection, and the three classic processes—invention, diffusion, and migration (Trigger, 1968a).

Inevitable Variation   This is somewhat similar to the well-known biological phenomenon of genetic drift. As people learn the behavior patterns of their society, inevitably some minor differences in learned behavior will appear from generation to generation; although minor in themselves, these differences accumulate over a long time, especially if the populations are isolated. Today we live in a far more complex society than people did even thirty years ago. The "snowball effect" of inevitable variation and slow-moving cultural evolution can be detected in dozens of prehistoric societies. For instance, the great variation in Acheulian hand ax technology throughout Europe and Africa between a million and 150,000 years ago can be explained in part by the effects of inevitable variation.

Inevitable variation is often the result of isolation, of a very low density of humans per square mile. It should not be confused with broad trends in prehistory that developed over long periods of time. The more and more complex burial rituals that developed in the Adena and Hopewell cultures of the American Midwest between 500 B.C. and A.D. 300 probably resulted from trends toward greater complexity in religious beliefs and rituals as well as in political and economic organization over a long period of time—not from isolation (Fagan, 1990). Inevitable variation is also quite different from what happens when a society recognizes that certain culture changes or inventions may be advantageous. Presumably, for example, many hunter-gatherer societies deliberately took up the cultivation of the soil once they saw the advantages it gave neighboring peoples, who had already adopted the new economies.

Cultural Selection   This concept is somewhat analogous to that of natural selection in biological evolution. It is the notion that human cultures accept or reject new traits—whether technological, economic, or intangible—on the basis of whether or not they are advantageous to society as a whole. Cultural selection results in cumulative cultural change, and it operates within the prevailing values of the society. This condition tends to make it harder for a society to accept social change as opposed to technological advance, which is less circumscribed by restrictive values. The state-organized societies in Mesopotamia and Mexico resulted from centuries of gradual social evolution, where centralized political and religious authority was perceived to be advantageous.

Invention   The first of the three classic processes that contribute to culture change involves creating a new idea and transforming it—in archaeological contexts—into an artifact or other tangible innovation. Unfortunately, many inventions, such as new religions or ideas, leave little tangible trace in the archaeological record. An invention implies either the modifying of an old idea or series of ideas or the creation of a completely new concept; it may come about by accident or by intentional research. The atom was split by long and patient investigation, with the ultimate objective of fragmentation; fire was probably the result of an accident. Inventions spread, and if they are sufficiently important, they spread widely and rapidly. The transistor is in almost universal use because it is an effective advance in electronic technology; plows had an equally dramatic effect on agriculture in prehistoric Europe. How inventions spread has been studied extensively by archaeologists and anthropologists, for the quality of inventiveness is an essential part of the human genius, as our society defines it.

In the early study of prehistory, people assumed that metallurgy and other major innovations were invented in only one place, a notion that led to the great diffusionist theories of a half century ago (Figure 17.3). But as people have come to understand the importance of environment and adaptation in prehistory, they have realized that many inventions have been made in several parts of the world, where identical adaptive processes occurred. Agriculture is known to have developed independently in the Near East, Southeast Asia, Mesoamerica, and Peru, quite apart from its supposed origins in northern China.

Diffusion   This model is defined as the processes by which new ideas or cultural traits spread from one person to another or from one group to

Figure 17.3 Iron-bladed dagger of the Egyptian pharaoh Tutankhamun, around 1340 B.C. This weapon was probably made of native hammered iron. The Egyptians tried, without success, to obtain iron tools from the Hittites after hearing of the revolutionary new metal.

another, often over long distances. Much modern research on diffusion is about how innovations that are new to the recipients spread to other areas. Diffusion can proceed through such diverse mechanisms as trade, warfare, frequent visits between neighboring communities, and migrations of entire communities. A key issue here is the formal or informal mechanisms of contact between the members of separate groups that account for the spread and acceptance of a new idea.

Just how are patterned stylistic trait distributions diffused from one area to another? The subject is rich in controversy and invalid assumptions (Davis, 1983). The growing popularity of evolutionary explanations in recent years has led to wholesale rejections of diffusion as a way of interpreting the past, so much so that archaeologists have tended to neglect it. Diffusion is, however, assuming new importance as large bodies of regional data are produced by large-scale cultural resource management surveys in such areas as the San Juan and Great Basins.

Current archaeological thinking about diffusion stems from pioneer work by early anthropologists Franz Boas and Alfred Kroeber and their contemporaries. They were interested in diffusion but argued that the symbolic value or prestige of a culture trait was a major factor in determining whether it was accepted and diffused to other societies. Archaeologists borrowed some of this thinking in the 1930s but found it impossible to establish the social context of culture traits from the archaeological record alone. They therefore assumed that acceptance of culture traits was directly proportional to the frequency with which people learned about an innovation. This simplistic approach, which often talked of culture "contact" instead of diffusion, collapsed in the face of more sophisticated archaeological and ethnographic studies showing that knowledge of an innovation did not necessarily mean that it would be adopted (Schiffer, 1979). A classic example occurs among the aborigines of northern Australia, who are well aware of agriculture among their neighbors but still remain hunter-gatherers themselves.

Diffusion research of this simplistic type is still found among some archaeologists, including those who study possible transatlantic and trans-pacific contacts between Old World and New (Riley, 1971). Were European or African crops diffused to the Americas? The researchers interested in this kind of topic concentrate not so much, as they should, on the social context of the innovations as on the archaeological criteria for establishing diffusion in the archaeological record.

Let us look at this sort of approach to diffusion more closely. Figure 17.4 diagrams a culture trait in space and time. Let us say that a new type of painted pot is invented in a village in about A.D. 1400. The advantages of this new pot are so great that villagers ten miles away learn about the vessel at a beer party five years later; within ten years their potters are making similar receptacles. In a short time the pot form is found not only in one village but in three within a ten-mile radius. By 1450 the pot form is so widely used that dozens of villages within a fifty-mile circle of the original settlement are making the same vessels. Plotting this development on paper yields the cone effect shown in Figure 17.4; that is the principle applied by culture historians looking at diffusion.

Under this topic, several criteria have to be satisfied before one can decide whether a series of artifacts in archaeological sites distant from one another are related in a historically meaningful way. First, the traits or objects must be sufficiently similar in design and typological attributes to indicate that they probably have a common origin. Second, it must be shown that the traits did not result from convergent evolution. The earlier development of the trait, perhaps as general as a form of architecture or the use of a domestic animal, must be carefully traced in both cultures. Third, distributions of the surviving traits must be carefully studied, as well as those of their antecedents. The only acceptable evidence for diffusion of a trait is a series of sites that show, when plotted on a map, continu-

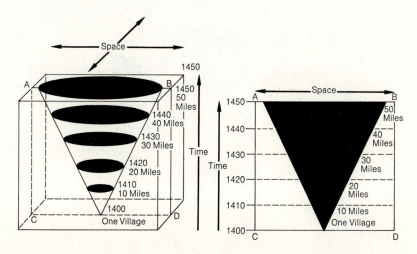

Figure 17.4 The spread of a culture trait in time and space: the *cone effect.*

ous distribution for the trait or, perhaps, a route along which it spread. Accurate chronological control is essential, with a time gradient from either end of the distribution or one from the middle. For many traits, the archaeological criteria may be difficult to establish; indeed, they are rarely satisfied, but the importance of reliable evidence is obvious. Theoretical speculations are all very well, but they may result in completely false conclusions, sometimes supported by uncritical use of scanty archaeological evidence (Thompson, 1956).

Instances of diffusion in prehistory are legion. There are innumerable cases wherein ideas or new technologies have spread widely from their place of origin, although none are as grandiose as Elliot Smith's schemes or Thor Heyerdahl's attempts to prove that the Egyptians colonized Mesoamerica. A well-documented instance is the religious beliefs of the Adena and Hopewell peoples of the Midwest, who held beliefs associated with death that spread far beyond the relatively narrow confines of the Midwest. Religious beliefs are expressed in the form of distinctive rituals, which for the Adena and Hopewell involved extensive earthworks and mound building. Such monuments are found far outside the Adena and Hopewell heartlands, as are the cult objects associated with Hopewell ritual (Figure 17.5).

During the 1960s and 1970s, the move away from normative explanations led to research into a number of basic assumptions about diffusion. Ethnoarchaeological studies of pottery making have shown just how important informal communication between potters is in spreading technological and stylistic changes (Longacre, 1974). Some basic research into the

Figure 17.5 A Hopewell craftsman cut this human hand from a sheet of mica. It was found in an Ohio burial mound with the body of its owner, who lived 370 miles from the nearest mica source. An example of the consequence of diffusion of religious beliefs, this hand probably had powerful shamanistic associations in the Hopewell society.

role of artifact style in reinforcing social identity and solidarity is important because it identifies factors that may have accelerated or prevented adoption of culture traits (Plog, 1980). Despite these efforts and a large body of diffusion research in other social sciences, many archaeologists are deeply suspicious of diffusion research, partly because a body of archaeological theory on the subject still does not exist. (For a valuable and comprehensive discussion, see Davis, 1983.)

Much of the unpopularity of diffusion stems from archaeologists using the term wrongly. Diffusion itself is not a cause of the spread or adoption of culture traits; it is a way of referring to a set of phenomena that have been caused by a wide range of cultural factors. To say that bronze sword-making diffused from one society to another is merely to describe what happened. It does not describe *how* the spread occurred. Under the culture-history title, diffusion has been invoked as a satisfactory explanation for distribution patterns of culture traits when in fact the factors behind the diffusion are still unexplained.

Migration   Migration as an explanatory concept suffers from many of the same disadvantages as diffusion. But this type of cultural change involves movement of entire populations, both large and small. Migration can be peaceful, or it can be the result of deliberate aggression, ending in invasion and conquest.

In every case, people deliberately decide to expand their sphere of influence into new areas. English settlers moved to the North American continent, taking their own culture and society with them; the Spanish occupied Mexico. Such population movements result not only in diffusion of ideas but also in a mass shift of people, with extensive social and cultural changes accompanying it.

For migration to be recognized in the archaeological record, one would need to find local sequences where the phases show a complete disruption of earlier cultural patterns by an intrusive new phase—not just of one tool type, or even several. Of course, some elements in earlier cultural traditions might survive and become an acculturated part of the peoples' new culture. Perhaps the classic instance of migration in world prehistory is that of the Polynesians, who settled the remote islands of the Pacific by deliberate voyaging from archipelago to archipelago (Kirch, 1984). Each time, the islands were discovered by an act of deliberate exploration, by voyagers who set out with every intention of returning. Hawaii, Easter Island, and Tahiti were first settled by deliberate colonization that was perforce a migration of a small number of people to a new, uninhabited landmass. The kind of total population movement, or in some cases, population replacement, that occurs with mass migrations of this type is rare in human prehistory. It will be reflected in the archaeological record either by totally new components and phases of artifacts or by skeletal evidence. When a total replacement is violent, a result of widespread warfare, the occurrence of such an event must be proved by excavation. It is not sufficient to find a few skeletons lying in confusion and then claim that a city was sacked, as Mortimer Wheeler did at Moenjo-daro in the Indus Valley (Wheeler, 1967).

A second type of migration, on a much smaller scale, occurs when a small group of foreigners moves into another region and settles there as an organized group. A group of Oaxacans may have done just that at Teotihuacán in the Valley of Mexico (Millon, 1973). They settled in their own special precinct of the city, tentatively identified by a concentration of Oaxacan potsherds and ornaments. The Oaxacan enclave lasted for centuries.

There are other forms of migration, too. Slaves and artisans wander as unorganized migrants. Artisans are an important source of diffusion of techniques and ideas. This type of unorganized migration is difficult to discern in the form of culture traits, for the individual migrant leaves little behind except, perhaps, some specialist artifacts, as bronzeworking migrant artisans did in prehistoric Europe. Finally, there are great warrior migrations, such as those of the eastern nomads in temperate Europe and the warlike Nguni tribes of southern Africa (Omer-Cooper, 1966). Each of these warrior bands swept over an indigenous, sedentary population, causing widespread disruption and population shifts. But within a few generations, the warrior newcomers had adopted the sedentary way of life of their neighbors and were virtually indistinguishable from them. Such migrations leave few traces in archaeological sites.

Noncultural Models

Cultural change triggered by alterations in the natural environment is an integral part of culture history. The model for this type of change is a simple one. Earlier models for the origins of agriculture in the Near East were based on the notion that the climate became progressively drier. Animal and human populations were forced into oases, where people started to domesticate animals and grow wild cereal grasses so that they could survive (Redman, 1978b). In other words, climatic changes caused cultural modifications. More recent research has shown, however, that actually a large number of highly complex variables were involved in the development of food production in this area, environmental change being only one of them.

Of course, human cultures can modify their environments, either accidentally or deliberately. Enormous areas of the Sahel regions of the southern Sahara have been stripped of vegetation by the overgrazing of goats and other domestic animals. These areas are now deserts, and the local people are starving as a result of their long-term cultural practices. One should emphasize the word *long-term,* for such modifications are not simply a phenomenon of recent times.

The most recent research in archaeology has focused heavily on specific details of the relationship between the environment and prehistoric cultures. The complex models that are growing from this research show that earlier models were far too general to explain these complex and ever-changing environment-culture relationships.

Reconstruction of culture history is a very difficult and complex descriptive process that depends on the availability of large amounts of basic data to be effective. In itself, inductive research of the type involved in culture history takes little account of the role of artifacts in the whole cultural system. Thus explanation of the cultural process requires far more complex models based on quite a different approach to archaeology. These are described in Chapter 18.

SUMMARY

- The study of culture history is based on inductive research methods and on a normative view of culture, which assumes that abstract rules govern what a given culture considers normal behavior.
- The process of constructing culture history begins with identifying a research area, with reconnaissance and surface surveys. These efforts yield at least a tentative chronological sequence for the area, which is based on attributes and artifact types that have been seriated in their correct order. Then carefully selected excavations are made to test, refine, and expand the sequence. The data are then analyzed and classified. Artifacts and structures are used as sensitive barometers of cultural change; they are divided into complexes, each of which is used to chronicle one aspect of technological and cultural change.
- The process of synthesis in culture history is based on constructing precise chronological sequences. Expanding these chronologies beyond one site or occupation layer is a cumulative process in which seriation and cross-dating have key roles.
- A series of arbitrary archaeological units are used to aid in this synthesis. Local chronological sequences lie at the core of all cultural-historical research. These are based on *phases*, which are cultural units in a local sequence that possess culture traits sufficient to distinguish them from all other phases. Normally, the boundaries of a phase are set arbitrarily. The term *component* describes a single manifestation of a phase at a single site.
- Archaeological regions are normally defined by natural geographic boundaries, but culture areas are much larger and coincide with major ethnographic culture areas; the American Southwest is an example.
- *Horizons* link a number of phases in neighboring areas, containing rather general cultural patterns, which are often distinguished by characteristic art styles, such as the Chavín of Peru. The term *tradition* describes a lasting artifact type—assemblages of tools, architectural styles, and so on that last much longer than a phase or even a horizon.

- The interpretation of culture history depends on analogy and descriptive cultural models that are used to identify variables that operate when culture change takes place.
- Some commonly accepted descriptive models of cultural change are inevitable variation, cultural selection, invention, diffusion, and migration. These in themselves, however, do not describe the factors that led to cultural change in the first place.

GUIDE TO FURTHER READING

Childe, V. Gordon. *Piecing Together the Past*. London: Routledge and Kegan Paul, 1956. Though dated, this is still an eloquent and easy-to-understand exposition of the basic principles of constructing culture history, European-style.

Rouse, Irving. *Introduction to Prehistory: A Systematic Approach*. New York: McGraw-Hill, 1972. A basic account, which is widely quoted, of archaeological units at the synthetic level.

Willey, Gordon R., and Philip Phillips. *Method and Theory in American Archaeology*. Chicago: University of Chicago Press, 1958. Often described as the culture historian's bible, this is a fundamental source on the methods of culture history, an essential part of the training of every professional archaeologist.

Chapter
18

Study of Cultural Process
Processual Archaeology

*P*rocessual archaeology, defined in Chapter 3, is a phenomenon of the 1960s and 1970s that stemmed from the research of W. W. Taylor, Albert Spaulding, and Lewis Binford, among many others (Binford, 1972). It provides a vehicle for closely examining the cultural process and a viable means of searching for explanations of culture change in prehistory (Plog, 1974). This chapter describes some of the applications of processual archaeology (Wylie, 1988).

PROCESSUAL APPROACH

Processual archaeology is based on a deductive research methodology that employs research design, formulation of explicit research hypotheses, and testing of these against basic data. Its methods are cumulative; that is, initial hypotheses are designed that propose a working model to explain culture change. These hypotheses are tested against basic data, and some are discarded, while others are tested again and again until the factors that affect cultural change are isolated in highly specific form. The synthesized archaeological data are interpreted on the basis of successive generations of working hypotheses that are tested many times.

The processual approach is firmly based on culture history and data obtained from inductive research. It has to be, for the chronological and spatial frameworks for prehistory come from descriptive methods developed over many years of arduous fieldwork and analysis. The difference between the two approaches lies in the *orientation* of the research. Processual archaeologists rely on deductive strategies that begin with for-

469

mulating testable hypotheses and proceed to the gathering of data to test them. Very often, however, the initial hypotheses are based on data derived from inductive culture history.

The early days of processual archaeology were marked by furious academic controversy not only between culture historians and those espousing processual methodology but also between proponents of different approaches to the study of cultural process (Flannery, 1973a; Meltzer and others, 1986). Two methods are commonly espoused: the deductive-nomological approach and the systems-ecological approach.

Deductive-Nomological Approach

Archaeologists who use this approach are firmly committed to a highly formal, scientific methodology, which is based on the work of Carl Hempel and other philosophers of science (Watson and others, 1984). Nomology is the study of general laws; a deductive-nomological approach is based on the philosophy of logical positivism. This philosophy considers the world to be composed of observable phenomena that act in an orderly way. It views the world as governed by general laws that can be identified by rigorous research methods. In other words, the world can be explained by predicting when a set of phenomena that indicate that a particular law is in operation will occur.

In archaeology, these general laws are derived from anthropology and other social sciences. Laws have been formulated about the relationships between human cultures and the environment, about ecological adaptation, and about cultural evolution (Sahlins and Service, 1960). Most of them are so generalized, however, that it is difficult to test them with specific data. Nevertheless, some archaeologists believe that archaeological data can be used to formulate and test hypotheses that identify the general and universal laws governing cultural processes.

At the heart of this approach to processual archaeology is the notion that there actually are general laws that govern human behavior. Proponents of the deductive-nomological approach also assume that formal scientific experiments, which can be repeated and can produce predictable results, can be used to identify instances when a particular law is in operation. Their explanations of cultural change are based on the predictability of these results. In other words, the hypothesis that allows accurate prediction of phenomena in one area, under circumstances similar to those elsewhere, is the one that can be justified as the best explanation.

The trouble is that archaeology is just not that sort of science. The deductive-nomological approach came to archaeology late in the 1960s, when to become a science was a desirable goal for archaeology. Physics had a theoretical rigor that was attractive to people who wanted more scientific rigor in archaeology. But physics has an essential metaphysical and abstract conception of reality that is quite different from that of archaeology, which concentrates so on change through time (Dunnell,

1982). The highly specific deductive methods applied to physics and other hard sciences are far less applicable to archaeological data, which are governed mainly by intangible variables such as values and beliefs. Deductive research is extremely valuable for the study of the past, provided that realistic account is taken of the uniqueness of archaeological data. If there is one scientific discipline that archaeology lies closest to, it is biology, for biologists are struggling with many similar theoretical problems connected with change (for a prolonged discussion, see Dunnell, 1982).

Systems-Ecological Approach

The second and more common processual approach deals with the ways in which cultural systems function, both internally and in relation to external factors, such as the natural environment. It involves three basic models of cultural change: *systems models,* which are based on general systems theory; *cultural ecology,* which provides complicated models of the interactions between human cultures and their environments; and *multilinear cultural evolution,* which combines both systems approaches and cultural ecology in a theory of the cumulative evolution of culture over long periods through complex adaptations to the environment (Gibbon, 1984).

The argument for using the systems-ecological approach was summarized by Kent Flannery (1973a) some years ago, when he wrote that archaeologists using these models are intent on "the search for the ways human populations (in their own way) do the things that other systems do."

General systems theory was first constructed in the sciences in the 1950s. It is a body of theoretical concepts that provides a way of searching for "general relationships" in the empirical world. By the same token, a system is defined as "a whole which functions as a whole by virtue of the interdependence of its parts" (Rapoport, 1968). Systems theory has been widely applied in physics and other hard sciences, where relationships between parts of a system can be defined with great precision. It has obvious appeal to archaeologists, for its believers assume that any organization, however simple or complex, can be studied as a system of interrelated concepts (Salmon, 1982). A change in one of these components will trigger reactions in many of the other parts. The notion of cultural systems, which was described in Chapter 4, is derived, in part, from systems theory.

Archaeologists took to systems theory with great enthusiasm as part of the great borrowing of concepts from the sciences that took hold in the 1960s and 1970s. They thought of human cultures as "open" systems, regulated in part by external stimuli. This general concept is most applicable to human cultures that interact intimately with the natural environment. For a while, everything was interpreted within rigid systems frameworks, as if human cultures were like systems in physics. So many intangibles affect the operation of human cultural systems, however, that the initial enthusiasm soon evaporated, to be replaced by the realization that systems theory was valuable as a general concept and little more. The advantage of systems theory is that it frees one from having to look at only one agent of cultural change, such as irrigation or diffusion, allowing one to focus instead on regulatory mechanisms and on the relationships between various components of a cultural system and the system as a whole and its environment. The systems approach is valuable to archaeology as it is to the study of ecology—as a general concept. But we must keep in mind that the data used to test the hypotheses derived to validate this model are acquired by the same methods used to acquire valuable culture-historical information.

CULTURAL ECOLOGY

As we saw in Chapter 3, processual archaeology relies not only on the concepts of systems theory but also on the study of cultural ecology (Gibbon, 1984). Cultural ecology is a way of obtaining a total picture of how human populations adapt to and transform their environments. These environments include not only the natural landscape but also vegetational and animal populations as well as other cultures.

This method is being hailed widely as a possible explanation for many major cultural changes in prehistory. Cultural ecologists see human cultures as subsystems interacting with other subsystems, all forming part of a total ecosystem with three major subsystems: human culture, the biotic community, and the physical environment. Thus the key to the cultural process lies in understanding the interactive relationships among the various subsystems. William Sanders has pointed out that every biological and physical environment presents problems for human use (Sanders and Price, 1968). Furthermore, the human response to different environments will be different and distinctive. Although the possibilities for human adaptation to an environment are almost unlimited, the number of probable adaptations to a specific environment is limited. Thus communities with very different cultures may occupy the same or similar environments, and the level of technological achievement and effectiveness of the hunting-gathering or food-producing economy involved naturally affects their responses in other aspects of culture. Some environments are inherently less productive than others, a factor that can limit population growth as well as other cultural responses.

The adaptation of any population is achieved primarily by effective subsistence strategies and technological artifices, but social organization and religious beliefs are important in ensuring cooperative exploitation of the environment as well as technological cooperation. Religious life provided an integrating force in many societies, not least among them the Maya and Sumerians. Human cultures are as dynamic as all other components of an ecological system, and any human culture can be thought of as what William Sanders and Barbara Price (1968) call "a complex of techniques adaptive to the problems of survival in a particular geographical region." Human culture is, ecologically speaking, a way in which human beings compete successfully with animals, plants, and other human beings. Sanders and Price point out that "the product of plant and animal evolution is more effective utilization of the landscape in competition with individuals of the same and other species. This effectiveness is usually expressed in population growth, and this growth can therefore be taken as a measure of success in a given area at a given point."

There are obvious difficulties in studying the interactions between people and their environment, especially when preservation conditions limit the artifacts and other data available for study. Fortunately, however, artifacts and other elements of the technological subsystem often survive. Because technology is a primary way in which different cultures adapt to their environment, detailed models of technological subsystems allow archaeologists to obtain a relatively comprehensive picture of the cultural system as a whole. It is in research of this type that the storage capacity of the digital computer has come into play. Cultural-ecological studies depend for their effectiveness on enormous quantities of basic data. Once these data are stored on the computer, one can use simulation techniques to model possible cultural outcomes by inserting hypothetical variables into the surviving cultural system. The techniques are somewhat like those used for business forecasting, but they are still in a highly experimental stage.

MULTILINEAR CULTURAL EVOLUTION

Anthropologist Julian Steward (1955) argued many years ago that people living in similar environments tend to solve the problem of adaptation in similar ways. This argument led him and others to develop the concept of *multilinear cultural evolution.* This is not the single-line evolutionary theory of the early evolutionists but a branching, cumulative process that results from cultural adaptations over long periods.

There was a stultifying inevitability about the earlier unilinear theories that put twentieth-century civilization at the pinnacle of human achievement. Multilinear evolutionary theory is far more flexible; it recognizes that there are many evolutionary tracks, from simple to complex, the differences resulting from individual adaptive solutions. Despite these variations, some broad evolutionary developmental stages can be recognized in the world's societies. The four-stage evolutionary classification of bands, tribes, chiefdoms, and state-organized societies was described in Chapter 16 (Service, 1971). These highly flexible stages are defined with reference to social complexity, subsistence strategy, and population size.

None of them are rigidly defined, for multilinear evolutionary theory recognizes that cultural adaptations are complex processes that are fine-tuned to local conditions, with long-term, cumulative effects.

Multilinear cultural evolution, then, is the vital integrative force that brings systems theory and cultural ecology together into a closely knit, highly flexible way of studying and explaining the cultural process (Sanders and Webster, 1978).

PROCESSUAL ARCHAEOLOGY APPLIED: ORIGINS OF LITERATE CIVILIZATION

Theoretical approaches are meaningless unless they are tested against actual field data. The models of processual archaeology have been applied successfully to many small-scale problems, and they have provided new means of studying major developments in world prehistory. The origins of literate civilization in the Near East some five thousand years ago illustrate the effectiveness of the processual approach very clearly.

Prime Movers

Early theories on the origins of cities and civilization in the Near East assumed that Sumerian civilization developed as a result of a major invention or technological advance, often called a *prime mover*, that was the ultimate cause of dramatic cultural change. Many people believed that the development of irrigation, with all its complex administrative problems, caused the growth of early civilization; others believed that population growth was the cause of the major changes in settlement patterns and agriculture that resulted in civilization. Warfare, trade, religious beliefs—all have been claimed as prime movers of early civilization. In truth, however, none of these prime-mover hypotheses is adequate to explain the complex cultural changes that preceded the emergence of the first civilizations. As Kent Flannery (1972) pointed out, "Complex societies are simply not amenable to the simple types of structural, functional, or 'culturological' analyses that anthropologists have traditionally carried out."

Multicausal Explanations

To replace the prime-mover hypotheses, Flannery proposed a many-sided approach to the origins of literate civilization. Instead of prime movers, he argued that there was a "whole series of important variables with complex interrelationships and variations between them" (Flannery, 1972). He said that, for example, the behavior of the people living in Mesopotamia at the time when the first city-states were formed was "a point of overlap (or articulation) between a vast number of systems, each of which encompasses both cultural and non-cultural phenomena—often much more of the latter."

Under this rubric, the rise of civilization should be thought of as a series of interacting and cumulative processes that were triggered by favorable cultural and ecological conditions and continued to develop cumulatively as a result of continual positive feedback. Just how complex the interactions may have been is shown in Figure 18.1 (Redman, 1978b). The process began with establishment of agricultural communities in the Mesopotamian delta about 7,300 years ago. These settlements triggered three processes that set up critical positive feedback relationships:

1. Slow but steady population growth within the delta region.
2. Increased specialization in food production by different groups within the society.
3. Demand for and acquisition of raw materials from outside the delta.

Each of these processes set off feedback reactions that became more and more complex as time went on. An increase in population led to either more extensive fields or more intensive cultivation of existing acreage. The need for increased agricultural production led to more centralized planning and administration of irrigation works and other communal food-producing activities. The inhabitants of the delta lived within a restricted area, and as populations rose, they were forced to live in larger, more densely populated settlements that took up the minimum of agricultural land and required extremely intensive exploitation of the closest fields. Finally, an administrative elite that controlled people's access to strategic agricultural resources eventually emerged. As Figure 18.1 shows, it is possible to develop a highly complex, multicausal model for emergence of Mesopotamian civilization that is based on logical, interlocking hypotheses. The problem is to test this model and its many hypotheses in the field.

Testing such a multicausal model is a difficult task, requiring the development not only of rigorous methodologies for identifying the variables in the archaeological record but also of comparative studies of these variables in regions where civilization emerged and where it did not and also in societies that flourished immediately before this development. Only in this way could one identify the crucial variables for the appearance of early civilization (Redman, 1978b).

William Sanders and David Webster (1978) point out that Flannery's approach relies heavily on cultural evolution and invokes a variety of universal processes that affected the formation of complex societies (see also Binford, 1983a). They argue that it seems a paradox to try to explain variability within human cultures by using universal, evolutionary processes that are in themselves unchanging. The one component of the scheme that does vary is environmental stimuli. In his classic study of the civilizations in the Basin of Mexico, Sanders shows how the Aztecs created and organized agricultural systems, huge acreages of swamp gardens that spread over the shallow waters of the basin's lakes. The variability of the

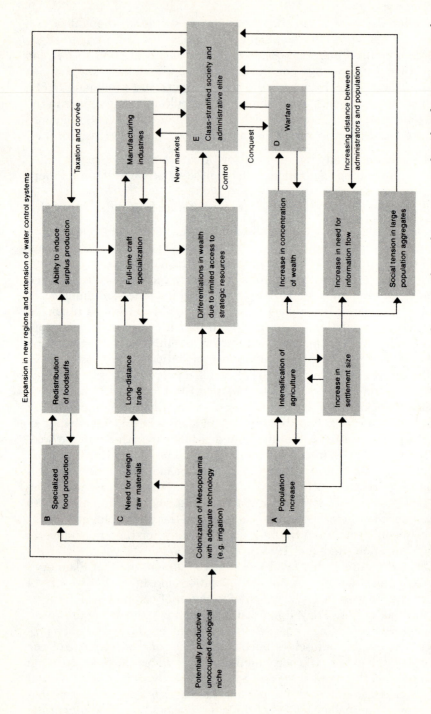

Figure 18.1 A tentative systems model that attempts to document the interrelationships among cultural and environmental variables leading the increasing stratification of class structure in Mesopotamian society between 5000 and 2000 B.C.

Expansion in new regions and extension of water control systems

Taxation and corvée

Manufacturing industries

E Class-stratified society and administrative elite

D Warfare

Conquest

Increasing distance between administrators and population

New markets

Control

Ability to induce surplus production

Full-time craft specialization

Differentiations in wealth due to limited access to strategic resources

Increase in concentration of wealth

Increase in need for information flow

Social tension in large population aggregates

B Specialized food production

Redistribution of foodstuffs

Long-distance trade

Intensification of agriculture

Increase in settlement size

C Need for foreign raw materials

Colonization of Mesopotamia with adequate technology (e.g. irrigation)

A Population increase

Potentially productive unoccupied ecological niche

basin environment meant that the Aztecs had to exploit every environmental opportunity afforded them; the state therefore organized large-scale swamp agriculture. By the time of the Spanish conquest (1519–1521), their agricultural systems were supporting a population of up to 250,000 people just in the Aztec capital, Tenochtitlán (Sanders and others, 1979).

SOME NEW ASSUMPTIONS

Ten years ago, archaeologists were talking about a "new archaeology," a revolutionary approach to the past that promised to overcome many limitations of the archaeological record. That talk has died down, for the "new" archaeology is far from new. In fact, it has failed to deliver on many of its promises. We are going through a prolonged period of theoretical fumbling, searching for a new body of archaeological theory that will truly provide us with new models for interpreting the past (Binford, 1986, 1989; Moore and Keene, 1983; Mithen, 1989).

Many scholars are searching for the meaning of the archaeological record, for ancient ideologies, for the structure of prehistoric societies. To do so, they have borrowed from cultural anthropology such theoretical ideas and models as structuralism, symbolic analysis, and Marxism (Leone, 1986). This has led to some interesting new directions in archaeology, which are based on a series of assumptions and emphases:

1. Culture is interactive. In other words, people are actors who create, use, and manipulate their symbolic capabilities to make and remake the world they live in.
2. Meaning is more important than materialism. No longer can one interpret the past in terms of purely ecological, technological, and other material considerations.
3. The past plays an active role in the society that is interested in it; the past is a vehicle for communicating meanings. Archaeology is not scientifically neutral, it is not objective, and it is not just a luxury. Structural archaeologists believe that the past is a social creation and that they must ask themselves the question, Why should our interpretation of the past be the only correct one? They regard archaeology as a social construct, as much a part of culture as language. In contrast, critical archaeologists agree with Karl Marx that history is always created in the service of "class interests." Archaeologists of this persuasion see history as ideology. They believe that by focusing on archaeology's ideological status, one can perhaps answer important questions.
4. It follows that archaeology cannot be "culture-free." To claim otherwise is to assert that we exist outside our culture. Thus the positivism that has been so important to archaeology in recent decades has a limited or even nonexistent role.

We must now explore briefly some of these new approaches to the past (an admirable summary appears in Leone, 1986).

FUNCTIONALISM AND STRUCTURAL ARCHAEOLOGY

Functionalism, the notion that a social institution within a society has a function in fulfilling all the needs of a social organism, is a concept that has been integral to much anthropological thinking since late in the nineteenth century. Hodder (1982a) uses the analogy of the stomach, which fulfills a function for the human body as a whole. Thus functionalists assess any aspect of a society according to its contribution to the total working of society. Functionalism has long been a controversial topic among anthropologists, but it is inextricable from the notion of systems and cultural systems, concepts that are fundamental tenets of processual archaeology. As Renfrew (1975) points out, to examine connections between cultural subsystems is to look at ancient society through a functionalist perspective. Processual archaeology proposes to identify relationships between variables in cultural systems, such as those that contributed to the beginnings of urban civilization (Gibbon, 1984; Salmon, 1978).

The functionalist approach to what was once called the new archaeology has been criticized by some archaeologists, who attack processual archaeologists of this school for their emphasis on equilibrium and the idea that most change has to come from outside the system (Hodder, 1982a). Function and utility are inadequate ways of explaining social and cultural systems, for many archaeologists distinguish between culture on the one hand and adaptive utility on the other. More extreme viewpoints reject any normative descriptions of cultural variation and seek to explain everything in terms of adaptive expedience. Under this title, material culture is simply seen as functioning at the interface between human organisms and the social and physical environment, as a means of allowing adaptation. Ian Hodder (1982a) writes:

> There is much more to culture than functions and activities. Behind functioning and doing there is a structure and content which has partly to be understood in its own terms, with its own logic and coherence. This applies as much to refuse distributions and "the economy" as it does to burial, pot decoration and art.

Not only that, but the processual school has stressed identification of variability in human culture and in so doing has tended to think of adaptation in general rather than adaptation in individual historical context. Systems are seen as in equilibrium or disequilibrium, populated by human beings who, as individuals, are minimally important. An impersonality about this form of processual archaeology is inclined to see things as cross-cultural statements of predictive value, even with the notion of predicting the past

(Thomas, 1974). It is within this context that ethnoarchaeology and concepts like middle-range theory have become fashionable. Prehistoric institutions were rational in dealing with their environments, assume archaeologists of this persuasion. Although there can be little doubt that they are partly right, recent theoretical argument has moved beyond functionalism into the realm of what is becoming known as "structural archaeology."

Structure in an archaeological context is defined by Ian Hodder (1982a) not as a set of relationships between components of a cultural system (a way in which it could be used, interchangeably with *system*) but as "the codes and rules according to which observed systems of interrelations are produced." Hodder argues that many studies of areas like the Peruvian coast or the American Southwest have explained the structure of human societies in terms of social functions and adaptive values. But they also hint that there is more to culture than observable relationships and functional utility. Hodder writes of a set of rules, a code, as it were, that he likens to those operating in chess or Monopoly, which are followed as people go about the business of survival, adaptation, and making a living.

Hodder calls this approach structural (or cognitive) archaeology. He associates his definition of a set of rules with three essential concepts:

1. *Artifacts, features, and other items*—signs in the archaeological record—occur in relation to one another to create patterns. The patterns resulting from this *interrelatedness* are the important thing, not the signs themselves.
2. *Language* is how the meaning of the world is communicated, in a sense the *code* to the structure.
3. *Transformation* is the notion that the patterns in the archaeological record are *generated* by underlying logic. Another important aspect of transformation is change through time. Hodder views cultural change as a manipulation of this logic by people through their intentional behavioral strategies.

Structural archaeology is an attempt to get at the active, social manipulation of *symbols,* objects as they are perceived by their owners—not merely at their use. Hodder himself studied the Nuba agriculturalists of the Sudan and showed that all aspects of their material culture, including burial customs, settlement patterns, and artifact styles, could be understood in the context of a set of rules that perpetuated their beliefs in "purity, boundedness, and categorization" (Hodder, 1982b). Thus Nuba society is the result of structured, symbolizing behavior and has fundamental utility. But it also has a logic of its own, which generated the material culture that is observed by the archaeologist. Structural archaeologists believe that although functionalist analyses can yield information on the underlying codes, explanations for them must be based not on function but on the logic behind them.

What structural archaeology is basically concerned with is the identification of the "idea of complex dimensions" (Leone, 1986). There are few examples of in-depth research that reveal such a structure. David Friedel and Linda Schele's (1987) research on Mayan iconography (Chapter 16) is one possible example, although the authors do not claim their study as a structural approach. They do show how ritual life, shrines, and temple structures helped shape people's lives. In other words, people think order into their world by using "central, powerful, and pliable symbols" (Leone, 1986).

Structural archaeology at its most general is the analysis of patterns and their transformations. It has probably arisen through frustration with the problems and limitations of spatial analysis (Chapter 15), where one confronts head-on the difficulties and frustrations of interpreting spatial patterns and the variables that affected their distribution. The concept is all very well in theory, but few archaeological studies have yet provided convincing accounts of the relationships between the "codes" and social and ecological organization. One reason is that we still lack a sound theory of structural archaeology, another that structural approaches deal with ideas that are separate from those of adaptation. Burial patterns in a cemetery are not just a reflection of human behavior and social patterns; they are structures in a highly emotional symbolic and social context. By the same token, pottery shapes and decoration can be used by their makers not just to distinguish different functional uses for pots but also to play out all manner of subtle social relationships.

On superficial examination, the notion of structural archaeology is not very different from the more traditional, normative approaches used by older generations of archaeologists in both the New and Old Worlds. Many of them realized that the material remains they studied had a little-understood social context. But it was difficult for them to move beyond chronology and artifacts, partly because they lacked the large bodies of data that are now available and also because they had no detailed descriptions of ethnographic contexts that would help them develop historical explanations. The new fascination with structural archaeology has flared at a time when these data are becoming available, when archaeologists are beginning to wrestle with the problems of developing a theory of social practice for understanding the relationships among structure, belief, action, and the material remains they ultimately generate (Hodder, 1982a). To some extent, structural archaeology is a reaction against the logicodeductive approach of much processual archaeology. But it is far more than that; it is an extension of the functionalist approach of processualists in that it reconsiders many of the basic issues about culture, ideology, and structure that worried earlier archaeologists just as much as their successors. Little more than a beginning has been made in developing the theory or carrying out the field studies to validate this new approach, but it is clear that the "new archaeology," with its systems and explicitly scientific approach, is about to undergo further exciting and radical change as archaeology begins to be a cultural and historical discipline that has the potential not only to contribute to our understanding of the past but also to contribute some highly original ideas to humanity's thinking about itself (Hodder, 1982b; for extended discussion, see Hodder, 1984, 1985; Leone, 1986).

COGNITIVE AND CRITICAL ARCHAEOLOGY

People are like actors, interacting with their culture—this concept is the major difference in approach between archaeologists using a materialist approach to the past and those who are concerned with symbolic meaning, structure, and the "rules" that once governed society.

Cognitive archaeology concerns itself with the patterns behind material culture. What are the links between large and diverse series of apparently unrelated artifacts? These artifacts manifested the changes in people's minds as time went on. The classic research is that of James Deetz on New England tombstones, which we described in Chapter 5. Deetz chronicles how housing and artifacts, as well as tombstone styles, changed as society became more individualist and the face-to-face community withered. For example, the impersonal, private urn-and-willow gravestone design replaced the earlier death's heads and cherubs, which had portrayed a human aspect of each individual and related that individual to the community of which he or she had once been a part (Deetz, 1983). This study drew heavily on historical research into folk housing and may prove to be a highly effective technique for use on historic sites.

Critical archaeology assumes that since archaeologists are actors in contemporary culture, they must have some active impact on our society (Shanks and Tilley, 1987a). Our reconstructions of the past have a social function, just as astronomy did in Mayan civilization. So archaeology may be more than a neutral, objective science. By engaging in critical analysis, an archaeologist can explore the relationship between a reconstruction of the past and the ideology that helped create that reconstruction. One extreme is the Marxist view of archaeology, which states that all knowledge is class-based, so archaeology composes history for class purposes (Spriggs, 1984). Much critical archaeology focuses on understanding the pasts of people who have been "denied" a history—women, blacks, the Third World, and so on. In other words, we should be concerned with the cultural roots of our work (Shanks and Tilley, 1987a, 1987b). In a sense, this approach to archaeology reproaches current archaeological practice and demands that archaeologists be socially and politically responsible in their research. Many archaeologists object to this thesis because of its strong critical and moral undertones, which, they feel, undermine basic method and theory in the discipline (Kristiansen, 1988).

Critical archaeology produces studies that assume a political and economic relationship between the past and interpretations of the past. This past can be interpreted archaeologically to provide insights into the impact of that relationship. So the research has two steps, well documented by Russell Handsman's research in western Connecticut (1981). He studied New England urban villages that appeared around 1800, communities that were "marked by an increase in the disparity of the distribution of wealth between many villages." The landscape changed from one of isolated farmsteads and occasional nuclear settlements to one of much larger villages. Analyzing artifacts found in a Canaan, Connecticut, tavern midden dating to between 1750 and 1850, Handsman argues that the homogeneous ceramics, glass vessels, and other objects of the earlier layers show an unchanging, homogeneous way of life. But after 1800 the artifacts become more individualized and fine-grained, as if individual wealth and status had become more important.

What are we to make of this research? Handsman shows that Canaan was constructed to provide a way in which the new, industrial elite could, by creating village communities, ground themselves and their great variations in wealth in an earlier farming era with different values. Handsman has given Canaan's early history an economic and political context through archaeological research. His critical approach establishes that Canaan came into being as a way of disguising the switch to an industrial society. He argues that New England society used settlement pattern and architecture to avoid knowledge of shifting family values and relations, new property rules, and wage relations. Research like this can contribute to a greater consciousness of modern society.

All these new approaches to the past are reactions to the feeling that modern archaeology has become too dehumanized, too divorced from its proper role in modern society—that it has no cultural context. Unfortunately, the very nature of much modern scientific archaeology is such that there is no conceptual basis for archaeologists to play a more active role in their own society (Trigger, 1984b). Some archaeologists are very worried about this (Meltzer and others, 1986), and it is interesting to see that some recent excavations opened to the public in places like Annapolis are not designed merely as justifications for spending public money or just to satisfy public curiosity. As Mark Leone (1986) says, they show that "we think up and with the past." This may be ideology of a sort, but it makes people understand that the past can be interpreted—and manipulated—in many ways. (For a full discussion, see Shanks and Tilley, 1987a, 1987b.)

In these new trends, we are perhaps seeing the beginning of a kind of redefinition of long-used conceptual frameworks and practices in archaeology. In a sense, this is a process of archaeologists becoming more critical of their own place in the unfolding intellectual development of Western scholarship (Trigger, 1989). As Bruce Trigger and others have pointed out, historical and archaeological research has gone through broad pendulum swings, from encasing data in broad, global frameworks such as Tylor's unilinear evolutionary scheme of the 1870s or Arnold Toynbee's celebrated world histories, to a greater concern with local examples and specifics, such as Boas's research among North American Indians. Functionalism and structuralism take somewhat middle-of-the-road positions.

To a great extent, these swings have been governed by much wider intellectual trends, by changes in economic patterns and ideological climates. Recently, for example, historians and anthropologists have been much concerned with the notion of world economic systems (Wolf, 1984). Perhaps it is no coincidence that the new interest in world systems coincides with a new, emerging global economic order.

At the moment, archaeology seems to be occupying a middle ground between the processualists and the postprocessualists, with evolutionary frameworks under attack and archaeologists of the processual persuasion arguing that there is no data-driven substance behind the theories of the structuralists and postprocessualists. In a sense, two polarized positions have been staked out, and a prolonged intellectual debate over the middle ground is about to begin. Much of this debate may well be focused outside the narrow confines of North American and European scholarship, in areas of the world where archaeology has important roles to play in national ideologies and where it really does provide the database and theoretical underpinning for national histories.

WHAT LIES AHEAD: EVOLUTIONARY ARCHAEOLOGY?

Where does the future lie? The answer can only be that archaeologists are uncertain. Clearly, both evolutionary theory and ecology will be important in the study of cultural change and the birth of complex societies. The term *postprocessual archaeology* has come to embrace a variety of criticisms of the use of evolutionary theory in archaeology (Shanks and Tilley, 1987a, 1987b; Hodder, 1982a). Many archaeologists find evolutionary theory useful, so one future direction of archaeological theory will lie in reconsidering the applications of evolutionary theory to our discipline (Mithen, 1989).

As Steven Mithen (1989) points out, *Homo sapiens sapiens* is a cultural animal, our capacity for culture a product of evolution in which natural selection played an important part. What is crucial for archaeologists is whether these same evolutionary processes had any consequences for the nature of human behavior. In other words, is culture independent of its biological roots and thus irrelevant to the study of human behavior?

The postprocessualists, with their strong criticisms of functionalism, seem to imply that culture *is* independent of biology. Thus evolutionary theory is irrelevant as a way of understanding human behavior (Shanks and Tilley, 1987b). This is less convincing than an alternative viewpoint, which supports the idea that natural selection produced culture by conferring some reproductive advantage on its bearers. So thought and action were channeled by natural selection in directions that were adaptive for an evolving *Homo sapiens sapiens*. The legacy of this is a tendency for humans to think and act in certain ways and not in others. The result is a strong tendency toward conformity in thought and action among very diverse human societies with very different institutions and beliefs. Archaeologists of this persuasion recognize that natural selection has constrained human thought and action, that the way in which people behave can be understood by understanding the constraints placed on the human mind by its long evolutionary heritage. It should be remembered, however, that the environment in which the human mind evolved is very different from that in which we live today and have lived in for many thousands of years.

Under this argument, the reality that *Homo sapiens sapiens* is a product of biological evolution, probably dominated by natural selection, underlies the ways in which we think and act. From the archaeological point of view, the existence of universal human psychological characteristics means that a link connects modern humans with prehistoric, anatomically modern characteristics (Mithen, 1989).

Intimately linked with the evolutionary approach is the notion of adaptation. Adaptation refers to the morphological, behavioral, and cognitive traits of any organism that increase its chances of survival and reproduction and those of its biological kin. By no means are all behavioral traits adaptive all the time or in all environments. One has to demonstrate how they allow the survival and reproduction of individuals in the past, a demonstration that requires considerable reasoning, for it is one thing to discover evidence of, say, more sea mammal hunting and quite another to show that this resulted in a variety of social consequences such as increased prestige. One must carry out research "armed with humility in the face of the complexity of human cognitive functioning and social systems" (Hinde, 1987).

By its very nature, archaeology tends to focus on groups rather than individuals, simply because of the anonymous nature of the archaeological record. Thus evolutionary approaches to archaeology have focused on group adaptation rather than the real unit of selection, the individual. Even the humblest and smallest of hunter-gatherer bands are made up of individuals, of different ages and sexes, knowledge and physique. This means that what may be adaptive behavior for one person is not for another. It is individuals who adapt, each in a personal way, to the challenges of their environment. Much of cultural ecology theory is built—erroneously—on notions of group behavior and adaptation. In the future, we are likely to see a greater concern with another evolutionary principle: that individuals adapt within groups.

Adaptation is a process, and archaeologists are concerned with studying the long-term cultural process through time. This process is the means by which an organism adopts behavioral patterns that have functional significance. We focus on prehistoric learning and decision making, the processes by which humans adapt to their ever-changing environments and make decisions about survival and reproduction. Studying decision making from the archaeological record is a very difficult task, partly because of the complex symbolism that surrounds every human society and the individuals within it. As the masterpieces of Upper Paleolithic art remind us, such symbolic environments are very hard to infer from archaeological data. In reality, however, people's actions tend to reflect ecological realities, to be based on information about their environments and their practical need to survive. Natural selection has created a tendency for people to repeat actions that result in feelings of satisfaction. These emotions are genetically programmed to occur when an individual is adapting successfully to the environment.

If one considers adaptation a process, the individuals doing the adapting are not passive, as some postprocessualists allege (Shanks and Tilley, 1987b). The evolutionary approach to archaeology considers adaptation as a process, with flexible behavior and creative thought on the part of individuals as the driving forces behind decisions to change social and physical environments. Nowhere can this be seen more clearly than in the case of the Khoi Khoi, cattle herders who lived at the Cape of Good Hope, the southernmost tip of Africa, in the fifteenth century. The Khoi Khoi were a society of individuals, each of whom pursued individual goals within the broad compass of a herder society. Their society disintegrated in the face of European colonization in the seventeenth and eighteenth centuries, largely because *individuals* made short-term decisions about selling off their breeding cows for immediate advantage. Within a generation or so, the long-term consequences were apparent: the loss of the ability to breed new stock and a loss of wealth in a society where cattle were the primary source of prestige and adaptation (Elphick, 1977). In short, reflective behavior is at the heart of the process of human adaptation, which accounts for our great cultural diversity in the present and in the past. The rich diversity of human society results from the interaction between universal psychological propensities of humankind and the unique circumstances that cause each individual to adapt to different social, ecological, and historical situations. It is the interaction between universals and individual adaptation that is important. Neither alone can explain the great differences and similarities between ancient or modern societies.

The most useful evolutionary perspective in archaeology, concerned as it is with change through time, is one that focuses on individuals as dynamic persons, constantly adjusting their behavior as their social and physical environments alter. These same individuals are people capable of creative thinking, a uniquely human characteristic. Thought is a driving force in cultural change, in decision making and learning, in the process of adaptation. There are, of course, limits on human knowledge—problems we cannot cope with, processes of comprehension that are beyond us, mistakes we can make through mental confusion. These limits place a premium on cooperation between individuals in the solving of problems, such as finding a way to kill large numbers of bison at one time.

Under this emerging rubric, evolutionary approaches in archaeology will be more concerned with "active individuals endowed with common psychological propensities to think and act in certain ways rather than others, taking decisions in ecological, social, and historical contexts which are unique to themselves" (Mithen, 1989). Until now, most evolutionary studies in archaeology have been more concerned with prehistoric subsistence and interaction with the natural environment and less focused on adaptations to the social environment. In the future, they may be more directed toward identifying the extent to which individual choices and the patterns in the archaeological record resulting from them can be explained in adaptive terms.

This form of evolutionary archaeology is very different from the type espoused by cultural ecology, which tends to focus on static group adaptation. It will involve developing new methodologies that integrate evolutionary ecology and human psychology and ways of relating short-term individual behavior to the inevitably generalized data from the archaeological record (Mithen, 1990). Many new and sometimes arcane approaches will characterize the next generation of evolutionary archaeology, everything from computer simulations to cost-benefit analysis. In recent years, mathematicians have developed some approaches and techniques that are very suitable to the study of the evolution and change of structures and frameworks. In many ways, the biologist and the archaeologist are facing the same problem: How do forms, whether living or cultural, emerge and stabilize?

Our knowledge of world prehistory grows more complex every day. We can discern some regularities, yet the more general relationships and processes that have led to these regularities are still little understood. The few general experiments in these new and unfolding areas of archaeology are tantalizing and highly technical. They lie, indeed, beyond the scope of this book and the technical competence of many professional archaeologists. But one can predict that future archaeologists may rely heavily on some mathematical studies of relationships, forms, and processes that enable us to explain how and why human societies have taken the forms and followed the courses they have. The objective will be not only to explain the patterns and variations of the archaeological record but also to examine the question of questions in our world, the exact place of humankind in the natural world. "Only with the reassessment of our place in nature—to which archaeology can make a significant contribution—will a true humanity emerge," concludes Steven Mithen (1989).

SUMMARY

- Processual archaeology is based on deductive research methodology that employs formal research design, explicit research hypotheses, and the testing of these against basic data. Its methods are cumulative; that is, synthesized archaeological data are interpreted on the basis of successive generations of working hypotheses that are tested again and again.

- The processual approach is based firmly on culture history and on data obtained from inductive research. The differences between it and the inductive approach lie in the orientation of the research, which is deductive rather than inductive.

- Processual archaeologists who use the deductive-nomological approach are committed to a highly formal, scientific methodology that is based on the study of general laws and the work of philosophers of science. They consider the world to be composed of observable phenomena that act in an orderly way. In other words, the world can be explained by predicting when a set of phenomena that indicate a particular law is in operation will occur.

- General laws governing human behavior are derived from anthropology and other social sciences. But many archaeologists reject the assumption that such general laws exist and believe that the highly specific, deductive scientific methods of physics and other sciences are inappropriate to archaeological data. They do, however, recognize the value of deductive research.

- Most processual archaeology embraces a systems-ecological approach that deals with the ways in which cultural systems function, both internally and in relation to external factors, such as the environment. This approach is based on general systems theory, cultural ecology, and multilinear cultural evolution.

- The systems approach provides a way of looking at the relationships of various traits within a cultural system. Archaeologists deal with open systems that are regulated, at least in part, by external stimuli. In cultural systems, these stimuli are the elements in the environment. The regulatory mechanisms that govern the system keep it in equilibrium and sometimes trigger further cultural change through positive feedback.

- Cultural ecologists see human cultures as subsystems interacting with other subsystems, all of which are part of a total ecosystem. Under this rubric, human culture is, ecologically speaking, a way in which human beings compete successfully with plants, animals, and other human beings.

- Multilinear cultural evolution recognizes that cultural adaptations are complex processes, fine-tuned to local conditions, with long-term cumulative effects. The four stages of the evolution of social organization described in Chapter 16 are defined in terms of social complexity, subsistence strategy, and population size, among other factors.

- Processual archaeology has proved effective in studying the origins of literate civilization, for explanations for cultural change are now couched in terms of multiple causes rather than single prime movers. The new multicausal models resulting from the systems-ecological approach require development of new, rigorous methodologies for data collection, comparative studies of cultural variables in the archaeological record, and the tracing of the development of these variables in the millennia immediately preceding the origins of civilization.

- Postprocessual archaeology is a reaction against the evolutionary and functionalist approaches and takes several forms. *Structural archaeology* tries to analyze the patterns of human culture and their transformations, while *critical archaeology* concerns itself with the patterns behind material culture and with the contemporary context of archaeological research.

- Evolutionary theory based on the interaction between individual adaptations and common behavioral characteristics of all humans is likely to unfold in the 1990s. It will involve developing new methodologies focused on examining social adaptations, as well as subsistence and adaptations to the natural environment.

GUIDE TO FURTHER READING

Binford, Lewis R. *An Archaeological Perspective.* New York: Seminar Press, 1972. Binford's autobiographical account of how he developed his ideas on processual archaeology. Polemical, but essential reading; the volume contains Binford's early papers.

Binford, Lewis R. *In Pursuit of the Past.* New York: Thames and Hudson, 1983. An essay on the archaeological record and archaeological interpretation.

Clarke, David L. *Analytical Archaeology.* London: Methuen, 1968. A massive discussion of processual archaeology written by an archaeologist that many scholars considered a genius. European orientation, but worth close attention by the serious student.

Flannery, Kent V., ed. *The Early Mesoamerican Village.* Orlando, Fla.: Academic Press, 1976. The "dialogues" that introduce each paper in this volume on settlement archaeology are a mine of entertaining and frank information on the uses and limitations of processual archaeology.

Gibbon, Guy. *Anthropological Archaeology.* New York: Columbia University Press, 1984. An essay on science in contemporary archaeology that highlights the confusion at the theoretical cutting edge of the discipline. For advanced readers.

Hodder, Ian, ed. *Symbolic and Structural Archaeology.* Cambridge: Cambridge University Press, 1982. Essays on symbolic and structural archaeology that grapple with the problems of reconciling normative and processual archaeology.

Mithen, Steven. "Evolutionary Theory and Post-processual Archaeology," *Antiquity* 63 (1989): 483–494. An eloquent, closely argued statement on evolutionary archaeology that sets a trend for the 1990s.

Shanks, Michael, and Christopher Tilley. *Reconstructing Archaeology: Theory and Practice.* Cambridge: Cambridge University Press, 1987.

Shanks, Michael, and Christopher Tilley. *Social Theory and Archaeology.* Albuquerque: University of New Mexico Press, 1987. Two very important discourses on postprocessual archaeology that epitomize some of the theoretical debates in the discipline today. Thought-provoking and well-argued essays.

Watson, Patti Jo, Steven A. Le Blanc, and Charles L. Redman. *Archaeological Explanation: The Scientific Method in Archaeology,* 2d ed. New York: Columbia University Press, 1984. A book that describes processual archaeology in a methodological context. For the advanced reader.

PART
Eight

CULTURAL RESOURCE MANAGEMENT

*W*e have now completed our journey through the complexities of contemporary archaeology, a journey that should leave you with some insights into the processes of archaeological research. Our discussion of contemporary archaeology would be incomplete, however, without considering cultural resource management, one of the most pressing and complex aspects of the discipline. A major crisis confronts archaeologists: destruction of finite resources. In the two chapters that follow we survey the problems of managing the world's archaeological resources and look at the various ways in which one can become involved in archaeology, both as a pastime and as a professional career.

Chapter
19

Management of the Past

*A*ll archaeological excavation is destruction, the destruction of a finite resource. But, though archaeologists themselves have destroyed thousands of sites in their research, far more damage has resulted from looting, treasure hunting, and modern agricultural and industrial activity (Fowler, 1982; Schiffer and Gumerman, 1977; King and others, 1977). In this chapter we look at ways in which archaeologists have sought to halt the destruction of sites by legislative means and at the practical problems of managing cultural resources.*

The inexorable destruction of archaeological sites has accelerated rapidly since the 1960s. Deep plowing, freeway construction, water control schemes, strip mining, and unprecedented urban development have all played havoc with the archaeological record. In many areas the situation has reached crisis proportions. It is estimated that less than 5 percent of the 1850s archaeological resource base in Los Angeles County is still undisturbed. Charles McGimsey estimated in 1972 that at least 25 percent of the sites that existed in Arkansas in 1750 had been destroyed by agricultural and other land use, to say nothing of looters, in the previous ten years. Archaeologists in Britain, worried about the wanton destruction of archaeological sites by industrial development and by treasure hunters using metal detectors, have formed an organization named RESCUE (Figure

*This chapter is concerned entirely with cultural resource management in North America, where most of our readership resides. Unfortunately, space precludes discussion of similar problems in other countries like Canada and Britain; in Japan, very different problems are encountered. Interested readers are referred to Henry Cleere's edited volume, *Approaches to the Archaeological Heritage* (1984).

19.1) that helps fight to save key sites and to prevent looting (Rahtz, 1974). Perhaps the most famous example of "rescue" archaeology was the international effort, sponsored by UNESCO, that resulted in moving the Abu Simbel temples in Egypt from the banks of the Nile behind the Aswan High Dam to a new site clear of the rising waters of Lake Nasser. The Aswan project also resulted in the discovery of hundreds of additional sites in the area to be flooded (Macquilty, 1965). (For worldwide surveys, see Cleere, 1984; Prott and O'Keefe, 1984.)

In this chapter we examine a vital branch of archaeology, the multifarious activities that come under the title cultural resource management (CRM). Because much of this work is done under contract to government agencies or private companies, it is sometimes called contract archaeology, to distinguish it from the management of the actual resources.

Cultural resources refers to both human-made and natural physical features associated with human activity. They are unique and nonrenewable resources and can include sites, structures, and artifacts significant in history or prehistory. Cultural resource management is the application of management skills to preserve important parts of our cultural heritage, both historic and prehistoric, for the benefit of the public. The concept of cultural resource management came into being in the mid-1970s but stemmed from long anxiety on the part of archaeologists and others over

Figure 19.1 RESCUE speaks for itself: "Tomorrow may be too late."

the destruction of archaeological sites and historic buildings. (For a survey covering both North and South America, see Wilson and Loyola, 1982.)

ANTIQUITIES LEGISLATION

People have worried about the destruction of archaeological sites for a long time. There were, for example, loud outcries as long ago as 1801, when Lord Elgin removed the stunning marbles that now bear his name from the Parthenon and bore them away to London (Bracken, 1975). The Greek government is still trying to get them back. The early proponents of historic preservation in the late nineteenth century included not only architects and historians but also anthropologists and archaeologists, who realized that American Indian societies and their forebears were vanishing almost without a trace in the face of colonization and vigorous industrial development (Lee, 1970). The Smithsonian Institution's Bureau of American Ethnology and other organizations struggled valiantly to stem the tidal wave of destruction that flattened prehistoric mounds all over eastern North America (Figure 19.2). They also fought a lucrative trade in brightly painted Pueblo pots in the Southwest. The first formal preservation of America's past began with the passage of the Antiquities Act of 1906. This extended some protection to archaeological sites on land owned or controlled by the United States government. There matters remained until the 1930s, when widespread and now classic archaeological surveys in areas threatened by federal dam projects yielded a mass of information on site distributions and key cultural sequences before the sites where they occurred vanished forever under human-made lakes. (For an extended discussion of conservation and legislation, see Fowler, 1986.)

Since World War II, an accelerating destruction of archaeological sites throughout North America has resulted in a jigsaw pattern of complicated but, alas, still inadequate legislation that serves as a framework for cultural resource management activity. This legislation is now so complex that we can do little more than summarize the key provisions of each act since 1960 in Box 19.1.

For a long time, federal legislation was concerned for the most part with site preservation as opposed to protection and management. This has now changed. In particular, the National Environmental Policy Act of 1969 (NEPA) developed requirements that made it essential for archaeologists to prepare and maintain extremely comprehensive information on archaeological resources on state, federal, and privately owned land. This would enable them to assess, at short notice, the potential effects of development on these resources. In addition, states have now developed historic preservations of their own, each headed by a state historic preservation officer, as required by the Historic Preservation Act of 1966. The result of all these changes was a dramatic explosion of archaeological

Figure 19.2 The Great Serpent Mound in Ohio, an early example of archaeological conservation. This remarkable monument, a depiction of a serpent devouring a burial mound, was saved by the efforts of Harvard archaeologist Frederick Putnam and a group of Boston ladies in 1886.

effort, much of it contracted by government agencies as well as private companies. It has also resulted in the emergence of cultural resource management as a sophisticated phenomenon, its practice surrounded by an elaborate framework of laws, regulations, and statutes, not only at the federal and state levels but also at the county, city, and Indian tribe level. Much of it is designed to amplify federal legislation and to adapt it to local conditions. Such local laws have become essential, to deal both with looting and vandalism and also with such issues as reburial of Native American skeletons and an explosion of urban development and urban archaeology throughout North America.

Underlying this jigsaw of legislation is one fundamental difference between United States law and that, for example, of many European nations. In many countries, antiquities are considered the property of the state, whereas American law is ambiguous. This is because of the Fifth Amendment to the Constitution, which forbids the seizure of public property for private use without just compensation. Private property is almost sacrosanct, and over the years, archaeological resources on private land have come to be thought of as part of that land and therefore the private property of the owner.

While many landowners take the preservation of archaeological resources on their land very seriously, others regard sites as sources of income. The damage done by pothunters to such sites has been incalculable. Often they lease sites for large sums of money and move in quite openly with earth-moving machinery and other sophisticated equipment. The objective is simple—to recover as many valuable artifacts as possible. This nefarious practice continues to this day: witness a recent case at Slack Farm, Kentucky, where an undisturbed Late Mississippian riverside cemetery and settlement were leased by a landowner to a group of pothunters. They dug for weeks before the state police moved in, leaving the site looking like a battlefield (Fagan, 1991a).

There have been several convictions under federal antiquities laws. In March 1983, two men were arrested on felony charges of illegally digging up tenth- and eleventh-century Anasazi artifacts and skeletons at Chimney Rock in southwestern Colorado. The artifacts were valued at $7,500, the damage done to the site at $75,000, and $25,000 was needed to restore the site. One offender was sentenced to five hundred hours of community service and ordered to pay $5,000 to the San Juan National Forest. His colleague was fined $500 and received a year's probation (Eddy and O'Sullivan, 1986).

MANAGING THE ARCHAEOLOGICAL RECORD

Cultural resource management, and the archaeological research that goes with it, is but one component of a much larger enterprise—the study of the effects of human activity on the total landscape (Adovasio and Carlisle, 1988). It is part of a much larger concern for the fragile ecology of North America, and the finite archaeological record is only part of the context in which decisions are made about projects that affect the landscape (Fowler, 1986). As we have learned more about ecology, scientists have come to realize that archaeological resources are part of the "public wealth" (Knudson, 1986). Recent legislation, especially the NEPA, reflects this realization, as well as the explicitly ecological approaches of archaeological research in recent years. Indeed, the NEPA provided the legal framework for environmental impact statements, the studies required for all major federal and state projects that can affect human life on earth. In this way, the NEPA may well override the notion of private ownership of archaeological sites.

A morass of laws and regulations at all levels and a growing body of legal opinions and court decisions provide an elaborate framework for

(text continues p. 501)

Box 19.1 ANTIQUITIES LEGISLATION IN THE UNITED STATES, 1960–1989

This is a summary of some of the key features of federal antiquities legislation, which built on the Historic Sites Act of 1935. This baseline act gave the National Park Service a broad mandate to identify, protect, and preserve cultural properties. It also meant that the federal government acknowledged broad responsibility for archaeological and historic sites on and off federally owned land.

It should be noted that numerous state and Native American tribal laws amplify and complicate this already complex legislative picture. We can summarize only the most basic provisions of each federal act in the space available.

RESERVOIR SALVAGE ACT OF 1960

This act authorized archaeologists to dig and salvage sites that were in danger of destruction. It was a last-ditch measure, but it did make possible some important surveys, as well as many rough-and-ready salvage operations literally under the blade of oncoming bulldozers (Figure 19.3). Two important surveys were the following.

Navajo Reservoir, New Mexico
The Navajo Reservoir flooded thirty-four square miles. The lake area was divided into nine sections and surveyed on foot and by jeep (Dittert and others, 1961). The archaeologists inventoried as many sites as possible, but they were never asked to recommend ways of saving sites, nor were they consulted about the siting of the water project so that archaeological considerations could be taken into account.

Glen Canyon, Utah
Glen Canyon lay on the Upper Colorado River in Utah and Arizona before Lake Powell came into being. Here the archaeologists had more time. They made a "total sampling of all cultures and all the periods to be found in the area" the first priority (Jennings, 1966). They placed great emphasis on accurate records and publication of results, for no one would be able to check their results in the field later. This was a highly effective form of salvage, but here again the archaeologists were not expected to make recommendations about *management* of resources.

HISTORIC PRESERVATION ACT OF 1966

This act set up a national framework for historic preservation, requiring the federal government to establish a nationwide system for identifying, protecting, and rehabilitating what are commonly called "historic places" (Schiffer and Gumerman, 1977). The act called for the establishment of the National Register of Historic Places (a "historic place" could include prehistoric and

Figure 19.3 Top: In Arkansas, four land-leveling machines work while archaeologists try to salvage the bottoms of trash pits and crushed burials exposed by the machines. Bottom: In California, emergency salvage in the wake of huge machinery recovers only scattered remnants of occupation.

historic archaeological sites) and required federal agencies to protect Register properties when development projects were planned.

NATIONAL ENVIRONMENTAL POLICY ACT OF 1969 (NEPA)

The NEPA laid down a comprehensive policy for government land use planning and resource management. It required federal agencies to weigh environmental, historical, and cultural values whenever federally owned land is modified or private land is modified with federal funds. The idea was that the nature, extent, and significance of archaeological resources should be inventoried, on the assumption that this information would affect land use planning in the future.

EXECUTIVE ORDER 11593

Some state surveys of archaeological and historical sites were conducted in the 1920s and 1930s. Then the Smithsonian Institution developed site inventories in the late 1940s as part of the river basin surveys. Executive Order 11593, promulgated in 1971, made it a *requirement* that such surveys be made. It was an attempt to develop a sensible federal policy on archaeological and historic preservation. It ordered all federal agencies to take the lead in historic preservation and to locate properties that might qualify for the National Register. They were also to develop programs to contribute to protection of important historic properties on nonfederal lands.

NEPA and Executive Order 11593 developed requirements that made it essential for archaeologists to prepare and maintain extremely comprehensive information on archaeological resources on state, federal, and privately owned land. This would enable them to assess, at short notice, the potential effects of development on these resources. In addition, the states had begun to develop historic preservation programs of their own, each headed by a state historic preservation officer, as required by the Historic Preservation Act of 1966.

AMENDMENT TO THE RESERVOIR SALVAGE ACT, 1974

This amendment authorized all federal agencies to provide funds for the preservation or salvage of sites endangered by federal projects.

ARCHAEOLOGICAL RESOURCES PROTECTION ACT OF 1979 (ARPA)

The ARPA gave more stringent protection to archaeological sites over one hundred years old on federal land. People removing archaeological materials from federal lands without a permit are committing a felony; they can be fined up to $10,000 and sentenced to a year in prison. The penalties rise sharply when more valuable finds are involved. This legislation is aimed at commercial vandals; it does not forbid individuals from removing arrowheads "located on the surface of the ground." Unfortunately, it gives no protection to archaeological resources on privately owned land.

AMENDMENTS TO THE NEPA, 1980

These amendments had made Executive Order 11593 law, rather than just an executive order, and also made provisions for the pass-through of some funds for historic preservation to certified local authorities. They also recognized that Indian tribes should have preservation programs and relationships with the National Park Service and State Historic Preservation offices.

Amendments to ARPA in recent years have tightened the definition of what constitutes an "archaeological resource" and have legislated far more severe penalties for violations of the original law.

ABANDONED SHIPWRECKS ACT OF 1988

This act extended protection to shipwrecks and defined ownership of abandoned vessels in state and federal waters more clearly. It is an important weapon in the fight against unauthorized looting of shipwrecks, looting that all too often masquerades as "underwater archaeology."

OTHER LEGISLATION

In 1989 important laws established a National Museum of the American Indian and charged the Smithsonian Institution both with setting up this museum and with developing policies for the repatriation of skeletal remains held by the institution. The reburial sections of this legislation are likely to have long-lasting effects on North American archaeology.

In addition, significant legislation covering the protection of archaeological sites on private lands and the reburial of Native American burials has been passed or is pending in many states.

long-term cultural resource management in American archaeology. This compliance process on even a medium-sized federal project is an attempt to see that cultural resources threatened by the project are properly managed—recorded, evaluated, protected, or, if necessary, salvaged (Fowler, 1982). Conflicting interests and regulations can lead to unforeseen problems, as, for example, when the local Indians insisted that the Chimney Rock Mesa skeletons disturbed by vandals be reburied. The archaeologists wanted to conserve and study the human remains, but they were overruled by the federal land manager on legal grounds. (For an admirable discussion of the complexities of management, see Eddy and O'Sullivan, 1986.)

The procedure of identification and management in the compliance process has three phases:

1. An *overview* of cultural resources in an area is compiled, ideally a description of the environment and the ethnographic background, a history of previous research, and a description of the known culture history of the area. Then the authors assess the research

potential of the area, identify important research problems, and make management recommendations.

2. An *archaeological assessment report* involves further inventory and assessment, including reexamination of known sites and surveys for new ones. These reports are especially important for areas where substantial modification of the land is likely to take place as a result of strip mining, dam building, and other such developments. The finished document discusses known cultural resources in the area and recommends additional research needed to evaluate their significance, to determine their eligibility for the National Register of Historic Places, and to establish suitable mitigation measures to protect them. The assessment report often forms a preliminary environmental impact report on the area.

3. A *management plan* proposes measures for protecting, preserving, interpreting, and using cultural resources. This is a formal part of the final environmental impact report. To be effective, a management plan should be regarded as a constantly evolving document, maintained and changed as archaeologists continue to manage and monitor the area.

The compliance process, even on simple projects, can be a nightmare, involving the archaeologist as it does in both recommending management strategies and conducting delicate negotiations with several government agencies at once. One of the most interesting examples of a management plan in action is that for the San Juan Basin in the Four Corners area of the American Southwest.

The San Juan Basin has been occupied since around 10,000 B.C. right up to modern times. Not only Anglos and Spanish-Americans but also several pueblo groups and Navajo, Apache, and Ute live in the region, which has been subjected to extensive energy development, including strip mining. Still more exploration and mining are planned. Not only that, but large numbers of people will start depending on the area for recreation—and archaeological sites are part of that recreation. At least seven federal, state, and local agencies have some CRM jurisdiction in the area, and several of them have joined in a cooperative management effort. The National Park Service carried out a preliminary assessment study in 1980. At the time, a database was compiled that contained more than 15,000 sites, with 15 categories of information on each one. An additional 4000 entries made up a survey file (Plot and Wait, 1982). At the time, it was estimated that this now inactive database contained about 70% of the known sites in the San Juan Basin. The database was conceived of as a management tool, with categories of information in it limited to those conceived of as having management potential.

The compliance process involves both federal and state agencies in other management duties as well. They have the responsibility for protecting sites against vandalism, a major problem in some areas. Then the value of each individual resource has to be assessed, either on account of its scientific value, established within the context of a valid research design, or because it merits preservation *in situ.* Agencies also have to consider how a site can be utilized for the public good. This responsibility means interpreting it for the public, who may either visit the location, as they do at, say, Mesa Verde, or learn about it through books, television programs, popular articles, and so on.

The main goal of cultural resource management in the United States has been preserving sites and artifacts for the information they have yielded or may yield. Experts in the field have confronted a number of management problems:

Because archaeological sites are a nonrenewable resource, which of them should be saved for future research rather than being investigated now?

Should data from sites acquired for conservation and planning be used for pure research as well?

How is the significance of archaeological resources to be established for legal compliance purposes?

MANAGEMENT PROBLEMS

Conservation

Obviously, the basic ethics of archaeology demand that as many sites as possible be preserved. Under ideal circumstances, the sites are not threatened by development, and the investigator can develop a research design based on purely scientific considerations. However, many other variables—budget, the public interest, possible design alternatives in the development project, and mitigation costs, to mention only a few—come into play when sites are threatened by imminent destruction. Then there is the problem of "secondary impacts," when unexpected spin-offs of the main project destroy resources outside the main project area. Don Fowler (1982) cites the monstrous MX missile project in the Great Basin that would have affected archaeological resources in no fewer than twenty-three valleys in the region. Although the project would have primarily affected sites in the lowlands, the archaeologists pointed out that most of the sites lay in the foothills and uplands nearby. These would have been disastrously affected by secondary activities such as seismic testing, survey work, and the sheer numbers of construction workers and military personnel brought into the area during the MX project. Whether effective ways of mitigating these secondary impacts would have been possible is questionable. Few, if any, agencies consider such impacts, often critical to archaeologists.

Management Versus Academic Research

The apparent conflict between resource management on the one hand and academic research in archaeology on the other comes down to a dilemma. Most CRM contracts involve collecting or developing scientifically useful data from a highly specific area such as the site of an oil-drilling pad or the sites of pylons along a hundred-mile power line. Are such activities meaningful unless tied to other cultural resources in the region? Though compliance requirements may be satisfied, scholarly needs often most emphatically are not (King, 1983; Renfrew, 1983). Although the Historic Preservation Act requires each state to have a state plan as a mechanism for management overviews of individual projects, only around half have allocated funds to create such plans.

One reason for the conflict between contract archaeology, with its emphasis on compliance and management, and academic archaeology, which concentrates on basic research, is that most contracting parties assume that archaeology is an inductive science (see Hester, 1981). Certainly the traditional methods of archaeological research have been inductive. That is, they assume that sufficient facts can eventually be collected to provide enough data for synthesis and inference from the data. Of course, inductive research is useful, especially in the sort of general exploratory work that is carried out in many large survey areas, such as the Cache River Valley in Arkansas (Schiffer and House, 1976). Until recently, most contracting agencies thought of archaeology as a discipline able to conduct piecemeal research. They assumed that the results from each small project would somehow eventually become part of a grand, final synthesis. Also until recently, the laws all related to specific projects. This type of archaeology was in fact attractive to people with some command of excavation techniques whose final objective was to produce a descriptive site report. Sites or areas were preselected by such criteria as imminence of destruction or availability of salvage funds.

In fact, the 1970s saw much archaeological research become deductive, and archaeologists were now viewing fieldwork and excavation as activities to be carried out only when a specific problem needed solving or a hypothesis needed testing. To these scholars, salvage archaeology for its own sake was an entirely inconsistent activity that simply did not mesh with the specific problem orientation of deductive research. There has been a dangerous and often unthinking tendency to segment archaeology into two broad camps—the academic, deductive researchers taking on specific problems on one side, the contract archaeologists involved with salvage, management, and compliance on the other. This insidious distinction is, of course, a gross simplification, for many distinguished academic archaeologists are deeply involved in cultural resource management. Thus there is often constant feedback between emerging archaeological theory and methodology and the realities of contract work, which is always funded on a project-by-project basis and never in a wider, say, regional, context. And in the final analysis, major cultural resource management projects are funded at a far higher level than even the most ambitious academic project—not only for just survey and excavation but for analysis and sometimes publication as well (Adovasio and Carlisle, 1988).

Can management and research needs be reconciled? Many CRM projects are small-scale operations, involving no more than a small plot of urban land or a simple inventory of a few acres. Such projects are usually undertaken by freelance archaeologists, as are many of the test excavations required for more significant sites. The reports on these operations are usually of relatively limited circulation and are basically descriptive, even if they are conducted within a sound intellectual context. With large-scale projects of regional or even broader scope, the marriage between management and research needs is much closer.

In recent years, many CRM projects have involved massive archaeological operations and the expenditure of millions of dollars in survey and excavation. The Texas-California pipeline, the Dolores Project in Colorado, and the Black Mesa project in the Southwest (Gumerman, 1984) have all yielded important methodological contributions and sometimes major theoretical perceptions. Most of these projects are conducted by larger private companies that specialize in environmental impact work or by CRM organizations with close ties to academic institutions. For instance, the Cultural Resource Management Program of the University of Pittsburgh has developed an elaborate archaeological organization with strong academic ties to the university that carries out major CRM projects in an academic setting. With their excellent technical resources and large project budgets, they are able to conduct detailed research and fine-grained field and laboratory investigations that are beyond the budgetary scope of all purely academic research projects.

For example, the program carried out a gas pipeline survey for a major Texas company, a project that involved close cooperation among the pipeline contractor, archaeologists, and government agencies and officials at all levels. As part of this work, they carried out major excavations at the Howorth-Nelson site in southwestern Pennsylvania, a large, multicomponent Late Woodland and Late Prehistoric site dating from around A.D. 1000 to 1650. The site could not be avoided by rerouting the gas line, so the right-of-way over the settlement was tested with hand-excavated pits, excavations that established that there were deep, undisturbed deposits at the site. Next, a resistivity survey was carried out, and the site was processed with a shallow disk before all surface artifacts and food remains and environmental data were mapped *in situ* with an automatic infrared mapping device. Using these data, a more comprehensive excavation was planned, an excavation that eventually uncovered 3,839 square feet of the site, including remains of houses, storage pits, burials, and other features (Figure 19.3).

This remarkable excavation was large by North American standards, even if it was confined by the nature of the contract to the pipeline right-of-way. It involved the use of sophisticated electronic technology as well as hand excavation, flotation methods, and carefully controlled screening, a combination of digging techniques that allowed a large dig to be completed in minimum time. That the investigation could be conducted at this level was a direct result of access to technology and excavation funds on a scale that far exceed those of any non-CRM excavation (Adovasio and Carlisle, 1988). The result was the recovery of remarkably fine-grained data for a Late Woodland occupation in southwestern Pennsylvania.

Virtually all federal and state agencies have strict requirements for the analysis and reporting of any archaeological data recovered from CRM projects. Such analysis is, of course, very expensive, and it is certain that significant advances in knowledge about the human past will come from major and well-funded CRM projects like the Howorth-Nelson site in Pennsylvania or the soon-to-be-published large-scale excavations and surveys conducted as part of the space shuttle launch pad construction operations at Vandenberg Air Force Base in California.

As Adovasio and Carlisle (1988) point out, CRM archaeology is the only viable way to identify and document rapidly vanishing archaeological resources in North America. It is also a primary means of assembling large bodies of basic archaeological data, the very kinds of data required to fulfill one of archaeology's major objectives, the explanation of cultural processes. Furthermore, CRM activities are also a primary way of gathering culture historical data, not only chronological sequences but also detailed records of individual sites and their environments.

"Nowhere else in contemporary archaeology can the methodological and theoretical challenges raised by the 'new archaeology' be realized with greater clarity than in CRM work," claim Adovasio and Carlisle (1988). As they point out, this is not only a matter of economic realities but also one of perceiving the opportunity to make major intellectual advances in archaeology while still meeting the requirements of individual contracts. No one can claim that all CRM work is good archaeology, but "good archaeology stands the best chance of answering the questions upon which reasonable management decisions about cultural resources depend."

In short, CRM archaeology offers unique opportunities for archaeologists to rest and refine basic operational theories in the field. Its legal mandate requires three-stage investigations. First is the inventorying and recording of all sites within a project area. Then important sites have to be tested. Finally, the most significant may be partly or wholly excavated. This three-stage process often provides unusual opportunities to refine existing models of ancient human behavior and to develop new ones. In the 1990s, CRM archaeology, especially when conducted on a large scale, offers unique opportunities for answering basic questions about the prehistoric past. The challenge is to grasp these opportunities and to exploit them to the fullest.

Research Designs

In the context of contract archaeology, the research design is best described as a "frame of reference"—plans in which basic assumptions, research goals, hypotheses, methodologies, and operating procedures are laid out (Fowler, 1982). Ideally, there should be a hierarchy of research designs. The Historic Preservation Act of 1966 required all states to prepare historic preservation plans. In 1976 the secretary of the interior developed regulations formulating these plans under professional supervision. The surveys, still incomplete, are to include nominations for the National Register of Historic Places and also inventories and *predictions* of where all forms of cultural resources may exist.

States are, of course, political rather than cultural entities, so the best overall research designs are those for regions, whether defined topographically, ecologically, or culturally. A good example of a region is the San Juan Basin in the Four Corners area of the Southwest.

Fowler (1982) lists six key elements for a successful research design:

1. A description of the resource base—an outline of current knowledge about the area and its culture history.
2. A statement of the implications of previous research, combined with a statement of basic assumptions, of the investigators' theoretical approach, whether ecological, materialist, or some other.
3. A statement of general areas of research interest, both general and specific problems to be worked on. These questions are the basis for specific hypotheses and related test implications.
4. A description of the kinds of data needed to complete the research design and specifics on maintaining the quality of the data and on the standards of data required.
5. A formulation of investigative strategies to acquire data of the quality needed. The vital element here is sampling strategies that reflect the realities of time, contract requirements, available funding, and size of the research area.
6. For specific project design, a statement of operating procedures from preliminary fieldwork right up to completion of the final report must be specified.

Research designs may be laid out in many ways, but the critical point is that they must be dynamic, ever-changing statements, not rigid dogma but state-of-the-art designs that keep up with new methodological advances and changing circumstances in the field and out of it. (For example, see Cordell and Green, 1983.) A large-scale CRM research design is far more than a plan for archaeological research; it is a management document, an administrative manifesto, and a high-quality control manual in the bargain. The administrative and legal skills required of a contract archaeologist aré much further-ranging than anything envisaged by an academic researcher.

Training and the Crisis of Quality

An archaeologist involved in contract archaeology and the management of cultural resources requires training in a battery of skills far from the halls of academe. A contract archaeologist must not only be thoroughly versed in academic archaeology but also have a background in the legal requirements of CRM, in antiquities and historic-preservation legislation, and in methods of administration and conservation. Even the beginning contract manager requires formidable archaeological and bureaucratic skills. The situation is somewhat similar to that in which geology and engineering found themselves some years ago. Archaeology is changing from a wholly academic discipline to what Fowler calls a real-world profession. But unlike geology, its product is not energy or more water but knowledge, much of which is not critical to the national interest by any stretch of the imagination.

No one is happy about the quality of training given contract archaeologists at this time. Some master's programs cater to fledgling contract archaeologists, but none achieves an ideal balance among academic, business, and management skills. It remains uncomfortably true that many of the archaeologists involved in CRM projects have received little or no formal training in anything more than basic archaeological method and theory—and that is simply not enough. We can, however, expect the situation to improve in the future as archaeology completes the transition undergone by academic geology some years ago. The curricula of the future should blend academic and practical management skills in graduate programs reflecting an employment picture that has most archaeologists working in government or business rather than in universities, colleges, and museums.

A number of organizations, most notably the Society of Professional Archaeologists (SOPA), have started to work on the thorny question of professional qualifications. The SOPA has drawn up basic ethical guidelines that focus on training and qualifications for archaeologists. But these ethical guidelines have drawn fire, partly on the grounds that they do not reflect the reality of carrying out archaeology under commercial conditions (Fitting and Goodyear, 1979). The SOPA guidelines appeared at a time when the academic discipline of archaeology was busy adjusting to a completely new environment, in which most financial support came from federal and state agencies and private companies involved with projects on government land (Wendorf, 1979).

With CRM now the dominant force in archaeological fieldwork in

North America, the problem of ensuring quality research is of major concern. Two basic strategies are used in CRM work:

The *conservation approach* regards preservation and protection of the archaeological record for humanistic and scientific purposes as the first priority (Lipe, 1970). This is a relatively theory-free and descriptive approach wherein management decisions are based on a representative sample of resources in an area.

The *problem-oriented approach* regards CRM as part of contemporary archaeology with all its sophisticated theoretical apparatus for studying and evaluating the past. In other words, the researcher relies on contemporary knowledge, belief, and concepts in archaeology to make management judgments about the content of the archaeological record in the future (Dunnell, 1985).

The debate about which of these approaches is the most appropriate rages at a high technical level. Much of the argument centers on the conflicting interests of management and pure research. Is one justified in using statistical models that predict the distribution of archaeological sites as a basis for deciding which areas are to be flooded and which are not? Could not one's predictions be so false that they might leave our descendants with a completely skewed archaeological record?

For all the debate about conflicting approaches, and, to be frank, a great deal of dubious research, CRM has brought extensive methodological benefits to basic research, among them a much greater emphasis on prehistoric settlement patterns, sampling procedures, computer applications, and, above all, remote sensing (Drager and Lyons, 1983). The San Juan Basin project and others are excellent examples of how sophisticated research designs and theoretical constructs are blended into a multitude of small contract projects. But among contract archaeology's worst products is that some agencies and contractors are even today quietly accepting second-rate reports and claiming that even minimal surveys are fulfilling both the requirements and the spirit of the law. Work of such poor quality led both the Society for American Archaeology and the SOPA to prepare ethical guidelines and certification procedures for archaeologists. These steps have helped mitigate the problem of quality somewhat. But the problem is so large and the amount of activity so great that the only long-term solution to the crisis of quality lies in a close relationship between the goals and research techniques of a sophisticated scientific archaeology on the one hand and the realities and demands of cultural management and contract archaeology on the other. (For discussion at a technical level, see Dunnell, 1984.)

The crisis of quality has taken a new twist in recent years. Proliferating contract archaeology and CRM have caused an explosion not only of raw data but also of publications and reports on completed projects (see Hester, 1981; Longacre, 1981). The essence of publishing archaeological data is, of course, to make them available to as wide an audience of archaeologists as needs access to them. This distribution is achieved with many books and national or international journals, even with regional periodicals such as *Plains Anthropologist,* most of which are little concerned with CRM. But most contract archaeology reports are either restricted-circulation documents buried in the files of government agencies or private companies or, at best, photocopied publications that have a severely limited circulation. Sometimes within months they are forgotten, even destroyed, and the vital data in them are as good as lost to science. The problem of failure to publish is enormous. Although efforts have been made to abstract CRM reports, the results have been patchy at best. The National Park Service's Archaeological Assistance Division is developing a national archaeological database, after intensive lobbying by the Society for American Archaeology. Ironically, now that awareness about destruction of the archaeological record is greater than ever before, the results of much of this anxiety are being buried, almost as effectively as if they had been destroyed, in inaccessible or temporary publications. The only solution appears to be some form of organization like a national microfilm archive, where copies of all reports are required to be deposited—by law. As yet, there is no sign that such an organization will be created.

Then there is the issue of what is called *curation,* the careful management of artifacts and other data recovered in the course of CRM activities. The National Park Service, for example, has issued regulations for the curation of federal collections, as required under the amendments to the NEPA of 1980. But curation is expensive, and the costs of providing permanent conservation and storage are prohibitive. Many museums and other designated repositories are grappling with seemingly insurmountable curation problems for the mountains of archaeological finds that pour in from CRM projects. There are simply not enough funds to pay the real costs of curation.

Protection and the Public

Although expenditures on contract archaeology may no longer be at the levels of the late 1970s, arguments rage about the worth of even a tenth of such expenditure. Though one can argue that knowledge in itself is valuable and is worth spending money on, one has to show at least something for the money beyond an abundance of technical and often inaccessible reports. To begin with, one has to convince people that the sites are worth preserving. Archaeologists may wax lyrical about the scientific significance of a site within a specific research design, but the public is much more interested in sites with humanistic significance. Gettysburg has a supreme place in our national heritage, as does Mesa Verde. Both are visited by tens of thousands of people each year. The protection afforded by the National Register of Historic Places covers both sites as in the "significant" category, a significance that provides a basis for management decisions about cultural resources.

Protection of archaeological sites proceeds through legislation, but until 1979 the United States had no laws forbidding the export of antiquities. The Archaeological Resources Protection Act of 1979 gives federal resource managers and prosecutors access to stringent criminal and civil penalties that may slow the destruction of sites on public lands. The Abandoned Shipwreck Act of 1988 has finally extended a degree of protection to shipwrecks in U.S. waters, though not before incalculable damage was done by professional treasure hunters and amateur divers.

Legislation is not the only protective tool available to archaeologists. The power of eminent domain, zoning, easements, and even tax incentives are tools that may be used to protect cultural resources on private land.

The Archaeological Conservancy is a bright hope, a privately funded membership organization that was formed in the early 1980s to purchase threatened archaeological sites and manage them as permanent archaeological preserves on hundred-year management plans. The sites that this organization has purchased include the Hopewell Mound group in Ohio; Savage Cave in Kentucky, a site with human occupation from Paleo-Indian to Mississippian times; and San Marcos Pueblo in New Mexico, a two thousand–room pueblo near Santa Fe. (You can join by writing to 415 Orchard Drive, Santa Fe, New Mexico 87501.)

A great deal of the effectiveness in protecting archaeological sites depends on public attitudes to the past. The basic question is easily stated: Is the public benefiting in practical ways from the expenditure of enormous funds on archaeology?

Public Involvement

Many people think of archaeology as a luxury and wonder how much taxpayer money is spent on cultural resource management. They are very ambivalent about protecting the past, let alone spending money on it. Yet thousands of other interested citizens have joined amateur archaeological societies in many parts of the country.

Ruthann Knudson, an expert on cultural resource management, points out (1986) that one problem revolves around the ownership of archaeological sites. Who actually owns them, the finds from them, even the records that detail the artifacts removed from them? Does the landowner have the right, or does a government agency? To put the question very simply, are archaeological sites and finds the property of individuals, or are they the property of the public, as represented by the state, and recognized as part of our common cultural heritage?

The answer to this question is clear-cut in countries like Australia, where the Crown owns all archaeological sites, even those on private land—just like mineral rights (Cleere, 1984). Ownership of archaeological sites tends to be in the hands of the state in countries where there is a direct tie between the current occupiers of the land and the people who lived at the site in earlier times. The situation is very different in the United States, where the dominant political community has no genetic relationship to prehistoric America (for a discussion, see Fowler, 1986; Trigger, 1986). Furthermore, the right of private ownership of land was established in the American Bill of Rights, the so-called taking clause of the Fifth Amendment: "Nor shall private property be taken for public use without just compensation." Since archaeological sites were virtually unknown in the eighteenth century, ownership of them passed to individuals by default.

Today, the legal philosophy about the ownership of America's resources is beginning to change, even if case law on the subject has yet to develop. These resources are increasingly being recognized as part of the public wealth, so their treatment is a matter of public concern. This is implicit in much federal legislation since the 1950s and is being addressed much more specifically in recent planning laws affecting everything from forests to archaeological sites. As things stand now, current legislation is beginning to reflect the belief of major policymakers and the people who elected them that archaeological resources have public significance. In the long run, all of us, archaeologists or not, will be accountable for the proper treatment of archaeological resources, regardless of who owns them.

But there is still a long way to go. Almost none of the vast sum spent on cultural resource management goes to public education and involvement in archaeology. A few projects provide excellent examples of how to reach a wider audience. A team of archaeologists in Annapolis has worked closely with historians and the local community to provide walking tours, lectures, and other educational programs that share with visitors to historic Annapolis the thinking of archaeologists about the past (Leone and Potter, 1984). In Pittsburgh, the Committee on Pittsburgh Archaeology and History is a nonprofit corporation of archaeologists, historians, geographers, archivists, and lay people that champions historic preservation and has promoted the founding of a Pittsburgh history center. The committee is working closely with the public on the preservation of Pittsburgh's canal system, an important part of the city's nineteenth-century industrial history (Adovasio and Carlisle, 1988).

American Indians

The American Indian Religious Freedom Act of 1978 states that it is "the policy of the United States to protect and preserve for American Indians their inherent freedom to believe, express, and exercise the traditional religions of the American Indian . . . including but not limited to access to sites, use and possession of sacred objects and the freedom to worship through ceremonials and traditional rites" (Fowler, 1982). The act guarantees access to sacred sites, requires federal agencies to adjust management policies to reflect its provisions, and recognizes the existence of sacred sites. This legislation is profoundly affecting American archaeology, for it often involves consultation with tribal and religious leaders if religious sites are to be disturbed.

Most archaeologists have thought of themselves as objective observers of the past or as favorably inclined toward Native Americans. But as Bruce Trigger points out (1986), many archaeologists have been influenced by popular stereotypes of indigenous peoples. Only recently have they become aware of the social significance of their studies. They have also realized that archaeology can no longer be undertaken independent of society. In recent years, for example, American Indians have protested strongly about archaeological excavations and surveys in sacred areas in many parts of the West and the Southwest. Recent legislation has given them considerable say in the conduct of CRM on public lands, and they have reacted strongly to development projects destined for sacred, privately owned lands as well.

The Reburial Issue   Many Indian communities are incensed by the excavation of prehistoric burials and have pushed for laws forbidding such activity and compelling reburial of previously excavated skeletons. In several states, archaeologists are now working closely with Indians to ensure proper recovery and reburial of skeletal remains when development threatens prehistoric cemeteries and burial places. In 1975, bulldozers threatened a prehistoric ossuary (a place where considerable numbers of people were buried together) on school grounds in Council Bluffs, Iowa. The Indians demanded immediate reburial of the remains, but when they heard that a bulldozer would be used to scoop up the bones, they agreed to archaeological excavation instead. Within nine days, the ossuary had been excavated carefully, and both bones and artifacts had been reburied in a local cemetery (Anderson, 1985).

Controversy over the reburial of Indian skeletal remains has reached fever pitch in recent years, fueled not only by increasingly activist policies by Native American groups but also by a growing public awareness of the complex moral issues involved. This awareness was heightened dramatically by the unprincipled ravaging of the Late Mississippian site at Slack Farm, Kentucky, which left a prehistoric cemetery looking like a battlefield. The few salvaged remains were reburied in an emotional ceremony amid widespread public outrage (Fagan, 1991a).

The reburial issue has international overtones, for native groups outside North America, notably the Australian aborigines, have striven for strict control of burial excavations. Increasingly, archaeologists and native peoples are working together to hammer out long-term agreements, or at minimum statements of principle, to cover reburials and burial excavations. On the international front, the executive committee of the World Archaeological Congress has recently adopted an accord that calls on archaeologists to be sensitive to the concerns of indigenous peoples. Named the Vermillion Accord, after the town of Vermillion, South Dakota, where it was drafted, the statement calls for respect both for the dead and for the wishes of the dead, as well as for the scientific research value of human remains. It establishes the principle that agreement on the disposition of human remains be established on the basis of mutual respect for the legitimate concerns for the correct burial of ancestors as well as those of science and education.

The reburial issue is a complex one in the United States, where the Native American Rights Fund estimates that there may be as many as 600,000 native human skeletons in museums, historical societies, universities, and private collections. There are some 18,500 in the Smithsonian Institution alone. Late in 1989, an act establishing the National Museum of the American Indian in Washington, D.C., contained language providing for the return of some skeletal remains to their documented descendants for reburial. This is one culmination of a long campaign by Native American groups to recover the remains of people removed from their basic cycles of life and death. This campaign has pitted them against scientists who point out that revolutionary new research techniques are beginning to yield a mine of new information about prehistoric North Americans. To rebury their database would deprive science of a vital resource, they argue. While the Smithsonian will examine each reburial application on a case-by-case basis, many states are considering reburial legislation and extending further protection to prehistoric sites, but they have no jurisdiction over federal lands. Many museums, universities, and other institutions are adopting specific reburial policies, and the Society for American Archaeology has drawn up a statement that defines the complex dimensions of the problem. Not that these efforts are doing much to dampen emotion on both sides of the issue. The Native Americans feel deeply about reburial for many complex reasons, if nothing else because they are concerned to preserve old traditions and values as a way of addressing current social ills. The scientists, for their part, are afraid that they will lose their database, which, from their perspective, is an intellectual crime.

There will be no quick resolution of the reburial issue, however promptly and sensitively archaeologists and their institutions respond to Native American concerns and to a controversy that hits at the very moral core of archaeological research. Only one thing is certain—no archaeologist in North America, and probably elsewhere, will be able to excavate a prehistoric or historic burial without the most careful and sensitive preparation. This involves working closely with native peoples in ways that archaeologists have not imagined until recently. And nothing but good can come of this.

American archaeologists have long regarded their work as a way of studying ancient American Indian lifeways, but the Indians themselves have displayed little interest in archaeology. As Fowler (1982) points out, Western intellectual traditions regard scholarly research as beneficial to the public. Other societies have entirely different cultural values, prohibiting desecration of sacred sites through study by outsiders, even if this activity adds to the common knowledge of the outside world (Johnson and others, 1977). For the first time, archaeologists have to forge a working partnership with American Indians. The influence of this change on archaeology remains to be seen.

Contract archaeology and cultural resource management have come of age. They dominate American archaeology and will continue to do so for the foreseeable future. Many of the prospective archaeologists who read this book will end up in contract archaeology. The problems of CRM are a leading issue in contemporary archaeology and will never disappear. All archaeologists are managers of a finite resource, which is banked in various ways—in the ground, within the pages of a report, or by finds and records in a museum storeroom. We as a nation have two alternatives for the future: either collect and interpret information about our cultural resources in a useful manner as an activity that contributes to the public good or take the easy way out and abandon the archaeological record to extinction.

SUMMARY

- In this chapter we surveyed the destruction of archaeological sites in the United States and outlined some of the federal legislation designed to protect antiquities.
- The 1960s saw the development of the concept of cultural resource management, overall strategies for conservation priorities and management of a finite resource, the archaeological record. New federal legislation, notably the National Environmental Policy Act of 1969 and the Archaeological Resources Protection Act of 1979, laid down regulations for land use and resource policies and also defined archaeological resources as any artifact more than a century old. These new laws had a dramatic effect on archaeology and led to a vigorous expansion of cultural resource management activity all over the United States.
- Much CRM activity is on a small scale. However, larger-scale projects often provide opportunities for major archaeological excavations and surveys that have important bearing on the development of archaeological methods and theories. CRM is having an increasingly important impact on the future direction of American archaeology, on account of both its large budgets and its unique opportunities for large-scale field and laboratory research. There are two basic approaches to cultural resource management: a conservation approach that is basically descriptive and a problem-oriented one that uses the latest methods of contemporary archaeology to make management decisions about the past. These approaches are the subject of much controversy.

- As a result of these conflicts, and of the crisis in general, the Society of Professional Archaeologists has developed a set of ethics for people engaged in field research. These guidelines have drawn criticism, especially from people who have failed to realize that archaeology, as an academic discipline, is adapting to completely new conditions; under these conditions, most research in North America is funded as part of a cultural resource management project.
- In recent years, Native American groups have demanded that many Indian skeletons in public and private collections be returned to them for reburial. This controversy has pitted native peoples against scientists not only in North America but in other parts of the world as well. In the future, American archaeologists will have to work closely with Indian communities when excavating sites where burials are likely to be found.

GUIDE TO FURTHER READING

Contract archaeologists and resource managers are still wrestling with the basic issues of their work and have yet to generate an extensive methodological and theoretical literature. Many of the best field reports are, for all intents and purposes, inaccessible to the general reader. Listed here are useful signpost publications to a complicated literature.

Cleere, Henry, ed. *Approaches to the Archaeological Heritage: A Comparative Study of World Cultural Resource Management Systems.* Cambridge: Cambridge University Press, 1984. A series of essays on CRM in different countries under radically different governments. A fascinating comparative exercise.

Fowler, Don D. "Cultural Resources Management," *Advances in Archaeological Method and Theory,* 5 (1982): 1–50. A superb essay on the basic issues of CRM in the early 1980s. Recommended also for its clear exposition and comprehensive references.

Fowler, Don D. "Conserving American Archaeological Resources," in David J. Meltzer, Don D. Fowler, and Jeremy A. Sabloff, eds., *American Archaeology Past and Future,* pp. 135–162. Washington, D.C.: Smithsonian Institution Press, 1986. An excellent account of conservation in North America.

Green, Ernestine, ed. *Ethics and Values in Archaeology.* New York: Free Press, 1984. A series of essays on the ethics of studying the past, with a strong emphasis on cultural resource management.

Knudson, Ruthann. "Contemporary Cultural Resource Management," in David J. Meltzer, Don D. Fowler, and Jeremy A. Sabloff, eds., *American Archaeology Past and Future,* pp. 395–413. Washington, D.C.: Smithsonian Institution Press, 1986. A brief statement on the state of the art and major issues, with an excellent bibliography.

Schiffer, Michael B., and George J. Gumerman, eds. *Conservation Archaeology.* Orlando, Fla.: Academic Press, 1977. Essays on basic problems of cultural resource management. The articles on research design are especially useful.

Chapter
20

Archaeology and You

We have two final questions to answer: How can I become an archaeologist? And even if I do not become one, what are my responsibilities as an informed citizen?

ARCHAEOLOGY AS A PROFESSION

Professional archaeologists are much more numerous than they were even a generation ago, mostly because the discipline now has many more career tracks. Archaeology is changing rapidly, from a purely academic discipline into more of a profession, with archaeologists performing a multitude of management, conservation, and environmental tasks. Until recently, most American archaeologists taught in universities and colleges and a few high schools. Once they also headed archaeology departments of national, state, city, or local museums all over the country or directed state archaeological surveys. But today, the majority of America's archaeologists work for the National Park Service or other federal, state, or local agencies in many activities that can be labeled loosely as cultural resource management. Others are employed by private firms undertaking environmental impact projects, both large and small, or are in business on their own doing similar work. The specialties of these archaeologists range from early Plains Indian settlement to historical sites in New England, from theoretical models of early agriculture to computer simulations. Although most North American archaeologists now work on the "applied" side of archaeology, a considerable number of academic archaeologists work abroad—in Africa, Europe, Mesoamerica, Peru, and even farther afield.

But a word of warning! Jobs in archaeology, except those involved in cultural resource management, are often hard to come by, even with a doctoral degree.

Qualifications

Most archaeological jobs, whether on a campus or in a museum, require an M.A. degree, but most often a Ph.D. is needed. The doctorate is a research degree requiring comprehensive seminar, course, and field training in graduate school followed by a period of intensive fieldwork that in written form constitutes the Ph.D. thesis. The average doctoral program takes between four and seven years to complete. The M.A. degree is normally completed in one or two years and provides broad, general training in the basic methods and theories of archaeology and world prehistory. In addition to this general knowledge, you will specialize in a local area or in cultural resource management. You may have to write a library thesis and obtain some digging experience as well. The M.A. does not give you as much access to research funds and opportunities as a Ph.D. However, you can do valuable work in cultural resource management or local archaeology.

Do *not* consider becoming a professional archaeologist unless you have these qualifications:

1. An academic record well above average, with in-depth coverage of anthropology and archaeology. An A-minus grade point average is a minimal requirement for good graduate schools.
2. Some field experience on a dig or survey.
3. Strong and *meaningful* support from at least two qualified archaeologists, who are able to write letters for you.
4. A strong motivation to become an archaeologist and, for the Ph.D., a specific research interest.
5. The type of personality that thrives on hard work and some discomfort, a mass of detail, and long hours of routine laboratory work.
6. The ability to face up to a very tight employment situation.
7. An interest in teaching or in resource management.
8. A moral commitment not to collect artifacts for profit or personal gain.

Gaining Digging Experience

Many people want to gain some digging experience, whether or not they intend to go to graduate school. The best way to learn is to take a course in field methods and then volunteer to dig for a time on a summer excavation. Details of these excavations are normally posted on anthropology department bulletin boards or at local museums. Some people elect to go to a university-sponsored field school and to obtain academic credit for their work. Many such schools are designed mainly for graduate students, but again, you should consult your own department. General field schools are worthwhile because they combine excavation, laboratory analysis, and academic instruction into one intensive experience. And the camaraderie among participants in such digs can be memorable.

Some people venture farther and join an excavation overseas for several weeks. By contacting such organizations as the Council for British Archaeology in London, it is possible to obtain details of excavations in progress where volunteers are needed. (Very few digs, either in this country or overseas, pay you to be an excavator.) At the other end of the spectrum are package travel tours that take students to such places as Israel to dig and learn archaeology under close supervision. These can be expensive experiences, often of variable academic quality. Whatever type of dig you choose, an excavation experience is a good way of testing your commitment to archaeology.

Undergraduate Degree

It is possible to get a low-level job in archaeology with a B.A. as a field-worker or a laboratory assistant. Some day, however, you will probably need further qualifications, and it is best to acquire these as soon as possible.

Most people who take a B.A. with a major in or emphasis on archaeology never become professionals. Nevertheless, they can enjoy the achievements and perspectives derived from archaeology for the rest of their lives. There are many ways to enjoy archaeology as a lay person. You can join a local archaeological society, participate in excavations and volunteer museum programs, and keep an eye on endangered sites in your neighborhood. Your background in archaeology will enable you to visit famous sites all over the world as an informed observer and to enjoy the achievements of prehistoric peoples to the fullest. I received a postcard mailed from Stonehenge by a former student: "Thank you for introducing me to archaeology," it read. "I enjoyed Stonehenge so much more after taking your course." His postcard made my day, for archaeology cannot survive without the involvement and interest of many people beyond professional archaeologists. And as an interested lay person, you have responsibilities.

RESPONSIBILITIES TO THE PAST

Professional archaeologists have ethical responsibilities as members of a demanding profession (Green, 1984). But everyone interested in archaeology has responsibilities, too. The world's archaeological sites are under attack from many sources: industrial development, mining, and agriculture, as well as treasure hunters, collectors, and professional tomb robbers. In these times of inflation, even modest antiquities fetch high prices on the antiquarian market. No government can hope to free the necessary funds to protect its antiquities adequately. And such countries as Egypt, Guatemala, and Mexico, with rich archaeological heritages, have almost overwhelming problems protecting even their well-known sites. As long as there is a demand for antiquities among collectors and we maintain our materialistic values about personal possessions, destruction of archaeological sites will continue unabated. Even the necessary legal controls to prevent destruction of archaeological sites are just barely in force in most parts of the world (McBryde, 1985; Layton, 1989).

Yet there is still hope, which stems from the enormous numbers of informed people who have gained an interest in archaeology from university and college courses or from chance encounters with archaeologists or the prehistoric past. If sufficient numbers of lay people can influence public behavior and attitudes toward archaeological sites and the morality of collecting, there is still hope that our descendants will have archaeological sites to study and enjoy.

Is there a future for the past? Yes, but only if we *all* help, not only by influencing other people's attitudes toward archaeology but also by obeying this simple code of ethics:

1. Treat all archaeological sites and artifacts as a finite resource.
2. Never dig an archaeological site.
3. Never collect artifacts for ourselves or buy and sell them for personal gain.
4. Adhere to all federal, state, local, and tribal laws that affect the archaeological record.
5. Report all accidental archaeological discoveries.
6. Avoid disturbing any archaeological site, and respect the sanctity of all burial sites.

SUMMARY

- Career opportunities for professional archaeologists can be found in universities, colleges, museums, government service, and private businesses both in the United States and abroad. Most archaeological jobs require at least an M.A. and very often a Ph.D.
- Do not consider becoming a professional archaeologist unless you have an above-average academic record, some field experience, strong support from your professors, and a moral commitment not to collect artifacts for profit.
- Even people who have no intention of becoming professional archaeologists can gain digging experience by attending a field school or by digging overseas.

- Archaeology can give you insight into the past and the potential for involvement as an informed lay person. It will also enable you to enjoy the major archaeological sites of the world in a unique way and to aid in archaeologists' attempts to preserve the past.
- All of us have ethical responsibilities to the past: *not to collect artifacts;* to report new finds; and to obey federal, state, and tribal laws that protect archaeological sites. Unless we all take our responsibility to the past seriously, the past has no future.

GUIDE TO FURTHER READING

Messenger, Phyllis M., ed. *The Ethics of Collecting Cultural Property.* Albuquerque: University of New Mexico Press, 1989. Some of the few essays on the international trade in antiquities and the ethics behind the controversy.

SOME USEFUL ADDRESSES

Here are three addresses from which you can obtain information about archaeological activities and excavations that need volunteers:

Archaeological Institute of America
Box 1901, Kenmore Station
Boston, MA 02215

The institute publishes the *Archaeological Fieldwork Opportunities Bulletin.* Members receive the journal *Archaeology.*

Society for American Archaeology
1511 K Street NW, Suite 716
Washington, DC 20005

Society members receive *American Antiquity,* a more technical journal. For excavation opportunities overseas, contact:

The Council for British Archaeology
112 Kennington Road
London SE11 6RE
England

This admirable organization publishes a monthly *Calendar of Excavations,* which you can obtain by airmail subscription. It contains complete details of volunteer excavations in Britain and sometimes in other parts of the world.

Information on archaeolgical field schools can be obtained from fliers that are posted on university department bulletin boards and also from the Society for American Archaeology. The American Anthropological Association publishes a summer field school list annually.

Glossary

This glossary is designed to give informal definitions of words and ideas in the text, particularly those that are theoretical. It is not a comprehensive dictionary of archaeology. Jargon is kept to a minimum, but a few technical expressions are inevitable. Terms such as *adaptation* and *mutation*, which are common in contexts other than archaeology, are not listed; a good dictionary will clarify these. Champion (1980) has published a good archaeological dictionary, Scarre (1988) an excellent atlas.

absolute dating Dating in calendar years before the present; chronometric dating.
activity area A pattern of artifacts in a site indicating that a specific activity, such as stone toolmaking, took place.
activity set A set of artifacts that reveals the activities of an individual.
alluvium Geological deposit laid down by the action of a river or stream.
analogy A process of reasoning whereby two entities that share some similarities are assumed to share many others.
analysis A stage of archaeological research that involves describing and classifying artifactual and nonartifactual data.
analytical type Arbitrary groupings that an archaeologist defines for classifying manufactured artifacts. Analytical types consist of groups of attributes that define convenient types of artifacts for comparing sites in space and time. They do not necessarily coincide with actual tool types used by prehistoric people.
anthropology The study of humanity in the widest possible sense. Anthropology studies humanity from the earliest times up to the present, and it includes cultural and physical anthropology and archaeology.
antiquarian Someone interested in the past who collects and digs up antiquities unscientifically, in contrast to the scientific archaeologist.

arbitrary sample unit A carefully defined unit of a total population of artifacts, or whatever is being sampled, selected by absolutely artificial criteria, without referring to cultural yardsticks. A typical example is a grid of squares laid out over a site.

archaeological context See *context*.

archaeological culture A group of assemblages representing the surviving remains of an extinct culture.

archaeological data Material recognized as significant as evidence by the archaeologist and collected and recorded as part of the research. The four main classes of archaeological data are artifacts, features, structures, and food remains.

archaeological reconnaissance Systematic attempts to locate, identify, and record the distribution of archaeological sites on the ground and against the natural geographic and environmental background.

archaeological theory A body of theoretical concepts providing both a framework and a means for archaeologists to look beyond the facts and material objects for explanations of events that took place in prehistory.

archaeological unit An arbitrary unit of classification set up by archaeologists to separate conveniently one grouping of artifacts in time and space from another.

archaeologist Someone who studies the past using scientific methods, with the motive of recording and interpreting ancient cultures rather than collecting artifacts for profit or display.

archaeology A special form of anthropology studying extinct human societies using the material remains of their behavior. The objectives of archaeology are to construct culture history, reconstruct past lifeways, and study cultural process.

archaeomagnetic dating Chronometric dating using magnetic alignments from buried features, such as pottery kilns, which can be compared to known fluctuations in the earth's magnetic field and produce a date in years.

Archaic In the New World, a period when hunter-gatherers were exploiting a broad spectrum of resources and may have been experimenting with agriculture.

area excavation Excavation of a large, horizontal area, normally used to uncover houses and prehistoric settlement patterns.

artifact Any object manufactured or modified by human beings.

assemblage All the artifacts found at a site, including the sum of all subassemblages at the site.

association The relationship between an artifact and other archaeological finds and a site level, or other artifact, structure, or feature in the site.

Assyriologist A student of the Assyrian civilization of Mesopotamia.

attribute A well-defined feature of an artifact that cannot be further subdivided. Archaeologists identify types of attributes, including form, style, and technology, in order to classify and interpret artifacts.

attribute analysis Analyzing artifacts using many of their features. Normally these attributes are studied statistically to produce clusters of attributes that can be used to identify statistical classes of artifacts.

attritional age profile The distribution of ages in an animal population that results from selective hunting or predation.

auger A drill, either hand- or power-driven, used to probe subsurface deposits.

Australopithecus Primate whose fossil remains have been found mainly in eastern and southern Africa. Thought to be closely related to the first human beings, who may indeed have evolved among *Australopithecus.*

band The simple form of human social organization that flourished for most of prehistory. Bands consist of a family or a series of families, normally with twenty to fifty people.

battleship curve A seriation graph formed by plotted points representing, for instance, the rise in popularity of an artifact, its period of maximum popularity, and its eventual decline.

biome Major biotic landscapes in which distinctive plant and animal communities live in harmony together.

biosphere All the earth's living organisms interacting with the physical environment.

blades Parallel-sided stone flakes, normally removed from a carefully prepared core, often by means of a punch.

bowsing Technique for detecting buried features by thumping the ground and sensing the differences between compacted and undisturbed earth.

bulbar surface The surface upon which the bulb of percussion occurs.

bulb of percussion The conelike effect caused by conchoidal fracture on siliceous rocks.

burin A blade tool, flaked on one or both ends to form a small chisel or grooving tool.

cambium A viscid substance under the bark of trees in which the annual growth of wood and bark takes place.

carrying capacity The number and density of people per square mile that a specified area of land can support, given a particular subsistence level.

catastrophic aging profile Distribution of ages in an animal population as a result of death by natural causes.

causes In archaeology, events that force people to make decisions about how to deal with new situations.

central-place theory A geographic theory applied to archaeology, stating that human settlements will space themselves evenly across a landscape as a function of the availability of natural resources and other factors. Eventually, these will evolve into a hierarchy of settlements of different size that depend on one another.

ceramics Objects of fired clay.

chiefdom A form of social organization more complex than a tribal society that has evolved some form of leadership structure and some mechanisms for distributing goods and services throughout the society. The chief who heads such a society and the specialists who work for the chief are supported by the voluntary contributions of the people.

chronological types Types defined by form that are time markers.

chronometric dating Dating in years before the present; absolute dating.

clan A group of people from many lineages who live in one place and have a common line of descent—a kin grouping.

class A general group of artifacts, like "hand axes," which will be broken down into specific types, like "ovates," and so on.

Classic In both Mesoamerica and Peru, the period of vigorous civilization characterized by numerous ceremonial centers and small states.

Classical archaeologist A student of the Classical civilizations of Greece and Rome.

classification The ordering of archaeological data into groups and classes, using various ordering systems.

closed system A system that is internally self-regulating and receives no feedback from external sources, a good example is a household heating and cooling system.

cluster analysis The process of analyzing clusters of sites in space.

cognitive archaeology See *structural archaeology.*

community In archaeology, the tangible remains of the activities of the maximum number of people who together occupy a settlement at any one period.

complex In archaeology, a chronological subdivision of different artifact types such as stone tools or pottery.

component An association of all the artifacts from one occupation level at a site.

conchoidal fracture A characteristic fracture pattern that occurs in siliceous rocks, such as obsidian and flint.

conchologist One who studies shells.

conservation archaeology Another name for *cultural resource management.*

context The position of an archaeological find in time and space, established by measuring and assessing its associations, matrix, and provenience. The assessment includes study of what has happened to the find since it was buried in the ground.

coprolite Excrement preserved by desiccation or fossilization.

core In archaeology, a lump of stone from which human-struck flakes have been removed.

core borer A hollow tubelike instrument used to collect samples of soils, pollens, and other materials from below the surface.

cranial Of or pertaining to the skull (cranium).

crop marks Differential growth in crops and vegetational cover that reveals the outlines of archaeological sites from the air.

cross-dating Dating of sites by means of objects or associated artifacts of known age.

cultural anthropology The aspects of anthropology focusing on cultural facets of human societies (a term widely used in the United States).

cultural ecology The study of the dynamic interactions between human societies and their environments. Under this approach, culture is the primary adaptive mechanism used by human societies.

cultural evolution A theory similar to that of biological evolution that argues that human cultures change gradually over time as a result of a number of cultural processes.

cultural process A deductive approach to archaeological research that is designed to study the changes and interactions in cultural systems and the processes by which human cultures change throughout time. Processual archaeologists use both descriptive and explanatory models.

cultural resource management (CRM) The conservation and management of archaeological sites and artifacts as a means of protecting the past.

cultural selection The process that leads to the acceptance of some cultural traits and innovations that make a culture more adaptive to its environment; somewhat akin to natural selection in biological evolution.

cultural system A perspective on culture that thinks of culture and its environment as a number of linked systems in which change occurs through a series of minor, linked variations in one or more of these systems.

cultural tradition In archaeology, a distinctive tool kit or technology that lasts a long time, longer than the duration of one culture, at one locality or several localities.

cultural transformations Changes in the archaeological record resulting from later human behavior, such as digging a rubbish pit into earlier levels.

culture A set of designs for living that help mold human responses to different situations. Culture is our primary means of adapting to our environment. In archaeology, a culture is an arbitrary unit applied to similar assemblages of artifacts found at several sites, defined in a precise context of time and space.

culture area An arbitrary geographic or research area in which general cultural homogeneity is found.

culture history An approach to archaeology that assumes that artifacts can be used to build up a generalized picture of human culture and descriptive models in time and space and that these can be interpreted.

cumulative recording Excavating and recording a trench in three dimensions, using both horizontal and vertical observations to reconstruct events at the site.

cuneiform The earliest known script from Mesopotamia, consisting of wedge-shaped markings (Greek, *cuneus,* "wedge").

curation Deliberate attempts by prehistoric peoples to preserve key artifacts and structures for posterity.

cybernetics General systems theory.

cylinder hammer technique Stone-flaking technique using a bone hammer that removes small, flat flakes from a core.

data universe A defined area of archaeological investigation, bounded in time and space, often a geographic region or an archaeological site.

datum point A location from which all measurements on a site are made. The datum point is tied into local survey maps.

debitage Waste byproducts resulting from the manufacture of stone tools.

deduction A process of reasoning that involves testing generalizations by generating hypotheses and trying them out with data. Deductive research is cumulative and involves constant refining of hypotheses. Contrasts with inductive approaches, which proceed from specific observations to general conclusions.

deductive-nomological reasoning A way of explaining observable phenomena by means of formal scientific methods, testing hypotheses generated from general laws governing human behavior. Some archaeologists believe that this is the appropriate way to explain cultural processes.

demography The study of population.

dendrochronology Tree-ring chronology.

descriptive types Types based on the physical or external properties of an artifact.

detritus Debris or droppings.

diffusion The spread of a cultural trait from one area to another by means of contact between people.

direct historical analogy An analogy using historical records or historical ethnographic data.

direct historical approach The archaeological technique of working backward in time from historic sites of known age into earlier times.

drift A glacial deposit laid down by ice or water in glacial streams, lakes, or arctic oceans.

ecofacts Archaeological finds that are of cultural significance but were not manufactured by humans, such as bones and vegetal remains. Not a commonly used term.

ecosystem An environmental system maintained by the regulation of trophic levels (vertical food chains) and by patterns of energy flow.

ecotone A transition zone between habitats.

Egyptologist A student of the cultures of ancient Egypt.

eolith A controversial artifact, identified by European archaeologists early in the twentieth century and claimed to be the earliest of human tools. Eoliths are now considered to be of natural origin.

epigrapher One who studies inscriptions.

epiphysis The articular end of a long bone, which fuses at adulthood.

escarpment A hill range or cliff (a geological term).

ethnoarchaeology Living archaeology, a form of ethnography that deals mainly with material remains. Archaeologists carry out living archaeology to document the relationships between human behavior and the patterns of artifacts and food remains in the archaeological record.

ethnography A descriptive study, normally an in-depth examination of a culture.

ethnohistory Study of the past using non-Western, indigenous historical records and especially oral traditions.

ethnology A cross-cultural study of aspects of various cultures, usually based on theory.

evolutionary archaeology An explanatory framework for the past that accounts for structure and change in the archaeological record.

excavation The digging of archaeological sites, removing the matrix and observing the provenience and context of the finds therein, and recording them three-dimensionally.

exchange system A system for exchanging goods and services between individuals and communities.

exogamy A rule requiring marriage outside a social or cultural unit (*endogamy* means the opposite).

experimental archaeology The use of carefully controlled modern experiments to provide data to aid in interpretation of the archaeological record.

extrasomatic Outside the body.

faience Glazed terra cotta.

feature An artifact such as a house or a storage pit that cannot be removed from a site; normally, it is recorded only.

feces Excrement.

feedback A concept in archaeological applications of systems theory reflecting the continually changing relationship between cultural variables and their environment.

fire setting Quarrying stone by using fire to shatter the outcrops of rock.

fission-track dating Observing accumulations of radioactivity in glass and volcanic rocks to produce absolute dates.

flake tools Stone tools made of flakes removed from cores.

flotation In archaeology, recovering plant remains by using water to separate seeds from their surrounding deposit.

focus Approximately equivalent to a *phase*.

form The physical characteristics—size and shape or composition—of any archaeological find. Form is an essential part of attribute analysis.

form analysis Analysis of artifacts based on the assumption that the shape of a pot or other tool directly reflects its function.

formation processes Humanly caused or natural processes by which an archaeological site is modified during or after occupation and abandonment.

Formative In Mesoamerica, the period when more complex societies and settlement patterns were coming into being; these led to the complex states of later times (contemporary with the rise of agriculture).

form types Artifact types based on the shape of an artifact.

formulation In archaeology, the process of making decisions about a research project as a preliminary to formal research design.

foot survey Archaeological reconnaissance on foot, often with a set interval between members of the survey team.

fuller A clothmaker.

function In an evolutionary context, the forms that directly affect the Darwinian fitness of the populations in which they occur.

functionalism The notion that a social institution within a society has a function in fulfilling all the needs of a social organism.

functional type Type based on cultural use or function rather than on outward form or chronological position.

general systems theory The notion that any organism or organization can be studied as a system broken down into many interacting subsystems or parts; sometimes called *cybernetics.*

geoarchaeology Archaeological research using the methods and concepts of the earth sciences.

geochronology Geological dating.

glacial eustacy The adjustments in sea levels and the earth's crust resulting from expansion and contraction of Pleistocene ice sheets.

habitat An area in the biome where different communities and populations flourish, each with specific locales.

half-life The time required for one-half of a radioactive isotope to decay into a stable element. Used as a basis for radiocarbon and other dating methods.

heuristic Serving to find out; a means of discovery.

hieroglyphs Ancient writing featuring pictographic or ideographic symbols; used in Egypt, Mesoamerica, and elsewhere.

historical archaeology The study of archaeological sites in conjunction with historical records. Sometimes called *historic sites archaeology.*

historiography The process of studying history.

history Study of the past through written records.

hominid A member of the family Hominidae, represented today by one species, *Homo sapiens.*

Homo erectus Human beings who evolved from Lower Pleistocene hominids. They possessed larger brains and made more elaborate stone tools than their predecessors and settled in much more extreme environments, as far apart as western Europe, Asia, and tropical Africa.

homotaxial Describing strata or cultures that have the same relationship to one another but are not necessarily contemporaneous.

horizon A widely distributed set of culture traits and artifact assemblages whose distribution and chronology allow one to assume that they spread rapidly.

Often, horizons are formed of artifacts that were associated with widespread, distinctive religious beliefs.

horizontal (area) excavation Archaeological excavation designed to uncover large areas of a site, especially settlement layouts.

household unit An arbitrary archaeological unit defining artifact patterns reflecting the activities that take place around a house and assumed to belong to one household.

hydrology The scientific study of water, its properties and laws.

ideology The knowledge or beliefs developed by human societies as part of their cultural adaptation.

induction Reasoning by which one proceeds from specific observations to general conclusions.

industrial archaeology The study of sites of the Industrial Revolution and later.

industry All the particular artifacts (bone, stone, wood) found at a site that were made at the same time by the same population.

inevitable variation The notion that cultures change and vary with time, cumulatively. The reasons for these changes are little understood.

inorganic materials Objects that are not part of the animal or vegetable kingdom.

interpretation The stage in research at which the results of archaeological analyses are synthesized and we attempt to explain their meaning.

interstadial A period of slightly warmer climate between two cold periods during a major glaciation.

kinship In anthropology, relationships between people that are based on real or imagined descent or, sometimes, on marriage. Kinship ties impose mutual obligations on all members of a kin group; these ties were at the core of most prehistoric societies.

knapper One who manufactures stone artifacts.

leaching Water seeping through the soil and removing the soluble materials from it.

Levallois technique Stoneworking technique that involves preparing a bun-shaped core from which one preshaped flake is removed.

limited-area reconnaissance Comprehensive door-to-door inquiries, supported by actual substantiation of claims that sites exist by checking on the ground. This method fails to give information on proportions of different sites in an area.

lineage A kinship that traces descent through either the male or female members.

lithic Of or pertaining to stone.

lithic experimentation Experimenting with the manufacture of stone tools. A useful analytical approach to the interpretation of prehistoric artifacts.

loess Windblown glacial soil.

lost-wax technique A method of bronzeworking employing a wax model of the object. The mold is assembled with wax in place of the artifact. The wax is then melted and replaced with molten bronze. The technique was much used by the Shang bronzeworkers of China.

lower-level theory A means of identifying site formation processes.

magnetometer A subsurface detection device that measures minor variations in the earth's magnetic field and locates archaeological features before excavation.

material culture Technology and artifacts.

matriarchal Characterized by family authority resting with the woman's family.

matrilineal Characterized by descent reckoned through the female line only.

matrilocal Characterized by married couples living with or near the wife's mother.

matrix The surrounding deposit in which archaeological finds are situated.

Mesolithic Rather dated name sometimes applied by Old World archaeologists to the period of transition between the Paleolithic and Neolithic eras. No precise economic or technological definition has even been formulated.

mica A mineral that occurs in a glittering, scaly form, widely prized for ornament.

midden A deposit of occupation debris, rubbish, or other by-products of human activity.

middle-range theory A way of seeking accurate means for identifying and measuring specified properties of past cultural systems.

midwestern taxonomic system A system of archaeological units developed before World War II to organize artifacts and sites in North America; still in widespread use in modified form.

mitigation In archaeology, measures taken to minimize destruction on archaeological sites.

model A theoretical reconstruction of a set of phenomena, devised to explain them better. Archaeological models can be descriptive or explanatory.

modified diffusionism A form of diffusionist theory, espoused by V. Gordon Childe and others, that allowed for some local cultural evolution.

monotheistic Recognizing only one god.

moraine A deposit of debris left by an advancing or retreating glacier.

multilinear cultural evolution A theory of cultural evolution that sees each human culture evolving in its own way by adaptation to diverse environments. Sometimes divided into four broad stages of evolving of social organization (band, tribe, chiefdom, and state-organized society).

natural transformations Changes in the archaeological record resulting from natural phenomena that occur after the artifacts are deposited in the ground.

natural type An archaeological type coinciding with an actual category recognized by the original toolmaker.

negative feedback A response to a system that lessens the chance of change.

Neolithic A dated Old World term referring to the period of the Stone Age when people were cultivating without metals.

niche The physical space occupied by an organism, its functional role in the community, and how it is constrained by other species and external forces.

nonarbitrary sample unit A sample unit chosen to conform with cultural and other factors, such as geographic proximity or layout of rooms in a pueblo. Such sample units are often clustered.

nonprobabilistic sampling Sampling using instinctual criteria, such as the archaeologist's experience, or factors affecting access to a research area.

normative view A view of human culture arguing that one can identify the abstract rules regulating a particular culture; a commonly used basis for studying archaeological cultures over time.

object clustering An approach to typology based on clusters of human artifacts that are seen as specific classificatory types.

obsidian Black volcanic glass.

obsidian hydration A dating method that measures the thickness of the hydration layer in obsidian artifacts. The hydration layer is caused by absorption of water on exposed surfaces of the rock.

open system In archaeology, cultural systems that interchange both energy and information with their environment.

oral tradition Historical traditions, often genealogies, passed down from generation to generation by word of mouth.

ordering In archaeology, the arranging of artifacts in logical classes and in chronological order.

organic materials Materials such as bone, wood, horn, or hide that were once living organisms.

ossification The fusion of a limb bone with its articular end. Implies calcification of soft tissue into bonelike material.

osteologist One who studies bones.

paleoanthropologist An archaeologist who studies the archaeology of the earliest human beings.

paleobotanist One who studies prehistoric botany.

paleoecology The modern study of past ecology.

Paleolithic The Old Stone Age.

paleontology The study of fossil (or ancient) bones.

palynology Pollen analysis.

parahistoric sites Archaeological sites of preliterate peoples who were contemporary with cultures that had writing.

patination Natural weathering on the surface of rocks and artifacts.

patrilineal Characterized by descent reckoned through the male line only.

patrilocal Characterized by married couples living with or near the husband's father.

patterns of discard Remains left for investigation after natural destructive forces have affected artifacts and food remains abandoned by their original users.

pedology The scientific study of soil.

perceived environment The physical environment as perceived by a human society; does not coincide with the archaeologist's perception of the same phenomenon.

periglacial Surrounding a glacial area.

period An archaeological unit defining a major stretch of prehistoric time; it contains several phases and pertains to a wide area.

permafrost Permanently frozen subsoil.

petrological analysis Examining thin sections of stone artifacts to determine the provenience of the rock used to make them.

petrology The study of rocks; in archaeology, analysis of trace elements and other characteristics of rocks used to make such artifacts as ax blades, which were traded over long distances.

phase An archaeological unit defined by characteristic groupings of cultural traits that can be identified precisely in time and space. It lasts for a relatively short time and is found at one or more sites in a locality or region. Its cultural traits are clear enough to distinguish it from other phases.

physical anthropology Basically, biological anthropology, which includes the study of fossil human beings, genetics, primates, and blood groups.

planimetric maps Maps used to record details of archaeological sites; they contain no topographic information.

Pleistocene The last major geological epoch, extending from about two million years ago until about 11,500 B.P. It is sometimes called the Quaternary or the Great Ice Age.

population In sampling methods, the sum of sampling units selected within a data universe.

positive feedback A system's response to external stimuli that leads to further change and reinforces it.

Postclassic A stage in Mesoamerican and Andean prehistory during which militarism arose, such as that of the Aztec and the Inca.

potassium argon dating An absolute dating technique based on the decay rate of potassium 40, which becomes argon 40.

potsherd A fragment of a clay vessel.

Preclassic See *Formative*.

prehistory The millennia of human history preceding written records. Prehistorians study prehistoric archaeology.

pressure flaking A stoneworking technique in which thin flakes are removed from a core or an artifact by applying hand or chest pressure.

primary context An undisturbed association, matrix, and provenience.

prime movers An early concept in the study of the origins of civilization, meaning a single, primary cause generating urban societies; many theorists considered irrigation a prime mover of Egyptian civilization.

probabilistic sampling Archaeological sampling based on formal statistical criteria. This method enables one to use probability statistics in analyzing data.

process In archaeology, the cultural change that takes place as a result of interactions between a cultural system's elements and the system and its environment.

provenience The position of an archaeological find in time and space, recorded three-dimensionally.

proximal Describing the end of a bone nearest to the skeleton's center line; opposite to *distal*.

pulse radar Use of a pulse induction meter that applies pulses of magnetic field to the soil; this method can be used to find graves, metals, and pottery.

quadrat A unit of spatial analysis used to divide an area into cells for analysis.

Quaternary Geological time since the beginning of the Pleistocene up to recent times. The exact date of its commencement is uncertain, but it is more than two million years ago.

radiocarbon dating An absolute dating method based on measuring the decay rate of the carbon isotope, carbon 14, to stable nitrogen. The resulting dates are calibrated with tree-ring chronologies, from radiocarbon ages into dates in calendar years.

random sampling Sampling based on a totally random selection of sample units to be investigated.

reciprocity In archaeology, the exchange of goods between two parties.

redistribution The dispersing of trade goods from a central place throughout a society, a complex process that was a critical part of the evolution of civilization.

refitting The reassembling of stone debitage and cores to reconstruct ancient lithic technologies.

region A geographically defined area in which ecological adaptations are basically similar.

relative chronology A time scale developed by the law of superposition or artifact ordering.

remote sensing Reconnaissance and site survey methods using such devices as aerial photography to detect subsurface features and sites.

research design A carefully formulated and systematic plan for executing archaeological research.

resistivity survey The measurement of differences in electrical conductivity in soils, used to detect buried features such as walls and ditches.

sample unit An arbitrary or nonarbitrary unit of the data universe, used for sampling archaeological data.

sampling frame Lists of chosen sampling units that form the sample of the population to be tested. Compiling as a means of proceeding to selection of units for investigation.

scanner imagery A method of recording sites from the air using infrared radiation that is beyond the practical spectral response of photographic film. Useful for tracing prehistoric agricultural systems that have disturbed the topsoil over wide areas.

science A way of acquiring knowledge and understanding about the parts of the natural world that can be observed. A disciplined and highly ordered search for knowledge carried out systematically.

seasonality Seasonal occupation.

secondary context A context of an archaeological find that has been disturbed by subsequent human activity or natural phenomena.

selective excavation Archaeological excavation of parts of a site using sampling methods or carefully placed trenches that do not uncover the entire site.

seriation Methods used to place artifacts in chronological order; artifacts closely similar in form or style are placed close to one another.

settlement pattern Distribution of human settlement on the landscape and within archaeological communities.

shadow sites Archaeological sites identified from the air, where oblique light can show up reduced topography of sites invisible on the ground.

site Any place where objects, features, or ecofacts manufactured or modified by human beings are found. A site can range from a living site to a quarry site, and it can be defined in functional and other ways.

site catchment analysis Inventorying natural resources within a given distance of a site.

site formation processes Cultural and noncultural phenomena that act on the formation of the archaeological record.

site plans Specially prepared maps for recording the horizontal provenience of artifacts, food remains, and features. They are keyed to topographic maps.

site survey The collection of surface data and evaluation of each site's archaeological significance.

slip A fine, wet finish applied to the surface of a clay vessel prior to its firing and decoration.

social anthropology The British equivalent of *cultural anthropology,* but emphasizing sociological factors.

sociocultural Combining social and cultural factors.

sodality A nonkinship organization within a society that cuts across kinship groups and lineages for specific purposes that add to the cohesiveness of that society.

sondage See *test pit.*

spectrographic analysis Chemical analysis that involves passing the light from a number of trace elements through a prism or diffraction grating that spreads out the wavelengths in a spectrum. This enables one to separate the emissions and identify different trace elements. A useful approach for studying metal objects and obsidian artifacts.

stage A technological subdivision of prehistoric time that has little chronological meaning but denotes the level of technological achievement of societies within it, such as the Stone Age.

stela (or stele) A column or stone slab, often with an inscribed or sculptured surface.

stratified sampling A probabilistic sampling technique used to cluster and isolate sample units, when regular spacing is inappropriate for cultural reasons.

stratigraphy Observing of the superimposed layers in an archaeological site.

stratum A single-deposited or cultural level.

structural archaeology A theoretical approach to archaeology based on the assumption that codes and rules produce observed systems of relations in human culture.

style In an evolutionary context, a means of describing forms that do not have detectable selective values.

stylistic analysis Artifact analysis that concentrates not only on form and function but also on the decorative styles used by the makers—a much-used approach to ceramic analysis.

stylistic attributes Attributes based on stylistic features.

stylistic type Type based on stylistic distinctions.

subarea The subdivision of an archaeological area, normally defined by geographic or cultural considerations.

subassemblage An association of artifacts denoting a particular form of prehistoric activity practiced by a group of people.

surface survey The collecting of archaeological finds from sites with the objective of gathering representative samples of artifacts from the surface. Surface surveys also establish the types of activity on the site, locate major structures, and gather information on the most densely occupied areas of the site that could be most productive for total or sample excavation.

synthesis The assembling and analyzing of data preparatory to interpretation.

systematics In archaeology, procedures for creating sets of archaeological units derived from a logical system for a particular purpose.

systematic sampling A refinement of random sampling in which one unit is chosen, then others at regular intervals from the first. Useful for studying artifact patterns.

taphonomy The study of the processes by which animal bones and other fossil remains are transformed after deposition.

taxonomy An ordered set of operations that results in the subdividing of objects into ordered classifications.

technological analysis The study of technological methods used to make an artifact.

technological attributes (technological types) Attributes based on technological features of an object.

tectonic Referring to the earth's crust; a tectonic movement is an earthquake.

telehistoric sites Sites far removed from written records; prehistoric sites.

tell A mound; used to refer to archaeological sites of this type in the Near East.

temper Coarse material such as sand or shell added to fine pot clay to make it bond during firing.

tempering A process for hardening iron blades, involving heating and rapid cooling. Also, material added to potter's clay.

test pit An excavation unit used to sample or probe a site before large-scale excavation or to check surface surveys.

thermoluminescence A chronometric dating method that measures the amount of light energy released by a baked clay object when heated rapidly. Gives an indication of the time elapsed since the object was last heated.

three-age system A technological subdivision of the prehistoric past developed for Old World prehistory in 1806.

topographic maps Maps that can be used to relate archaeological sites to basic features of the natural landscape.

total excavation Complete excavation of an archaeological site. Normally confined to smaller sites, such as burial mounds or campsites.

trace elements Minute amounts of chemical elements found in rocks that emit characteristic wavelengths of light when heated to incandescence. Trace element analysis is used to study the sources of obsidian and other materials traded over long distances.

tradition A persistent technological or cultural pattern identified by characteristic artifact forms. These persistent forms outlast a single phase and can occur over a wide area.

transformational processes Processes that transform an abandoned prehistoric settlement into an archaeological site through the passage of time. These processes can be initiated by natural phenomena or human activity.

tribe A larger group of bands unified by sodalities and governed by a council of representatives from the bands, kin groups, or sodalities within it.

trypanosomiasis Sleeping sickness.

tsetse A fly that carries trypanosomiasis. Belts of tsetse fly country in Africa prevent inhabitants from raising cattle.

tuff Solidified volcanic ash.

type In archaeology, a grouping of artifacts created for comparison with other groups. This grouping may or may not coincide with the actual tool types designed by the original manufacturers.

type fossil A tool characteristic of a particular "archaeological era," a dated concept borrowed from geology.

typology The classification of types.

unaerated Not exposed to the open air.

underwater archaeology The study of archaeological sites and shipwrecks beneath the surface of the water.

uniformitarianism The doctrine that states that the earth was formed by the same natural geological processes that are operating today.

unilinear cultural evolution A late-nineteenth-century evolutionary theory envisaging all human societies as evolving along one track of cultural evolution, from simple hunting and gathering to literate civilization.

unit In archaeology, an artificial grouping used for describing artifacts.

use-wear analysis Microscopic analysis of artifacts to detect signs of wear through use on their working edges.

varves Annual clay deposits made by retreating and melting glaciers. Used to measure recent Pleistocene geological events.

vertical excavation Excavation undertaken to establish a chronological sequence, normally covering a limited area.

votive Intended as an offering as a result of a vow.

zooarchaeology The study of animal remains in archaeology.

Bibliography

This Bibliography is not intended as a comprehensive reference guide to method and theory in archaeology. Rather, it is a compilation of both the majority of the sources used to compile this book and a cross-section of the most important methodological and theoretical research. Readers interested in probing even more deeply into the literature should consult the Guide to Further Reading at the end of each chapter.

Adams, C. E. 1983. "The Architectural Analogue to Hopi Social Organization and Room Use and Implications for Prehistoric Northern Southwestern Culture," *American Antiquity* 48: 44–61.

Adams, R. E. W. 1975. "Stratigraphy," in T. R. Hester, R. F. Heizer, and J. A. Graham, eds., *Field Methods in Archaeology,* 6th ed., pp. 147–162. Palo Alto, Calif.: Mayfield.

Adams, R. E. W., and others. 1981. "Radar Mapping, Archaeology, and Ancient Maya Land Use," *Science* 213 (4515): 1457–1462.

Adams, R. M. 1974. *The Uruk Landscape.* Chicago: University of Chicago Press.

Adovasio, J. M. 1979. *Basketry Technology: A Guide to Identification and Analysis.* Hawthorne, N.Y.: Aldine.

Adovasio, J. M., and R. C. Carlisle. 1988. "Some Thoughts on Cultural Resource Management Archaeology in the United States," *Antiquity* 62: 72–87.

Adovasio, J. M., and J. D. Gunn. 1977. "Style, Basketry, and Basketmakers," in J. Hill and J. D. Gunn, eds., *The Individual in Prehistory,* pp. 137–154. Orlando, Fla.: Academic Press.

Adovasio, J. M., J. D. Gunn, J. Donahue, and R. Stuckenrath. 1975. "Excavations at Meadowcroft Rockshelter, 1973–74," *Pennsylvania Archaeologist* 45: 1–30.

Adovasio, J. M., and others. 1984. "Paleoenvironmental Reconstruction at Meadowcroft Rockshelter, Washington County, Pennsylvania," in J. I. Mead and D. J. Meltzer, eds., *Environments and Extinctions: Man in Late Glacial North America,* pp. 73–110. Oroco, Maine: Center for the Study of Early Man.

Aikens, C. M. 1970. *Hogup Cave.* University of Utah Anthropological Papers, No. 93.

———. 1978. "The Far West," in J. D. Jennings, ed., *Ancient Native Americans,* 2d ed., pp. 131–182. New York: Freeman.

Aitken, M. J. 1984. *Thermoluminescence Dating.* London: Academic Press.

Akazawa, T., and C. M. Aikens. 1986. *Prehistoric Hunter-Gatherers in Japan.* Tokyo: University Museum, Bulletin 27.

Aldendorfer, M. S., and C. A. Hale-Pierce, eds. 1984. "The Small Scale Survey," *American Archaeology* 4: 4–53.

Alexander, J. 1970. *The Directing of Archaeological Excavations.* New York: Humanities Press.

Allan, W. 1965. *The African Husbandman.* Edinburgh: Oliver and Boyd.

Alva, W. 1988. "Discovering the New World's Richest Unlooted Tomb," *National Geographic,* April, pp. 510–555.

Ambler, J. R. 1984. "The Use and Abuse of Predictive Modeling in CRM," *American Archaeology* 4: 140–145.

Ammerman, A. J. 1981. "Surveys and Archaeological Research," *Annual Review of Anthropology* 10: 63–88.

Ammerman, A. J., and G. D. Schaffer. 1981. "Neolithic Settlement Patterns in Calabria," *Current Anthropology* 22: 430–432.

Anawalt, P. 1981. *Indian Clothing Before Cortés.* Norman: University of Oklahoma Press.

Anderson, Duane. 1985. "Reburial: Is It Reasonable?" *Archaeology* 38 (5): 48–51.

Anderson, D. G., and G. T. Hanson. 1988. "Early Archaic Settlement in the Southeastern United States," *American Antiquity* 53: 262–286.

Anderson, J. E. 1969. *The Human Skeleton: A Manual for Archaeologists.* Ottawa: National Museum of Canada.

Anton, F. 1988. *Ancient Peruvian Textiles.* London: Thames and Hudson.

Arnold, D. E. 1985. *Ceramic Theory and Cultural Process.* Cambridge: Cambridge University Press.

Arnold, J. R., and W. F. Libby. 1949. "Age Determinations by Radiocarbon Content," *Science* 110: 678–680.

Asaro, F., and I. Perlman. 1967. *Determination of Provenience of Pottery from Trace Element Analysis.* Berkeley, Calif.: Lawrence Radiation Laboratory.

Asch, D. L. 1975. "On Sample Size Problems and the Uses of Non-probabilistic Sampling," in J. A. Mueller, ed., *Sampling in Archaeology,* pp. 170–191. Orlando, Fla.: Academic Press.

Asch, N. B., R. I. Ford, and D. L. Asch. 1972. *The Paleoethnobotany of the Koster Site: The Archaic Horizon.* Springfield: Illinois State Museum.

Asher, R. 1961. "Analogy in Archaeological Interpretation," *Southwestern Journal of Anthropology* 17: 317–325.

Atkinson, R. J. C. 1953. *Field Archaeology*. London: Methuen.

———. 1957. "Worms and Weathering," *Antiquity* 31: 46–52.

———. 1969. "Moonshine on Stonehenge," *Antiquity* 43: 212–216.

Avebury, Lord (Sir John Lubbock). 1865. *Prehistoric Times*. London: Williams and Norgate.

Aveni, A. F., and G. Brotherston, eds. 1983. *Calendars in Mesoamerica and Peru: Native American Computations of Time*. Oxford: British Archaeological Reports International Series.

Avery, G., and L. G. Underhill. 1986. "Seasonal Exploitation of Seabirds by Late Holocene Coastal Foragers," *Journal of Archaeological Science* 13: 339–360.

Bahn, P., and J. Vertut. 1988. *Images of the Ice Age*. London: Windward.

Bailey, G. N., ed. 1981. *Hunter-Gatherer Economy in Prehistory*. Cambridge: Cambridge University Press.

———. 1983. "Concepts of Time in Quaternary Prehistory," *Annual Review of Anthropology* 12: 165–192.

Bailey, G. N., M. R. Deith, and N. J. Shackleton. 1982. "Oxygen Isotope Analysis and Seasonality Determinants: Limits and Potential of a New Technique," *American Antiquity* 48: 390–398.

Baillie, M. G. L. 1982. *Tree-Ring Dating and Archaeology*. Chicago: University of Chicago Press.

Baker, C. M. 1978. "The Size Effect: An Explanation of Variability in Surface Artifact and Assemblage Content," *American Antiquity* 43: 288–293.

Bannister, B., and W. J. Robinson. 1975. "Tree Dating in Archaeology," *World Archaeology* 7: 210–225.

Bannister, R. 1969. "Dendrochronology," in D. R. Brothwell and E. Higgs, eds., *Science in Archaeology*, pp. 191–205. London: Thames and Hudson.

Bareis, C. F., and J. W. Porter, eds. 1984. *American Bottom Archaeology*. Urbana: University of Illinois Press.

Barker, P. 1983. *Techniques of Archaeological Excavation*. New York: Humanities Press.

———. 1986. *Understanding Archaeological Excavation*. London: Batsford.

Bartel, B. 1982. "A Historical Review of Ethnological and Archaeological Analyses of Mortuary Practice," *Journal of Anthropological Archaeology* 1: 32–58.

Bass, G. F. 1966. *Archaeology Under Water*. New York: Praeger.

———, ed. 1970. *A History of Seafaring from Underwater Archaeology*. London: Thames and Hudson.

———, ed. 1988. *Ships and Shipwrecks of the Americas*. London: Thames and Hudson.

Bass, W. M. 1971. *Human Osteology: A Laboratory and Field Manual of the Human Skeleton*. Columbia: Missouri Archaeological Society.

Bayard, D. T. 1972. "Early Thai Bronze: Analysis and New Dates," *Science* 196: 1411–1412.

Beadle, G. 1981. "The Ancestry of Corn," *Scientific American,* January, pp. 96–103.

Beattie, O., and J. Geiger. 1986. *Frozen in Time: The Fate of the Franklin Expedition.* London: Bloomsbury Publications.

Beck, H., and J. F. Schofield. 1958. "Beads," in R. Summers, ed., *Inyanga,* pp. 267–291. Cambridge: Cambridge University Press.

Begler, E. B., and R. W. Keatinge. 1979. "Theoretical Goals and Methodological Realities: Problems in the Reconstruction of Prehistoric Subsistence Economies," *World Archaeology* 11: 208–226.

Bennett, W. J. 1974. *Basic Ceramic Analysis.* Eastern New Mexico University Contributions in Anthropology, vol. 6, no. 1.

Berry, M. S. 1984. "Sampling and Predictive Modeling on Federal Lands in the West," *American Antiquity* 49: 842–853.

Bettinger, R. L. 1980. "Explanatory/Predictive Models of Hunter-Gatherer Adaptations," *Advances in Archaeological Method and Theory* 3: 189–256.

———. 1986. "Archaeological Approaches to Hunter-Gatherers," *Annual Review of Anthropology* 16: 121–142.

Biddle, M. 1961. "Nonsuch Palace, 1959–60: An Interim Report," *Surrey Archaeological Collections* 58: 1–20.

Biddle, M., and B. Kjølbye-Biddle. 1969. "Metres, Areas, and Robbing," *World Archaeology* 2: 208–219.

Binford, L. R. 1962. "Archaeology as Anthropology," *American Antiquity* 28: 217–225.

———. 1964. "A Consideration of Archaeological Research Design," *American Antiquity* 29: 425–441.

———. 1968. "Archaeological Perspectives," in S. R. Binford and L. R. Binford, eds., *New Perspectives in Archaeology,* pp. 5–32. Hawthorne, N.Y.: Aldine.

———. 1972. *An Archaeological Perspective.* New York: Seminar Press.

———, ed. 1977. *For Theory Building in Archaeology.* Orlando, Fla.: Academic Press.

———. 1978. *Nunamiut Ethnoarchaeology.* Orlando, Fla.: Academic Press.

———. 1980. "Willow Smoke and Dog's Tails: Hunter-Gatherer Settlement Systems and Archaeological Site Formation," *American Antiquity* 45: 4–20.

———. 1981a. "Behavioral Archaeology and the Pompeii Premise," *Journal of Archaeological Research* 37: 195–208.

———. 1981b. *Bones: Ancient Men and Modern Myths.* Orlando, Fla.: Academic Press.

———. 1983a. *In Pursuit of the Past.* New York: Thames and Hudson.

———. 1983b. *Working at Archaeology.* Orlando, Fla.: Academic Press.

———. 1984. "An Alyawara Day: Flour, Spinifex Gum, and Shifting Perspectives," *Journal of Anthropological Research* 40: 157–257.

———. 1986. "In Pursuit of the Future," in D. J. Meltzer, D. D. Fowler, and J. A. Sabloff, eds., *American Archaeology Past and Future,* pp. 459–479. Washington, D.C.: Smithsonian Institution Press.

———. 1989. *Debating Archaeology.* Orlando, Fla.: Academic Press.

Binford, L. R., and J. A. Sabloff. 1982. "Paradigms, Systematics, and Archaeology," *Journal of Anthropological Research* 38: 137–153.

Bishop, R. L., R. L. Rands, and G. R. Hedley. 1982. "Ceramic Compositional Analysis in Archaeological Perspectives," *Advances in Archaeological Method and Theory* 5: 275–331.

Bisson, M. S. 1977. "Prehistoric Copper Mining in North West Zambia," *Archaeology* 29: 242–247.

Blanton, R. E. 1978. *Monte Alban: Settlement Patterns at the Ancient Zapotec Capital.* Orlando, Fla.: Academic Press.

Boardman, J., and L. R. Palmer. 1963. *On the Knossos Tablets.* Oxford: Clarendon Press.

Bobrowsky, P. T. 1984. "The History and Science of Gastropods in Archaeology," *American Antiquity* 49: 77–93.

Bohrer, V. L. 1981. "Methods of Recognizing Cultural Activity from Pollen in Archaeological Sites," *Kiva* 46 (3): 13.

Bordaz, J. 1970. *Tools of the Old and New Stone Age.* Garden City, N.Y.: Natural History Press.

Bordes, F. 1968. *The Old Stone Age.* New York: McGraw-Hill.

Boserup, E. 1965. *Conditions of Agricultural Growth: The Economics of Agrarian Change Under Population Pressure.* Hawthorne, N.Y.: Aldine.

Boulton, T. W., and others. 1984. "Stable Carbon Isotope Ratios as Indicators of Prehistoric Human Diet," *American Chemical Society Symposium Series* 258: 191–204.

Brace, C. L. 1979. *The Stages of Human Evolution,* 2d ed. Englewood Cliffs, N.J.: Prentice-Hall.

Bracken, C.P. 1975. *Antiquities Acquired.* Newton Abbott, England: David and Charles.

Bradford, J. 1957. *Ancient Landscapes: Studies in Field Archaeology.* London: Bell.

Braidwood, R. J., and B. Howe. 1962. "Southwestern Asia Beyond the Lands of the Mediterranean Littoral," in R. J. Braidwood and G. R. Willey, eds., *Courses Toward Urban Life,* pp. 132–146. New York: Viking Penguin.

Braidwood, R. J., and L. Braidwood, eds. 1983. *Prehistoric Archaeology Along the Zagros.* Chicago: University of Chicago Press.

Brain, C. K. 1967. "Hottentot Food Remains and Their Bearing on the Interpretation of Fossil Bone Assemblages," *Scientific Papers of the Namib Desert Research Station* 32 (6): 1–7.

———. 1981. *The Hunters or the Hunted: An Introduction to African Cave Taphonomy.* Chicago: University of Chicago Press.

Breiner, S. 1973. *Applications Manual for Portable Magnetometers.* Sunnyvale, Calif.: Geometrics.

Brill, R.H. 1964. "Applications of Fission-Track Dating to Historic and Prehistoric Glasses," *Archaeometry* 7: 51–57.

Bronitsky, G. 1986. "The Use of Materials Science Techniques in the Study of Pottery Construction and Use," *Advances in Archaeological Method and Theory* 10: 209–276.

Brothwell, D. R. 1982. *Digging Up Bones,* 3d ed. London: Oxford University Press and the British Museum.

Brown, J. A., ed. 1971. *Approaches to the Social Dimensions of Mortuary Practices.* Memoirs of the Society for American Archaeology, vol. 25.

———. 1981. "The Search for Rank in Prehistoric Burials," in R. Chapman, I. Kinnes, and K. Randsborg, eds., *The Archaeology of Death,* pp. 25–38. Cambridge: Cambridge University Press.

———. 1982. "On the Structure of Artifact Typologies," in R. A. Whallon and J. A. Brown, eds., *Essays on Archaeological Typology,* pp. 176–190. Evanston, Ill.: Center for American Archaeology.

Brown, J. A., and S. Struever. 1973. "The Organization of Archaeological Research: An Illinois Example," in C. L. Redman, ed., *Method and Theory in Current Archaeology,* pp. 261–280. New York: Wiley Interscience.

Brumfiel, E. O. 1976. "Regional Growth in the Eastern Valley of Mexico," in K. V. Flannery, ed., *The Early Mesoamerican Village,* pp. 243–247. Orlando, Fla.: Academic Press.

Brumfiel, E. O., and T. K. Earle, eds. 1987. *Specialization, Exchange, and Complex Societies.* Cambridge: Cambridge University Press.

Bryant, V. M. 1974. "Prehistoric Diet in Southwest Texas: The Coprolite Evidence," *American Antiquity* 39: 407–420.

Bryant, V. M., and R. G. Holloway. 1983. "The Role of Palynology in Archaeology," *Advances in Archaeological Method and Theory* 6: 191–224.

Bryant, V. M., and G. Williams-Dean. 1975. "The Coprolites of Man," *Scientific American* 232: 100–109.

Buikstra, J. 1984. "The Lower Illinois River Region: A Prehistoric Context for the Study of Ancient Diet and Health," in M. N. Cohen and G. J. Armelagos, eds., *Paleopathology at the Origins of Agriculture,* pp. 217–236. Orlando, Fla.: Academic Press.

Burghardt, A. F. 1959. "The Location of Towns in the Central Lowland of the United States," *Annals of the Association of American Geographers* 49: 305–323.

Burleigh, R., and D. R. Brothwell. 1978. "Studies on Amerindian Dogs," *Journal of Archaeological Science* 5: 355–362.

Butzer, K. W. 1974. *Environment and Archaeology,* 3d ed. Hawthorne, N.Y.: Aldine.

———. 1982. *Archaeology as Human Ecology.* Cambridge: Cambridge University Press.

Byers, D. S., ed. 1967. *The Prehistory of the Tehuacán Valley.* Austin: University of Texas Press.

Cahen, D., and L. H. Keeley. 1980. "Not Less than Two, Not More than Three," *World Archaeology* 12: 166–180.

Campbell, B. G. 1985. *Humankind Emerging,* 4th ed. Boston: Little, Brown.

Campbell, J. B. 1977. *The Upper Palaeolithic of Britain.* Oxford: Oxford University Press.

Cann, J. R., and A. C. Renfrew. 1964. "The Characterization of Obsidian and Its Application to the Mediterranean Region," *Proceedings of the Prehistoric Society* 30: 111–133.

Carr, C. 1982. *Handbook on Soil Resistivity.* Evanston, Ill.: Center for American Archaeology Press.

Cartailhac, E. 1901. "Les Cavernes Ornées de Dessins: La Grotte d'Altamira. Mea Culpa d'un Sceptique," *L'Anthropologie* 12: 671.

Carter, H., and others. 1923–1933. *The Tomb of Tutankhamun.* London: Cassell.

Casteel, R. W. 1976. *Fish Remains in Archaeology and Paleo-environmental Studies.* Orlando, Fla.: Academic Press.

Ceci, L. 1984. "Shell Midden Deposits as Coastal Resources," *World Archaeology* 16: 62–74.

Ceram, C. W. 1953. *Gods, Graves, and Scholars.* New York: Knopf.

Cernych, E. N. 1978. "Aibunar: A Balkan Copper Mine of the Fourth Millennium B.C.," *Proceedings of the Prehistoric Society* 44: 203–218.

Champion, S. 1980. *A Dictionary of Terms and Techniques in Archaeology.* Oxford: Phaidon.

Champion, T., and others. 1984. *Prehistoric Europe.* Orlando, Fla.: Academic Press.

Chang, K. C., ed. 1968. *Settlement Archaeology.* Palo Alto, Calif.: National Press.

Chang, K. C. 1984. *The Archaeology of Ancient China,* 3d ed. New Haven, Conn.: Yale University Press.

Chaplin, R. E. 1971. *The Study of Animal Bones from Archaeological Sites.* New York: Seminar Press.

Chapman, R., I. Kinnes, and K. Randsborg, eds. 1981. *The Archaeology of Death.* Cambridge: Cambridge University Press.

Chartkoff, J. L. 1978. "Transect Interval Sampling in Forests," *American Antiquity* 43: 46–53.

Charton, T. H. 1981. "Archaeology, Ethnohistory, and Ethnology: Interpretative Interfaces," *Advances in Archaeological Method and Theory* 4: 129–176.

Childe, V. G. 1925. *The Dawn of European Civilization.* London: Routledge and Kegan Paul.

———. 1942. *What Happened in History.* Baltimore: Pelican.

———. 1956. *Piecing Together the Past.* London: Routledge and Kegan Paul.

———. 1958. "Retrospect," *Antiquity* 32: 69–74.

Chippendale, C. 1983. *Stonehenge Complete.* London: Thames and Hudson.

Chisholm, B. S., and others 1983. "Marine and Terrestrial Protein in Prehistoric Diets on the British Columbia Coast," *Current Anthropology* 24: 396–398.

Chisholm, M. 1968. *Rural Settlement and Land Use.* London: Hutchinson.

Chittick, H. N. 1974. *Kilwa.* Nairobi: British Institute in Eastern Africa.

Christaller, W. 1933. *Die Zentralen Orte in Süddeutschland.* Jena, East Germany: Karl Zeiss.

Ciolek-Torrello, R. 1984. "An Alternative Model of Room Function from Grass-hopper Pueblo, Arizona," in A. Hietala, ed., *Intrasite Spatial Analysis in Archaeology,* pp. 127–153. Cambridge: Cambridge University Press.

Clark, C. M. 1987. "Trouble at t'Mill: Industrial Archaeology in the 1980s," *Antiquity* 61: 169–179.

Clark, G. A. 1982. "Quantifying Archaeological Research," *Advances in Archaeological Method and Theory* 5: 217–274.

Clark, J. D. 1958. "The Natural Fracturing of Pebbles from the Batoka Gorge, Northern Rhodesia, and Its Bearing on the Kafuan Industries of Africa," *Proceedings of the Prehistoric Society* 24: 64–77.

———. 1959. *The Prehistory of Southern Africa.* Baltimore: Pelican.

———. 1960. "A Note on Early Fishing-Craft and Fishing Practices in Southeast Africa," *South African Archaeological Bulletin* 15: 77–79.

Clark, J. D., and S. Brandt, eds. 1984. *From Hunters to Farming.* Berkeley: University of California Press.

Clark, J. G. D. 1932. *The Mesolithic Age in Britain.* Cambridge: Cambridge University Press.

———. 1939. *Archaeology and Society.* New York: Barnes and Noble.

———. 1952. *Prehistoric Europe: The Economic Basis.* Stanford, Calif.: Stanford University Press.

———. 1954. *Star Carr.* Cambridge: Cambridge University Press.

———. 1970. *Aspects of Prehistory.* Berkeley: University of California Press.

———. 1972. *Star Carr: A Case Study in Bioarchaeology.* Reading, Mass.: Addison-Wesley.

———. 1975. *The Early Stone Age Settlement of Scandinavia.* Cambridge: Cambridge University Press.

———. 1978. *World Prehistory in New Perspective,* 3d ed. Cambridge: Cambridge University Press.

Clark, R. 1935. "The Flint Knapping Industry at Brandon," *Antiquity* 9: 38–56.

Clark, R. M. 1975. "A Calibration Curve for Radiocarbon Dates," *Antiquity* 49: 251–266.

Clarke, D. L. 1968. *Analytical Archaeology.* London: Methuen.

———, ed. 1977. *Spatial Archaeology.* Orlando, Fla.: Academic Press.

Clarke, J. E. 1982. "Manufacture of Mesoamerican Prismatic Blades: An Alternative Technique," *American Antiquity* 47: 355–375.

Clay, R. B. 1976. "Typological Classification, Attribute Analysis, and Lithic Variability," *Journal of Field Archaeology* 3: 303–311.

Cleere, H., ed. 1984. *Approaches to the Archaeological Heritage: A Comparative Study of World Cultural Resource Management Systems.* Cambridge: Cambridge University Press.

Clutton-Brock, J. 1981. *Domesticated Animals from Early Times.* Austin: University of Texas Press.

Clutton-Brock, J., and J. Grigson. 1985. *Early Herders and Their Flocks.* Oxford: British Archaeological Reports.

Coe, M. D. 1967. *Tikal: A Handbook of the Ancient Maya Ruins.* Philadelphia: University Museum.

———. 1976. *The Maya,* 2d ed. New York: Praeger.

———. 1984. *Mexico,* 2d ed. New York: Thames and Hudson.

Coe, M. D., and R. A. Diehl. 1980. *In the Land of the Olmec.* Austin: University of Texas Press.

Coe, W. 1982. *Introduction to the Archaeology of Tikal, Guatemala.* Philadelphia: University Museum, University of Pennsylvania.

Cole, J. H. 1980. "Cult Archaeology and Unscientific Method and Theory," *Advances in Archaeological Method and Theory* 3: 4–37.

Coles, Bryony, and Coles, John. 1989. *People of the Wetlands.* New York: Guild Publishing.

Coles, B., and Coles, J. M. 1986. *Sweet Track to Glastonbury.* New York: Thames and Hudson.

Coles, J. M. 1972. *Field Archaeology in Britain.* London: Heinemann.

———. 1973. *Archaeology by Experiment.* London: Heinemann.

———. 1984. *The Archaeology of the Wetlands.* Cambridge: Cambridge University Press.

Coles, J. M., and A. F. Harding. 1979. *The Bronze Age in Europe.* London: Methuen.

Coles, J. M., S. V. E. Heal, and B. J. Orme. 1978. "The Use and Character of Wood in Prehistoric Britain and Ireland," *Proceedings of the Prehistoric Society* 44: 1–45.

Coles, J. M., and B. J. Orme. 1983. *"Homo sapiens* or *Caster Fiber?" Antiquity* 57: 95–102.

Collins, H. B. 1937. *The Archaeology of St. Lawrence Island.* Washington, D.C.: Smithsonian Institution.

Collins, M. B. 1975. "Lithic Technology as a Means of Processual Inference," in E. Swanson, ed., *Lithic Technology: Making and Using Stone Tools,* pp. 13–54. Hawthorne, N.Y.: Aldine.

Collis, J. 1984. *The European Iron Age.* London: Batsford.

Colwell, R. N., ed. 1983. *Manual of Remote Sensing,* 2d ed. Falls Church, Va.: American Society of Photogrammetry.

Conkey, M. W. 1981. "A Century of Palaeolithic Cave Art," *Archaeology* 34 (4): 20–28.

Conrad, G. W., and A. A. Demarast. 1984. *Religion and Empire: The Dynamics of Aztec and Inca Expansion.* Cambridge: Cambridge University Press.

Cook, D. C. 1984. "Subsistence and Health in the Central Illinois Valley: Osteological Evidence," in M. N. Cohen and G. J. Armelagos, eds., *Paleopathology at the Origins of Agriculture,* pp. 237–270. Orlando, Fla.: Academic Press.

Cook, S. F. 1972. *Prehistoric Demography.* Reading, Mass.: Addison-Wesley.

Cordell, L., and D. L. Green. 1983. *Theory and Model Building: Refining Survey Strategies for Locating Prehistoric Heritage Resources, Trial Formulations for Southwestern Forests.* Albuquerque, N.M.: USDA Forest Service.

Covey, C. 1984. "The Earth's Orbit and the Ice Ages," *Scientific American,* February, pp. 58–77.

Cowgill, G. L. 1982. "Clusters of Objects and Associations Between Variables: Two Approaches to Archaeological Classification," in R. A. Whallon and J. A. Brown, eds., *Essays in Archaeological Typology,* pp. 30–55. Evanston, Ill.: Center for American Archaeology.

———. 1986. "Archaeological Applications of Mathematical and Formal Methods," in D. J. Meltzer, D. D. Fowler, and J. A. Sabloff, eds., *American Archaeology Past and Future,* pp. 369–394. Washington, D.C.: Smithsonian Institution Press.

Cowgill, G. L., and others. 1984. "Spatial Analysis of Teotihuacán: A Mesoamerican Metropolis," in A. Hietala, ed., *Intrasite Spatial Analysis in Archaeology,* pp. 154–195. Cambridge: Cambridge University Press.

Crabtree, D. E. 1972a. *An Introduction to Flintworking.* Pocatello: Idaho State Museum.

———. 1972b. "A Stoneworker's Approach to Analysing and Replicating the Lindenmeier Folsom," *Tebiwa* 9: 3–39.

Crabtree, R. M. 1963. "Archaeological Investigations at Batiquitos Lagoon, San Diego County," in *California Archaeological Survey Annual Report,* pp. 319–462.

Crawford, O. G. S. 1953. *Archaeology in the Field.* New York: Praeger.

Crawford, O. G. S., and A. Keiller. 1928. *Wessex from the Air.* Oxford: Clarendon Press.

Croes, D. R., and J. O. Davis. 1977. "Computer Mapping of Idiosyncratic Basketry Manufacturing Techniques in the Prehistoric Ozette House, Cape Alava, Washington," in J. N. Hill and J. D. Gunn, eds., *The Individual in Prehistory,* pp. 155–166. Orlando, Fla.: Academic Press.

Curtis, G. H. 1975. "Improvements in Potassium-Argon Dating, 1962–1975," *World Archaeology* 7: 198–209.

Dalrymple, G. B., and M. A. Lamphere. 1970. *Potassium Argon Dating.* New York: Freeman.

Dancey, W. S. 1981. *Archaeological Field Methods: An Introduction.* Minneapolis: Burgess.

Daniel, G. 1962. *The Idea of Prehistory.* London: Watts.

———, ed. 1967. *The Origins and Growth of Archaeology.* Baltimore: Pelican.

———. 1976. "Stone, Bronze, and Iron," in J. V. S. Megaw, ed., *To Illustrate the Monuments,* pp. 35–42. London: Thames and Hudson.

———. 1981. *A Short History of Archaeology.* New York: Thames and Hudson.

Däniken, E. von. 1970. *Chariots of the Gods?* New York: Bantam Books.

———. 1971. *Gods from Outer Space.* New York: Bantam Books.

Darrah, W. C. 1938. "Technical Contributions to the Study of Archaeological Materials," *American Antiquity,* 3: 269–270.

Dart, R. A. 1957. *The Osteodontokeratic Culture of Australopithecus Prometheus.* Pretoria: Transvaal Museum.

Darwin, C. 1859. *On the Origin of Species.* London: John Murray.

———. 1881. *The Formation of Vegetable Mould Through the Actions of Worms with Observations on Their Habits.* London: Faber and Faber. (Republished in 1945.)

David, N. C. 1971. "The Fulani Compound and the Archaeologist," *World Archaeology* 3: 111–131.

Davidson, J. 1984. *The Prehistory of New Zealand.* London: Longman.

Davis, D. D. 1983. "Investigating the Diffusion of Stylistic Innovation," *Advances in Archaeological Method and Theory* 6: 53–89.

Davis, S. J. M. 1987. *The Archaeology of Animals.* London: Batsford.

Dawson, E. W. 1969. "Bird Remains in Archaeology," in D. R. Brothwell and E. Higgs, eds., *Science in Archaeology,* pp. 359–375. London: Thames and Hudson.

Deagan, K. 1982. "Avenues of Inquiry in Historical Archaeology," *Advances in Archaeological Method and Theory* 5: 151–178.

———. 1983. *Spanish Saint Augustine: The Archaeology of a Colonial Creole Community.* Orlando, Fla.: Academic Press.

Dean, J. S. 1970. "Aspects of Tsegi Phase Soil Organization," in W. A. Longacre, ed., *Reconstructing Prehistoric Pueblo Societies.* Albuquerque: University of New Mexico Press.

Deetz, J. 1967. *Invitation to Archaeology.* Garden City, N.Y.: Natural History Press.

———. 1977. *In Small Things Forgotten.* Garden City, N.Y.: Anchor/Doubleday.

———. 1983. "Scientific Humanism and Humanist Science," *Geoscience and Man* 23: 27–34.

———. 1988. "American Historical Archaeology: Methods and Results," *Science* 239: 362–367.

Deith, M. R. 1983. "Molluscan Calendars," *Journal of Archaeological Science* 10: 423–440.

Dekin, A. 1987. "Sealed in Time," *National Geographic,* June, pp. 824–836.

De Niro, M. J., and M. J. Schoeringer. 1983. "Stable Carbon and Nitrogen Isotope Ratios of Bone Collagen," *Journal of Archaeological Science* 10: 199–203.

Dennell, R. W. 1979. "Prehistoric Diet and Nutrition: Some Food for Thought," *World Archaeology* 11: 121–135.

De Perthes, B. 1841. *De la Création: Essai sur l'Origine et la Progression des Êtres.* Abbeville, France.

De Roche, C. D. 1983. "Population Estimates from Settlement Area and Number of Residences," *Journal of Field Archaeology* 10: 187–192.

Dethlefsen, E., and J. Deetz. 1966. "Death's Heads, Cherubs, and Willow Trees: Experimental Archaeology in Colonial Cemeteries," *American Antiquity* 31: 502–510.

Deuel, L. 1969. *Flights into Yesterday.* London: Macdonald.

————. 1977. *Memoirs of Heinrich Schliemann.* New York: Harper and Row.

De Viro, B., and S. Epstein. 1978. "Dietary Analysis from $^{12}C/^{13}C$ Ratios of Carbonate and Collagen Fractions of Bone," *U.S. Geological Survey Open File Report,* 78–701: 90–91.

Dibble, H. 1987. "Penn Anthropologist Adapts Laser and Computers to Speed Archaeological Exploration," *SAA Bulletin,* March, p. 5.

Digby, B. 1926. *The Mammoth and Mammoth-Hunting in North-East Siberia.* London: Macmillan.

Dimbleby, G. W. 1985. *The Palynology of Archaeological Sites.* London: Academic Press.

Dincauze, D. 1987. "Strategies for Paleoenvironmental Reconstruction in Archaeology," *Advances in Archaeological Method and Theory* 11: 255–336.

Dittert, A. E., Jr., J. J. Hester, and F. W. Eddy. 1961. *An Archaeological Survey of the Navajo Reservoir District of Northwestern New Mexico.* Monographs of the School of American Research and Museum of New Mexico, No. 23.

Doran, J. E. 1987. "Formal Methods and Archaeology," *Journal of Field Archaeology* 18: 21–37.

Doran, J. E., and F. R. Hodson. 1975. *Mathematics and Computers in Archaeology.* Cambridge, Mass.: Harvard University Press.

Dorrell, P. 1989. *Photography in Archaeology and Conservation.* Cambridge: Cambridge University Press.

Dowman, E. A. 1970. *Conservation in Field Archaeology.* London: Methuen.

Drager, D. L., and T. R. Lyons. 1983. *Remote Sensing in CRM: The San Juan Basin Project.* Washington, D.C.: National Park Service.

Drennan, R. D. 1976. "Religion and Social Evolution in Formative Mesoamerica," in K. V. Flannery, ed., *The Early Mesoamerican Village,* pp. 345–363. Orlando, Fla.: Academic Press.

Drucker, P. 1966. *Cultures of the North Pacific Coast.* New York: Harper and Row.

————. 1972. *Stratigraphy in Archaeology: An Introduction.* Reading, Mass.: Addison-Wesley.

Dumond, D. E. 1987. *The Eskimos and Aleuts,* 2d ed. London: Thames and Hudson.

Dunn, M. E. 1983. "Phytolith Analysis in Archaeology," *Midcontinental Journal of Archaeology* 8: 287–297.

Dunnell, R. C. 1970. "The Seriation Method and Its Evaluation," *American Antiquity* 35: 305–319.

————. 1971. *Systematics in Prehistory.* New York: Free Press.

————. 1977. "Science and Archaeology: When the Saints Go Marching In," *American Antiquity* 42: 33–49.

————. 1978. "Style and Function: A Fundamental Dichotomy," *American Antiquity* 43: 192–202.

————. 1980. "Evolutionary Theory and Archaeology." *Advances in Archaeological Method and Theory* 3: 38–99.

———. 1982. "Science, Social Science, and Common Sense: The Agonizing Dilemma of Modern Archaeology," *Journal of Anthropological Research* 38: 1–25.

———. 1984. "The Americanist Literature for 1983: A Year of Contrasts and Challenges," *American Journal of Archaeology* 88: 489–513.

———. 1985. "Americanist Archaeology in 1984," *American Journal of Archaeology* 89: 585–611.

———. 1986a. "Five Decades of American Archaeology," in D. J. Meltzer, D. D. Fowler, and J. A. Sabloff, eds., *American Archaeology Past and Future,* pp. 23–52. Washington, D.C.: Smithsonian Institution Press.

———. 1986b. "Methodological Issues in Americanist Artifact Classification," *Advances in Archaeological Method and Theory* 10: 149–208.

Dunnell, R. C., and W. S. Dancey. 1983. "The Siteless Survey: A Regional Scale Data Collection," *Advances in Archaeological Method and Theory* 6: 267–288.

Dymond, D. P. 1974. *Archaeology and History.* London: Thames and Hudson.

Earle, T. K. 1976. "A Nearest Neighbor Analysis of Two Formative Settlement Systems," in K. V. Flannery, ed., *The Early Mesoamerican Village,* pp. 196–224. Orlando, Fla.: Academic Press.

Earle, T. K., and J. E. Ericson, eds. 1977. *Exchange Systems in Prehistory.* Orlando, Fla.: Academic Press.

Ebert, J. I. 1984. "Remote Sensing Applications in Archaeology," *Advances in Archaeological Method and Theory* 7: 293–362.

Ebert, J. I., and J. Hitchcock. 1980. "Locational Modeling in the Analysis of the Prehistoric Road System at and Around Chaco Canyon, New Mexico," in T. R. Lyons and F. J. Mattison, eds., *Remote Sensing in Cultural Resource Management,* pp. 169–208. Washington, D.C.: National Park Service.

Eddy, F. W., and C. O'Sullivan. 1986. "The Federal Management of Archaeological Resources in the American West," *Archaeology* 39 (6): 48–52.

Eliade, M. 1954. *The Myth of the Eternal Return.* New York: Pantheon.

Elphick, R. 1977. *Kraal and Castle.* New Haven, Conn.: Yale University Press.

Ericson, J. E., and T. K. Earle, eds. 1982. *Contexts of Prehistoric Exchange.* Orlando, Fla.: Academic Press.

Ericson, J. E., and B. A. Purdy, eds. 1984. *Prehistoric Quarries and Lithic Production.* Cambridge: Cambridge University Press.

Erickson, C. L. 1985. "Applications of Prehistoric Andean Technology: Experiments in Raised Field Agriculture," in I. S. Farrington, ed., *Prehistoric Intensive Agriculture in the Tropics,* pp. 209–222. Oxford: British Archaeological Reports.

Evans, J. 1849. "On the Date of British Coins," *Numismatic Chronicle* 12: 127.

———. 1860. "On the Occurrence of Flint Implements in Undisturbed Beds of Gravel, Sand, and Clay," *Archaeologia* 38: 280–308.

Evans, J. D. 1978. *An Introduction to Environmental Archaeology.* London: Paul Elek.

Fagan, B. M. 1967. *Iron Age Cultures in Zambia,* vol. 1. Atlantic Highlands, N.J.: Humanities Press.

——. 1969. "Early Trade and Raw Materials in South Central Africa," *Journal of African History* 10: 1–26.

——. 1975. *The Rape of the Nile.* New York: Scribner.

——. 1977. *Elusive Treasure.* New York: Scribner.

——. 1978. *Quest for the Past.* Reading, Mass.: Addison-Wesley.

——. 1979. *Return to Babylon.* Boston: Little, Brown.

——. 1984a. *The Aztecs.* New York: Freeman.

——. 1984b. *Clash of Cultures.* New York: Freeman.

——. 1985. *The Adventure of Archaeology.* Washington, D.C.: National Geographic Society.

——. 1987. *The Great Journey.* New York: Thames and Hudson.

——. 1989. *People of the Earth,* 6th ed. Glenview, Ill.: Scott, Foresman Little, Brown.

——. 1990. *Ancient North America.* London: Thames and Hudson.

——. 1991a. *Archaeology: A Brief Introduction,* 4th ed. New York: Harper Collins.

——. 1991b. *The Journey from Eden.* London: Thames and Hudson.

Fagan, B. M., and F. Van Noten. 1971. *The Hunter-Gatherers of Gwisho.* Tervuren, Belgium: Musée Royal de l'Afrique Centrale.

Fell, B. 1977. *America B. C.* New York: Viking Penguin.

Fitting, J. F., and A. C. Goodyear. 1979. "Client-oriented Archaeology: An Exchange of Views," *Journal of Field Archaeology* 6: 352–360.

Fitzhugh, W., ed. 1988. *Crossroads of Continents.* Washington D.C.: Smithsonian Institution Press.

Fladmark, K. R. 1982. "Microdebitage Analysis: Initial Considerations," *Journal of Archaeological Science* 9: 205–220.

Flannery, K. V. 1968. "Archaeological Systems Theory and Early Mesoamerica," in B. J. Meggers, ed., *Anthropological Archaeology in the Americas,* pp. 67–87. Washington: Anthropological Society of Washington.

——. 1972. "The Cultural Evolution of Civilizations," *Biennial Review of Ecology and Systematics,* 399–426.

——. 1973a. "Archaeology with a Capital A," in C. L. Redman, ed., *Research and Theory in Current Archaeology,* pp. 337–354. New York: Wiley Interscience.

——. 1973b. "The Origins of Agriculture," *Biennial Review of Anthropology* 12: 271–310.

——, ed. 1976. *The Early Mesoamerican Village.* Orlando, Fla.: Academic Press.

——. 1982. "The Golden Marshalltown: A Parable for the Archaeology of the 1980s," *American Anthropologist* 84: 265–278.

Flannery, K. V., and J. Marcus, eds. 1983. *The Cloud People.* Orlando, Fla.: Academic Press.

Flannery, K. V., and M. C. Winter. 1976. "Analyzing Village Activities," in K. V. Flannery, ed., *The Early Mesoamerican Village,* pp. 34–44. Orlando, Fla.: Academic Press.

Flannery, K. V., and others. 1989. *The Flocks of the Wamani.* Orlando, Fla.: Academic Press.

Fleischer, R. L. 1975. "Advances in Fission Track Dating," *World Archaeology* 7: 136–150.

Fleming, S. J. 1976. *Dating in Archaeology.* New York: St. Martin's Press.

———. *Dating Methods in Archaeology.* New York: St. Martin's Press.

———. 1979. *Thermoluminescence Techniques in Archaeology.* Oxford: Clarendon Press.

Flenniken, J. J. 1984. "The Past, Present, and Future of Flintknapping: An Anthropological Perspective," *Annual Review of Anthropology* 13: 187–203.

Fontana, B. L. 1968. "Bottles, Buckets, and Horseshoes: The Unrespectable in American Archaeology," *Keystone Folklore Quarterly* 13: 171–184.

Fontana, B. L., W. J. Robinson, C. W. Cormack, and E. E. Leavitt. 1962. *Papago Indian Pottery.* Seattle: University of Washington Press.

Forbes, R. J. 1955–1958. *Studies in Ancient Technology.* The Hague: Brill.

Ford, J. A. 1962. *A Quantitative Method for Deriving Cultural Chronology.* Washington, D.C.: Pan American Union.

Ford, J. A., and G. R. Willey. 1941. "An Interpretation of the Prehistory of the Eastern United States," *American Anthropologist* 43: 325–363.

Ford, R. I. 1979. "Paleoethnobotany in American Archaeology," *Advances in Archaeological Method and Theory* 2: 286–336.

———. ed. 1985. *Early Food Production in North America.* Ann Arbor: University of Michigan Museum of Anthropology.

Fowler, D. D. 1982. "Cultural Resources Management," *Advances in Archaeological Method and Theory* 5: 1–50.

———. 1986. "Conserving American Archaeological Resources," in D. J. Meltzer, D. D. Fowler, and J. A. Sabloff, eds., *American Archaeology Past and Future,* pp. 135–162. Washington, D.C.: Smithsonian Institution Press.

———. 1987. "Uses of the Past: Archaeology in the Service of the State," *American Antiquity* 52: 229–248.

Fox, C. 1932. *The Personality of Britain.* Cambridge: Cambridge University Press.

Frankfort, H. 1951. *The Birth of Civilization in the Near East.* Garden City, N.Y.: Doubleday.

Frazer, J. 1980. *The Golden Bough.* London: Macmillan.

Friedel, D. A., and J. A. Sabloff. 1984. *Cozumel: Late Maya Settlement Patterns.* Orlando, Fla.: Academic Press.

Friedel, D. A., and L. Schele. 1987. "Symbol and Power: A History of the Lowland Maya Cosmogram," in E. P. Benson and G. Griddin, eds., *Maya Iconography.* Princeton, N.J.: Princeton University Press.

Friedman, I., and F. Trembour. 1983. "Obsidian Hydration Update," *American Antiquity* 48: 544–547.

Frison, G. 1978. *Prehistoric Hunters of the High Plains.* Orlando, Fla.: Academic Press.

Fritts, H. C. 1976. *Tree Rings and Climate.* Orlando, Fla.: Academic Press.

Garlake, P. 1973. *Great Zimbabwe.* London: Thames and Hudson.

Garrod, D. A. E., and D. Bate. 1937. *The Stone Age of Mount Carmel,* vol. 1. Cambridge: Cambridge University Press.

Gibbon, G. 1984. *Anthropological Archaeology.* New York: Columbia University Press.

Gifford, D. P. 1981. "Taphonomy and Paleoecology: A Critical Review of Archaeology's Sister Discipline," *Advances in Archaeological Method and Theory* 4: 365–437.

Gifford, J. C. 1976. *Prehistoric Pottery Analysis and the Ceramics of Barton Ramie in the Belize Valley.* Cambridge, Mass.: Peabody Museum, Harvard University.

Gilbert, R. I., and others, eds. 1985. *Analysis of Prehistoric Diet.* Orlando, Fla.: Academic Press.

Gillespie, R., and others, 1984. "Radiocarbon Dating of Bone by Accelerator Mass Spectrometry," *Journal of Archaeological Science* 11: 165–170.

Gish, J. W. 1979. "Palynological Research at Pueblo Grande Ruin," *Kiva* 44: 159–177.

Glob, P. V. 1969. *The Bog People.* London: Faber and Faber.

Goodyear, A. C., L. M. Raab, and T. C. Klinger. 1978. "The Status of Archaeological Research Design in Cultural Resource Management," *American Antiquity* 43: 159–173.

Gould, R. H. 1977. *Puntutjarpa Rockshelter.* New York: American Museum of Natural History.

———, ed. 1978. *Explorations in Ethnoarchaeology.* Albuquerque: University of New Mexico Press.

———. 1980. *Living Archaeology.* Cambridge: Cambridge University Press.

———, ed. 1983. *Shipwreck Archaeology.* Albuquerque: University of New Mexico Press.

Gould, R. H., and M. B. Schiffer. 1981. *Modern Material Culture: The Archaeology of Us.* Orlando, Fla.: Academic Press.

Gould, R. H., and P. J. Watson. 1982. "A Dialogue on the Meaning and Use of Analogy in Ethnoarchaeological Reasoning," *Journal of Anthropological Archaeology* 1: 355–381.

Gowlett, J. A. J. 1987. "The Archaeology of Radiocarbon Accelerator Dating," *Journal of World Prehistory* 1: 127–170.

Grange, R. T. 1972. "Pawnee Potsherds Revisited: Formula Dating of a Non-European Ceramic Tradition," *Conference on Historic Site Archaeology Papers* 7: 318–336.

———. 1981. "Ceramic Dating Formula of the Arikara," in A. E. Johnson and L. J. Zimmerman, eds., *Method and Theory in Plains Archaeology.* Vermillion: South Dakota Archaeological Society.

Grasiozi, P. 1960. *Palaeolithic Art.* New York: McGraw-Hill.

Grayson, D. K. 1979. "On the Quantification of Vertebrate Archaeofaunas," *Advances in Archaeological Method and Theory* 2: 200–238.

———. 1980. "Vicissitudes and Overkill: The Development of Explanations of Pleistocene Extinctions," *Advances in Archaeological Method and Theory* 3: 357–404.

———. 1981. "A Critical View of the Use of Archaeological Vertebrates in Paleoenvironmental Reconstruction," *Journal of Ethnobiology* 1: 28–38.

———. 1983. *The Establishment of Human Antiquity.* Orlando, Fla.: Academic Press.

———. 1984. *Quantitative Zooarchaeology.* Orlando, Fla.: Academic Press.

———. 1986. " 'Eoliths,' Archaeological Ambiguity, and the Generation of 'Middle Range' Research," in D. J. Meltzer, D. D. Fowler, and J. A. Sabloff, eds., *American Archaeology Past and Future,* pp. 77–134. Washington, D.C.: Smithsonian Institution Press.

Green, E. L., ed. 1984. *Ethics and Values in Archaeology.* New York: Free Press.

Griffin, J. B. 1946. "Culture Change and Continuity in the Eastern United States," in F. Johnson, ed., *Man in Northeastern North America.* Andover, Mass.: Peabody Foundation.

Grinsell, L. V., P. A. Rahtz, and D. P. Williams. 1970. *The Preparation of Archaeological Reports.* London: John Baker.

Grootes, P. M. 1978. "Carbon-14 Time Scale Extended: Comparison of Chronologies," *Science* 200: 11–15.

Grossman, J. W. 1982. *Raritan Landing: The Archaeology of a Buried Port.* New Brunswick, N.J.: Rutgers Archaeological Survey Office.

Guidon, N., and G. Delibrias. 1986. "Carbon 14 Dates Point to Man in the Americas 32,000 Years Ago," *Nature* 321: 769–771.

Gumerman, G. J. 1984. *A View from Black Mesa: The Changing Face of Archaeology.* Tucson: University of Arizona Press.

Gumerman, G. J., and R. C. Euler. 1976. *Papers on the Archaeology of Black Mesa, Arizona.* Carbondale: Southern Illinois University Press.

Hally, D. J. 1981. "Plant Preservation and the Content of Paleobotanical Samples: A Case Study," *American Antiquity* 46: 723–742.

Hamblin, D. J. 1970. *Pots and Robbers.* New York: Simon and Schuster.

Hammond, N. 1982. *Ancient Maya Civilization.* New Brunswick: Rutgers University Press.

Hammond, N., and C. H. Miksicek. 1981. "Ecology and Economy of a Formative Maya Site at Cuello, Belize," *Journal of Field Archaeology* 8: 259–269.

Handsman, R. G. 1981. "Early Capitalism and the Center Village of Canaan, CT," *Artifacts* 9: 1–21.

Hardesty, D. 1977. *Ecological Anthropology.* New York: Wiley.

———. 1980. "The Use of General Ecological Principles in Archaeology," *Advances in Archaeological Method and Theory* 3: 158–188.

Hardin, M. A. 1977. "Individual Style in San José Pottery Painting: The Role of Deliberate Choice," in J. N. Hill and J. D. Gunn, eds., *The Individual in Prehistory*, pp. 109–136. Orlando, Fla.: Academic Press.

Harlan, J. 1967. "A Wild Wheat Harvest in Turkey," *Archaeology* 20: 197–201.

Harp, E., Jr. 1978. *Photography for Archaeologists*. Orlando, Fla.: Academic Press.

Harrington, J. C. 1948. "Evidence of Manual Reckoning in the Cittie of Raleigh," *North Carolina Historical Review* 33: 1–8.

Harris, E. C. 1989. *Principles of Archaeological Stratigraphy*, 2d ed. Orlando, Fla.: Academic Press.

Harris, M. 1968. *The Rise of Anthropological Theory*. New York: Crowell.

Harrold, F. B., and R. A. Eve, eds. 1987. *Cult Archaeology and Creationism*. Iowa City: University of Iowa Press.

Hassan, F. 1981. *Demographic Archaeology*. Orlando, Fla.: Academic Press.

Hatch, E. 1973. *Theories of Man and Culture*. New York: Columbia University Press.

Hawkes, J. G. 1983. *The Diversity of Crop Plants*. Cambridge, Mass.: Harvard University Press.

Hayden, B., ed. 1979. *Lithic Wear Analysis*. Orlando, Fla.: Academic Press.

———, ed. 1987. *Lithic Studies Among the Contemporary Highland Maya*. Tucson: University of Arizona Press.

Heizer, R. F. 1969. "The Archaeology of Great Basin Coprolites," in D. R. Brothwell and E. Higgs, eds., *Science in Archaeology*, pp. 244–250. London: Thames and Hudson.

Hess, J. L. 1974. *The Grand Acquisitors*. Boston: Houghton Mifflin.

Hesse, B., and P. Wapnish. 1985. *Animal Bone Archaeology*. Washington, D.C.: Taraxacum.

Hester, T. R. 1981. "CRM Publication: Dealing with Reality," *Journal of Field Archaeology* 8: 493–496.

Hester, T. R., and R. F. Heizer. 1973. *Bibliography of Archaeology, Volume 1: Lithic Technology and Petrography*. Reading, Mass.: Addison-Wesley.

Hester, T. R., H.J. Shafer, and R. F. Heizer. 1987. *Field Methods in Archaeology*. Palo Alto, Calif.: Mayfield.

Heyerdahl, T. 1950. *The Kon-Tiki Expedition*. New York: Random House.

Hietala, H., ed. 1984. *Intersite Spatial Analysis in Archaeology*. Cambridge: Cambridge University Press.

Hill, J. N. 1970. *Broken K Pueblo: Prehistoric Social Organization in the American Southwest*. Tucson: University of Arizona Press.

———, ed. 1977. *Explanation of Prehistoric Change*. Albuquerque: University of New Mexico Press.

Hill, J. N., and J. D. Gunn, eds. 1977. *The Individual in Prehistory*. Orlando, Fla.: Academic Press.

Hinde, R. 1987. *Individuals, Relationships, and Culture*. Cambridge: Cambridge University Press.

Hodder, I., ed. 1978. *Simulation Studies in Archaeology*. Cambridge: Cambridge University Press.

————, ed. 1982a. *Symbolic and Structural Archaeology*. Cambridge: Cambridge University Press.

————, ed. 1982b. *Symbols in Action*. Cambridge: Cambridge University Press.

————. 1984. *The Present Past*. New York: Pica.

————. 1985. "Postprocessual Archaeology," *Advances in Archaeological Method and Theory* 8: 1–26.

Hodder, I., and M. Hassell. 1972. "The Non-random Spacing of Romano-British Walled Towns," *Man* 6: 391–407.

Hodder, I., G. L. Isaac, and N. Hammond. 1981. *Patterns in the Past: Studies in Honor of David Clarke*. Cambridge: Cambridge University Press.

Hodder, I, and C. Orton. 1976. *Spatial Analysis in Archaeology*. Cambridge: Cambridge University Press.

Hogg, A. H. A. 1980. *Surveying for Archaeologists and Other Professionals*. New York: St. Martin's Press.

Hole, F. 1984. "Analysis of Structure and Design in Prehistoric Ceramics," *World Archaeology* 16: 326–347.

Hole, F., K. V. Flannery, and J. A. Neely. 1969. *The Prehistory and Human Ecology of the Deh Luran Plain*. Ann Arbor: University of Michigan Museum of Anthropology.

Hole, F., and R. F. Heizer. 1973. *An Introduction to Prehistoric Archaeology*, 3d ed. Fort Worth: Holt, Rinehart and Winston.

Hole, F., and M. Shaw. 1967. "Computer Analysis of Chronological Seriation," *Rice University Studies* 53 (3).

Holly, G. A., and T. A. Del Bene. 1981. "An Evaluation of Keeley's Microwear Approach," *Journal of Archaeological Science* 8: 337–352.

Holmes, W. H. 1919. *Handbook of Aboriginal American Antiquities, Part 1: Introductory: The Lithic Industry*. Bureau of American Ethnology, Bulletin No. 60.

Hope-Simpson, R. 1984. "The Analysis of Data from Surface Surveys," *Journal of Field Archaeology* 11: 115–116.

Horne, P. D. 1985. "A Review of the Evidence of Human Endoplasm in the Pre-Columbian New World Through the Study of Coprolites," *Journal of Field Archaeology* 12: 299–310.

Howard, H., 1929. "The Avifauna of Emeryville Shellmound," *University of California Publications in Zoology* 23: 378–383.

Hudson, C. M. 1979. *Black Drink: A Native American Tea*. Athens: University of Georgia Press.

Hudson, K. 1982. *World Industrial Archaeology*. Cambridge: Cambridge University Press.

Huss-Ashmore, R., A. H. Goodman, and G. J. Armelagos. 1982. "Nutritional Inference from Paleopathology," *Advances in Archaeological Method and Theory* 5: 395–476.

Huxley, T. 1863. *Man's Place in Nature*. London: Macmillan.

INAH. 1980. *Atlas Arquelógico del Estado de Yucatán.* Mexico City.

Ingersoll, D., J. E. Yellen, and W. Macdonald, eds. 1977. *Experimental Archaeology.* New York: Columbia University Press.

Isaac, G. L. 1983. "Review: *Ancient Men and Modern Myths,"American Antiquity* 48: 416–419.

Isaac, G. L., and B. Isaac. 1989. *The Archaeology of Human Origins.* Cambridge: Cambridge University Press.

Isaac, G. L., and E. McKown, eds. 1977. *Human Origins: Louis Leakey and the East African Evidence.* Menlo Park, Calif.: Benjamin.

Iversen, J. 1941. "Land Occupation in Denmark's Stone Age," *Danmarks Geologiske Undersøgelse* 66: 70–76.

Jarman, H. N., A. J. Legge, and J. A. Charles. 1972. "Retrieval of Plant Remains from Archaeological Sites by Froth Flotation," in E. S. Higgs, ed., *Essays in Economic Prehistory,* pp. 39–48. Cambridge: Cambridge University Press.

Jennings, J. D. 1966. *Glen Canyon: A Summary.* Salt Lake City: University of Utah Anthropological Papers.

———. 1973. *The Prehistory of North America,* 2d ed. New York: McGraw-Hill.

———, ed. 1983. *Ancient Native Americans,* 2d ed. New York: Freeman.

Jett, S., and P. B. Moyle. 1986. "The Exotic Origins of Fishes Depicted in Prehistoric Mimbres Pottery from New Mexico," *American Antiquity* 51: 688–720.

Jewell, P. A., and G. W. Dimbleby. 1966. "The Experimental Earthwork at Overton Down, Wiltshire, England," *Proceedings of the Prehistoric Society* 32: 313–342.

Jochim, M. A. 1979. "Breaking Down the System: Recent Ecological Approaches in Archaeology," *Advances in Archaeological Method and Theory* 2: 77–119.

Johnson, E., and others. 1977. "Archaeology and Native Americans," in C. R. McGimsey and H. A. Davis, eds., *The Management of Archaeological Resources,* pp. 90–96. Washington, D.C.: Society for American Archaeology.

Johnson, F., and others. 1942. "The Boylston Street Fishweir," *Papers of the R. S. Peabody Foundation for Archaeology* 2.

Johnson, L. 1968. *Item Seriation as an Aid for Elementary Scale and Cluster Analysis.* Eugene: University of Oregon.

Johnson, L. L. 1978. "A History of Flint Knapping Experimentation, 1838–1976," *Current Anthropology* 19: 337–372.

Jones, P. R. 1980. "Experimental Butchery with Modern Stone Tools and Its Relevance for Palaeolithic Archaeology," *World Archaeology* 12: 153–165.

Joukowsky, M. 1981. *Complete Manual of Field Archaeology.* Englewood Cliffs, N.J.: Prentice-Hall.

Judge, J. W., and J. Dawson. 1972. "Paleo-Indian Settlement Technology in New Mexico," *Science* 176: 1210–1216.

Kaczor, M. J., and J. Weymouth. 1981. "Magnetic Prospecting: Results of the 1980 Field Season at the Toltec Site, 3LN42," *Proceedings of the South-East Archaeological Conference* 24: 118–123.

Keatinge, R. W., ed. 1988. *Peruvian Prehistory.* Cambridge: Cambridge University Press.

Keeley, L. H. 1980. *Experimental Determination of Stone Tool Uses.* Chicago: University of Chicago Press.

Keene, D. 1985. *Survey of Medieval Winchester.* Oxford: Clarendon Press.

Keesing, R. M. 1974. "Theories of Culture," *Annual Review of Anthropology* 3: 71–97.

Kelley, J. H., and M. P. Hanan. 1988. *Archaeology and the Methods of Science.* Albuquerque: University of New Mexico Press.

Kelso, W. M. 1984. *Kingsmill Plantation.* Orlando, Fla.: Academic Press.

———. 1986. "Mulberry Row: Slave Life at Thomas Jefferson's Monticello," *Archaeology* 39 (5): 28–35.

Kemp, B. 1989. *Ancient Egypt: Anatomy of a Civilization.* London: Routledge and Kegan Paul.

Kent, S. 1984. *Analyzing Activity Areas: An Ethnoarchaeological Study of the Use of Space.* Albuquerque: University of New Mexico Press.

Kidder, A. V. 1924. *An Introduction to the Study of Southwestern Archaeology.* New Haven, Conn.: Yale University Press.

Killingley, J. S. 1981. "Seasonality of Mollusk Collecting Determined from 0–18 Profiles of Midden Shells," *American Antiquity* 46: 152–158.

King, C., T. Blackburn, and E. Chandonet. 1968. "The Archaeological Inventory of Three Sites on the Century Ranch, Western Los Angeles County, California," *California Archaeological Survey Annual Report* 10: 12–161.

King, M. E. 1978. "Analytical Methods and Prehistoric Textiles," *American Antiquity* 43: 89–96.

King, T. F. 1971. "Resolving a Conflict of Values in American Archaeology," *American Antiquity* 36: 255–262.

———. 1983. "Professional Responsibility in Public Archaeology," *Annual Review of Anthropology* 12: 143–164.

King, T. F., P. Hickman, and G. Berg, eds. 1977. *Anthropology in Historic Preservation: Caring for Culture's Clutter.* Orlando, Fla.: Academic Press.

Kirch, P. V. 1980. "The Archaeological Study of Adaptation: Theoretical and Methodological Issues," *Advances in Archaeological Method and Theory* 3: 101–155.

———. 1984. *The Evolution of Polynesian Chiefdoms.* Cambridge: Cambridge University Press.

Kirk, R. 1974. *Hunters of the Whale.* New York: Morrow.

Klein, J., and others. 1982. "Calibration of Radiocarbon Dating: Tables Based on the Consensus Data of the Workshop on Calibrating the Radiocarbon Time Scale," *Radiocarbon* 22: 103–153.

Klein, R. G., 1969. *Man and Culture in the Late Pleistocene.* New York: Harper and Row.

———. 1977. "Environment and Subsistence of Prehistoric Man in the Southern Cape Province, South Africa," *World Archaeology* 5: 249–284.

———. 1983. "The Stone Age Prehistory of South Africa," *Annual Review of Anthropology* 12: 25–48.

Klein, R. G., and K. Cruz-Uribe. 1983. "The Computation of Ungulate Age (Mortality) Profiles from Dental Crown Heights," *Paleobiology* 9: 70–78.

———. 1984. *The Analysis of Animal Bones from Archaeological Sites.* Chicago: University of Chicago Press.

Klepinger, L. L. 1984. "Nutritional Assessment from Bone," *Annual Review of Anthropology* 13: 75–96.

Kluckhohn, C. 1940. "The Conceptual Structure in Middle American Studies," in A. M. Tozzer, ed., *The Maya and Their Neighbors.* Norwalk, Conn.: Appleton and Lang.

———. 1943. "Bronislaw Malinowski, 1884–1942," *Journal of American Folklore* 56: 208–219.

Knudson, R. 1986. "Contemporary Cultural Resource Management," in D. J. Meltzer, D. D. Fowler, and J. A. Sabloff, eds., *American Archaeology Past and Future,* pp. 395–413. Washington, D.C.: Smithsonian Institution Press.

Kramer, C. 1982. *Village Ethnoarchaeology: Rural Iran in Archaeological Perspective.* Orlando, Fla.: Academic Press.

———. 1983. "Ceramic Ethnoarchaeology," *Annual Review of Anthropology* 14: 77–102.

Krause, R. A. 1985. *The Clay Sleeps: An Ethnoarchaeological Study of Three African Potters.* Birmingham: University of Alabama Press.

Kristiansen, K. 1988. "The Black and the Red: Shanks and Tilley's Programme for a Radical Archaeology," *Antiquity* 62: 473–482.

Kroeber, A. L., and C. Kluckhohn. 1952. *Culture: A Critical Review of Concepts and Definitions.* Cambridge, Mass.: Harvard University, Peabody Museum of American Archaeology and Ethnology.

Kroeber, T. 1965. *Ishi in Two Worlds.* Berkeley: University of California Press.

Kuhn, T. S. 1970. *The Structure of Scientific Revolutions,* 2d ed. Chicago: University of Chicago Press.

Kurten, B. 1968. *Pleistocene Mammals in Europe.* Hawthorne, N.Y.: Aldine.

Lamberg-Karlovsky, C. C. 1970. *Excavations at Tepe Yahya, Iran, 1967–1969.* Cambridge, Mass.: American School of Prehistoric Research.

———. 1975. "Third Millennium Modes of Exchange and Modes of Production," in J. A. Sabloff and C. C. Lamberg-Karlovsky, eds., *Early Civilization and Trade,* pp. 341–368. Albuquerque: University of New Mexico Press.

Lambrecht, F. L. 1964. "Aspects of the Evolution and Ecology of Tsetse Flies and Trypanosomiasis in the Prehistoric African Environment," *Journal of African History* 5: 1–24.

Larsen, C. S. 1987. "Bioarchaeological Interpretations of Subsistence Economy and Behavior from Human Skeletal Remains," *Advances in Archaeological Method and Theory* 10: 27–56.

Laville, H., and others. 1980. *Rockshelters of the Perigord.* New York: Academic Press.

Layard, A. H. 1849. *Nineveh and Its Remains.* London: John Murray.

Layton, R. 1989. *Who Needs the Past?* London: Unwin Hyman.

Leakey, L. S. B. 1951. *Olduvai Gorge, 1931–1951.* Cambridge: Cambridge University Press.

———. 1971. *Olduvai Gorge,* vol. 1. Cambridge: Cambridge University Press.

Leakey, M. D. 1973. *Olduvai Gorge,* vol. 3. Cambridge: Cambridge University Press.

Le Blanc, S. A. 1975. "Microseriation: A Method for Fine Chronologic Differentiation," *American Antiquity* 40: 22–30.

Lee, R. B. 1979. *The !Kung San.* Cambridge: Cambridge University Press.

Lee, R. B., and I. De Vore, eds. 1976. *Kalahari Hunter-Gatherers.* Cambridge, Mass.: Harvard University Press.

Lee, R. F. 1970. *The Antiquities Act of 1906.* Washington, D.C.: National Park Service.

Legge, A. J., and P. A. Rowley-Conwy. 1987. "Gazelle Killing in Stone Age Syria," *Scientific American* 257: 76–83.

Leone, M. P. 1978. "Time in American Archaeology," in C. L. Redman, and others, eds., *Social Archaeology,* pp. 25–36. Orlando, Fla.: Academic Press.

———. 1982. "Childe's Offspring," in I. Hodder, ed., *Structural Archaeology,* pp. 179–184. Cambridge: Cambridge University Press.

———. 1986. "Symbolic, Structural, and Critical Archaeology," in D. J. Meltzer, D. D. Fowler, and J. A. Sabloff, eds., *American Archaeology Past and Future,* pp. 415–438. Washington, D.C.: Smithsonian Institution Press.

Leone, M. P., and P. B. Potter. 1984. *Archaeological Annapolis.* Annapolis, Md.: Historical Annapolis Inc.

Lepper, B. T. 1983. "Fluted Point Distributional Patterns in the Eastern United States," *Midcontinental Journal of Archaeology* 8: 269–285.

Leroi-Gourhan, A. 1967. *Treasures of Prehistoric Art.* New York: Abrams.

Leute, U. 1987. *Archaeometry.* Weinheim, West Germany: VCH.

Lewarch, D. E., and M. J. O'Brien. 1981. "The Expanding Role of Surface Assemblages in Archaeological Research," *Advances in Archaeological Method and Theory* 4: 297–343.

Lewis-Williams, J. D. 1981. *Believing and Seeing: Symbolic Meanings in Southern San Rock Paintings.* Orlando, Fla.: Academic Press.

Lewis-Williams, J. D., and J. H. N. Loubser. 1986. "Deceptive Appearances: A Critique of Southern African Rock Art Studies," *Advances in World Archaeology* 5: 203–290.

Libby, W. F. 1955. *Radiocarbon Dating.* Chicago: University of Chicago Press.

Lightfoot, K. G., and R. M. Cerrato. 1988. "Prehistoric Shellfish Exploitation in Coastal New York," *Journal of Field Archaeology* 15: 141–149.

Limbrey, S. 1972. *Soil Science in Archaeology.* New York: Seminar Press.

Lipe, W. D. 1970. "A Conservation Model for American Archaeology," *Kiva* 3: 213–243.

Lloyd, S. 1963. *Mounds of the Near East.* Hawthorne, N.Y.: Aldine.

Loew, J. J., and M. J. C. Walker. 1985. *Reconstructing Quaternary Environments.* White Plains, N.Y.: Longman.

Longacre, W. 1970. *Archaeology as Anthropology.* Tucson: University of Arizona Press.

————. 1974. "Kalinga Pottery Making: The Evolution of a Research Design," in M. J. Leaf, ed., *Frontiers of Anthropology,* pp. 51–67. New York: Van Nostrand.

————. 1981. "CRM Publication: A Review Essay," *Journal of Field Archaeology* 8: 487–490.

Lubbock, Sir John (Lord Avebury). 1865. *Prehistoric Times.* London: Williams and Norgate.

Lumley, H. de. 1969. "A Palaeolithic Camp at Nice," *Scientific American* 220: 42–50.

Lyman, R. L. 1982. "Archaeofaunas and Subsistence Studies," *Advances in Archaeological Method and Theory* 5: 332–394.

Lyons, T. R., ed. 1981. *Remote Sensing: Multispectral Analysis of Cultural Resources in Chaco Canyon and Bandelier National Momument.* Washington, D.C.: National Park Service.

Lyons, T. R., and T. Avery. 1977. *Remote Sensing: A Handbook for Archaeologists and Cultural Resource Managers.* Washington, D.C.: National Park Service.

MacNeish, R. S., ed. 1970. *The Prehistory of the Tehuacán Valley,* vol. 3. Austin: University of Texas Press.

————. 1978. *The Science of Archaeology?* North Scituate, Mass.: Duxbury Press.

Macquilty, W. 1965. *Abu Simbel.* London: Macmillan.

Madsen, D. P., and J. F. O'Connell, eds. 1982. *Man and Environment in the Great Basin.* Washington, D.C.: Society for American Archaeology.

Mangelsdorf, P. C. 1974. *Corn: Its Origin, Evolution, and Improvement.* Cambridge, Mass.: Belknap Press.

Marcus, J. 1976. "The Size of the Early Mesoamerican Village," in K. V. Flannery, ed., *The Early Mesoamerican Village,* pp. 79–88. Orlando, Fla.: Academic Press.

Marquardt, W. H. 1978. "Advances in Archaeological Seriation," *Advances in Archaeological Method and Theory* 1: 28–64.

Marsden, B. M. 1984. *Pioneers of Prehistory.* Ormskirk, England: Heskett.

Marshack, A. 1972. *The Roots of Civilization.* New York: McGraw-Hill.

Martin, P. S., and F. T. Plog. 1973. *The Archaeology of Arizona.* Garden City, N.Y.: Doubleday.

Martin, P. S., and Klein, R. G., eds. 1984. *A Pleistocene Revolution.* Tucson: University of Arizona Press.

Matson, F. R. 1965. *Ceramics and Man.* New York: Viking Penguin.

McBryde, I., ed. 1985. *Who Owns the Past?* Melbourne, Australia: Oxford University Press.

McEwen, B. G., and J. M. Mitchum. 1984. "Indian and European Acculturation in the Eastern United States as a Result of Trade," *North American Archaeologist* 5: 271–285.

McGimsey, C. 1972. *Public Archaeology.* New York: Seminar Press.

McGimsey, C., and H. Davis. 1977. *The Management of Archaeological Resources.* Washington, D.C.: National Park Service.

McHargue, G., and M. Roberts. 1977. *A Field Guide to Conservation Archaeology in North America.* Philadelphia: Lippincott.

McKern, W. C. 1939. "The Midwestern Taxonomic System as an Aid to Archaeological Culture Study," *American Antiquity* 4: 301–313.

McManamon, F. P. 1984. "Discovering Sites Unseen," *Advances in Archaeological Method and Theory* 7: 223–292.

McNairn, B. 1980. *The Theory and Method of V. Gordon Childe.* Edinburgh: Edinburgh University Press.

Meehan, B. 1982. *Shell Bed to Shell Midden.* Canberra: Australian Institute of Aboriginal Studies.

Meeke, N. D., and others. 1982. "Gloss and Use-Wear Traces on Flint Sickles and Similar Phenomena," *Journal of Archaeological Science* 9: 317–340.

Meighan, C. W. 1983. "Obsidian Dating in California: Theory and Practice," *American Antiquity* 48: 600–609.

Mellaart, J. 1975. *The Neolithic of the Near East.* London: Thames and Hudson.

Meltzer, D. J. 1983. "The Antiquity of Man and the Development of American Archaeology," *Advances in Archaeological Method and Theory* 6: 1–51.

Meltzer, D. J., D. D. Fowler, and J. A. Sabloff, eds., 1986. *American Archaeology Past and Future.* Washington, D.C.: Smithsonian Institution Press.

Messenger, P. M., ed. 1989. *The Ethics of Collecting Cultural Property.* Albuquerque: University of New Mexico Press.

Meyer, K. 1977. *The Plundered Past.* 2d ed. Baltimore: Pelican.

Michael, H. N., and E. K. Ralph, eds. 1971. *Dating Techniques for the Archaeologist.* Cambridge, Mass.: MIT Press.

Michels, J. W. 1973. *Dating Methods in Archaeology.* Orlando, Fla.: Academic Press.

Michels, J. W., and R. Tsong. 1980. "Obsidian Hydration," *Advances in Archaeological Method and Theory* 3: 233–271.

Milanich, J. T., and Milbrath, S., eds. 1987. *First Encounters.* Gainesville: University of Florida Press.

Miller, D., and C. Tilley, eds. 1983. *Ideology, Power, and Prehistory.* Cambridge: Cambridge University Press.

Millon, R. 1973. *The Teotihuacán Map: Urbanization of Teotihuacán, Mexico,* vol. 1. Austin: University of Texas Press.

———. 1981. "Teotihuacán: City, State, and Civilization," in J. A. Sabloff, ed., *Supplement to the Handbook of Middle American Indians,* pp. 198–243. Austin: University of Texas Press.

Mithen, S. 1989. "Evolutionary Theory and Postprocessual Archaeology," *Antiquity* 63: 483–494.

———. 1990. *Thoughtful Foragers: A Study of Prehistoric Decision Making.* Cambridge: Cambridge University Press.

Monks, G. C. 1981. "Seasonality Studies," *Advances in Archaeological Method and Theory* 4: 177–240.

Moore, A. M. T. 1983. "Agricultural Origins in the Near East: A Model for the 1980s," *World Archaeology* 14: 224–236.

———. 1985. "Neolithic Societies in the Near East," *Advances in Archaeological Method and Theory* 4: 1–69.

———. 1989. "The Transition from Foraging to Farming in Southwest Asia: Present Problems and Future Directions," in D. Harris and G. Hillman, eds., *Foraging and Farming*, pp. 620–631. London: Unwin Hyman.

Moore, J. A., and K. S. Keene, eds. 1983. *Archaeological Hammers and Theories*. Orlando, Fla.: Academic Press.

Morgan, J. W. W. 1975. "The Preservation of Timber," *Timber Grower* 8: 55.

Morgan, L. 1877. *Ancient Society*. Fort Worth: Holt, Rinehart and Winston.

Morlan, R. E. 1978. "Early Man in Northern Yukon Territory: Perspectives as of 1977," in A. L. Bryan, ed., *Early Man in America*, pp. 78–95. Edmonton, Canada: Archaeological Research International.

Mortillet, G. de. 1867. *Promenades Préhistoriques à l' Exposition Universelle*. Paris.

Movius, H. L. 1974. "The Abri Pataud Program of the French Upper Paleolithic in Retrospect," in G. R. Willey, ed., *Archaeological Researches in Retrospect*. Cambridge, Mass.: Winthrop.

———. 1977. *Excavation of the Abri Pataud, Les Eyzies (Dordogne)*. Cambridge, Mass.: Peabody Museum.

Muckelroy, K. 1978. *Maritime Archaeology*. Cambridge: Cambridge University Press.

Mueller, J. A. 1974. *The Use of Sampling in Archaeological Survey*. Washington, D.C.: U.S. Government Printing Office.

———, ed. 1975. *Sampling in Archaeology*. Tucson: University of Arizona Press.

Muhly, J. D. 1980. "The Bronze Age Setting," in J. D. Muhly and T. A. Wertime, eds., *The Coming of the Age of Iron*, pp. 25–68. New Haven, Conn.: Yale University Press.

Muhly, J. D., and T. A. Wertime, eds. 1980. *The Coming of the Age of Iron*. New Haven, Conn.: Yale University Press.

Murdock, G. P. 1949. *Social Structure*. New York: Macmillan.

Nance, J. D. 1983. "Regional Sampling in Archaeological Survey: The Statistical Perspective," *Advances in Archaeological Method and Theory* 6: 289–356.

Nash, C. H. 1968. *Residence Mounds: An Intermediate Middle Mississippian Settlement Pattern*. Memphis, Tenn.: Memphis State University Anthropological Research Center.

Nelson, N. C. 1914. *Pueblo Ruins of the Galisteo Basin, New Mexico*. New York: Macmillan.

Netting, R., and others, eds. 1984. *Households*. Berkeley: University of California Press.

Nilsson, T. 1983. *The Pleistocene*. Stuttgart, West Germany: Ferdinand Enke.

Nir, D. 1983. *Man: A Geomorphological Agent.* Boston: Reidd.

Noël Hume, I. 1969. *Historical Archaeology.* New York: Knopf.

———. 1982. *Martin's Hundred.* New York: Knopf.

Oakley, K. P. 1969. *Frameworks for Dating Fossil Man,* 2d ed. Hawthorne, N.Y.: Aldine.

O'Connell, J. 1975. *The Prehistory of Surprise Valley.* Ramona, Calif.: Ballena Press.

Odell, G. H., and Cowan, F. 1986. "Experiments with Spears and Arrows on Animal Targets," *Journal of Field Archaeology* 13: 195–212.

Odell, G. H., and F. Odell-Vereechea. 1980. "Verifying the Reliability of Lithic Use-Wear: The Lower Power Approach," *Journal of Field Archaeology* 7: 87–120.

Olin, J. S., and A. D. Franklin, eds. 1982. *Archaeological Ceramics.* Washington, D.C.: Smithsonian Institution Press.

Olsen, S. J. 1978. *Fish, Amphibian, and Reptile Remains from Archaeological Sites.* Cambridge, Mass.: Peabody Museum.

———. 1979a. "Osteologically, What Constitutes an Early Domesticated Animal?" *Advances in Archaeological Method and Theory* 2: 175–197.

———. 1979b. *Osteology for the Archaeologist,* rev. ed. Cambridge, Mass.: Peabody Museum.

Omer-Cooper, J. 1966. *The Zulu Aftermath.* London: Heinemann.

Organ, R. M. 1968. *Design for Scientific Conservation of Antiquities.* Washington, D.C.: Smithsonian Institution Press.

Orme, B. 1979. *Thermoluminescence Techniques in Archaeology.* Oxford: Clarendon Press.

———. 1981. *Anthropology for Archaeologists.* Ithaca, N.Y.: Cornell University Press.

Ortner, D. J., and W. G. J. Putschar. 1982. *Identification of Pathological Conditions in Human Remains.* Washington, D.C.: Smithsonian Institution Press.

O'Shea, J. M. 1984. *Mortuary Variability: An Archaeological Investigation.* Orlando, Fla.: Academic Press.

Pallottino, M. 1968. *The Meaning of Archaeology.* New York: Abrams.

Parmalee, P., and W. E. Klippel. 1974. "Freshwater Mollusca as a Prehistoric Food Resource," *American Antiquity* 39: 421–434.

Parrington, M. 1983. "Remote Sensing," *Annual Review of Anthropology* 12: 105–124.

Parson, J. A., and B. J. Price. 1971. *Mesoamerican Trade and Its Role in the Emergence of Civilization.* Berkeley: University of California Press.

Paul, A., and S. A. Turpin. 1986. "The Ecstatic Shaman Theme of Paracas Textiles," *Archaeology* 39 (5): 20–27.

Pavlish, L. A., and E. B. Banning. 1980. "Revolutionary Developments in Carbon 14 Dating," *American Antiquity* 45: 290–296.

Pearsall, D. 1989. *Paleoethnobotany: A Handbook of Procedures.* Orlando, Fla.: Academic Press.

Petersen, J. B., and others. 1984. "Netting Technology and the Antiquity of Fish Exploitation in Eastern North America," *Midcontinental Journal of Archaeology* 9: 199–226.

Petrie, F. 1889. "Sequences in Prehistoric Remains," *Journal of the Royal Anthropological Institute* 29: 295–301.

Phillips, P. 1988. "Traceology (Microwear) Studies in the USSR," *World Archaeology* 19: 111–125.

Phillipson, D. W. 1969. "Gunflint Manufacture in North-western Zambia," *Antiquity* 43: 301–304.

Piggott, S. 1965. *Ancient Europe.* Hawthorne, N.Y.: Aldine.

————. 1979. *Ruins in a Landscape.* Edinburgh: Edinburgh University Press.

Piperno, D. R. 1988. *Phytolith Analysis: An Archaeological and Geological Perspective.* Orlando, Fla.: Academic Press.

Pires-Ferreira, J. 1976. "Obsidian Exchange in Formative Mesoamerica," in K. V. Flannery, ed., *The Early Mesoamerican Village,* pp. 293–305. Orlando, Fla.: Academic Press.

Pitcher, J. R., and others. 1984. "A 7272-Year Tree-Ring Chronology for Western Europe," *Nature* 312: 150.

Plenderleith, H. J., and A. E. A. Werner. 1973. *The Conservation of Antiquities and Works of Art,* 2d ed. London: Oxford University Press.

Plog, F. T., ed. 1974. *The Study of Prehistoric Change.* Orlando, Fla.: Academic Press.

————. 1978. "Cultural Resource Management and the 'New Archaeology,' " in C. L. Redman, and others, eds., *Social Archaeology,* pp. 421–429. Orlando, Fla.: Academic Press.

Plog, F. T., and W. Wait, eds. 1982. *The San Juan Tomorrow.* Santa Fe, N.M.: National Park Service.

Plog, S. 1976a. "Measurement of Prehistoric Interaction Between Communities," in K. V. Flannery, ed., *The Early Mesoamerican Village,* pp. 255–272. Orlando, Fla.: Academic Press.

————. 1976b. "Relative Efficiencies of Sampling Techniques for Archaeological Surveys," in K. V. Flannery, ed., *The Early Mesoamerican Village,* pp. 136–158. Orlando, Fla.: Academic Press.

————. 1980. *Stylistic Variation in Prehistoric Ceramics.* New York: Cambridge University Press.

————. 1983. "Analysis of Style in Artifacts," *Annual Review of Anthropology* 12: 125–142.

Polyani, K. 1975. "Traders and Trade," in J. A. Sabloff and C. C. Lamberg-Karlovsky, eds., *Early Civilization and Trade,* pp. 133–154. Albuquerque: University of New Mexico Press.

Pope, S. T. 1923. *Hunting with the Bow and Arrow.* San Francisco: James H. Barry.

Prott, L., and P. J. O'Keefe. 1984. *Law and the Cultural Heritage.* Abingdon, England: Professional Books.

Purdy, B., ed. 1988. *Wet Site Archaeology*. Caldwell, N.J.: Telford Press.

Raab, L. M., and A. C. Goodyear. 1984. "Middle Range Theory in Archaeology: A Critical Review of Origins and Applications," *American Antiquity* 49: 255–268.

Rahtz, P. A. 1974. *RESCUE Archaeology*. Baltimore: Pelican.

Rapoport, A. 1968. "Foreword," in W. Buckley, ed., *Modern Systems Research for the Behavioral Sciences*. Hawthorne, N.Y.: Aldine.

Rappaport, R. A. 1968. *Pigs for the Ancestors*. New Haven, Conn.: Yale University Press.

———. 1971. "Ritual, Sanctity, and Cybernetics," *Current Anthropology* 73: 59–76.

Rathje, W. H. 1970. "Socio-political Implications of Maya Lowland Burials," *World Archaeology* 1: 359–374.

———. 1971. "The Origin and Development of Lowland Classic Mayan Civilization," *American Antiquity* 36: 275–285.

———. 1974. "The Garbage Project: A New Way of Looking at the Problems of Archaeology," *Archaeology* 27: 236–241.

———. 1979. "Modern Material Culture Studies," *Advances in Archaeological Method and Theory* 2: 1–38.

Rathje, W. H., and W. McCarthy. 1977. "Regularity and Variability in Contemporary Garbage," in S. A. South, ed., *Method and Theory in Historical Archaeology*. Orlando, Fla.: Academic Press.

Rathje, W. H., and C. K. Ritenbaugh, eds. 1984a. *Household Refuse Analysis: Theory, Method, and Applications in Social Science*. Newbury Park, Calif.: Sage.

———, eds. 1984b. "House Refuse Analysis," *American Behavioral Scientist* 28: 47–55.

Rathje, W. H., and M. B. Schiffer. 1982. *Archaeology*. Orlando, Fla.: Harcourt Brace Jovanovich.

Raven-Hart, R. 1967. *Before Van Riebeeck*. Cape Town: Struik.

Read, D. W., and S. A. Le Blanc. 1978. "Descriptive Statistics, Covering Laws, and Theories in Archaeology," *Current Anthropology* 19: 307–335.

Redman, C. L., ed. 1973. *Research and Theory in Current Archaeology*. New York: Wiley Interscience.

———. 1974. *Archaeological Sampling Strategies*. Reading, Mass.: Addison-Wesley.

———. 1978a. "Mesopotamian Urban Ecology: The Systemic Context of the Emergence of Urbanism," in C. L. Redman, and others, eds., *Social Archaeology*, pp. 329–348. Orlando, Fla.: Academic Press.

———. 1978b. "Multivariate Artifact Analysis: A Basis for Multidimensional Interpretations," in C. L. Redman, and others, eds., *Social Archaeology*, pp. 159–192. Orlando, Fla.: Academic Press.

———. 1978c. *The Rise of Civilization*. New York: Freeman.

————. 1985. *Qsar es-Seghir: An Archaeological View of Medieval Life.* Orlando, Fla.: Academic Press.

————. 1987. "Surface Collection, Sampling, and Research Design: A Retrospective," *American Antiquity* 52: 249–265.

Redman, C. L., and others, eds. 1978. *Social Archaeology.* Orlando, Fla.: Academic Press.

Redman, C. L., and P. J. Watson. 1970. "Systematic, Intensive Surface Collection," *American Antiquity* 35: 279–291.

Reed, C. A., ed. 1977. *The Origins of Agriculture.* The Hague: Mouton.

Renfrew, A. C. 1971. *Before Civilization.* New York: Knopf.

————. 1975. *The Emergence of Civilization.* London: Methuen.

————. 1979. "Transformations," in A. C. Renfrew and K. L. Cooke, eds., *Transformations: Mathematical Applications to Cultural Change,* pp. 3–44. Orlando, Fla.: Academic Press.

————. 1983. "Divided We Stand: Aspects of Archaeology and Information," *American Antiquity* 48: 3–16.

Renfrew, A. C., and A. Shennan, eds. 1982. *Ranking, Resources, and Exchange.* Cambridge: Cambridge University Press.

Renfrew, A. C., J. E. Dixon, and J. R. Cann. 1966. "Obsidian and Early Cultural Contact in the Near East," *Proceedings of the Prehistoric Society* 32: 1–29.

Renfrew, J. 1973. *Paleoethnobotany.* London: Methuen.

Reynolds, B. 1967. *The Material Culture of the Gwembe Tonga.* Manchester, England: Manchester University Press.

Reynolds, P. J. 1979. *Iron Age Farm.* London: British Museum.

Rice, P. C. 1981. "Prehistoric Venuses: Symbols of Motherhood or Womanhood," *Journal of Anthropological Research* 3: 402–414.

Rice, P. C., and A. L. Peterson. 1985. "Cave Art and Bones: Exploring the Interrelationships," *American Anthropologist* 87: 94–100.

Rice, P. M. 1984. *Pots and Potters: Current Approaches in Ceramic Archaeology.* Los Angeles: UCLA Institute of Archaeology.

Rice, P. M. 1987. *Pottery Analysis: A Sourcebook.* Chicago: University of Chicago Press.

Richards, A. I. 1937. *Land, Labor, and Diet Among the Bemba of Northern Rhodesia.* Oxford: Clarendon Press.

Riley, C. L. 1971. *Man Across the Sea.* Austin: University of Texas Press.

Riley, D. N. 1987. *Air Photography and Archaeology.* London: Duckworth.

Rindos, D. 1983. *The Origins of Agriculture: An Evolutionary Perspective.* Orlando, Fla.: Academic Press.

Roper, D. C. 1979. "The Method and Theory of Site Catchment Analysis: A Review," *Advances in Archaeological Method and Theory* 2: 120–142.

Rosen, A. M. 1986. *Cities of Clay.* Chicago: University of Chicago Press.

Rouse, I. 1939. *Prehistory in Haiti: A Study in Method.* New Haven, Conn.: Yale University Press.

————. 1972. *Introduction to Prehistory: A Systematic Approach.* New York: McGraw-Hill.

Rovner, I. 1983. "Plant Opal Phytolith Research: Major Advances in Archaeobotanical Research," *Advances in Archaeological Method and Theory* 6: 225–266.

Rudenko, S. I. 1961. "The Ancient Cultures of the Bering Sea and the Eskimo Problem," in *Arctic Institute of North America: Anthropology of the North, Translations from Russian Sources,* vol. 1, pp. 163–164. Toronto: University of Toronto Press.

————. 1970. *Frozen Tombs of Siberia: The Pazyryk Burials of Iron Age Horsemen.* Trans. by M. W. Thompson. Berkeley: University of California Press.

Rye, O. S. 1981. *Pottery Technology.* Washington, D.C.: Taraxacum.

Sabloff, J. A. 1975. *Excavations at Seibal: Ceramics.* Cambridge, Mass.: Harvard University, Peabody Museum of American Archaeology and Ethnology.

————, ed. 1981. *Simulation in Archaeology.* Albuquerque: University of New Mexico Press.

————. 1989. *The Cities of Ancient Mexico.* London: Thames and Hudson.

Sabloff, J. A., and C. C. Lamberg-Karlovsky, eds. 1975. *Early Civilization and Trade.* Albuquerque: University of New Mexico Press.

Sabloff, J. A., and W. L. Rathje, eds. 1975. *A Study of Pre-Columbian Commercial Systems: The 1972–1973 Seasons at Cozumel, Mexico.* Cambridge, Mass.: Harvard University, Peabody Museum.

Sackett, J. 1966. "Quantitative Analysis of Upper Paleolithic Stone Tools," *American Anthropologist* 68: 356–394.

————. 1977. "The Meaning of Style in Archaeology," *American Antiquity* 43: 369–382.

————. 1981. "From de Mortillet to Bordes: A Century of French Upper Paleolithic Research," in G. Daniel, ed., *Towards a History of Archaeology,* pp. 85–99. London: Thames and Hudson.

————. 1982. "Approaches to Style in Lithic Archaeology," *Journal of Anthropological Archaeology* 1: 59–112.

Sahlins, M., and E. Service, eds. 1960. *Evolution and Culture.* Ann Arbor: University of Michigan Press.

Salmon, M. 1978. "What Can Systems Theory Do for Archaeology?" *American Antiquity* 43: 174–183.

————. 1982. *The Philosophy of Archaeology.* Orlando, Fla.: Academic Press.

Sanders, W. T., J. R. Parsons, and R. S. Santley. 1979. *The Basin of Mexico: Ecological Processes in the Evolution of a Civilization.* Orlando, Fla.: Academic Press.

Sanders, W. T., and B. J. Price. 1968. *Mesoamerica: Evolution of a Civilization.* New York: Random House.

Sanders, W. T., and D. Webster. 1978. "Unilinealism, Multilinealism, and the Evolution of Complex Societies," in C. L. Redman, and others, eds., *Social Archaeology,* pp. 249–302. Orlando, Fla.: Academic Press.

Scarre, C., ed. 1988. *Past Worlds: The Times Atlas of Archaeology.* London: Times Books.

Schele, L., and M. E. Miller. 1986. *The Blood of Kings: Dynasty and Ritual in Maya Art.* Fort Worth: Kimbell Art Museum.

Schiffer, M. B. 1976. *Behavioral Archaeology.* Orlando, Fla.: Academic Press.

———. 1979. "A Preliminary Consideration of Behavioral Change," in A. C. Renfrew, ed., *Transformations: Mathematical Approaches to Culture Change,* pp. 353–368. Orlando, Fla.: Academic Press.

———. 1983. "Towards the Identification of Site Formation Processes," *American Antiquity* 48: 675–706.

———. 1987. *Site Formation Processes of the Archaeological Record.* Albuquerque: University of New Mexico Press.

Schiffer, M. B., and G. J. Gumerman, eds. 1977. *Conservation Archaeology.* Orlando, Fla.: Academic Press.

Schiffer, M. B., and J. H. House. 1976. *The Cache River Archaeological Project.* Fayetteville: Arkansas Archaeological Survey.

———. 1977. "Cultural Resource Management and Archaeological Research: The Cache Project," *Current Anthropology* 18: 43–68.

Schiffer, M. B., A. P. Sullivan, and T. C. Klinger. 1978. "The Design of Archaeological Surveys," *World Archaeology* 10: 1–28.

Schuyler, R. L., ed. 1978. *Historical Archaeology: A Guide to Substantive and Theoretical Contributions.* Farmingdale, N.Y.: Baywood.

Scudder, T. 1962. *The Ecology of the Gwembe Tonga.* Manchester, England: Manchester University Press.

Selkirk, A., and W. Selkirk. 1970. "Winchester: The Brooks," *Current Archaeology* 2: 250–255.

Semenov, S. A. 1964. *Prehistoric Technology.* Trans. by M. W. Thompson. London: Cory, Adams, and MacKay.

Service, E. 1971. *Primitive Social Organization.* New York: Random House.

Sever, T., and J. Wiseman. 1985. *Remote Sensing and Archaeology: Potential for the Future.* Picayune, Miss.: NASA Earth Sciences Laboratory.

Shackleton, N. J., and N. D. Opdyke. 1973. "Oxygen Isotope and Paleomagnetic Stratigraphy of Equatorial Pacific Ocean Core V28-238," *Quaternary Research* 3: 38–55.

Shackley, M. L. 1975. *Archaeological Sediments.* New York: Wiley.

———. 1985. *Environmental Archaeology.* London: Batsford.

Shanks, M., and C. Tilley. 1987a. *Reconstructing Archaeology: Theory and Practice.* Cambridge: Cambridge University Press.

————. 1987b. *Social Theory and Archaeology.* Albuquerque: University of New Mexico Press.

————. 1989. "Archaeology into the 1990s." *Norwegian Archaeological Review* 22: 1–54.

Sharer, R. J., and W. Ashmore. 1987. *Archaeology: Discovering the Past.* Palo Alto, Calif.: Mayfield.

————. 1988. *Discovering Our Past.* Palo Alto, Calif.: Mayfield.

Shaw, T. 1960. "Early Smoking Pipes in Africa, Europe, and America," *Journal of the Royal Anthropological Institute* 90: 272–305.

————. 1969. "Tree Felling by Fire," *Antiquity* 43: 52.

Shawcross, F. C. 1967. "Prehistoric Diet and Economy on a Coastal Site at Galatea Bay, New Zealand," *Proceedings of the Prehistoric Society* 33(7): 125–130.

Sheets, P. D., and G. R. Muto. 1972. "Pressure Blades and Total Cutting Edge," *Science* 175: 632–634.

Shennan, S. 1988. *Quantifying Archaeology.* Orlando, Fla.: Academic Press.

Shepard, A. O. 1971. *Ceramics for the Archaeologist,* 2d ed. Washington, D.C.: Smithsonian Institution.

Sheridan, A., and G. Bailey. 1981. *Economic Archaeology.* Oxford: British Archaeological Reports.

Shipman, P. 1981. *Life History of a Fossil: An Introduction to Taphonomy and Paleoecology.* Cambridge, Mass.: Harvard University Press.

Shipman, P., and J. Rose. 1983. "Early Hominid Hunting, Butchering, and Carcass Processing Behaviors: Approaches to the Fossil Record," *Journal of Anthropological Archaeology* 2: 57–98.

Sillen, A. and others. 1989. "Chemistry and Paleodietery Research: No More Easy Answers," *American Antiquity* 54: 504–512.

Silverberg, R. 1968. *The Mound Builders of Ancient America.* New York: New York Graphic Society.

Slotkin, J. S., ed. 1965. *Readings in Early Anthropology.* New York: Viking Penguin.

Smith, B. D. 1974. "Middle Mississippian Exploitation of Animal Populations: A Predictive Model," *American Antiquity* 39: 274–291.

Smith, B. D. 1986. "The Archaeology of the Southeastern United States: From Dalton to de Soto, 10,500–500 B.P.," *Advances in World Archaeology* 5: 1–92.

Smith, E. G. 1911. *The Ancient Egyptians.* London: Macmillan.

Smith, P. E. L. 1966. *Le Solutréen en France.* Paris: Payot.

Snodgrass, A. M. 1987. *An Archaeology of Greece: The Present State and Future Scope of a Discipline.* Berkeley: University of California Press.

Snow, D. 1976. *The North American Indians.* New York: Viking Penguin.

Soffer, O. 1985. *The Upper Palaeolithic of the Central Russian Plain.* Orlando, Fla.: Academic Press.

Sollas, W. J. 1911. *Ancient Hunters.* London: Macmillan.

Soren, D., and J. James. 1988. *Kourion: The Search for a Lost Roman City.* Garden City, N.Y.: Anchor/Doubleday.

South, S. 1972. "Evolution and Horizon as Revealed in Ceramic Analysis in Historical Archaeology," *Conference on Historic Sites Archaeology Papers* 6(2): 71–106.

————, ed. 1977. *Method and Theory in Historical Archaeology.* Orlando, Fla.: Academic Press.

South, S., and R. Widmer. 1977. "A Subsurface Strategy for Archaeological Reconnaissance," in S. South, ed., *Method and Theory in Historical Archaeology.* Orlando, Fla.: Academic Press.

Spaulding, A. C. 1953. "Statistical Techniques for the Study of Artifact Types," *American Antiquity* 18: 305–313.

————. 1960a. "The Dimensions of Archaeology," in G. E. Dole and R. L. Carneiro, eds., *Essays in the Science of Culture in Honor of Leslie A. White,* pp. 437–456. New York: Crowell.

————. 1960b. "Statistical Description and Comparison of Artifact Assemblages," in R. F. Heizer and S. F. Cook, eds., *Quantitative Methods in Archaeology,* pp. 60–92. New York: Viking Penguin.

————. 1973. "Archaeology in the Active Voice: The New Anthropology," in C. L. Redman, ed., *Research and Theory in Current Archaeology,* pp. 337–354. New York: Wiley Interscience.

Spencer, H. 1855. *Social Statistics.* London: Macmillan.

Speth, J. D. 1983. *Bison Kills and Bone Counts: Decision Making by Ancient Hunters.* Chicago: University of Chicago Press.

Spooner, B., ed. 1972. *Population Growth: Anthropological Implications.* Cambridge, Mass.: MIT Press.

Spriggs, M., ed. 1984. *Marxist Perspectives in Archaeology.* Cambridge: Cambridge University Press.

Spuhler, J. N. 1985. "Anthropology, Evolution, and 'Scientific Creationism'," *Annual Review of Anthropology* 14: 103–133.

Stark, B. L. 1984. "An Ethnoarchaeological Study of a Mexican Pottery Industry," *Journal of Northwest Archaeology* 6(2): 4–14.

Stark, B. L., and D. L. Young. 1981. "Linear Nearest Neighbor Analysis," *American Antiquity* 46: 284–300.

Starki, E. 1982. "Advances in Urban Archaeology," *Advances in Archaeological Method and Theory* 5: 97–150.

Steffy, R. 1985. "The Kyrenia Ship: A Preliminary Report," *American Journal of Archaeology* 125: 1–36.

Stein, J. K. 1983. "Earthworm Activity: A Source of Potential Disturbances of Archaeological Sediments," *American Antiquity* 48: 277–289.

————. 1987. "Deposits for Archaeologists," *Advances in Archaeological Method and Theory* 11: 337–398.

Stephens, J. L. 1841. *Incidents of Travel in Central America, Chiapas, and Yucatán.* New York: Harper and Row.

Steponaitis, V. P., and J. P. Brain. 1976. "A Portable Differential Proton Magnetometer," *Journal of Field Archaeology* 3: 455–463.

Steward, J. 1938. *Basin-Plateau Aboriginal Sociopolitical Groups.* Washington, D.C.: Smithsonian Institution.

———. 1955. *A Theory of Culture Change.* Urbana: University of Illinois Press.

Steward, J., and F. M. Setzler, eds. 1977. *Evolution and Ecology.* Urbana: University of Illinois Press.

Stimmell, Carole, and others. 1982. "Indian Pottery from the Mississippi Valley: Coping with Bad Raw Materials," in J. S. Olin and A. D. Franklin, eds., *Archaeological Ceramics,* pp. 219–228. Washington, D.C.: Smithsonian Institution Press.

Stirland, A. 1987. *Human Bones in Archaeology.* Aylesbury, England: Shire Press.

Stocking, G. 1968. *Race, Culture, and Evolution.* New York: Free Press.

Stoltman, J. B., and D. A. Barreis. 1983. "The Evolution of Human Ecosystems in the Eastern and Central United States," in H. E. Wright, ed., *Late Quarternary Environments of the United States,* pp. 252–268. Minneapolis: University of Minnesota Press.

Strong, W. D. 1935. *An Introduction to Nebraska Archaeology.* Washington, D.C.: Smithsonian Institution.

Struever, S. 1968. "Woodland Subsistence-Settlement Systems in the Lower Illinois Valley," in S. R. Binford and L. R. Binford, eds., *New Perspectives in Archaeology,* pp. 285–312. Hawthorne, N.Y.: Aldine.

———. 1971. "Comments on Archaeological Data Requirements and Research Strategy," *American Antiquity* 36: 10.

Struever, S., and F. A. Holton. 1979. *Koster.* Garden City, N.Y.: Anchor/Doubleday.

Struever, S., and G. L. Houart. 1972. "An Analysis of the Hopewell Interaction Sphere," *Anthropological Papers of the University of Michigan* 46: 47–79.

Suess, H. E. 1965. "Secular Variations of the Cosmic-Ray-Produced Carbon 14 in the Atmosphere and Their Interpretations," *Journal of Geophysical Research* 70: 23–31.

Sullivan, A. P., and K. C. Rozen. 1985. "Debitage Analysis and Archaeological Interpretation," *American Antiquity* 50: 755–779.

Summers, R. 1969. *Ancient Mining in Rhodesia.* Salisbury: National Museums of Rhodesia.

Swanson, E., ed. 1975. *Lithic Technology: Making and Using Stone Tools.* Hawthorne, N.Y.: Aldine.

Taylor, R. E., and C. W. Meighan, eds. 1978. *Chronologies in New World Archaeology.* Orlando, Fla.: Academic Press.

Taylor, W. W. 1948. *A Study of Archaeology.* Menasha, Wis.: American Anthropological Association.

Terrell, J. 1967. "Galatea Bay: The Excavation of a Beach-Stream Midden Site on Ponju Island in the Hauraki Gulf, New Zealand," *Transactions of the Royal Society of New Zealand* 2(3): 31–70.

Thomas, D. H. 1969. "Regional Sampling in Archaeology: A Pilot Great Basin Research Design," *UCLA Archaeological Survey Annual Report* 11: 87–100.

———. 1973. "An Empirical Test for Steward's Model of Great Basin Settlement Patterns," *American Antiquity* 38: 155–176.

———. 1974. *Predicting the Past.* Fort Worth: Holt, Rinehart and Winston.

———. 1978. "The Awful Truth About Statistics in Archaeology," *American Antiquity* 43: 231–244.

———. 1983a. *The Archaeology of Monitor Valley,* vols. 1 and 2. New York: Anthropological Papers of the American Museum of Natural History.

———. 1983b. "On Steward's Models of Shoshonean Sociopolitical Organization: A Great Bias in the Basin," in E. Tooker, ed., *The Development of Political Organization in Native North America,* pp. 56–68. Washington, D.C.: American Ethnological Society.

———. 1986. "Contemporary Hunter-Gatherer Archaeology in America," in D. J. Meltzer, D. D. Fowler, and J. A. Sabloff, eds., *American Archaeology Past and Future,* pp. 237–276. Washington, D.C.: Smithsonian Institution Press.

———. 1988. *Archaeology,* 2d ed. Forth Worth: Holt, Rinehart and Winston.

———. 1989. *Refiguring Anthropology.* Prospect Heights, Ill.: Waveland Press.

Thomas, M. N., and M. K. Lewis. 1961. *Eva: An Archaic Site.* Knoxville: University of Tennessee Press.

Thompson, J. E. S. 1972. *Maya Hieroglyphs Without Tears.* London: British Museum.

Thompson, M. W. 1977. *General Pitt-Rivers.* London: Moonraker Press.

Thompson, R. H. 1956. "The Subjective Element in Archaeological Inference," *Southwestern Journal of Anthropology* 12: 327–332.

Thomsen, C. J. 1836. *Ledestraad til Nordisk Oldkyndighed.* Trans. by Lord Ellesmere in 1848 as *A Guide to the Northern Antiquities.* Copenhagen.

Tite, M. S. 1972. *Methods of Physical Examination in Archaeology.* Orlando, Fla.: Academic Press.

Tobias, P. V. 1971. *Olduvai Gorge,* vol. 2. Cambridge: Cambridge University Press.

Torrence, R. 1986. *Production and Exchange of Stone Tools.* Cambridge: Cambridge University Press.

Toth, N. 1985. "The Oldowan Reassessed: A Close Look at Early Stone Artifacts," *Journal of Archaeological Science* 12: 101–120.

Townsend, W. H. 1969. "Stone and Steel Tool Use in a New Guinea Society," *Ethnology* 8: 199–205.

Traling, D. H. 1983. *Paleomagnetism: Principles and Applications in Geology, Geophysics, and Archaeology.* London: Chapman and Hall.

Trigger, B. G. 1968a. *Beyond History: The Methods of Prehistory.* Forth Worth: Holt, Rinehart and Winston.

———. 1968b. "The Determination of Settlement Patterns," in K. C. Chang, ed., *Settlement Archaeology,* pp. 53–78. Palo Alto, Calif.: National Press.

———. 1971. "Archaeology and Ecology," *World Archaeology* 2: 321–336.

———. 1978. *Time and Tradition*. Edinburgh: Edinburgh University Press.

———. 1980. *Gordon Childe: Revolutions in Archaeology*. London: Thames and Hudson.

———. 1984a. "Alternative Archaeologies: Nationalist, Colonialist, Imperialist," *Man* 19: 355–370.

———. 1984b. "Archaeology at the Crossroads: What's New," *Annual Review of Anthropology* 13: 275–300.

———. 1985. "The Past as Power: Anthropology and the American Indian," in I. McBryde, ed., *Who Owns the Past?* pp. 11–40. Melbourne, Australia: Oxford University Press.

———. 1986. "Prehistoric Archaeology and American Society," in D. J. Meltzer, D. D. Fowler, and J. A. Sabloff, eds., *American Archaeology Past and Future*, pp. 187–216. Washington, D.C.: Smithsonian Institution Press.

———. 1989. *A History of Archaeological Interpretation*. Cambridge: Cambridge University Press.

Tringham, R. 1971. *Hunters, Fishers, and Farmers of Southeastern Europe, 6000 to 300 B.C.* London: Hutchinson.

Turner, B. L., and P. D. Harrison. 1983. *Pulltrouser Swamp: Ancient Maya Habitat, Agriculture, and Settlement in Northern Belize*. Austin: University of Texas Press.

Tylecote, R. F. 1972. *Metallurgy in Antiquity*. London: Edward Arnold.

———. 1980. "Furnaces, Crucibles, and Slags," in J. D. Muhly and T. A. Wertime, eds., *The Coming of the Age of Iron*, pp. 183–228. New Haven, Conn.: Yale University Press.

Tylor, E. B. 1871. *Primitive Culture*. London: John Murray.

Ucko, P. J. 1962. "The Interpretation of Prehistoric Anthropomorphic Figurines," *Journal of the Royal Anthropological Institute* 92: 38–54.

Ucko, P. J., and G. W. Dimbleby, eds. 1969. *The Domestication and Exploitation of Plants and Animals*. London: Duckworth.

United States Department of the Interior. 1976. "National Register of Historic Places: Criteria for Statewide Surveys and Plans," *Code of Federal Regulations*, Title 36, Chapter 1, Part 60. Washington, D.C.: GPO.

Valliant, C. G., and J. C. Vogel. 1978. "^{13}C Content of Human Collagen as a Measure of Prehistoric Diet in Woodland North America," *Nature* 276: 815–816.

Van der Merwe, N. J., 1982. "Carbon Isotopes, Photosynthesis, and Archaeology," *American Scientist* 70: 596–606.

Vaughan, C. J. 1986. "Ground Penetrating Radar Surveys Used in Archaeological Investigations," *Geoscience* 51: 595–605.

Vaughan, P. 1985. *Use-Wear Analysis of Flaked Stone Tools*. Tucson: University of Arizona Press.

Villa, P. 1982. "Conjoinable Pieces and Site Formation Processes," *American Antiquity* 47: 276–290.

———. 1983. *Terra Amata and the Middle Pleistocene Archaeological Record of Southern France*. Berkeley: University of California Press.

Villa, P., and J. Courtin. 1983. "The Interpretation of Stratified Sites: A View from Underground," *Journal of Archaeological Science* 10: 267–281.

Vinnecombe, P. 1960. "A Fishing Scene from the Tsoelike River, Southwestern Basutoland," *South African Archaeological Bulletin* 15: 15–19.

Vita-Finzi, C. 1978. *Archaeological Sites in Their Setting.* London: Thames and Hudson.

Vita-Finzi, C., and E. G. Higgs. 1970. "Prehistoric Ecology in the Mount Carmel Area of Palestine: Site Catchment Analysis," *Proceedings of the Prehistoric Society* 36: 1–37.

Vogt, E. Z. 1967. *A Maya Community in the Highlands of Chiapas.* Cambridge, Mass.: Belknap Press.

———, ed. 1974. *Aerial Photography in Anthropological Field Research.* Cambridge, Mass.: Harvard University Press.

Waselkov, G. 1987. "Shellfish Gathering and Shell Midden Archaeology," *Advances in Archaeological Method and Theory* 10: 112–167.

Watson, P. J. 1974. *Archaeology of the Mammoth Cave Area.* Orlando, Fla.: Academic Press.

———. 1976. "In Pursuit of Prehistoric Subsistence: A Comparative Account of Some Contemporary Flotation Techniques," *Mid-continental Journal of Archaeology* 1: 77–100.

Watson, P. J., S. A. Le Blanc, and C. L. Redman. 1984. *Archaeological Explanation: The Scientific Method in Archaeology.* New York: Columbia University Press.

Watson, R. A. 1976. "Inference in Archaeology," *American Antiquity* 41: 58–66.

Wauchope, R. 1972. *Lost Tribes and Sunken Continents.* Chicago: University of Chicago Press.

Webb, W. S. 1939. *An Archaeological Survey of Wheeler Basin on the Tennessee River in Northern Alabama.* Washington, D.C.: Smithsonian Institution, Bureau of American Ethnology.

Webster, D., and N. Gordon. 1988. "Household Remains of the Humblest Maya," *Journal of Field Archaeology* 15: 169–180.

Wells, C. 1964. *Bones, Bodies, and Disease.* London: Thames and Hudson.

Wendorf, F. 1979. "Changing Values in Archaeology," *American Antiquity* 44: 641–643.

Wendorf, F., and others. 1968. *The Prehistory of Nubia.* Dallas: Southern Methodist University Press.

Wenke, R. J. 1981. "Explaining the Evolution of Cultural Complexity: A Review," *Advances in Archaeological Method and Theory* 4: 979–1028.

Weymouth, J. W. 1986. "Geophysical Methods of Archaeological Site Survey," *Advances in Archaeological Method and Theory* 10: 311–396.

Whalen, M. A. 1976. "Zoning Within an Early Formative Community in the Valley of Oaxaca," in K. V. Flannery, ed., *The Early Mesoamerican Village,* pp. 75–78. Orlando, Fla.: Academic Press.

———. 1981. "Excavations at Santo Domingo Tomaltepec: Evolution of a Formative Community in the Valley of Oaxaca, Mexico," *Memoirs of the University of Michigan Museum of Anthropology* 6: 12–25.

Whallon, R. A., and J. A. Brown, eds. 1982. *Essays in Archaeological Typology.* Evanston, Ill.: Center for American Archaeology.

Wheat, J. B. 1972. *The Olsen-Chubbock Site: A Paleo-Indian Bison Kill.* Washington, D.C.: Smithsonian Institution, Society for American Archaeology.

Wheatley, P. 1971. *The Pivot of the Four Quarters.* Hawthorne, N.Y.: Aldine.

Wheeler, A., and A. K. G. Jones. 1989. *Fishes.* Cambridge: Cambridge University Press.

Wheeler, R. E. M. 1943. *Maiden Castle.* London: Society of Antiquaries.

———. 1954. *Archaeology from the Earth.* Oxford: Clarendon Press.

———. 1967. *The Indus Civilization.* Cambridge: Cambridge University Press.

Wheeler, T. S., and R. Madden. 1980. "Metallurgy and Ancient Man," in J. D. Muhly and T. A. Wertime, eds., *The Coming of the Age of Iron,* pp. 99–126. New Haven, Conn.: Yale University Press.

White, E. M., and L. A. Hannus, 1983. "Chemical Weathering of Bones in Archaeological Soils," *American Antiquity* 48: 316–332.

White, J. P. 1974. *The Past Is Human.* New York: Taplinger.

White, J. P., and J. O'Connell. 1982. *A Prehistory of Australia, New Guinea, and Sahul.* Orlando, Fla.: Academic Press.

White, J. P., and D. H. Thomas. 1972. "What Mean These Stones?" in D. L. Clarke, ed., *Models in Archaeology,* pp. 275–308. London: Methuen.

White, L. 1949. *The Evolution of Culture.* New York: McGraw-Hill.

White, R. 1986. *Dark Caves, Bright Images.* New York: American Museum of Natural History.

White, T. 1953. "Observations on the Butchery Techniques of Some Aboriginal Peoples," *American Antiquity* 19: 160–164.

Wildeson, L. E. 1982. "The Study of Impacts on Archaeological Sites," *Advances in Archaeological Method and Theory* 5: 51–96.

Willey, G. R. 1953. *Prehistoric Settlement Patterns in the Virú Valley, Peru.* Washington, D.C.: Smithsonian Institution, Bureau of American Ethnology.

———. 1962. "The Early Great Styles and the Rise of the Pre-Columbian Civilizations," *American Anthropologist* 64: 1–14.

———. 1966. *An Introduction to American Archaeology, Volume 1: North America.* Englewood Cliffs, N.J.: Prentice-Hall.

———. 1971. *An Introduction to American Archaeology, Volume 2: Middle and South America.* Englewood Cliffs, N.J.: Prentice-Hall.

———. ed. 1974. *Archaeological Researches in Retrospect.* Cambridge, Mass.: Winthrop.

Willey, G. R., and P. Phillips. 1958. *Method and Theory in American Archaeology.* Chicago: University of Chicago Press.

Willey, G. R., and J. A. Sabloff. 1980. *A History of American Archaeology,* 2d ed. New York: Freeman.

Wilson, D. R. 1983. *Air Photo Interpretation for Archaeologists.* New York: St. Martin's Press.

Wilson, R., and G. Loyola, eds. 1982. *Rescue Archaeology: Papers from the First New World Conference on Rescue Archaeology.* Washington, D.C.: Preservation Press.

Winter, M. C. 1976. "The Archaeological Household Cluster in the Valley of Oaxaca," in K. V. Flannery, ed., *The Early Mesoamerican Village,* pp. 25–30. Orlando, Fla.: Academic Press.

Winterhalder, B., and E. A. Smith, eds. 1981. *Hunter-Gatherer Foraging Strategies.* Chicago: University of Chicago Press.

Winters, H. D. 1969. *The Riverton Culture.* Urbana: Illinois Archaeological Survey.

Wolf, E. 1984. *Europe and the People Without History.* Berkeley: University of California Press.

Wolfman, D. 1984. "Geomagnetic Dating Methods in Archaeology," *Advances in Archaeological Method and Theory* 7: 363–458.

Wood, J. J. 1978. "Optimal Location in Settlement Space: A Model for Describing Location Strategies," *American Antiquity* 43: 258–270.

Wood, M. 1985. *The Search for Troy.* New York: BBC Publications.

Wood, W. R., and D. L. Johnson. 1978. "A Survey of the Disturbance Processes in Archaeological Site Formation," *Advances in Archaeological Method and Theory* 1: 112–146.

Woodbury, J. C. 1980. "The First Archaeological Appearance of Iron," in J. D. Muhly and T. A. Wertime, eds., *The Coming of the Age of Iron,* pp. 69–98. New Haven, Conn.: Yale University Press.

Woolley, C. L. 1943. *Ur Excavations. Volume 2, The Royal Cemetery.* Philadelphia: University of Pennsylvania Museum.

———. 1954. *Excavations at Ur.* New York: Barnes and Noble.

Worsaae, J. J. A. 1843. *Danmarks Oldtid.* Copenhagen.

Wright, T. 1852. "Wanderings of an Antiquary: Part VII," *Gentleman's Magazine,* October, p. 569.

Wylie, A. 1985. "The Reaction Against Analogy," *Advances in Archaeological Method and Theory* 8: 63–111.

———. 1988. *The New Archaeology: Tensions in Theory and Practice.* Orlando, Fla.: Academic Press.

Yellen, J. E. 1977. *Archaeological Approaches to the Present: Models for Predicting the Past.* Orlando, Fla.: Academic Press.

Zeist, W. V., and W. A. Casparie, eds. 1983. *Plants and Ancient Man: Studies in Paleoethnobotany.* Rotterdam: A. Balkema.

Zubrow, E. 1976. *Demographic Anthropology: Quantitative Approaches.* Albuquerque: University of New Mexico.

Illustration Credits

Chapter 1: *Fig. 1.2,* The Bettmann Archive; *Fig. 1.3,* Courtesy of the Peabody Museum, Harvard University; *Fig. 1.4,* The Metropolitan Museum of Art, bequest of Joseph H. Durkee, gift of Darius Mills, and gift of C. Ruxton Love, by Exchange, 1972 (1972.11.10); *Fig. 1.5,* Hester A. Davis, "Is There a Future for the Past?" *Archaeology* 24:4. Copyright © 1971, Archaeological Institute of America; *Fig. 1.6,* George Holton/Photo Researchers, Inc.; *Fig. 1.7,* Courtesy of the Colonial Williamsburg Foundation; *Fig. 1.8,* Courtesy of Dr. Braidwood and the Oriental Institute, University of Chicago.

Chapter 2: *Fig. 2.1,* Reproduced by permission of the Werner Forman Archive; *Fig. 2.2,* George Gerster/Photo Researchers, Inc.; *Fig. 2.4,* Courtesy of the Royal Anthropological Institute of Great Britain and Ireland. Redrawn from "The Swanscombe Skull: A Survey of Research on a Pleistocene Site" (Occasional Paper No. 20, Fig. 26.3); *Fig. 2.5,* The Bettmann Archive; *Fig. 2.6,* Robert Lackenbach/Black Star; *Fig. 2.7,* Photo by J. Oster. Courtesy of the Musée de l'Homme, Paris.

Chapter 3: *Fig. 3.1,* DeVore/Anthro-Photo.

Chapter 4: *Fig. 4.1,* By courtesy of Electa Editrice, Milano; *Fig. 4.2,* Richard Lee/Anthro-Photo; *Fig. 4.3,* Courtesy of the Trustees of the British Museum; *Fig. 4.5,* Courtesy of the Society of Antiquaries of London; *Fig. 4.6,* From Deetz, *Invitation to Archaeology,* 1967. Reprinted by permission of Natural History Press/Doubleday & Company, Inc., New York; *Fig. 4.7,* Courtesy of the University Museum, University of Pennsylvania.

Chapter 5: *Fig. 5.3,* Redrawn from John Alexander, *The Directing of Archaeological Excavations,* Fig. 16a, London: A & C Black (Publishers) Ltd., 1970. After Kenneth P. Oakley, *Frameworks for Dating Fossil Man,* Chicago: Aldine Publishers and London: Weidenfeld & Nicholson, 1964; *Fig. 5.4,* From John Alexander, *The Directing of Archaeological Excavations,* Fig. 36, London: A & C Black (Publishers) Ltd., 1970; *Fig. 5.5,* After Sir John Evans from J. G. D. Clark, *Archaeology and Society,* Fig. 18, London: Methuen and Company, 1939. Reprinted by Barnes and Noble, New York; *Fig. 5.7,* From James Deetz, *Invitation to Archaeology,* illustrated by Eric G. Engstrom. Copyright © 1967 by James Deetz. Reproduced by permission of Doubleday & Company, Inc.; *Fig. 5.8,* Adapted from R. S. MacNeish, *The Prehistory of the Tehuacan Valley,* Vol. 3, Figs. 2 and 3. Copyright © 1970 by The University of Texas Press, Austin; *Fig. 5.9,* Reprinted with permission of Macmillan Publishing Company from *Foundations of Archaeology* by Jason W. Smith. Copyright © 1976 by Jason W. Smith; *Fig. 5.10,* From N. J. Shackleton and N. D. Opdyke, "Oxygen Isotope and Paleomagnetic Stratigraphy of Equatorial Pacific Ocean Core V28-238," *Quaternary Research* 3: 38–55. Reprinted by permission; *Fig. 5.11,* From O. Soffer, *The Upper Paleolithic of the Central Russian Plain,* Fig. 2.67, San Diego: Academic Press, 1985. Reprinted with permission; *Fig. 5.12,* After J. G. D. Clark, *Star Carr,* Fig. 27b, New York: Cambridge University Press, 1954. Used by permission; *Fig. 5.13,* Adapted from Kenneth P. Oakley, *Frameworks for Dating Fossil Man,* Fig. 7, Chicago: Aldine Publishers and London: Weidenfeld & Nicholson, 1964; *Fig. 5.14,* After J. G. D. Clark, *Star Carr,* Fig. 27b, New York: Cambridge University Press, 1954. Used by permission.

Chapter 6: *Fig. 6.2,* By permission of Phillip V. Tobias, University of Witwatersrand, Johannesburg, South Africa; *Fig. 6.3,* Courtesy of the University Museum, University of Pennsylvania; *Fig. 6.4,* Adapted from D. R. Brotherwell and Eric Higgs, *Science in Archaeology,* London: Thames & Hudson Ltd.; *Fig. 6.5,* After Joseph W. Michels, *Dating Methods in Archaeology,* Fig. 40, New York: Seminar Press, 1973; *Fig. 6.6,* Courtesy of the University Museum, University of Pennsylvania; *Fig. 6.7,* Redrawn from Ivor Noël Hume, *The Artifacts of Colonial America,* Fig. 9. Copyright © 1969 by Ivor Noël Hume. Reprinted by permission of the publisher, Alfred A. Knopf, Inc., and Curtis Brown Ltd.

Chapter 7: *Fig. 7.1,* Courtesy of the Danish National Museum; *Fig. 7.2,* John Coles, Somerset Levels Project; *Fig. 7.3,* Ruth Kirk with Richard D. Daugherty, *Hunters of the Whale,* 1974, New

York: William Morrow & Company; *Fig. 7.4,* Ruth Kirk with Richard D. Daugherty, *Hunters of the Whale,* 1974, New York: William Morrow & Company; *Fig. 7.5,* Dr. Owen Beattie, University of Alberta, Edmonton.

Chapter 9: *Fig. 9.1,* Courtesy of Lesley Newhart; *Fig. 9.2,* Courtesy of University of Colorado Museum, Joe Ben Wheat photo; *Fig. 9.3,* Courtesy of the Peabody Museum, Harvard University; *Fig. 9.4,* Michael Moseley/Anthro-Photo; *Fig. 9.5,* Cambridge University Collection. Copyright reserved; *Fig. 9.6,* Courtesy of Aero Service Division, Western Geophysical Company of America; *Fig. 9.7,* Courtesy of Fondazione Lerici Prospezioni Archeologiche, Rome; *Fig. 9.8,* From John Coles, *Field Archaeology in Britain,* Fig. 7. Copyright © 1972 Methuen & Company, London; *Fig. 9.9,* Courtesy of Norman Hammond; *Fig. 9.10,* Courtesy of Arizona State Museum.

Chapter 10: *Fig. 10.1,* Photograph by Barny Cuniliffe. Courtesy of Oxford University, England; *Fig. 10.2,* Courtesy of the Center for American Archaeology, Kampsville, Illinois; *Fig. 10.3,* Redrawn from Stuart Streuver and James A. Brown, "The Organization of Archaeological Research: An Illinois Example," Fig. 1, p. 278 in Charles L. Redman, *Research and Theory in Current Archaeology,* New York: John Wiley and Sons, 1973. Also courtesy of the Center for American Archaeology, 1911 Ridge Avenue, P.O. Box 1499, Chicago, Illinois 60204; *Fig. 10.4,* Courtesy of the University Museum, University of Pennsylvania; *Fig. 10.5,* Courtesy of Sir Mortimer Wheeler and the Society of Antiquaries of London; *Fig. 10.6,* Courtesy of the Historic St. Augustine Preservation Board; *Fig. 10.7,* Courtesy of J. A. Tuck, Memorial University of Newfoundland; *Fig. 10.8,* Redrawn from Ivor Noël Hume, *Historical Archaeology,* Fig. 10. Copyright © 1968 by Ivor Noël Hume. Redrawn by permission of the author, the publisher, Alfred A. Knopf, Inc., and Curtis Brown Ltd.; *Fig. 10.10,* Courtesy of the Peabody Museum, Harvard University; *Fig. 10.11,* Photo by A. L. Smith. Courtesy of the Peabody Museum, Harvard University; *Fig. 10.12,* Carl W. Blegan and Marion Rawson, *The Palace of Nestor at Pylor in Western Mesenia,* Vol. 1, Part 2, Fig. 9. Plates copyright © 1966 Princeton University Press. Reproduced by permission of Princeton University Press and the University of Cincinnati; *Fig. 10.13,* Redrawn from Ivor Noël Hume, *Historical Archaeology,* Fig. 15. Copyright © 1968 by Ivor Noël Hume. Redrawn by permission of the author, the publisher, Alfred A. Knopf, Inc., and Curtis Brown Ltd.; *Fig. 10.14,* Courtesy of Mesa Verde National Park/National Park Service; *Fig. 10.15,* Courtesy of the Society of Antiquaries, London; *Fig. 10.16,* Copyright © H. T. Bunn, University of California at Berkeley; *Fig. 10.17,* Courtesy of the R. S. Peabody Foundation for Archaeology, Andover, Mass.; *Fig. 10.18,* Wilfred Shawcross; *Fig. 10.20,* Courtesy of the Winchester Excavations Committee, Winchester, England.

Chapter 11: *Fig. 11.1,* Courtesy of the Society of Antiquaries, London; *Fig. 11.2,* Courtesy of Lowie Museum of Anthropology, University of California at Berkeley; *Fig. 11.3,* From James Deetz, *Invitation to Archaeology,* illustrated by Eric G. Engstrom. Copyright © 1967 by James Deetz. Reproduced by permission of Doubleday & Company, Inc.; *Fig. 11.4,* After J. G. D. Clark, *Star Carr,* Fig. 35, New York: Cambridge University Press, 1954. Used by permission; *Fig. 11.5,* Reproduced by permission of the Trustees of the British Museum (Natural History); *Fig. 11.6,* Courtesy of Lesley Newhart.

Chapter 12: *Fig. 12.1,* Redrawn from M. D. Leakey, *Olduvai Gorge,* Vol. III, New York: Cambridge University Press, 1971. Used by permission; *Fig. 12.2,* Courtesy of the University of Chicago Press. From Kenneth P. Oakley, *Man the Tool-maker,* 6th edition, published by the British Museum of Natural History, 1972, p. 10, Fig. 4; *Fig. 12.4, Life Nature Library/Early Man.* Copyright © 1965, 1973 by Time, Inc.; *Fig. 12.5,* Courtesy of Pitt-Rivers Museum, Oxford, England; *Fig. 12.6,* From J. M. Coles and E. S. Higgs, *The Archaeology of Early Man,* London: Faber and Faber Ltd. Reprinted by permission of the publisher; *Fig. 12.7,* Adapted from F. Bordes, *The Old Stone Age,* Fig. 34, London: Weidenfeld & Nicholson, 1968; *Fig. 12.8a and 12.8b,* Adapted from F. Bordes, *The Old Stone Age,* Figs. 54 and 55, London: Weidenfeld & Nicholson, 1968; *Fig. 12.8d,* After G. H. Bushnell, *The First Americans: The Pre-Columbian Civilizations,* Fig. 12, London: Thames & Hudson Ltd. and New York: McGraw-Hill. Copyright © 1968 by Thames & Hudson and McGraw-Hill; *Fig. 12.9,* Courtesy of Robert Edwards, Aboriginal Arts Board; *Fig. 12.10,* Photo by Wyatt Davis. Courtesy Museum of New Mexico (Negative No. 44191); *Fig. 12.11,* Photo by Carmelo Guadagno. Courtesy of the Museum of the American Indian, Heye Foundation, New York; *Fig. 12.12,* Courtesy of the Art Institute of Chicago; *Fig. 12.14,* Courtesy of the Ohio Historical Society; *Fig. 12.15,* From G. H. Bushnell, *The First Americans: The Pre-Columbian Civilizations,* p. 132, London: Thames & Hudson Ltd. and New York: McGraw-Hill. Copyright © 1968 by Thames & Hudson and McGraw-Hill; *Fig. 12.16,* Courtesy of Michael S. Bisson; *Fig. 12.18,* From K. C. Chang,

The Archaeology of Ancient China, New Haven: Yale University Press, 1971. Also courtesy of the Smithsonian Institution; *Fig. 12.19,* Photograph by Jean Vertut taken at the British Museum; *Fig. 12.20,* Courtesy of the University of Alaska Museum. Used by permission; *Fig. 12.21,* Ruth Kirk with Richard D. Daugherty, *Hunters of the Whale,* New York: William Morrow & Company, 1974. Photograph by Harvey Rice; *Fig. 12.22,* Courtesy of the Trustees of the British Museum (Natural History).

Chapter 13: *Fig. 13.1,* From J. G. D. Clark, *Star Carr,* New York: Cambridge University Press, 1954. Used by permission; *Figure 13.2,* Adapted from S. J. M. Davis, *The Archaeology of Animals.* London: Batsford, 1987, Figure 1.1. Reprinted by permission; *Fig. 13.4,* Reproduced by permission of Blackwell Scientific Publications; *Fig. 13.5,* Courtesy of Richard Klein and the University of Chicago; *Fig. 13.6,* University Museum of Archaeology and Ethnology, Cambridge, England. Copyright reserved; *Fig. 13.7,* From Richard G. Klein, *The Analysis of Animal Bones from Archaeological Sites.* Chicago: The University of Chicago Press, 1984, Fig. 5.4; *Fig. 13.8,* Copyright © 1970 by the Regents of the University of California. Reprinted by permission of the University of California Press; *Fig. 13.9,* Reproduced by permission of the Trustees of the British Museum (Natural History); *Fig. 13.10,* Photograph by Roger W. Brucker. Courtesy of the Cave Research Foundation Archaeological Project; *Fig. 13.11,* University Museum of Archaeology and Ethnology, Cambridge, England. Copyright reserved; *Fig. 13.12,* Redrawn from J. G. D. Clark, *Prehistoric Europe: The Economic Basis,* Fig. 44. Copyright © 1952 by J. G. D. Clark. Reproduced by permission of Stanford University Press and Methuen and Company Ltd.; *Fig. 13.13,* Redrawn from J. G. D. Clark, *Prehistoric Europe: The Economic Basis,* Fig. 44. Copyright © 1952 by J. G. D. Clark. Reproduced by permission of Stanford University Press and Methuen and Company Ltd.; *Fig. 13.15,* Patricia Vinnecombe, "A Fishing Scene from the Tsoelike River, South-Eastern Basutoland," *South African Archaeological Bulletin* 15:57, March 1960, p. 15, Fig. 1; *Fig. 13.16,* Photograph by Fred Stimson; private collection; *Fig. 13.17,* Courtesy of Vaughn M. Bryant.

Chapter 14: *Fig. 14.1,* Courtesy of the Smithsonian Institution. Photo No. T13301; *Fig. 14.2,* Courtesy of the Society of Antiquaries, London; *Fig. 14.3,* Redrawn from Richard Lee and Irven DeVore, *Kalahari Hunter Gatherers,* Cambridge, Mass.: Harvard University Press, 1976. Used by permission; *Fig. 14.4,* Richard A. Gould, "The Archaeologist as Ethnographer," *World Archaeology,* 1971, pp. 143–177, Fig. 18; *Fig. 14.5,* Photographs by Lewis R. Bindord, from Gordon R. Willey and Jeremy A. Sabloff, *A History of American Archaeology,* 2nd edition, New York: W. H. Freeman and Company, 1980. Reproduced by permission of the authors and the publisher; *Fig. 14.6,* Reconstruction by Nelson Reed, courtesy of Illinois State Museum.

Chapter 15: *Fig. 15.2,* Carl Frank/Photo Researchers, Inc.; *Fig. 15.4,* Redrawn from Marcus C. Winter, "Analyzing Household Activities," Fig. 2.17, in Kent V. Flannery, ed., *The Early Mesoamerican Village,* San Diego: Academic Press, 1976; *Fig. 15.5,* From Marcus C. Winter, "The Archaeological Household Cluster in Oaxaca," Fig. 2.1, in Kent V. Flannery, ed., *The Early Mesoamerican Village,* San Diego: Academic Press, 1976; *Fig. 15.6,* Redrawn from E. Z. Vogt, *Zinacantan,* Cambridge, Mass.: The Belknap Press of Harvard University Press, 1969. Used by permission; *Fig. 15.7a,* Melvin Konner/Anthro-Photo; *Fig. 15.7b,* Reproduced by permission of the Trustees of the British Museum; *Fig. 15.8,* Lee Boltin; *Fig. 15.9,* After Karl Butzer, *Archaeology as Human Biology,* p. 16, New York: Cambridge University Press, 1982. Used by permission; *Fig. 15.10,* After Karl Butzer, *Archaeology as Human Biology,* p. 31, New York: Cambridge University Press, 1982. Used by permission; *Fig. 15.11,* After Karl Butzer, *Archaeology as Human Biology,* p. 83, New York: Cambridge University Press, 1982. Used by permission; *Fig. 15.12,* From J. G. D. Clark, *Star Carr,* Fig. 8, New York: Cambridge University Press, 1954. Used by permission; *Fig. 15.13,* Redrawn from Kent V. Flannery, "Empirical Determination of Site Catchments in Oaxaca and Tehuacan," Fig. 4.6, in Kent V. Flannery, ed., *The Early Mesoamerican Village,* San Diego: Academic Press, 1976; *Fig. 15.15,* Redrawn from Hodder and Orton, *Spatial Analysis in Archaeology,* p. 461, New York: Cambridge University Press and the Royal Anthropological Institute of Great Britain and Ireland, 1976; *Fig. 15.16,* After Karl Butzer, *Archaeology as Human Biology,* p. 296, New York: Cambridge University Press, 1982. Used by permission; *Fig. 15.17,* After Karl Butzer, *Archaeology as Human Biology,* p. 238, New York: Cambridge University Press, 1982. Used by permission.

Chapter 16: *Fig. 16.1,* Courtesy Department of Library Services, American Museum of Natural History (Neg. No. 312721); *Fig. 16.3,* Courtesy of the Museum of the American Indian, Heye Foundation, New York; *Fig. 16.4,* Courtesy of the Peabody Museum, Harvard University; *Fig. 16.5,* After Renfrew in J. S. Sabloff and C. C. Lamberg-Karlovsky, eds., *Ancient Civilization and Trade,*

Index

Note: Italicized page numbers indicate a page on which an illustration appears.